# Gone!

## Yorkshire's Long Lost Football Teams

### Rob Grillo

All rights reserved. No part of this publication may be reproduced, stored in a retrieval system, or transmitted in any form or in any means, electronic, mechanical, photography, recording or otherwise without the permission of the copyright holders. Nor be otherwise circulated in any form or binding other than in which it is published without a similar condition being imposed on the subsequent publisher.

© Rob Grillo, 2021

# Contents

|  | Page |
|---|---|
| **1. Association Football in Yorkshire - The Beginnings…From Teams to Clubs** | 7 |
| **2. The Bullcroft Colliery Affair** | 16 |
| **3. Former Football League Teams** | |

| | | |
|---|---|---|
| Middlesbrough Ironopolis | 1889-1894 | 18 |
| *'The other team in town'* | | |
| Rotherham Town | 1877-1896 | 26 |
| *'Football by moonlight'* | | |
| Scarborough | 1879-2007 | 33 |
| *'The seasiders'* | | |
| Hunslet & Leeds City | 1877-1927 | 48 |
| (also including Leeds Harehills & Leeds United) | | |

**4. Almost Made It - The Old Midland League Teams**

| | | |
|---|---|---|
| Mexborough | 1876-1936 | 59 |
| *'Boom and bust'* | | |
| Castleford Town | 1905-1936 | 72 |
| *'The team that nearly got into the Football League'* | | |
| Wakefield City | 1920-1928 | 79 |
| *'Brave failures'* | | |
| Wath Athletic | 1885-1935 | 85 |
| *'Stern fighters'* | | |

**5. Past Yorkshire League & Amateur Teams**

| | | |
|---|---|---|
| Attercliffe | 1870-1933 | 98 |
| *'From bible class to giant slayers'* | | |
| Beverley Church Institute | 1893-1901 | 111 |
| *'Beverley's forgotten club'* | | |
| Boothtown | 1905-1955 | 116 |
| *'Half a century of success'* | | |

|  |  | *Page* |
|---|---|---|
| Bradford Rovers<br>*'Bradford's third best team'* | 1899-1977 | 121 |
| Bridlington Trinity<br>*'Brid's other team'* | 1913-1990 | 128 |
| Grimethorpe<br>*'More than just a brass band'* | 1899-2003 | 134 |
| Heeley<br>*'Both goals stand on two hills'* | 1862-1899 | 140 |
| Hull Brunswick<br>*'The oldest team in Hull'* | 1894-1973 | 148 |
| Hull Town<br>*'Forerunners of Hull City'* | 1879-1898 | 153 |
| Kilnhurst<br>*'First champions of the Sheffield League'* | 1877-1951 | 159 |
| Leeds Ashley Road<br>*'Ralph Naylor's Lads'* | 1928-1983 | 168 |
| Leeds Malvern<br>*'Lesser lights'* | 1896-1924 | 175 |
| Luddendenfoot<br>*'Don't mention the FA Cup'* | 1911-1984 | 180 |
| Manningham Mills<br>*'The mill team'* | 1909-1988 | 186 |
| Methley Perseverance<br>*'In the dock'* | 1908-1929 | 193 |
| Mirfield United<br>*'If it wasn't for that team from down the road'* | 1897-1914 | 199 |
| Portsmouth Rovers<br>*'The team that didn't reach the First Round of the FA Cup'* | 1887-1928 | 204 |
| Rowntree's<br>*'Relegated champions'* | 1897-2013 | 210 |
| Scarborough Penguins<br>*'Seaside rivals'* | 1921-1929 | 215 |
| Sutton United<br>*'Noisy neighbours'* | 1903-1956 | 218 |
| Wombwell<br>*'A tale of two teams'* | 1880-1933 | 226 |
| York City<br>*'Versions one and two'* | 1868-1915 | 238 |

## 6. Women's Football

| | | |
|---|---|---|
| Women's Football Pioneers of the 1920s | | 243 |
| Brontë Ladies | 1968-1996 | 250 |

## 7. Other Notable Clubs                          *Page*

| | |
|---|---|
| Acomb | 255 |
| Airedale | 256 |
| Batley | 257 |
| Bowling and Bowling Albion | 258 |
| Dewsbury & Savile | 259 |
| Gargrave | 264 |
| Girlington | 270 |
| Goole Loco | 271 |
| Guardhouse Sports Club | 272 |
| Guiseley Celtic | 273 |
| Haworth | 276 |
| Hebden Bridge | 280 |
| Heckmondwike | 283 |
| Horsforth | 287 |
| Ingrow United | 290 |
| Menston | 291 |
| Monckton Athletic | 292 |
| Morley | 297 |
| Mytholmroyd | 299 |
| Oakworth Albion | 302 |
| Pontefract *(AFC, Garrison, United)* | 305 |
| Selby   *(AFC, Mizpah & Olympia)* | 307 |
| Upton Colliery | 310 |

## 8. Gallery /Ardath Photocards                  316

## 9. Bibliography                                  330

---

*Leeds Mercury,*
Monday 2nd December 1929
'FOWL' PLAY. 'When the Scarborough Yorkshire League football team played Pontefract Borough on Saturday, they kept their opponents so much in their own half that at one time half a dozen fowls strayed on to the field and peacefully hunted for scraps in the Scarborough penalty area.'

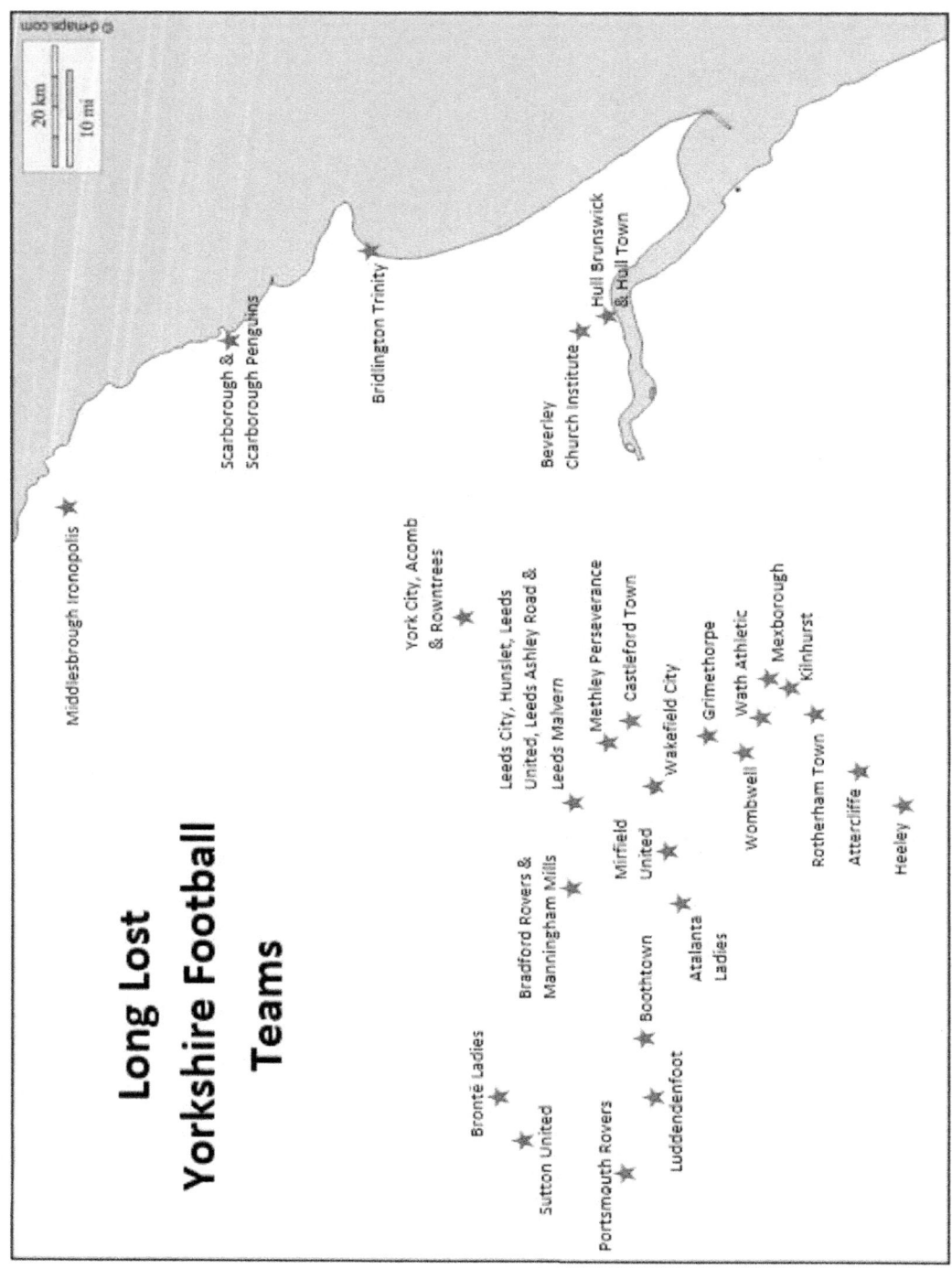

# Association Football in Yorkshire
# The Beginnings…From Teams to Clubs

Yorkshire, at nearly 12,000 square kilometres, is a vast and diverse part of the United Kingdom. Its landscape is as varied as perhaps any other part of the country, with vast rolling hills in the Pennines, the Yorkshire Dales, and North York Moors national parks, which contrast with the sprawling conurbations of West and South Yorkshire. Similarly, its local industries, from steelmaking, to fishing, textiles and traditional cottage industries are most varied, and each has played its part in the social and domestic lives of the people that live amid these communities.

The traditional forms of 'mob' football, played by large groups of men on feast days, or as inter village rivalry are well documented in history. The evidence suggests that this was very much the case in Yorkshire where 'Foot-ball' was being played throughout the early and mid-1800s, in various unregulated forms, and ranging from small sided to large-sided challenges. These were played by what we call 'teams' in the loosest possible sense, as games were more akin to one large group of individuals taking on another large group of individuals. There were informal knock-abouts that have of course continued to the present day, but there were also organised challenges, particularly in the area south of Huddersfield which went on to the play a big part in the development in the 1850s of what is now association football in Sheffield.

The historian Francis Magoun recorded football as being played in Yorkshire during the Seventeenth Century in Penistone (two games in 1648) and in Richmond (1668). In addition, the *Leeds Intelligencer* referred in its Tuesday 2nd March 1773 issue to a *'grand foot-ball match'* played the previous Tuesday between the married gentlemen and bachelors of Walton, near Wetherby, for the sum of twenty guineas. *'The success of the game was obstinately disputed for upwards of an hour, and many falls and broken shins given on each side'*. One female spectator, upon *'seeing her husband hard pressed, entered the field to his assistance, when instead of being intimidated with seeing him fall by the superior strength of his antagonist, like a true Amazon she pursued the ball and soon determined the victory'*.

The violent form that such games could take was referred to in Robert Holmes' *Keighley Past & Present* (1858), who recorded that football *'was sometimes carried to a riotous and dangerous extent, township being arrayed against township and village against village'*, and that *'much excitement and alarm were often created by the great set matches between the Town and Parish of Keighley'*.

Local villagers were pitted against those from another local village, with 'goals' in each village and a rural expanse in between on which to play. There were no formal rules, the object being merely to place the 'ball', in whichever form it took into the 'goal' of the opposing village. These 'goals' could be the village green or another well-known area where people were known to congregate, the church gates for instance.

Further evidence to corroborate that foot-ball was played in this particular part of the county comes from Elizabeth Gaskill's *The Life of Charlotte Brontë*, who referred to the esteemed Reverend William Grimshaw who sought to call out a religious life among his parishioners. Many of these *'had been in habit of playing at football on Sunday, using stones for this purpose; and giving and receiving challenges from other parishes.'*

However, after Grimshaw's time, as Gaskell goes on to say, *'The games of football on Sundays, with the challenges to the neighbouring parishes, were resumed, bringing in an influx of riotous strangers to fill the public houses.'* Once the game was over, the festivities began. Such infidels, the football hooligan element of its day, were to become associated with football in various forms throughout the sport's history.

William Cudworth, in *Round About Bradford*, published in 1876, also refers to football in his description of that district. *'Thornton used to be the scene of many a good tussle at football, and that too on a large scale, when Haworth met Clayton, or either township challenged Thornton.'*

Those matches around Keighley and the Worth Valley seem to have naturally died a death in the district without having been subjected to any particular prohibitions, but such team games gradually became confined to distinct playing areas, as opposed to 'goals' being located in different villages. John Goulstone, in *Football's Secret History,* refers to the villagers of Footstone (Fulstone), near Holmfirth, offering, in January 1884, to meet those from Bolton across the border in Lancashire at 12-a-side for any sum between £25 and £50, or, if this offer was not accepted, six of them would meet a similar number from Thurlstone for £5 a side.

The *Leeds Times*, on 17th September 1842, bemoaned the fact that many of the field games of old England had almost entirely passed away, become obsolete and forgotten, but the evidence from local reports suggested that 'foot-ball' itself was still being played, albeit to a lesser extent.

According to *huddersfieldheritage.co.uk* the earliest reference to a football match in the Huddersfield district is of a match played near Whinney Bank, Holmfirth in 1848, between Holmfirth and Hepworth. The stakes were £5 and each side deposited half this sum. According to reports the game was well contested and *'exhibited the usual amount of contusions, bloody noses, etc'*, with the Hepworth lads emerging victors.

The Holmfirth district was another early hot-bed of challenge matches, Goulstone also referred to Holmfirth players who had arranged to play those from Enderby (Leicester) at 10 or 12-a-side over two or three games at Sheffield's Hyde Park cricket ground on Good Friday, 1852. The West Yorkshire 'team' merely required the fee of £5 to be sent to Mr J Batty's, Red Lion Inn at Jackson Bridge, Holmfirth for the matches to take place. Whether these matches were ever played is unknown.

The role of the public house can never be underestimated. The relationship between pubs and sportsmen was mutually beneficial. Publicans were happy to host sportsmen, as this attracted customers. As such, some publicans would also sponsor sporting events.

Whitsuntide Festivities often included the playing of 'foot-ball', of which mention was increasingly made in local and regional newspapers from the late 1850s. These were less competitive games than the inter-village challenges.

## The Sabbath

Sabbath desecration often resulted in outcry, particularly if a regular event. This is none-more-so illustrated in the letter printed in the *Bradford Observer* on Thursday 28th January 1858, and the corroboration of such events in the form of the editorial comment that followed.

*SIR – You would oblige me by inserting this short letter in your valuable paper. In looking from my window, which commands a view of Spinkwell Bridge, I have seen for the last two successive Sundays, a number of young men, I think between twenty and thirty, playing at football in a field adjoining the canal, some appear to have on white smocks, and others to be without coats, and from the great earnestness manifested by all, I inferred that it was not mere pastime, but a regular 'set game'. They generally congregate about 10 o'clock and leave the field about 12. Hoping that this information will come to the knowledge of the authorities, and that they put a stop to such a disgraceful desecration of the Sabbath,*

*I beg Sir, to subscribe myself, Yours respectfully, A.S.*

*[We can corroborate the statements of A.S in every particular. Further, we know that scenes similar to those he describes are of weekly occurrence in other localities around the suburbs. We do not like to trench on the pastimes of the people, but when it comes to the desecration of the Sabbath, it is surely time for the strong arm of the law to be wielded, and we hope to hear of a number of active police-officers being appointed to the special duty of scouring the suburbs and putting down this nuisance. It is evil that will grow if not nipped in the bud. We should also advise the police to keep a sharp eye on the streets running from Wakefield Road to Manchester Road. On Sunday afternoon a number of rough lads were busily engaged in some game there, and their language was anything but fit to be put into type. We hope that our active police superintendent will attend to these matters REP B.O.]*

It is no surprise that playing on a Sunday was such a big deal, but this was the one day of the week when many working people would have had free time in which to take part in sports and pastimes. It wasn't until 1850 that a Factories Act was passed that enabled workers to leave work at 2pm on a Saturday (although conversely the working week was increased by 2 hours, from 58 to 60 hours per week).

The *Bradford Observer* ran an article on Thursday 11th February 1847, which suggests that foot-ball was actually played as a matter of course on a Sunday;

*SABBATH DESECRATION - During several Sundays, a large number of young persons have almost incessantly amused themselves with football playing, shindying, gambling, etc. The place selected for the exhibition of these sports is a croft situated in a densely populated portion of the west end of the town, and quite adjacent to a chapel occupied by a respectable congregation. To a peaceful assembly of worshippers, shouts, yells, and other discordant noises repeatedly greeting their ears must be anything but agreeable...now that the authorities have resolved to grapple with the grave matters of sewers and other sanitary improvements, it is hoped that it is only necessary to point out this Sabbatical nuisance to ensure its immediate suppression.*

## Football in the Street

The law was also used to make it harder for young men to play 'foot-ball'. The Lighting, etc., of Parishes (England) Act 1830 was passed, one which was *'to make provision for the lighting, watching, cleansing and paving of parishes in England and Wales'*, in which it was made an offence for any person *'to fly any kite, drive any hoop, or play football or any other game or games, to the annoyance of any passenger or traveller'* was an example.

The 1835 Highway Act further hardened the authorities stance against the playing of football on public highways, with a maximum penalty of forty shillings for those flouting the new laws, and local by-laws allowed for the punishment of those who were caught playing foot-ball in specified areas. This prevented the working classes from disrupting the business classes from going about their way, and paved the way – so to speak – for football to return to local fields and pastures from whence it came.

By 1868, footballs were available to buy in local shops, at least those in the south Huddersfield district

It is also interesting to note that in this case this was not an example of a rural sport, but one which was played in one of the more populous areas of Yorkshire. Of course kicking a ball around the street can hardly be classed as a 'team' sport, but the formation of formally organised teams was inevitable given the increasing levels of social organisation during the mid-1800s.

### Evidence of Early 'Foot-ball' fields

The *Bradford Observer* included a lament for the loss of recreational land in a rapidly growing industrial town, in its Thursday 12th November 1840 issue, *'For ourselves, we protest against that grasping allotment of waste lands to landlords and farmers, which deprives the rustic of his ox-gang, sheep-walk and goose-gate, and the artisan and labourer of their foot-ball, quoits, and their knorr and spell, their bandy, bowls, and cricket…from the poor is taken the little all which he possesses'*.

There is evidence of early pastures that were likely used for foot-ball challenges. These are those fields with 'foot-ball' in their titles (fields were given with their names up to the mid-1800s). While many matches would have been played on common ground, the field names given in tithe reports give us evidence that they were on private enclosures, and no doubt held with permission of the landowners.

The *Leeds Intelligencer,* on Monday 7th September 1807, carried details of the *'The farmhouse and lands currently inhabited by one Ann Fletcher in the township of Northowram'*. Two of the nine enclosures (fields), among others with names such as *Dub Croft, Whinney Brow* and *Whinney Croft,* were known as *Football Field*.

As new housing spread outwards from Leeds, land at Yeadon was offered for sale on 27th September 1842 included a *Football Close* as part of land occupied by a J Brayshaw (this was indicated on the 1858 tithe map of the area). It is perhaps no co-incidence that there were other 'foot-ball' enclosures in nearby villages. In nearby Rawdon, the village tithe map from 1858 shows two adjacent *'Foot Ball'* fields just to the north of the main turnpike, the current Town Street. The site is now covered by Billington Avenue and a Primary School.

### Football 'Teams' Around the County

Adrian Harvey, in Football, *The First Hundred Years,* has identified nineteen active football 'teams' in Yorkshire in the period 1830-1859, more than in any other part of the UK, and just ahead of Lancashire. Many of these teams were from communities south of Huddersfield, close to Sheffield, which was the first part of the UK to really experience a 'boom' in competitive, club-based football. These were 'teams'- representing their village, and in some cases, school - as distinct from what we now call properly organised 'clubs'. To this list can be added the villages of Haworth, Thornton, and Clayton (Bradford). Unlike some other places around the country, there were no teams discovered that represented workplaces at this time in Yorkshire.

Of the nineteen that Harvey discovered, those in West Yorkshire were: Leeds Grammar School (1851), Foolstone (Fulstone) (1844), Holmfirth (1845 & 1852), Thurstonland (1843), Totties (1843), Hepworth (1845),

The following were Sheffield district teams, which was then part of the West Riding: Hoylandswaine (1844), Thurlstone (1843-45), Thurlstone Upper End (1844), Penistone (1844), Hallam (1857), and Sheffield (1857). The final two in this list were certainly the two first distinct 'clubs'.

In the north of the county, three teams were identified by Harvey, all from educational institutions: Bramham School (1855), Richmond Grammar School (1854), St Peter's School, York (1856)

Those with an unknown location are: Bilkerstone (1844), Southouse (1845)

Harvey also made reference to a Denby (1844). The location of this particular could well have been Denby Dale (near Huddersfield), but other 'Denby' possibilities do exist.

As large, expanding urban areas based around Leeds and Bradford, Sheffield, and Middlesbrough in the north, came to dominate, it was inevitable that sport and recreation would take off as the population burgeoned. Each of those local industries was woven into the fabric of the area, and had a huge influence on the sporting interests of the communities they served.

Cricket experienced phenomenal growth from the 1850s, due massively to that 1850 Factories Act. It meant that Saturday afternoons, for the first time, were left for the worker to do what he pleased. Aspiring sportsmen were free to not only take part in a sport of their choice, but it also gave them the opportunity to watch their local heroes or teams in action on the field of play. Others chose to set up organise and administer local teams in a range of sports, some of which had been the domain of the middle classes only. Rugby prevailed as a winter pastime in West Yorkshire, Cleveland, and the Hull region, while the handling code was more or less eschewed in the south of the region as what would become association football prevailed. Gate receipts spiralled and previously exclusive town clubs were suddenly experiencing four-figure crowds on a weekly basis. Public open spaces were laid down, and these were the venues for informal sporting activities as well as pleasant days out and local galas.

Further to this, the railway boom made travel to seaside resorts and sports events much easier, and from the early 1880s horse-drawn trams ran in the streets, making journeys from town to town far easier.

## The emergence of Football Clubs

Organised football started in Yorkshire in Sheffield in 1857 with the birth of Sheffield FC and the creation of Sheffield Rules. No longer were football players member of 'teams', they were members of specifically organised clubs, ones that were formed with an intention of playing organised matches between club members or against other clubs. These clubs organised their own teams according to the rules that governed each club, and the matches took place on prescribed areas of play. The era of village teams taking on other villages with few rules and any number of players all-but died out, making way for challenge matches played initially under a number of different codes.

Local mills and industrial companies began to organise sports clubs, which in turn organised teams in different sports; cricket teams, and then rugby and Association football for instance. It kept their workforce happy, and a happy workforce would be far more productive. The church recognised the value of promoting sporting clubs too. The same religious institutions that had objected to the supposed violence and lawlessness of the early forms of football around the country were prime movers behind the new 'Muscular Christianity', which encouraged the playing of physical sport, partly through a need to closely establish young men in their community with the local church, and also to gain spiritual fulfilment through 'manly' exercise. If you didn't go to church on Sunday, you would not be selected to play the following Saturday. It worked, even if many of the church-based teams didn't conduct themselves particularly well on the sporting field.

The early history of organised association football in Yorkshire is by no means uniform. The old West Riding covered the Sheffield district as well as what we now know as West Yorkshire, yet the footballing histories of these two districts are very, very different and quite distinct. Similarly, Middlesbrough's history is more in line with what was going on in the north-east of England, while the Hull district had its own battles with the oval ball game.

By the early 1860s there were as many as twenty clubs in the Sheffield area, although it wasn't until 1867 that the Sheffield Football Association was founded. Harry Chambers, secretary of Sheffield FC, served as its first President. The Association issued its first set of rules on 6th March 1867, just days after the conclusion of the first competitive football tournament.

This one-off tournament was the Youdan Cup, which was named after a local theatre owner, Thomas Youdan. Ties took place between February and March of 1867, and was competed for by most of the Sheffield Association's member clubs. The following year, the Cromwell Cup, offered this time by Oliver Cromwell (the manager at the Alexandra Opera House, rather than the historical figure), was played under the auspices of the Association. This competition was only open to teams under two years old and was won by The Wednesday.

The first annual competition, the Sheffield Association Challenge Cup, was introduced in the 1876/77 season. This was joined by the Wharncliffe Charity Cup two years later. Both were won by The Wednesday, who had quickly become the dominant force in local football. It wasn't until 1878 that the Sheffield Rules were unified with those in use by the English Football Association.

Most of the clubs that sprung up during the sport's formative years are no more, some lasting only a few matches, with others establishing themselves in local circles before folding, often due to financial reasons - which gradually became more important as the game became more organised – or through the loss of players or a major benefactor. Many of the short lived 'teams' in the late nineteenth century were just that, a group of players from one street or locality organising a team from a nearby locality, with a team name agreed or imposed by the 'captain' or organiser, and a basic field procured for the means of playing. Very rarely would a shared football kit have been use, similar colour caps at best, and there may not have been any proper goalposts – other than two pieces of wood at each end - or pitch markings. The same lads might have got together another week for a similar match, or turned out for a different team entirely. There was no club to pay a subscription to, no conditions of membership, just a set of lads playing a football match.

In July 1885, professionalism was made legal but the Sheffield Association, led by Charles Clegg and William Peirce Dix remained firm opponents of professionalism in football.

In 1877 a rival association, the 'Sheffield New Association' was established in protest at the Sheffield FA's decision not to allow any club under two years old to become a member. It later changed its name to the Hallamshire Football Association but in the summer of 1887 merged with the Sheffield FA. Clegg took charge of the new association with Dix employed as secretary.

Member clubs of the Sheffield FA in 1877 included Hallam, Sheffield, and The Wednesday, all of which are still very much in existence. The other members were Albion, Artillery & Hallamshire Rifles, Attercliffe, Brightside, Brincliffe, Broomhall, Crookes, Exchange, Exchange Brewery, Fir Vale, Gleadless, Heeley, Kimberworth, Millhouses, Norfolk, Norfolk Works, Owlerton, Oxford, Parkwood Springs, Philadelphia, Rotherham, Surrey, and Thursday Wanderers.

### The Emergence of League Competition

Following the success of the Football League, established in 1888, George Willey, a member of the Sheffield & Hallamshire FA, was the man behind the founding of the Sheffield & District Football League for the 1889/90 season, which was the first such competition in the Sheffield area. The eight founding members were: Attercliffe, Clinton, Eckington Works, Exchange, Owlerton, Walkley, Kilnhurst, and

Ecclesfield. The latter two clubs topped the table with 18 points, Ecclesfield, having played one more game than Kilnhurst, who were considered champions in the local press. No trophy was awarded though as only two teams completed their full fixture schedule. None of these clubs survives today.

Willey donated a trophy for the league's second campaign, appropriately named the *'George Willey Sheffield & District Football League Challenge Shield.'* It was a wooden shield covered in red hide with a metal centre showing a football scene.

A decision was taken to disband the league at a general meeting on 18th July 1895, not due to a lack of support, but because it was felt that the original purpose of the league, assumed to be to provide clubs with competitive football or to encourage new clubs to play the sport, had been achieved.

However, by the time the league disbanded, there were over twenty leagues in operation throughout the Sheffield & Hallamshire FA region, with one in almost every town. It was decided that the best eight teams in the district would enter the Wharncliffe Cup – which took its name from the Earl of Wharncliffe, with the aim of raising money for local good causes - with the rest taking part in a new league administered by the Sheffield & Hallamshire FA.

This did not happen for the following season, 1895/96. However, the Sheffield & Hallamshire FA did start its own league in 1896, known as the Sheffield Association League. The league ran under this name until 1960, and with a merger with the Hatchard League along the way, now takes the form of the Sheffield & Hallamshire County Senior League.

With league competition came more rules and regulations, and there was no opportunity for an informal 'team' to be able to join any of the local competitions that emerged. Properly constituted clubs were welcome, given that there needed to be uniformity among league members. In the early 1900s, so many leagues and clubs appeared, and many of the latter could only just be described as 'clubs', having some written rules as governance, and a small committee, a condition of league membership. However, with regular league fees, subscriptions, and fines there needed to be at least some order to these clubs.

## Catching Up

The area around what is now modern day West Yorkshire was much slower in adopting the round ball game. The reason for the non-appearance of competitive Association football at this time was down to the enormous strength and power of the region's rugby clubs. It was not only their strength on the field of play, but also the strength they wielded off the field, and the strategies they used, that maintained their position as the leading sporting representatives of the towns they served.

Despite some of the first clubs in the district hailing from the Leeds district, it was in the Bradford area that the game really began to take off. In both, it took the adoption and take-off of the code in schools to really kick-start the game after several failed attempts to establish it in the region. Similarly, in the Heavy Woollen region, south of the two major towns, industrial growth helped the sport grow.

The West Riding coal fields were a hotbed of early forms of football, with the 1842 Royal Commission on Children in Mines and Manufactories reporting that the sport was widespread here, mainly due to migrants to the area from areas such as Stoke-on-Trent, who had experience of the game in their homelands, and who wished to continue playing while based in West Yorkshire. However, it was the rugby codes that came to dominate.

Other towns, such as Harrogate, saw the sport played almost entirely in local schools and colleges before senior clubs of any note were formed. The influence of local schoolteachers was profound here as well as in Leeds and Bradford. The church, as we shall see, also had no small part to play in the growth of the sport.

However, for many years the association football game didn't just 'take-off' as it had done around the country. It took West Yorkshire much longer to take to association football in the numbers needed for it to sustain itself.

Aspirational association teams became heavily reliant on the Northern Union (Rugby League) clubs for a base, illustrating the large disparity between the codes. The Hunslet association club, the strongest in the district, was for a time reliant on the rugby club of the same name and, at Bradford's Park Avenue, the association side initially played on the ground when first team rugby was not scheduled. The Bradford club, Girlington AFC, moved to Valley Parade to accommodate the demands associated with their rising status while other clubs, such as Featherstone, were allowed the use of a ground by the rugby club there and could play there when their hosts had a fixture away from home. Association cup finals and exhibition games were also staged at the grounds of Northern Union clubs and, in other instances, soccer teams jumped into the fields vacated by defunct junior rugby clubs. That relationship could work the other way, however, as in the summer of 1905, association football was dropped at Fartown, Huddersfield, in favour of the rugby club's second team, despite the association team's strong showing in the West Yorkshire League the previous season. The same thing had already happened, controversially, at Park Avenue, Bradford.

What the local association scene in the West Riding really lacked was a successful and well-organised county league that would enable successful and ambitious clubs to progress, should they choose to do so. The Yorkshire Rugby Union had organised league competition, against the wishes of the national body, and yet the county Football Association was unable to do so despite support from the national body. Other areas had benefitted from such competition: the Midland, Northern and Lancashire leagues had all come into being in 1889, and all served to produce future Football League teams over the years. Very few West Riding clubs were able to progress beyond county level due to this, and those that did had to go down the Midland League (and in one case Southern League) route. Despite this, local league competitions were in abundance within just a few years of the introduction of the Football League, but this didn't solve the problem of the lack of a county league competition for the stronger and more ambitious clubs.

In the East Riding of Yorkshire, association football also had rugby to content with. The Hull FA organised its own senior cup competition for the 1896/97 season, although it was without a trophy for the winning team until the editor of the *Hull Times* - a newspaper that had already donated a rugby trophy – stepped forward in October and donated a brand new cup.

The East Riding FA was founded on 1st May 1902, following Football Association recommendations. Before the formation of the County FA, football in the area was under the jurisdiction of a Hull & District FA and the Scarborough & East Riding FA, the former of which took over the running of the new East Riding FA. Hull teams were originally members of the Scarborough FA although by August 1898 there were 60 affiliated clubs in Hull, with barely one-third of that number in Scarborough.

In both the East Riding and the West Yorkshire regions, the local press referred to rugby playing clubs as 'football club', with 'association football club' for those using the round ball. However, it was different in Sheffield, where rugby never had the same hold. A 'football club' here would be in reference to an association club.

Over in the North Riding, a Cleveland Cup competition came into being in 1881, competed for mainly by Middlesbrough district clubs, as well as teams from towns such as Whitby, on the coast.

A York & District League was founded in 1897 with ten clubs in two sections; Acomb, Easingwold, Ebor Wanderers, Groves Wesley, Heworth, Rowntree's, Selby, St Clement's, Sycamore, and Ulleskelf. C M Rawes & A Lumley were instrumental in the formation of the league, which of course is still in existence today. York's J A McGregor, a life member of the West Yorkshire Association of Referees, was another prominent figure in local association circles.

A York & District Football Association was formed in 1900, its two knock-out cup competitions quickly established as the Riley Smith Cup (Junior Cup), and the Faber Cup (Senior Cup). There was also a Half Holiday League, with fixtures played on Wednesdays, founded around this time. Rowntree's – a name that would feature many, many times over the years in York football honours - was initially the top club in the city.

Among the many thousands of long-gone teams that have graced God's Own Country since the mid-1880s, this book contains the histories of just a few. Those featured are from all over Yorkshire, and in many cases have quite diverse stories. There are those which graced the Football League; the short-lived Middlesbrough Ironopolis, near neighbours and great rivals of the Middlesbrough AFC; Leeds City, the forerunners of the current Leeds United with a history that goes back to the days of Hunslet AFC; Rotherham Town and County, forerunners of today's Rotherham United.

There are the teams that were at one time, in effect, just one step away from the Football League. Mexborough and Wath clubs were arguably punching above their weight in the old Midland League, although Castleford and the highly unsuccessful Wakefield City could be said to have underachieved at this level.

The names of Hull City and York City were prominent among local teams, before their namesakes went on to achieve Football League (and in Hull's case Premier League) status, yet the histories of these early and relatively short-lived City clubs have largely escaped the attention of sports historians through the decades. I've avoided the temptation of including the original pre-1903 Bradford City clubs as they are covered in detail in my previous publication *Late To The Game*.

Other clubs, Attercliffe, Beverley Church Institute, Bradford Rovers, Bridlington Trinity, Hull Brunswick, Methley Perseverance, Mirfield United, Portsmouth Rovers (from Todmorden). Scarborough Penguins, Sutton United, Wombwell, and others experienced very different histories, as did Bronte and Manningham Ladies clubs, the latter two in very different eras.

But as diverse as these club histories might be, there is a common thread running through many of them, and that is of the dangers of overstretching in an era when it was common for teams in senior league to pay players a basic wage for their services. The Bullcroft Colliery affair in the following section, underlines the dangers that every club that aspired to be successful faced.

I feel it is important to note that, although some women's teams are featured here, the history of women in football is largely an untold one. Behind each of the teams featured in this book there will have been an organising committee that consisted of both male and female members. Many behind the scenes activities were organised by women for example, particularly fund raising events, so it is perhaps wrong to assume that women's football history is not that marked. Women's football teams might not have been great in number, but the number of women working behind the scenes was. Those hidden influences are at last being acknowledged by sports historians, both in academic and non-academic circles.

# The Bullcroft Colliery Affair

There are many reasons why the football clubs in this book ceased to exist. Financial problems account for many of them, a loss of funding from its parent company, an enforced move away from its traditional base, internal problems, or the success of a local rival leading to others to go to the wall.

One common theme is the fact that many of what we would today class as semi-professional clubs folded after having experienced financial problems, or at least experienced financial problems on one or a number of occasions during their existence.

The problems, in many cases, were caused when the football club overstretched. This certainly applies to several of the Colliery-based teams in the Sheffield and Hallamshire district and village teams in the West Yorkshire region. By overstretching, this involved the paying of 'professionals', which of course needed paying from gate receipts, the main source of income for these teams. However, the clubs were often unable to cover players wages, which were paid on a weekly basis, rather than by match. It was rare for a team to be successful in a senior league by playing local amateurs only. In order to compete with the best, players from out with the community needed to be brought in. This may have been a short-term benefit to the club, but was clearly unsustainable.

The 'Bullcroft Colliery affair' from November 1926 best sums up the problems facing football clubs that strove for success, despite their limited means. The club was made an example of by the Sheffield & Hallamshire Football Association. It was doing nothing that its rivals were not doing, which is worth bearing in mind when reading some of the short written histories of the lesser clubs that follow in this volume.

*Star Green 'Un,* Saturday 6th November 1926

**BULLCROFTS BIG FINE. Colliery Clubs and Their Professionals. THE SECRETARY EXPLAINS.**

*There has been a first-class football sensation in the Doncaster district this week, provided the FA fining Bullcroft Main for £50 for a breach of rules in not paying one of their professionals, W Chappell, the requisite minimum of 10s a week.*

*It is not the amount of the fine, writes W M, that provides the sensation, it the attack on a recognised practice among minor clubs which the FA decision serves to illuminate. Those well versed in the management of junior football contend that if the FA mean to stick strictly to rules, then a great proportion of colliery and works clubs in the country are likely to go out of existence.*

*The Bullcroft position, Mr G Stevens, the secretary, tells me is this:*

*Like many other colliery and works clubs, they sought to run a good class team for the workmen at the pit. To do so it became necessary to bring in professionals. Some were youngsters with ambitions, others were recognised players temporarily off form, and others were players with a good record.*

For a variety of reasons these players sought to retain their professional status, and strictly speaking ought to be paid 10s week. How many Junior clubs could do that?

Take an average of eight professionals to a team. This means £4 a week in wages. Bullcroft, as members of the Doncaster Senior League, could not play a home match every week, there were insufficient clubs, and consequently it meant that at least £10 was necessary out of every home match to pay professionals if the FA rule was to be rigidly carried out.

Mr Stevens tells me that what Bullcroft did when a footballer came along, was to explain the financial position of the club. The man was told the club had not the money for actual payment, but if he cared to accept the minimum wages as part of his wages for working at the pit, then well and good. These conditions were explained to the men before they joined Bullcroft.

### The Understanding

Many were ready to accept, for as often as not favourable facilities for earning big money in the pit were forthcoming.

These terms applied at Bullcroft in the case of W Chappell, a promising outside-right, who some time ago went on trial with Bradford Park Avenue. He returned, and went on trial with Sunderland. He returned again and sought to join a Nottinghamshire club.

Inquiries were made, and Chappell denied receiving payment from Bullcroft. The facts were reported to the FA with the aforementioned outcome. The fine has to be paid by November 13th, and Mr Stevens says unless an appeal brings relief there is nothing but to pack up, as there is not sufficient money to meet the fine.

With such an action an end would come to a distinguished Doncaster district club, which has been existence for seventeen years, and which has turned out well-known players like Boyle (Sheffield United), S Cowan (Manchester City), Slicer (Huddersfield), Allen (Denaby and Scunthorpe), and others who have gone further afield.

Inquiries among other Doncaster clubs find that few of them are able to actually pay the 10s weekly minimum. One club gets over the difficulty by having signed agreements with players that they agree to the club owing the money and paying when in a financial position to do so. But it is a long time since players received a full week's pay. In fact, it is not now expected, with financial conditions as they are.

Due in part to the local coal stoppage, the club could not afford to pay the fine, and was therefore suspended by the Sheffield & Hallamshire FA on 22nd November 1926. It was a sad end for the club that had been formed in 1909 and which had finished runner-up in the Doncaster Senior League the previous season.

Bullcroft Colliery was a coal mine situated by the village of Carcroft, north of Doncaster, from 1908 until it was merged with Brodsworth Colliery in 1970. Prior to the events of 1926, its football club had spent one single season in the Yorkshire League, finishing in twelfth place in a sixteen-team division in the 1924/25 season. The paying of professional players was permitted (hence the number of reserve and third teams of professional Football League clubs in the league), and it was rare for a club not to do so. In debt, the club had dropped back into the Doncaster League, but even at this level a club needed to provide incentives to its players if it was to be successful.

# Middlesbrough Ironopolis 1889-94
## *'The other team in town'*

Only two teams can claim the unenviable distinction of having spent just one season in the Football League. One, Bootle AFC on Merseyside has been reformed at a much lower level, but the other, the uniquely-named Middlesbrough Ironopolis, hailing from the far north of Yorkshire has vanished into obscurity as its major rival for top team in the town has gone on to establish itself in the higher echelons of the game.

The area around Middlesbrough was largely rural, agricultural land until the early 1800s. The coal industry, and resulting iron and steelworks that developed around the area drove demand for labour. Large numbers of Welsh and Irish settlers swelled the population. By the late 1800s, steel production and ship building had also become primary producers. By 1851, the population had grown to over 7,500 residents, a number that was to mushroom over the ensuing decades, reaching 90,000 by 1900.

Middlesbrough AFC was founded in response to the sporting interests of this booming population in 1876, and by the 1879/80 season had moved to an old cricket ground in Linthorpe Road. There was a split early in the 1889/90 season over the issue of professionalism, which resulted in the formation of the Ironopolis club. The Middlesbrough AFC membership numbered around 400, but upon a vote in May 1889 it was left to the casting vote of W Cochrane to decide the club's future progress – the decision *'the Club to remain unchanged'*, which was to remain amateur.

That was far from the end of the matter though, as the club made a very poor start to the season, and then six of its eleven first team players threatened to strike in late September / early October until the club agreed to remunerate them for their services, thought to be 10s for a victory and 7s 6d for a draw or defeat, rather than merely paying expenses for away fixtures. An impasse was reached whereby the players involved would play on, if the club made an application to the English Football Association to adopt a rule which would enable Middlesbrough AFC to pay its players for loss of time in taking part in matches whilst still retaining its amateur status.

However, those involved in the sport in the town that wanted full professionalism took their own action, with a meeting at the town's packed Temperance Hall, with a Mr Malcolm McDonald in the Chair, on 29th October 1889. The event was attended by around 2,000 interested locals, and was reported in detail in the likes of the *Northern Echo* and Middlesbrough's *Daily Gazette*, as was the resulting decision to form a breakaway club. Former Middlesbrough AFC committee-member J Wood was one of those behind the new club, arguing *'Football was now a money-making affair, and the players had an equal right to share the money with anyone else'*. It was also argued that the paying of players would stimulate them into giving better performances on the field, particularly apt given that Middlesbrough AFC had made such a torrid start to the season.

The new professional club was launched with some 150 £1 shares towards the new company being sold, towards a target of £1000. Those who committed to two or more shares would be granted free access to home fixtures, with season tickets sold for 5s for those without shares. The *Northern Echo* reported that *'The meeting caused the liveliest interest in the town, and for hours after its close it was the topic of animated conversation in knots of enthusiasts'*.

With the club being founded during the late Victorian industrial boom - during which time Middlesbrough was a centre of iron and steel production - then the nickname 'Ironopolis' (iron-city) was adopted in order to emphasise this. Hence one of the club nicknames *The Nops* was based on 'Ironopolis'. The other nickname for the club was *The Washers*. At an early meeting of the club, a shipyard worker is said to have stated that *'If you want professionals you must put your washers together'*. Washers meaning 'coins'.

The headquarters of the newly formed team was the Swatters Carr Hotel, the club later relocating to the County Hotel in Newport Road, which was almost opposite the old North Riding Infirmary.

A field formerly used by a local rugby club was rented, becoming known as 'The Paradise Ground', and which was close to the main entrance to the Royal Albert Park and Middlesbrough Union Workhouse, south of the town centre. Although it offered open seating area and some covered accommodation by the time Football League status had been achieved, it was not as well equipped as the Linthorpe Road ground, and almost certainly offered no shower or refreshment facilities for players or spectators.

*The only known photograph of Middlesbrough Ironopolis AFC, from 1892/93*

Three Middlesbrough AFC players - W Hopewell, T Cronshaw, and J Taylor (all of whom were part of six threatening strike action) - went to the new club, with six coming from Scotland via Arthurlie (three players), Dundee Strathmore (two players), and Dundee Harp. There were 140 applications from professional players in total.

Ironically, despite having initially planned to pay expenses only for the 1889/90 season, in a dramatic about-turn, Middlesbrough AFC itself turned professional in November 1889 and played its first professional match before the Ironopolis had played its first match. Had the club committee come to this decision only weeks earlier then there would have been no break-away club.

The first ever Ironopolis game was on 14th December 1889 at home to Gainsborough Trinity, a 1-1 draw the result, Seymour equalising for *The Washers* before half-time. An estimated 4,000 spectators attended the game. The first ever Ironopolis line up was: *Goal: G Smart, Backs: T Anderson, J Matthew, Half Backs: J A Elliot, R F Thompson, W Hopewell, Forwards: T Cronshaw, J M M'Gregor, T J Morrisey, J Taylor, T Seymour.* Middlesbrough AFC went down 0-7 at Darlington the same day. Two wins came from the eight matches played by Ironopolis before the New Year, against Northern League clubs South Bank and Darlington St Augustine's, the latter of which ended the season as league champions.

Middlesbrough AFC declined an invitation to play the new club early in 1890, but to be fair, defeat could have spelt the death knell of the better established club, a suggestion certainly alluded to in the local press at the time. In the event Ironopolis could have been merged back into Middlesbrough AFC, given that both teams were following the same path now, although the suggestion that each shareholder of the Ironopolis club should be paid £650 if the clubs were to merge put paid to any chances of that happening at the time. The teams did finally meet, on 26th April 1890, a goal-less draw resulting, in front of a crowd of 12,000 at Linthorpe Road in a Cleveland Charity Cup Final tie (beneficiaries being the North Riding Infirmary and North Ormesby Cottage Hospital). The replay, at the Paradise Ground, was won by Ironopolis 2-0.

Other opponents that first season included West Bromwich Albion, Notts County, Sheffield Wednesday, Sunderland, and Aston Villa, with 20 of the club's 36 matches being won, with a further eight resulting in draws. One of the most interesting fixtures of the season took place on Thursday 6th February 1890, a friendly fixture at home to Sheffield FC under artificial gas-light. The novelty, one of several played around the country around this time, attracted several thousand spectators to the Paradise Ground. The Northern Echo reported, *'The night was dark and cloudy, but by the aid of the Wells's light the game was carried on with but slight disadvantage, as the nine powerful lights disposed round the ground enabled the ball to be easily distinguished except in the centre of the field, where the darkness was not so completely dispelled.'* The result of this friendly fixture was secondary to the spectacle itself, but for the record, the home team won 10-2.

Ironopolis was elected to the Northern League for the 1890/91 season, alongside the likes of Middlesbrough, Sunderland Albion (itself a break-away club of Sunderland), and the two senior Newcastle teams, West End and East End. The club's opening league fixture, on 10th September 1890 resulted in a 0-3 loss at Sunderland Albion's Blue House Fields ground, in a match that was completed in near darkness due to the non-appearance of the appointed referee. However, the club had only three days to wait for its first victory, a 5-1 success at home to Newcastle West End, followed by a massive 8-0 home victory against the East End club one week later.

A crowd of almost 10,000, at that time a record for the Northern League, packed into Linthorpe Road for the Middlesbrough derby on Saturday 1st November 1890, bringing with them receipts of £200. A 2-2 draw ensued. Ironopolis won the return fixture by a single goal later in season, and despite heavy defeats at home to Stockton and at Darlington, won the title at its first attempt, just a point clear of local rivals Middlesbrough AFC.

A first foray into the FA Cup produced a run through three qualifying rounds before a First Round tie at home to the cup holders, Blackburn Rovers. A narrow 1-2 home loss was the result in front of 10,000 spectators (£230 receipts) on Saturday 17th January 1891, but a successful appeal by Ironopolis over the state of the ground saw the match replayed. Blackburn won again, 3-0 and went on to retain the cup. A 6-0 victory over Darlington was also overturned, for the same reason, in the previous round, with Ironopolis winning the re-played match 3-0.

Several Football League teams were also played in friendly fixtures this season, notably Sunderland, Preston North End, and Everton, as well as founder members of the newly formed Scottish League, Cowlairs, who were thrashed 9-0. A massive 52 fixtures were played throughout the season, with 36 won and 4 drawn. The Cleveland Charity Cup was retained with a 2-0 victory over Darlington in the final, and a reserve team was established to enable a bigger, and stronger, squad of players. But all was not rosy, with a deficit of over £513 on the season. As a result, since its inception, the club was now over £1,090 in the red.

While Middlesbrough AFC continued to draw its main support from the middle and upper classes of the town, Ironopolis were very much the team of the working man. Evidence for this comes from the occupations listed on the register of investors who bought £1 shares in 1891.

### Northern League tables featuring Ironopolis
*(Including the team's results against other teams in the final two columns)*

| 1890/1891 | P | W | D | L | F | A | Pts | H | A |
|---|---|---|---|---|---|---|---|---|---|
| **Middlesbrough Ironopolis** | 14 | 9 | 2 | 3 | 37 | 24 | 20 | -- | -- |
| Middlesbrough | 14 | 8 | 3 | 3 | 33 | 17 | 19 | 1-0 | 2-2 |
| Sunderland Albion | 14 | 7 | 3 | 4 | 33 | 16 | 17 | 3-2 | 0-3 |
| Stockton | 14 | 8 | 1 | 5 | 38 | 19 | 17 | 1-4 | 2-1 |
| Darlington | 14 | 7 | 0 | 7 | 25 | 29 | 14 | 2-1 | 1-4 |
| Newcastle East End | 14 | 5 | 2 | 7 | 25 | 39 | 12 | 8-0 | 2-0 |
| Newcastle West End | 14 | 3 | 4 | 7 | 21 | 38 | 10 | 5-1 | 2-2 |
| Darlington St. Augustine's | 14 | 0 | 3 | 11 | 14 | 44 | 3 | 6-3 | 2-1 |
| **1891/1892** | | | | | | | | | |
| **Middlesbrough Ironopolis** | 16 | 14 | 1 | 1 | 49 | 13 | 29 | -- | -- |
| Middlesbrough | 16 | 13 | 0 | 3 | 33 | 13 | 26 | 1-0 | 2-0 |
| Sheffield United | 16 | 10 | 2 | 4 | 49 | 21 | 22 | 2-1 | 2-2 |
| Newcastle East End | 16 | 9 | 2 | 5 | 37 | 20 | 20 | 3-0 | 1-4 |
| Stockton | 16 | 6 | 2 | 8 | 31 | 34 | 14 | 5-1 | 1-0 |
| Sunderland Albion | 16 | 5 | 0 | 11 | 36 | 38 | 10 | 5-2 | 4-2 |
| South Bank | 16 | 3 | 2 | 11 | 21 | 50 | 8 | 4-1 | 3-0 |
| Newcastle West End | 16 | 4 | 0 | 12 | 21 | 56 | 8 | 6-0 | 5-0 |
| Darlington | 16 | 2 | 3 | 11 | 17 | 49 | 7 | 4-0 | 1-0 |
| **1892/1893** | | | | | | | | | |
| **Middlesbrough Ironopolis** | 10 | 9 | 1 | 0 | 22 | 6 | 19 | -- | -- |
| Newcastle United * | 10 | 5 | 1 | 4 | 30 | 19 | 11 | 3-2 | 2-1 |
| Sheffield United * | 10 | 4 | 2 | 4 | 18 | 16 | 10 | 1-0 | 0-0 |
| Middlesbrough | 10 | 4 | 0 | 6 | 17 | 17 | 8 | 1-0 | 2-0 |
| Stockton | 10 | 3 | 1 | 6 | 24 | 27 | 7 | 3-2 | 2-0 |
| Darlington | 10 | 2 | 1 | 7 | 11 | 37 | 5 | 4-1 | 4-0 |

*(\*Sheffield United also played in the Football League Second Division this season, Newcastle East End changed its name to Newcastle United in December 1892)*

The 1891/92 season saw Ironopolis win 14 of its 16 league fixtures, this time with a three point cushion between itself and its local rivals at the top of the table. There were also victories in the Cleveland Cup (later known as the North Riding Senior Cup, 4-0 v Middlesbrough in the final), and the Cleveland Charity Cup (2-1 v Middlesbrough AFC in the final), as well as the Cleveland Amateur Cup, won by its reserve team which played in the Teeside League (3-1 v Port Clarence in the final). The club once again made it through the qualifying rounds of the FA Cup which included a 7-0 thrashing of Whitby Town and defeats of both Stockton (in a replay), and Darlington (again) before becoming unstuck by six goals to nil at First Division giants Preston North End in what was in effect a replay following a 0-0 draw on a quagmire of a pitch on the scheduled date. The original match was deemed a 'friendly fixture', but not until the final whistle had been blown by the referee.

A report in the *Northern Echo* on 26th August 1892 on the club's AGM indicates that finances were at that stage causing further concern. Unexpected financial losses in several key fixtures alongside the Durham miners' strike had hit income hard and they ended the season with another deficit, of over £379

Cleveland Cup ties had resulted in losses of £110, and the FA Cup run also saw the club a further £50 in arrears. It was also reported that qualifying round opponents Hurworth had been 'paid off' in October, suggesting that it was more financially prudent for Ironopolis NOT to have played the tie against opposition that would not have attracted a good gate (The Washers reserve team defeated Hurworth in a Cleveland Cup tie later in the month).With Middlesbrough AFC also struggling financially an amalgamation of the two clubs was again proposed. On 7th May 1892, officials representing the two clubs met to present a joint application for membership of the Football League. As a result, for just a few weeks, there was just one senior club in town: 'Middlesbrough and Ironopolis AFC'.

Sadly the application failed, as did that of Newcastle East End (both teams receiving just one vote each), while Sheffield United - third in the Northern League that season – were elected with five votes, alongside Burton Swifts, who gained two. There was a suspicion that both Middlesbrough clubs had been poaching players from Football League clubs during the season, an act that led to an agreement that banned this practice between the Football League and Northern Leagues. It has been suggested that the suspicion surrounding the Middlesbrough teams could have led to the poor show of support for the 'merged' club's application.

However, an opportunity was provided to join the new Second Division of the Football League instead. This opportunity was passed on, on account of the additional costs that would result, as well as reduced gates from fewer local derbies. In the event, the two clubs involved chose to go their own ways again rather than continue as a merged club in the Northern League again for the 1892/93 campaign.

The short-lived merger between the two Middlesbrough clubs fell apart over disagreements over which ground would be used, and over the composition of the club committee. Two separate clubs may not have been good for the town of Middlesbrough but it was for the Northern League, which, despite the playing strength of its members, was by now down to six clubs. Sheffield United retained a first team in the league despite also competing in the Football League, while Newcastle East End (which had also turned down the chance to play in the Football League's Second Division) absorbed its cross town rival to create a new unified Newcastle United during the season.

There was no mistaking The Washers' supremacy this time around, with only Sheffield United managing to take a point off the three-time Northern League champions. Although five of the club's nine league victories were by a single-goal margin, the points difference between Ironopolis and Newcastle United was a huge eight points.

The club was given exemption to the first round proper of the FA Cup this season, and victory over non-league Marlow, following a giant-killing defeat of First Division Notts County saw Ironopolis amazingly through to the quarter-final of the competition, with Preston North End again lying in wait, after having only played two ties. A record 14,000 crowd saw the underdogs snatch a 2-2 draw on Saturday 18th February 1893 after having taken the lead in the fifth minute, but sadly the replay a week later ended in a 0-7 defeat in front of a crowd of 8,000 at Preston.

In late September 1892, the club staged a Bazaar at Middlesbrough Town Hall, with proceeds intended to be used for a possible move to a new ground on the Ayresome Grange estate, which would also contain facilities for athletics, cycling and other community sporting uses. However, the event, postponed from an earlier date in March, was not a huge success, as the club's financial position was becoming ever more critical. Despite donations to local charities, totalling £400, the Ironopolis club was struggling to reach the break-even figure of between £60 and £70 per week at the gate. Another loss, of £246, was made on the season, certainly an improvement on the past two seasons but one which plunged the club further into the red. A move to the new ground was no closer to fruition, and in the event, would never happen. There was serious consideration given to reverting to amateur status for the following season but Ironopolis would continue as a professional concern.

The club's penultimate season saw 53 matches played, resulting in 33 wins and 6 draws. The Cleveland Charity Cup was won for the third successive season, with Middlesbrough AFC defeated 2-0 in the final, which was played at Linthorpe Road, although the club lost its grasp on the other two Cleveland Cup competitions it had won twelve months previously. It is interesting to note that cricket and baseball teams bearing the Ironopolis name were also in existence at this time.

The Football League expanded its Second Division by four teams in the summer of 1893, with Newcastle United among those elected. However, when founder members Accrington later chose to compete in the Lancashire League instead of being demoted from the First Division, then a further vacancy was created. Despite its previous reluctance to play in the Football League's second tier twelve months previously, and not without misgivings over club finances, the Ironopolis committee made an immediate application to fill the vacancy, and on 2nd August, at the Football League's management committee meeting at Birmingham, the club was accepted into the competition.

Alongside Ironopolis were the likes of Liverpool, Woolwich Arsenal (now of course without the Woolwich prefix) and Small Heath (now Birmingham City). In fact The Washers' debut in the Football League was at home to Liverpool on 2nd September 1893 in front of a *'large and enthusiastic crowd'*. A 0-2 loss resulted, with the club's first victory coming in its fourth match of the season, a 2-0 revenge victory over Ardwick (now Manchester City), a team that had thrashed them 1-6 two weeks earlier. However, that first victory was watched by a crowd of only 800. The visit of Newcastle United on Christmas Day was attended by only 2,000, due to the inclement weather and it was obvious that life in the Football League with an average attendance of only 1,450 over the season just wasn't viable.

As a Football League club, Ironopolis was exempt from FA Cup qualifying round ties in the 1893/94 season. A First Round tie at home to Luton Town was won 2-1 on Saturday 27th January 1894, before defeat at First Division Nottingham Forest two weeks later.

Among the Ironopolis squad that season were: *G Watts, J Elliott, Philip Bach, Thomas Seymour,*

### Middlesbrough Ironopolis – Complete Record in the 1893/94 Football League Second Division
*(see Rotherham Town section for league table)*

| 1893 | Opponents | Venue | Result | Score |
|---|---|---|---|---|
| Sat Sep 2 | Liverpool | H | L | 0-2 |
| Sat Sep 9 | Ardwick | A | L | 1-6 |
| Mon Sep 18 | Burslem Port Vale | A | L | 0-4 |
| Sat Sep 23 | Ardwick | H | W | 2-0 |
| Sat Sep 30 | Crewe Alexandra | A | L | 0-5 |
| Sat Oct 7 | Liverpool | A | L | 0-6 |
| Sat Oct 21 | Walsall Town Swifts | A | L | 0-1 |
| Sat Oct 28 | Burton Swifts | H | W | 2-1 |
| Sat Nov 4 | Notts County | A | L | 0-3 |
| Sat Nov 11 | Grimsby Town | H | L | 2-6 |
| Sat Nov 25 | Small Heath | H | W | 3-0 |
| Sat Dec 9 | Rotherham Town | H | W | 6-1 |
| Sat Dec 16 | Notts County | H | D | 0-0 |
| Sat Dec 23 | Small Heath | A | L | 1-2 |
| Mon Dec 25 | Newcastle United | H | D | 1-1 |
| Tue Dec 26 | Lincoln City | A | W | 3-2 |
| Sat Dec 30 | Walsall Town Swifts | H | D | 1-1 |
| **1894** | | | | |
| Mon Jan 1 | Burslem Port Vale | H | W | 3-1 |
| Tue Jan 2 | Newcastle United | A | L | 2-7 |
| Sat Jan 6 | Crewe Alexandra | H | W | 2-0 |
| Sat Jan 13 | Lincoln City | H | D | 0-0 |
| Sat Feb 3 | Grimsby Town | A | L | 1-2 |
| Sat Feb 24 | Woolwich Arsenal | H | L | 3-6 |
| Sat Mar 3 | Northwich Victoria | H | W | 2-1 |
| Wed Mar 7 | Burton Swifts | A | L | 0-7 |
| Sat Mar 10 | Woolwich Arsenal | A | L | 0-1 |
| Sat Apr 7 | Northwich Victoria | A | L | 1-2 |
| Sat Apr 14 | Rotherham Town | A | L | 1-4 |

*Robert Chatt, R Nicholson, J Hill, Archibald M Hughes, Thomas McCairns, P Coupar, Wallace McReddie.*

The club finished 11th out of 15 clubs, recording impressive wins in succession at home to Small Heath, 3-0, and Rotherham Town, 6-1, but the club's financial position was by now beyond repair, as gate receipts did not cover the cost of players' wages and the costs of travelling to fixtures outside the North-East of the country. As early as December 1893 there were doubts as to whether the club could complete the season. In February 1894 all the professional players were served notice of the plans to liquidate the team, with the club's final game a 1-1 draw against South Bank on 30th April 1894. Ironopolis resigned from the Football League the following month and was wound up. When the Paradise Ground was repossessed by the landlord at the end of the season, this resulted in the Ironopolis cricket and baseball teams also having to find a new location for home fixtures. Ironically, both were accommodated by Middlesbrough AFC at Linthorpe Road.

Middlesbrough AFC had reverted to amateur status for the 1893/94 season, and this ploy in effect saved the club from going the same way as Ironopolis. Six years later having turned professional again after having improved its fortunes, winning the FA Amateur Cup in 1895 and 1898, the club was itself elected to the Football League.

As a postscript, having entered the FA Cup for the 1894/95 season, the defunct Ironopolis was drawn away at Mickley in the Preliminary round of the competition, giving its opponents a bye into the first qualifying round.

The Paradise ground disappeared soon after the demise of Ironopolis, but a good deal of the site was later covered by the new Ayresome Park stadium that was finally opened by Middlesbrough AFC in 1903 following their relocation from Linthorpe Road, itself located near the junction of Gresham Road and Portman Street.

The Ironopolis kit was, in 1889/90, maroon and bright green halves, with a possible alternative kit being a dark blue with a white sash. In January 1891, *No-Side* wrote in the *Northern Echo* that prior to a match with Cambuslang, '*Alderman R Weighill, a well-known owner of racehorses, and proprietor of the Cleveland Bay Inn and Oxford Music Hall, presented the team with jerseys of his racing colours (cherry with white stripes)*'. The club's old maroon and green tops were retained as an alternative. In February 1893 cherry red shirts with a white sash were also adopted by the club.

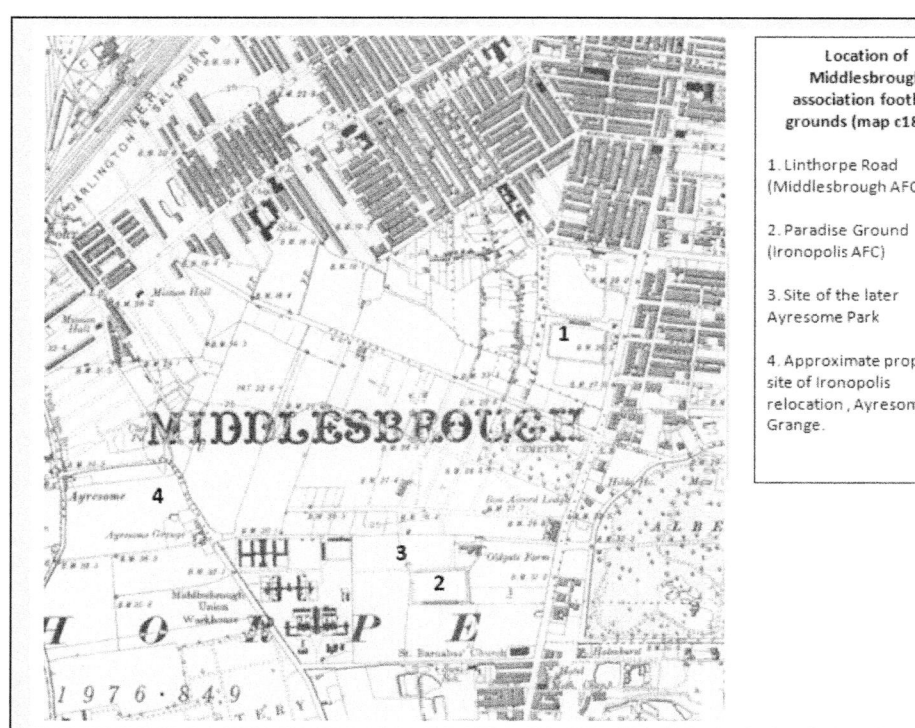

# Rotherham Town
# 1877-96
*'Football by moonlight'*

Anyone researching the origins of the current Rotherham United (and there have been a few outstanding historians in that field) will have come across a myriad of linked clubs. In particular, the names of Rotherham Town and Rotherham County are prominent, both names having appeared in the Football League before the birth of the United club. However, the original Rotherham Town that existed in the late nineteenth century can arguably be considered a separate club, as it was a re-formed Rotherham Town that went on to become one half of the current Rotherham United.

A Rotherham Football Club first came into being in 1870 playing at the Clifton Lane cricket field but this group, which was founded by the local cricket club itself, was defunct by 1877. It is known to have moved to a field opposite Eastwood House on Doncaster Road for home games, a ground that continued to be used for association football in future years.

The original Rotherham Town club was founded as Lunar Rovers, its name deriving from the fact that in its early days the club often played under moonlight, due to fact that it had been formed by a group of shopkeepers, and, as they did not have afternoons off were forced to play their games much later in the day than usual. Many sources state 1878 as the founding date of Lunar Rovers (as match reports in the local press first appeared at this time), although Martin Westby, in *A History of Sheffield Football*, has traced the club back to 1875 when it is possible that the club was playing its moonlit fixtures on an informal basis.

In an era when the registration of players was not necessary, Lunar players would also turn out for other local clubs, such as the Rotherham Wesleyans. The club joined the Sheffield New Association (later the Hallamshire FA) in 1879, and a second team was also up and running by 1880. There was no shortage of opponents for the Lunar teams, with the Sheffield district of course an early hotbed of association football.

The club's early years were spent on the Middle Lane / Clifton Grove area, before a short move to the same Doncaster Road / Middle Lane ground, opposite Eastwood House, that the original Rotherham club had used. A move to the Clifton Lane cricket ground followed soon after that, with the Lunar club building up a reputation as a tough team to beat, although a 2-6 loss to Thornhill at the end of January 1890 was significant in that both teams would later, in different guises, play in the Football League.

Match reports featuring the club dried up at the end of 1880, suggesting that club had become dormant, but what is known is the fact that Lunar Rovers had morphed into 'Rotherham' by the start of the

1881/82 season, with the eventual Sir Charles Stoddart becoming club president, and Walter Musson taking over as club captain. Match reports were again regularly featured in the local press from then on.

The marriage with the cricket club at Clifton Lane was not always a happy one, with the footballers making temporary moves to Cocker's Field, Sherwood Crescent (off Wellgate) where there was a pronounced slope and then the West End ground near Ickles. Neither venue offered the benefits of the cricket ground – a suitable playing surface and good accessibility – so the footballers returned there. The permanency of their latest stay here was underlined with the building of a new stand at Clifton Lane, which could accommodate up to 500 spectators.

By 1887 the club had added the 'Town' suffix to its title, underlining the fact that it was by now considered the most senior team in the town. The strength of the team was evident when, in 1887/88, it reached the Wharncliffe Charity Cup final, at the time one of the region's most prestigious knock-out competitions. Town lost 0-2 to The Wednesday in the final, on a pitch that had to be cleared of snow beforehand.

The 1888/89 season saw Rotherham Town win its first piece of silverware. Despite losing 0-1 to Staveley in the Wharncliffe Charity Cup final at Olive Grove, then the home of The Wednesday, Town defeated the same club 2-1 to win the Sheffield & Hallamshire Challenge Cup at Bramall Lane at the end of March 1889. Wednesday had won the cup for the previous six years, but had chosen not to enter that season. Rotherham Town also hosted Preston North End that season, 4,000 spectators seeing the Football League champions win 3-1.

The Sheffield & Hallamshire Cup was retained the following season when Sheffield United were defeated 1-0 at Clifton Lane, following a goal-less draw at Bramall Lane.

**Rotherham Town in the FA Cup**

The club was keen to establish itself beyond local competition, so entry was made to the English FA Cup competition for the first time in the 1883/84 season, defeating Chesterfield Spital in the First Round, before defeat at Lockwood Brothers FC, a club that would make a name for itself in this competition. The 1884/85 season saw the Rotherham club drawn at home against Nottingham Forest. However, Town were to receive £17 10s (plus dinner at the Maypole Hotel in Nottingham) to switch their second round tie to the ground of their opponents. Forest won the tie 5-0. The following season Notts County paid the club £30 to switch grounds before defeating them 15-0 in the first round. Those results apart, there were other high scoring FA Cup results in Town's favour through the years, with Doncaster thrashed 9-1 in 1888 and again 7-0 in 1895, the latter a welcome result in an otherwise horrendous season.

The 1889/90 season saw a promising run to the Fourth Qualifying Round of the competition, which was becoming increasingly popular in terms of media attention, crowd numbers, and the number of clubs entering. Doncaster were defeated (only 2-1 this time) before an 8-1 defeat of Redcar, and then local rivals Rotherham Swifts, who took Town to replay before succumbing 2-1. Sheffield United were then taken to a replay by Town before themselves winning by the same score.

Long Eaton Rangers defeated Rotherham Town 2-1 at the same stage in the 1890/91 competition, although Town had defeated Sheffield FC 13-0 in a previous round. The Fourth Qualifying Round was reached again in 1895/96 when, after wins over Barnsley St Peter's (7-3 away from home, in a replay), Doncaster Rovers, and then Gainsborough Trinity, 2-0, the run was ended at Grimsby Town

***

In 1889 the club became a founder member of the Midland League. Its first fixture in the competition was on 14th September 1889, and resulted in a 3-1 home victory against Sheffield.

The final game played at Clifton Lane was a single-goal victory over Burnley on 18th April 1891, the club making a further ground move – stands and all - to Clifton Grove, which was in a residential area just off Middle Lane, and opposite what is now Gladys Street. This could well have been the same field that the club used in its formative years. The move was necessitated through problems with the renewal of its tenancy, not least an inability to arrange home fixtures in September due to cricket, and to a loss of key fixture dates brought on by the ground owners The Racing Company wanting to use the area for parking for the nearby racecourse. The club had reduced its overall debt from £247 in January 1891 to just £64 by the end of the season but it was hoped that the ground move would enable the club to be in a much stronger financial position.

Ironically, the first fixture to be played at Clifton Grove on Saturday 5th September 1891 was a match between a Hallamshire League team by the name of Rotherham United and Ecclesfield, which was won 3-1 by the former. Rotherham United was, in fact, the Town reserve team that played in a competition that contained Sheffield Strollers (United's second team) and Wednesday Wanderers (also of course a second team). The United team moved to the Sheffield & District League the following season.

The ground had not yet been fully completed, with one of the stands still lacking its roof. However, 3,000 spectators witnessed the first competitive match on the new ground for Town's first team, a 2-2 draw with Grantham Rovers on Saturday 26th September. Although gates were not usually this high, a massive 4,000 were in the ground to see Wednesbury Old Athletic defeated 4-1 in the last match of the season, a result that brought with it a first league title for the club.

A profit of £158 was made on the 1891/92 season, and a number of ground improvements included a cycle track around the ground.

Rotherham Town were champions of the Midland League again the following season, 1892/93, this time with a seven point advantage over its closest challengers, Burton Wanderers. Liverpool FC played its first ever fixture against the club on 1st September 1892 in a friendly game. Liverpool won 7-1, but the first ever opponent to score at

### Rotherham Town in the Midland League

| 1889/1890 | P | W | D | L | F | A | Pts |
|---|---|---|---|---|---|---|---|
| Lincoln City | 20 | 16 | 2 | 2 | 75 | 19 | 34 |
| Derby Midland | 19 | 11 | 3 | 5 | 41 | 30 | 25 |
| **Rotherham Town** | 20 | 11 | 3 | 6 | 44 | 27 | 25 |
| Burton Wanderers | 20 | 11 | 3 | 6 | 42 | 40 | 25 |
| Staveley | 20 | 9 | 4 | 7 | 46 | 28 | 22 |
| Warwick County | 20 | 9 | 4 | 7 | 36 | 28 | 22 |
| Gainsborough Trin | 19 | 8 | 5 | 6 | 47 | 32 | 21 |
| Derby Junction | 18 | 7 | 2 | 9 | 32 | 49 | 16 |
| Leek | 20 | 3 | 2 | 15 | 26 | 64 | 8 |
| Notts Rangers | 15 | 1 | 4 | 10 | 11 | 36 | 6 |
| Sheffield | 19 | 2 | 2 | 15 | 19 | 66 | 6 |

| 1890/1891 | | | | | | | |
|---|---|---|---|---|---|---|---|
| Gainsborough Trin | 18 | 10 | 4 | 4 | 58 | 21 | 24 |
| Long Eaton Rgrs | 18 | 10 | 2 | 6 | 50 | 33 | 22 |
| Lincoln City | 18 | 7 | 6 | 5 | 34 | 21 | 20 |
| Derby Midland | 18 | 8 | 4 | 6 | 28 | 28 | 20 |
| Sheffield United | 18 | 8 | 3 | 7 | 32 | 25 | 19 |
| Burton Wanderers | 18 | 7 | 4 | 7 | 25 | 33 | 18 |
| **Rotherham Town** | 18 | 7 | 4 | 7 | 20 | 28 | 18 |
| Burslem Port Vale | 18 | 7 | 2 | 9 | 35 | 43 | 16 |
| Derby Junction | 18 | 5 | 5 | 8 | 18 | 30 | 15 |
| Staveley | 18 | 2 | 4 | 12 | 19 | 57 | 8 |

*Kidderminster withdrew during the season*
*Warwick County expelled for failing to fulfil fixtures*

| 1891/1892 | | | | | | | |
|---|---|---|---|---|---|---|---|
| **Rotherham Town** | 20 | 13 | 1 | 6 | 70 | 41 | 27 |
| Gainsborough Trin | 20 | 12 | 2 | 6 | 49 | 31 | 26 |
| Burslem Port Vale | 20 | 11 | 1 | 8 | 49 | 33 | 23 |
| Wednesbury O Ath | 20 | 9 | 5 | 6 | 49 | 41 | 23 |
| Burton Wanderers | 20 | 10 | 2 | 8 | 48 | 32 | 22 |
| Doncaster Rovers | 20 | 8 | 5 | 7 | 30 | 36 | 21 |
| Grantham Rovers | 20 | 6 | 6 | 8 | 29 | 37 | 18 |
| Loughborough Tn | 20 | 8 | 1 | 11 | 42 | 46 | 17 |
| Long Eaton Rgrs | 20 | 5 | 7 | 8 | 32 | 46 | 17 |
| Derby Junction | 20 | 4 | 5 | 11 | 21 | 41 | 13 |
| Leicester Fosse | 20 | 5 | 3 | 12 | 21 | 56 | 13 |

*Staveley withdrew during the season*

| 1892/1893 | | | | | | | |
|---|---|---|---|---|---|---|---|
| **Rotherham Town** | 24 | 19 | 3 | 2 | 80 | 28 | 41 |
| Burton Wanderers | 24 | 15 | 4 | 5 | 49 | 33 | 34 |
| Loughborough Tn | 24 | 15 | 3 | 6 | 64 | 30 | 33 |
| Leicester Fosse | 24 | 12 | 3 | 9 | 50 | 37 | 27 |
| Doncaster Rovers | 24 | 11 | 4 | 9 | 47 | 44 | 26 |
| Gainsborough Trin | 24 | 12 | 1 | 11 | 51 | 34 | 25 |
| Kettering | 24 | 11 | 3 | 10 | 48 | 41 | 25 |
| Grantham Rovers | 24 | 10 | 2 | 12 | 46 | 43 | 22 |
| Wednesbury O Ath | 24 | 8 | 3 | 13 | 41 | 51 | 19 |
| Long Eaton Rgrs | 24 | 6 | 6 | 12 | 34 | 53 | 18 |
| Mansfield Town | 24 | 7 | 2 | 15 | 26 | 70 | 16 |
| Newark | 24 | 6 | 3 | 15 | 34 | 62 | 15 |
| Derby Junction | 24 | 3 | 5 | 16 | 32 | 76 | 11 |

## Rotherham Town in the Second Division of the Football League

| 1893/94 | P | W | D | L | F | A | Pts |
|---|---|---|---|---|---|---|---|
| Liverpool | 28 | 22 | 6 | 0 | 77 | 18 | 50 |
| Small Heath | 28 | 21 | 0 | 7 | 103 | 44 | 42 |
| Notts County | 28 | 18 | 3 | 7 | 70 | 31 | 39 |
| Newcastle United | 28 | 15 | 6 | 7 | 66 | 39 | 36 |
| Grimsby Town | 28 | 15 | 2 | 11 | 71 | 38 | 32 |
| Burton Swifts | 28 | 14 | 3 | 11 | 79 | 61 | 31 |
| Burslem Port Vale | 28 | 13 | 4 | 11 | 66 | 64 | 30 |
| Lincoln City | 28 | 11 | 6 | 11 | 59 | 58 | 28 |
| Woolwich Arsenal | 28 | 12 | 4 | 12 | 52 | 55 | 28 |
| Walsall Tn Swifts | 28 | 10 | 3 | 15 | 51 | 61 | 23 |
| Middlesbro'Ironop | 28 | 8 | 4 | 16 | 37 | 72 | 20 |
| Crewe Alexandra | 28 | 6 | 7 | 15 | 42 | 73 | 19 |
| Ardwick | 28 | 8 | 2 | 18 | 47 | 71 | 18 |
| **Rotherham Town** | 28 | 6 | 3 | 19 | 44 | 91 | 15 |
| Northwich Victoria | 28 | 3 | 3 | 22 | 30 | 98 | 9 |
| **1894/95** | | | | | | | |
| Bury | 30 | 23 | 2 | 5 | 78 | 33 | 48 |
| Notts County | 30 | 17 | 5 | 8 | 75 | 45 | 39 |
| Newton Heath | 30 | 15 | 8 | 7 | 78 | 44 | 38 |
| Leicester Fosse | 30 | 15 | 8 | 7 | 72 | 53 | 38 |
| Grimsby Town | 30 | 18 | 1 | 11 | 79 | 52 | 37 |
| Darwen | 30 | 16 | 4 | 10 | 74 | 43 | 36 |
| Burton Wanderers | 30 | 14 | 7 | 9 | 67 | 39 | 35 |
| Woolwich Arsenal | 30 | 14 | 6 | 10 | 75 | 58 | 34 |
| Manchester City | 30 | 14 | 3 | 13 | 82 | 72 | 31 |
| Newcastle United | 30 | 12 | 3 | 15 | 72 | 84 | 27 |
| Burton Swifts | 30 | 11 | 3 | 16 | 52 | 74 | 25 |
| **Rotherham Town** | 30 | 11 | 2 | 17 | 55 | 62 | 24 |
| Lincoln City | 30 | 10 | 0 | 20 | 52 | 92 | 20 |
| Walsall Tn Swifts | 30 | 10 | 0 | 20 | 47 | 92 | 20 |
| Burslem Port Vale | 30 | 7 | 4 | 19 | 39 | 77 | 18 |
| Crewe Alexandra | 30 | 3 | 4 | 23 | 26 | 103 | 10 |
| **1895/96** | | | | | | | |
| Liverpool | 30 | 22 | 2 | 6 | 106 | 32 | 46 |
| Manchester City | 30 | 21 | 4 | 5 | 63 | 38 | 46 |
| Grimsby Town | 30 | 20 | 2 | 8 | 82 | 38 | 42 |
| Burton Wanderers | 30 | 19 | 4 | 7 | 69 | 40 | 42 |
| Newcastle United | 30 | 16 | 2 | 12 | 73 | 50 | 34 |
| Newton Heath | 30 | 15 | 3 | 12 | 66 | 57 | 33 |
| Woolwich Arsenal | 30 | 14 | 4 | 12 | 58 | 42 | 32 |
| Leicester Fosse | 30 | 14 | 4 | 12 | 57 | 44 | 32 |
| Darwen | 30 | 12 | 6 | 12 | 72 | 67 | 30 |
| Notts County | 30 | 12 | 2 | 16 | 57 | 54 | 26 |
| Burton Swifts | 30 | 10 | 4 | 16 | 39 | 69 | 24 |
| Loughborough Tn | 30 | 9 | 5 | 16 | 40 | 66 | 23 |
| Lincoln City | 30 | 9 | 4 | 17 | 53 | 75 | 22 |
| Burslem Port Vale | 30 | 7 | 4 | 19 | 43 | 78 | 18 |
| **Rotherham Town** | 30 | 7 | 3 | 20 | 34 | 97 | 17 |
| Crewe Alexandra | 30 | 5 | 3 | 22 | 30 | 95 | 13 |

Anfield was Rotherham striker Charlie Leatherbarrow. The title was secured despite attendances having been affected by the Midland League's insistence on a 'fourpenny' gate (which was considered an excessive amount for many working class football fans), although there were an estimated 6,000 at Clifton Grove to see the title secured with a 3-1 victory over Loughborough Town.

Rotherham Town was subsequently elected to an expanded Second Division of the Football League in 1893. However, the club's League tenure – and indeed its future existence - lasted just three seasons.

The first home fixture in the Football League was on Saturday 9th September 1893, resulting in a narrow 4-3 victory over Grimsby Town. The fixture was in doubt right up until kick-off due to a cholera epidemic in Grimsby, and there were attempts by local magistrates to have the fixture cancelled amid worries that the special train from Grimsby might bring the disease to Rotherham. The team endured poor season both on and off the field, and finished 14th of 15 teams at the end of the season. It was disappointing however, when the club was not re-elected at the Football League AGM, with Ardwick (20 votes) Leicester Fosse (20), Bury and Burton Wanderers (both 17) elected in their place. Rotherham just missed out, with 15 votes, well ahead of Blackpool (8), Loughborough (8), Accrington (7), and Rossendale, the latter of which received no votes. Fortunately for the Rotherham club, Middlesbrough Ironopolis resigned its membership of the league on 11th June and Town was accepted back into the competition.

Finances had again been of concern that season, with total match-day receipts only one half of what they had been the previous season, attendances affected by the miners strike in the region. The lack of playing strength was attributable to the fact that players' wages had also been halved.

The 1894/95 season was an improvement, with the club not having to apply for re-election, finishing 12th of the 16 teams in the Second Division, but this was only temporary respite as the following campaign was the club's last.

At the end of the 1895/96 season Rotherham Town did not even apply for re-election after having finished 15th and second-bottom of the league, and the club subsequently folded. It is unlikely that the club would have been re-elected anyway, given its financial problems, and an inability to raise a full team for several of its league fixtures in the final weeks of the season. Had it not been for some modicum of success in the qualifying rounds of the FA Cup then the club might not have seen out the season.

On the field, only a single point was picked up away from home, and the team suffered a 2-10 thrashing at Darwen in January 1896 and a 1-10 rout at Liverpool the following month. The latter fixture saw Town only able to raise 10 players for the match, a situation repeated in its following match away at Grimsby Town and its final two Football League fixtures in April at Leicester Fosse (a 0-8 defeat) and Loughborough. The home fixture with Loughborough on March 14th had seen only nine Rotherham men take the field – somehow winning 4-0. The same nine men managed to hold Lincoln City to a 2-2 draw just two days later in the club's final home match, watched by a crowd that numbered just 300, around one third of those hailing from Lincoln.

*Arthur Wharton*

Despite an appeal for subscriptions to keep the club afloat a benefit performance at the Theatre Royal, a Grand Ball and a special benefit match, the Town club only just managed to complete its fixtures. The club had taken just £550 at the gate during the season, yet with wages alone accounting for £470, then a loss of £77 was made during its final season. Most of those players that were left at the club dispersed among other Football League teams. Edlington man, Arthur Wharton, widely regarded as the first ever black professional footballer, played in goal for the club from 1889 to 1894 (19 appearances) and then 1895/96 (14 appearances) after a season at Sheffield United. He moved to Stalybridge Rovers, and later Stockport County. On a few occasions, Wharton played on the wing! From 1891 he was also landlord of the town's Albert Tavern.

The *Sheffield Daily Telegraph* was clear about who it considered responsible for the club's demise, *'Rotherham people have only themselves to thank for the present unhappy state of affairs. Had they offered even a moderate amount of support the present crisis would not have come; it is their lukewarmness which is to blame.'*

A final meeting of shareholders of the Rotherham Town Football and Athletic Company Limited was held on Tuesday 11th August 1896, at the town's Ship Inn. Only seven persons directly associated with the company showed up, well short of its quorum of 20, highlighting the apathy now being shown towards the club.

On Wednesday 4th November 1896 auctioneer W H Sheldon sold all the Clifton Grove stands, hoardings and other fixtures belonging to the defunct club on behalf of the executors of the estate of the late R J Bentley, the ground landlords, who were owed rent. At the time, it was expected that the land would be laid out in building plots, but luckily this never came to pass.

The second, re-formed Rotherham Town had its source in 1899 when Rotherham Casuals and Rotherham Grammar School combined to form Rotherham Club FC, turning semi-professional, and moving to Clifton Lane. On becoming a limited company in 1904 a new name of Rotherham Athletic (reflecting the fact it was now part of the Rotherham Athletic Company Limited) was adopted, and a year later it changed name again, to Rotherham Town. In 1903 the new club joined the Midland League, where it remained until 1925, until a merger with Third Division North neighbours Rotherham County to form Rotherham United.

The club had won the Sheffield Association League in the 1902/03 season, ahead of Thornhill United – which itself renamed itself Rotherham County in 1905. As a result, both clubs were elected to the Midland League the same season.

The Thornhill United club had been founded in 1877, as Thornhill FC. Its first recorded fixtures taking place in October 1877 and its home ground was a basic field on Greasbrough Road, which remained in use until a move to the Red House Ground in 1882. This enclosure was situated close to the junction of Henley Grove Road and Park Street, with the adjacent Red House Inn used as dressing rooms. Gerry Somerton, in *Still United* describes the old centre spot as being roughly where the current roundabout is located where Henley Rise meets the ring road dual carriageway. The ground was said to have been very cramped, reported in local circles as being '*devoid of natural or artistic beauty,*' with the ball continually having to be recovered from the back yards of the adjacent houses. In 1907 a further move was made to Millmoor, described at the time as '*a grass plot of not much practical utility*'.

Thornhill joined the Midland League in 1903, and stayed in that competition until it was abandoned for World War I. The club won the Midland League title for four consecutive seasons, from 1911-15. After the War, it was elected to the Football League when the league expanded from 40 clubs to 44 in 1919. In 1925 the merger with local rivals Rotherham Town resulted in the present day Rotherham United.

*Rotherham Town, 1910*

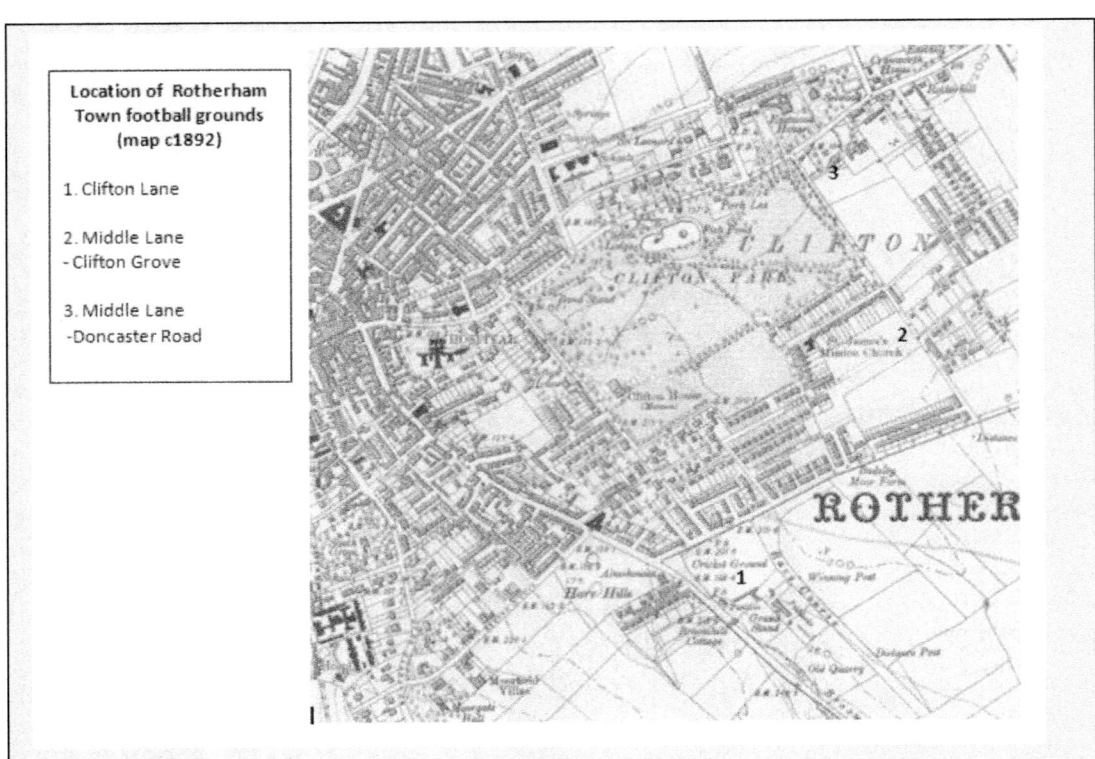

# Scarborough
# 1879-2007
*'The seasiders'*

Of all the clubs featured here, Scarborough FC was not only the longest surviving, but also the most recent to go to the wall. The club's demise will still be in many people's memory, as will the goal that sent the club out of the Football League back in 1999. Despite surviving several financial crises through the years, its luck finally ran out in 2007.

Scarborough Football Club was founded in February 1879 by members of the local cricket club, based at North Marine Road, who wished to play a sport during the winter months. Lord Londesborough was a pivotal figure in getting the club off the ground (he also donated the Scarborough and East Riding Challenge Cup to the Scarborough FA in 1882) and it was he who helped organise the first inter-club matches, which were played under rugby rules. The first of these was at home to Hull on Saturday 1st March when opponents Hull turned up with only eleven players due to that club also having another engagement on the same day. The lack of numbers did not stop the visitors from winning the match, however.

Bridlington provided the opposition for the club's first association football match, played on Thursday 6th November 1880 at the Cricket Ground, with Scarborough winning 2-1 after trailing at half time. The first ever Scarborough XI was:- *Wheater, Bolland, Baynes, Land, Frank, Dixon, Cresser, Calvert, Jackson, Newton, and the captain, W Sanderson.* Sanderson was a master at the town's Oliver's Mount School, early pioneers of football in the region. The Football Club continued to play both rugby and association codes for the time being, although it was the latter that quickly became the favourite.

The Scarborough & District Football Association was founded in 1882, with Sanderson himself becoming its first chairman. With league competition still a few years away, the only opportunity to win silverware was in cup competition, and therefore during the early half of the 1880s the side played in the Scarborough & East Riding County Cup competition, which was organised by the Scarborough FA.

The club won its first trophy in the 1885/86 season, when it 'defeated' the holders, Hull, in the County Cup final. The initial final, played in Hull, ended 4-4, but Hull refused to attend the replay, scheduled for 17th April 1886, which was switched to the Oliver's Mount ground on Oriel Crescent, at the last minute after the Castle Hill ground in Scarborough was commandeered by the army for military training (the cricket ground was unavailable that day). Therefore Scarborough was awarded the cup by default. At Christmas 1885, the club had formally changed its name to Scarborough Cricketers FC in order to reinforce its links with its hosts. The following season Whitby defeated the club 3-2 in the final of the same cup competition.

*Possibly the first photograph taken of Scarborough FC, 1885*

By the summer of 1887, the club had reverted to the name Scarborough FC again, having moved to its own ground, known as the Recreation Ground, which was adjacent to the cricket field. During its stay there, the ground was regularly criticized by opposing teams for being too small, being enclosed inside an existing cycle track.

The 1887/88 season ended in success. On Saturday 31st March, a crowd of 5,000 at the North Marine Road cricket ground saw Scarborough avenge its County Cup final defeat the previous season, thrashing its fierce rivals Whitby 6–1 in the final.

*Yorkshire Post*, 2nd April 1888

SCARBOROUGH V. WHITBY, *Played in the Scarborough Cricket Field, in the presence a very large number of spectators. The respective teams have frequently met, Whitby in every instance proving victorious, and consequently the present struggle was productive of the greatest among the lovers of the game. Whitby kicked off against the wind, and soon afterwards Scarborough was attacking their goal vigorously, and succeeded in scoring two goals. Whitby by an inadvertence of the home goal keeper dribbled one through the posts, and then Scarborough followed by four goals more in quick succession before half time, the game then being Scarborough six goals to their opponents one. On the resumption of play Scarborough acted almost strictly on the defensive, and succeeded in preventing their opponents scoring again. When time was called Scarborough had won six goals to Whitby's one. Lady Ida Sitwell subsequently presented the silver bowl to the winners.*

The County Cup was won again in 1888/89, with Whitby again defeated in the final on Saturday 30th April on the ground of the Kirkbymoorside club. 2,000 spectators saw Scarborough win the match 4-0.

However, the intense rivalry culminated in a riot during a fixture between the teams at Scarborough on Friday 10th January 1890 game after a disagreement about over a goal. Whitby players were attacked on the pitch by Scarborough fans, one of whom was nineteen-year-old Albert Drabble. He died the following month of a heart attack, and although there were tenuous links between the incidents, his death cast a large shadow over fixtures between the clubs.

The County Cup was recaptured on Saturday 28th March 1891 when Kirkbymoorside were defeated 3-0 at the Recreation Ground. The same opponents were defeated 2-1 in the final the following season, with Duncombe Park beaten 3-0 at the Recreation Ground in the 1892/93 final. The next Scarborough win in the final of the competition was a 4-1 victory over Hull, at Malton, at the conclusion of the 1896/97 season.

Scarborough's reserve team was also successful during this period, winning the Scarborough Junior Bowl three times in succession between 1891-93. The second team were

*Scarborough FC Baines Shield*

founder members of the Scarborough & District League in the 1892/93 season, but the competition was declared null and void after half of the twelve clubs involved either dropped out or were expelled.

Scarborough became one of nine founding members of the Cleveland Amateur League in the 1893/94 season, but the club was expelled soon after Christmas for having failed to fulfil its fixtures. The Scarborough committee had already bemoaned the fact that beaten visitors to the Recreation Ground would complain to the league in order to get the result overturned due to the size of the playing area.

The club withdrew from the Scarborough and East Riding FA at the end of the 1897/98. Scarborough had been suspended twice during the season, once following fighting on the pitch between players from Grimsby All Saints and its own players, and then for refusing to play a re-played County Cup final against Leeds on a date suggested by the organisers as another fixture had been scheduled for that date. This was huge loss at the time for the Scarborough & East Riding FA, but to the advantage of the Cleveland FA, with which the club affiliated. The club continued to take part in the local Scarborough Hospital Charity Cup however, a trophy it would win with regularity.

After patching things up, Scarborough did return to the County FA in the 1900/01 season, and promptly won the County Cup for a seventh time, defeating local rivals Scarborough Peasholme 3-1 in a replayed final at Seamer Road on Wednesday 27th March 1901.

In the 1898/99 season Scarborough took a huge step up in status by joining the Northern League, this following two unsuccessful previous applications to join this prestigious competition. This was without doubt the strongest amateur competition in the north of England featuring the likes of Bishop Auckland, and the reserve teams of Newcastle United, Sunderland and Middlesbrough. The club played in the league's second tier for its first two seasons, until the league reverted to a single division.

Scarborough played in the Northern League in two spells, 1898-1910 & 1914-26 (albeit with a war enforced break), twenty seasons in total, and not once did the club finish in the top half of the table. Four of those seasons saw Scarborough at the bottom of the table, with nine further placings in the bottom three, this despite the goalscoring exploits of Ocky Johnson, who scored at least 245 goals for the club. Ironically, the club's first match in their new league, on Saturday 10th September 1898 had resulted in a fine 4-0 home win over West Hartlepool, but results such as this proved the exception in an unsuccessful period for the club.

1898 was also significant in that Scarborough made its final ground move, to a new site on Seamer Road. With the Recreation Ground sold for building purposes, the new owners allowed the club to play there for free while its new ground was being built. The first game played at the new Athletic Ground, on Saturday 22nd October 1898, was a 1-1 draw with Loftus in a Cleveland Senior Cup tie.

A disagreement over the headquarters of the club saw the club torn in two in the summer of 1899, with half of the players and staff staying with the club, which had relocated from the County Hotel to the Albermarle Temperance Hotel. Those that broke away formed a new club, Scarborough Utopians FC, which would play, with a good deal of success, in the Beckett League and local cup ties until its demise in the summer of 1903.

The first of 19 wins in the North Riding Senior Cup was achieved on 10th April 1910, when Grangetown were defeated 2-0 in front of 2,000 spectators at York.

Scarborough resigned from the Northern League in the summer of 1910 in order to become a member of the Yorkshire Combination, finishing runner-up in its first season to the dominant Bradford City reserves. The general feeling at the club was that travelling costs would be reduced in the new league, and that Yorkshire opposition might increase takings at the gate. In its four seasons in this competition,

Scarborough did not finish outside the top half of the table, reflecting a slightly lower standard of football.

However, the Combination itself folded in 1914, necessitating Scarborough's move back to the Northern League, where it struggled on until 1926, despite Ocky Johnson's continued presence in the team.

Scarborough sat out World War One, but in 1919 was able to purchase its ground from Scarborough Corporation following the expiry of its 14 year lease. Unfortunately this did not guarantee improvement on the field, and a record 1-16 loss at South Bank on Saturday 15th November 1919 illustrated the fact that the club had a long way to go before it could reach its potential. An embarrassing FA Amateur Cup defeat to Scarborough League side Whitby Whitehall Swifts on Saturday 28th October 1922 showed that turning around its fortunes was not going to be an easy task.

1926 proved to be a major turning point for the club, when it adopted professionalism, which necessitated another move from the strictly amateur Northern League. Entry was made to the Yorkshire League, which had been formed in 1920 as a professional competition, alongside its neighbours Scarborough Penguins *(see later chapter on this club)*.

The club's first ever professional match at Bridlington Town was won 3-1, but the season was not a success, with the final table showing the club in tenth place in a 16 team division, and trailing its town rivals, who finished in fifth place. A loss of £167 was made on the season, despite good support at the gates, a significant part of this loss being the payment of wages to players. However, with greater resources and a much higher support, the club's potential was still much higher than that of the less established Penguins club.

The clubs in the Midland League, a step higher than the Yorkshire League, recognised this potential and were happy to accept Scarborough's application to join that competition in the summer of 1927. Despite having the burden of having to rebuild the main stand at the Athletic Ground, which had been burned down on the morning of 22nd May 1927 (children playing with matches was the cause, but luckily the stand was insured), the club finished runner-up to Gainsborough Trinity in its debut season in the league. This was a huge improvement on previous seasons, reflecting the strength of the new playing squad, led by Harry Lovatt who scored 42 goals in league and cup fixtures.

Local rivals Scarborough Penguins merged with Scarborough at the end of 1928, becoming Scarborough's reserve team in the process and retaining its place in the Yorkshire League. Also significant, in 1929, was the fact that the fifty year old Scarborough club became a limited liability company.

Despite losing Lovatt to First Division Leicester City and player-coach James McGraham to Boston United in the summer of 1928, the following season proved the club's most successful to date. Under the tutelage of trainer Arthur Price, and with Billy Clayson leading the way, Scarborough were crowned champions of the Midland League at the end of the 1929/30 season. The team scored a massive total of 143 goals in its 50 league matches, finishing six points clear of Barnsley reserves in a massive 26 team league.

The title came at a cost however, with the running costs of the club now at an unsustainable level. Despite various donations, fund-raising and cost cutting exercises, the entire championship winning squad was made available for transfer, with many of them going on to play with Football League sides. Additionally, Scarborough council stepped in to help the club, repurchasing the Athletic Ground back from the club for a sum of £3,000.

Only five years after having been champions, the Seasiders finished at the foot of the Midland League, having won just two if its 30 league fixtures in the 1934/35 season. The cash strapped club had continued to survive by selling its better players to Football League clubs but had itself made a surprise bid to join the Football League in the summer of 1933. Despite being the only club to apply for membership that season, the club polled only four votes at the league AGM, well short of the 47 awarded to Darlington and New Brighton, both of which were applying for re-election.

By the time World War Two had broken out, the club had improved its fortunes considerably, with a third place finish in the league at the end of the 1937/38 season behind Shrewsbury Town and Grantham.

Unfortunately Scarborough was unable to take part in the first post-war Midland League season because the Athletic Ground had been requisitioned for military training during the war, and as a result the playing surface was in poor condition. The club did return to the competition for the 1946/47 season, however. In the mean-time, a squad of local players was entered into the Scarborough & District League for the 1945/46 season, with the league title duly won.

Scarborough almost dropped out of the Midland League due to another financial crisis during the 1950/51 season. However a prestige friendly match against Hull City - one of several such matches during the years, played in order to boost the club's funds - was organised to help the club, with famous players such as Don Revie and Raich Carter turning out for Hull, who won 2-0.

Despite the poor financial situation at the club during the 1950s, the club did enjoy having the likes of Peter Cook and Alan Parkinson in its team during that time, both being consistent goal-scorers who helped keep the club stay off the bottom of the table. Despite a sixth place finish at the end of the 1951/52 season, the following five seasons saw the club struggling badly at the wrong end of the table, before a massively improved 1957/58 season, which saw the club finish seventh.

Ironically, it was the Midland League's turn to find itself in trouble following an exodus of its Football League reserve teams, who had moved to the new North Regional League and Football Combination competitions at the end of the 1957/58 season, as well as four others joining the Southern League. With the North Eastern League folding due to the same problem, its eight remaining clubs joined the Midland League, giving the competition a very different look.

Scarborough FC was able to buy back the Athletic Ground from Scarborough Corporation in 1960. This was due in no small part to the club's Supporters Club, which paid the initial £1,500 deposit. A mortgage was taken out on the rest of the balance.

The Midland League collapsed in the summer of 1960 as another mass exodus of clubs, this time due to their own financial problems, made the competition unviable. The Seasiders therefore had to find another league in which to play. An initial application to play in the lesser Central Alliance was unsuccessful, but there was space in the newly formed Northern Counties League instead. This competition was organised specifically for the north eastern teams that had been members of the Midland League, and initially had only ten clubs, leading to separate league and league cup competitions where teams played each other home and away. The second season saw an increase to 13 clubs, Scarborough finishing in mid-table in both campaigns.

Following the collapse of the Northern Counties League in the summer of 1962, Scarborough joined a re-formed North Eastern League, for the 1962/63 season, lifting the league title during its only season in the competition, ahead of a whole host of clubs that Scarborough had continued to play against over the seasons in its previous two league competitions; the likes of South Shields, North Shields, Blyth Spartans, and Ashington. A 7-1 victory at home to Stockton on Wednesday 15th May 1963, in front of a crowd of 2,800 was enough to see the club finish just one point ahead of South Shields at the head of the table. The League Cup was also won that year. With Scarborough heading the table, the competition was abandoned due to poor weather in order to allow league fixtures to be completed instead, with the league committee declaring Scarborough the winners.

At this point, Scarborough chose to return to the Midland League, which had been revived in 1961. The Seasiders finished as runners-up in its first year back in the competition, albeit well behind a dominant Grantham Town at the top of the table. However, such a promising league position was overshadowed when manager Eddy Brown left after a dispute with the board.

The club played for five more seasons in the Midland. Now one of the leading sides in the league, Scarborough went on to become founding members of the Northern Premier League in 1968. This was a competition that brought together the best non-league clubs in the north of England (with the exception of those in the all-amateur Northern League, which wanted nothing to do with the new league).

Despite a disappointing 17$^{th}$ position in a twenty-team division in the 1968/69 season, Scarborough finished every one of the following ten seasons in the Northern Premier League in the top five places without ever winning the title. A runner-up position behind Boston United achieved in the 1972/73 season, with Colin Appleton at the helm, was its best placing. It is interesting to note that in third place, just one point behind, was Wigan Athletic, followed by Altrincham and Bradford Park Avenue. On top of such consistent performances in the league, the Seasiders were also making a name for itself in cup competitions (see later section).

The 1976/77 was overshadowed by the death of 21-year-old local lad, Tony Aveyard. Just two days after helping his club win the FA Trophy for a third time in five seasons. He died from head injuries sustained in a league match with Boston United at the Athletic Ground. He had been married for less than a year, and the Scarborough players donated their entire cup final winnings and bonus fund to a fund for his 19-year-old widow.

The club celebrated its centenary year in 1979, as well as becoming founder members of another league. In this case it was the Alliance Premier League, later the Conference, which is of course now known as the National League. The league brought together the top clubs in the Northern Premier and Southern Leagues, and although Isthmian League (a Southern based league on a par with those two leagues) clubs were initially not interested in becoming involved, it marked the beginning of the first 'national' league in England since the late 1800s to sit below the Football League.

With ground improvements undertaken, and a squad consisting of several with Football League experience, Scarborough finished third in its second season in the league, behind defending champions Altrincham, and Kettering Town. The goals of Colin Williams, who was the top scorer in the Alliance Premier League for two seasons in a row, enabled the club to achieve what would be its best position in the league until the momentous 1986/87 season.

However, by this time match day attendances were in steady decline, averaging well under 1,000 for home games by the middle of the decade, leading to the Scarborough reserve team being withdrawn from the Northern Counties East League in the summer of 1984, a competition it had joined upon its formation in 1982 after having re-joined the Yorkshire League in 1949. The club did take on a nursery team for a short-time though, in the form of Teeside League side Scarborough Athletic.

Fan favourite and former team captain Harry Dunn, who had played around 900 games for the club, returned for a spell as manager, after having played in all four of his clubs FA Trophy finals, guiding the side to a sixth-place finish during 1984/85. Dunn had initially signed on a part-time basis due to a lack of money at the club, but he was surprisingly sacked following the 1985/86 season, which had seen the side struggle due to a horrendous injury list at the club.

New chairman Barry Adamson, who died during the season aged just 47, brought in Neil Warnock as manager for the 1986/87 season, and this proved to be a huge turning point for the club. Scarborough went on a run of 22 games unbeaten during the season, and four days after beating Sutton United 2-0, the club was declared champions and promoted to The Football League at last, finishing six points ahead of runners-up, Barnet, and a massive 18 points ahead of third-placed Maidstone United. The last match of the season, a 2-1 victory at home to Weymouth on Saturday 2nd May 1947, was watched by a crowd of over 5,600, a huge increase on the 806 that attended the club's first home match of the season against Boston United the previous August.

Scarborough's first Football League fixture was against Wolverhampton Wanderers on Saturday 15th August 1987. Over 7,300 spectators witnessed a thrilling 2-2 draw. The club finished the season in mid-table but it was the 1988/89 season, its second in the Football League, that the club achieved its highest ever placing. Scarborough reached the promotion play-offs after finishing fifth, but lost out to Leyton Orient. After losing the first leg 0-2 down in London, the Seasiders could only win 1-0 in the return, leaving them just short of a place in the final.

The first season in the Football league, while certainly not being a disaster on the field, almost brought the club to its knees financially. It took the intervention of Leeds businessman Geoffrey Richmond, who became a major shareholder of the club in June 1988, and club Chairman a few weeks later, to guarantee the club's short-term financial future  Richmond also helped to forge deal with McCain (UK) Ltd, which saw the Athletic Ground renamed The McCain Stadium.

However, with the club going well on the field, Neil Warnock sensationally announced his resignation following the club's 2-1 victory over Crewe Alexandra on New Year's Eve 1988, citing *'intolerable interference in managerial matters by the chairman.'* Richmond denied this. Five days later Warnock was installed as manger of Notts County, and Richmond appointed player-coach Colin Morris as his replacement at Scarborough.

### Scarborough - Football League record

| Season | Division | P | W | D | L | F | A | Pts | Pos |
|---|---|---|---|---|---|---|---|---|---|
| 1987/88 | Four | 46 | 17 | 14 | 15 | 56 | 48 | 65 | 12/24 |
| 1988/89 | Four | 46 | 21 | 14 | 11 | 67 | 52 | 77 | 5/24 |
| 1989/90 | Four | 46 | 15 | 10 | 21 | 60 | 73 | 55 | 18/24 |
| 1990/91 | Four | 46 | 19 | 12 | 15 | 59 | 56 | 69 | 9/24 |
| 1991/92 | Four | 42 | 15 | 12 | 15 | 64 | 68 | 57 | 12/22 |
| *Division Four renamed Division Three in the summer of 1992* | | | | | | | | | |
| 1992/93 | Three | 42 | 15 | 9 | 18 | 66 | 71 | 54 | 13/22 |
| 1993/94 | Three | 42 | 15 | 8 | 19 | 55 | 61 | 53 | 14/22 |
| 1994/95 | Three | 42 | 8 | 10 | 24 | 49 | 70 | 34 | 21/22 |
| 1995/96 | Three | 46 | 8 | 16 | 22 | 39 | 69 | 40 | 23/24 |
| 1996/97 | Three | 46 | 16 | 15 | 15 | 65 | 68 | 63 | 12/24 |
| 1997/98 | Three | 46 | 19 | 15 | 12 | 67 | 58 | 72 | 6/24 |
| 1998/99 | Three | 46 | 14 | 6 | 26 | 50 | 77 | 48 | 24/24 |

After a disappointing 1988/89 season, the Seasiders improved again to finish 9th the following season, before  three mid-table finishes in the fourth tier (Division Four was renamed Division Three in the summer of 1992, due to the formation of the FA Premier League). During that time, a crowd of only 625 attended the club's home match with Wrexham on Friday 7th Dember 1990. There were then two seasons of struggle at the foot of the league, with the club finishing just one place off the bottom in the 1994/95 and 1995/96 seasons.

Richmond went on to become chairman of Bradford City on 27th January 1994, when he and the outgoing chairman of City, David Simpson switched positions.

An improvement was made in the 1996/97 season, when Scarborough finished mid-table, but the 1997/98 was a season in which Scarborough, under manager Mick Wadsworth, could well have been promoted. Had the club gone up then its short-term history would have so very different.

Torquay defeated Scarborough 7-2 on aggregate, winning 3-1 at Scarborough and then 4-1 at home, to consign the North Yorkshire side to another season in Division Three. In the event it would be club's last ever season at that level.

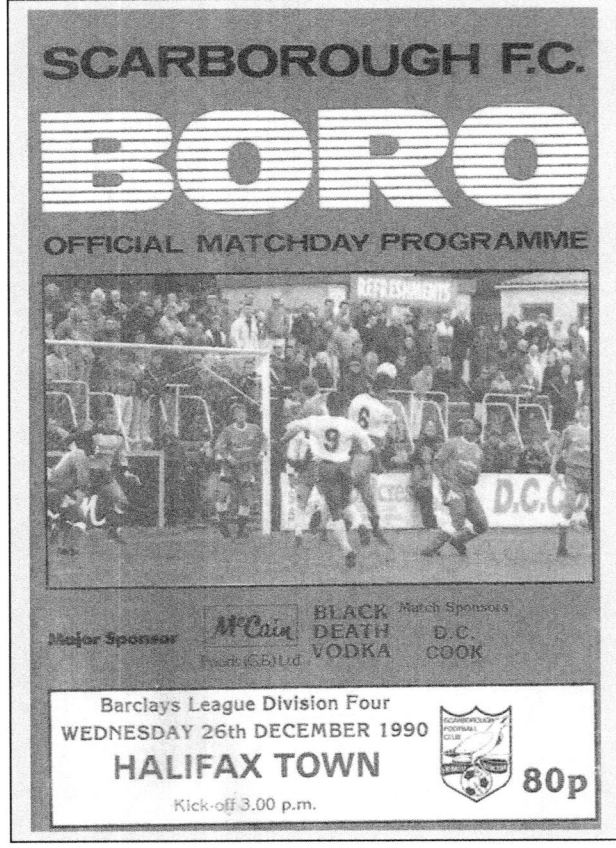

Just twelve months after having failed to be promoted via the play-offs, Scarborough FC suffered relegation from the Football League, and it could not have been in more dramatic circumstances.

Scarborough was stuck at the bottom of the table for most of the 1998/99 season, with Colin Addison taking over from Wadsworth as manager during the season. The team finally managed to move off bottom place after its penultimate match of the season, but in a dramatic ending to the season, were relegated in the final minute of the season when Carlisle United's on-loan goalkeeper Jimmy Glass scored the winner for his team against Plymouth to take them back above Scarbough at the death. Scarborough, who had drawn 1-1 with Peterborough United that day, finished with a points total of 48, the highest for a club finishing bottom of any division in the Football League at that time. This was the first relegation in the history of the club, and it would ultimately prove to be the beginning of a downward spiral that would end in the club's demise.

Hopes of a quick return to The Football League were dashed when the club could only finish fourth on its return to the Conference, behind Kidderminster Harriers, Rushden & Diamonds, and Morecambe. After that, the club never made a challenge at the top of the table, it's best being 7th pace in the 2002/03 season, and despite going through the whole season unbeaten at home in the 2004/05 season, could only finish down in 13th in the final table that season.

With finances worsening, the club found it harder to stay afloat and put out a side capable of achieving success at this level. It was surprise therefore when the 2005/06 season saw Scarborough struggling at the foot of the table. Despite finishing bottom of the pile at the end of the season, the club was not initially relegated, as Canvey Island resigned from the league and Altrincham were deducted 18 points for fielding an ineligible player, which meant that the Manchester club occupied bottom position instead.

However, with finances in such a precarious state, Scarborough did not fulfil the Conference's financial guidelines and was therefore relegated to Conference North.

Placed in administration, the club started its first, and ultimately final, season in Conference North with a ten point deduction. Scarborough finished 20th in the 22 team division, which would have brought a possible relegation back to the Northern Premier League, its last game being on Saturday 28th April 2007, a 1-0 win at Hucknall Town.

Scarborough had hoped to move to a new stadium on the outskirts of town by the start of the 2009/10 season. Proceeds from the sale of the McCain Stadium to a housing developer would, it was hoped, wipe out the club's debts in addition to providing the finance to build the new ground. However, a covenant existing on the stadium that dated back to the days when it was first established as the Athletic Ground, restricted its use only to sporting activities. In order to have this covenant removed Scarborough would have to convince Scarborough Borough Council that its proposals were realistic. This the club sadly failed to do. Despite an initial eight eight-day stay of execution', Scarborough Football Club was wound up at Leeds High Court on Wednesday 20th June with debts of around £2.5 million, thus ending its 128-year old existence.

However, the winding up of Scarborough FC initially led to the formation of two clubs representing the Seaside town, one of which has already folded.

Scarborough Athletic was founded by a supporters' trust named The Seadog Trust, which took on the same red kit, nickname, motto, and official club logo from the original club. The Trust successfully applied for membership of the North Riding County FA and the Northern Counties East League on 25th June 2007, just five days after the dissolution of Scarborough FC, but due to the unavailability of any suitable grounds in the town, was forced to ground-share at Bridlington Town. The 2017/18 season saw Scarborough Athletic return to the town in a newly built stadium after ten years in exile, while, in 2017, the site of the McCain Stadium became a Lidl supermarket.

Scarborough Town was also founded following the demise of Scarborough FC. The club's former Centre of Excellence, youth team and Football in the Community sections moved, with some assistance from Sheffield United, to the George Pindar Community Sports College, south of the town, in Eastfield. An open-age team was admitted to the Teesside League for the 2008/09 season, winning the league's second division title with ease with an unbeaten record. In 2009/10 Scarborough Town moved up into the Wearside League, scoring a massive 140 goals in its 36 league fixtures as the club won the championship, six points ahead of Ryhope Colliery Welfare. On Monday 3rd May 2010, Town also won the league's Sunderland Shipowners Cup, defeating Teeside Athletic , who finished in third place in the league, 3-2 in the
final. The club was then forced to take a year out when issues over floodlights at ground left it with no league to play in, having initially been accepted into the Northern Counties East League. Town returned, in the second tier of the Humber Premier League, for the 2011/12 season, but after two years in that league, having failed in its bid to upgrade facilities at its home ground, the club folded in June 2013. This left Scarborough Athletic as the sole successor to Scarborough FC.

## Scarborough FC finishing positions

### Northern League Division Two
- 1898/99  8/10
- 1899/00  6/8

### Northern League
- 1900/01  6/11
- 1901/02  9/10
- 1902/03  11/13
- 1903/04  11/13
- 1904/05  12/13
- 1905/06  13/14
- 1906/07  12/12
- 1907/08  12/12
- 1908/09  8/12
- 1909/10  7/12

### Yorkshire Combination
- 1910/11  2/10
- 1911/12  4/14
- 1912/13  6/13
- 1913/14  5/10

### Northern League
- 1914/15  7/9
- 1919/20  14/14
- 1920/21  14/14
- 1921/22  12/14
- 1922/23  12/14
- 1923/24  10/15
- 1924/25  10/15
- 1925/26  11/14

### Yorkshire League
- 1926/27  10/16

### Midland League
- 1927/28  2/23
- 1928/29  7/26
- 1929/30  1/26
- 1930/31  16/24
- 1931/32  6/24
- 1932/33  5/23
- 1933/34  8/17
- 1934/35  20/20
- 1935/36  13/21
- 1936/37  21/22
- 1937/38  3/22
- 1938/39  9/22

### Scarborough League
- 1945/46  1/11

### Midland League
- 1946/47  14/22
- 1947/48  17/22
- 1948/49  19/22
- 1949/50  14/24
- 1950/51  11/22
- 1951/52  6/22
- 1952/53  20/24
- 1953/54  19/24
- 1954/55  22/24
- 1955/56  18/24
- 1956/57  23/24
- 1957/58  7/24
- 1958/59  9/19
- 1959/60  13/17

### Northern Counties League
- 1960/61  6/10
- 1961/62  6/13

### North Eastern League
- 1962/63  1/12

### Midland League
- 1963/64  2/22
- 1964/65  5/22
- 1965/66  11/22
- 1966/67  6/22
- 1967/68  7/21

### Northern Premier League
- 1968/69  17/20
- 1969/70  4/20
- 1970/71  3/22
- 1971/72  4/24
- 1972/73  2/24
- 1973/74  5/24
- 1974/75  5/24
- 1975/76  3/24
- 1976/77  5/23
- 1977/78  4/24
- 1978/79  4/23

### Alliance Premier / Conference
- 1979/80  11/20
- 1980/81  3/20
- 1981/82  7/22
- 1982/83  9/22
- 1983/84  13/22
- 1984/85  6/22
- 1985/86  15/22
- 1986/87  1/22

### Football League
- 1987-99 - *See separate box*

### Conference
- 1999/00  4/22
- 2000/01  10/22
- 2001/02  12/22
- 2002/03  7/22
- 2003/04  15/22
- 2004/05  13/22
- 2005/06  21/22

### Conference North
- 2006/07  20/22

## Local Cup Successes

**North Riding Senior Cup** winners 19 times: 1908/09, 1928/29, 1938/39, 1947/48, 1955/56, 1958/59, 1960/61, 1961/62, 1968/69, 1972/73, 1973/74, 1976/77, 1977/78, 1980/81, 1981/82, 1984/85, 1986/87, 1991/92, & 2003/04, (Scarborough Athletic were winners in 2018/19)

**Scarborough & East Riding Challenge Cup** winners 6 times: 1887/88, 1888/89, 1890/91, 1891/92, 1892/93, 1896/97, & 1900/01

**Scarborough Hospital Cup** winners 9 times: 1896/97, 1899/1900, 1900/01, 1901/02, 1903/04, 1907/08, 1908/09, 1909/10, & 1910/11. Scarborough dominated this competition in its later years, winning the 1910 final 12-0 against the West Yorkshire Regiment army team, and the 1908 final 7-1 against St Mary's. The club's domination over its rivals is obvious when looking at its list of results in the competition between February 1908 and April 1911: 14-0, 8-0, 7-1, 15-0, 3-2, 16-2, 6-2, 2-0, 12-0, 3-0, 4-1 & 3-0.

## Scarborough in FA Competitions

Scarborough FC made a name for itself many times over the years with its famous cup runs, particularly during the 1970s when the club made four Wembley appearances in five years. Details of the more senior competitions that the club appeared in are detailed below.

## FA Cup

Scarborough first entered the FA Cup in the 1887/88 season, losing 3-5 at home to Shankhouse in a First Qualifying Round tie. Very little success was achieved in the first few years of entry, a 0-11 loss at

Middlesbrough in the 1890/91 season being a low point, as was a 1-13 rout at Darlington twelve months later (at least Hartlepool NER had been defeated in the previous round that season).

The club returned to the competition in 1901/02, although it wasn't until the 1925/26 season that any real progress was made. That year, the likes of Normanby Magnesite, Stockton Malleable Institute, Eston United (in a replay), and Guisborough Belmont were defeated before Horden Athletic won 5-2 in front of 4,000 spectators at their own ground in the Fourth Qualifying round.

The 1930/31 season brought Scarborough national headlines. Now exempt to the Fourth Qualifying round, victories over West Stanley (in a replay), and Rhyl Athletic (6-0) brought a Second Round tie with Football League side Lincoln City. The tie, played on Saturday 13th December 1930 was at the time considered the greatest ever played at the Athletic Ground, when 6,318 supporters saw the home team come from behind to beat its higher-placed opponents in dramatic circumstances. The Seasiders trailed 0-2 after five minutes, and 2-4 at half time, before producing a sensational second-half comeback to win 6-4. Grimsby Town put paid to further progress with a 2-1 home win in the Third Round but the memories produced by that defeat of Lincoln City lived long in the memory in the Seaside town.

*Athletic News,* **Monday 15th December 1930**

*LINCOLN FALL TO PIECES. Despairing Tactics in Face of Defeat. SCARBORO'S PLUCK.*

*Scarborough 6 Lincoln City 4 (Half-time: 2-4)*

HISTORY *was made by the Scarborough club on Saturday, the club never having been so successful before in the English Cup competition before.*

*Sheer pluck and hard work would seem to have a great deal to do with their victory, for after Cartwright and Lax had scored for Lincoln in the first five minutes Scarborough were facing heavy odds at half time, Dinsdale having scored two further goals, against a couple by Palfreyman and Hickman.*

*Rand (2), Hickman and Hill scored for Scarborough in the second half.*

*During the opening stages Scarborough seemed over-excited. The second half, however, found their old confidence restored, and the half-backs broke up the Lincoln forwards' movements with deadly precision, while the Lincoln defence, which had previously seemed impregnable, now seemed unable to hold the Scarborough forwards.*

*As the possibility of a draw changed into certainty of defeat, Lincoln seemed to break up. Their shooting became wild and clockwork-like movements became erratic.*

*Lax, on the Lincoln left wing, showed a brilliant turn speed and was often prominent, whilst Cartwright, a native of Scarborough and an old Scarborough player, also came in for favourable comment, as did Dinsdale On the Scarborough side the half backs were excellent. Palfreyman, at centre-forward, worked very hard but was rather slow, whilst both full-backs endangered their goal more than once by faulty clearances.*

*Both sides had penalty kicks granted in the second half, but the goalkeepers saved cleverly.*

*Scarborough: – Turner; Severn, Betton, Maskill, Robinson, Wallis; Small, Rand, Palfreyman, Hill, and Hickman.*

The club made it to the Second Round in the 1935/36 season, losing to Brighton & Hove Albion following victories over Stockton, Bridlington Town, Smith's Dock, South Bank St Peter's, Shildon, and Darwen.

There was a huge crowd of 11,162 at the Athletic Ground for the Third Round home tie with Luton Town on 8th January 1938. The match was drawn 1-1, but Scarborough lost the replay 1-5 in front of 11,750 in what was the club's tenth match in the competition. The run that season had started in the Preliminary

Round, with victory over South Bank. Further victories over Stockton, South Bank St Peter's, Whitby United (in a replay, following an abandoned tie), North Shields, Darlington, and Bromley followed.

Appearances in the First Round Proper of the competition were achieved regularly, with the Second Round reached in 1948/49 (losing 0-3 to Gateshead), 1964/65 (losing 1-2 at home to Doncaster Rovers in a replay), and 1972/73 (another 1-2 home loss to Doncaster Rovers). One year later, Port Vale defeated Scarborough 2-1 at the same stage.

Scarborough had two significant runs in the latter part of the 1970s which saw the club reach the Third Round in each case. In the 1975/76, season Scarborough knocked out Morecambe, and then Football League side Preston North End before losing 2–1 to eventual semi-finalists Crystal Palace. Harry Dunn had given Scarborough a first half lead in the Preston tie, before their Division Three opponents hit back to lead 2-1 at half-time. However, goals from John Woodall and Sean Marshall, the latter in the 89th minute, saw the home team win through.

Brighton & Hove Albion knocked out Scarborough 3-0 at the same stage in the 1977/78 season. This followed victory over two Football League teams, Rochdale (4-2 at home), and Crewe Alexandra (2-0 at home, following a 0-0 draw).

As a Football League club, the Third Round was reached in the 1994/95 season, with Watford winning a replay 2-0 at Vicarage Road.

Following its relegation from the Football League, the final time the club made it beyond the qualifying rounds was in the 2003/04 season when a fine run took the club to a Fourth Round tie with Chelsea, which was narrowly lost by a single goal from John Terry. The match brought back memories of Scarborough's shock victory over their London rivals in the Football League Cup back in the October 1989 *(see below)*. The run began with a 3-1 home win over Hinckley United in the Fourth Qualifying Round, and this was followed by victories over three Football League sides, Division Three champions-elect Doncaster Rovers (1-0 at home), Division Two promotion aspirants Port Vale (1-0, away from home), and then Southend United, also from Division Three (1-0 at home, following a 1-1 draw).

**Football League Cup**

Scarborough's best run in the competition was in the 1992/93 season, when the competition was known as the Coca-Cola Cup. Scarborough made the Fourth Round – the last 16 – following defeats of Bradford City and Coventry City (both over two legs) and Plymouth Argyle (in a replay) before losing 0-1 to Arsenal on Wednesday 6th January 1993. A crowd of over 6,200 saw Nigel Winterburn score the only goal for the Premier League team that evening.

However, Scarborough's finest moment in the competition came in the 1989/90 season, when, on 4th October 1989, Chelsea were defeated 3-2 in what was at the time known as the Littlewoods Cup. The first leg at Stamford Bridge had ended 1-1, but in the return tie a crowd of just over 5,000 saw Chelsea leading 2-0 with just twenty minutes remaining. However, in an incredible spell of football, Scarborough scored three times in just seven minutes, through Tommy Graham, 18-year-old Paul Robinson and then Martin Russell, from the penalty spot, to see the Yorkshire team win 4-3 on aggregate. Sadly, the team was thrashed 0-7 at Oldham Athletic in the Third Round, but the Chelsea victory remains one of the club's finest results.

## FA Amateur Cup

Scarborough was among the entrants in the competition's first year, losing 2-4 to Loftus in the Second Qualifying Round 1893/94 season. The team waited until the 1897/98 season before entering again, but was thrashed 0-6 at South Bank in a Third Qualifying Round tie. Defeats to Whitby, and Mickley followed in subsequent competitions, before a first win was achieved, and that was at home to West Hartlepool in the Third Qualifying Round in the 1900/01 season. The club actually negotiated another round that season when it was awarded a win following Skinningrove Ironworks' refusal to play extra time at the Athletic Ground. Grimsby All Saints ended the run with a 3-1 victory in Scarborough.

A place in the Second Round was achieved in the 1905/06 season, following wins over Whitby (3-2), Skinningrove United (3-0) and Old Xaverians (2-1) before a 2-4 home loss to South Bank.

The 1907/08 season was notable for Scarborough's 16-1 rout of Leeds Amateurs at home on 9th November 1907. This came after a 7-3 home victory over Beverley Town. Spennymoor ended hopes of further progress with a 1-0 victory on the Athletic Ground.

The only other runs of note in the competition were in 1908/'09, 1920/21 and 1925/26. In the former, Beverley Town and York City were both defeated in replays, followed by a 1-0 win at Knaresborough in the Fourth Qualifying Round. Sadly the team was thrashed 2-8 at West Hartlepool in front of a crowd of 4,000 in the first round proper.

The 1920/21 cup run saw Acomb WMC, Bridlington Town, and Hornsea defeated, before a Second Round loss to Loftus Albion.

Local rivals Scarborough Penguins were defeated 2-1 in front of a crowd of 4,000 at the Athletic Ground in the 1925/26 season. This was followed by three resounding victories over Whitby Town (10-0), Carlin How (9-4) and South Bank (7-2). In the Second Round, Stockton ended Scarborough's hopes with a 3-1 away victory.

Also worth noting is the team's experience in the 1909/10 season. A 1-0 Third Round victory over Preston Winckley was later awarded to Preston Winckley after Scarborough were controversially disqualified. The club had hosted a charity match for Lionel Charlwood, who was suffering from a serious illness and would never play again, the previous December. As he was still registered as a player then the FA deemed the payment paid to Charlwood as technically breaking the rules of amateurism, therefore expelling the club from the competition.

## FA Trophy

Non-league's premier knock-out competition was dominated by Scarborough during the mid-1970s, when Wembley almost became a second home for the club. The Trophy was introduced for the 1969/70 season, one in which Scarborough started at the First Qualifying Round. Its Second Round replay defeat at home to Mossley was the team's eighth tie in the competition.

Scarborough appeared in four Wembley finals in the space of five years. These are listed below.

1972/73: Wigan Athletic were defeated 2-1 in the final on Saturday 28th April 1973, in front of a crowd of 23,000. Scarborough went ahead in the 12th minute through Malcolm Leask but a late, late Wigan equaliser sent the game into extra-time. Malcolm Thompson's winner, however, saw Scarborough win the trophy for the first time.

1974/75: Scarborough finished as runners-up this season, losing heavily, to Matlock Town on Saturday 26th April. Despite having the lions-share of possession, the Seasiders lost 0-4.

1975/76: Twelve months later, Scarborough were winners for a second time, with a 3-2 victory over Stafford Rangers on Saturday 24th April 1976. Goals from Woodall, Abbey and then a late Sean Marshall penalty in extra-time saw the Staffordshire team narrowly edged-out, in front of a crowd of 21,000.

1976/77: Scarborough were winners for a third and final time, on Saturday 14th May 1977. Dagenham were defeated 2-1 in front of 20,000 fans. Harry Dunn (penalty) and Abbey were the goal-scorers. Scarborough's two legged semi-final with Altrincham finished level, necessitating two replays before being decided in Scarborough's favour.

Scarborough only once more made it to the Quarter Final stage, and that was in the 1981/82 season, when the team went out 2-4 at Enfield.

**Scarborough FA Trophy results - Selected seasons**

**1972-73**
| | | | |
|---|---|---|---|
| 1 | Macclesfield Town | H | 3-1 |
| 2 | Sandbach Ramblers | A | 3-0 |
| 3 | Mexborough Town | A | 3-1 |
| QF | Chelmsford City | H | 2-0 |
| SF | Ashford Tn (Kent) | N2 | 1-0 |
| F | Wigan Athletic | N1 | 2-1 |

**1974-75**
| | | | |
|---|---|---|---|
| 1 | Gateshead United | H | 4-0 |
| 2 | Boston United | A | 1-1 |
| 2r | Boston United | H | 1-0 |
| 3 | Enfield | H | 2-1 |
| QF | Wimbledon | H | 1-0 |
| SF(1) | Bedford Town | H | 3-1 |
| SF(2) | Bedford Town | A | 3-1 |
| F | Matlock Town | N1 | 0-4 |

**1975-76**
| | | | |
|---|---|---|---|
| 1 | Willington | H | 3-2 |
| 2 | Goole Town | A | 1-1 |
| 2r | Goole Town | H | 3-1 |
| 3 | Dagenham | H | 3-0 |
| QF | Tooting & Mitcham United | H | 1-0 |
| SF1 | Enfield | H | 1-0 |
| SF2 | Enfield | A | 0-0 |
| F | Stafford Rangers | N1 | 3-2 |

**1976-77**
| | | | |
|---|---|---|---|
| 1 | Frickley Athletic | H | 3-1 |
| 2 | Walthamstow Ave | A | 0-0 |
| 2r | Walthamstow Ave | H | 2-1 |
| 3 | Hitchin Town | A | 0-0 |
| 3r | Hitchin Town | H | 3-1 |
| QF | Nuneaton Boro | H | 1-1 |
| Qfr | Nuneaton Boro | A | 1-0 |
| SF(1) | Altrincham | H | 2-0 |
| SF(2) | Altrincham | A | 0-2 |
| SFr | Altrincham | N3 | 0-0 |
| SFr2 | Altrincham | N4 | 2-1 |
| F | Dagenham | N1 | 2-1 |

N1 = at Wembley
N2 = at Peterborough United
N3 = at Doncaster Rovers
N4 = at Rotherham United
r = replay

## Anglo-Italian Cup

Scarborough played in the Anglo-Italian Cup, a competition of semi-professional teams, which allowed the fielding of 'guest' players, in Scarborough's case from Gordon Banks and Alan A'Court.

The 1976 tournament was played during May and June, the Seasiders defeating Udinese 4–0 at home, losing the away match 0-1, also drawing 0-0 at home to Monza, but losing 0-1 in the return.

The 1977 saw home games played in April – 2-2 with Teramo, and 1-0 against Parma, before playing two ties in Italy in June against Lecce and Cremonese – both of them resulting in 1-1 draws.

## Other cup competitions

Scarborough lifted the Bob Lord Trophy, the league cup competition of the Alliance Premier League, in the 1983/84 season, defeating Barnet in the final. Ties were played over two legs, with the Seasiders defeating Boston United, Frickley Athletic, and Yeovil Town en-route to the final. Barnet were defeated 2-0 at the Athletic Ground on Monday 16th April 1984, thanks to goals from Wiggan and Bowman, with the second leg at Barnet ending 1-0 to the home team.

## Other Scarborough teams in FA Competitions

A number of other long, gone Scarborough teams have played in FA Cup and FA Amateur Cup competitions. The Scarborough Penguins club is featured in a later chapter.

Scarborough Rangers entered both competitions, but failed to play a single match in either. In the FA Cup, the club entered in the 1892/'93 season, but scratched from its First Qualifying Round tie at Rothwell, near Leeds. In the Amateur Cup, Rangers was also to have played in the inaugural competition in the 1893/94 season, but scratched from its tie at Whitby.

Scarborough Juniors played seven ties in the FA Amateur Cup from 1934/35 to 1938/39, although only two of those were won and the club made no impact beyond the early qualifying rounds in the competition. The club also played four FA Cup ties between 1937-39.

Scarborough Junior Imperial, a separate club to Scarborough Juniors, played four FA cup ties, between 1934/35 and 1937/38, but lost on each occasion.

*There is plenty of information online regarding Scarborough FC and its history, as well as a number of books on the subject. Steve Adamson's excellent official club history, published in 1999 (see bibliography at the end of this book) is an outstanding and detailed source of information.*

# Hunslet & Leeds City
# 1877-1927
## ...also including Leeds Harehills & Leeds United

The first ever Hunslet AFC existed between 1877-1883. It is said to have been founded by Sam Gilbert, a Sheffield cricketer by the bringing together two junior clubs, Hunslet Excelsior and Hunslet Albion, under the auspices of the Woodhouse Hill cricket club in Leeds. The two clubs had played friendly fixtures under rugby rules before this, and in fact continued to do so afterwards, so it seems that the Hunslet Association club was a separate entity, made up on players who played for the two rugby teams rather than being a merger of the two.

> **HUNSLET ASSOCIATION FOOTBALL CLUB.**
> —Two Grand Football Matches at Woodhouse Hill Cricket Ground: On Monday, Dec. 24th, Hunslet v. Holmes; on Thursday, Dec. 27th a Grand Exhibition Match, White v. Blues of Sheffield. Kick off 2.15 p.m. Admission each day, 3d.

Hunslet AFC played its first-ever home match against a team called Holmes, from Kimberworth, near Rotherham, on Christmas Eve, 1887 at the Woodhouse Hill ground. A report appeared in the *Leeds Mercury* two days later, '*The first half of the game was exceedingly good, but a little in favour of Hunslet, who obtained one goal, which was disputed on account of the offside rule. The second half was in favour of Holmes, who obtained one goal. Ogden, Mills and Frith played exceedingly well for Hunslet, Holmes proving victorious by one goal to nil.*' The Hunslet team that day was: *J Coates, J Clarke, A Mills, W Hill, F Hinde, W H Stacey, J B Ogden, F Firth, C Shaw, R Hudson, and W Gilston.*

Two days earlier, on Saturday 22nd December, a Hunslet team defeated Holbeck by three 'goals' to one, although little else is known about this fixture, which was played at Holbeck. It may well have been played under rugby rules.

Three days after the Holmes match, on Boxing Day 1877, the club hosted a match that had been organised by Fred Sanderson, president of the Sheffield New Football Association, under Sheffield Rules. The match was advertised as '*Whites v Blues*', according to the *Leeds Times*, although other sources indicate that, in reality, this this was a fixture between Hallam FC and Hunslet. However, the Sheffield Independent reported the match as being between two teams made up of representative players of the Sheffield New Association, which had been founded earlier in the year as a breakaway of the Sheffield FA.

The Hallam / New Association team was happy to bring a ball, umpires, and even its own set of posts for the occasion, which was switched to the Holbeck Recreation Ground, one assumes due to the interest shown in the game. However, despite an entertaining match, takings were disappointing, as the ground was deep in snow, and the wind made it difficult to both play and watch the game. On top of that, the majority of those present to see the game were Holbeck Football Club season ticket holders who had got in without paying. For the record, the Whites' won 4-3. Team names were not always as important as the event itself in this day, and age. The same day as the match at Holbeck, Sheffield Alliance FC played 'A Nottingham team' at the Forest ground, Nottingham.

The Hunslet club, with its headquarters at the George IV, in the absence of any governing body in West Yorkshire, affiliated with the Sheffield FA. Sadly, there was a complete lack of support and finance available to sustain a successful Association club in Leeds at the time, and the first Hunslet AFC faded away quietly around 1883, by which time other local teams such as Hunslet Wesleyans had begun to play the game in the immediate vicinity.

> HUNSLET FOOTBALL CLUB will be glad to arrange home and home games (Association rules) with any club round about Leeds, first or second teams.—Address F. W. BRIGHAM, 2, Newport St.; or George the Fourth, Hunslet.

The name would be revived when employees at Leeds Steelworks formed a club in 1889, rechristened as Hunslet AFC when it joined the newly formed West Yorkshire League in 1894 (although the name of Leeds Steelworks would re-appear in local football in later years). Hunslet, known locally as *'The Twinklers'*, initially played at the Laburnum Grounds, which was shared with the West Hunslet Cricket Club. The man behind the club, W Nicholson went on to donate a trophy to the Leeds League, which was used for its league competition.

Hunslet became West Yorkshire's first 'super' club, winning the West Yorkshire Cup four times and reaching the FA Amateur Cup Quarter-Final twice, including one celebrated victory over the mighty past winners and six-time finalists, Old Etonians. Yet it could not compete with the best of the teams from the Sheffield district, despite its prominence locally. It is this particular Hunslet club that eventually morphed into the Football League club, Leeds City.

The Old Etonians match came during a wonderful cup run which saw Hunslet defeat West Hartlepool, Loftus, and Buxton to earn a home tie with the famous club in the Second Round proper of the Amateur Cup on 15th February 1896. There were few who gave Hunslet any chance of progressing, and when they fell 2-0 behind within seven minutes it looked like a heavy defeat would follow. However, the Yorkshiremen fought back with an inspiring display to earn a shock 3-2 victory, with one of the goals coming from 'Tipper' Heffron, a winger who went on to play for Leeds City. Hunslet sadly lost to Darlington in the next round and ended the season with a loss of £35, which demonstrated the size of the financial challenge facing football in Yorkshire.

The club's first West Yorkshire League season saw the club finish 6th of the eleven finishers (Castleford Albion having dropped out early in the season following some heavy defeats), before finishing joint top of the table with Bradford at the end of the 1895/96 season. The teams were declared joint champions.

The league fell apart in the summer of 1896 as the West Yorkshire FA felt it was unable to organise a competition for its best sides, although it had no problem organising a West Yorkshire Junior League instead.

Instead, a West Yorkshire Cup was organised for the 1896/97 season for the district's senior teams instead, and at this point Hunslet began its domination of the game in the district. After a number of designs were considered, the one chosen for the winners of the competition was that from Messrs. Fattorini and Sons from Bradford. Hallmarked silver, the cup weighed 75oz and was of a *'bold Grecian design, without lid'*. One side of the trophy featured the West Yorkshire Arms and bore the inscription *'West Yorkshire Association Challenge Cup. Established 1896.'* The reverse showed a group of footballers representing the five named teams who had sponsored the cup, namely Leeds, Huddersfield, Bradford, Halifax and Hunslet. The base of the cup featured a white rose of Yorkshire and the arms of the five clubs. The cup was also *'decorated with raised flutings and acanthus leaves in bold relief, and presents a very handsome appearance.'* according to the *Leeds Mercury*.

Hunslet defeated Halifax 4-2 in the first final, on 10th April 1897, with the game played in fine conditions at Valley Parade, Bradford. According to the *Yorkshire Evening Post*, Hunslet winning the game was due in large measure to their forwards, who *'played with far greater dash and combination than their opponents'*. Two weeks later *The Twinklers*, defeated the same opposition 4-1 in the Leeds Hospitals Cup final at the same venue. Hunslet might well have won the 1900/01 competition had it entered, preferring to let another team get its hands on the cup.

The first four West Yorkshire Cup competitions were won by Hunslet, the finals being;
1896/97: Hunslet…4   Halifax…2, at Valley Parade, Bradford
1897/98: Hunslet…1   Harrogate…0, at Elland Road, Leeds
1898/99: Hunslet…3   Huddersfield…1, at The Victoria Ground, Savile Town, Dewsbury
1899/1900: Hunslet…5   Altofts…2, at Elland Road, Leeds

Hunslet dominated the Leeds Hospital Cup also, achieving four wins on the bounce in what was the area's most prestigious competition before the introduction of the West Yorkshire Cup. Hunslet's 1897/98 replay win over Leeds in front of a crowd of around 4,000 was dwarfed by the massive crowd of 7,000 for their initial drawn game. Their fourth and final victory in the competition was a much harder effort and it needed three games before Huddersfield were defeated 2-1 at the Leeds Parish Church rugby ground (this following 1-1 and 0-0 draws). The replayed 1901/02 final between Hunslet and Altofts was to be held over to the start of the following season due to a suitable date not being found, but unfortunately Hunslet had folded in the meantime, and the cup was withheld for twelve months.

Leeds Hospital Cup finals featuring Hunslet were as follows:
1896/97: Hunslet…4   Halifax… 1
1897/98: Hunslet…4   Leeds…1, in a replay
1898/99: Hunslet…1   Huddersfield…0
1899/1900: Hunslet…2   Huddersfield…1, in a second replay
1901/02 Cup withheld. Altofts & Hunslet drew twice.

In 1897, Hunslet was among the leading local clubs which formed the Yorkshire League. Leeds, Bradford, Huddersfield and Halifax, were the other West Yorkshire clubs. The club finished in 6th place in both of its first two seasons, well clear of the other West Yorkshire teams, but well adrift of the South Yorkshire clubs with which it could not compete.

The league more or less broke up in the summer of 1899 when the latter clubs withdrew due to the lack of competition the league was providing, leaving just five West Yorkshire clubs in the competition. Hunslet tied with Huddersfield at the top of the table, and moved into the Sheffield & Hallamshire League in 1900.

The club was by now receiving substantial attention in the local press. The *Leeds Mercury* on 12th August 1898 had this to say: *'When the Association game was first introduced at Hunslet, and only a moderate exhibition of football was provided, the attendances at the matches were very small, and there was but little encouragement for the promoters to continue their venture. However, they stuck to their task, and have been so far rewarded as to* be able to boast of a team that is qualified to hold its own against the best of amateur combinations, and not to be disgraced when opposed by professionals.'

As the new century dawned, Hunslet was undisputedly the leading side in West Yorkshire. Many of the side's players were said to have learnt the game outside the district, although the pick of the players in Leeds were keen to join in the success the club was having. The team was formidable when faced with local opposition, and good enough to hold a Blackburn Rovers XI to a 1-1 draw on Easter Tuesday 1900. Hunslet's team included Harold Lemoine, who became one of the best goalkeepers in the country, winning three amateur caps for England between 1908 and 1910.

As powerful a club as Hunslet was, however, it had no ground of its own and as a result its very existence was a precarious one. The club had moved from the Wellington Ground in Low Road back to the Laburnum Ground at Parkside, just off Dewsbury Road, and with only a narrow strip of land separating the pitch from the Hunslet rugby club's pitch, the facilities on the site were shared. Hunslet's final home was at the Nelson Ground in Low Road. The club was all ready to join the reformed West Yorkshire League in 1902 - following an unsuccessful two seasons in the Sheffield league - but it lost the lease on the ground, and, as the committee could not find an alternative base in time, sadly disbanded. However, a 'Hunslet' team did defeat Upper Armley Christ Church, a strong local club, in April 1903, with no other intention than to keep the name alive should there be a need to revive it at a time in the near future. However, that didn't happen, and it seemed that Leeds would, once again, fail in its attempts to create an association club that could fly the flag for the city. But all was not lost.

Following Bradford City's elevation to the Football League in 1903, officials linked to the Hunslet club were at the forefront of a new attempt to form a team to represent the city of Leeds, and it was then that Leeds City AFC was born.

Between 1882 and 1898 there had been no less than four failed Leeds AFC clubs and, given that Bradford City was elected straight into the Football League in 1903, it only served to reinforce the growing divide between the industrial rivals.

## Leeds City AFC

However, the former officials and supporters of Hunslet AFC had not simply given up the ghost and walked away, and it was they that were behind the formation of Leeds City AFC in the summer of 1904. The sports pages of the local newspapers were full of encouragement for the venture, convinced that a Leeds team could, and should, be playing in the Football League sooner rather than later.

The first meeting, of what would become the new club's committee, under the presidency of Frederick Waterhouse, was held at the Royal Exchange Hotel, Hunslet on 17th June, and its formation was rubber-stamped following a further meeting at the Griffin Hotel, Boar Lane on 30th August 1904, with the club already admitted to the West Yorkshire League for the 1904/05 season. Norris R Hepworth would succeed Waterhouse as club president in November.

*Old Ebor*, writing in his column for the Manchester-based *Athletic News* on 4th September that year, was all too aware of the need for a Leeds team to be formed, *'In my opinion, there is not only room but an actual necessity for a representative Association club in Leeds. Within the past few years Leeds Parish Church, Wortley, Kirkstall and now Holbeck – all Northern Union clubs with a good following of the public – have become defunct, and it is certain that all who used to support them do not follow the Leeds and Hunslet clubs, the only two Northern Union clubs of note that remain in Leeds.'* He continued, *'The Leeds City Association club…ought to 'go' and its promoters have not only my good wishes but a willingness to render the movement all the assistance in my power. There is room for two – even three – codes of football in Leeds with its unrivalled means of communication with all* parts of the kingdom, and its greater contiguity to large centres of population than any other town in the North possesses.' Old Ebor was able to put his words of support into action not long later.

*Flaneur*, of the *Leeds Mercury*, was far more guarded, *'I have no antipathy to the Association game, but I cannot imagine anyone brought up to the Rugby code forsaking his original love for socker, provided he gets the best class of Rugby'*. By the end of the decade, *Flaneur* had been completely won over by the round-ball game.

Despite a lowly position of 11th out of fourteen clubs in that first season (Bradford City reserves won the title), there was much to be happy about for the club. Several prestigious friendly fixtures against Football League clubs were played, which resulted in Leeds City fielding under-strength teams for some league games, and a suitable ground was procured for the early weeks of the season, namely the old Wellington Ground on Low Lane where Hunslet AFC had previously played. One wonders why Hunslet was denied the use of this ground in 1902 because this was virtually the same organisation making use of Low Lane as the defunct club. One explanation for this is that Low Lane had been secured by another club at the time of Hunslet's demise.

Leeds City's first fixture was away at Morley on 1st September 1904, less than 48 hours after the Griffin Hotel meeting (the result, a 2-2 draw), and the following month a move was made to the Elland Road enclosure that had just been vacated by Holbeck FC. The annual rent was set at £75, with an option to buy the ground for no more than £5,000 the following April. To make the pitch large enough for association football, an embankment needed to be removed before any games could be played there. This is surprising, as the ground had been used for association football prior to that, with amateur team Leeds Woodville playing on it on alternate weeks to Holbeck. The ground was just a one penny tram ride from the city centre, closer than the Headingley stadium, and was easily accessible from the south. Ironically, the club's first ever opponents, Morley, would fold less than a decade later, citing the popularity of Leeds City in that town as the main reason for its financial problems.

There were many complaints regarding the conduct of City, however, with its apparent undermining of league fixtures, and had the club not been elected to the Football League one wonders whether it would have been able to continue in the county league in future years. A move to the Midland Counties League would have been a probable outcome had it suffered expulsion from the West Yorkshire League.

Leeds City 1905/06

*1907 Wills Scissors cigarette card showing Leeds City club colours (Dark blue, with orange collar)*

There was no cup success that first season, with South Yorkshire side Rockingham Colliery denying Leeds City in the FA Cup, Bradford City's reserve team the West Yorkshire Cup, and Upper Armley Christ Church the Leeds Hospitals Cup. While disappointing, the club committee was working hard behind the scenes to improve the club's standing with those it would depend on at the end of the season. And how things would change within the space of a few months.

Following twelve months of trying to win over its member clubs, Leeds City was elected in May 1905 to an expanding Football League. It topped the poll with 25 votes, ahead of Burslem Port Vale (21 votes), Chelsea (20) and Hull City (18), proving its efforts successful. In addition, a reserve team was formed, and entered into the Midland Counties League for the 1905/06 season, a competition in which it remained until 1915.

In preparation for its move into the professional game, the club became a limited company on 5th June 1905, with 1,000 x £1 shares on offer. The first chairman of the new company was the club president, Hepworth, an established local clothier, with Ralph Younger, landlord of the nearby Peacock Hotel and AW Pullin, 'Old Ebor', joining Hepworth as the main shareholders. Meanwhile, the pitch was extended further to 115 yards in length and 72 in width and a new 75-yard stand erected on the Elland Road side of the ground. Terracing replaced the old stand on the north side of the ground, with a special 'sod laying ceremony' held in May 1906 to celebrate the relaying of the playing area itself. Season tickets were charged at 10s for entry to the ground only, or a guinea for entry to the stand.

Leeds City AFC had not been elected to the Football League due to its prowess, nor was this a result of the abandonment of Northern Union at Elland Road (Holbeck Football Club's folding merely provided an opportunity for 'socker' to take over at the ground), but in the first instance, it did mirror the franchising element of providing new clubs to the national league. Leeds was, at the time, the largest city in the country without a Football League team. The financial rewards to the Football League and its clubs were considerably higher with a team from Leeds in it.

Under the tutelage of secretary-manager Gilbert Gillies, the attendance for City's first Football League home game was 6,802 for the

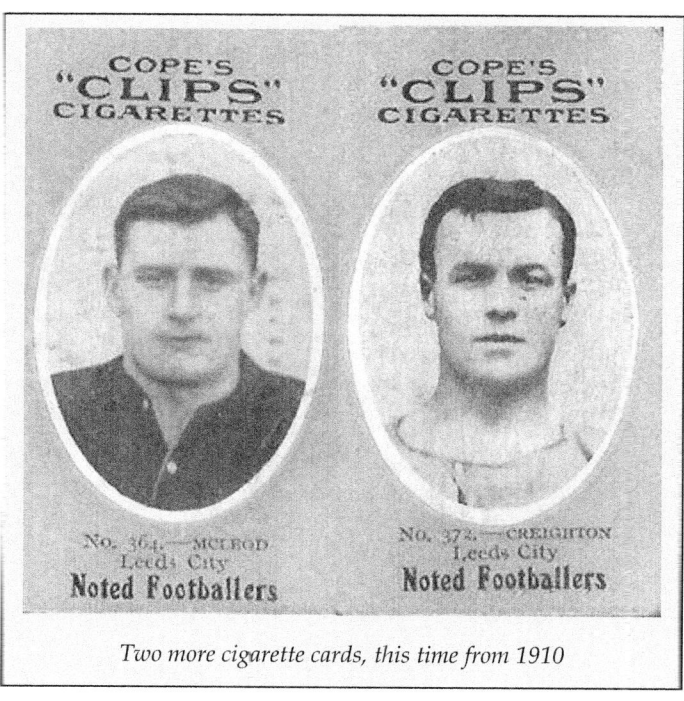

*Two more cigarette cards, this time from 1910*

visit of West Bromwich Albion, but only 3,000 were present two days later when Lincoln City arrived in town. But attendances improved considerably after that as the locals bought into the new club, with 22,000 attending for the derby with Bradford City in late December eclipsing the 20,000 for the Chelsea game the previous month.

Interestingly the gates at Headingley, for Leeds Northern Union games, slumped from an average of just over 9,000 during the 1904/05 season to 5,632 the following season, City's first in the Football League. By now there was no doubt which was the biggest sport in the city.

But it was proving expensive to run a competitive, professional team. A Leeds City Emergency General Meeting in April 1912 saw the club at breaking point due to its increasing financial problems. With liabilities of nearly £16,000, the club was close to going out of business, kept afloat only due to the generosity of Hepworth, who ploughed in some £15,000 of his own money. Ironically, Leeds Cricket, Football & Athletics Club offered to take on the ailing club and relocate it to Headingley. Fourteen years had passed since the old Leeds AFC had been more or less forced to fold by the Headingley club, who cancelled its tenancy of the ground, but now that Association Football had outgrown both codes of rugby and COULD be made to pay, then the situation had clearly changed. City finished second bottom of the Second Division that year, having previously established itself as a mid-table second-tier club, but it was easily re-elected by member clubs. In the meantime, Tom Coombes was placed as the club's receiver, and he would run the club for the near future.

After being saved, the club, under new manager Herbert Chapman, made great strides over the next two seasons, with finishing positions of 6th, and then 4th in the 1913/14 season - just two points away from promotion. In August that summer the club was finally taken over by a consortium of Leeds sportsmen led by Joseph Connor, the then President of the West Riding Football Association. Despite a lowly 15th place the following season, there was optimism within the club that promotion to the First Division would be secured sooner rather than later, which would then put the club at the same level as

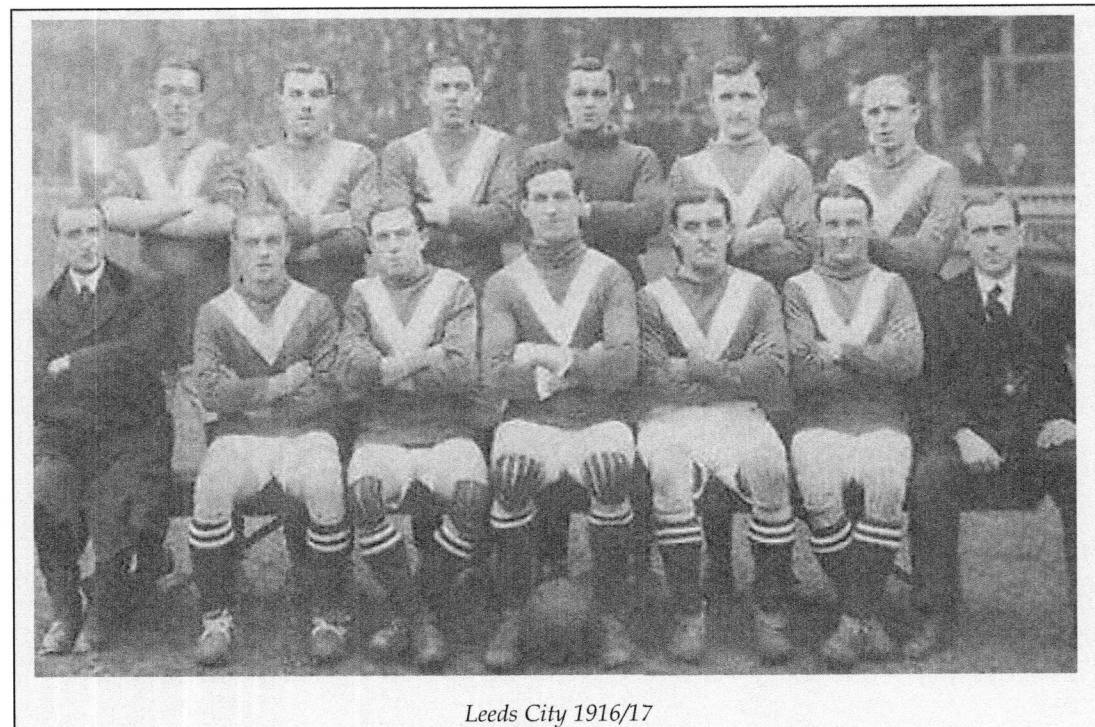

*Leeds City 1916/17*

Bradford's two professional clubs. Alas, the Leeds City story would end just eight games after normal League operations were resumed in 1919 when the club was expelled from the League for illegal payments to players during the war. Charlie Copeland, who had been with Leeds City since 1912, fell out with the club over the issue of a pay rise. As a result, he made allegations about illegal payments made to guest players during the war. Although this practice was widespread, it had been simply ignored by the Football Association and the Football League, but Copelard's allegations now made it impossible for the authorities to simply sweep the matter under the carpet. Officials of the club were summoned to a meeting of an FA Commission at Manchester on 26th September 1919, chaired by the Football Association Chairman John Charles Clegg, where they were ordered to turn over their books. Officials of Leeds City replied they were not in a power to do so, but were nevertheless ordered to produce the documents by 6th October.

*A rare Baines Shield depicting Jack White, a full-back who made 60 appearances for Leeds City between 1908-10*

Two days before the Commission's deadline, Leeds City won 4-2 at Wolves, ironically giving a lift home on the team coach to none other than Charlie Copeland. The Wolves fixture proved to be Leeds City's last ever game, with the documents failing to be produced.

The team's next fixture against South Shields was suspended as the enquiry team later met at the Russell Hotel in London. The result, Leeds City were expelled from the Football League. There was no firm evidence that Leeds City had actually done anything wrong, but it is believed that with the club failing to produce the documents then this was an admission of guilt. Port Vale replaced Leeds City in the league and went on to finish in 13th position after inheriting Leeds City's points that had been accumulated to date.

## Leeds United

There had been two previous Leeds United clubs in existence before the current club was formed from the ashes of Leeds City. Neither of them completed its first season.

The first Leeds United appeared in the 1898/99 season, playing on the well-established Cardigan Fields site at Kirkstall, and it disappeared as quickly as it had appeared, dropping out of the West Yorkshire League in mid-January 1899 after claiming that it had been treated badly by other clubs in the league. The *Yorkshire Evening Post* reported that, *'difficulties and dissensions'* had cropped up, with several of the team having already signed for other clubs. The club was in second place in the league at the time, albeit having played more games than most of its rivals, so its folding affected the final positions in a marked way.

A second Leeds United, with lofty ambitions, was founded in May 1911, and immediately applied for membership of the West Riding Football Association, the FA Cup (its' one tie in the competition resulted in a 1-3 loss at Morley in the Preliminary Round) and the FA Amateur Cup (withdrawing from its Second

Qualifying Round tie at Hull St. George's), as well as the Yorkshire Combination league. Like the previous club of that name, this club also played home games at Cardigan Fields. A reserve team was also formed, playing in the Leeds & District League's Senior Division. Sadly, both teams failed to complete their fixtures. For the first team, a 0-15 home defeat to Bradford Park Avenue's reserve team in September, and 1-7 defeat at home to York City the following month, reflected the fact that the newly formed club was out of its depth at this standard of competition. By March the club had officially disbanded.

## A New Leeds City

A new Leeds City appeared in 1924, but this was not a new club, it was through a name change of the well-established Leeds Harehills AFC, which had been in existence for over twenty years and had achieved success at a local level before stepping up to the Yorkshire League.

In September 1903, the *Yorkshire Evening Post* was carrying an advert for 'Leeds Harehills AFC (affiliated)', which had a few open dates for friendly fixtures. Those interested should apply to a Mr Powell, Darfield Street, Leeds.

In the 1904/05 season, Leeds Harehills amicably shared a ground on Foundry Lane with another junior club, Cameron Trinity although, with both teams enjoying success, Harehills, playing in the Leeds & District League's Junior A Division (winning the divisional title), was forced to play some home games on alternative grounds instead. The following season, Harehills appear to have been in the short-lived Leeds Central League.

Harehills played regular friendly fixtures during the latter half of the 1906/07 season and for the 1907/08 season was accepted into the Leeds League. However, during the summer the club became a founder member of the Leeds Amateur League instead, later moving from its current open Military Field ground at Roundhay to Avenue Road, Roundhay Road in the summer of 1913. The club stayed in the Amateur League until the summer of 1922, by which time it was playing on a ground off Harehills Avenue.

Harehills was then a founder member of the West Yorkshire Amateur League, alongside the likes of Knaresborough Town, Guiseley, Yeadon Celtic, East End Park WMC, several clubs having broken away from the Leeds Amateur League to become members. Armley AFC withdrew prior to the league's first season after having lost its Pasture Hills Ground, but the new competition proved a success. However, the 1922/23 campaign was the club's only season in this company. After having lost out to Leeds Malvern in the final table, the team lost 0-2 to Yeadon Celtic

### 1907/08 Leeds Amateur League

| | P | W | D | L | F | A | Pts |
|---|---|---|---|---|---|---|---|
| Yeadon Amateurs | 20 | 17 | 1 | 2 | 56 | 24 | 35 |
| **Leeds Harehills** | 20 | 16 | 2 | 2 | 72 | 29 | 34 |
| Hunslet United | 20 | 14 | 3 | 3 | 50 | 22 | 31 |
| Lodge Lane Albion | 20 | 11 | 0 | 9 | 42 | 40 | 22 |
| Wortley Clarendon | 20 | 9 | 4 | 7 | 47 | 47 | 20 |
| Wortley Temp | 20 | 9 | 1 | 10 | 49 | 41 | 19 |
| Silver Royd Hill | 20 | 6 | 5 | 9 | 45 | 44 | 17 |
| St.Margaret's | 20 | 8 | 2 | 10 | 24 | 39 | 16 |
| Watsons Ltd. | 20 | 3 | 3 | 14 | 28 | 49 | 9 |
| Princes Field | 20 | 4 | 0 | 16 | 24 | 80 | 8 |
| Yorkshire Post | 20 | 2 | 1 | 17 | 11 | 33 | 5 |

### 1912/13 Leeds Amateur League

| | P | W | D | L | F | A | Pts |
|---|---|---|---|---|---|---|---|
| **Leeds Harehills** | 22 | 17 | 3 | 2 | 62 | 22 | 37 |
| Royal Horse Art | 22 | 16 | 3 | 2 | 66 | 27 | 37 |
| Leeds Churchville | 22 | 13 | 2 | 7 | 59 | 32 | 28 |
| Silver Royd Hill | 22 | 11 | 7 | 4 | 50 | 18 | 27 |
| Leeds Univ YMI | 22 | 10 | 2 | 10 | 58 | 58 | 22 |
| Leeds St. Clements | 22 | 8 | 5 | 9 | 43 | 48 | 21 |
| Holbeck Leam'ton | 22 | 10 | 2 | 10 | 39 | 32 | 20 |
| Quarry Hill St Mary | 22 | 6 | 6 | 10 | 49 | 40 | 18 |
| Kirkstall St. Steph | 22 | 6 | 3 | 13 | 47 | 60 | 15 |
| RAMC (T) | 22 | 4 | 4 | 14 | 30 | 77 | 12 |
| Beeston Hill Par Ch | 22 | 4 | 3 | 15 | 32 | 66 | 11 |
| Farnley Loco | 22 | 4 | 4 | 14 | 34 | 85 | 10 |

*Royal Horse Artillery defeated Leeds Harehills 1-0 in a replay in a play-off for the title*

### 1922/23 West Yorkshire Amateur League

| | P | W | D | L | Pts |
|---|---|---|---|---|---|
| **Leeds Malvern** | 26 | 18 | 4 | 4 | 40 |
| **Leeds Harehills** | 26 | 19 | 2 | 5 | 40 |
| Yeadon Celtic | 26 | 18 | 3 | 5 | 39 |
| Morley St.Andrews | 26 | 13 | 9 | 3 | 35 |
| Garforth Athletic | 26 | 16 | 3 | 7 | 35 |
| East End Pk WMC | 24 | 13 | 4 | 7 | 30 |
| Rawdon | 25 | 13 | 3 | 9 | 29 |
| Guiseley | 24 | 8 | 3 | 13 | 19 |
| Monkbridge Sports | 23 | 6 | 6 | 11 | 18 |
| Otley Parish Ch | 25 | 5 | 8 | 12 | 18 |
| Leeds St.Hildas | 24 | 6 | 5 | 13 | 17 |
| Knaresborough Tn | 25 | 4 | 6 | 15 | 14 |
| Starbeck Athletic | 24 | 3 | 3 | 18 | 9 |
| Harrogate Amats | 24 | 1 | 4 | 19 | 6 |

*Armley w/d pre-season*

in the league's 'Shield' play-off final, before successfully applying to move up to the Yorkshire League.

The club had been successful through the years, having won the Leeds Amateur League title in the 1911/12 season, and finishing runner-up in the 1910/11 and 1912/13 seasons, the latter of which saw the team defeated 1-0 in a replay in a play-off for the title by Royal Horse Artillery. Some consolation that season was a 3-1 defeat of Silver Royd Hill in the Leeds Amateur Cup final.

The opening of the club's new home ground, at Bracken Edge (now the home of Yorkshire Amateurs, who at this time were playing at Harehills Avenue) was on Saturday 22nd September 1923, with a crowd of 3,000 witnessing an exciting 2-2 draw with York City reserves in the Yorkshire League.

Eighth place in an 18-strong division in 1923/24 was a really good start to Yorkshire League life for the Harehills club, which, with the higher standard of football being offered, chose to change its name to Leeds City in June 1924.

Three more seasons were spent in the Yorkshire League as Leeds City, the club finishing 6th out of 16 in the 1924/25 season, 4th out of 15 in 1925/26, and then 11th out of 16 in 1926/27, by which time it was playing on a new ground at Hunslet Nelson, having lost the use of its Bracken Edge home. The Nelson cricket club was located on Low Road, and the football field could well have been the same used by Hunslet AFC in the late 1800s/very early 1900s.

The team folded in the summer of 1927, and its passing was hardly noticed. Its demise could by no means be put down to its playing record, as the club did not struggle on the pitch, and is likely to be down to finance, which could have explained the ground move twelve months earlier. There were no reports of the club's passing in the local press, although Bracken Edge has of course continued to be used as a football ground.

Of course, the name of Leeds City has been revived more than once in recent times, and the current – entirely unrelated club – plays in the Yorkshire Amateur League, following several successful years in the West Yorkshire League.

## Hunslet in FA Competitions

Hunslet took part in both FA Cup and FA Amateur Cup competitions, with its best run in the former competition in the 1899/1900 season, when it reached the Fourth Qualifying Round. Much more success was achieved in the Amateur Cup competition however, with Quarter Final appearances in both 1895/96 and 1900/01. As referred to earlier, the mighty Old Etonians were defeated en-route to the last eight in the latter, before a heavy defeat at Darlington. The run to the same stage in 1900/01 was far shorter, as the club had been exempt from the qualifying stages. North-eastern teams were played in all three ties that season, with defeat coming at home to Bishop Auckland, who also defeated Hunslet in its last ever tie in the Amateur Cup the following season.

**FA Cup**
1896/97: 2Q (H) Attercliffe 3-1, 3Q (A) Barnsley St. Peter's 2-3
1897/98: 1Q (A) Parkgate United 1-1 (H) 1-2
1898/99: 1Q (A) Wath-upon-Dearne 0-0(H) 1-1 (N) 3-3, (N) 1-2
1899/1900: 1Q (H) Altofts 3-0, 2Q (A) Wombwell Town 2-1, 3Q (A) Denaby United 2-2 (H) 1-1 (N) 4-3,
    4Q (A) Chesterfield 0-6
1900/01: 1Q (A) Royston United 2-1, 2Q (H) Wath Athletic 4-1, 3Q (A) Chesterfield 3-8
1901/02: 1Q (H) Royston United 1-1, withdrew from replay

**FA Amateur Cup**

1895/96: 3Q West Hartlepool NER (A) 4-6v (H) 8-1, 4Q (H) Loftus 5-4, 1R (H) Buxton 3-1, 2R Old Etonians (H) 3-2, QF (A) Darlington 0-6
1896/97: 2Q (A) Derby Constitutional 1-0, 3Q (A) Bradford 2-0, 4Q (H) Peterborough 8-1, 1R (A) Old Wilsonians 6-0, 2R (A) Bishop Auckland 0-4
1897/98: 1R (A) Darlington 1-4
1898/99: 2Q (H) Sheffield 4-2, 3Q (H) Liverpool Casuals 1-0, 4Q (A) Grimsby All Saints 1-2
1899/1900: 1R (H) Thornaby 4-0, 2R (A) Grimsby All Saints 2-3
1900/01: 1R (H) Tow law 6-1, 2R (A) Thornaby Utopians 3-1, QF (H) Bishop Auckland 0-3
1901/02: 1R (A) Bishop Auckland 1-5

## Leeds City in the FA Cup

1904/05: PR (A) Rockingham Colliery 1-3
1905/06: 1Q (H) Morley 11-0, 2Q Mexborough Town (H) 1-1 (A) 1-1 (H) 3-1, Q3 Hull City (A) 1-1 (H) 1-2
1906/07: 1R (A) Bristol City 1-4
1907/08: 1R (A) Oldham Athletic 1-2
1908/09: 1R (A) Oldham Athletic 1-1 (H) 2-0, 2R (H) West Ham United 1-1 (A) 1-2
1909/10: 1R (A) Sunderland 0-1
1910/11: 1R (A) Brighton & Hove Albion 1-3
1911/12: 1R (H) Glossop 1-0, 2R (A) West Bromwich Albion 0-1
1912/13: 1R (H) Burnley 2-3
1913/14: 1R (A) Gainsborough Trinity 4-2, 2R (H) West Bromwich Albion 0-2
1914/15: 1R (A) Derby County 2-1, 2R (A) Queens Park Rangers 0-1

## Leeds Harehills / City in the FA Amateur Cup

1921/22: 1Q (A) Leeds Malvern 0-1
1922/23: 1Q (A) Morley St Andrew's 3-1, 2Q (H) Rawdon 4-2, 3Q (H) Apperley Bridge 4-4, (A) 0-1
1923/24: PR (H) East End Park 2-1, 1Q (A) Starbeck Athletic 7-1, 2Q (H) Calverley 2-0, 3Q (H) Cleckheaton 4-1, 4Q (H) Rawdon 0-0, (A) 0-2
1924/25: 1Q Rothwell Athletic (H) 2-1, 2Q (H) Otley 8-1, 3Q (A) Cleckheaton 3-4

# Mexborough
# 1876-1936
## 'Boom and bust'

Mexborough Football Club is a prime example of one that for many years proved too strong for local football, yet, for a town of less than 20,000 throughout most of the late 1800s and early 1900s, wasn't large enough for it to compete with those from larger towns at a regional level. For some of that time, Mexborough's football team was able to punch above its weight, but could never maintain its lofty position at the head of the Midland League.

Throughout the 18th, 19th and much of the 20th Centuries Mexborough's economy was based around coal mining, quarrying, brickworks, and the production of ceramics. Glassmaking was also big business, with the Phoenix Glassworks, established in 1850, providing employment for hundreds of local workers. For over a hundred years, the railway locomotive maintenance and stabling depot, 'Mexborough Locc' was also a major employer. The South Yorkshire, Doncaster and Goole Railway arrived in Mexborough in 1850, with extensive coal traffic generated by the local collieries and it soon became a busy railway junction.

According to the 1887 Football Annual, the football club was founded 1876, with dressing rooms located at the town's Commercial Hotel, High Street. This would coincide with the Mexborough cricket club's move to the ground, which had been covered by allotment gardens before being secured by the club, which had itself been founded a few years earlier. It is almost certain that the football club was formed as a winter pastime by the cricketers, initially with informal games played between members.

The football section soon became established as a separate organisation and early competitive games were played against other local teams such as Parkgate Rising Star, who were defeated 3-1 on 1st November 1879. There were a few informal teams operating in the Mexborough district at the same time, such as Mexborough White Rose, which played other local clubs in and around 1877. These teams had no ambition to become Mexborough's 'town' club, being, in the main, a group of lads experimenting with the new, rapidly growing code.

By 1887, the Mexborough AFC club colours were red and white, with the secretary being one W Sayer of Garden Street, Mexborough. The 1886/87 season proved to be fairly successful, with 14 matches won, and one drawn from 29 completed fixtures. In addition, the Mexborough reserve team had won eleven and drawn four of its 18 matches. One of the team's early stars was Jimmy Sayer, who played with club in 1880 and soon went on to play 24 times for Stoke, and once for England, in a 7-0 win over Ireland in 1887. Dubbed '*Greyhound*' by Stoke fans due to his pace, he returned to play for Mexborough after leaving that club in 1890.

The football club organised its own feast sports at the Hampden Road cricket ground, those over three days in June 1887 involving the usual footraces, as well as potty-races, obstacle races, a six-a-side football contest, and donkey races.

A few years later, *the Sheffield Evening Telegraph,* on 10th January 1907 referred to a past incident occurring at a football match in Mexborough, and one can assume that this refers to a certain relative of Sayer, *'the mother of a popular player, who afterwards wore an international cap, was invariably conspicuous in her strenuous approval or condemnation of incidents of the game. Indeed, on one occasion, her partisanship led her to heartily belabour a player with her umbrella, an incident that is still recording reminiscences of local football,'*

*Tip Bennett (left), and Walter Bennett*

Another player of note in the club's early years was Walter Bennett, who went on to play for Sheffield United (195 appearances, 59 goals) and Bristol City (48 appearances, 22 goals), and gained two international caps, playing for England against Wales and Scotland in the 1901 Home International Championship. After leaving Bristol City he moved to Denaby Main, where he took a job as a miner and played for the colliery team there. He was tragically killed in April 1908, aged 33, following a roof fall at the colliery as he was making his way back to the surface after his shift, leaving a widow and four children.

'Cocky', as he was nicknamed, was also one of the best all-rounders in the Mexborough and District Cricket League. He was not alone in his family in being a top-class footballer.

His eldest brother William, or 'Micky', also started his career at Mexborough before going on to play for The Wednesday as centre-forward. Harry E Bennett, better known as *Tip,* was captain of the Mexborough team when Walter, as a youngster of 17, joined it. Subsequently he went to Barnsley, where he became club captain, as a right-half. Another brother, George, also played for Sheffield United and Barnsley.

Later in 1908, another Mexborough footballer lost his life. Full-back, Arthur W Windle, succumbed to injuries received on the 12th of September, when he broke his leg during a match between his team and Barnsley reserves at Oakwell. The cause of death was exhaustion and heart failure due to lockjaw. The saddest aspect his death was the fact that Windle had only married three months earlier.

*** 

The first piece of silverware won by Mexborough football club was the Sheffield & Hallamshire Senior Cup in 1885/86, after having reached the Semi Final stage the previous season. The final saw the favourites, Heeley, defeated 2-1 at the Old Forge Ground, Newhall on 10th April 1886 in front of 2,000 spectators.

In on Friday 20th September 1889 the *Sheffield Daily Telegraph* reported on an amalgamation of the football and cricket clubs in Mexborough. It was believed that funds would be forthcoming for much-needed ground improvements that would benefit both football and cricket sections. However, the cricket section retained the lease on the ground, which would cause problems further down the line.

By 1890/91 the club became a member of the Sheffield & District League, a competition that had been founded the season before. The Football League itself had been founded in 1888, which quickly gave rise to a number of other national, regional, and local league competitions, such as those that appeared in the Sheffield district.

The Shefield League, in its various guises, improved in strength during the early 1890s, containing the likes future Football League teams Barnsley (St Peter's), and Chesterfield, as well as the current Kivetor Park, and, later, several reserve teams from professional clubs. It was, in effect, a South Yorkshire League competition.

Mexborough was a leading light in the league, with a third-place finish in its first season in the competition. The title was very nearly won twelve months later, when, despite leading the league in its final stages, a 1-2 defeat at Chesterfield in front of 4,000 spectators in its final fixture allowed the Derbyshire club to take the 1891/92 title itself. The following season it was The Wednesday reserves who narrowly pipped Mexborough for the title.

For the season 1893/94 season, the Sheffield & District League had morphed into the Sheffield Challenge Cup League, and at last Mexborough won the title, thanks a 3-1 victory over Sheffield United Strollers in its final match. The team was afterwards driven through the town accompanied by a brass band. However, the Sheffield & District League did continue in a reduced format, with two groups of five teams. Mexborough achieved the double, defeating Sheffield Wednesday reserves 1-0 in the league's play-off final.

The Sheffield & District League ran a single 'top' division called the 'Wharncliffe Charity Cup League' from the 1894/95 season, with ten others in a two division Shield competition. Mexborough regained the title, which made up somewhat for its failure to successfully defend the Sheffield Challenge Cup League title.

Mexborough's final season in the Sheffield Leagues resulted in it regaining the Sheffield Challenge Cup League, winning 24 of its 28 matches and remaining unbeaten (The club's first 22 league matches were all won). Although the Wharncliffe League title was not retained, the club, at least on the field, couldn't have been in a better position to move up to the Midland League, which sat just one level below the Football League. The 1895/96 season was in fact the last time that the Sheffield Challenge Cup was organised on a league basis, reverting to a knock-out competition the following season. As a result, the Sheffield Association League was introduced for 1896/97.

Mexborough had been invited to apply for membership of the Midland League, and on Monday 4th May 1896 a special general meeting was held at the town's Royal Oak, Bank Street, where that invitation was accepted. The club was just about breaking even at this stage, with a small financial deficit just about wiped out during the season.

Eventual champions Doncaster Rovers were visitors on Mexborough's debut in the competition, winning 1-0, and the gulf between the Sheffield and Midland leagues was underlined when the club finished 13th in its first season. Just Worksop Town and Grantham finished below Mexborough in the final table. Adverse weather affected gates during the season, and the club, despite having paid its share on a new stand, was behind with its rent to the cricket club to the tune of £14. The club AGM on Monday 10th May 1897 passed a resolution that the team would be paid 7s per player for a loss, 8s for a draw and 10s for a victory, although it was accepted that results would have to improve if the club was to be able to sustain itself in the future.

Things could not have been more different the following season, as 1897/98 campaign was the most successful in the club's history, winning the Midland League title as well as finishing runners-up in the Yorkshire League and reaching the 5th Qualifying Round of the FA Cup. In what was a decisive match, a 4-2 victory over Barnsley early in April saw the club climb to the top of the table, and by the season's end just two points separated the new champions from Barnsley themselves. The reverse fixture in December had ended early due to fog with the score a 2-2, with the league committee ordering the final ten minutes to be played on 3rd February before a Yorkshire League fixture between the teams, with the score remaining unaltered.

The ten-team Yorkshire League was a new competition that lasted just three seasons. It brought together the best of the teams from what is now West Yorkshire, with the second teams of South Yorkshire clubs. The latter proved far too strong, Mexborough finishing runner-up behind Sheffield United reserves. In theory, this was a Mexborough first team, but precedence was given to Midland League fixtures.

However, the club's finances were still of concern, and it was clear that wages and travelling expenses were not being met at the gate, despite the outstanding football on offer at Hampden Road. Several players moved on to other clubs during the summer as Mexborough FC looked to reduce its debts.

Unsurprisingly, in light of its financial woes, the club struggled during the 1898/99 season, although it was a surprise to see Mexborough finish at the foot of the table in the Midland League this time around. As well as the Yorkshire League team, a reserve team was entered into the South Yorkshire League, with only one league match being lost all season in that competition. By the season's end, Mexborough AFC was over £99 in debt, and sufficient support through the turnstiles was still not forthcoming. With a working-class fan-base, many of whom were in the coal mining profession, money was tight and despite a successful football team there were few people who could invest in the club. The only bright spot during the season was victory in the Mexborough Montagu Charity Cup final – a

---

*Mexborough and Swinton Times, 6th May 1898*

*For the last, last time this season,*
*I'm privileged to write*
*How plucky little Mexborough*
*Have conquered in the fight*
*For the last, last time, their efforts*
*In song I must applaud,*
*And once again for the last, last time,*
*Must vict'ry I record.*

*Hurrah! For the game eleven*
*Whose season is now done!*
*Who've finished in the fashion*
*They gallantly begun.*
*Hurrah! For the plucky players –*
*Lads it is far confessed,*
*Where'er you next discover,*
*Are gamest, and aye, the best!*
    *G R Tennyson-Sims*

competition which is still in existence today - when Tip Bennett captained the team to a 3-1 defeat of Wath in the final, played at Kilnhurst. Mexborough's Montagu Cottage Hospital had been officially opened in January 1890 on Bank Street, Mexborough and the competition was organised initially to raise much needed funds for this.

Despite an initial intention to continue in the Midland League, the Mexborough club's committee decided that there no other option but to revert to more local football in the summer of 1899, joining the Sheffield Association League, ultimately without success, and the Wharncliffe Charity League, in which it struggled at the foot of the table all season. (in addition, the Yorkshire League fell apart when the South Yorkshire Clubs withdrew en-masse). An end of season general meeting, held on Thursday 3rd May saw the reading of the statement of accounts for the club, and it was decided to find some way to wipe those debts before the club could be resuscitated. Debts by now totalled £113 11s, with £15 9s 9d incurred in the season just past. Rent arrears to the cricket club were £25 (rent was £20 per annum), and indeed the cricket club was threatening to form its own association team should Mexborough AFC not be in a position to pay off its debt. Players' wages had been suspended in January 1900, which had saved the club around £70.

Sadly, those debts could not be wiped out before the following season, so therefore, the 1900/01 season began with the name of Mexborough AFC missing. All was not lost though, as the *Sheffield Daily Telegraph* reported, on Thursday 3rd January 1901 that progress had been made, with the chief creditor having called together others owed money and an agreement being made whereby an agreement was made to accept half their accounts in full settlement. Furthermore, the cricket club reduced its debt to just £10, and a fund-raising archery tournament organised for Easter.

However, the club was not reformed during the summer of 1901, with junior side Mexborough St John's representing the town in the FA Cup instead. It wasn't until 1903 when a new Mexborough Town was formed, again playing at the cricket ground, and also going on to play in the Midland League. Mexborough West End also tried its luck in the FA Cup in the 1903/04 season, eventually bring knocked out in the second qualifying round by the new Mexborough Town. Town itself continued until 1936, ten years after having changed its name to Mexborough Athletic. Subsequent teams representing the town have also been based at the cricket club.

### Mexborough in the FA Cup (1)

The club only featured in the First Round proper of the English Cup on one occasion, and that, in the absence of qualifying round ties, was in its first entry into the competition in the 1885/86 season. Following a 1-1 draw at Staveley, Mexborough scratched from the replay, although no reason was given for this in the local press

The club's best performance was in the 1897/98 season, which included eight ties, four of them against Doncaster Rovers. Following three 2-1 victories over Leeds, Kilnhurst, and Barnsley, there were three drawn ties with Doncaster, before another 2-1 Mexborough victory in the third replay, played at Barnsley. Gainsborough Trinity ended the cup run in the Fifth Qualifying Round with a 1-0 win at Hampden Road.

### Mexborough FC League record 1896-99

| | P | W | D | L | F | A | Pts | Pos |
|---|---|---|---|---|---|---|---|---|
| **1896/97** | | | | | | | | |
| Midland | 28 | 7 | 7 | 14 | 39 | 50 | 21 | 13/15 |
| **1897/98** | | | | | | | | |
| Midland | 22 | 15 | 3 | 4 | 53 | 30 | 33 | 1/12 |
| Yorkshire | 18 | 12 | 2 | 4 | 51 | 22 | 26 | 2/10 |
| **1898/99** | | | | | | | | |
| Midland | 26 | 8 | 3 | 15 | 33 | 54 | 19 | 14/14 |
| Yorkshire | 18 | 11 | 2 | 5 | 40 | 28 | 24 | 5/10 |

### 1897/1898 Midland League

| | P | W | D | L | F | A | Pts |
|---|---|---|---|---|---|---|---|
| Mexborough Town | 22 | 15 | 3 | 4 | 53 | 30 | 33 |
| Barnsley St. Peter's | 22 | 14 | 3 | 5 | 47 | 29 | 31 |
| Chesterfield | 22 | 11 | 7 | 4 | 54 | 23 | 29 |
| Ilkeston Town | 22 | 9 | 6 | 7 | 37 | 39 | 24 |
| Burslem Port Vale | 22 | 10 | 3 | 9 | 46 | 32 | 23 |
| Rushden Town | 22 | 9 | 5 | 8 | 35 | 44 | 23 |
| Kettering | 22 | 7 | 5 | 10 | 19 | 28 | 19 |
| Long Eaton Rgrs | 22 | 7 | 5 | 10 | 26 | 44 | 19 |
| Glossop North End | 22 | 8 | 2 | 12 | 41 | 47 | 18 |
| Doncaster Rovers | 22 | 5 | 6 | 11 | 33 | 35 | 16 |
| Burton Wanderers | 22 | 5 | 6 | 11 | 31 | 44 | 16 |
| Wellingborough | 22 | 5 | 3 | 14 | 21 | 48 | 13 |

## A New Mexborough Town

*South Yorkshire Times and Mexborough & Swinton Times*, Friday 14th August 1903

### Mexboro' Town Football Club

The resuscitation of the old Mexboro' Town Football Club, which, one memorable season, won such high honours in the Midland League, and whose decadence was all too rapid, has given great satisfaction to local followers of the great winter game, who have some reason for their hopes that the club once again destined to win further honours in the football world. Mr E Mountford has been appointed secretary, and his energetic interest, together with the efforts of a strong working committee, should ensure the management success of the club, whilst the strong string of players signed on should see the team more often than not victorious on the field. The decline of the old club was namely due to the tremendous expense entailed in the long journeys to meet the then clubs of the Midland League, but the progress of time has been responsible for a considerable alteration in the constitution of that competition, which now includes such teams in the near locality as the United and Wednesday reserves of Sheffield, Rotherham, Thornhill, and Doncaster football clubs, giving the Mexboro' Town Club every inducement to do so well this season as to next year be able to apply with success for admission once again to the Midland League. And to do this good and consistent form must be shown this winter. The competitions entered are the Sheffield Association League, the Sheffield Challenge Cup, the Mexboro' Montagu Hospital Charity Cup, and, breathe it gently, the English Cup. Thus, the followers of the club are promised some rare, good games. The players engaged are as follows – C Tayles and J Wommack, goal; W Westwood, M Hobson and J Turner, backs; J E Shaw, C E Coates, W Scholey, T Darby, and J Hilton, half backs; W Biggs, J T Hakin, W Groves, Tim Roper, A McNeil, G E Groves. H Whiteley, H Whitworth, T Hall, W Newton, J Cronshaw, and W Whitham, forwards. That these players may top a league, and win a cup or two, is the desire of hundreds who want to see the name of Mexboro' once again famous in football circles.

*Now, lads!*
*'Set the ball s-rolling*
*'Play up' the people call*
*Dribbling, kicking, shooting, tricking,*
*Always on the ball'*

The club's return turned out to be very successful, with the Sheffield Association League title won at the first attempt, ahead of some strong reserve teams from Midland League sides. In celebration, players and officials, as well as several enthusiastic supporters, enjoyed a dinner at the Bulls Head, when medals were also presented. It was suggested that Midland League football might return to the town the following season, but in the event, there was to be another season at local level first, one in which Mexborough Town just missed out on defending its league title. However, the 1904/05 season did see a good run in the FA Cup, with a run to the Fifth Qualifying Round before defeat at Gainsborough Trinity in a replay (there were two preliminary rounds and an intermediate round as well as six qualifying rounds that season, making nine qualifying rounds before the First Round proper!). That run did the club no harm in its application to the Midland League, which this time was successful. Thirty-one of the 52 fixtures played by the first team were won that season, and importantly, the club at this point had no debt, with over £79 in the bank.

Mexborough Town won the Montagu Cup in 1904 and 1905. Finals of the competition were usually staged at Hampden Road, but were switched when Town reached the final – as it had been in 1899 – in order not to give the club an unfair advantage. Rotherham Town reserves were defeated 4-1 at Denaby in a 1904 replay (following a 3-3 draw at Clifton), with South Kirkby defeated 1-0 in 1905, in a final staged at Bolton upon Dearne. With entry to the Midland League, Town's first team did not enter the Montagu Cup competition again, although its reserve team reached the final in 1910, losing 0-2 to Hickleton Main at Bolton.

With Midland League football again on the horizon, the main point of discussion at Mexborough Town FC during the summer of 1905 was which venue would serve as club headquarters in the following years. The club was divided into two camps, 'Bulls Headers' and 'Royal Oakites', as the *South Yorkshire Times* put it, and it was this debate that dominated proceedings at the club AGM in May 1905 rather than club finances and other important matters. Both inns had helped the club a great deal since its revival, and there had been an informal understanding that each inn would serve as headquarters on alternative years. This was not acceptable to all, so an extra meeting was held the following month when the Bulls Head won the vote by 93 votes to 90 – subsequent votes being held each year, which meant that the landlords, Mr Venables and Mr Biggs, both of had contributed so much to the club during the years could both continue to do so. By 1908, the Montagu Arms Hotel was also being used. Meanwhile, and of importance to the battling innkeepers, keen to pull in the punters, the team had been elected to the Midland League.

*Mexborough Town, 1906/07*

Despite a fine first season in the Midland League - a fifth place finish – financial matters took another turn for the worse, with a loss of over £55 over the season reported at the 1906 AGM. The club had also performed reasonably well in the Wharncliffe Charity and Sheffield Association leagues, but it was recognised that it was unable to compete with some of the reserve teams of Football League sides in the Midland League that were able to pay players as professionals, as opposed to the semi-professional status of the Mexborough team. The arrears had risen slightly to £70 one year later.

The 1908 AGM was another fractious one that reflected a return to desperate times for the club, which seemed to lurch from boom (at least on the field) to bust, as once again the move upwards had proved financially challenging, and the fact that the club's playing fortunes had taken a turn for the worst. With a new pavilion on the ground by 1910, finances were stretched, and by 1913 the club owed over £287, and although other clubs in the league owed just as much to its' debtors, things were becoming more alarming. In fact, in 1913, local rivals Denaby United dropped out of the Midland League in order to regroup, after having also struggled financially.

In April 1914 Mexborough Town hosted a public meeting in the cricket pavilion, in order to ascertain whether there was a public desire for the club to continue. Support from local tradesmen as well as paying supporters was much needed, with the club by now almost £370 in the red, and a number of local gentlemen had lent the club money totalling £245 which could not possibly be paid back yet. Wages were owed to the tune of £4 and the club had struggled to provide train fares for away fixtures. Benefit performances to aid club funds were said to be in the pipeline, and there were hopes of a grant being obtained from the Football Association's Benevolent Fund, but in the event there was an even bigger challenge facing the club, and indeed the local community, in the outbreak of War. One more season was completed, with Mexborough again in the lower reaches of the league, before activities were curtailed.

Very little football was played during the World War One, although match was played by a Mexborough Town XI and a Doncaster Army Veterans Corps XI at Hampden Road in October 1915. It was organised by Major Skinner, an army recruiting officer for the Mexborough district.

**Mexborough in the FA Cup (2)**

The club was back in the English Cup competition in the 1903/04 season, although its secretary forgot to send in the club's entry for the 1906/07 season. Mexborough's best performance was in the 1904/05 and 1909/10 seasons, when it reached the Fifth Qualifying Round.

The 1904/05 run began at home to Thornhill United, in a tie which was won 1-0, and that was followed by wins at Sheffield (in a replay), Denaby United, Doncaster Rovers (also after a replay), and Blackwell (6-2), before a 1-1 draw with Gainsborough Trinity. A crushing 0-7 defeat followed in the replay. There were two more qualifying rounds to negotiate that season before the first round could be reached.

The 1910/11 season cup run nearly ended in the Preliminary Round, when Allerton Bywater Colliery took Mexborough to a replay. Once a successful replay had been negotiated then Castleford Town (5-0), Grimsby Town (6-1), Denaby United (in a second replay) and Doncaster Rovers (in a replay) were overcome, before Mexborough went out in a replay to Carlisle United, just one stage prior to the First Round Proper.

Other notable FA Cup victories included a 9-0 rout of Leeds side Upper Armley Old Boys in a Second Qualifying Round tie in the 1905/06 season, and an 8-0 win at Acomb WMC (York) in the Preliminary Round in 1914/15.

*\*\*\**

On Sunday 9th March 1919, a well-attended meeting at the Royal Oak saw Mexborough AFC (minus the 'Town' part of the name) revived, with hopes of entering a team, hopefully with more success than the pre-War club, into the Midland League. It was proposed to use more local players, which would elicit more local support for the club, and arrangements were made with the cricket club to again use the field for home fixtures. The league readily accepted Mexborough back into the fold.

Sheffield Wednesday reserves were the first visitors to Hampden Road on 30th August 1919 as Mexborough resumed its Midland League career. A 3-0 victory for the home team couldn't have been a better start, and the good form continued as the side finished the season in fifth place.

There was a spirit of optimism at the 1920 AGM, although there was talk whether the club should continue to operate from the cricket club or to find a new ground of its own – one on a field off Swinton

> *South Yorkshire Times* – 20th April 1904
> ### The Ballad of The Montagu Cup
>
> *Go talk of your Manchester City,*
> *And the Wanderers of Bolton who 'Trot,'*
> *Cup finalists are they? I wouldn't*
> *Give more than a fig for the lot,*
> *The teams that do set an example*
> *To whom all the rest may look up,*
> *Is the plucky eleven of Mexboro',*
> *Who've captured the Montagu Cup.*
>
> *With talk about class I've no patience.*
> *'Nor of science and style and such rot,*
> *Let them keep such expensive gymnastics*
> *To the fight for the old English pot.*
> *Instead of the team that manoeuvres*
> *Like eleven old elephants tame,*
> *Give me that which goes hot for goal-scoring,*
> *And play with their heart in the game.*
>
> *Be hanged to your crossing and passing,*
> *On a daught board, may be, it looks well,*
> *But upon the true lover of football*
> *'Tis certain to pull in a spell*
> *I prefer the eleven that isn't*
> *An elegant composite whole,*
> *And rushes a bit, if it happens*
> *Their energy gets them to goal.*
>
> *For 'tis goals that win matches, not waltzing,*
> *And football is played in a field,*
> *And not on the floor of a ballroom,*
> *Where to elegance, vigour might yield:*
> *The player who, like the professor*
> *Indulges in 'twiddeldy bits,'*
> *If he plays in a cup-tie is certain*
> *To suffer a series of fits.*
>
> *But the lad, who, like Rodgers, McArthur,*
> *Drops science, and goes for the goal*
> *Is the player who'll bring an eleven*
> *Out safe on top of the poll;*
> *When O'Roper, McHakin, and Biggy*
> *Back up the McR. It's a cert*
> *That somebody's pretty goal record*
> *Is seriously going to get hurt.*
>
> *Well, the Montagu Cup has been captured,*
> *Mexboro' Town have secured it again.*
> *And now, if they're anxious to keep it*
> *Their rivals may covet in vain*
> *'Tis a custom on all such occasions,*
> *Champagne from the goblet to sup –*
> *Millionaires may now make application*
> *For the honour of filling the cup*
>
> G R Tennyson-Sims

Road being suggested. In the event, ground improvements were made at Hampden Road instead, with a Ground Improvement Committee formed from the members of football, cricket and bowling clubs based there.

In 1923 the cricket club handed over the Hampden Road property to the present Mexborough Athletic Club, which was formed to administer a grant of £5,500 from the Miners' Welfare Fund. The *South Yorkshire Times* stated, 'It is possible but for the stimulus of this fund the Mexborough athletic ground, celebrated in the local annals of sport as it is, would have continued shabby, dilapidated and poverty-stricken to the end of time. for it cried out for so much improvement and the means were so scanty, that it seemed hardly worth-while to attempt anything.'

The football section of the new entity continued officially as Mexborough AFC until the summer of 1926 when it became 'Mexborough Athletic'. The club, at the time, was on a high after becoming league champions for the first time since 1898, ahead of favourites Mansfield Town and local rivals Denaby United and Wath Athletic.

The championship trophy was handed to the Mexborough captain, Rob Hill by the league president at the conclusion of a rather dull, meaningless 1-0 home victory against Mansfield Town on Thursday 29th April - the match being a champions versus runners-up fixture. The title had been secured on the 21st of that month with a 2-2 draw at Loughborough Corinthians, after the team had won its previous ten fixtures.

Although undoubtedly one of the top non-leagues in the country, there was never any chance of the club applying to join the Football League, with the Athletic ground being nowhere near the standard required and on top of the lack of finance, it was always going to be a battle to maintain the standard set in this particular season.

The following season, despite losing its grip on the title, finishing in fifth place again, Mexborough Athletic reached the First Round of the FA Cup for the only time as a reformed club, losing 1-2 at Chesterfield in controversial circumstances.

Sadly, the club was never able to achieve those heights again, as its nine remaining seasons in that company proved to be a struggle, with the team languishing in the lower reaches of the Midland League in each of those seasons. In seven of those seasons over 100 goals were conceded in total, and at the close of the 1935/36 season the team was left propping up the rest.

Mexborough Athletic had actually resigned from the league in April 1932, with liabilities of around £350. The guarantors who had seen the club through the previous three years had chosen not to undertake the responsibility further and it seemed that the club would not be able to continue. However, following a public appeal for assistance and a public meeting, the Mexborough committee withdrew that resignation and in June an entirely new management committee of 24 members was elected, with both Mr T Ford, president and Mr A Marklew, secretary, elected unanimously. The football club was now no longer associated with the Athletic Club, although it continued to carry its name.

Despite the will to carry on, the end came in May 1936, precisely ten years after the team had won the Midland League title. The new committee had come to a decision that it could no longer support a football team, and as such it was disbanded. It was announced in the local press that the football ground was up for rental for any suitable sporting event, gala, flower show or even band contest.

However, on Saturday 28th January 1939 the *Sheffield Daily Telegraph* reported that there would be a new Mexborough Town club formed in time for the following season

*'Next season, after a lapse of four years, Mexborough will have its own football club, run under the title of Mexborough Town. The club will take over the fixtures of Barnsley 'A' (its third team)* in the Yorkshire League, *the whole of the Barnsley 'A' team players will be transferred to Mexborough Town, and the club will be administered by a local committee. This season Barnsley 'A' have operated on the Mexborough ground. The club, it is understood, will be maintained under a financial arrangement with Barnsley, and the Oakwell club will have first claim on the players.'*

In the event, these plans never came to pass, as Barnsley 'A' itself began the aborted 1939/40 season, and the Hampden Road ground was also used by other teams such as Manvers Colliery FC until the onset of World War Two. The town would have to wait until 1962 for a new 'Mexborough

### 1925/26 Midland League

|  | P | W | D | L | F | A | Pts |
|---|---|---|---|---|---|---|---|
| **Mexborough** | 40 | 25 | 7 | 8 | 111 | 53 | 57 |
| Mansfield Town | 40 | 23 | 7 | 10 | 120 | 54 | 53 |
| Boston Town | 40 | 21 | 10 | 9 | 98 | 43 | 52 |
| Lincoln City | 40 | 20 | 10 | 10 | 102 | 57 | 50 |
| Denaby United | 40 | 20 | 7 | 13 | 95 | 63 | 47 |
| **Wath Athletic** | 40 | 19 | 9 | 12 | 98 | 72 | 47 |
| Scunthorpe United | 40 | 19 | 9 | 12 | 86 | 78 | 47 |
| Newark Town | 40 | 16 | 9 | 15 | 94 | 88 | 41 |
| Alfreton Town | 40 | 17 | 7 | 16 | 99 | 102 | 41 |
| Loughborough Corinth | 40 | 17 | 5 | 18 | 86 | 82 | 39 |
| Worksop Town | 40 | 14 | 10 | 16 | 82 | 82 | 38 |
| **Wombwell** | 40 | 14 | 9 | 17 | 73 | 89 | 37 |
| Long Eaton | 40 | 14 | 8 | 18 | 82 | 94 | 36 |
| Grantham | 40 | 15 | 6 | 19 | 71 | 94 | 36 |
| Sutton Town | 40 | 15 | 6 | 19 | 68 | 102 | 36 |
| **York City** | 40 | 14 | 7 | 19 | 74 | 94 | 35 |
| Gainsborough Trinity | 40 | 13 | 4 | 19 | 58 | 85 | 34 |
| Shirebrook | 40 | 14 | 8 | 22 | 81 | 106 | 32 |
| Ilkeston United | 40 | 12 | 7 | 21 | 57 | 91 | 31 |
| Frickley Colliery | 40 | 11 | 7 | 22 | 61 | 99 | 29 |
| **Castleford Town** | 40 | 10 | 2 | 28 | 62 | 130 | 22 |

### Midland League record

|  | P | W | D | L | F | A | Pts | Pos |
|---|---|---|---|---|---|---|---|---|
| 1905/06 | 34 | 16 | 8 | 10 | 73 | 45 | 40 | 5/18 |
| 1906/07 | 38 | 20 | 7 | 11 | 71 | 51 | 47 | 6/20 |
| 1907/08 | 38 | 12 | 7 | 19 | 57 | 78 | 31 | 17/20 |
| 1908/09 | 38 | 13 | 8 | 17 | 57 | 88 | 34 | 12/20 |
| 1909/10 | 42 | 15 | 3 | 24 | 67 | 101 | 33 | 20/22 |
| 1910/11 | 38 | 13 | 10 | 15 | 70 | 65 | 36 | 10/20 |
| 1911/12 | 36 | 15 | 8 | 13 | 54 | 66 | 38 | 9/19 |
| 1912/13 | 38 | 11 | 3 | 24 | 42 | 77 | 25 | 19/20 |
| 1913/14 | 34 | 10 | 4 | 20 | 41 | 85 | 24 | 17/18 |
| 1914/15 | 38 | 10 | 8 | 20 | 37 | 89 | 28 | 17/20 |
| 1919/20 | 34 | 18 | 6 | 10 | 60 | 45 | 42 | 5/18 |
| 1920/21 | 38 | 10 | 11 | 17 | 39 | 61 | 31 | 17/20 |
| 1921/22 | 42 | 19 | 9 | 14 | 67 | 40 | 47 | 6/22 |
| 1922/23 | 42 | 11 | 13 | 18 | 44 | 63 | 35 | 18/22 |
| 1923/24 | 42 | 22 | 7 | 13 | 78 | 64 | 51 | 4/22 |
| 1924/25 | 28 | 9 | 9 | 10 | 49 | 49 | 27 | 8/15 |
| 1925/26 | 40 | 25 | 7 | 8 | 111 | 53 | 57 | 1/21 |
| *As Mexborough Athletic* | | | | | | | | |
| 1926/27 | 38 | 20 | 6 | 12 | 97 | 81 | 46 | 5/20 |
| 1927/28 | 44 | 14 | 9 | 21 | 84 | 112 | 37 | 17/23 |
| 1928/29 | 50 | 15 | 12 | 23 | 81 | 105 | 42 | 20/26 |
| 1929/30 | 50 | 14 | 12 | 24 | 90 | 132 | 40 | 20/26 |
| 1930/31 | 46 | 13 | 8 | 25 | 84 | 129 | 34 | 20/24 |
| 1931/32 | 46 | 18 | 5 | 23 | 92 | 121 | 41 | 16/24 |
| 1932/33 | 44 | 11 | 6 | 27 | 73 | 139 | 28 | 21/23 |
| 1933/34 | 32 | 10 | 2 | 20 | 53 | 85 | 22 | 16/17 |
| 1934/35 | 38 | 14 | 4 | 20 | 69 | 96 | 32 | 15/20 |
| 1935/36 | 40 | 7 | 8 | 25 | 46 | 117 | 22 | 21/21 |

Town', a team that would also achieve Midland League status before folding in 1993. Since then, several other less prominent teams have represented the town, all playing at the same Hampden Road ground, the latest being Mexborough Athletic, who have joined the Sheffield & Hallamshire County Senior League for the 2021/22 season.

## Mexborough in the FA Cup (3)

The 1926/27 cup run, alluded to earlier, brought an initial tie with Methley Perseverance in the Preliminary Round, and a 7-2 victory. Liversedge (4-0), Denaby United (2-0, in a replay), Wath Athletic 2-0, and Brodsworth Main Colliery (2-1, following a 4-4 draw) were overcome in further qualifying rounds, before the narrow defeat at Chesterfield, of Division Three North, on Wednesday 1st December 1926, in the First Round. Mexborough had led 1-0 at one point, but the match was marred by events that followed Chesterfield's winning goal. The referee, C M Overton, had sent off Mexborough's R Hill for laying out the Chesterfield player Shirley Abbott. In the melee that followed, the Mexborough trainer Matt Morallee was also ordered from the field after remonstrating with the official. When he refused to leave, a police officer was summoned from the touchline. The referee then insisted that Morallee was escorted out of the ground, and was forcibly removed by two police officers.

At the end of the month, The Football Association suspended Hill for two months, but Morallee was suspended from all football until the end of the season.

The 1929/30 season saw Mexborough score seven in two consecutive rounds, against Altofts and Methley Perseverance but made it no further than the Third Qualifying Round. This was the last time that the club progressed past the First Qualifying Round.

MEXBORO FOOTBALL CLUB. SEASON 1919-1920.

Mexboro' F.C. Season 1922-23

*Mexborough, seasons 1919/20 & 1922/23*

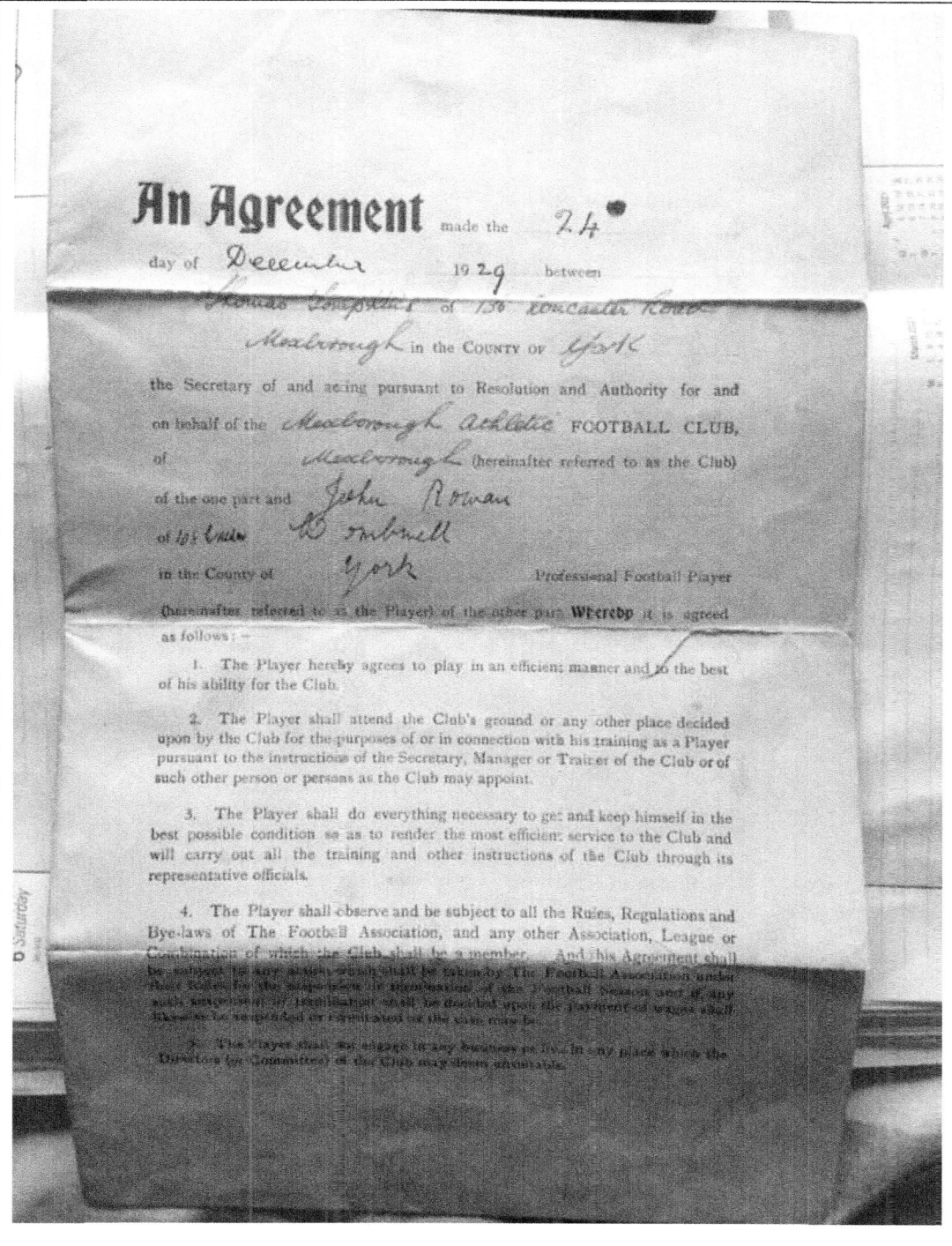

*Courtesy of John Rowan, whose great uncle signed for Mexborough Athletic in 1929*

# Castleford Town
# 1905-1936
*'The team that nearly got into the Football League'*

In the days before automatic promotion to the competition, Castleford Town was one of only two West Yorkshire football clubs (along with Wakefield City) to fail in its application to join the Football League, although its playing record did not always match the club's ambitions.

An early Castleford AFC competed in the first two West Yorkshire League seasons, finishing runner-up in the 1894/95 season, and a disappointing ninth place the following season. A Castleford Albion was also entered in the first season, but clearly out of its depth, it folded as early as October after a string of heavy defeats, including a 0-14 loss to Pontefract Garrison, and a 1-13 loss to Normanton. Not much more has been discovered about the Albion club. A rugby team of that name was in existence until late 1891 when match results ended suddenly in the local press, and a Castleford Albion cycling club was also active from the early 1890s. One possible link is the Albion Hotel in the town, although the club could equally have been linked to the Albion Glassworks in town, a major employer, which was owned by Sykes, MacVay & Co.

The original Castleford AFC has been reported as not being related to the town's rugby club, refusing an offer to amalgamate with the Northern Union team in March 1896. However, it would appear that there was indeed a merger. By January 1897, though, the club had applied to withdraw from the West Yorkshire FA cup competition owing to its financial difficulties – a debt of £16 – made worse by poor attendances for home fixtures, the local populace being tempted by the rugby football game instead. It was stated at the meeting that the association club was a section of the Northern Union club that was responsible for their debts. The previous month, the *Sheffield Daily Telegraph* reported that the club had raised only 1s 7d from the gate of their previous home fixture, with public patronage falling off. Conversely the Northern Union team was filling its ground every other week. At that point, the plug was pulled, and the association section folded.

A new Castleford club, fully independent of the Northern Union club, advertised for fixtures in September 1899 (Interested parties were to apply to A Waddington, 54 Carlton Street), but was not down to compete in the West Yorkshire League as expected, and failed to make any impact before it, too, folded after only a short time.

Castleford Town emerged in 1905, in the Leeds & District League's Senior Division. Ambitious from the outset, a move was made to the West Yorkshire League in the summer of 1907, the club agreeing to play at the ground of Castleford Rugby Union club for the 1907/08 season, one of the grounds on Lock Lane (see later note), and one which would be suitable for its new league.

The two years spent in this competition proved successful. Following a runner-up spot behind Heckmondwike, Castleford Town were champions in the 1908/09 season, prompting a further upward move for the semi-professional club. The short-lived Leeds & District League team, Castleford Dragons AFC had also applied to play in the West Yorkshire League for the 1908/09 season alongside Castleford Town but was not successful in its application. This club had only spent one season in the Leeds competition and re-emerged as Castleford United in the summer of 1908.

Castleford's move to the Midland League was keenly anticipated. Sheffield's *Star Green 'Un* reported, on Saturday 28th September 1909, '*The elevation of Castleford Town AFC to the Midland League has aroused intense interest. The local sportsmen have arisen from their torpidity, and things begin to be reminiscent of the days when the town was second to none in the country for love of sport. Even the devotees of Rugger – now dead as a door-nail – are beginning to talk, read, and study Soccer on the principle of 'makkin' 't best o' what yer con got, if yo conna get what yo want.'*

It was also reported that club officials were sparing neither cash, time, nor brains to secure a team which would do them credit. The article also went on to say that '*the committee, which is composed of practical men, not figure heads, deserve, and doubtless will secure a good measure of success.*' Several players with Football League experience were signed on, including William MacMillan, who had played over 170 times for Lincoln City.

Castleford Town, competed in the Midland League between 1909-26 (war years apart), initially taking the place of Newark, who resigned prior to the 1909/10 season. Despite a difficult first season, the club held its own in this much higher standard of competition, finishing in 8th place three times, and seventh once. The club's best period, after the war, coincided with two applications to join the Football League in 1921 and 1922, missing out by a small margin in 1921 when there was an expansion to include a new Division Three North, but receiving no votes at all the following season. With a population of just over 24,000 at the time, Castleford would have been one of the smallest towns to host a Football League team. Additionally as a town at the heart of a declining coal industry, it would certainly have been hard to sustain a team at that level.

The failed application, on 5th May 1921, must have been particularly galling for the club. Wigan Borough, Halifax Town, Southport, and Stalybridge Celtic were all elected to the Football League. Castleford polling the fifth highest score, ahead of teams that included Rotherham Town and Doncaster Rovers. Despite being promised a place in the league should one of these clubs subsequently drop out, this never happened and the three Castleford directors, along with solicitor A E Masser returned to the town bearing the bad news.

The 1922 application yielded not a single vote, disappointing given the club's near miss the previous year. Doncaster Rovers (nine votes) and York City (one vote) were also among the unsuccessful applicants. Expectations had not been as high however, with support for home matches having been disappointing, and the proceeds from a shilling fund raising only £30 having been well below that hoped for.

A move to Wheldon Road was made soon after Midland League football commenced in the town, although the club did see its ground suspended for two weeks in November 1912, following unruly crowd incidents during a match with Rotherham County on 19th October. The ground itself was often referred to as the 'Wheldale Lane enclosure', however. This was because much of the current Wheldon Road was called Wheldale Lane at this time.

Arthur Robins, the team's manager at the time and formerly with Sheffield United, was reputed to be the fastest professional footballer in the country, having won the professional footballer's championship cup (one can assume over 110 yards) – valued at 50 guineas - in 1911.

Robins returned to Castleford Town in 1919 where he played a further season as player-manager before retiring from playing in 1920, remaining as manager until his death on 18th March 1924. The winger passed away at The Railway Hotel, Bridge Street in the town, where he was licensee, following an eleven-week illness. His former Castleford Town team-mate Harold Gough was at his side when he passed. He was interred at Castleford Cemetery, with Gough one of the four bearers.

Castleford's final season in the Midland League, 1925/26, was a torrid one. The side finished at the foot of the league, and endured some embarrassing defeats, including 0-11 at Boston Town in February, and 1-10 at Mansfield Town a month earlier. In May 1926, the club announced that it had no option but to drop down to the Yorkshire League due to increasing costs associated with playing in the competition, particularly as there had been a southern extension of the league. Additionally, the club had also lost the use of the Wheldon Road ground to the town's revived professional rugby league club, which had just been elected to the Rugby League. The ground had been rented to Town by J D Bland of Kippax, whose agent gave the newly professional rugby club the option of purchasing it. The uncertainty surrounding this over the final few weeks of the season did nothing to help matters

*Arthur Robins*

On Tuesday 18th May 1926, the *Yorkshire Evening Post* reported that the rugby and association teams would swap grounds, Town therefore moving to the established Lock Lane enclosure, possibly the same one used in its West Yorkshire League days, although the club soon ended up at the Miners Welfare Ground at Hightown.

The first season back in the Yorkshire League saw a marked improvement on the field for Castleford Town, with runner-up spot achieved the end of the 1926/27 campaign, just three points behind Harrogate. This, however, proved to be a false dawn.

Over 100 goals were conceded in just 30 league fixtures during the 1928/29 season, during which the club had returned to Lock Lane to share with the recently formed rugby union team. Castleford and Allerton United FC, which had just dropped out of the Yorkshire League had also been using the ground. There had been a suggestion that the two soccer clubs should merge in the summer of 1928, but nothing was ever confirmed in the local press, although Castleford & Allerton did leave the league at the end of the season. The move to the Welfare Ground by Castleford Town had been deemed a failure, with the Town club over £1000 in debt and crowds having dropped off further at the ground.

On a more positive note, Town had won its first silverware, the Castleford & District Embleton Cup, on 5th May 1928 at Lock Lane, with a 2-0 victory over Selby Town.

The move back to Lock Lane was in vain. In debt, the club folded for the first time in July 1929 as the company was liquidated, just seven years after its second application to join the Football League. Liabilities to trade creditors were said to be around £300, and with no assets and nobody to rescue the club, there was no option but to close down. The shareholders appointed Mr Frank William Hansor, Jessop Street, Castleford as the liquidator.

Following attempts to re-establish soccer in the town, and the staging of two local cup finals at Lock Lane in April 1934, a brand-new Castleford Town returned to the Yorkshire League, as a purely amateur team, for the 1934/35 season. Former Barnsley and Stockport County goalkeeper Tommy Gale was manager of the revived club, having started his career with Town back in 1920. The club's first league fixture was a 4-2 home success against Brodsworth Main, with Gale turning out for the club for the first time at home to Sheffield United reserves the following month (a 2-2 draw the result). An eventual thirteenth place in an 18-team division was a disappointment, with some heavy defeats along the way, but one bright spot was winning the Embleton Cup, again on 4th May, when Leeds United reserves were defeated 5-2 in the final at Lock Lane. This was not a taste of what was to come though.

*Tommy Gale, pictured in 1922*

The 1935/36 season saw Castleford struggle badly, with only perennial strugglers Sheffield University finishing below Town, who conceded 157 goals in its 38 league matches (The University team conceded a massive 193, and withdrew from the league during the summer).

By December 1936 the club was rock bottom of the league, having lost all of its fixtures. The club chairman, W Walkington, was left to run the club practically by himself, after all but one of the club committee resigned. It was felt that since the club had re-formed inclement weather had prevented good gates for its more attractive matches and there was little enthusiasm among the locals for it to continue. In reality, poor performances on the field had hardly inspired the local populace to part with its hard-earned money.

Therefore, the club resigned from the Yorkshire League again at Christmas during the 1936/37 season, folding straight after its final match at home to Sheffield United on 19th December, which was lost 0-8. The previous month, the side had conceded twelve goals at Goole. Ollerton Colliery, a team that had narrowly failed to be elected to the league at the start of the season, took over Town's remaining fixtures.

The name of Castleford Town has been revived since then, notably in the 1960s when a team played in the lower reaches of the West Yorkshire League, playing on a

| Castleford Town League Record |||||||||
|---|---|---|---|---|---|---|---|---|
| Midland League |||||||||
|  | P | W | D | L | F | A | Pts | Pos |
| 1909/10 | 42 | 9 | 12 | 21 | 46 | 101 | 30 | 22/22 |
| 1910/11 | 38 | 14 | 3 | 21 | 72 | 110 | 31 | 15/20 |
| 1911/12 | 36 | 15 | 7 | 14 | 66 | 58 | 37 | 10/19 |
| 1912/13 | 38 | 12 | 9 | 17 | 55 | 56 | 33 | 16/20 |
| 1913/14 | 34 | 15 | 4 | 15 | 54 | 51 | 34 | 8/18 |
| 1914/15 | 38 | 9 | 9 | 20 | 50 | 103 | 27 | 18/20 |
| 1919/20 | 34 | 14 | 8 | 12 | 53 | 46 | 36 | 8/18 |
| 1920/21 | 38 | 17 | 6 | 15 | 61 | 56 | 40 | 8/20 |
| 1921/22 | 42 | 18 | 11 | 13 | 69 | 54 | 47 | 7/22 |
| 1922/23 | 42 | 15 | 6 | 21 | 61 | 70 | 36 | 16/22 |
| 1923/24 | 42 | 8 | 5 | 29 | 39 | 116 | 21 | 21/22 |
| 1924/25 | 28 | 9 | 6 | 13 | 47 | 61 | 24 | 11/15 |
| 1925/26 | 40 | 10 | 2 | 28 | 62 | 130 | 22 | 21/21 |
| Yorkshire League |||||||||
| 1926/27 | 30 | 20 | 5 | 5 | 87 | 37 | 45 | 2/16 |
| 1927/28 | 24 | 17 | 2 | 5 | 89 | 74 | 36 | 4/13 |
| 1928/29 | 30 | 8 | 7 | 15 | 77 | 100 | 23 | 13/16 |
| 1934/35 | 34 | 11 | 3 | 20 | 74 | 114 | 25 | 13/18 |
| 1935/36 | 38 | 4 | 5 | 29 | 61 | 157 | 13 | 19/20 |
| 1936/37 | 16 | 0 | 0 | 16 | 17 | 91 | 0 | w/d |

ground near Whitwood College, with the Alma Inn, Hightown doubling as dressing rooms, and headquarters. There was another club formed at the end of the 1980s, but that club did not survive long.

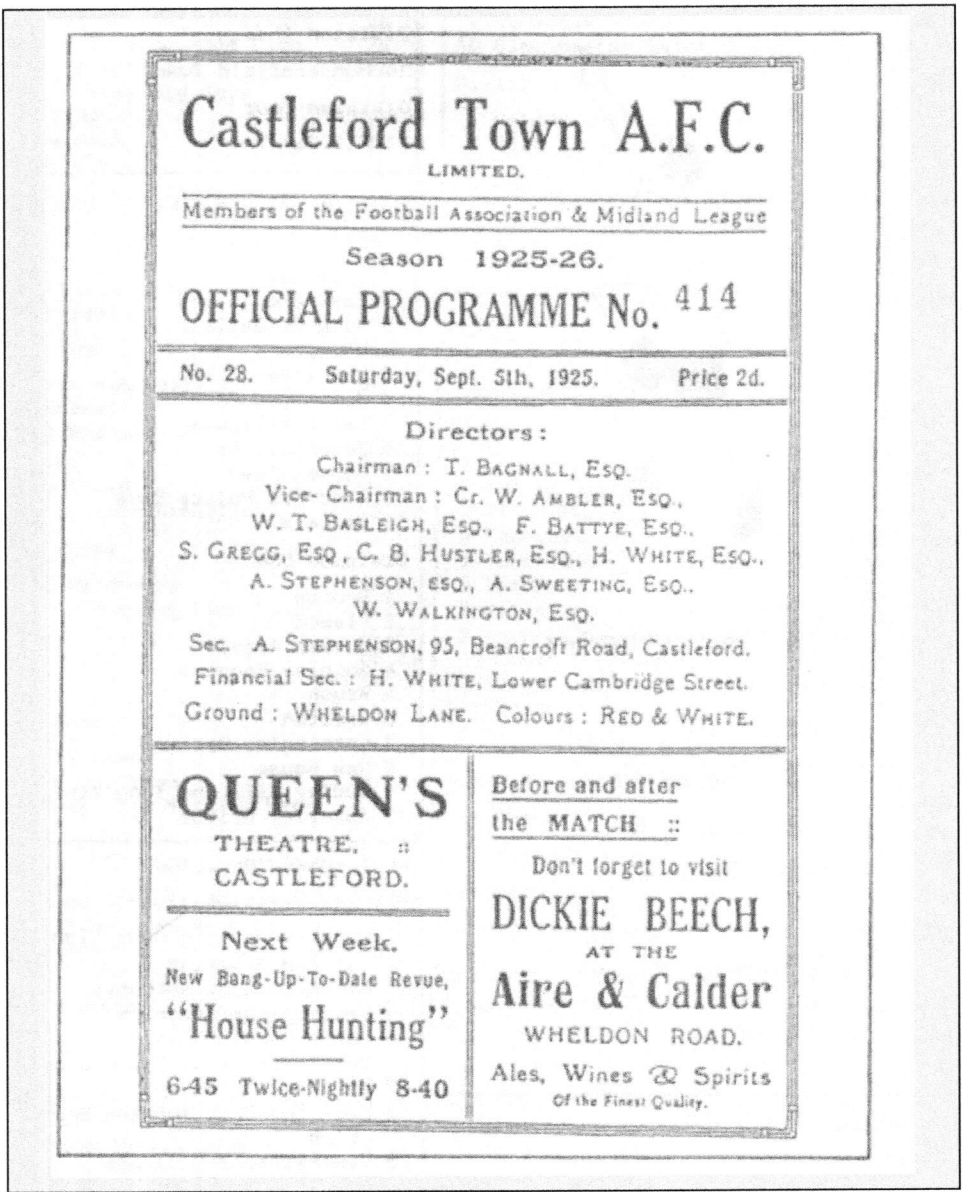

*Above, a Castleford Town programme from the 1925/26 season. This was for an FA Cup Extra Preliminary Round tie at home to Yorkshire Amateurs, which was won 7-0. Monckton Athletic & Frickley Colliery were defeated in the following rounds, before defeat came at the hands of York City.*

## Castleford Town in the FA Cup

The Castleford club first entered the FA Cup in the 1906/07 season, whilst still in the Leeds and District League. The team made it to the Second Qualifying Round, losing at that stage to Heckmondwike Town following a 4-1 home defeat of Rockingham Colliery. The following season Castleford made it to the Fourth Qualifying Round after defeating Doncaster St James, Goole Town, and Denaby United, before a narrow 3-4 defeat at Worksop Town. Mexborough Town defeated them in the Third Qualifying Round in the 1908/09 season, following defeats of Doncaster Rovers and the long-gone Grimsby Rangers.

The 1911/12 season saw Castleford's best run in the competition before the War, with a run through to the Fifth Qualifying Round. An excellent 8-1 win at Grimsby St John's in the Preliminary Round was followed by wins against Doncaster Rovers, Cleethorpes Town, Mexborough Town, and Morley (in a replay) before a narrow 1-2 home defeat to Reading on 2nd December 1910 in front of 7,000 spectators. Castleford's Brandon had equalised late in the second half, only for Reading to regain the lead in rapidly fading light with just five minutes remaining.

Another run took Castleford to the Fourth Qualifying round the following year, when Hartlepools United defeated them by a single goal.

The first competition following World War One saw Castleford achieve its best ever run, through to the Second Round proper of the competition. No less than seven qualifying victories over Calverley, Halifax Town, Leeds Steelworks, South Kirkby Colliery, Lintz Institute (of the Northern Alliance League, after a replay), Cleethorpes Town, and London Caledonians took them to the First Round for the first time. Hednesford Town, then of the Birmingham & District League were defeated 2-0 at Wheldrake Lane before a narrow 2-3 defeat at First Division Bradford Park Avenue on Saturday 31st January 1920.

The *Leeds Mercury* covered the match the following Monday,

> BRADFORD JUST SCRAPE HOME. CASTLEFORD TOWN'S GREAT FIGHT.

*Scorers:- Bradford; McLean (2), Little, Castleford Town; Howson, Dyer.*

*Castleford Town put up a great fight at Park Avenue, and after being two goals down they twice brought an equaliser within sight. Bradford only won by the odd goal in five, and the issue could not be held to be decided until the whistle had finally blown, for Castleford fought with a determination which called forth every effort on the part of the winning team.*

*There were 10,600 spectators present, who paid £690 at the turnstiles, and the rapid fluctuation in the score, together with the clever display of the Midland League team, made it a game which never flagged in interest for a moment. Particularly attractive was the work of Duffield, who was the most polished back on the field. Indeed, the Town backs and halves, including Albert Bartlett, the former Bradford City player, gave a sterling display. The forwards were very clever mid-field, but rather lacked finish in front of goal.*

*Bradford should have had another goal in the first half, for Bauchop failed to convert a golden opportunity. Bauchop and McCandless did excellent work in the first half, and Little's passing was always judicious. The halves were very much occupied with defence, Hovie being a redoubtable defender.*

*Blackham was a strength in the rear-guard, and it was rarely that the Castleford forwards were allowed to settle on the ball near goal. The Bradford forwards certainly had the better chances of scoring, and the superior experience and higher average merit of the team told in the long run. But it was a narrow squeak. Castleford Town are to be congratulated on their fine performance, which was worthy of a team in higher circles.*

The club did not progress beyond the early qualifying rounds in each of the subsequent seasons it entered the FA Cup. Its last appearance on 5th September 1936, a 1-5 defeat at Ravensthorpe in the Extra Preliminary Round in front of just a few dozen spectators.

***

Had Castleford Town been admitted to the Football League in 1921, then its subsequent history might well have been very different, but its rapid decline after that date would suggest that financially the club was not sustainable enough to hold its own at that level. Nevertheless, for many years after its demise, Castleford Town AFC was referred to as *'The team that nearly got into the Football League'*.

The Lock Lane ground is still in use today, the rugby pitch now at 90 dgrees to what it was during Castleford Town's time there. This ground lies on the east side of Lock Lane, although there was a football ground on the west of Lock Lane, close to William Street, which has caused much confusion in the past to those researching local football and rugby histories, and which may well have been the earlier pre-1907 ground of Castleford AFC.

# Wakefield City
# 1920-28
## *'Brave failures'*

Of all the teams that applied unsuccessfully to join the Football League – before the days of automatic promotion – few, if any, will have had such a poor record on the field of play as Wakefield City. This was a then an ambitious Yorkshire League club that neither caused a stir before, or after, its failed bid, but one which seized an opportunity to be one of a number of new clubs that would join an expanding Football League in 1921.

The Wakefield Trinity Football Club was founded in 1873, moving to its current ground at Belle Vue in 1879, the same year that the Yorkshire Challenge Cup was won for the first time. The *T'Owd Tin Pot* would be won three more times by 1887, and since then no other sporting club has really challenged its dominance in the city. Several Wakefield association football teams have tried, and failed to attract the attention of the local sporting public, without any degree of success, and Wakefield remains one of the largest urban areas not to have a team in the higher echelons of the national league system.

When the nearby Barnsley Football Union was founded in April 1891, the first Wakefield AFC, one of the earliest in the county to be affiliated to the English FA, expressed interest in joining despite no delegates attending the meeting. In the event, it passed on the opportunity for competitive football and gradually faded away, failing to generate any interest in the sport Wakefield itself. The club did at least have the use of Belle Vue at the time, and its results there included a 3-1 victory over Huddersfield, who turned up a man short, on 18th January 1890.

That original association club appears to have folded by around 1892, withdrawing from a First Qualifying Round match in the FA Cup at Port Clarence.

As Trinity followed a new path in the Northern Union following the great rugby schism of 1895 which led to the formation what is now known as Rugby League, another Wakefield AFC emerged in December 1896. This followed a meeting at the Graziers' Hotel, where R G L Anderson, of the York Street Academy, presided. The team played in chocolate and amber shirts and blue 'knickerbockers' and was based on the ground of the former Thornes rugby club. The club joined the West Yorkshire League in January 1897 (half-way through the season) before resigning from the competition - and presumably disbanding - only twelve months later.

The first Wakefield City AFC appeared in the 1899/1900 season, initially playing friendly fixtures against other teams. The following season, despite having fulfilled all twelve of their away fixtures, the club bemoaned the fact that half of its twelve home fixtures were cancelled through the non-appearance of their opponents, four of which occurred after the City team had finally affiliated to the County FA in order to ensure that such matters would not arise. Saying that, the club's opponents were very much minor it status (for example, a 1-1 draw was played away from home at Silcoates School on Saturday 17th November 1900). The club was, like its predecessor, lucky enough to be able to make use of the Wakefield Trinity rugby ground at Belle Vue, which enabled it to join the established Leeds & District League for the 1901/02 season. However, the club was expelled from the league prior to the start of the following season due to the non-payment of fines and that was the end of another failed football venture.

A new Wakefield City was founded in 1907, following an initial meeting at the Woolpack Hotel on 27th February. The meeting was chaired by E Dacre Makin (late captain of the previous club), and the club was elected to the West Yorkshire League for the 1907/08 season. The new club planned to take the Elm Tree ground of the Belle Vue Association club, opposite the ground of Wakefield Trinity - although some West Yorkshire League games were played at the Belle Vue stadium itself. Club shirts were green, with red neck-band, cuffs and trim, with white shorts (the reserve team kit had the green and red colours reversed), and from the outset the club adopted professionalism. E A Brotherton the local MP, agreed to be its first president, and according to the local press a number of influential gentlemen had signified their willingness to be vice presidents. However, the *Athletic News* reported early in January 1908 that both the West Yorkshire League and the Leeds & District League (where their reserves played) had allowed them '*to discharge their obligations*' as the club was unable to meet the costs of running teams in each league. Support for the club was obviously not forthcoming, and neither, it would seem, were performances on the field, with the club's one appearance in the FA Cup resulting in a 0-13 home defeat to Denaby United. This was now the fourth unsuccessful attempt to establish a senior team in Wakefield, and a fifth would not come until over a decade later, following the end of World War One.

It is perhaps no surprise that several years passed before the next attempt, as Wakefield Trinity at this time experienced something of a purple patch, winning the Challenge Cup in the 1908/09 season, the Yorkshire League title in 1909/10 and 1910/11 (a competition that ran alongside the Northern Union championship), and also the Yorkshire Cup in the latter season. Ironically, just ten miles or so down the road, Barnsley was by now an association stronghold, along with the whole of the Sheffield district. None of this fervour for the round-ball game managed to infiltrate Wakefield, just up the road.

The name of Wakefield City was again revived as a professional club in 1920, playing at Thornes Lane, and elected straight into the newly formed Yorkshire League. Some seventy enthusiasts convened at a meeting on Wednesday 17th March at the George Hotel, Wakefield in order to get the ball rolling, although the original intention had been to enter either the Midland League or Lancashire Combination. However, with the Yorkshire League being founded that summer then the Lancashire league idea was quickly shelved. The new club had the support of other local teams in its application, nearby Castleford Town for example, and there were applications from over 100 players to play for the club.

Early home matches were played on an established football ground on Coach Road in Outwood. This site still exists, although the ground's perimeter fence was removed many years ago, and it is hard to imagine the site being able to hold up to 10,000 spectators, which were the claims at the time. On 17th April 1920, the club's first match was played, a friendly, against a 'Mr Maley's XI'. Tom Maley was the secretary/manager of Bradford Park Avenue, and he included several players from his own club in his team, which won 4-1 in front of a crowd of 1,300. Friendly fixtures were also played against Leeds United and Huddersfield Town, both also ending in defeat. Despite having announced that Coach Road would be its home ground the following season, it wasn't to be, possibly due to its distance from the centre of Wakefield.

The 1920/21 season would be first full season for Wakefield City. The *Wakefield Advertiser & Gazette* ran a very positive story on Tuesday 31st August 1920,

'WAKEFIELD'S 'SOCCER' CLUB. It is not given to any person or Association to command success, but certainly the efforts put forth by the promoters of the newly formed Wakefield City Association Football Club have deserved it. The Club is in the Yorkshire League and played its opening match with Dewsbury on Saturday, and everything seems to indicate that the venture will prove a success, strong support having been secured, and a fine set players.

Thornes Lane, the ground, is situate five minutes from Kirkgate Station, and only eight minutes from the top of Westgate. The post of player-manager has been accepted by Harry Tufnell, the famous Barnsley player, and amongst a large number of promising lads who have signed on may be mentioned: White, a left half-back who played for Barnsley last season; Bedford, a left-outside winger, who played for Leeds United last season; Mitchell, a promising centre half-back from Darton; Senior (Thornhill), goalkeeper; William Taylor, an experienced right half from Leeds; and Silvester (Ossett), who is looked upon as one of the finest backs in the district.'

Given the description of the location of the ground, this could well have been the cricket ground adjacent to the railway, not far off Thorn Lane and accessed via what was then Mark Lane (now part of New Brunswick Street). Fox/Turner Way now covers the exact site of the cricket ground.

Bradford Park Avenue's second team won the inaugural Yorkshire League season, while Wakefield held its own in the competition, leading the table early in the season, and finally finishing sixth in the 13-team division.

**PUBLIC COMPANY.**
10th October, 1921.
WAKEFIELD CITY ASSOCIATION FOOTBALL CLUB LIMITED, (177143).

"Smith's Arms," Thornes Lane, Wakefield. Registered 5th October, 1921 to promote and carry on the business of a Football Club. Nominal Capital £3,000 in 6,000 shares of 10/- each; Minimum subscription, £500. Directors Messrs. R. Caven, 2 Oakland Terrace, Sandal, Wakefield; A. Depledge, Mount Pleasant, Haigh Lane, Barnsley; T. E. Catterall, "Ryburn," St. John's, Wakefield; A. Cooper, "Smith's Arms," Thornes Lane, Wakefield; and 7 others. Qualification of Directors, £10. (From the Daily Register compiled by Jordan and Sons, Ltd., Company Registration Agents, Chancery Lane, W.C.2).

*Wakefield Advertiser & Gazette*
*Tuesday 18 October 1921*

The club became a limited company in October 1921, with a capital of £3000, and 6,000 shares on offer at 10 shillings each. This was intended to put Wakefield City on a sound financial footing for its foray into a higher league

The team, along with Wombwell, Wath and Harrogate (Second, third, and fourth, in the Yorkshire League) moved up to the Midland League for the 1921/22 season, but not before having made its audacious bid to join the Football League.

It had been decided to create a Division Three (North) to complement Division Three (South), which had been formed the previous year. The Football League Management Committee proposed 14 clubs for consideration. These attended a meeting in March 1921, and were all elected after having stated their cases. They were: Lincoln City, Accrington Stanley, Rochdale, Walsall, Chesterfield Town, Crewe Alexandra, Nelson, Tranmere Rovers, Ashington, Hartlepools United, Darlington, Durham City, Barrow, Wrexham

The division was to have twenty clubs, so at the Football League AGM, *Grimsby Town* was transferred to the northern section, and a relegated club - *Stockport County* - took another place. This left four places available: Those elected were: *Wigan Borough 34, Halifax Town25, Southport 25, Stalybridge Celtic 25,*

Those not elected were: *Castleford Town 18, Rotherham Town 13, Blyth Spartans 9, Gainsborough Trinity 8, Doncaster Rovers 6, West Stanley 6, Wakefield City 4, Lancaster Town 3, Scunthorpe & Lindsey United 3, South Liverpool 1.*

Wakefield City only ever had an outside chance of gaining entry to the league, although it had received support from the Football League itself in 1921, given that the league wished to attract clubs from the Northern Union heartlands. But following that failed venture, there was no chance that another application could be made given the club's subsequent complete lack of success.

The 1921/22 Midland League campaign was disastrous, with only Lincoln City reserves below Wakefield, who conceded over 100 goals in its 42 league matches, at the end of the season. With such a lack of success on the field, and a succession of disappointing crowds then there was little choice but to drop back into the county league, where costs – including players wages – would be far less, and hopefully more sustainable.

Wakefield City's reserve team had replaced its first team in the Yorkshire League for the 1921/22 the season, avoiding the wooden spoon thanks to the form of York YMCA, a club which was way out of its depth for the second successive season in the semi-professional competition. City had been put in a difficult position when its resignation from the Yorkshire League in 1921 was not accepted by the league's management committee – possibly because the club had agreed to stay in the competition for more than one season – and so, in order to avoid any further problems, it had been decided to place a second team there instead. By May 1923, the club was reported to have wiped out £200 of its liabilities, and that the past season it had at least paid its way.

The Wakefield City team was managed by Harry Tufnell during the 1920/21 season. Tufnell had appeared 199 times for Barnsley, scoring 61 goals for the club, including the winner in the 1912 FA Cup final, so his appointment as manager was certainly met with enthusiasm. Sadly, he left at the end of that first season to manage Doncaster Rovers.

*Two renowned Wakefield City FC managers, Harry Tufnell (above), and Jimmy McDonald (below)*

Jimmy McDonald, who had played over 200 times for Bradford City (including the 1911 FA Cup final) and captained the team before World War One, was brought in to replace Tufnell as coach, but he failed in his bid to create a winning team, no doubt due to the lack of finance available. He did not last long at the club, and by the following season he was with the Keighley Parkwood club.

Wakefield City's only foray into the FA Cup came during its Midland League season. Bradford team Apperley Bridge was defeated 3-1 at Thornes Lane in a Preliminary Round tie, followed by a 3-0 defeat of Rothwell Athletic in the next round. The mini run was ended in a Second Qualifying Round replay at home to Castleford & Allerton United, 0-2, following a 1-1 draw.

A further move to Westgate Common for the 1926/27 season followed, but by now the club was receiving very little coverage in the local press and was attracting very few spectators. The club struggled on until folding in the summer of 1928 after finishing bottom of the Yorkshire League for the second successive season. In its final two seasons in the competition, only one match was won, and over 250 goals were conceded. Even at county league standard, Wakefield City AFC was clearly out of its depth.

The final mention of the club came in the Yorkshire Post on Thursday 30th August 1928, *'The Wakefield City Association Football Club, which came into existence soon after the war, playing in the Yorkshire League, have this season arranged no fixtures.'*

Wakefield has still never had a team that has come close to Football League status. Emley's rebrand into Wakefield & Emley, and then Wakefield AFC between 2002-2014 ultimately failed, and this apart, West Yorkshire League and, latterly, Sheffield County Senior League football is the best that the city has been able to achieve.

**Wakefield City League Record**

| Season | League | P | W | D | L | F | A | Pts | Pos |
|---|---|---|---|---|---|---|---|---|---|
| 1920-21 | Yorkshire | 24 | 10 | 6 | 8 | 41 | 33 | 26 | 6/13 |
| 1921-22 | Midland | 42 | 9 | 9 | 24 | 39 | 103 | 27 | 21/22 |
| 1922-23 | Yorkshire | 30 | 11 | 11 | 8 | 53 | 39 | 33 | 6/16 |
| 1923-24 | Yorkshire | 34 | 15 | 5 | 14 | 51 | 54 | 35 | 9/18 |
| 1924-25 | Yorkshire | 30 | 7 | 9 | 14 | 38 | 48 | 23 | 14/16 |
| 1925-26 | Yorkshire | 28 | 6 | 4 | 18 | 35 | 71 | 16 | 14/15 |
| 1926-27 | Yorkshire | 30 | 0 | 4 | 26 | 24 | 123 | 4 | 16/16 |
| 1927-28 | Yorkshire | 24 | 1 | 0 | 23 | 31 | 134 | 2 | 13/13 |

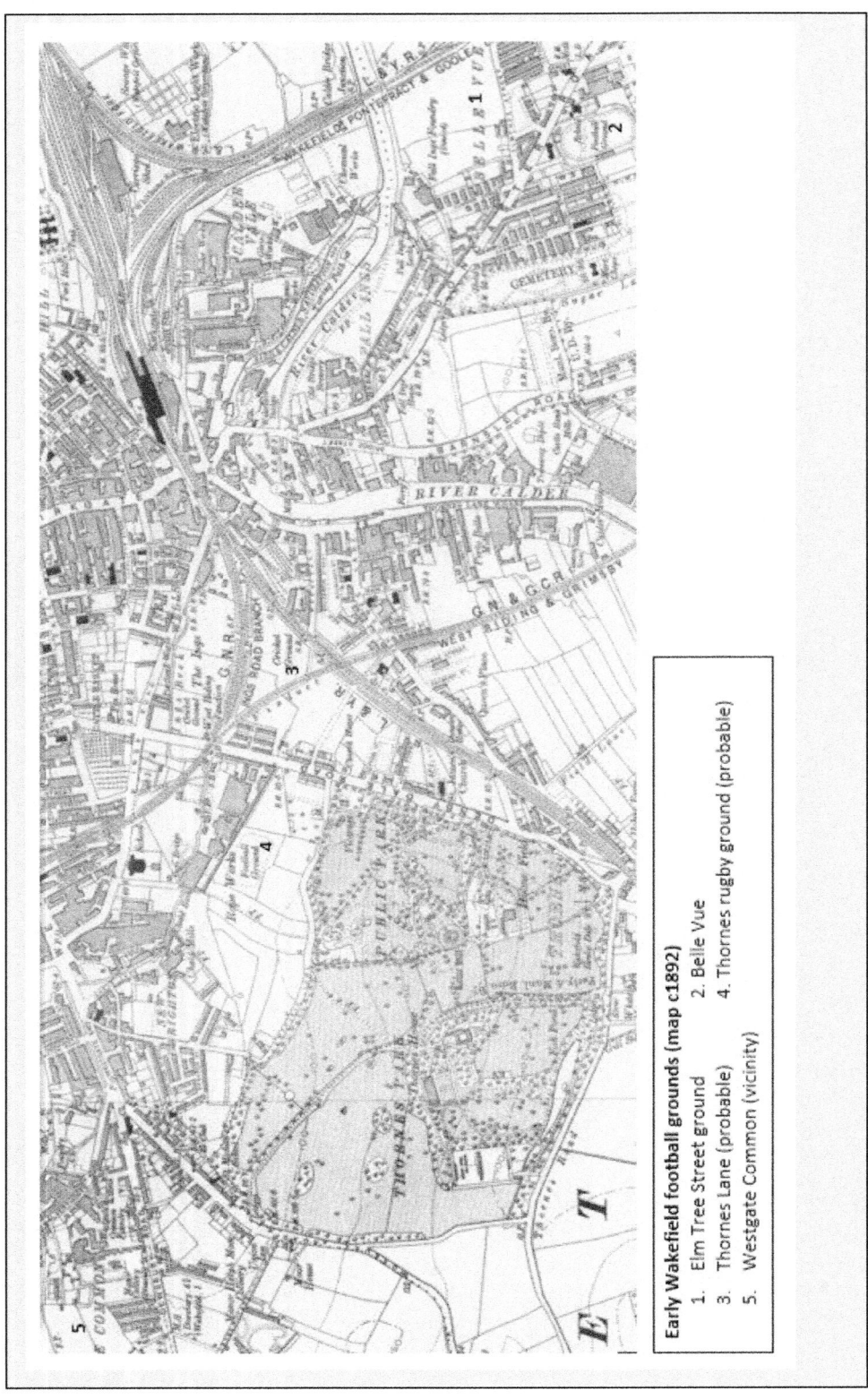

Early Wakefield football grounds (map c1892)
1. Elm Tree Street ground
2. Belle Vue
3. Thornes Lane (probable)
4. Thornes rugby ground (probable)
5. Westgate Common (vicinity)

# Wath Athletic
# 1884-1935
### *'Stern fighters'*

Wath Upon Dearne, around five miles north of Rotherham was part of the extensive coal mining district of what was then Yorkshire's West Riding. It also became an important rail-freight terminal after 1907, but with a population of under 10,000 until the early 1920s its football team was very much punching above its weight when it achieved Midland League status, just one step away from the Football League.

Wath FC and Wath Rangers were among the first association football clubs to emerge from the town, late in 1882, playing fixtures against other junior teams such as Barnsley Park Road and Mexborough Britain Star, most of which were very short-lived. Relationships between local clubs were not always cordial, illustrated by a short spat in the local press in 1884. The *South Yorkshire Times*, on Friday 7th November 1884, reported that an Elsecar correspondent had complained that on a least five occasions since the start of the season the Wath club had failed to turn up for away fixtures, including a fixture against his own club. This was refuted in the same newspaper the following week by a Wath correspondent, who claimed that the club had not arranged that many fixtures so early in the season. Similar letters between officials and supports of local clubs enlightened the local readership with regularity.

Wath FC began to come to prominence in 1888, and entered the Sheffield Minor Cup for the first time in the 1888/89 season. Its president was S

*Rare football cards from the early 1900s. The top card was produced by J Baines, Bradford, and the bottom one by W H Sharpe, also of Bradford.*

Stables of the Star Inn, which was obviously used as club headquarters, with one F Stables also on the committee. However, it was the club secretary Edward Scorah who tirelessly served the club in its early years, and indeed he was recognised by Wath FC for his efforts in June 1891.

For the 1889/90 season, Wath entered the local Heeley Challenge Cup, Sheffield Minor Cup and Mexborough Times Challenge Cups. The season couldn't have got off to a better start, with with a 10-1 rout of Rotherham Baptists. The good form continued, and in the 1890/91 season the team won 33 out of the 40 fixtures it played. On Saturday 18th April 1991 the club won the Sheffield Minor Cup, with a narrow 3-2 defeat of Heeley, in front of 1,500 spectators in the final, which was played at Bramall Lane. The match was described in the press as a *'close and exciting contest.'* Not long after, an athletics festival in connection with the Wath cricket and football clubs was held in a field adjoining the Midland Station on Thursday 20th August 1891, illustrating the rising status of the sports clubs in the town.

*Sheffield Independent,* Monday 20th April 1891

*SHEFFIELD MINOR CUP. FINAL TIE. HEELEY v. WATH.*

*This postponed final, which aroused great interest, was played at Bramall lane on Saturday, before about 1500 spectators, the attendance being very good considering the counter attraction at Olive Grove and the fact that rain fell during the time play was in progress. Both the visitors and Heeley had shown good form in the previous rounds, and the chances of either team were strongly fancied by their respective supporters, who did not forget to demonstrate their opinions.*

*Heeley winning the toss, Lovatt started the ball rolling towards Bramall lane at three o'clock. After an incursion into Heeley territory had been repelled by Harrison the homesters forced a corner, from which Wiggett nearly scored. Play thus early on was of a fast description, and a pass by E. Hutchinson to Lunn gave that player a chance, but he wildly shot outside. Just afterwards J T Ellis put in a good screw, which the local custodian only partly got away, and then J Ellis just shot wide. After Hobson and Hunt had nullified an attack upon their citadel Wath began to bring pressure on the Heeley goal, but their shots were too high or wide of the mark, and F Shaw had not much to do. When the game was about 18 minutes old a foul against Heeley resulted in J Ellis scoring the first goal. This aroused the homesters, and Hobson saved cleverly on two occasions, one shot in particular from Wiggett, who was close in, being a scorcher. He was soon afterwards called upon again, but Simmonite cleared. Play was very fast, and a free kick against E. Nicholson gave Wragg an opportunity, which he availed himself of, the score thus being made even at the end of 25 minutes' play. Heeley were now showing the best football, their passing being superior to that of the villagers, but the defence of Hunt and Simmonite was too good to be broken through. From a flag-kick in favour of Wath, the visitors drew ahead again, but Heeley alleged that the ball had not been played. The referee ruled, however, that F Shaw had touched it with his hand. J T Ellis, on the visitors' right wing, showed good form, and just before the interval Gambles sent in a good shot, which many thought had gone through, but no score was allowed, half-time arriving with Wath leading by 2 to 1.*

*On resuming a free kick in favour of the Sheffielders was safely disposed of, and after the Heeley end had been visited a good cross by Gambles forced Hobson to concede a corner, which, however, was got away. A miskick by one of the home backs followed, and Bamforth getting through scored the third goal, which Heeley appealed against for off-side, but the decision was in favour of the visitors. This reverse infused new vigour into the local men, and after a bully near the Wath goal Wiggett shot through, but the goal was not allowed on account of the off-side rule having been infringed. Play then ruled rather rough, and more attention was paid to the man than to the ball. Hague was playing a good game, and from a long kick by Robinson the locals bothered the Wath backs, making clearing a very difficult matter. Heeley were now attacking strongly, Hague, Gambles, Hill, Wiggett, and Clarke each sending in shots. A foul to Heeley was taken by Wiggett, and Robinson shooting in Hunt headed out, but Hill pouncing on the leather sent in a splendid fast shot which bent Hobson. Good play by Hill and Wragg sent the ball right across, and E Hutchinson was somewhat lucky in clearing. Several corners were nicely dropped by Hill, one of which Gambles inadvertently fouled. The visitors afterwards caused the Heeley defence some trouble, and then*

A Shaw only just shot over the bar. Play was now very exciting, and once Gambles was in a splendid position for shooting, but he missed what appeared an easy chance. A run to the other end resulted in Bamforth putting the ball past F Shaw, but he was clearly off-side, and no goal was allowed. Heeley tried desperately hard to draw level, Gambles just grazing the bar, and Hill sending in a splendid low shot, which Hobson stopped rather luckily, but to no purpose, and 'time' was signalled with the ball in the visitors quarter, leaving Wath the winners of a sternly-fought end even game. Result : – Wath 3 goals. Heeley 2 goals.

Heeley – F Shaw (goal), J Clarke, E Harrison, A Shaw, Hague, A Robinson, W Hill, C Wragg, T Dungworth, F Wiggett, and F Gambles. Wath – Hobson (goal), B Hunt, H. Simmonite, T. Hutchinson, F Hargreaves. E Hutchinson, J T Ellis, J Ellis, W Lovatt, W Bamforth, and S Lunn. Umpires, Messrs. J W Fox and R B Middleton; referee, Mr H Muscroft.

Wath became founder members of the Hallamshire League in the 1891/1892 season, and finished runner-up behind Sheffield Strollers (United reserves) on goal average. Wednesday Wanderers also finished on the same number of points at the top of the league, in what was an exciting conclusion to the season.

The season was certainly not without its success, however, with a resounding 4-0 victory over Thornhill in the final of the Rotherham Charity Cup, held on the Rotherham Town ground on Clifton Grove on Saturday 16th April 1892.

By the end of the season, the club had a balance in hand of over £4 11d, a figure that had risen to £7 7s twelve months later.

There was a move up into the Sheffield & District League in 1892. This was the area's strongest league competition, and one which in the next few years would go through a number of transformations and name changes. The club also fielded a first team in the Wharncliffe Charity Cup League, following a season in the Wharncliffe Shield (which was in effect a second division of the former).

The English FA Cup was also entered for the first time, in the 1893/94, although entry was made under the name 'Wath upon Dearne FC'. That season the Rotherham Charity Cup final against Thornhill United on Saturday 7th April 1894 resulted in a 1-1 draw in front of around 2,500 spectators. The replay, in heavy rain (resulting in an attendance of only 1,000) on Monday 16th April saw Wath win 2-1. However, Thornhill successfully protested against the inclusion of Early of Wath, who was actually suspended at the time. Therefore the teams met for the third time on 30th April, with Thornhill finally lifting the cup with a narrow 3-2 victory.

Life in the Sheffield Association League saw the club finish in mid-table in each of seasons between 1892-1898. In the 1894/95 Wharncliffe Charity Shield the club won the North Division section, only to lose out in a replay by a single goal to Eckington Works, the South division winners, in a play-off for the Shield.

The club's AGM on Tuesday 19th May 1896 was possibly its most significant yet. A deficit of £34 had been reported, and there was a debate as to whether Wath FC should continue to operate as a professional club. It was decided, for the time being, to continue this way the following season, although a new committee was to be elected to take over the running of the club. However, twelve months later the club announced that it would revert to amateur status, at a lower level of football in order to avoid the possibility of being wound up. This was despite an excellent cup run, through to the final of the Sheffield & Hallamshire Senior Cup, losing the 1896/97 final 0-3 to Sheffield United reserves at Olive Grove in front of a disappointing attendance of 2,000 on Saturday 10th April 1897. Wretched weather and meagre gates had hampered the club all season, with the total debt in June 1897 being almost £64 Despite that, the club had finished well up the league table, and again held its own in the Wharncliffe

Charity League. It was decided to pay expenses only, as well as proportion of gate money to the players, which, it was hoped, might keep the club's head above water.

By the 21st of August 1899, the Wath committee was expecting the club to have paid off its debt soon, despite continuing poor attendances, and they were in the process of making plans for a new brick stand with dressing rooms and a corrugated iron roof, which would be built by a Mr J H Kelley at its new ground. By now, club headquarters was at the Cross Keys Hotel, with a T Wade acting as club secretary. Club colours were unchanged, being red and white.

The new ground was the Athletic Ground, a short distance from the headquarters. It had taken twelve months to prepare, and was part of a piece of land 17 acres in area purchased by Spedding Whitworth of Wath, six of which were set aside for the football and cricket club. As a result, the club became known as 'Wath Athletic'. The newly named club promptly finished in third place in the Sheffield League that season, narrowly trailing Worksop Town and Parkgate United who shared the title.

The 1899/1900 season saw the first team still playing in the Wharncliffe Cup league and Sheffield Association League, with the reserve team in the South Yorkshire League (winning the league title) and Hatchard Cup. The club was £50 out of pocket over the season, but by now there was clearly much more confidence in the club's ability to compete at this level. That debt had been reduced to just £11 by the close of the 1900/01 season, despite the fact that the first team had finished rock bottom of the Sheffield League.

Sadly, Wath's poor form on the field did not change the following season, with the club again at the bottom of the Sheffield Association League at the end of the 1901/02 campaign. The league reduced to just nine teams for the 1902/03 season, with Wath performing much better and finishing third, behind Rotherham and Thornhill United. However, these heady heights were only temporary as the team slipped to second bottom in a 14-team league at the end of the 1903/04 season.

On Wednesday 27th April 1904, a decision to withdraw the football club from all competitions was made. There had been a deficit of between £7 and £8 on the season, and smoking concerts and dances were to be organised to wipe off that debt, while a newly formed Wath Thursday FC secured the football field for their midweek league fixtures for the following season. The rest of the Wath Athletic club seemed to be doing much better, with cricket thriving, regular athletics events, and a newly formed Harriers pack all on offer to the local sporting community.

***

The club was resuscitated, debt free, three years later and was immediately accepted back into the Sheffield Association League for the 1907/08 season, winning the league title with ease at the first time of asking as the club - which had been advertising for players towards the end of the 1906/07 season - began what could be classed its 'golden era'.

The club AGM at the clubhouse, The Red Lion Inn, on Wednesday 6th May 1908 was well attended, with a balance of £16 7s in the bank and healthy home attendances reported. The possibility of Midland League football was discussed, but the club committee wisely put that to one side for the time being.

The club preferred, for now, to live within its means in the Sheffield League, and remained a leading side in the competition. Denied third place only on goal average at the end of the 1908/09 season, and denied the title the following year also on goal difference (to Monckton Athletic), the club remained a force in the local game.

However, performances on the field improved further, and the club went on to lift the league title three years in succession. The Wath AGM reported a balance of £30 for the 1910/11 season, despite expenses being higher and gates being slightly lower. With ground facilities now being almost up to Midland League standard the decision to try at the higher level was again passed. The following season a loss of £26 was made, despite the league title being won again (on goal average from Frickley Colliery) with a positive balance of nearly £6 in 1913, illustrating the precarious nature of running a football club even at this level of football. However, it should be pointed out that with the football club now having amalgamated with several others as part of the Athletic Club then each season would start with a clean financial slate. Saying that, excessive or persistent debts could quite easily have led to the athletic club shutting down the football section should it feel it necessary.

Financial considerations aside, a third successive title was achieved at the close of the 1912/13 season, but the bubble burst and a position in the bottom half of the table was all the team could muster one year later. The final season before shutting down for the war, 1914/15, saw a much-improved performance, denied runner-up spot on goal average only, but it was one which resulted in a loss of £43 for the football team, and with that in mind, and the problems of fielding a competitive eleven the section went into hibernation.

Despite finishing behind Bentley Colliery in the Sheffield Association League at the end of the 1919/20 season, the signs were encouraging enough for the club to make, at last, a step up. The move was made to the newly formed Yorkshire League for the 1920/21 season, in which the club performed well enough to gain third place in the thirteen-team division. Such was the ambition shown by the Yorkshire League's founder clubs, four of the top five, including Wath, moved on to the Midland League for the 1921/22 season (Wath keeping a reserve team in the Yorkshire League for just one more season).

Now just one step below the Football League, it was obvious that the Athletic team would have to be fully professional if it was to hold its own in the Midland League.

The club spent nine seasons in the competition, finishing in the top half in four of those. Although its highest league finish (fourth) came in 1926/27, the club had arguably its most successful season a year earlier when it reached the first round of the FA Cup for the only time.

In fact the 1925/26 season was certainly a year of cup runs for Athletic, with a resounding 4-0 victory over Hemsworth West End in the final of the Sheffield & Hallamshire Senior Cup final at Denaby on Saturday 13th March 1926.

**Wath Athletic League Record**

Yorkshire League

| Season | P | W | D | L | F | A | Pts | Pos |
|---|---|---|---|---|---|---|---|---|
| 1920-21 | 24 | 15 | 4 | 5 | 56 | 29 | 34 | 3/13 |

Midland League

| Season | P | W | D | L | F | A | Pts | Pos |
|---|---|---|---|---|---|---|---|---|
| 1921-22 | 42 | 13 | 8 | 21 | 50 | 71 | 34 | 18/22 |

Reserves 10th of 17 in Yorkshire League

| Season | P | W | D | L | F | A | Pts | Pos |
|---|---|---|---|---|---|---|---|---|
| 1922-23 | 42 | 18 | 10 | 14 | 59 | 38 | 46 | 7/22 |
| 1923-24 | 42 | 14 | 8 | 20 | 57 | 85 | 36 | 17/22 |
| 1924-25 | 28 | 10 | 4 | 14 | 43 | 49 | 24 | 10/15 |
| 1925-26 | 40 | 19 | 9 | 12 | 98 | 72 | 47 | 6/21 |
| 1926-27 | 38 | 21 | 4 | 13 | 76 | 63 | 46 | 4/20 |
| 1927-28 | 44 | 24 | 4 | 16 | 94 | 74 | 52 | 6/23 |
| 1928-29 | 50 | 16 | 12 | 22 | 97 | 104 | 44 | 19/26 |
| 1929-30 | 50 | 4 | 6 | 40 | 55 | 177 | 14 | 26/26 |

*South Yorkshire Times*, Friday 19th March 1926

*SHEFFIELD CHALLENGE CUP (OPEN COMPETITION: FINAL ROUND).*

*SHAW, THE MASTER. ANOTHER TROPHY FOR WATH. (Wath Athletic 4 Hemsworth West End 0).*

*Dick Shaw, of Wath, received a special cheer at Denaby on Saturday at the end of the match when he went to receive his cup winner's medal. He had led Wath to victory. Playing coolly throughout, when others were slightly suffering from cup-tie excitement, he soon had Wath playing their normal game.*

*Cup tie enthusiasm was let loose on the ground at the outset, and for a time there was pandemonium. With Wath attacking, Shaw had only Kirk to beat when, just outside the penalty area, he was badly tripped. The referee astonished everyone by awarding a corner, which was cleared. Breedon served his wingers with good passes, but nothing came of them owing to Wath's resolute defence. The ever dangerous Shaw hit the crossbar with a strong* header and Hemsworth were given a chance to show that defensive power which has won them all their sixteen matches in the Barnsley League, in which they have given away less than a goal a match.

More was expected from forwards with an average of nearly four goals a match, but the Wath halves showed their power. In the first half-hour Kirk had several shots to deal with, but Whittaker only once handled. Kirk brought off one wonderful save from Clegg. A free kick to Wath on the right set Moore going. His centre was taken by SHAW, who calmly manoeuvred for position and shot into the net after 37 minutes. Five minutes later another free kick led to Wath's second goal. DAWBER met the pass as it was going away to the right and headed out of Kirk's reach.

After the interval Hemsworth, with the breeze behind them, promised to make a fight, but though they tried hard they did not get so near as Wath had got. Carver and Scott were busy on the left, and Glasbey tried a shot, and for a few minutes Wath were penned in. Breedon tried an overhead pull and Massey shot hard. The siege was raised and after that Hemsworth's hopes went. The best shot of the match was from Scott, but Whittaker saved brilliantly. Wath advanced and Dennis put the ball into the goalmouth for CLEGG to dash in and bang it past Kirk. Again Hemsworth advanced and Breedon made a terrific shot which Whittaker did well to put over the bar. During the scuffle from the resultant corner a Wath player handled. Rowbotham took the penalty kick. which was a hard straight shot. Whittaker stopped it but before he could clear, Rowbotham dashed and, kicking at the ball, got the man. Fortunately Whittaker was only slightly hart. From the free-kick Wath rot away, and RIPPON completed the scoring by a fine individual effort.

After the match Mr H Parkin, a member of the Council of the Sheffield and Hallamshire Association handed the cup to Hargreaves, saying that Wath had handsomely won it, and there was no doubt that they had been the better team on the day. Whittaker received an ovation.

Teams:- Wath; Whittaker, Bratley, Wheatley, Dawber, Watson, Dennis, Moore, Rippon, Clegg, Shaw, Hargreaves. Hemsworth West End: Kirk, Rowbotham, Horbury, Cartwright, Glasbey, Glynn, Purcell, Massey, Breedon, Scott. Carver. Referee: J Whitham, Sheffield.

Later that month there was a runner-up spot in the Wharncliffe Cup, Athletic losing 0-2 to Sheffield United on Monday 29th March in what was described as a *'stern fight'* in the final. A balance in hand of £594 was reported at the club AGM in June 1926, despite the first two rounds of the FA Cup having lost the club nearly £50. Dark clouds were on the horizon, however, and within a decade the club would be no more.

A position in the top half of the Midland League could not be sustained by the club, with attendances falling and the club's financial position worsening as the nation sunk into economic depression. By 1929/30, Athletic was fielding a purely amateur side with its players having had little or no Midland League experience. The club policy that season was to build a good quality team which would play in local competition the following season.

Wath Athletic left the Midland League in 1930 after finishing bottom of the 26-team table, and returning to the Sheffield Association League. They Association League was won again – for the fifth time - in 1931/32, with a 2-0 defeat of South Kirkby Colliery in the league decider at the end of April 1932, thus depriving that team of a third successive title. Despite this, the football club lost around £130 over the season. Poor support was one of the main reasons, crowds for home matches being disappointingly low for a team that enjoyed such a successful season. The following season the club finished fifth, but as costs were further cut, and interest in the club waned, a drop into the Rawmarsh Junior and Minor Leagues, alongside the likes of Wath Main FC, was made. Two seasons were spent in the local league before Wath Athletic quietly faded away in the summer of 1935.

Several clubs have represented the town of Wath since then, none of them progressing beyond Sheffield county league competitions.

*The pavilion at the Wath Athletic Ground*

## Wath in the FA Cup

The club's first FA appearance in the national competition was during the 1893/94 season, a 3-2 win at Ardsley in the First Qualifying Round being followed by a 1-3 home defeat to Worksop Town.

Wath's early record in the FA Cup was not particularly impressive, with few decent runs in the competition. The best of those took place in the 1925/26 season when the First Round proper was achieved.

The cup run had started in the Extra Preliminary Round, and a 6-1 win at Brodsworth Main. This was followed by a 3-1 success at Cudworth Village, before a 2-0 home success against Denaby United in the First Qualifying Round. A narrow 3-2 success at Mexborough followed (this after a 2-2 draw at Wath), before a resounding 4-1 success against York City in the Third Qualifying Round. Northamptonshire team Rushden Town were expected to provide strong opposition in the final qualifying round, and for the first twenty minutes they did. However, once the home team went ahead the game became very one-sided as Athletic stormed to a stunning 7-3 success (Shaw scoring six teams as well as missing a penalty in the game) in front of 2,500 spectators, to set up a tie against Chesterfield in the First Round proper. The run came to an end that day as the Football League side ran out easy 5-0 winners at the Athletic Ground, in front of 4,200 spectators, gate receipts totalling nearly £232.

Earlier, during the 1922/23 season, Wath had played nine FA Cup ties, although they were then two stages from the First Round proper. Fryston Colliery (after a replay), Liversedge (7-2), Frickley Colliery (also after a replay), Doncaster Rovers (also after a replay), and Alfreton Town were defeated en-route to the Fifth Qualifying Round against Mansfield Town, who put paid to further progress with a 1-0 victory.

Despite its drop in status, Wath Athletic still entered for the FA Cup in its final season, but a 0-7 loss to Doncaster district team Owston Park Rangers in the Extra Qualifying Round was perhaps not a high point in its long history. The season before, Guiseley had also thrashed the team 7-1.

### Past Players

A number of players have played in the Football League either before or after playing for Wath Athletic, Eric Brook being the most notable. He played for Wath during the 1925/26 season, before going on to play for Barnsley (78 appearances, 18 goals) and Manchester City (450 appearances, 158 goals). He also made 18 appearances for England between 1929 and 1937, scoring on 10 occasions as an outside left. In later life he became a coach driver in the Mexborough area, and a barman in Halifax. He died at his home in Wythenshawe, Manchester, in March 1965, aged 57.

Among the others, the much-travelled Albert Pape played as a forward for the likes of Rotherham County, Notts County, Clapton Orient, Manchester United, Fulham, Hartlepools United, and Halifax Town, although his early days were spent with the Wath and Bolton on Dearne clubs. Born in Elsecar, he joined Rotherham County from Wath in 1919. Jack Wilkinson began his career as a youth with the Wath and Dearne Valley Old Boys, before going on to likes of Sheffield Wednesday, Newcastle United, Lincoln City & Hull City).

Other Football League players include John Addenbrooke (Chesterfield), Jack Angus (Exeter City), Walter Moore (Nelson), Bernard Radford (Nelson, Sheffield United, Northampton Town), Pip Rippon (Grimsby Town & Lincoln City), Harold Watson (Stoke City & Brighton).

*Eric Brook (above) & Albert Pape (below), two of Wath Football Club's finest players*

# Final League Tables For Competitions Involving Featured Sheffield & District Clubs

*(Where available. Please bear in mind that many tables don't 'add up', but these are those published in the local press or other sources. Mike Blakeman has recently 'updated' some of these tables by tallying up results, and researching 'missing' matches )*

### 1890/91 Sheffield & District League

| | P | W | D | L | F | A | Pts |
|---|---|---|---|---|---|---|---|
| Kilnhurst | 14 | 8 | 4 | 2 | 68 | 19 | 20 |
| Ecclesfield | 14 | 8 | 3 | 3 | 40 | 27 | 19 |
| **Mexborough** | 14 | 6 | 5 | 3 | 33 | 24 | 17 |
| Eckington Works | 14 | 5 | 4 | 5 | 32 | 37 | 14 |
| Carbrook Church | 14 | 5 | 3 | 6 | 24 | 39 | 13 |
| Barnsley St Peter's | 14 | 3 | 4 | 7 | 22 | 38 | 10 |
| Owlerton | 14 | 2 | 6 | 6 | 20 | 44 | 10 |
| Montrose | 14 | 2 | 5 | 7 | 31 | 42 | 9 |

### 1891/92 Sheffield & District League

| | P | W | D | L | F | A | Pts |
|---|---|---|---|---|---|---|---|
| Chesterfield | 18 | 14 | 2 | 2 | 63 | 34 | 30 |
| **Mexborough** | 18 | 12 | 2 | 4 | 97 | 23 | 26 |
| Barnsley St Peter's | 18 | 11 | 2 | 5 | 50 | 37 | 24 |
| **Kilnhurst** | 18 | 10 | 4 | 4 | 51 | 35 | 24 |
| Kiveton Park | 18 | 9 | 2 | 7 | 68 | 37 | 20 |
| Ecclesfield | 18 | 8 | 2 | 8 | 34 | 50 | 18 |
| Eckington Works | 18 | 7 | 2 | 9 | 35 | 51 | 16 |
| Melville | 18 | 4 | 4 | 10 | 34 | 65 | 12 |
| Carbrook Church | 18 | 2 | 2 | 14 | 27 | 67 | 6 |
| Owlerton | 18 | 2 | 0 | 16 | 21 | 81 | 4 |

### 1891/92 Hallamshire League

| | P | W | D | L | F | A | Pts |
|---|---|---|---|---|---|---|---|
| Sheffield Strollers | 14 | 11 | 0 | 3 | 73 | 26 | 22 |
| **Wath** | 14 | 9 | 4 | 1 | 50 | 22 | 22 |
| Wednesday Wdrs | 14 | 10 | 2 | 2 | 53 | 26 | 22 |
| **Rotherham Utd** | 14 | 7 | 4 | 3 | 41 | 36 | 18 |
| **Heeley** | 14 | 5 | 0 | 9 | 41 | 46 | 10 |
| Ardsley | 14 | 4 | 1 | 9 | 38 | 48 | 9 |
| Sheepbridge Works | 14 | 4 | 1 | 9 | 30 | 49 | 9 |
| Wentworth | 14 | 0 | 0 | 14 | 6 | 100 | 0 |

### 1892/93 Sheffield & District League

| | P | W | D | L | F | A | Pts |
|---|---|---|---|---|---|---|---|
| Wednesday Wdrs | 26 | 18 | 2 | 6 | 98 | 34 | 38 |
| **Mexborough** | 26 | 16 | 4 | 6 | 110 | 53 | 36 |
| **Attercliffe** | 26 | 17 | 2 | 7 | 67 | 36 | 34 |
| Barnsley St Peter's | 26 | 15 | 3 | 8 | 84 | 45 | 33 |
| Chesterfield Town | 26 | 14 | 4 | 8 | 59 | 34 | 32 |
| **Rotherham United** | 26 | 15 | 4 | 7 | 85 | 64 | 32 |
| Eckington Works | 26 | 14 | 4 | 8 | 63 | 60 | 32 |
| **Kilnhurst** | 26 | 13 | 2 | 11 | 60 | 51 | 28 |
| **Wath** | 26 | 12 | 4 | 10 | 68 | 68 | 28 |
| Sheepbridge Works | 26 | 9 | 2 | 15 | 62 | 84 | 20 |
| Kiveton Park | 26 | 9 | 2 | 15 | 54 | 85 | 20 |
| Worksop Town | 26 | 6 | 2 | 18 | 50 | 93 | 14 |
| Ecclesfield | 26 | 4 | 3 | 19 | 33 | 89 | 11 |
| Penistone Athletic | 26 | 0 | 2 | 24 | 40 | 121 | 2 |

### 1892/93 Hallamshire League
*Division One*

| | P | W | D | L | F | A | Pts |
|---|---|---|---|---|---|---|---|
| **Heeley** | 14 | 13 | 0 | 1 | 88 | 21 | 26 |
| Rotherwood Rovers | 14 | 12 | 0 | 2 | 74 | 23 | 24 |
| Norton Woodseats | 14 | 11 | 0 | 3 | 63 | 17 | 22 |
| Oughtibridge | 14 | 6 | 1 | 7 | 34 | 58 | 13 |
| Hallam | 14 | 6 | 0 | 8 | 31 | 49 | 12 |
| Darnall Congs | 14 | 4 | 1 | 9 | 29 | 52 | 9 |
| Channing Rovers | 14 | 2 | 0 | 12 | 17 | 74 | 4 |
| St George's Athletic | 14 | 1 | 0 | 13 | 33 | 72 | 2 |

**Championship final:** Rotherwood 1 Heeley 0

### 1892/93 Sheffield & District Alliance
*Division One*

| | P | W | D | L | F | A | Pts |
|---|---|---|---|---|---|---|---|
| Elsecar | 12 | 9 | 1 | 2 | 37 | 9 | 19 |
| **Wombwell Main** | 12 | 7 | 4 | 1 | 41 | 16 | 18 |
| Hoyland Town | 12 | 7 | 2 | 3 | 34 | 29 | 16 |
| Staincross | 12 | 6 | 3 | 4 | 26 | 27 | 15 |
| Birdwell | 12 | 4 | 1 | 7 | 27 | 24 | 9 |
| Hoyland Silkstone | 12 | 3 | 1 | 8 | 21 | 45 | 7 |
| Barnsley Swifts | 12 | 0 | 1 | 11 | 12 | 48 | 1 |

### 1893/94 Sheffield Challenge Cup League

| | P | W | D | L | F | A | Pts |
|---|---|---|---|---|---|---|---|
| **Mexborough** | 26 | 20 | 4 | 2 | 98 | 25 | 44 |
| United Strollers | 26 | 20 | 2 | 4 | 85 | 28 | 42 |
| Wednesday Wdrs | 26 | 17 | 6 | 3 | 78 | 31 | 40 |
| Barnsley St Peter's | 26 | 15 | 5 | 6 | 67 | 50 | 35 |
| Worksop Town | 26 | 11 | 5 | 10 | 59 | 63 | 27 |
| Chesterfield Town | 26 | 11 | 4 | 11 | 65 | 49 | 26 |
| **Wath** | 26 | 10 | 4 | 12 | 60 | 55 | 24 |
| Sheepbridge Works | 25 | 10 | 3 | 12 | 50 | 60 | 23 |
| Eckington Works | 26 | 10 | 3 | 13 | 39 | 60 | 23 |
| **Attercliffe** | 26 | 8 | 3 | 15 | 46 | 59 | 19 |
| Ardsley | 26 | 9 | 0 | 17 | 42 | 68 | 18 |
| **Rotherham United** | 25 | 7 | 3 | 15 | 40 | 79 | 17 |
| **Kilnhurst** | 26 | 7 | 2 | 17 | 38 | 77 | 16 |
| Sheffield Club | 26 | 4 | 0 | 22 | 35 | 96 | 8 |

### 1893/94 Sheffield & District League
*Division One*

| | P | W | D | L | F | A | Pts |
|---|---|---|---|---|---|---|---|
| Wednesday Wdrs | 8 | 6 | 0 | 2 | 28 | 13 | 12 |
| United Strollers | 8 | 4 | 2 | 2 | 16 | 11 | 10 |
| **Attercliffe** | 8 | 4 | 1 | 3 | 11 | 8 | 9 |
| Worksop Town | 8 | 2 | 2 | 4 | 10 | 19 | 6 |
| Sheffield Club | 8 | 1 | 1 | 6 | 12 | 26 | 3 |

*Division Two*

| | P | W | D | L | F | A | Pts |
|---|---|---|---|---|---|---|---|
| **Mexborough** | 8 | 6 | 1 | 1 | 20 | 5 | 13 |
| Barnsley St Peter's | 8 | 4 | 3 | 1 | 19 | 11 | 11 |
| **Wath** | 8 | 3 | 1 | 4 | 12 | 17 | 7 |
| **Kilnhurst** | 8 | 3 | 0 | 5 | 11 | 19 | 6 |
| Ardsley | 8 | 1 | 1 | 6 | 4 | 17 | 3 |

**Championship final:** Mexborough 1 Wednesday 0

### 1894/95 Sheffield Challenge Cup League

| Team | P | W | D | L | F | A | Pts |
|---|---|---|---|---|---|---|---|
| Wednesday res | 28 | 23 | 1 | 4 | 106 | 26 | 47 |
| Sheff United res | 28 | 20 | 4 | 4 | 83 | 29 | 44 |
| Chesterfield Town | 28 | 17 | 3 | 8 | 68 | 44 | 37 |
| **Mexborough** | 28 | 15 | 5 | 8 | 80 | 42 | 35 |
| Barnsley St Peter's | 28 | 17 | 3 | 8 | 67 | 43 | 35 |
| **Wath** | 28 | 14 | 5 | 9 | 65 | 53 | 33 |
| Eckington Works | 28 | 15 | 2 | 11 | 78 | 67 | 32 |
| Worksop Town | 28 | 12 | 4 | 12 | 62 | 56 | 28 |
| Ardsley | 28 | 9 | 6 | 13 | 64 | 62 | 24 |
| Sheepbridge Works | 28 | 10 | 3 | 15 | 51 | 68 | 23 |
| Rotherham res | 28 | 10 | 2 | 16 | 49 | 87 | 22 |
| **Kilnhurst** | 28 | 6 | 5 | 17 | 48 | 77 | 17 |
| Ecclesfield | 28 | 7 | 1 | 20 | 41 | 111 | 15 |
| **Attercliffe** | 28 | 5 | 4 | 19 | 35 | 84 | 14 |
| Sheffield Club | 28 | 5 | 2 | 21 | 44 | 92 | 12 |

### 1894/95 Wharncliffe Charity Cup League

| Team | P | W | D | L | F | A | Pts |
|---|---|---|---|---|---|---|---|
| **Mexborough** | 10 | 6 | 3 | 1 | 27 | 14 | 15 |
| Chesterfield Tn | 10 | 5 | 0 | 5 | 14 | 15 | 10 |
| Doncaster Rovers | 10 | 3 | 3 | 4 | 16 | 15 | 9 |
| Barnsley St Peter's | 10 | 4 | 1 | 5 | 19 | 21 | 9 |
| Wednesday res | 10 | 4 | 1 | 5 | 17 | 31 | 9 |
| Sheff United res | 10 | 3 | 2 | 5 | 24 | 21 | 8 |

### 1894/95 Wharncliffe Charity Shield

*North Division*

| Team | P | W | D | L | F | A | Pts |
|---|---|---|---|---|---|---|---|
| **Wath** | 8 | 6 | 1 | 1 | 25 | 14 | 13 |
| Ardsley | 8 | 4 | 0 | 4 | 19 | 15 | 8 |
| **Attercliffe** | 8 | 4 | 0 | 4 | 15 | 14 | 8 |
| **Kilnhurst** | 8 | 2 | 2 | 4 | 14 | 20 | 6 |
| **Wombwell Town** | 8 | 2 | 1 | 5 | 11 | 21 | 5 |

*South Division*

| Team | P | W | D | L | F | A | Pts |
|---|---|---|---|---|---|---|---|
| Eckington Works | 6 | 5 | 0 | 1 | 24 | 8 | 10 |
| Worksop Town | 6 | 4 | 0 | 2 | 27 | 5 | 8 |
| Sheepbridge Works | 6 | 2 | 0 | 4 | 10 | 12 | 4 |
| Staveley | 6 | 1 | 0 | 5 | 1 | 37 | 2 |

*Kiveton Park w/d*
Eckington defeated Wath 1-0 in a replay to win the Shield competition.

### 1895/96 Sheffield Challenge Cup League

| Team | P | W | D | L | F | A | Pts |
|---|---|---|---|---|---|---|---|
| **Mexborough** | 28 | 24 | 4 | 0 | 124 | 29 | 52 |
| Sheff United | 28 | 20 | 4 | 4 | 88 | 24 | 44 |
| Wednesday res | 28 | 19 | 2 | 7 | 129 | 47 | 40 |
| Chesterfield Town | 28 | 16 | 3 | 9 | 71 | 37 | 35 |
| Sheepbridge Works | 27 | 15 | 4 | 8 | 79 | 66 | 34 |
| **Kilnhurst** | 28 | 14 | 5 | 9 | 41 | 47 | 33 |
| Worksop Town | 27 | 13 | 6 | 8 | 53 | 34 | 32 |
| **Wath** | 28 | 12 | 5 | 11 | 54 | 65 | 29 |
| **Wombwell Town** | 28 | 12 | 1 | 15 | 53 | 64 | 25 |
| **Attercliffe** | 28 | 8 | 5 | 15 | 45 | 67 | 21 |
| Sheffield Club | 28 | 8 | 5 | 15 | 33 | 77 | 21 |
| Staveley | 28 | 8 | 2 | 18 | 51 | 71 | 18 |
| Ardsley | 28 | 4 | 5 | 19 | 31 | 102 | 13 |
| Eckington Works | 28 | 5 | 4 | 19 | 33 | 124 | 12 |
| Rotherham res | 28 | 2 | 3 | 25 | 23 | 75 | 7 |

### 1895/96 Wharncliffe Charity Cup League

| Team | P | W | D | L | F | A | Pts |
|---|---|---|---|---|---|---|---|
| Barnsley St Peter's | 10 | 7 | 0 | 3 | 25 | 12 | 14 |
| Sheff United res | 10 | 7 | 0 | 3 | 27 | 13 | 14 |
| Wednesday res | 10 | 4 | 2 | 4 | 15 | 16 | 10 |
| **Mexborough** | 10 | 4 | 1 | 5 | 18 | 23 | 9 |
| Chesterfield | 10 | 3 | 2 | 5 | 18 | 25 | 8 |
| **Wath** | 10 | 2 | 1 | 7 | 16 | 31 | 5 |

### 1895/96 South Yorkshire League

| Team | P | W | D | L | F | A | Pts |
|---|---|---|---|---|---|---|---|
| Wombwell R S | 24 | 17 | 3 | 4 | 63 | 35 | 37 |
| Swinton Town | 24 | 16 | 4 | 4 | 73 | 29 | 36 |
| Newhill (Wath) | 24 | 12 | 2 | 10 | 60 | 47 | 26 |
| Hexthorpe W | 24 | 11 | 4 | 9 | 50 | 35 | 26 |
| Eastwood M | 24 | 10 | 6 | 8 | 42 | 40 | 26 |
| Thornhill United | 23 | 11 | 4 | 8 | 52 | 44 | 26 |
| Doncaster RR | 24 | 10 | 3 | 11 | 57 | 45 | 23 |
| Darfield Old | 23 | 10 | 2 | 11 | 50 | 53 | 22 |
| Conisbrough Tn | 23 | 9 | 3 | 11 | 51 | 38 | 21 |
| Sandhill | 23 | 8 | 3 | 12 | 48 | 69 | 19 |
| Rawmarsh Par Ch | 24 | 7 | 4 | 13 | 52 | 54 | 18 |
| Denaby Parish Ch | 24 | 5 | 8 | 11 | 31 | 57 | 18 |
| Greasbrough | 24 | 4 | 2 | 18 | 50 | 87 | 10 |

### 1896/97 Sheffield Association League

| Team | P | W | D | L | F | A | Pts |
|---|---|---|---|---|---|---|---|
| Sheffield Utd res | 18 | 14 | 3 | 1 | 53 | 9 | 31 |
| Wednesday res | 18 | 11 | 3 | 4 | 54 | 18 | 25 |
| **Wath** | 18 | 11 | 3 | 4 | 51 | 24 | 25 |
| Sheepbridge | 18 | 10 | 2 | 6 | 47 | 28 | 22 |
| Sheffield Club | 18 | 10 | 2 | 6 | 42 | 23 | 22 |
| **Kilnhurst** | 18 | 6 | 1 | 11 | 23 | 31 | 13 |
| Birdwell | 18 | 5 | 3 | 10 | 34 | 44 | 13 |
| Staveley | 18 | 5 | 1 | 12 | 17 | 52 | 11 |
| **Attercliffe** | 18 | 4 | 2 | 12 | 21 | 54 | 10 |
| **Wombwell Town** | 18 | 4 | 0 | 14 | 20 | 64 | 8 |

### 1897/98 Yorkshire League

| Team | P | W | D | L | F | A | Pts |
|---|---|---|---|---|---|---|---|
| Sheffield United res | 18 | 11 | 5 | 2 | 55 | 15 | 27 |
| Mexborough res | 18 | 12 | 2 | 4 | 51 | 22 | 26 |
| Barnsley St P res | 18 | 11 | 3 | 4 | 62 | 27 | 25 |
| Doncaster Rvrs res | 18 | 11 | 2 | 5 | 61 | 26 | 24 |
| The Wednesday res | 18 | 11 | 1 | 6 | 56 | 26 | 23 |
| **Hunslet** | 18 | 7 | 5 | 6 | 32 | 38 | 19 |
| Leeds | 18 | 5 | 1 | 12 | 26 | 52 | 11 |
| Halifax | 18 | 4 | 3 | 11 | 26 | 54 | 11 |
| Bradford | 18 | 3 | 3 | 12 | 26 | 72 | 9 |
| Huddersfield | 18 | 2 | 1 | 15 | 14 | 77 | 5 |

### 1897/98 Sheffield Association League

| Team | P | W | D | L | F | A | Pts |
|---|---|---|---|---|---|---|---|
| Parkgate United | 22 | 15 | 2 | 5 | 52 | 26 | 32 |
| **Wombwell Town** | 22 | 14 | 4 | 4 | 49 | 38 | 32 |
| Worksop | 21 | 12 | 5 | 4 | 60 | 21 | 29 |
| **Kilnhurst** | 21 | 10 | 6 | 5 | 52 | 32 | 26 |
| Owlerton Swifts | 22 | 11 | 3 | 8 | 54 | 37 | 25 |
| Thornhill United | 22 | 9 | 5 | 8 | 40 | 47 | 23 |
| **Wath** | 22 | 7 | 5 | 10 | 41 | 43 | 19 |
| **Attercliffe** | 22 | 6 | 4 | 12 | 29 | 46 | 16 |
| Swinton Town | 20 | 5 | 5 | 10 | 29 | 46 | 15 |
| Hoyland | 22 | 6 | 3 | 13 | 28 | 63 | 15 |
| Channing Rovers | 22 | 5 | 5 | 12 | 30 | 55 | 15 |
| Rotherham Ch Inst | 22 | 5 | 3 | 14 | 26 | 49 | 13 |

### 1898/99 Yorkshire League
| | | | | | | | |
|---|---|---|---|---|---|---|---|
| **Wombwell Town** | 18 | 13 | 4 | 1 | 48 | 11 | 30 |
| Doncaster Rvrs res | 18 | 13 | 1 | 4 | 78 | 20 | 27 |
| Sheffield Utd res | 18 | 12 | 2 | 4 | 55 | 20 | 26 |
| The Wednesday res | 18 | 12 | 1 | 5 | 58 | 27 | 25 |
| **Mexborough res** | 18 | 11 | 2 | 5 | 40 | 28 | 24 |
| **Hunslet** | 18 | 7 | 3 | 8 | 38 | 27 | 17 |
| Bradford | 18 | 4 | 1 | 13 | 25 | 49 | 9 |
| Sheffield | 18 | 4 | 1 | 13 | 36 | 65 | 9 |
| Huddersfield | 18 | 4 | 1 | 13 | 15 | 73 | 9 |
| Dewsbury | 18 | 1 | 2 | 15 | 10 | 78 | 4 |

### 1899/1900 Yorkshire League
| | | | | | | | |
|---|---|---|---|---|---|---|---|
| **Hunslet** | 8 | 5 | 2 | 1 | 26 | 8 | 12 |
| Huddersfield | 8 | 5 | 2 | 1 | 14 | 3 | 12 |
| Featherstone | 8 | 3 | 2 | 2 | 23 | 22 | 8 |
| Ossett | 8 | 2 | 1 | 5 | 5 | 22 | 5 |
| Dewsbury | 8 | 1 | 1 | 6 | 13 | 21 | 3 |

*Huddersfield & Hunslet tied for the title.*

### 1899/1900 Sheffield Association League Division One
| | | | | | | | |
|---|---|---|---|---|---|---|---|
| Wednesday res | 16 | 14 | 1 | 1 | 54 | 9 | 29 |
| Worksop | 16 | 12 | 2 | 2 | 65 | 16 | 26 |
| Royston | 16 | 8 | 1 | 7 | 34 | 33 | 17 |
| **Attercliffe** | 16 | 8 | 1 | 7 | 34 | 38 | 17 |
| **Mexborough** | 16 | 6 | 5 | 5 | 26 | 35 | 17 |
| **Wath Athletic** | 15 | 6 | 3 | 6 | 31 | 41 | 15 |
| Sheffield Club | 16 | 5 | 3 | 8 | 18 | 35 | 13 |
| **Wombwell** | 15 | 5 | 0 | 10 | 24 | 26 | 10 |
| Pyebank | 16 | 2 | 0 | 14 | 17 | 58 | 4 |

### 1900/01 Sheffield Association League
| | | | | | | | |
|---|---|---|---|---|---|---|---|
| Wednesday res | 28 | 23 | 3 | 2 | 110 | 25 | 49 |
| Sheffield Utd res | 28 | 22 | 2 | 4 | 115 | 34 | 46 |
| Thornhill United | 28 | 21 | 2 | 5 | 96 | 48 | 44 |
| Monk Bretton | 28 | 16 | 4 | 8 | 69 | 51 | 36 |
| Royston | 28 | 15 | 4 | 9 | 53 | 48 | 34 |
| Rotherham | 28 | 11 | 7 | 10 | 64 | 46 | 29 |
| **Hunslet** | 28 | 11 | 4 | 13 | 59 | 68 | 26 |
| Denaby United | 28 | 9 | 8 | 11 | 44 | 56 | 26 |
| **Wombwell Town** | 28 | 9 | 6 | 13 | 44 | 46 | 24 |
| Sheffield Club | 28 | 8 | 6 | 14 | 36 | 71 | 22 |
| Montrose Works | 27 | 8 | 5 | 14 | 36 | 59 | 21 |
| Gainsborough Tres | 28 | 9 | 2 | 17 | 54 | 73 | 20 |
| Swinton | 27 | 7 | 5 | 15 | 32 | 66 | 19 |
| **Attercliffe** | 28 | 5 | 7 | 16 | 27 | 56 | 17 |
| **Wath Athletic** | 28 | 3 | 4 | 21 | 24 | 99 | 10 |

### 1901/02 Sheffield Association League
| | | | | | | | |
|---|---|---|---|---|---|---|---|
| Barnsley reserves | 24 | 16 | 5 | 3 | 80 | 31 | 37 |
| Denaby United | 23 | 14 | 4 | 5 | 53 | 30 | 32 |
| Royston | 23 | 12 | 6 | 5 | 46 | 28 | 30 |
| Thornhill United | 24 | 13 | 1 | 10 | 48 | 44 | 27 |
| Rotherham | 22 | 11 | 4 | 9 | 53 | 33 | 26 |
| Gainsborough T res | 23 | 11 | 2 | 10 | 39 | 28 | 24 |
| Monk Bretton | 24 | 10 | 4 | 10 | 44 | 48 | 24 |
| Roundell | 24 | 10 | 4 | 10 | 54 | 46 | 24 |
| **Attercliffe** | 23 | 10 | 3 | 10 | 60 | 43 | 23 |
| **Hunslet** | 23 | 7 | 5 | 11 | 30 | 64 | 19 |
| Doncaster Rvrs res | 24 | 7 | 4 | 13 | 43 | 51 | 18 |
| Sheffield Club | 24 | 5 | 1 | 18 | 38 | 73 | 11 |
| **Wath Athletic** | 23 | 3 | 3 | 17 | 26 | 88 | 9 |

### 1902/03 Sheffield Association League
| | | | | | | | |
|---|---|---|---|---|---|---|---|
| Rotherham | 16 | 12 | 3 | 1 | 44 | 12 | 27 |
| Thornhill United | 15 | 11 | 1 | 3 | 41 | 13 | 23 |
| **Wath Athletic** | 16 | 10 | 2 | 4 | 36 | 24 | 22 |
| Roundell | 16 | 8 | 3 | 5 | 39 | 31 | 19 |
| **Attercliffe** | 16 | 4 | 4 | 8 | 21 | 30 | 12 |
| Sheffield Club | 16 | 4 | 3 | 9 | 25 | 39 | 11 |
| Royston | 16 | 3 | 4 | 9 | 21 | 34 | 10 |
| Denaby United res | 16 | 2 | 6 | 8 | 19 | 41 | 10 |
| Hemsworth | 15 | 4 | 2 | 9 | 13 | 33 | 10 |

### 1903/04 Sheffield Association League
| | | | | | | | |
|---|---|---|---|---|---|---|---|
| **Mexborough Town** | 26 | 21 | 4 | 1 | 105 | 21 | 46 |
| Thornhill Utd res | 26 | 16 | 6 | 4 | 65 | 37 | 38 |
| Rotherham Tn res | 26 | 15 | 6 | 5 | 49 | 31 | 36 |
| Doncaster Rvrs res | 25 | 16 | 3 | 6 | 58 | 32 | 35 |
| Mexboro' West End | 26 | 12 | 5 | 9 | 65 | 41 | 29 |
| Worksop Town res | 26 | 11 | 3 | 12 | 46 | 67 | 25 |
| Thorpe Hesley | 26 | 11 | 2 | 13 | 48 | 50 | 24 |
| Sheffield Club | 26 | 10 | 3 | 13 | 55 | 59 | 23 |
| **Attercliffe** | 26 | 10 | 2 | 14 | 44 | 48 | 22 |
| Denaby United res | 25 | 7 | 6 | 12 | 26 | 53 | 20 |
| Rawmarsh Albion | 26 | 7 | 3 | 16 | 38 | 55 | 17 |
| South Kirkby | 26 | 7 | 3 | 16 | 34 | 75 | 17 |
| **Wath** | 26 | 5 | 6 | 15 | 32 | 54 | 16 |
| Holmes | 26 | 5 | 4 | 17 | 38 | 77 | 14 |

### 1904/05 Sheffield Association League
| | | | | | | | |
|---|---|---|---|---|---|---|---|
| Thornhill Utd res | 12 | 8 | 2 | 2 | 30 | 18 | 18 |
| **Mexborough Town** | 12 | 8 | 0 | 4 | 28 | 17 | 16 |
| South Kirkby | 12 | 4 | 3 | 5 | 20 | 18 | 11 |
| **Highthorn** | 12 | 4 | 3 | 5 | 24 | 27 | 11 |
| Rotherham Tn res | 12 | 3 | 5 | 4 | 18 | 17 | 10 |
| Rawmarsh Albion | 12 | 4 | 1 | 7 | 18 | 28 | 9 |
| **Kilnhurst** | 12 | 4 | 1 | 7 | 19 | 32 | 9 |

### 1904/05 Wharncliffe Charity Cup League
| | | | | | | | |
|---|---|---|---|---|---|---|---|
| Wednesday res | 14 | 10 | 1 | 3 | 42 | 11 | 21 |
| Denaby United | 14 | 10 | 1 | 3 | 36 | 17 | 21 |
| Rotherham Town | 14 | 8 | 1 | 5 | 19 | 15 | 17 |
| **Mexborough Town** | 14 | 7 | 2 | 5 | 25 | 22 | 16 |
| Sheffield United res | 14 | 6 | 2 | 6 | 28 | 20 | 14 |
| Barnsley reserves | 14 | 6 | 0 | 8 | 23 | 33 | 12 |
| Thornhill Utd | 14 | 3 | 3 | 8 | 18 | 27 | 9 |
| Sheffield Club | 14 | 0 | 2 | 12 | 16 | 66 | 2 |

### 1905/06 Sheffield Association League
| | | | | | | | |
|---|---|---|---|---|---|---|---|
| South Kirkby | 24 | 18 | 3 | 3 | 60 | 28 | 39 |
| Denaby United res | 24 | 16 | 5 | 3 | 57 | 29 | 37 |
| Rawmarsh Albion | 24 | 11 | 9 | 4 | 45 | 33 | 31 |
| Rotherham Tn res | 23 | 12 | 4 | 7 | 65 | 29 | 28 |
| Rotherham Main | 24 | 10 | 6 | 8 | 52 | 40 | 26 |
| Rotherham Co res | 24 | 10 | 6 | 8 | 50 | 42 | 26 |
| Mexborough Tn res | 24 | 10 | 5 | 9 | 53 | 49 | 25 |
| Catcliffe | 24 | 9 | 4 | 11 | 59 | 46 | 22 |
| Hallam | 24 | 9 | 3 | 12 | 48 | 47 | 21 |
| **Kilnhurst Town** | 24 | 6 | 9 | 9 | 53 | 64 | 21 |
| Wycliffe | 24 | 5 | 5 | 14 | 27 | 48 | 15 |

| | | | | | | | |
|---|---|---|---|---|---|---|---|
| Sheffield Club | 23 | 4 | 6 | 13 | 35 | 75 | 14 |
| Doncaster St James' | 24 | 3 | 3 | 18 | 32 | 77 | 9 |

### 1905/06 Wharncliffe Charity Cup League

| | | | | | | | |
|---|---|---|---|---|---|---|---|
| Wednesday res | 14 | 12 | 0 | 2 | 39 | 5 | 24 |
| Sheffield Utd res | 14 | 8 | 2 | 3 | 24 | 13 | 20 |
| Mexborough Tn res | 14 | 7 | 3 | 4 | 17 | 24 | 17 |
| Barnsley res | 14 | 7 | 1 | 6 | 25 | 29 | 15 |
| Rotherham Tn res | 14 | 6 | 0 | 8 | 24 | 22 | 12 |
| Rotherham Co res | 14 | 5 | 2 | 7 | 23 | 21 | 12 |
| Denaby United res | 14 | 5 | 0 | 9 | 13 | 25 | 10 |
| Rawmarsh Albion | 14 | 0 | 2 | 12 | 8 | 42 | 2 |

### 1906/07 Sheffield Association League

| | | | | | | | |
|---|---|---|---|---|---|---|---|
| South Kirkby | 24 | 18 | 4 | 2 | 84 | 21 | 40 |
| Rotherham Tn res | 24 | 17 | 2 | 5 | 56 | 27 | 36 |
| Rawmarsh Albion | 23 | 12 | 5 | 6 | 54 | 29 | 29 |
| **Kilnhurst Town** | 23 | 13 | 1 | 9 | 61 | 41 | 27 |
| Tinsley Club | 24 | 12 | 3 | 9 | 46 | 42 | 27 |
| Rotherham Co res | 24 | 11 | 4 | 9 | 53 | 54 | 26 |
| Rotherham Main | 24 | 12 | 1 | 11 | 46 | 41 | 25 |
| Catcliffe | 22 | 11 | 2 | 9 | 50 | 35 | 24 |
| Parkgate United | 24 | 9 | 3 | 12 | 42 | 54 | 21 |
| Denaby United | 24 | 6 | 5 | 13 | 36 | 62 | 17 |
| Doncaster Rov res | 24 | 6 | 3 | 15 | 33 | 60 | 15 |
| Sheffield Club | 24 | 5 | 2 | 17 | 36 | 84 | 12 |
| Mexborough Tn res | 24 | 4 | 1 | 19 | 38 | 77 | 9 |

### 1906/07 Wharncliffe Charity Cup League

| | | | | | | | |
|---|---|---|---|---|---|---|---|
| Sheffield Utd res | 14 | 8 | 2 | 4 | 27 | 16 | 18 |
| Rotherham Co res | 14 | 6 | 4 | 4 | 23 | 21 | 16 |
| South Kirkby | 14 | 6 | 3 | 5 | 20 | 15 | 15 |
| Rotherham Tn res | 14 | 6 | 2 | 6 | 16 | 19 | 14 |
| Mexborough Tn res | 14 | 6 | 2 | 6 | 20 | 24 | 14 |
| Rawmarsh Albion | 14 | 4 | 5 | 5 | 11 | 14 | 13 |
| Wednesday res | 14 | 4 | 3 | 7 | 24 | 23 | 11 |
| Barnsley reserves | 14 | 3 | 3 | 8 | 14 | 26 | 9 |

### 1907/08 Sheffield Association League

| | | | | | | | |
|---|---|---|---|---|---|---|---|
| **Wath Athletic** | 30 | 24 | 3 | 3 | 97 | 18 | 51 |
| South Kirkby | 29 | 21 | 2 | 6 | 98 | 24 | 44 |
| Denaby United res | 30 | 17 | 7 | 6 | 73 | 34 | 41 |
| Rawmarsh Albion | 29 | 15 | 9 | 6 | 67 | 45 | 39 |
| Rotherham Town | 29 | 14 | 10 | 5 | 84 | 45 | 38 |
| Rotherham County | 29 | 15 | 4 | 10 | 69 | 49 | 34 |
| Doncaster Rov res | 29 | 13 | 4 | 12 | 51 | 59 | 30 |
| Parkgate & Raw U | 30 | 11 | 4 | 15 | 73 | 56 | 26 |
| Grimethorpe ILP | 30 | 9 | 6 | 15 | 65 | 101 | 24 |
| Hickleton Main | 28 | 10 | 4 | 14 | 51 | 97 | 24 |
| Rother Vale | 29 | 9 | 5 | 15 | 41 | 98 | 23 |
| Mexborough Tn res | 30 | 9 | 5 | 16 | 49 | 66 | 23 |
| **Kilnhurst Town** | 29 | 10 | 1 | 18 | 55 | 90 | 21 |
| Rotherham Main | 30 | 6 | 7 | 17 | 39 | 85 | 19 |
| Tinsley | 30 | 7 | 5 | 18 | 33 | 50 | 19 |
| Sheffield Club | 30 | 7 | 3 | 20 | 51 | 85 | 17 |

### 1908/09 Sheffield Association League

| | | | | | | | |
|---|---|---|---|---|---|---|---|
| Denaby United res | 28 | 19 | 6 | 3 | 83 | 40 | 44 |
| South Kirkby | 28 | 19 | 2 | 7 | 68 | 36 | 40 |
| **Monckton Athletic** | 28 | 18 | 2 | 8 | 82 | 38 | 38 |
| **Wath Athletic** | 28 | 17 | 4 | 7 | 67 | 40 | 38 |
| Rotherham County | 28 | 17 | 3 | 8 | 60 | 45 | 37 |
| Rawmarsh Albion | 28 | 14 | 3 | 11 | 51 | 37 | 31 |
| Mexborough Tn res | 28 | 12 | 5 | 11 | 58 | 59 | 29 |
| Rotherham Tn res | 28 | 11 | 5 | 12 | 60 | 63 | 27 |
| Worksop Town | 28 | 11 | 4 | 13 | 64 | 76 | 26 |
| Doncaster Rov res | 28 | 8 | 7 | 13 | 53 | 54 | 23 |
| Hickleton main | 29 | 9 | 3 | 16 | 42 | 68 | 21 |
| Silverwood Colliery | 28 | 7 | 6 | 15 | 32 | 65 | 20 |
| Parkgate &Raw Utd | 28 | 8 | 3 | 17 | 45 | 64 | 19 |
| Rotherham Main | 27 | 4 | 4 | 19 | 38 | 68 | 12 |
| **Kilnhurst Town** | 27 | 4 | 4 | 19 | 35 | 93 | 12 |

*Rother Vale expelled*

### 1909/10 Sheffield Association League

| | | | | | | | |
|---|---|---|---|---|---|---|---|
| **Monckton Athletic** | 26 | 19 | 2 | 5 | 83 | 30 | 40 |
| **Wath Athletic** | 26 | 18 | 4 | 4 | 64 | 25 | 40 |
| Parkgate &Raw Utd | 26 | 18 | 1 | 7 | 78 | 44 | 37 |
| South Kirkby | 26 | 15 | 3 | 8 | 55 | 39 | 33 |
| Rotherham Tn res | 26 | 12 | 7 | 7 | 49 | 35 | 31 |
| Doncaster Rov res | 26 | 13 | 4 | 9 | 53 | 59 | 30 |
| Denaby United res | 26 | 12 | 2 | 12 | 51 | 89 | 26 |
| Mexborough Tn res | 26 | 11 | 3 | 12 | 47 | 48 | 25 |
| Hickleton Main | 26 | 10 | 5 | 11 | 56 | 63 | 25 |
| Darfield United | 26 | 10 | 4 | 12 | 47 | 51 | 24 |
| Rawmarsh Albion | 26 | 5 | 5 | 16 | 36 | 61 | 15 |
| Silverwood Colliery | 26 | 5 | 4 | 17 | 36 | 74 | 14 |
| Worksop Town | 26 | 5 | 3 | 18 | 35 | 83 | 13 |
| **Kilnhurst Town** | 26 | 3 | 6 | 17 | 32 | 70 | 12 |

### 1910/11 Sheffield Association League

| | | | | | | | |
|---|---|---|---|---|---|---|---|
| **Wath Athletic** | 26 | 21 | 2 | 3 | 99 | 28 | 44 |
| Rotherham County | 26 | 17 | 3 | 6 | 75 | 30 | 37 |
| Darfield United | 25 | 13 | 6 | 6 | 58 | 38 | 32 |
| Doncaster Rov res | 26 | 12 | 7 | 7 | 60 | 39 | 31 |
| Silverwood Colliery | 26 | 14 | 3 | 9 | 50 | 38 | 31 |
| Frickley Colliery | 25 | 13 | 4 | 8 | 71 | 46 | 30 |
| Hickleton Main | 25 | 11 | 5 | 9 | 51 | 36 | 27 |
| South Kirkby | 26 | 12 | 1 | 13 | 61 | 53 | 25 |
| Conisbro' St Peter's | 25 | 10 | 4 | 11 | 50 | 58 | 24 |
| **Kilnhurst Town** | 26 | 8 | 7 | 11 | 45 | 61 | 23 |
| Rotherham Amat | 26 | 8 | 5 | 13 | 46 | 66 | 21 |
| Parkgate &Raw Utd | 26 | 6 | 4 | 16 | 47 | 75 | 16 |
| Mexborough Tn res | 26 | 4 | 3 | 19 | 36 | 99 | 11 |
| Brodsworth Main | 26 | 3 | 2 | 21 | 29 | 109 | 8 |

### 1911/12 Sheffield Association League

| | | | | | | | |
|---|---|---|---|---|---|---|---|
| **Wath Athletic** | 30 | 24 | 1 | 5 | 82 | 21 | 49 |
| Frickley Colliery | 30 | 24 | 1 | 5 | 96 | 31 | 49 |
| South Kirkby | 30 | 22 | 3 | 5 | 114 | 28 | 47 |
| Hickleton Main | 30 | 19 | 7 | 4 | 96 | 47 | 45 |
| Silverwood Colliery | 30 | 13 | 5 | 12 | 53 | 55 | 31 |
| Doncaster Rovers | 30 | 14 | 2 | 14 | 49 | 47 | 30 |
| Rotherham County | 30 | 13 | 4 | 13 | 57 | 56 | 30 |
| Rawmarsh Town | 30 | 12 | 3 | 15 | 85 | 86 | 27 |
| Rotherham Tn res | 30 | 10 | 5 | 15 | 41 | 59 | 25 |
| Bentley Colliery | 30 | 10 | 5 | 15 | 44 | 72 | 25 |

| | | | | | | | |
|---|---|---|---|---|---|---|---|
| Mexborough Tn res | 30 | 10 | 4 | 16 | 48 | 65 | 24 |
| **Kilnhurst Town** | 30 | 11 | 2 | 17 | 47 | 74 | 24 |
| Conisbro' St Peter's | 30 | 9 | 5 | 16 | 53 | 81 | 23 |
| Parkgate &Raw Utd | 30 | 9 | 3 | 18 | 55 | 104 | 21 |
| Brodsworth Colliery | 30 | 8 | 3 | 19 | 32 | 71 | 19 |
| Denaby United res | 30 | 7 | 3 | 20 | 42 | 87 | 17 |

### 1912/13 Sheffield Association League

| | | | | | | | |
|---|---|---|---|---|---|---|---|
| **Wath Athletic** | 28 | 20 | 4 | 4 | 90 | 32 | 44 |
| South Kirkby | 28 | 18 | 6 | 4 | 38 | 40 | 42 |
| Gainsborough T res | 28 | 19 | 3 | 6 | 36 | 43 | 41 |
| Kilnhurst Town | 28 | 17 | 5 | 6 | 55 | 41 | 39 |
| Silverwood Colliery | 28 | 16 | 5 | 7 | 30 | 43 | 37 |
| Hickleton Main | 28 | 16 | 5 | 7 | 59 | 44 | 37 |
| Bentley Colliery | 27 | 14 | 4 | 9 | 74 | 40 | 32 |
| Rotherham Amat | 28 | 11 | 6 | 11 | 46 | 54 | 28 |
| Rawmarsh Town | 28 | 9 | 4 | 15 | 43 | 83 | 22 |
| Conisbro' St Peter's | 28 | 9 | 3 | 16 | 47 | 78 | 21 |
| Frickley Colliery | 28 | 8 | 4 | 16 | 43 | 59 | 20 |
| Doncaster Rov res | 28 | 9 | 1 | 18 | 52 | 62 | 19 |
| Brodsworth Main | 27 | 8 | 3 | 16 | 45 | 67 | 19 |
| Denaby United res | 28 | 5 | 5 | 18 | 40 | 109 | 15 |
| Mexborough T res | 28 | 2 | 2 | 24 | 19 | 94 | 6 |

### 1913/14 Sheffield Association League
(as at April 27th, 1914)

| | | | | | | | |
|---|---|---|---|---|---|---|---|
| South Kirkby | 29 | 21 | 7 | 1 | 124 | 36 | 49 |
| Gainsboro' Trin res | 30 | 19 | 2 | 9 | 104 | 47 | 40 |
| Bentley Colliery | 27 | 14 | 8 | 5 | 53 | 37 | 36 |
| Denaby United | 29 | 15 | 5 | 9 | 59 | 52 | 35 |
| Rawmarsh Town | 27 | 10 | 12 | 5 | 51 | 42 | 32 |
| Brodsworth Main | 30 | 12 | 8 | 10 | 47 | 45 | 32 |
| Hickleton Main | 30 | 12 | 7 | 11 | 52 | 44 | 31 |
| Silverwood Coll | 30 | 14 | 1 | 15 | 38 | 65 | 29 |
| Rotherham Tn res | 30 | 12 | 4 | 14 | 53 | 78 | 28 |
| **Wath Athletic** | **29** | **10** | **7** | **12** | **49** | **34** | **27** |
| Rotherham Amat | 27 | 10 | 4 | 13 | 57 | 61 | 24 |
| Darfield United | 28 | 10 | 4 | 14 | 45 | 48 | 24 |
| Bolton Collingwood | 30 | 8 | 7 | 15 | 49 | 77 | 23 |
| **Kilnhurst Town** | **28** | **8** | **5** | **15** | **40** | **80** | **21** |
| Conisbro' St Peter's | 30 | 8 | 4 | 18 | 56 | 113 | 20 |
| Frickley Colliery | 30 | 4 | 3 | 23 | 31 | 102 | 11 |

### 1914/15 Sheffield Association League

| | | | | | | | |
|---|---|---|---|---|---|---|---|
| Rotherham County | 24 | 15 | 6 | 3 | 91 | 34 | 36 |
| Bentley Colliery | 23 | 15 | 2 | 6 | 78 | 38 | 32 |
| **Wath Athletic** | 24 | 15 | 2 | 7 | 51 | 36 | 32 |
| South Kirkby | 24 | 15 | 1 | 8 | 51 | 38 | 31 |
| Denaby United | 23 | 14 | 0 | 9 | 42 | 34 | 28 |
| **Kilnhurst Town** | 23 | 11 | 2 | 10 | 45 | 56 | 24 |
| Hickleton Main | 22 | 10 | 2 | 10 | 50 | 43 | 22 |
| Silverwood Colliery | 24 | 9 | 2 | 13 | 50 | 52 | 20 |
| Frickley Athletic | 23 | 9 | 2 | 12 | 40 | 54 | 20 |
| Brodsworth Main | 24 | 8 | 4 | 12 | 38 | 54 | 20 |
| Darfield United | 24 | 8 | 2 | 14 | 40 | 69 | 18 |
| Gainsborough T res | 23 | 6 | 2 | 15 | 30 | 70 | 14 |
| Rotherham Amat | 23 | 2 | 3 | 18 | 29 | 74 | 7 |

### 1915/16 Sheffield Association League

| | | | | | | | |
|---|---|---|---|---|---|---|---|
| Hoyland Town | 10 | 7 | 1 | 2 | 17 | 8 | 15 |
| Rotherham County | 10 | 5 | 1 | 4 | 14 | 10 | 11 |
| Parkgate CC | 10 | 5 | 0 | 5 | 25 | 11 | 10 |
| Mexborough Town | 9 | 4 | 1 | 4 | 17 | 15 | 9 |
| **Kilnhurst Town** | 10 | 3 | 3 | 4 | 11 | 15 | 9 |
| South Kirkby | 9 | 2 | 0 | 7 | 4 | 29 | 4 |

*Hickleton Main, Silverwood Colliery & Darfield United, all w/d*

### 1915/16 Wharncliffe Charity League

| | | | | | | | |
|---|---|---|---|---|---|---|---|
| Worksop Town | 12 | 9 | 2 | 1 | 28 | 11 | 20 |
| Rotherham County | 12 | 8 | 1 | 3 | 32 | 20 | 17 |
| Doncaster Rovers | 9 | 6 | 0 | 3 | 29 | 11 | 12 |
| Mexborough Town | 10 | 4 | 2 | 4 | 34 | 29 | 10 |
| Dinnington Main | 12 | 3 | 1 | 8 | 18 | 27 | 7 |
| South Kirkby | 12 | 3 | 1 | 8 | 15 | 37 | 7 |
| **Kilnhurst Town** | 11 | 2 | 1 | 8 | 13 | 34 | 5 |

# Attercliffe
# 1870-1933
### *'From bible class to giant slayers'*

Attercliffe, a predominantly industrial suburb of northeast Sheffield, on the south bank of the River Don, has made its mark in local footballing circles. It quickly became a hotbed of football in an area that had taken to the sport in a much bigger way than any other district in the county, and from the late 19th Century until the mid-1920's there were several league and cup competitions centred around the area, and a whole host of teams that won local silverware.

While Sheffield has always had a proud and significant footballing history, the leading lights of Wednesday and Sheffield United began to dominate the local sporting press, with a good deal of coverage given to the senior professional clubs in the Midland League. However, the Attercliffe name became synonymous with success at amateur league level during the mid-1920s, on a national as well as regional level.

### Attercliffe FC 1870-1904

An early reference to an Attercliffe football club came with the organisation of its inaugural athletic sports event held on 3rd October 1864, hosted by the Attercliffe Cricket & Football Club (The cricket club itself was founded around 1856), which also went by the name of Attercliffe Christ Church Cricket & Football Club. References in the local press referred to the two different titles, although it is clear that the local team represented the church. The Christ Church Cricket Club had opened its new ground in Monday 4th May 1863 with a match against Attercliffe United, and it is likely that it was this field that was used for the sports event. However, by 1867 the event was advertised as being organised by the cricket club, with no mention of 'football'. Neither are any competitive football fixtures reported for the Christ Church club, it is likely that the sport was played on an informal basis during the winter by cricket club members.

The football section of the club was properly organised in 1870 when Christchurch (Attercliffe) FC began playing friendly matches with other local sides. The club's first match was on Wednesday 30th November that year when an inexperienced side played The Wednesday, the more experienced team fielding a mixed team of players for what was, for them, a relatively minor local fixture. Wednesday won 2-0.

The following day, the *Sheffield Daily Telegraph* reported, 'On behalf of the Christ Church Club, the Rev. G Osborne and B Shaw, Esq, more particularly distinguished themselves by their superior and plucky play. After the match the players were very hospitably entertained by Dr Shaw, at his residence, a kindness that was very highly appreciated. The following gentlemen composed the Christ Church Club:- B Shaw, Esq., captain, Dr Douglass, Rev. G Osborne, W Naylor, W Widdowson, F Twigg, C Bridgman, C Malpas, R England, R Crookes, J Lee C Kingrose, E Beardshaw; Umpire, J Lee.'

Sadly the club lost its captain in February 1871, when he passed away suddenly. The *Sheffield Daily Telegraph* printed the following tribute to one of club's founder members, 'The deceased was the second son of the late Mr Shaw, many years surgeon, of Attercliffe. He was educated at Caius College, Cambridge, where he graduated as BA. in 1867. In proof of the esteem in which he was held by fellow collegians, both as young man of amiable and gentlemanly disposition and as an individual of remarkable physical development and muscular power, we may mention that he was elected captain of his college boat club. In 1870 he passed the last examination and received his diploma as member the Royal College Surgeons of London. Since then he has been assisting his brother, Mr Geo. Shaw, surgeon, of Attercliffe, was captain of the Attercliffe Christ Church Football Club, and played in a match exactly a previous to his death. The first fifteen of the club have requested permission to attend his funeral. He was universally esteemed as a man extreme good nature and kindliness of heart; and all of the brother's patients whom he visited speak of him in the highest terms of admiration and respect. He was engaged to be married to Miss Mary Jessop, of Endcliffe, and will be buried in their new tomb at Ecclesall at the side of the late Mr Sydney Jessop.'

The club, having joined the Sheffield FA in 1871, was officially rechristened 'Attercliffe Football Club' in 1873. By the time of its affiliation it had around 70 members, but by the end of the decade this had grown to 200.

Although the club at first comprised of local men, by 1875 many of the leading footballers in Sheffield had become members. The football ground by now was in all probability in a different location to the cricket club, with a ground on Shirland Lane, close to the Attercliffe railway station, being reported. The church itself (now long-gone) was just under a mile away from the station, on Attercliffe Road.

Mrs Bingley's Coach & Horses Hotel was used for club meetings and social events from the mid-1870s (1876), the club making use of Mr Webster's Fox House before that (in 1873) as well as The Attercliffe Boys' School on Church Street (1874 & 1875).

The 1877/78 season was a successful one, with 23 wins coming from 27 matches (two were drawn, and two were lost), scoring 55 goals and conceding only six. In the course of two seasons the side had scored 131 goals. The team, which played in blue and white striped shirts, white shorts, and blue socks, reached the final of the Sheffield FA Senior Cup for the first time, at Bramall Lane on Saturday 2nd March, in front of almost 4,000 spectators (although some newspapers claimed that up to ten thousand were present). Despite the weather being really good, the pitch was in a fairly poor state due to heavy rain the night before, making the field slippery and treacherous. The red-hot favourites and holders of the cup, The Wednesday, adapted better to the conditions and ran out 2-0 winners again.

By 1879 the athletic sports were advertised as being organised by 'Attercliffe Football Club', and held on the Old Forge Cricket Ground, Newhall Road, close to Brightside Lane. The Old Forge ground was by now being used by the football club, and in time it became regarded as one of the best grounds in Sheffield.

Attercliffe achieved a semi-final place in the Wharncliffe Charity Cup, losing 2-4 to The Wednesday on Saturday 3rd March 1883. At the end of the month, The Wednesday defeated Pyebank 4-0 in the final. The Charity Cup itself later became a league competition.

An interesting Sheffield Association Cup tie on Saturday 12th January 1884 saw Attercliffe lose 2-3 at home to Middlesbrough despite being 2-0 up. There were no boundary limitations to entry to the competition so the north-eastern team took advantage of this, enabling it to experience stronger competition than it would have by playing friendly fixtures against local competition. Attercliffe protested that Jackson Ewbank should not have played for the winners due to his residential status, but this was over-ruled when Middlesbrough were able to prove that Ewbank had worked in the town for several years, and that he had been one of the principal members of the club since its commencement.

On Thursday 18th December 1884 the Old Foundry ground was used for a representative fixture between the famous Corinthians club and Sheffield FC. Due to the wretched weather conditions, play only lasted for one hour, with the Corinthians winning 2-1.

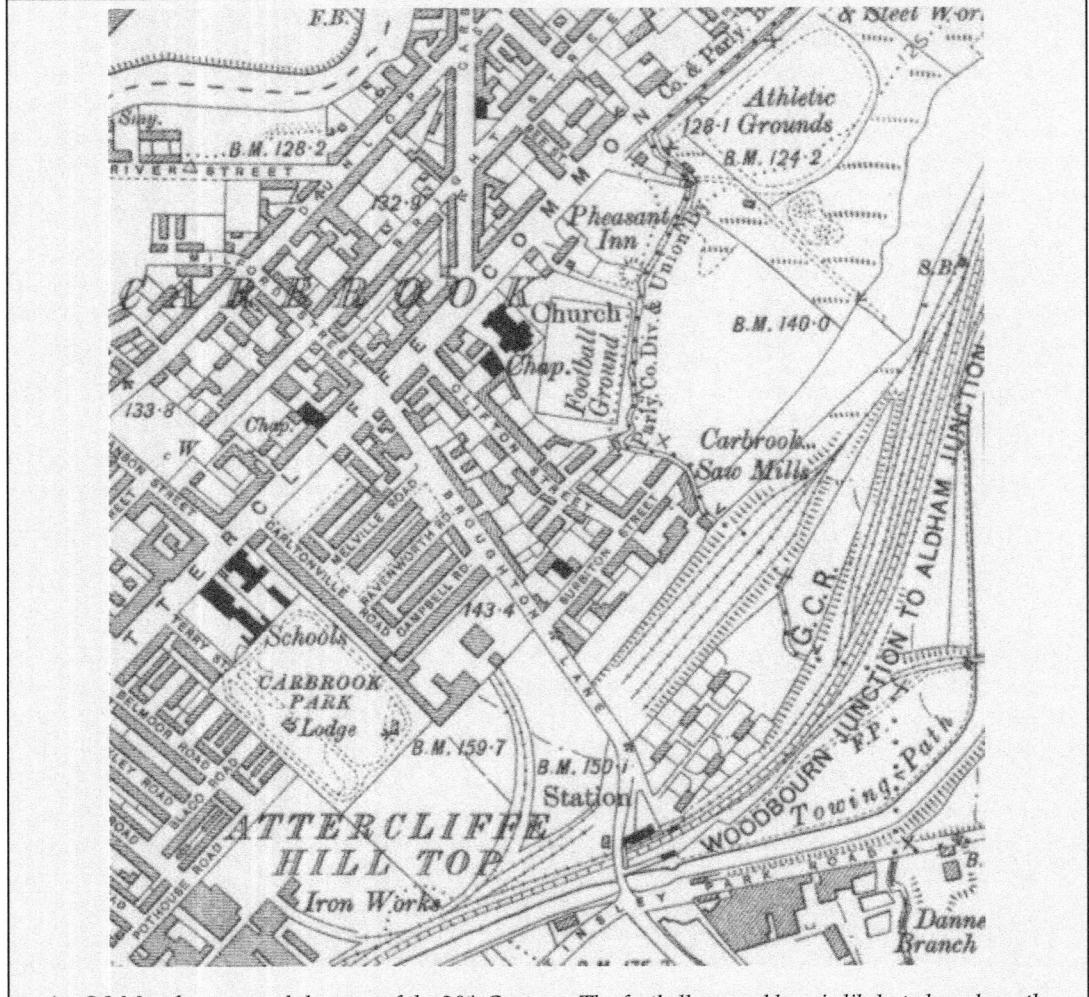

*An OS Map from around the turn of the 20th Century. The football ground here is likely to have been the one used by Attercliffe FC from 1891.*

*The later Attercliffe United played several cup final ties on what was then called the 'Pheasant Inn Ground', and which is shown as the 'Athletic Grounds' at the top of the map. The revived Attercliffe FC also played on this ground from 1923.*

First four seasons of the Sheffield Minor Cup competition all went the same way, with Attercliffe proving victorious in each season;

1883/84: Played at the Queen's Grounds on Saturday 5th April 1884. Won 2-0 v Heeley, with goals from Reach & Platts.

1884/85: Played at Bramall Lane on Saturday 21st February 1885. Won 6-1 v Clarence.

1885/86: Played at the Newhall Grounds on Saturday 3rd April 1886. Won 1-0 v Eckington Works, in front of 1,500 spectators.

1886/87: Played at Bramall Lane on Saturday 2nd April 1887. Won 1-0 v Melville, in front of 3,000 spectators.

The Attercliffe and Kilnhurst clubs played out an epic series of ties in the Sheffield & Hallamshire Challenge Cup during the 1889/90 season, with Attercliffe finally winning 2-0 in January. The Second Round tie took seven matches to decide following a series of drawn games, although later reports in the local press have differed in the number of ties being played - six and eight also being suggested. Either way, Attercliffe's reward for finally seeing off its opponents was a 0-6 defeat to Sheffield United on Monday 27th January 1890 in the Third Round.

The club AGM at the Coach & Horses on Wednesday 11th July 1888 was significant in that there was a discussion regarding a possible change of status for the club in turning professional. The matter was put on the table, to be discussed at a later date, and true to the committee's word later discussions led to the club announcing that it would indeed be turning professional in July 1889. Several players were signed on, including W & J Ellis, J Bloom, and A Hemingfield from Eccleshall FC, but the venture did not prove successful and by the following July the club announced that it was releasing all but five of its players in an attempt to build a stronger team for the upcoming season.

There is little doubt that by the time the club joined its first league competition, money would still have been paid from gate money to team members. Attercliffe joined the Sheffield & District League in 1891/92, where payments to players was the norm, and there would have little chance of a purely amateur club finishing in third place in the 14-team league. The club's home ground was by now on a new enclosure at Carbrook, although the reasons for the ground-move, which occurred right at the start of 1891 has not been explained, as the Old Forge Ground remained in use as football ground for many years after Attercliffe's departure. It is likely that the Carbrook ground was the same, established ground that was already being used by Carbrook Church FC. The site is now covered by modern warehousing adjacent to the current Surbiton Street.

*Tommy Crawshaw*

One of Sheffield's most famous footballing sons, Tommy Crawshaw, played for Attercliffe at this time. After starting out with the local Park Grange club, he was an Attercliffe player between 1891 and 1893, before going on to play for Lancashire team Heywood Central and then Sheffield Wednesday, who he helped to two league titles and two FA Cup wins. He made 418 appearances for Wednesday, before moving to Chesterfield, and also played ten times for England, scoring once in a 3-0 win at The Dell, Southampton against Ireland on Saturday 9th March 1901.

In later years, Crawshaw would go on to play for Castleford Town, and by 1911 has was licensee at the Shrewsbury Hotel, on South Street in Sheffield, later moving to the Sportsman near Hillsborough and then The Yorkshireman in Sheffield City Centre. He passed away in 1960, aged 87. Between his tenancies at the Shrewsbury and Sportsman, Tommy owned a newsagent's shop on Bramall Lane.

For the 1892/93 season Attercliffe's league competition was known as the Sheffield Challenge Cup League, with a slip to 10th place in the final league table. A small five team Sheffield & District League Division One ran simultaneously, with the team finishing 3rd in that. The 1894/95 season saw the team down to 14th in the 15-team Sheffield league, also finishing third of five teams in the North division of the Wharncliffe Charity Shield (which was in effect a 'second division' of the Wharncliffe Charity Cup league).

The local football association was unable to organise a new senior league in time for the 1895/96 season, but late in the season eight clubs got together to form a 'New League', with two groups of four organised. Attercliffe won its division, and went on to defeat the winners of the other division, Kilnhurst 5-1 in a re-played final. On Saturday 25th January 1896, the team achieved possibly its record victory, thrashing Ardsley 16-0 at home. Due to the poor weather that day, very few spectators were witness to the rout. The first goal was scored in the first 60 seconds, and the home team were seven goals to the good by half time.

From the 1896/97 season the top Sheffield league was known simply as the Sheffield Association League, with Attercliffe occupying a bottom half place in the table in most seasons leading up to the end of the 1903/04 season, when the club left the competition. Ironically, the club had just experienced a reasonable season by its standards when the decision was made to disband, given its apparent worsening financial position.

In 1898/99 the side reached the final of the Sheffield FA Senior Cup for the second time, losing 5-2 to Sheffield United reserves in a replay at Bramall Lane on Saturday 15th April, in front of 2,000 spectators in what were described in heavy, slippery conditions. Exactly two weeks earlier, the sides had drawn 1-1 on the Carbrook ground in front of an estimated crowd of 3,000.

**Attercliffe in the FA Cup**

Attercliffe made an inauspicious start to their FA Cup adventures, losing 0-7 at Staveley in the 1886/87 season, and then 0-9 at Sheffield Heeley the following season, both being First Round ties. Qualifying rounds were introduced from the 1888/89 season, but the club rarely managed to progress beyond the first stage. Whitby were defeated 5-0 in a First Qualifying Round tie on Saturday 5th October 1889. However, the Whitby team successfully protested the result, on the grounds that the field was below the minimum length. The 'replay' the following week saw Whitby win 6-0 on their own ground. The club managed to play three ties on only one occasion, which was the 1899/1900 season, and that was due to a replayed First Qualifying Round match against Mexborough, which was lost. Earlier, Montrose Works had been defeat 3-0 in a Preliminary Round tie, which - discounting the void victory over Whitby – was Attercliffe's best result in an FA Cup tie.

The club's final season of entry into the FA Cup was the 1903/04 season, when the team drew 3-3 at home to Mexborough West End in a Preliminary Round tie, before losing the replay 1-2.

## Attercliffe FC revival 1923-27

A newly re-formed Attercliffe AFC entered the Sheffield Association League for the 1923/24 season, and in a hark back to the start of Attercliffe's football history, the club, in conjunction with the Sheffield United Harriers, hosted its first sports meeting on Saturday 23rd August 1924 on the Pheasant Inn Grounds, which was again used for home matches in the league. Sadly the event was ruined by the rain, although the events reported did result in some close finishes, which gave those attending plenty to cheer about. However, despite the club finishing well up the league in its first season, it was the Attercliffe United club that was receiving all of the attention locally. The Tinsley Charity Cup was won by Attercliffe FC, however. The 1923/24 final saw a 4-1 win against the successful Attercliffe Victory club on Saturday 10th May 1924 after having gone behind early in the game.

| Sheffield Association League 1924/25 | | | | | | | |
|---|---|---|---|---|---|---|---|
| | P | W | D | L | F | A | Pts |
| Attercliffe | 28 | 21 | 5 | 2 | 91 | 32 | 47 |
| Beighton MW | 28 | 18 | 4 | 6 | 87 | 40 | 40 |
| Denaby United res | 28 | 17 | 5 | 6 | 74 | 34 | 39 |
| South Kirkby Coll | 28 | 14 | 9 | 5 | 59 | 33 | 37 |
| Maltby Main | 27 | 14 | 6 | 7 | 58 | 47 | 34 |
| Rotherham Amat | 28 | 15 | 4 | 9 | 51 | 43 | 34 |
| Bullcroft Colliery | 28 | 14 | 4 | 10 | 68 | 51 | 32 |
| Eckington Works | 27 | 12 | 2 | 13 | 49 | 69 | 26 |
| Treeton RR | 28 | 10 | 2 | 16 | 50 | 53 | 22 |
| Brodsworth Main | 28 | 10 | 1 | 17 | 42 | 67 | 21 |
| Rossington Main | 28 | 6 | 7 | 15 | 34 | 52 | 19 |
| Goldthorpe United | 28 | 7 | 5 | 16 | 42 | 61 | 19 |
| Dinnington Main | 28 | 7 | 4 | 17 | 44 | 69 | 18 |
| New Stubbin Coll | 28 | 7 | 3 | 18 | 37 | 73 | 17 |
| Silverwood Coll | 28 | 6 | 1 | 21 | 53 | 108 | 13 |

The club's second season was different, however, as the 'new' Attercliffe became the 1924/25 Sheffield Association League champions. Amazingly, this was the first time in 24 years that a club from Sheffield itself had won the league title, The Wednesday reserves having been the last such team to do so in 1901. The team also won the Tinsley Charity Cup in the 1924/25 season.

The following two seasons saw the club finish out of the leading places in the competition, but Attercliffe FC also entered the Wragg League, winning the championship of that league in 1926, when Mosborough WMC were defeated 3-2 in the final on Saturday 17th April, and the following season finished runner-up to Ecclesfield United who defeated them 2-1 in a re-played 1927 final at High Green early in May.

However, all was not well, and the *Sheffield Daily Telegraph* reported, on Wednesday 13th July 1927 that the Attercliffe Football Club was to be wound up. The club AGM the evening before was attended by just three members, H Vickers (President) H Barrett (Hon. Secretary), and H Dyson, and in view of the apathy shown, coupled with serious ground and financial issues, the three agreed that the club should be disbanded.

This wasn't quite the end of Attercliffe in the Sheffield Association League, however, as Attercliffe United stepped in to take its place in this competition, as well as in the Wragg League.

## Attercliffe United 1919-1928

At a time when the country was recovering from the devastating effects of World War One, there was huge upsurge in number of teams playing in local competition, and minor competitions such as the Attercliffe League thrived. One of the clubs that emerged during this time was one of several to use the Attercliffe name, and that was Attercliffe United.

The origins of the club relate to a group of boys who kicked a ball about in Hazell's Park, Darnall, in 1909. A year later, church officials and many of the same boys who were members of the Attercliffe Unitarian Church Bible Class founded the team, which originally took the name of the church, which was located on Shirland Lane.

The club eventually turned to competitive football in 1912/13, spending a season in the Sheffield Bible Class League before re-emerging in the 1914/15 Sheffield Friendlies League. At this time the club was known as Attercliffe '*Units*' in short – but was also often referred mistakenly to as Attercliffe United. Despite seven members of the team signing-up en-bloc to the Rifle Brigade, the club continued and gradually grew in strength. The league title was won at the end of the 1918/19 season, following a runners-up position two years earlier. No trophy or medals were awarded to the club or its players as the Friendlies League which ran until 1987, had a policy of not awarding such prizes, as it was a competition that promoted friendly rivalry.

The team played in dark blue jerseys, which had a six-inch belt of sky-blue, white cuffs and white collars. The reason for this choice of kit was the fact that the club secretary at the time discovered that a local sports outfitter had a surplus set of jerseys of the Sheffield University Rugby Club for sale at a cheap price.

> *Star Green 'Un*, Saturday 20th November 1920
>
> *There's luck for you! Last week W Booth of Attercliffe Units turned out at the last minute to complete the team against Deep Pits; in fact the game had commenced when he went on the field. Five minutes later he had broken a leg!*

A step up was made when the team entered into the Sheffield City League for 1919/20. Incidentally, an unrelated Attercliffe United is also known to have existed in the 1920/21 season, playing 'minor' (under 16s or under 18s) fixtures across the city. From the 1921/22 season, *the Units* were formally renamed Attercliffe United and also fielded a team in the top division of the Sheffield Junior League at this time.

The 1920s were a particularly successful time for United, eventually gaining national prominence. In addition to its good form in the Friendlies League, successes included:

*Darnall Medical Aid Cup winners* in 1918/19, 1920/21, and 1922/23, runners up 1921/22. The 1918/19 final saw Woodhouse defeated 4-1 on Saturday 26th April, 1920/21 while Darnall Old Boys were defeated 1-0 on Tuesday 29th March at the Wellington Cricket Ground before 3,000 spectators in the 1920/21 final. Darnall Church Institute were defeated 1-0 in the 1922/23 final at Owlergreave Road (which was in the area close to where the current Prince of Wales Road lies) in what was Attercliffe's third final in the space of five days. In what had also proved a hectic schedule over the final weeks of the season, the 1921/22 Darnall Cup final against Darnall Old Boys was one step too far. The initial final on Craven's Sports Ground finished goal-less in front of 4,000 spectators on Thursday 11th May 1922. The replayed final on the same ground five days later was attended by 5,000, who saw Darnall win 2-0.

*Wragg League runners-up* in 1919/20, losing 0-1 to Darnall Old Boys in a replay Saturday 15th May at Sanderson Sports Ground, Manor Lane, the teams having drawn 0-0 the week before, and 1922/23, 1-3 to Treeton Reading Room on Saturday 5th May.

*City League winners* 1919/20, 1920/21, and 1921/22. Unitarians won its first City League title when Norwood Amateurs were defeated 4-2 in the league final on Saturday 1st May 1920 on 'Craven's Ground'. It took six hours for Unitarians to defeat Malin Bridge Old Boys the following season, however. A second replay was won 4-3 at the Midland Athletic Ground on Saturday 7th May, that tie itself lasting 2½ hours, with extra-extra time played in order to bring the tie to a conclusion. The initial final on the Handsworth WMC ground had ended 1-1 on Saturday 30th April, the replay on the Cammell Sports ground on Tuesday 3rd May also ending 1-1. The team was just as successful the following season. On Saturday 29th April 1922 it defeated Malin Bridge Old Boys in the final for the second successive season. It was much easier this time around, United winning 4-1.

***Sheffield Minor League winners*** 1922/'23. There were 3,000 spectators present on Saturday 21st April 1923 to see Attercliffe draw 3-3 with Rawmarsh Athletic. The replay played five days later ended in a 0-0 draw. A second replay on Thursday 3rd May was won 3-1 by Attercliffe after extra time. This was another final that took six hours to determine a winner. All three games were played at the Pheasant Inn Ground, Carbrook.

***Tinsley Charity Cup winners*** 1921/22 and 1922/23. On Monday 22nd May 1922, United defeated Park Grange 1-0 in the Tinsley Cup final replay at Hyde Park, thanks to a goal from W Watts in the closing stages of extra-time. The following season, Industry Sports were defeated finalists, Attercliffe winning 3-0 on Saturday 12th May 1923 at the Pheasant Inn Ground.

The club joined the Sheffield Amateur League for the 1923/24 season, alongside neighbours Attercliffe Victory FC. Placed in Division Two, the team finished in a play-off position. However, the league championship final was lost, to Norton Woodseats, who won 4-1 on Saturday 26th April 1924 at Shiregreen.

However, this was the season in which the club produced one of the greatest FA Amateur Cup upsets of all time by defeating the Northern Nomads club in the FA Amateur Cup, and then repeated its giant-killing exploits by beating three-time winners Stockton in the very next round.

Attercliffe United played on a ground at Waverley Cottages, Handsworth. Its capacity was said to have been around 5,000 prior to the club's FA Amateur Cup match against Northern Nomads, but cup ties apart, this number was obviously rarely, if ever, tested. The area is still used for football to this day.

The club continued to field teams in several local leagues, re-joining the Sheffield Friendlies League for the 1924/25 season, as well as fielding a team in the Wragg League. The Sheffield Amateur League was still the main source of competition for the first team. The Division One title of the league was won in the 1924/25 season, although the club lost in the championship play-off semi-final to Atlas & Norfolk on Saturday 4th April 1925.

By now, Attercliffe Victory FC, founded in 1921, and originating from the Attercliffe Victory club in the city was quickly making a name for itself. The team had also won the Sheffield Junior League championship (for under 18s teams) in its first two seasons, and had then added the Sheffield & Hallamshire Junior Cup in the 1923/24 season.

It was this club that lifted more silverware rather than United at the end of the 1925/26 season. Victory had stepped up to open-age football and became the Amateur League champions after winning the play-offs - both they are United played in Division Two that season - and also added the Tinsley Charity Cup, defeating Brightside Congs in the final on Friday 30th April 1926. This was the fifth year in succession that an Attercliffe club had won the competition.

Both United and Victory were in 'Division One' again for the 1926/27 season as United introduced its reserve team into the league, although by now many of the players that had enabled the club to make a name for itself had moved on. It should be noted that in some local competitions, such as the Sheffield Amateur League, teams were allocated divisions, with the winners playing off for the championship, rather than having divisions based on ability.

The summer of 1927 was significant in terms of football in Attercliffe. The senior Attercliffe FC withdrew from the Sheffield Association League after only three seasons, while the successful Attercliffe Victory team was also disbanded. This left United to fly for the flag for this part of Sheffield (although there were still several other small clubs in the minor leagues around the city), and a decision was made to join the Sheffield Association League, as well as the Wragg League in which the disbanded Attercliffe

FC had competed. At the same time, a side was left in the Sheffield Amateur League. Hallam, another club with an excellent FA Amateur Cup record, was accepted into the Association League at the same time. The team finished in mid-table in the 1927/28 but this was to be Attercliffe United's final season under that title, changing its name to Handsworth in the summer of 1928. The club continued in the same competitions, but struggled on the field, later dropping down to the league's new second tier, and also off the field as it struggled to attract support. The sad decision to disband the club was made in May 1933.

### Attercliffe United in the FA Amateur Cup

Not many Sheffield Amateur League sides could hope to enjoy a successful run in the national amateur competition, but Attercliffe United did just that, reaching the last 16 of the 1923/24 competition - it's first year of entry – and causing two huge cup upsets along the way.

The cup run began with a 3-1 First Qualifying Round win at Bolsover Colliery, and this was followed by a narrow 1-0 home victory over Youlgrave, a team that went on to win the Matlock & District League that season. Further qualifying round wins followed, 1-0 at Rotherham Amateurs and 5-0 at home to Hallam. Neither of these ties attracted much attention outside of Sheffield.

However, the victory over Hallam set up a fascinating home tie with the great Northern Nomads club in the First Round proper. The following match report sums up the occasion nicely.

*Sheffield Daily Telegraph,* Monday 7th January 1924

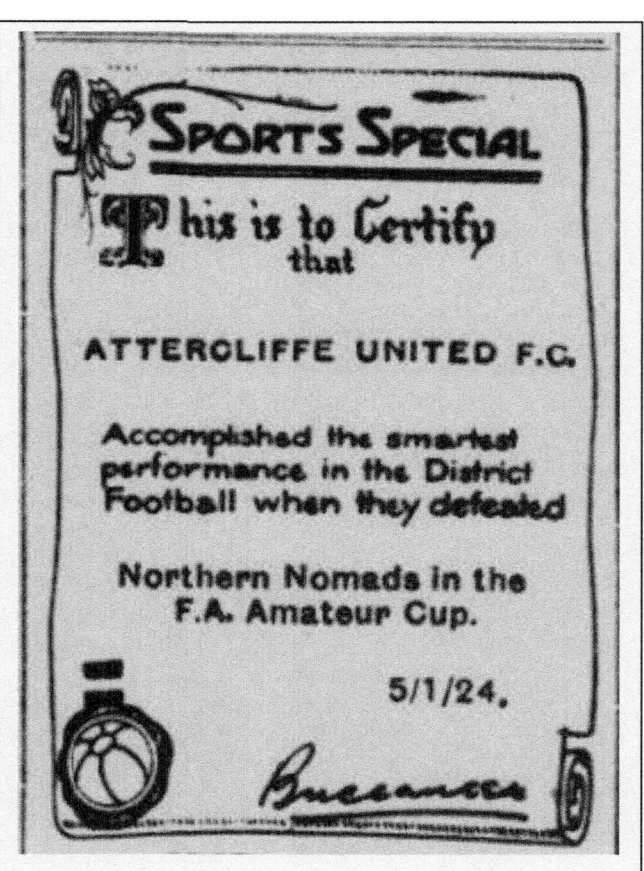

**FA AMATEUR CUP.**
***Attercliffe United Rise to the Occasion.***
**GREAT WIN OVER NOMADS.**
*Attercliffe United made the Great Adventure on Saturday, and to the huge delight not only of the one thousand people who saw the game at Waverley Cottages, Handsworth, but of all who have interests of Sheffield amateur football at heart, they won through into the second round of the FA Amateur Cup. It took the Attercliffe lads some time realise that the great Northern Nomads were only mortals like themselves, and just prone to make mistakes, but once that fact had become uppermost in their minds, the result was never in doubt, and in every sense of the word they were worthy winners. So many people had made up their minds that Attercliffe were certain to make their exit against the famous Merseyside combination, which fields Amateur Internationals and players with League experience in profusion, that even the bulk of the spectators were dumbfounded when they found the home team not only standing*

up to their visitors, but actually beating them at their own game. Instead of becoming disheartened at the missing of many chances in the first half, and the concession of penalty, which was converted by Ravale, Attercliffe buckled to after the interval, and, within a short space of time, Lill had obtained both the equaliser and what proved to be the winning goal.

**A True Captain in Every Sense.** In the first half it had been shown that neither of the Nomads backs was reliable under pressure, so the Attercliffe forwards played like demons, and with such success that Robertson and Beswick, two of the best amateur half-backs in the country, spent the whole of the second half in an often vain endeavour to curb the enthusiasm of the brothers Rodgers and their virile inside forwards. The man behind the scenes — the prompter of the numerous attacks — was 'Ken' Bannister, and later, when the Nomads forwards, desperate by the passing of time, made many dangerous breakaways, it was he again who, time and time again, stemmed the tide and fell back to help his resolute, but outweighted backs. Cox, Roebuck, and Bannister gave a splendid exhibition of defensive play in the second half against two inside forwards, Randle, and Mokhtar, the Egyptian, who were very wily. Never has the experience of 'Ken' Bannister stood Attercliffe United in such good stead as it did on Saturday. Inspired by their captain's display, the whole team rose to the occasion. The Nomads had no excuses to make after the match. They were beaten by the better side, and the ground, they said, played much better than it looked. Attercliffe United were a very good side on Saturday, and if fortune favours them in the draw, they will go far in the FA Amateur Cup competition.

The former winners fielded an experienced team that day, one which included J E Beswick (Stoke), Woodwiss (Derby County), Moktar (Tranmere Rovers), Robertson (New Brighton), Royle (Manchester City/ New Brighton, and a northern sprint champion). The Attercliffe team was an entirely local one.

Attercliffe proved that the result was no fluke when north-eastern side Stockton was defeated on Saturday 19th January in the Second Round. Again, the local press was on hand to report the team's stunning victory.

*Sheffield Daily Telegraph*, Monday 21st January 1924

### AMATEUR CUP TRIUMPH. Attercliffe United Dismiss Notable Stockton Eleven.

*Stockton thrice winners of the FA Amateur Cup, and six times finalists, were beaten 1-0 by Attercliffe United on Saturday in the second round of this season's competition, and Sheffield amateurs are delighted with the progress made. In the first round the Northern Nomads were beaten. Both games were played at Handsworth.*

*Attercliffe deserved their victory over Stockton for the goal by H Unwin was a good one; nevertheless they missed many chances. The Stockton forwards, however, were worse offenders in that respect. Longstaff, the visitors' centre-forward, had a glorious opportunity on one occasion, but he tapped the ball into the goalkeeper's hands when a shot would probably have been successful. K Bannister played an inspiring game at centre half-back for Attercliffe, and N Rodgers was a clever outside-right. On the other wing R Baptie was a hard-working player, his only fault being that did not lift his centres better. Marsh, the Attercliffe goalkeeper started shakily, but was soon confident and reliable.*

*For Stockton, Bullock and Oates, especially the latter, played well back, and their left half-back, Conway, set the forwards going splendidly. The left-wing forwards, Brownlee, and Shute, were the best forwards on the field, and combined prettily. Result - Attercliffe United 1 Stockton 0.*

After the match Stockton protested against the result, having mistaken Attercliffe's K Bannister for his brother, who had been a professional with the Darlington and Sheffield United clubs. The protest was dismissed and the United secretary, Mr Bailey, later announced that the Stockton club had apologised to both Bannister and the Attercliffe club for the inconvenience caused by the misinformation it had received.

The remarkable run ended in the Third Round (last 16) when another famous old team, Dulwich Hamlet, previous Amateur Cup winners, ran out winners in another tie played on the Attercliffe ground.

*Sheffield Daily Telegraph*, Monday 18th February, 1924

*DOWN WITH COLOURS FLYING* **Attercliffe United Give Famous Londoners Close Game.**

The most interesting and exciting part of the FA Amateur Cup (Third Round) tie between Attercliffe United and Dulwich Hamlet (Cup winners in 1919-20), the Waverley Cottages ground, at Handsworth, Sheffield, was the last ten minutes, when the United, by a mighty effort, suddenly pulled themselves together, scored, and were exceedingly unlucky not equalize. Yet, taking the game as a whole, the noted Isthmian League team were, on merits, entitled to their 2-1 victory. It was game of fluctuations: a frankly disappointing scramble; an unscientific tussle; but the ground being in very trying condition, through melted snow, must have had a good deal to do with the quality of the play. Dulwich had three internationals in their side – Coleman (goal). Brooker (right back), and Kail (inside-right). The United also had a full team, including their sparse-haired centre-half, Bannister, the captain, who, now in his nineteenth season of football, played a very creditable game.

**Men of Stature.** Until the first goal was scored (in surprising fashion, by Nicol, inside-left for Dulwich) after 27 minutes play, Attercliffe were having the better of the exchanges, but always found it difficult to get past two backs, who were conspicuous amongst team of men of stature that appeared quite above the average, and noticeably superior that of the Sheffield men. From then until twelve minutes of the second half had gone the Hamlet proved themselves rather cleverer, but no means great side. At the time mentioned. Kail, their most conspicuous forward, made the score 2-0. He was rather fortunate, however, to catch a half-back and Cox (left-back) off the alert, for he went from the halfway line to beat Marsh, the goalkeeper, in a somewhat lucky manner; the ball rolled timidly just the inside of the post, and then stopped.

It was Rodgers who, by a particularly bright individual effort, scored the best goal of the day, and after that there was tearing struggle for an equaliser, Coleman once being lucky to get the ball over the bar in very inexpert way. Throughout, the goalkeepers did not have a great deal to do; Coleman revealed nothing of that form which gained him international fame. The Attercliffe defence was really splendid - halves and backs; but the forwards failed to reproduce that form that enabled them to go through all the qualifying rounds of the competition, and then knock-out such formidable opponents as the Northern Nomads and Stockton. However, the United left the competition in a manner no way discreditable to them. The club had the satisfaction of securing a record 'gate', 3,600 paid £120. Hundreds of people broke into the ground and hundreds more watched from a high bank outside.

The *Yorkshire Post* actually reported that there were 8,000 spectators present that day, although other newspapers, both local and national, were more in line with the figure given by the *Sheffield Daily Telegraph*.

Attercliffe United was not able to repeat its run in the FA Amateur Cup in subsequent seasons. The club was rewarded for its efforts the previous season with a bye to the First Round proper in the 1924/25 season, when a 1-0 victory at Hull Young People's Institute enabled the club face local rivals Hallam at the next stage. Despite a goal-less draw in the away leg, a 1-3 loss at home ended hopes of another run to the later stages.

The 1925/26 season saw a 2-5 loss at Nottingham team Basford United in the First Round, which meant that Attercliffe would have to negotiate the qualifying rounds in future. The final of the competition that season, incidentally, saw Northern Amateurs defeat Stockton 7-1.

A 2-6 home loss in the first qualifying round to Rotherham Amateurs in the 1926/27 season was a far cry from events three years earlier. A final entry came in 1927/28, when, following a 6-1 home win over Sheffield Municipal Officers (following a 3-3 draw) in the Second Qualifying Round was followed by a heavy 3-7 loss at Warmsworth at the next stage.

**Attercliffe Victory** also entered the FA Amateur Cup in the 1926/27 season. They drew local side Norfolk Amateurs in the First Qualifying Round, drawing 3-3 at home, before losing 2-3 in the replay.

Attercliffe United's name change to **Handsworth** in 1927, meant that the club entered the Amateur Cup under its new name between 1927-33. The club came close to making it to the First Round proper in the 1930/31 season. Exempt until the third qualifying round, a 3-2 home victory over Sheffield was followed by a 3-3 draw at home to Norton Woodseats at the final qualifying stage. Sadly a 4-2 Norton victory ended hopes for that year.

Handsworth's final entry in the competition saw a 5-4 home success against Humber United in the Second Qualifying Round in the 1932/33 season. The Norton Woodseats club was then defeated 5-3 at home, before a final qualifying round tie at Nether Edge Amateurs, another club from Sheffield which resulted in a 1-4 defeat.

## Attercliffe Radicals

One more Attercliffe team is worth a mention in this chapter, and that is one which achieved almost all of its success during World War Two, and that is the almost uniquely titled Attercliffe Radicals club.

Attercliffe Radical Club, or *'The Rads'* as it was nicknamed, was located on Roundel Street, opening originally in the 1920s as Attercliffe Non-Political Club & Institute Ltd, but later becoming The Attercliffe Radical Working Men's Club. Its sports and social teams were always known as 'Attercliffe Radicals'.

The club was very popular amongst the local community, often hosting piano nights, discos, bingo, and drag acts on its large stage.

The football club played in the Sheffield Sports & Athletic League between 1937-40, following a season in the Attercliffe Alliance, winning its first silverware in the 1938/39 season. That first success was in the Tinsley Charity Cup, a competition that had brought so much success to Attercliffe's football clubs right at the start of the previous decade. The Radicals club actually won the cup more times than any of its predecessors, five times in total.

The 1938/39 Tinsley Charity Cup final resulted in a 3-0 win against Aqueduct WMC on Monday 24th April 1939 on the Tinsley Park Colliery MW ground in front of *'a big crowd.'* The trophy presentation evening was actually held at the Radical club itself on Tuesday June 20th. The Tinsley Charity Cup was also won in the 1939/40, 1941/42, 1942/'43, and 1943/44 seasons, when coverage of local sporting events in the local press was very limited.

The Attercliffe Charity Cup was won in the 1940/41 season, ironically the one season which the club failed to win the Tinsley Charity Cup.

Other successes during this period included the following:

*Sheffield & Hallamshire Junior Cup:* This was won in the 1941/42 and 1942/43 seasons, after having lost the 1940/41 final 0-4 to Grimethorpe Sports at Millmoor, Rotherham, on Saturday 5th April 1941.

*Sheffield & Hallamshire Senior Invitation Cup*: Radicals lost the 1941/42 final 1-6 to Royal Army Signals Corps, the Sheffield Association League side that swept all before it in the local game during the War.

*Sheffield City Amateur League* – this was a wartime amalgam of the Sheffield City and Amateur Leagues – the club being champions in the 1942/43 season.

Attercliffe Radicals FC seems to have been defunct by the time that organised football was back on its feet, and given that the Sheffield public had more important things to think about during the war, the team wasn't really missed, although to be fair, few outside local circles would have even noticed it in the first place. Little else is known about the team, but it does deserve a mention given the considerable amount of success achieved in a short space of time.

# Beverley Church Institute
# 1893-1901
## *'Beverley's forgotten club'*

Beverley, a market town in the East Riding of Yorkshire, is best known for Beverley Minster and its racecourse, but not for its association football teams. There have been some significant football clubs in the town through the years, but one that is very rarely referred to is the long-gone Beverley Church Institute club, which, despite being successful in East Riding competitions, disappeared practically overnight and was quickly replaced another town club.

The origins of the club go back to Monday 26th November 1886 when a meeting was held in the town's Guild Hall to consider the desirability of forming a Church Institute in Beverley. The incumbent minister, Reverend J B Birtwhistle moved *'that in the opinion of this meeting it is desirable to form an association, to be called the Beverley Church Institute, to have for its object the uniting of members of the Church of England, and to cultivate a desire for literature and science amongst its members in subordination to religion.'* The motion was carried, and the inauguration evening took place on Tuesday 29th January 1887 at a soiree at the Norwood Assembly Rooms, with some 300 attendees.

With several sports already being catered for, an association football section was founded in 1892. The football club's first opponents were the likes of Hull Blue Star, Middleton, and the strong Oliver's Mount School (Scarborough), the latter of which defeated *The Beavers*, as they were often referred to in the local press, 4-1 on their own ground amid the open pastures of Westwood, on the edge of the town.

The 1894/85 season saw Beverley Church Institute playing friendly fixtures against the likes of Bridlington Town, Grimsby Rovers, Barton Town, and Scarborough, which were more established names than those encountered the previous season. With Rev W B Stillman as club captain, and Rev W Gell vice-captain at that time, this illustrated the fact that the club was not just linked to the church in name only

The club, representing a town that had grown steadily to a population of around 12,500 by now, also had a busy fixture list for its second team. It became a member of the early Scarborough & East Riding FA at its meeting at the Station Hotel, Scarborough on Saturday 4th October 1884, and was drawn to play away at the Scarborough Post Office club on 10th December in the first round of the Association's Cup competition. The match was played on the Scarborough Cricket Club ground on North Marine Road, and resulted in a 3-0 win for the home team. Beverley continued to enter that competition, without success, although it did reach the semi-final in 1901, losing 3-5 to Scarborough.

The *Yorkshire Gazette* reported, on Saturday 2nd October 1896, that the club was *'in a prosperous position'*, and that Colonel George Cussons was club President (although reports in the local press continued to refer to him as 'Major', a title he had been known by until his promotion in 1893). Church Institute FC was sharing the Westwood field with the local rugby club by 1892, with goal posts often placed just in front of the rugby posts when association games were played on the field.

The 1895/96 season saw *The Beavers* enter the Hull & District Junior League, and this competition did provide the club with success.

By the 1896/97 season, Beverley Thursday Association Club came to prominence, with the same George Cussons also acting as its President. The club was run as a separate entity to the Church Institute club, but also claimed a formation date of 1893, which would suggest that the two were run by the same committee.

Cussons himself was a highly respected member of the community. He was the son of Thomas Cussons, who hailed from the Coxwold area, north of York, and who had established a well-known Tannery in the town in 1834. He was also Mayor of Beverely in 1863/64. George himself was a local Commission of the Peace, Church Warden for the Minister, and played various roles in the local corporation. He was also an influential governor the Minister Schools in the locality.

From 1896 both Saturday and Thursday teams had moved again, to a ground on Molescroft Road that had previously been used by the town's Brittania football club. Both clubs played in black and white from this season, with '*university knickers,*' and both now ran both a first and reserve team as association football continued to grow in popularity in the town. Of the other teams around town, Beverley Buffaloes was a notable name, while Beverley Grammar School also played association fixtures.

In the Hull & District Junior Cup, the Church Institute drew the inaugural 1896/97 final 1-1 with local rivals East Yorkshire Regiment (Beverley Barracks) reserves on Saturday 3rd April 1897 on the Kingston Amateurs ground, in front of around 300 spectators. The replay, at the Station Ground in Beverley two weeks later, was won by the Church Institute, 2-0 in poor conditions. The club had also finished runner-up in the Hull Junior League table that season.

*Eastern Morning News - Monday 19th April 1897*

HULL JUNIOR CUP. FINAL TIE. *The re-played final tie in connection with the above cup was decided on Saturday afternoon at Beverley. There was a good gate, despite the heavy downpour of rain, but this was in anticipation of a good and close game as was witnessed at Hull. Both teams put on their best players, each being imbued with a sense of superiority, though in a narrow scope. The Institute, unfortunately, had to dispense with the service of Golding at hack, the substitution being undertaken by Ramshaw. The ground was in a wretched condition, and surely it would have been justifiable for the officials responsible to have postponed the fixture, not only in their own interests, but in the interests of the players themselves, and, in addition, the comfort of the spectators.*

### 1898/99 Hull & District League

**Senior Division**

| | P | W | D | L | F | A | Pts |
|---|---|---|---|---|---|---|---|
| **Beverley C I** | 14 | 11 | 2 | 1 | 44 | 13 | 24 |
| Dairycoates NER | 14 | 10 | 1 | 3 | 28 | 16 | 21 |
| Beverley Barracks | 14 | 9 | 2 | 3 | 30 | 20 | 20 |
| Kingston Amat | 14 | 8 | 1 | 5 | 39 | 26 | 17 |
| **Brunswick Wes** | 14 | 6 | 1 | 7 | 25 | 35 | 13 |
| St Paul's | 14 | 4 | 3 | 7 | 23 | 42 | 11 |
| Holmes | 14 | 1 | 3 | 10 | 19 | 30 | 5 |
| Holborn | 14 | 0 | 1 | 13 | 5 | 32 | 1 |

**Division Two**

| | P | W | D | L | F | A | Pts |
|---|---|---|---|---|---|---|---|
| **Beverley CI res** | 14 | 11 | 2 | 1 | 34 | 5 | 24 |
| Driffield CI | 14 | 10 | 1 | 3 | 33 | 16 | 21 |
| Sculcoates Amats | 14 | 9 | 1 | 4 | 27 | 22 | 19 |
| Dairycoates res | 14 | 5 | 3 | 6 | 19 | 15 | 13 |
| Harlequins | 14 | 2 | 8 | 4 | 4 | 4 | 12 |
| Beverley Barr res | 14 | 5 | 2 | 7 | 19 | 14 | 12 |
| Holborn res | 14 | 2 | 3 | 9 | 1 | 35 | 7 |
| St Paul's res | 14 | 1 | 3 | 10 | 7 | 35 | 5 |

Goals for & against for some teams in the above table are highly questionable

Brunswick Wesleyan reserve team finished 3rd out of 8 teams in division 3 (see later section on that club)

**Thursday League**

| | P | W | D | L | F | A | Pts |
|---|---|---|---|---|---|---|---|
| Beverley Thursday | 7 | 5 | 2 | 0 | 38 | 9 | 12 |
| Hull Thursday | 7 | 4 | 2 | 1 | 20 | 8 | 10 |
| Hull Botanic | 8 | 2 | 4 | 2 | 20 | 16 | 8 |
| Central Hull | 8 | 3 | 2 | 3 | 18 | 15 | 8 |
| Hairdressers | 8 | 0 | 0 | 8 | 2 | 39 | 0 |

The following were the teams:— Church Institute: Goal, Day; backs, Gooding and Ebden; half-backs, Grieves, Laws, and Caunt; forwards, Edwards, Beezley, Warner, Bristow, and Lee.

E.Y.R.: Goal, Wells; backs, Ramshaw and Witty; half-backs, Campy, Nolan. &Whitton; forwards, Whitehead, Kilpatrick, Galliger, Drury, and Cairns. Referee, Percy E Harrison. Linesmen, Messrs A E Spring and R C Preston.

The Institute men started the game in a heavy downpour of rain, and had certainly the best of the passing in the initial stages. The game from the very commencement became exciting, and after a splendid burst by the Barrack men the Institute forwards by splendid combination and passing came down with a rush. Whitehead, from a near pass, sent through, but a penalty kick was awarded the Institute for valuable hands in front of goal. Galliger took the kick, and scored easily amidst enthusiasm.

The excitement was new intensified, both teams strenuously endeavouring to improve their position, but, despite the praiseworthy efforts adopted, play remained principally in neutral territory. A free kick for the Soldiers placed them in a good position, yet they appeared to lack combination to improve their advance, the Institute defence being too strong for them. A strong run by the Institute forwards brought the game into their opponents' territory, and here Ebden, endeavouring to save, sent through his own goal, but the point was not allowed on account of a corner having been previously conceded. The place kick was put in well, but nothing resulted. By dint of hard kicking, though rather rash, the Barrack men transferred hostilities, but had to return to the defence by a free kick being awarded to the Institute. With equal rapidity the sphere was taken to the opposite end, and a corner was awarded to the Soldiers, but Ebden sent a bye. The Barrack men, however, were not dismayed, and returned sharply to the attack, Warner just, sending over the bar. Immediately afterwards Bristow, observing an opening, put in a long swift shot, which only just missed the uprights. Luck, however, appeared against the Barrack men, for twice in succession Edwards hit the uprights, the ball going a bye on each occasion. Still they stuck manfully to the game, and gave the Institute defence a remarkably warm time of it, and on several occasions the ball just grazed the uprights and went past. Wells saved many good shots sent in by the occupants of the Barracks, and it seemed as though the soldiers were unable to surmount their ill-luck. Nothing further was scored, half-time being called with the scores reading:- Church Institute, 1 goal, East Yorkshire Regiment, nil.

Recommencing, the Institute men, now aided with the wind, pressed hard, taxing the Soldiers' defence to the utmost. Several smart runs were made by the forwards, but the shooting was somewhat erratic. The Soldiers, however, were not downhearted, and repeatedly endeavoured to break through. The Institute's defence was good, and really too strong for them. A free kick for the Soldiers changed the venue, but Witty, closely watching his opponents, repelled each attack. The Barracks appeared from now to be somewhat demoralised, but whether from being outplayed or completely done up was not apparent. With a good run down, the Institute made matters very warm for their opponents, and when right in front of goal, Whitehead, with a stinging shot, scored the second goal for them. The game from now appeared solely in the hands of the Institute, who tried hard to still add to the score, but were too confident. Final: — Beverley Church Institute, 2 goals, East Yorkshire Regiment, nil.

Tuesday 3rd May 1898, a special meeting was held regarding the ownership of the Hull & District Junior Cup itself, which the club had refused to return to Hull Association on account of the local FA not providing sufficient proof that it had actually purchased the trophy.

C I were founder members of the Hull & District Senior League in the 1897/98, and finished runners-up behind the Beverley Barracks first team. However the following season took some beating, as all three teams became champions of their respective divisions. The first team, led by Frank Barnes was beaten only once in its 14 matches, a record that the second string – led by a Mr Meadley – matched. The Thursday team, meanwhile, managed to complete its fixtures unbeaten.

The 1897/98 season had also seen the winning of another cup. On Thursday 28th April 1898 the Thursday team won the Sir Seymour King's Challenge Cup, defeating Beverely Barracks on the 'Locos' ground Despite trailing at half time, the team hit back to win 3-1.

On top its phenomenal league success, the 1898/99 season saw Beverley C I finish runners up in the East Riding Cup, losing 1-3 to Hull Kingston Amateurs on the Malton Swifts ground on Saturday 25th March 1899, the winners scoring two late goals to take the cup south of the river. Beverley were also losing finalists in the *Hull Times* Charity Cup, losing 2-3 to the favourites, Grimsby All Saints in front of a large crowd at The Boulevard, Hull on Saturday 22nd April. The reserves won the Division Two league cup, to make up for those defeats. That season the club had moved in with the Beverley Cricket Club, which was then located on Mill Lane, close to the town's Cottage Hospital.

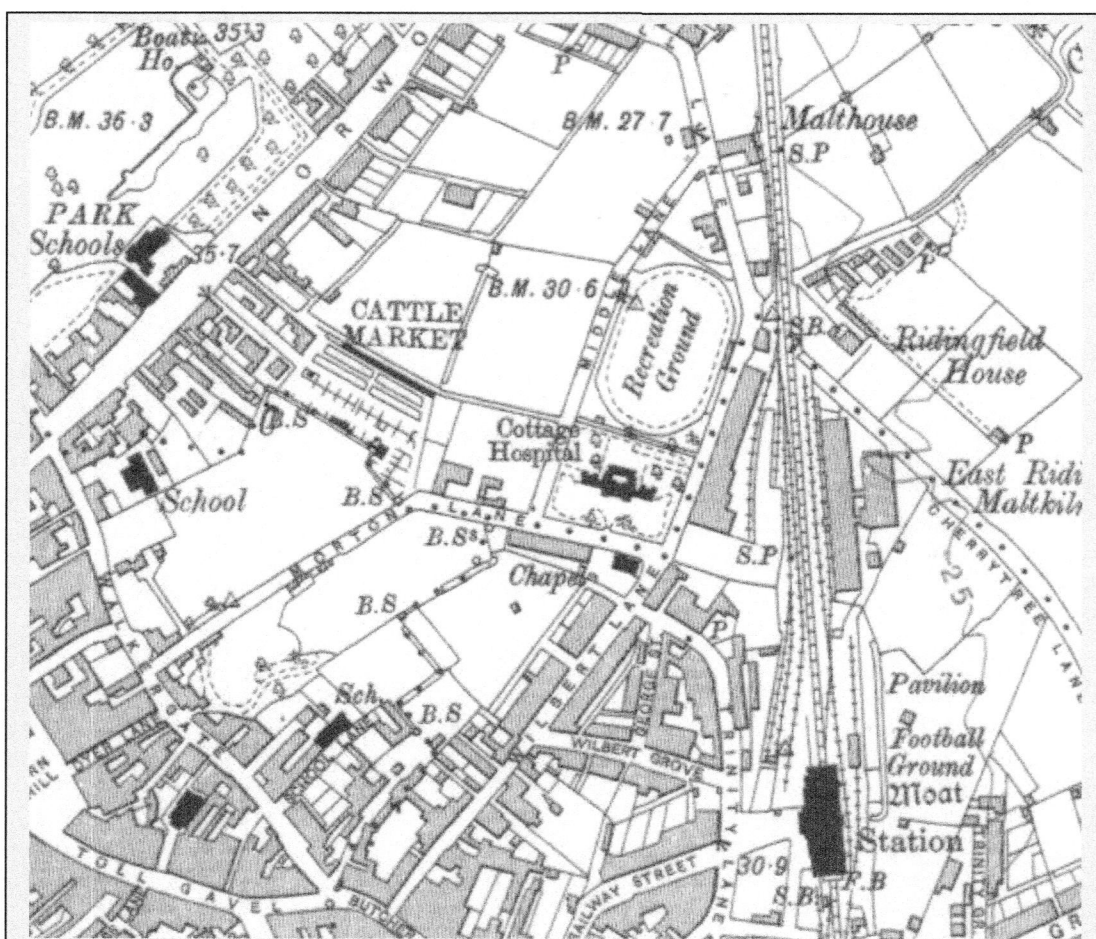

*An old OS map showing two former grounds of the Beverley Church Institute Club, both now covered by housing. The Mill Lane Recreation Ground was the home of Beverley Cricket Club until 1908, and was also used for other sports such as athletics, cycling and tennis. To the right, is the Station Ground, labelled here as 'football ground'.*

Grimsby All Saints also defeated Beverley in the club's only FA Amateur Cup tie, winning 4-1 on the Beverley ground early in the season. It was reported that seven or eight of the strong All Saints team had previously turned out for Grimsby Town. A brass band turned out for the occasion, but the home team was unable to rise to the occasion.

Success continued into the 1899/1900 season, with the Senior League title retained, although the *Hull Times* Charity Cup final was lost 0-4 to the club's bogey team, Grimsby All Saints on Hull's Craven Street ground on Saturday 21st April 1900.

With the cricket club denying them the use of the Recreation Ground for the 1900/01 season, a new field was procured on Kitchen Lane, in the south of the town, which was not of the standard experienced in previous seasons. The inaugural Stanley Wilson Beverley Hospital Cup competition was won with a relatively easy 4-0 defeat of East Hull in the final on the Station Ground on Saturday 27th April 1901, following victories over Comet and Withernsea in earlier rounds. The league title was not retained, however.

Incredibly, the club committee failed to find a suitable ground for the 1901/02 season, and as a result the Beverley Church Institute Association Football Club was forced to disband. The East Riding League's senior division – in which the team would have competed - continued with just three teams, which included the army team from Beverley Barracks.

The final season of 1900/01 had seen Harold W Mackrill taking on the roll of captain. Mackrill, who had previously played for other local clubs such as Old Hymerians, where he was also captain, was one of four Cottingham brothers (his brother Oscar was also a renowned local player). After the Beavers demise he went on to play soccer with the Hull Comet Club.

Harold went on to make a mark in the local sporting world. He also played, rugby union as wing three-quarter for the Hull & East Riding club and Yorkshire, and was also a keen tennis player, later becoming president of the Yorkshire Lawn Tennis Association. A knee injury in 1906 curtailed his football and rugby career, but he continued to make a mark playing tennis circuit, with several tournament victories. He also played golf at the Newland Golf Club at Cottingham Hill from its inception in 1906. Mackrill was also involved in local politics as a Conservative and subsequently Independent councillor, chairing the Beverley Rural District Council.

***

The 1902/03 season saw seven teams competing in the East Riding's Senior division, one of which was a new Beverley AFC.

The new club was formed as a section of the Beverley Rugby Football Club at that club's AGM on Friday 1st August 1902, and initially played on the Station Road ground. The new club finished sixth of the seven teams in the 1902/03 season, behind the Barracks club, but was certainly not out of its depth. A new grandstand was erected on the ground during the summer of 1903. However, there was a motion at the Football club's 1904 AGM to disband the association section, and although this was not carried, the association team was renamed Beverley Town AFC.

Beverley Town won the East Riding Senior Cup in 1905/06, and went on to play in the FA Amateur Cup between 1907-09, and FA Cup in the 1914/15 and 1919/20 seasons. A ground on Pighill Lane was later used by the club, which has had several incarnations since that time.

George Cussons died after a short illness at his home, Keldgate House, on the day of his daughter's wedding, 3rd September 1913, aged 78. He had collapsed previous evening and the wedding itself was moved forward to 8am in the morning, with Cussons passing away at noon.

# Boothtown AFC
# 1903-55
*'Half a century of success'*

Boothtown (more often referred to a 'Booth Town' before World War Two) is a suburb to the north of Halifax that includes the former model village of Ackroydon, with its gothic housing provided for the workers at the textile mills of Edward Ackroyd. Boothtown United was the first football club in the area, playing rugby by 1889 and into the 1900s. By 1901 it had been joined by other clubs such as Booth Town New Road

The 1900/01 football season saw association friendlies played by 'Booth Town' although this may well have been the established rugby side of the time playing experimental games, opponents in September 1900 being the likes of Ovenden, another well-known local rugby team. The famous old Boothtown club that did emerge is said to have emerged around 1901, and this may have been the same set of players who chose to found their own club which was separate to the rugby football club.

Booth Town Council School was also playing regular association fixtures against other Elementary schools in the district by now. The following season a Booth Town Old Boys, another rugby team, was also playing friendly association fixtures in addition to its regular rugby fixtures.

Booth Town AFC first came to prominence in the Salterhebble & District League in the 1903/04 season, after having played friendly fixtures before then. The league title was won with ease in its first two years in the competition, and in fact the second of those successes was part of a 'triple triumph'.

In the league, the side won 13 of its 18 matches, drawing four and losing just one (2-5 at Lightcliffe), although several games were conceded by opposition teams. In the league cup, Warley St John's, King Cross WNC and Queens Road were defeated en-route to a final against Holywell Green at the St Augustine's ground on Easter Monday. The game ended 1-1, leading to a replay at Southowram St Anne's ground the following day. A single goal by Robertshaw was enough to win the game.

### 1903/04 Salterhebble & District League
*(inaccurate, as published in the Halifax Courier 21/3/04)*

|  | P | W | D | L | F | A | Pts |
|---|---|---|---|---|---|---|---|
| **Booth Town** | 22 | 21 | 0 | 1 | 84 | 21 | 42 |
| Pellon Church res | 22 | 16 | 1 | 5 | 62 | 19 | 33 |
| Lee Mount Albions | 21 | 14 | 2 | 5 | 55 | 24 | 30 |
| King Cross reserves | 22 | 11 | 4 | 7 | 34 | 32 | 26 |
| Southowram | 22 | 12 | 2 | 8 | 39 | 38 | 26 |
| Dry Clough | 22 | 10 | 5 | 7 | 37 | 39 | 25 |
| East Ward | 22 | 7 | 5 | 10 | 28 | 32 | 19 |
| Highroad Well res | 22 | 7 | 4 | 11 | 65 | 28 | 18 |
| Hollins Mills | 22 | 5 | 6 | 11 | 15 | 66 | 16 |
| Wellington Mills | 22 | 4 | 5 | 13 | 19 | 32 | 13 |
| Parish Church | 22 | 3 | 2 | 17 | 16 | 34 | 8 |
| Siddal Amateurs | 22 | 1 | 2 | 19 | 12 | 71 | 4 |

### 1908/09 Halifax & District League Division One

|  | P | W | D | L | F | A | Pts |
|---|---|---|---|---|---|---|---|
| **Booth Town** | 16 | 14 | 1 | 1 | 64 | 13 | 29 |
| Sowerby Bridge | 16 | 10 | 3 | 3 | 45 | 18 | 23 |
| West Vale Ramblers | 16 | 8 | 4 | 4 | 44 | 27 | 20 |
| Stump Cross | 16 | 6 | 4 | 6 | 36 | 28 | 16 |
| Eastwood | 16 | 6 | 3 | 7 | 28 | 35 | 15 |
| Halifax Trinity | 16 | 5 | 3 | 8 | 35 | 31 | 13 |
| Hebden Bridge | 16 | 5 | 1 | 10 | 28 | 60 | 11 |
| Technical College | 15 | 3 | 3 | 9 | 18 | 36 | 9 |
| Mytholmroyd | 15 | 3 | 0 | 12 | 13 | 62 | 6 |

In the Booth Town Cup, essentially a competition for players of 18 years and under, Heptonstall (5-0), Mytholmroyd (2-1), and local rivals Booth Town United (6-0) were defeated before Luddenden Albions were beaten 2-1 in the final.

It seems that as those that played in the previous season's successful side moved on, a younger team was retained in the Second Division of the Salterhebble League for the 1905/06 season. However, in 1906 the team entered the Halifax & District League, a big step up in standard, initially spending two seasons as a leading club in the Second Division. Promotion was granted in the summer of 1908. The move up was entirely successful, with the club becoming 1908/09 Halifax & District League champions, at the first attempt, and followed that up with third place the following season.

Boothtown were Halifax & District Cup winners in the 1908/09 season, defeating Hebden Bridge 4-0 in the final, on Saturday 24th April 1909 on the Pheasant Ground at Pellon. Miller, Bliss and Greenwood scored first half goals, before the club captain, Longbottom added a fourth before the end of the game. Hebden Bridge actually had more of the play in the game, but poor finishing - including a missed penalty – let them down.

A surprising move into the Bradford & District League was made in 1910, this competition held was held in a higher regard than the Halifax League, having been formed a few years earlier. A reserve team continued to play in the top division of the Halifax League for a little longer though. While there were no league titles won by the club at this time, the first team did win the 1910/11 Bradford Hospitals Cup for the first time, at Valley Parade, the home of Bradford City AFC.

Boothtown were winners of the Halifax Charity Cup, in 1912/13, defeating Lee Mount 3-1 in a replayed final on Wednesday 9th April 1913, through goals from Miller (in the first half), Lawton and Haigh (both in the second half). The teams had drawn 1-1 the previous Saturday at Halifax Town's Sandhall ground, with Haigh having scoring a second half equaliser for the eventual winners. Boothtown made the final again two years later, but were defeated by the holders, Norland.

The Bradford competition was revived as the Bradford Football Association League in 1919, and Boothtown continued where it left off in 1914. Ground improvements at its Grantham Road ground during the summer of 1920 saw drainage improved and the pitch being partially returfed and enclosed. The work

## Boothtown AFC - League Record

1903-06 Salterhebble & District League
1906-10 Halifax & District League
1910-14 Bradford & District League
1919-22 Bradford FA League

### West Riding County Amateur League record

| Season | P | W | D | L | F | A | Pts | Pos |
|---|---|---|---|---|---|---|---|---|
| 1922/23 | 30 | 17 | 4 | 9 | 83 | 45 | 38 | 4th |
| 1923/24 | 30 | 17 | 5 | 8 | 64 | 41 | 39 | 4th |
| 1924/25 | 26 | 8 | 4 | 14 | 42 | 51 | 20 | 8th |
| 1925/26 | 24 | 11 | 3 | 10 | 59 | 53 | 25 | 4th |
| 1926/27 | 21 | 16 | 1 | 4 | 82 | 41 | 33 | 2nd |
| 1927/28 | 22 | 7 | 10 | 5 | 70 | 61 | 24 | 6th |
| 1928/29 | 26 | 20 | 4 | 2 | | | 44 | 1st |
| 1929/30 | 22 | 12 | 1 | 9 | | | 25 | 5th |
| 1930/31 | 26 | 15 | 5 | 6 | 69 | 48 | 35 | 3rd |
| 1931/32 | 20 | 10 | 4 | 6 | 57 | 39 | 24 | 4th |
| 1932/33 | 22 | 6 | 5 | 11 | 45 | 62 | 17 | 10th |
| 1933/34 | 22 | 13 | 5 | 4 | 64 | 27 | 31 | 2nd |
| 1934/35 | 22 | 7 | 8 | 7 | 49 | 62 | 22 | 9th |
| 1935/36 | 22 | 10 | 3 | 9 | 65 | 53 | 23 | 7th |
| 1936/37 | 22 | 8 | 1 | 13 | 57 | 68 | 17 | 8th |
| 1937/38 | 26 | 14 | 7 | 5 | 79 | 50 | 35 | 3rd |
| 1938/39 | 20 | 11 | 6 | 3 | | | 25 | 3rd |

1939/40 *not known*
1940-46 *did not operate, due to war.*
1946/47 *not known*
1947/48 *not known*

| Season | P | W | D | L | F | A | Pts | Pos |
|---|---|---|---|---|---|---|---|---|
| 1948/49 | 26 | 14 | 10 | 2 | | | 38 | 2nd |
| 1949/50 | 26 | 14 | 4 | 8 | | | 32 | 5th |
| 1950/51 | 26 | 17 | 3 | 6 | | | 37 | 4th |
| 1951/52 | 26 | 14 | 4 | 8 | | | 32 | 5th |
| 1952/53 | 26 | 7 | 2 | 17 | | | 16 | 12th |
| 1953/54 | 21 | 3 | 2 | 16 | | | 8 | 11th * |
| 1954/55 | 22 | 6 | 4 | 12 | | | 16 | 11th * |

(* 1953-55 in Division A. In all the other seasons the league operated a single division.

### 1928-29
### West Riding County Amateur League

| | P | W | D | L | Pts |
|---|---|---|---|---|---|
| **Boothtown** | 26 | 20 | 4 | 2 | 44 |
| Yeadon Celtic | 26 | 17 | 4 | 5 | 38 |
| **Manningham Mill** | 26 | 14 | 4 | 8 | 32 |
| Farsley Celtic | 26 | 12 | 6 | 8 | 30 |
| **Haworth** | 26 | 12 | 5 | 9 | 29 |
| Wibsey | 26 | 12 | 4 | 10 | 28 |
| Guiseley | 26 | 11 | 6 | 9 | 28 |
| Birkenshaw | 26 | 8 | 10 | 8 | 26 |
| Keighley Parkwood | 26 | 10 | 3 | 13 | 23 |
| Southowram | 26 | 8 | 5 | 13 | 21 |
| Idle | 26 | 7 | 4 | 15 | 18 |
| Blythwick | 26 | 5 | 6 | 15 | 16 |
| Apperley Bridge | 26 | 7 | 2 | 17 | 16 |
| **Horsforth** | 26 | 6 | 3 | 13 | 15 |

was completed voluntarily by the club committee and supporters, although problems with drainage would continue right through the club's existence.

In 1922, Boothtown became founder members of West Riding County Amateur League, a competition founded with the intention of bringing together the best amateur teams in what is now West Yorkshire. Although dominated by Bradford clubs, with the league having its headquarters in the city, other clubs joined from the area south of Bradford, with Boothtown initially the only one from the Halifax district. The formation of the league was all part of the battle of supremacy between the Bradford and Leeds football associations, the former backing other 'county' competitions, including the formation of the current West Yorkshire League.

What was possibly the club's finest achievement was the lifting of the County Amateur League title at the end of the 1928/29 season. Captained by Gilbert Feavers, the club finished six points clear of Yeadon Celtic (runners-up for the second successive season), and a massive twelve clear of Bradford side Manningham Mills (a team that had dropped just one point in the whole of the previous season) at the head of the table.

*Boothtown AFC, photographed around 1930, in front of the club pavilion at Grantham Road*

Although 1928/29 was the only time that the league title was won, the club remained a major force in the competition right up until the early 1950s. The team finished runners up in 1926/27 (behind Liversedge), 1933/34 (behind Guiseley) and 1948/49 (behind Thackley), finishing in the top five on at least 15 occasions.

Among the club's successes was the 1931/32 Bradford Hospitals Cup, won for a second time, defeating Wyke Old Boys 5-1 in the final, and a league cup final success in the 1947/48 season. Huddersfield side Meltham Mills were defeated in that final, 2-1 in a replay on Wednesday 29th April 1948. Boothtown had gone behind early in the second half, but struck back to win with goals from Longbottom and Williams.

Earlier that month, a league encounter with Guiseley at Grantham Road attracted the headline makers. The *Halifax Evening Courier* reported, its correspondent stopping short of laying direct blame at the hands of the match official, 'What should have been a good game…degenerated into a complete farce. Players from both sides deserve praise for trying to play the game in spite of questionable decisions, and the spectators too, who got past the annoyed stage and saw the funny side of things. Guiseley got 9 goals, and Booth Town 5, and three of the local team's goals were penalty kicks. In the circumstances it would be difficult offering criticism of any of the players.'

Boothtown AFC dominated the Halifax Association Cup, winning it four years in succession in the late 1930s and early 1940s. After having lost the 1935/36 final to Northowram FC, Luddendenfoot were defeated in the 1936/37 final, albeit after in a replay after a 1-1 draw at the Shay on Thursday 22nd April 1937. The replay, which ended 4-1, took place on Saturday 1st May on the Northowram ground. The same opposition was encountered the following year when a last-minute long-range effort by H Charnock proved the difference between the teams at the Shay on Friday 29th April 1938. In the 1938/39 season, the defeated cup final opponents were Bourillion, a team from Todmorden, who were completely outclassed 8-0 at The Shay on Friday 28th April.

In the 1939/40 final, also played at The Shay, Elland Wesleyans put up a much better fight, leading 2-1 at one point before going down 3-2 on Friday 3rd May 1940. Boothtown's scorers that day were I Charnock, Gough, and Ward. It was the club's sixth win in the competition by that time.

It should be noted, however, that the Halifax FA ran more than one cup competition at the time, and the local newspapers quite often did not differentiate between the two, or between these and the Halifax League's cup competition, with all three being referred to as the 'Halifax Association Cup'.

The pavilion on the Boothtown ground was regarded as one of the best in the County Amateur League. However, it was in the news for the wrong reason on Friday 10th July 1953, the *Halifax Evening Courier* reporting that 'A nine-year-old boy was sent to an approved school and his two companions aged eight and nine were put on probation for 12 months, at Halifax Borough Juvenile Court yesterday, when they admitted breaking into the pavilion belonging to Boothtown Football Club and stealing cups worth 7s. The youngest lad said he smashed the cups.'

The club's final two seasons in the West Riding County Amateur League were its least successful, with only eight points being won in the 1953/54 season. Relegation to the league's new 'B' division was narrowly avoided. Twice as many points were obtained in the 1954/55 season, although the club finished in the same position, 11th out of 12. Harrogate Town could only muster only two points all season, finishing way adrift at the foot of the table. Both Harrogate and Boothtown were missing from the league the following season. The long-term future of these two struggling clubs could not have been more marked.

The first ten games of Boothtown's 1954/55 season had to be played away from home due to the ongoing works at the Grantham Road site, on behalf of the Halifax Markets & Parks Committee (the site having been purchased in 1951 by Halifax Corporation). The club's first home match was therefore delayed until late November. However, dark clouds were on the horizon.

The *Halifax Evening Courier* on Thursday 9th June 1955 brought sad news from the club AGM, held the previous evening at the club's ground. A proposition by Ernest Dracup, and seconded by Harold Lees that the club was to be wound up was passed. This did not come as a complete surprise as the club's problems had been widely reported in the local press. It was sad to see a club that been integral in the local community for more than half a century fold, particularly as it was not in debt. The problem was twofold. One was financial backing, or lack of it, with the club being fully independent and not being run as a nursery for a Football League club, which several other sides in the league were.

In existence for around 54 years, and by now the oldest in the Halifax district, the club was also hindered by ground issues. £180 had recently been spent on a new drainage system for the field, which was in as bad a state as ever, and there were conditions in the club's new lease of the ground relating to its maintenance that were not acceptable to the Boothtown club, which cost around £5 a week to run. With Halifax Corporation having recently taken on the ownership of the ground, this now prevented the club from sub-letting it or organising its popular end-of-season Workshops competition for unaffiliated teams, as the area around the football field was being developed as a children's playground. The club had played on the field for over 40 years, but this was no longer 'their' ground, it was merely a football pitch that they were allowed the use of. Although a loss of £27 on the past season was reported, the club still had £30 in the bank, and these funds were used to pay off all the club's liabilities. A similar meeting had been held the previous August – widely reported on - at the Boothtown Conservative Club, when it had been decided to keep the club going. Ten months on, all enthusiasm for keeping it going had all but gone.

A winding-up meeting was held the following Tuesday, and the club was no more. The local authority advertised in the Halifax press for an amateur team to take over the lease of the ground, but in the event it was Halifax Rugby League Club that took up the option in June 1956, for use by its Under 21 team.

The name 'Boothtown AFC' has been revived in local football since then, but has been unrelated to the old club, the most recent incarnation having played at Savile Park. That club rose through the ranks of the Halifax & District League during the 1980s and by 1993 was playing in the league's top division before folding a few seasons later. The original club's Grantham Road site is still used for rugby, but is no longer enclosed, and the pavilion owned by the football club has long since gone.

Former Boothtown players who went on to play in the Football League included Clem Longbottom (Halifax Town, Huddersfield & Bradford Park Avenue), G Green (Huddersfield Town & Reading), and Frank 'Tiny' Williams (Halifax Town).

Percy Abbott, who died in 1959, aged 63, was a member of the club since its early days. However, after having served in World War One, he went on to become the club's secretary, as well as a sports correspondent for over 40 years for local newspapers.

### Boothtown in FA Competitions

The club first entered the **FA Amateur Cup** in the 1922/23 season, defeating Leeds-based Monkbridge Sports 4-1 at home in a Preliminary Round tie, following a 1-1 away draw. This was followed by a 1-0 victory at Scholes Athletic, before a 0-1 home loss to Wibsey, of Bradford, in the Second Qualifying Round. Its entries to the 1927/28 & 1928/29 competitions resulted in defeat to Farsley Celtic on both occasions.

Ten **FA Cup** ties were played by Boothtown, its only victory before World War One was its first game in the competition, a 1-0 victory at home over West Vale Ramblers in a 1912/13 Preliminary Round tie. The team went down 1-2 to South Kirkby Colliery in the following round. The 1920/21 season saw Boothtown lose 2-5 at newly formed Leeds United in an Extra Preliminary Round tie on 11th September 1920, in front of 3,000 spectators. FA Cup rules dictated that a club had to be two years old before being exempt from the qualifying rounds, meaning that United had to start at the first qualifying stage. The side that the Elland Road club put out consisted entirely of reserves, given that a Football League fixture at Leicester City was also played on that date.

The following season, the club's last in the FA Cup resulted in a 5-2 win at home to York side Acomb WMC in the Extra Preliminary Round. This was followed by a 2-1 success against another York side, Rowntrees. This took the club into the First Qualifying Round, and a 1-3 home defeat to Frickley Colliery.

# Bradford Rovers
# 1899-1977
### *'Bradford's third best team'*

The period between 1899-1977 actually encompasses several different Bradford Rovers clubs, two of which certainly made their mark in local and regional football circles.

A Bradford Sun Rovers rugby football club existed in the 1885/86 season, and then from August 1886 there was a Bradford Rovers rugby football club. These two teams are likely to have been one and the same. This organisation played regular fixtures against other local teams until the summer of 1899, when the first Bradford Rovers association football team emerged. It is highly likely that the Rovers switched codes, which was not uncommon at the time with the round ball game finally making inroads in a district that was a rugby football stronghold.

The club is not thought to be linked to the Bradford Rovers cricket club, one which predated the football teams, and which existed into the 1920s. This club took on other sides from around the country in 'friendly' challenge matches and was made up predominantly of middle class gents who played for other clubs in the town.

The Rovers association football team was originally based at Spier Fields, which was on Moorside Road, Fagley, but by 1904 the club had progressed sufficiently to merit tenancy at Greenfield, Dudley Hill, an enclosed multi-use sporting ground in the south of the city. The ground had previously been used by a number of association football teams, most noticeably the first Bradford City AFC. The Spier Fields

*Greenfield, Dudley Hill, Bradford in later years, during its use as a greyhound stadium*

ground was later occupied by the Airedale AFC club which went on to play in the West Yorkshire League after having pipped Bradford City to the Bradford & District League title in the 1901/02 season.

*Recognition appeared in the Yorkshire Sports newspaper on 23rd January 1904*

Rovers initially restricted itself to playing friendly fixtures for its first two seasons, not yet competitive enough to take part in the Bradford & District League. As the round ball game began to make further inroads and the number of tiny, local teams rose exponentially, several other local league competitions also emerged in Bradford. Rovers made its league debut in the Fourth (bottom) Division of the Bradford & District League for the 1901/02 season, but the side struggled and instead played in the Third Division of the Bradford Alliance between 1902-04. In the summer of 1904, having strengthened its team, there was a jump back into the Bradford & District League, with the team winning the Second Division title.

The following season, saw Rovers one of only eight teams left in the league, which ran a single division. The club's promotions to higher divisions - 1904/05 excepted - had not really been down to its playing strength, and was more to do with the number of teams switching between different local leagues, some of which became more popular than others.

On Thursday 27th April 1905, Rovers took part in its first final, that of the Bradford Hospitals Cup. The tie was lost 0-2 to Four Lane Ends at Valley Parade, before *'a large assembly of spectators'* according to the *Bradford Daily Telegraph*.

Despite its size, the Bradford & District League still contained the area's strongest clubs. The *Yorkshire Evening Post*, on Saturday 14th October 1905, reported that Bradford Rovers was the most *'poached on'* club in the district so it is clear that the club was growing in prestige (although in February 1907 Rovers themselves were accused of poaching two players by the junior Bradford St Chrysostom's club).

*Advertisement for the 1905 Bradford Charity Cup final*

The club's next move was very much an upward one. Rovers chose to compete in the recently introduced Second Division of the West Yorkshire League for the 1906/07 season, along with several other Bradford district teams, and in this company it spent two fairly unspectacular seasons. This was very much what we would now call a 'semi-professional' competition, with players receiving, at the very least, match fees. The expense of competing in the league proved too much for the majority of the second tier teams, a good number of which were from Wharfedale, and many of them folded within a couple of years of joining the competition, having overstretched themselves financially. Bradford Rovers was sadly one of them, and in the summer of 1908 the club dropped out of the competition and folded.

It wasn't too long before the Bradford Rovers name was revived however, this time as a purely amateur concern, in the summer of 1912. The revived club was admitted into the top division of the Bradford Amateur League, where it spent four seasons. The 1913/14 season saw runners-up position achieved - behind champions Bolton United - after defeating Baildon Woodbottom 1-0 in a play-off for the runner-up medals at Greenfield. It is not known if Greenfield was still being used for home matches. The club folded up again in the summer of 1916, half-way through World War One.

After the war, Rovers initially only entered local cup competitions, but re-entered the Bradford Amateur League in 1923, staying there until 1929. Its final two seasons saw the league title won, with the final season itself - 1928/29 – also seeing success in local cup competition. The Bradford Hospitals Charity Cup was won for the first time, with victory over Bingley Temperance (although no report of that final has been uncovered), with Rovers also reaching the Bradford & District Cup final, losing 0-2 to Acton Athletic, the team that Rovers had narrowly overcome to win the league title.

The team broke up in the summer of 1929 and it seems that the club took a year out to regroup. Ground problems may also have necessitated that decision. However, when the club returned, initially in the Bradford Industrial League (1930/31), the Bradford FA League (1931-33 – champions in the first of the two seasons in the league, and third the following season), and then the Bradford Amateur League (1933/34, finishing third), it quickly established itself as one of the strongest amateur teams in the district.

The West Riding County Amateur League was joined in 1934 when a vacancy was created by the withdrawal of another Bradford side, Marshfield Athletic, and this is where the club stayed until its demise in 1977. In that time, it became one of the district's - and the league's - most successful amateur clubs of all time, with a remarkable and consistent string of success, captained by stalwarts Harry Clapham and then Stanley Ham.

Rovers were by now playing on a ground on Lower Lane, one which was said to be one of the best in the city, and were indebted to Fred Braithwaite, the club president, whose enthusiasm drove the club forward. Ronnie Wharton, in *The Best of Bradford Amateur Football*, has researched this part of the club's history in detail, and the full story of the

**BRADFORD FOOTBALLER.**

T. Worsman, of Bradford Rovers. He has been a member of the club for four seasons, and his trickiness with the ball has earned for him the name of the "Wizard."

*A 1916 player feature*

sustained run of success would fill a book all by itself. A season-by-season look at Bradford Rovers between 1934 and the 1943 shows that the club won at least one piece of silverware in eight of those nine seasons.

*1934/35:* Rovers finished in fourth place in the league, but were Bradford & District Cup winners, with a 4-2 defeat of Wyke Old Boys in the final at Valley Parade on Monday 29th April 1935

The *Yorkshire Post* reported on the final the following day, *'The first goal was scored by Ogden (Wyke centre forward) making good use the pass he received from Heath on the left wing, but soon after Brown, the Rovers centre forward, bundled the goalkeeper into the net along with the ball to equalise and two minutes later King, inside left, put Rovers in the lead. Early In the second half. Turner, at right back for Wyke, put Rovers further ahead when he was unlucky enough put the ball through his own goal. Shortly afterwards Ogden again scored, but the issue was settled when a misunderstanding between Wyke's goalkeeper and right back enabled a shot from Hamm (Rovers left half) to find its way into the net. The Lord Mayor of Bradford (Alderman W Hodgson) presented the cup to the winners and also medals to the players of both teams.'*

*1935/36:* The club were league champions. The title was sealed with a 2-1 victory over reigning champions Guiseley late in April. However, due to fixture congestion, Rovers had another league fixture later the same day. This one was lost to Yeadon Celtic.

Rovers were Bradford & District Cup winners again, with a 5-2 victory against Laisterdyke WMC in the final, on Monday 27th April 1936 at Park Avenue. Rawson scored a hat-trick that day.

| 1927/28 Bradford Amateur League | | | | | |
|---|---|---|---|---|---|
| *Senior Division* | P | W | D | L | Pts |
| **Bradford Rovers** | 16 | 14 | 0 | 2 | 28 |
| Acton Athletic | 16 | 13 | 1 | 2 | 27 |
| Crag Road United | 16 | 9 | 1 | 6 | 19 |
| Low Moor Hotspurs | 16 | 8 | 1 | 7 | 17 |
| Bradford City Band | 16 | 8 | 1 | 7 | 17 |
| Morley Carr WMC | 16 | 6 | 1 | 9 | 13 |
| Blythwick reserves | 16 | 3 | 2 | 11 | 8 |
| Fairweather Green | 16 | 3 | 2 | 11 | 8 |
| Low Moor LMS | 16 | 3 | 1 | 12 | 7 |
| *Drighlington, Undercliffe, Low Moor AFC all w/d* | | | | | |

| 1928/29 Bradford Amateur League | | | | | |
|---|---|---|---|---|---|
| *Senior Division* | | | | | |
| **Bradford Rovers** | 16 | 11 | 4 | 1 | 26 |
| Acton Athletic | 16 | 11 | 3 | 2 | 25 |
| Midland Mills | 16 | 9 | 1 | 6 | 19 |
| Marshfield Athletic | 16 | 7 | 2 | 7 | 16 |
| Bingley Temperance | 16 | 8 | 0 | 8 | 16 |
| Cashmere Works | 16 | 5 | 3 | 8 | 13 |
| Thornton United | 16 | 5 | 2 | 9 | 12 |
| Windhill Crag | 16 | 4 | 3 | 9 | 11 |
| Bank Top | 16 | 2 | 2 | 12 | 6 |
| *Swaine House w/d* | | | | | |

*1936/37:* The Lower Lane side were League champions again, four points ahead of Farsley Celtic, and another four ahead of East Bierley. Only six points were dropped all season.

*1937/38:* The club finished in sixth place in the league, well behind runaway champions East Bierley, but were Bradford & District Cup winners for the third time in four seasons, winning 2-0 against arch-rivals, Salts on Friday 6th May at Valley Parade.

*1938/39:* Rovers finished runner-up, behind Guiseley, in the league. However, they were West Riding County Cup winners for the first time, coming from a goal down at half time to defeat Salts again at Valley Parade on Monday 24th April 1939. The final score this time was 3-2, thanks to goals from King (twice) and Futter. The match was *'fast and keenly contested'* according to the *Bradford Observer*, and he cup was presented to the victorious team by the Deputy Mayor of Bradford, Mr H J White.

However, one final was lost that season, and that was the league cup final, to Guiseley.

*1939/40:* With the league continuing to operate during World War Two, Bradford Rovers was able to continue in the same competition, although was obviously affected, as all clubs were, when many of its players went off to fight for their country. The club achieved the 'grand slam' of league title and cup wins this season. On top of the West Riding County Amateur league championship was another County Cup final appearance, this time resulting in a 5-2 defeat of Kippax on Saturday 27th April 1940. Kippax had been defeated by Rovers at the semi-final the previous season, but with several players having had

Football League experience, were favourites to win the final this year. The Rovers goals were scored by Futter (twice), King, Pickles and Pedley. The Bradford & District Cup was also won, with a convincing 6-1 defeat of East Bierley at Valley Parade, on Monday 13th May 1940. In a hectic end to the season, Rovers also won the County Amateur League Cup.

*1940/41:* Bradford Rovers were again league champions again, and also West Riding County Cup winners, defeating Huddersfield Town reserves in the final at Valley Parade, on Friday 11th April 1941. The club therefore became only the second team (After Altofts) to win the cup three years in succession. Huddersfield Town reserves gained revenge for that defeat the following month, beating Rovers 2-1 in the League Cup final.

*1941/42*: No trophies were won this season, but the local press reported that Fred Braithwaite was keeping the name of the club going in the absence of many of its players, who were overseas.

*1942/43:* The West Riding County Amateur League title was won again, as was the Bradford & District FA Cup.

Unfortunately, with the land needed for buildings during World War Two the Lower Lane ground became unavailable towards the end of the 1941/42 season and a new ground was needed. Remaining home fixtures that season were played on the East Bierley ground, before a permanent move to a new pitch located on Parry Lane, right on its junction with Lower Lane itself, and a stone's throw from the club's former home. This ground was shared with the Bradford Park Avenue's 'A' team and was brought up to standard with the money given as compensation for the loss of the Lower Lane ground.

After the County Cup win of 1941, it took 25 years for Rovers to win that competition again, at the end of the 1965/66 season. In that time, the league title had been won a further six times. The club captain by 1966 was Keith Perkins, and it was leading goalscorer Malcolm Emmett whose goal saw Rovers take that fourth County Cup title, defeating Armthorpe Welfare at Bracken Edge, the home of Yorkshire Amateur FC.

Queensbury provided stern opposition in the 1967/68 Bradford & District Cup final, Rovers eventually winning 4-2 thanks to two late goals. Rovers also defeated Firth Sports 3-0 in the League Cup final to achieve a 'treble', as the league title had also been won for the first time in seven seasons.

Despite winning the league for the twelfth and final time in the 1969/70 season, Rovers lost two big cup finals that season. They went down disappointingly to Westwood in the Bradford & District Cup final, and also lost to Liversedge in the County Cup final and League Cup semi-final.

The County Cup was won for the final time at the end of the 1970/71 season, but it took a replay, and a 2-1 victory, over Leeds Athletic to win the trophy. The club was again losing finalist in the District Cup though, going down to Clayton FC in the final. When the Bradford & District Cup final was won at the end of the 1971/72 season, it was the last time that the name of Bradford Rovers would figure in the winners lists. Westwood were defeated in the tie by two extra time goals.

Unfortunately, by the 1970s, Rovers had been eclipsed by the likes of Thackley and Guiseley, who had moved on to the Yorkshire League. Rovers remained staunchly amateur, but the costs of maintaining their Parry Lane ground, and problems raising a team saw the club resign from the West Riding County Amateur League in the summer of 1977.

Its place in the Premier Division for 1977/78 was given to Manningham Mills, who played home fixtures at Scotchman Road. Ironically, when Manningham Mills folded in 1988, its ground was initially used by Dubrovnic FC, a team named after a local hotel, and which renamed itself Bradford Rovers in the summer of 1992. The club played in the lower divisions of what was by then a much larger West Riding County Amateur League, but folded during the 1995/96 season.

Parry Lane is still used today, as Dudley Hill amateur rugby league club moved in following Rovers' demise.

## Bradford Rovers Roll of Honour

*West Riding County Cup:*
Winners five times: 1938/39, 1939/40, 1940/41, 1965/66, 1970/71
*Bradford & District FA Cup:*
Winners seven times: 1934/35, 1935/36, 1937/38, 1939/40, 1942/43, 1967/68, 1971/72
*Bradford & District FA Junior Cup* – Bradford Rovers reserves:
Winners twice: 1941/42, 1963/64,
*West Riding County Amateur League:*
Champions twelve times: 1935/36, 1936/37, 1939/40, 1940/41, 1942/43, 1945/46, 1949/50, 1950/51, 1957/58, 1959/60, 1967/68, 1969/70,
League Cup Winners six times: 1939/40, 1945/46, 1949/50, 1958/59, 1959/60, 1967/68,

## Bradford Rovers in FA Competitions

The club entered the English **FA Cup** competition for three successive seasons between 1937-40, knocked out at the Extra Preliminary Round on each occasion, and each time away from home. Midland League side Frickley Colliery narrowly defeated them 2-1 in the 1937/38 season. Goole Town defeated Rovers more easily the following season, 4-1, while the 1939/40 campaign saw Brodsworth Main Colliery edge home 4-3.

Bradford Rovers entered the **FA Amateur Cup** three times before World War Two, and were then regular entrants between 1946-1973 (only missing the 1966/67 competition).

The club's first ever match in the FA Amateur Cup was in the 1934/35 season, and it couldn't have gone any better, with a resounding 13-0 victory over Heptonstall Red Star, at home in the First Qualifying Round on 6th October 1934. Centre-forward Footer scored six goals in the tie, with Sutcliffe also bagging a hat-trick. However, Farsley Celtic put paid to any further progress in the following round, winning 2-1.

One year later, East Bierley were thrashed 7-3 on their home ground on Hunsworth Lane in the First Qualifying Round, with Ravensthorpe this time ending Rovers hopes in the following round with a 3-2 home victory. The 1936/37 season saw East Bierley defeated on their own ground again, this time 4-2 in a Preliminary Round tie that was a much tighter game than the previous season. Ravensthorpe were this time held to a 1-1 in the First Qualifying Round, before a 6-2 success for Rovers in the replay. A 4-1 win at Golcar followed, before a hefty 0-4 defeat for Rovers on Merseyside against Earle in the Third Qualifying Round, just two rounds from the First Round proper. After that fine run the club surprisingly chose not to enter the following year, a run in the competition not always proving financially beneficial, and it wasn't until the 1946/47 season that entry was again made.

Bradford Rovers FA Amateur Cup ties could certainly never be called dull. The return to the competition saw Old Hullensians defeated 11-0 on their own ground on 28th September 1946 in a Preliminary Round tie, before a narrow home defeat for Rovers at the hands of Brigham & Cowans, the Hull side winning 5-4. Rovers trailed 0-3 at the break, hit back to lead 4-3, only to throw the game away late on.

The 1948/49 season might not have seen Rovers progress beyond the Third Qualifying Round, but again the goals flowed. Hull Nomads were thrashed 8-1, Brunswick Institute defeated 5-4, before a 5-5 draw with local rivals Salts. Salts won the replay 4-3 – only seven goals being scored in this tie. A least those present would have got their moneys-worth for their entrance fee

The 1956/57 season saw Rovers come very close to making the First Round proper. Ossett Albion (2-1), Methley United (4-2), and East End Park WMC (3-2) were defeated, before a 2-2 draw at Yorkshire Amateur in the final qualifying round. The replay, at home, was lost 3-4, although their victors didn't make it past the first round.

The 1969/70 season saw the side again almost reach the First Round proper. Wins at Salts (2-0), at Knaresborough (3-2) and at Norton Woodseats in a replay was followed by a narrow 0-1 loss at Loughborough Colleges. The club's last entry into the competition ended in a 0-3 home defeat in a Preliminary Round replay to local rivals Thackley in the 1972/73 season, the penultimate season of the national competition before it was effectively replaced by the FA Vase.

# Bridlington Trinity
# 1913-1990
### 'Brid's other team'

Bridlington Trinity FC was founded in 1935 but its roots stretch back to the Bridlington Excelsior club, which itself was founded in 1913. Trinity, and the current Bridlington Town FC (itself founded in time for the 1920/21 season) were by no means among the first clubs to emerge from the seaside town though. Bridlington Athletic were early entrants in the FA Amateur Cup (in 1909/10) and Bridlington Albion the FA Cup (in 1912/13), and other clubs included Bridlington Wanderers, which played in the Flamborough Road part of town. Bridlington Albion played from an open ground off Bessingby Road, adjacent to the Grammar School. Many local clubs went on to play in the Driffield & District League, which was founded in 1902, as well as the more local Bridlington & District League. Bridlington Rovers was another local club of note. That team won the Wolds League title in 1907, which was a minor, short-lived competition.

| 1906/07 Wolds League | | | | | | | |
|---|---|---|---|---|---|---|---|
|  | P | W | D | L | F | A | Pts |
| Bridlington Rovers | 8 | 6 | 0 | 2 | 23 | 8 | 12 |
| Market Weighton Town | 8 | 5 | 1 | 2 | 29 | 9 | 11 |
| Market Weighton CI | 8 | 4 | 1 | 3 | 6 | 8 | 9 |
| Driffield White Star res | 8 | 4 | 0 | 4 | 17 | 18 | 8 |
| Holme Rangers | 8 | 0 | 0 | 8 | 8 | 40 | 0 |

Bridlington Excelsiors FC was playing in the Bridlington & District League in the 1913/14 season, and in the 1920/21 season won the Driffield & District League title before changing its name for the 1924/25 season to Bridlington Trinity Excelsior. The club was playing on a ground at Priory Close before World War One. In December 1924 an advert was placed in the *Hull Daily Mail* for a match in Hull on Boxing Day, stating that the team had an average age of nineteen. Potential opponents were asked to apply to C Earnshaw, of 'Timor', North Street, Bridlington. By October 1928, G H Chambers, of Marlborough Terrace in the town had been appointed the new club secretary.

Winning the Driffield League title in 1927/28 and 1928/29 as Bridlington Excelsior, the club was included in the in East Riding Senior Cup by 1930, after having previously played in the county Junior Cup and it played in the top division of the East Riding Amateur League from 1930, alongside local rivals Bridlington Central United, as well as the likes of Brunswick Institute, Brunswick Avenue Old Boys, Reckitt's, Hull Nomads and Hedon United. Confusingly, the club was also referred to without the 'Excelsior' part of its title at times, but by the mid-1930s was referred to as plain Excelsiors FC again, and still sat in the top division of the County Amateur League

| 1930/31 East Riding Amateur League | | | | | |
|---|---|---|---|---|---|
| Division One | P | W | D | L | Pts |
| Municipal Sports | 20 | 16 | 2 | 2 | 34 |
| National Radiator | 20 | 14 | 1 | 5 | 29 |
| Kingston Recs | 20 | 12 | 2 | 6 | 26 |
| Old Cravonians | 20 | 11 | 2 | 7 | 24 |
| **Bridlington Trin** | 20 | 10 | 3 | 7 | 23 |
| YPI | 20 | 10 | 3 | 7 | 23 |
| St Peter's | 20 | 9 | 5 | 6 | 23 |
| Sandringham | 20 | 9 | 0 | 11 | 18 |
| Old Grammarians | 20 | 3 | 1 | 16 | 7 |
| BAM Co | 20 | 3 | 1 | 16 | 7 |
| Shell Mex | 20 | 2 | 2 | 16 | 6 |

Bridlington Trinity United was founded in 1935, around the same time that Bridlington Trinity Excelsior became commonly known as plain Excelsiors. It's not inconceivable then that Trinity United was a break-away club from Excelsiors, or even a de-facto second team. By 1938, United was one division below Excelsior in the league.

From its formation until its demise in 1990, Trinity (United) shared the home ground of Bridlington Town, Queensgate, although after World War Two, Bridlington Central United (formed in the mid-1930s) also played at the ground.

In a short time, Central became a stronger side than Trinity, lifting the East Riding Amateur League title at the end of the 1938/39 season. From 1920, when the Bridlington Town club was founded, competition for top club in town had become even more intense.

Bridlington Town initially played on what was known as the Moorfield Road Ground in 1920, along with Bridlingtonians FC, who folded in 1924. The Discharged Soldiers & Sailors FC was also incorporated into the new club, which took on the Bridlington Grammar School Old Boys club as it's reserve team. Bridlington YMCA FC also played on the Moorfield pitch. The club later made the short move across to Queensgate, which is just to the north of Moorfield site.

Following the war, and with the backing of the East Riding County FA, Trinity organised a 'Bridlington Victory Cup' competition, which was played in April and May 1946. The winning team was presented with a cup provided by prominent townspeople, with a Mr J Porter donating a smaller one for the team that finished runner-up. Nafferton, a scratch side put together just for this competition won the cup, defeating Hunmanby 5-2 in the final on 11th May, although it would be an understatement to say that the beaten finalists would have been a little jaded having played Bridlington Trinity twice (on the Monday and Wednesday) and Kilham (on the Friday, the day before the final) that week. Gone are those days when cup ties could be played at 24 hours notice. It is worth repeating the comments in the *Driffield Times* the Saturday after that final, referring to the Nafferton team, *'Some of the players are well into the veteran stage, and it was pathetically humorous to see the see the bald and partly bald heads in the side on Saturday evening. Judging by their stamina, however, they are still far beaten by Father Time, and the old-stagers were the best men on the field.'*

Bridlington Trinity, meanwhile, gradually gained the upper hand over Central United, and at the end of the 1948/49 season – its most successful to date - had achieved runner-up spot in the league (behind Hull's Brunswick Institute), and victory in the Hull British Legion Senior Cup. Its reserve team lifted the East Riding County Junior Cup, (defeating Hull College of Commerce in the final) and were runner-up in the league's Junior Cup (to Wheeler White Star) and their division in the league, as well as losing out to Hull City Juniors in the Hull & East Riding Institute for the Blind Cup.

Trinity's reserves continued to be successful during this time, being Junior league cup runners up (losing 2-6 to Central United in the final) in the 1949/50 season, as well as being the winners of Division 3A. Bridlington Town dominated the East Riding League during the 1950s, winning the title in five consecutive seasons.

Having dropped the 'United' part of the club's name, the club made an unsuccessful attempt to join the Northern League in the summer of 1959. Jack Major, a former right winger with Hull City had just been appointed as coach and team manager, but the league, as expected, chose to re-elect both Penrith and Whitley Bay, it's bottom two clubs. The move to a higher standard of competition was only twelve months away, however.

Instead, Trinity became a major force in the Yorkshire League when it stepped up from the East Riding Amateur League just twelve months later. The Division Two title was won at the second attempt, in the 1961/62 season, before becoming Yorkshire League champions in 1963/64, again in only its second season at that level. The 1964/65 season brought league cup success, with Scarborough reserves defeated 4-2 at Bootham Crescent, York, on 28th April 1965.

The club finished runners up to their local rivals Bridlington Town, on goal difference only, in 1966/67, but the championship trophy stayed at Queensgate when Trinity won its second Yorkshire League title the following season. In fact, the league double was done as Hull Brunswick were defeated 2-1 in the league cup final (Trinity had lost 0-3 to Farsley Celtic in the previous season's final).

The club became members of the Midland League in 1972, despite having endured a torrid season in the Yorkshire League the previous season. However, rather than suffering relegation to second division, the club was in effect promoted instead when its application to join the Midland League had been accepted.

After taking a while to find its feet in the higher standard of competition, Trinity finished runners up in the Midland League in the 1979/80 season, and went on to become founder members of the Northern Counties East League in 1982 when the Midland and Yorkshire Leagues merged.

Eight seasons were spent in the Premier Division of the Northern Counties East League. Six of the first seven of these were spent in the lower reaches of the table, but in the 1989/90 season the side had improved massively and finished 4th in an eighteen-strong division.

However, that season proved to be its last. Bridlington Town, who held the lease at Queensgate, were taken over by businessman Ken Richardson, who became their President. He was already the Chairman of Doncaster Rovers.

Richardson paid for ground improvements at Queensgate, but controversially he changed Trinity's tenancy arrangements at the termination of their previous lease, leaving the club with no home. With no alternative ground to play on, Trinity was forced to fold in the summer of 1990. Ironically it was not long before Bridlington Town also folded (although it has since been revived), after having been relocated to Doncaster's Belle Vue stadium in order to meet ground

**Bridlington Trinity
League Record 1960-1990**

**Yorkshire League**

| Season | Div | P | W | D | L | F | A | Pts | Pos |
|---|---|---|---|---|---|---|---|---|---|
| 1960/61 | Div2 | 36 | 18 | 10 | 8 | 80 | 53 | 46 | 5/19 |
| 1961/62 | Div2 | 26 | 19 | 4 | 3 | 73 | 23 | 42 | 1/14 |
| 1962/63 | Div1 | 30 | 12 | 7 | 11 | 69 | 70 | 31 | 6/16 |
| 1963/64 | Div1 | 30 | 18 | 6 | 6 | 76 | 42 | 42 | 1/16 |
| 1964/65 | Div1 | 30 | 16 | 5 | 9 | 70 | 62 | 37 | 6/16 |
| 1965/66 | Div1 | 30 | 16 | 2 | 12 | 85 | 60 | 34 | 6/16 |
| 1966/67 | Div1 | 32 | 21 | 5 | 6 | 83 | 43 | 47 | 2/17 |
| 1967/68 | Div1 | 32 | 24 | 4 | 4 | 90 | 42 | 52 | 1/17 |
| 1968/69 | Div1 | 34 | 19 | 7 | 8 | 68 | 41 | 45 | 5/18 |
| 1969/70 | Div1 | 34 | 20 | 8 | 6 | 70 | 44 | 48 | 2/18 |
| 1970/71 | Div1 | 26 | 9 | 4 | 13 | 43 | 50 | 22 | 9/14 |
| 1971/72 | Div1 | 30 | 9 | 7 | 14 | 33 | 43 | 25 | 15/16 |

**Midland League**

| Season | | P | W | D | L | F | A | Pts | Pos |
|---|---|---|---|---|---|---|---|---|---|
| 1972/73 | | 34 | 9 | 5 | 20 | 58 | 74 | 23 | 14/18 |
| 1973/74 | | 32 | 12 | 3 | 17 | 50 | 62 | 27 | 13/17 |
| 1974/75 | | 34 | 6 | 7 | 21 | 31 | 61 | 19 | 18/18 |
| 1975/76 | | 34 | 18 | 6 | 10 | 56 | 36 | 40 | 5/18 |
| 1976/77 | | 34 | 12 | 8 | 14 | 43 | 51 | 32 | 10/18 |
| 1977/78 | | 32 | 7 | 10 | 15 | 30 | 55 | 24 | 13/17 |
| 1978/79 | | 36 | 16 | 11 | 9 | 76 | 43 | 43 | 5/19 |
| 1979/80 | | 34 | 19 | 9 | 6 | 56 | 34 | 47 | 2/18 |
| 1980/81 | | 34 | 15 | 10 | 9 | 63 | 40 | 40 | 4/18 |
| 1981/82 | | 34 | 10 | 9 | 15 | 48 | 56 | 29 | 13/18 |

**Northern Counties East League**
*Premier Division*

| Season | | P | W | D | L | F | A | Pts | Pos |
|---|---|---|---|---|---|---|---|---|---|
| 1982/83 | | 38 | 10 | 3 | 25 | 39 | 89 | 23 | 17/20 |
| 1983/84 | | 34 | 7 | 9 | 18 | 40 | 60 | 23 | 16/18 |
| 1984/85 | | 36 | 16 | 5 | 15 | 71 | 67 | 53 | 9/19 |
| 1985/86 | | 38 | 4 | 14 | 20 | 34 | 85 | 26 | 19/20 |
| 1986/87 | | 36 | 6 | 11 | 19 | 46 | 76 | 29 | 17/19 |
| 1987/88 | | 32 | 8 | 9 | 15 | 52 | 68 | 33 | 13/17 |
| 1988/89 | | 32 | 6 | 7 | 19 | 40 | 72 | 25 | 16/17 |
| 1989/90 | | 34 | 18 | 6 | 10 | 82 | 44 | 60 | 4/18 |

grading requirements. Richardson's era at Doncaster ended when he was convicted, and jailed, over his arrangements to have Rovers' Belle Vue Ground burnt down, that after his secret arrangements to sell the ground were uncovered.

## Bridlington Trinity in FA Competitions

### FA Cup

Bridlington Trinity made its FA Cup debut in the 1950/51 season, with a Preliminary Round tie at South Bank East End. The match was drawn 1-1 with Trinity winning 4-2 in the replay. A 2-7 defeat at Scarborough in the First Qualifying Round put paid to any further progress.

A 1-9 loss at North Skelton in the 1954/55 season was its last appearance in the FA Cup until the 1964/65 season, when Selby Town were overcome 5-1 at their own ground in the First Qualifying Round, before local rivals Bridlington Town put them out with a 3-1 win, following a 4-4 draw. Town were defeated two seasons later at the same stage, but Goole Town put paid to further progress that season.

With teams playing in regional qualifying rounds, several teams provided regular opposition for Trinity. In 1970/71, following a win over Farsley Celtic, the Goole club was finally defeated in a third replay, before going out in a replay at the third qualifying stage to Scarborough.

That stage was only achieved once more, and that was the 1985/86 season when Bishop Auckland put Trinity out. The club's last entry, the 1989/90 season saw Trinity thrown out of the competition after being locked out of its ground prior to its Preliminary Round tie with Darlington Cleveland Bridge on 2nd September 1989. This was due to a disagreements regarding Trinity's use of the ground, a problem which of course led to the downfall of the club at the end of the season.

### FA Amateur Cup

Both Bridlington Trinity United and its rivals Bridlington Central United were regular entrants to the Amateur Cup in between 1948 and 1960. Both teams entered for the first time in the 1948/49 season and of course were drawn to play each other in the Extra Preliminary Round. Trinity won 6-1 before defeating Head Wrightson's, the team representing the large industrial works at Thornaby. Sadly a 0-4 home defeat to Middlesbrough side Cargo Fleet in the First Qualifying Round put paid to further progress that season.

Central's best run in the competition came in the 1953/54 season when it reached the fourth, and final qualifying round, ironically a season that Trinity chose not to enter. However, they were back for the 1954/55 season and as luck would have it, the sides were again drawn to play each other again in the Preliminary Round – Trinity winning easily again, this time 4-1. Unfortunately a heavy 0-6 loss at South Bank followed in the next round.

The 1955/56 season saw Trinity's best win in the Amateur Cup, a 10-0 home success against Whitby Albion in another Preliminary Round tie, before Port Clarence SS, from Stockton-on-Tees were thumped 4-1 in the First Qualifying Round. South Bank were the next opponents, this tie at home, but there was no difference in the outcome, with Trinity going down 1-7.

High scoring games followed in the 1956/57 season too, a 7-1 thumping of 7-1 Skinningrove Works followed by a 2-7 loss to Whitby Town, both ties played at Queensgate.

Central United gained revenge for its two earlier defeats to finally get the better of Trinity in the 1958/59 season, winning 2-1 in a First Qualifying Round tie, before going out to Whitby in the Third Qualifying

Round. Trinity made it one step further the following year, after defeats of Wensleydale Wanderers (5-1), West View Albion (3-1) and Newcastle team Highgate United (5-1), before a 0-4 loss to Sheffield FC in its final game in the competition. Bridlington Town also played its one and only FA Amateur Cup that season, losing 0-4 at home to Redcar Albion in a First Qualifying Round tie.

**FA Trophy**

The 1980/81 season was marked by the fact that Bridlington Trinity played no less than seven ties against Netherfield (now Kendal Town) in the Second Qualifying Round, which ended in a 0-2 defeat in the sixth replay, played at Goole early in December 1980. At the time it was believed to be the longest cup tie in FA history, having taken 13 hours to conclude. However, over the seven ties, the aggregate attendance came to just 918.

The initial tie at Netherfield ended 0-0, the replay at Bridlington finished 1-1, and the second replay at Goole was all-square at 2-2. The third and fourth replays were both staged at Chorley, and both finished 1-1. The fifth replay at Netherfield finished 2-2, before the deciding sixth replay at Goole finished 2-0 to Netherfield.

Trinity played in the Trophy from the 1969/70 season – that competition's inception – before dropping into the FA Vase. That season Selby Town, Wombwell Sporting Association (after a replay), and Fleetwood were overcome before defeat, in a replay, at Worcester City.

The 1973/74 season saw Barton Town, Horden Colliery Welfare and Denaby United overcome in the qualifying rounds, before a 0-2 defeat at Bangor City in the First Round. The club failed to reach that stage again, with its final tie in the competition a 2-3 defeat at Accrington Stanley in the Preliminary Round.

**FA Vase**

The club played in the FA Vase during the last three years of its existence, but achieved only one victory in the four ties it played, that a 5-3 home win against north-eastern side Annfield Plain in a Preliminary Round tie in the 1989/90 season. Dunston Federation Brewery defeated Trinity at the following stage of the competition.

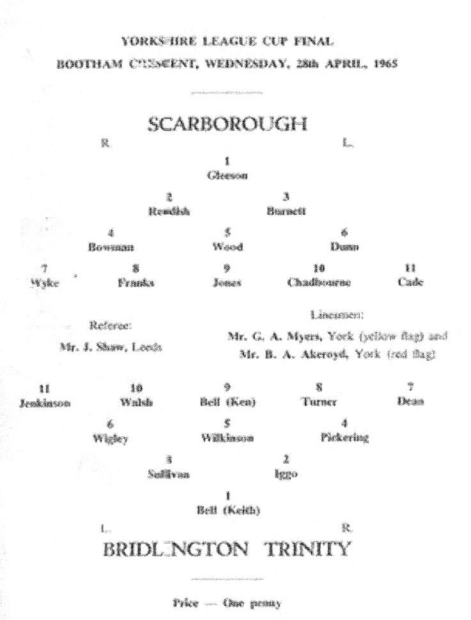

*Bridlington Trinity matchday programmes*

*Top left, from 1963, top right from 1965, bottom from the FA Cup replay in 1968*

# Grimethorpe
# 1899-2003
## *'More than just a brass band'*

The Colliery village of Grimethorpe, some four miles north-east of Barnsley, and perhaps best known for its Brass Band (and, in fact, the location for the film *Brassed Off*) has been represented by a number of association football teams since 1899. The village is not to be confused with the similarly named Grimesthorpe, in Sheffield, which did actually have an association club during earliest years of Sheffield's football history.

A Grimethorpe AFC was down to compete in the 1899/1900 Barnsley Minor League Division One, but by the end of September had already withdrawn. A much better effort to establish a club in the village was that of Grimethorpe United, which played in the 1901/02 Barnsley & District Junior Football Cup League. The team's first match was an easy 6-1 win over Hemsworth on Saturday 14th September 1901, the Hemsworth goal, according to the *South Yorkshire Times*, being scored *'out of sheer pity by the acting manager of the team.'* The team was eventually pipped for the title in the eleven-team league by Birdwell reserves.

The Grimethorpe United team stepped up to the Barnsley Minor Cup League in 1902. This was a step higher than the town's Junior League, and just one below the Barnsley Challenge Cup League, and the team was again challenging for honours, finishing third, behind champions Hoyland Town in a competition that finished with twelve clubs (two having dropped out during the season). The 1903/04 season saw United finish fourth in a nine-club division. In a tight finish to the league, Grimethorpe made the league final, but did not win the title. Grimethorpe's reserve team was by now playing in the Junior Cup competition.

The team did make the league final twelve months later, finishing runners-up to Wombwell Main in the 1904/05 season. The teams drew the initial tie 0-0 on Friday 28th April 1905 at Oakwell, necessitating a rather lengthy replay at the same venue the following day. At ninety minutes, the score stood at 1-1. After fifteen minutes each way in extra-time the score was 2-2. Therefore, the sides played another ten minutes each way, with no score, another five minutes each way, then another quarter hour each way, followed by ten more minutes each way, with Wombwell Main finally scoring a third, and decisive goal to become champions.

A 10-0 victory over Mitchell Main on Saturday 2nd September certainly signalled a great start to the 1905/06 season in the Barnsley Minor Cup, but for the first time the club found itself way off the pace and ended the season in 8th place from eleven teams.

In the 1906/07 season sixteen teams started out (three of which later dropped out) in the Barnsley Minor League, with Grimethorpe United once again challenging for honours. This time the club finished clear at the top but again lost the championship final to Wombwell Main in a replay. The same club defeated them 4-0 in the Barnsley Challenge Cup final, in front of almost 3,000 spectators at Oakwell.

Grimethorpe United did not trouble the top positions of the league again, and when the league was rebranded as the Barnsley Association League in time for the 1909/10 season the club found itself at the foot of the nine-team table.

A better start was made to the 1910/11 season, but the club struggled to fulfil its programme of league fixtures and was forced to withdraw from the league in February 1911. It seemed that the club was far from dead, however, as it was back in the competition for the 1911/12 season. However, by March the club had again resigned from the league, after having fulfilled just four of its 11 fixtures.

There seems to have been no Grimethorpe club during the 1912/13 season, but there was another return, and it was back in the Barnsley Association League the following season. The re-formed club was known as Grimethorpe Colliery Institute, although often referred to as plain 'Grimethorpe' in the local press. It played through to 1930 in the local Barnsley league competitions, the Senior League, and Minor League, along with other short-lived local sides such as Grimethorpe WMC.

Between 1930-34 the Colliery Institute team played in the Sheffield Association League, as well as retaining a team in local Barnsley competitions, but by the 1934/35 season it too seems to have folded, the team having scratched from the FA Cup and having dropped out of the league during the summer.

There is little doubt that the early Grimethorpe clubs were linked either directly, or indirectly – through the fielding of local mineworkers – to the local colliery, which had itself opened in 1894.

Between 1935-37 the village was represented by Grimethorpe Juniors in the Barnsley Association League, after the club had stepped up from the Junior League, while in 1937/38 a Grimethorpe Rovers club was in the top division of the Barnsley Nelson League, in the absence of Grimethorpe Juniors.

In August 1938, Grimethorpe Rovers asked for the suspension of the Grimethorpe Colliery Institute ground by the Sheffield & Hallamshire FA to be lifted, as they sought permission to revive senior football on the ground. This strongly suggest that the previous tenants had indeed folded, with unpaid debts. The request was granted, and the Rovers club moved up to the Barnsley Junior League, while retaining a team in the Nelson League. Rovers finished runner-up to Hoyland Law in the eleven-team Junior League (in which a phenomenal number of goals were scored, and conceded by each team), which led to a move to the much stronger Sheffield Association League for the 1939/40 season. Although there was no league success, Rovers made it through to the final of the Mexborough Montagu Cup, losing heavily to Manvers Main 8-0 in the final on Good Friday 22nd March 1940. The attendance that day was an impressive 3,868 but Grimethorpe were thoroughly outplayed and were handicapped by the injuries to two key players during the game. Ironically the teams met in a league fixture the following day, with Grimethorpe winning 5-0!

### 1938/39 Barnsley Junior League

| | P | W | D | L | F | A | Pts |
|---|---|---|---|---|---|---|---|
| Hoyland Law | 20 | 18 | 0 | 2 | 112 | 23 | 36 |
| **Grimethorpe Rov** | 20 | 16 | 0 | 4 | 120 | 42 | 32 |
| Lundwood WMC | 20 | 13 | 2 | 5 | 80 | 47 | 28 |
| Dearne Grove | 20 | 10 | 4 | 6 | 88 | 47 | 24 |
| Redfearn Sports | 20 | 12 | 0 | 8 | 76 | 73 | 24 |
| Barnsley WW | 20 | 9 | 4 | 7 | 63 | 42 | 22 |
| Worsbro' Br Ath | 20 | 10 | 1 | 9 | 71 | 57 | 21 |
| Ardsley Wel | 20 | 5 | 3 | 12 | 47 | 73 | 13 |
| Swallow Hill Utd | 20 | 5 | 2 | 13 | 48 | 64 | 12 |
| Darton | 20 | 2 | 0 | 18 | 19 | 124 | 4 |
| Darton Main | 20 | 2 | 0 | 18 | 21 | 145 | 4 |
| *Barugh Coalite w/d* | | | | | | | |

The same two teams met in the following years' Montagu Cup final too, with Manvers again winning, a *'lively and entertaining'* match, 2-1, with all the goals coming from headers in the second half.

With the World War Two causing such disruption, a team was put into just the Barnsley Minor League for the 1940/41 season, with that team finishing top of a six team 'Section A', but by 1941/42 it was back in the Sheffield Association League. The team began a period of success from hereon, with a resounding 9-0 rout of Sheffield United reserves in a Wharncliffe Charity Cup tie in April 1942 underlining the strength of the team being put out by the club. That season, Grimethorpe won the Barnsley & District Cup, defeating Barnsley League champions, Shipcroft United at Oakwell 1-0 on Saturday 9th May 1942, and by the end of the season had also won Barnsley Hospitals Cup.

Following the war, the club was renamed Grimethorpe Athletic in 1947, reflecting that fact that the club's home ground, along with that of the adjacent cricket field, was known as the Athletic grounds.

As Athletic, the club won the Sheffield Association League championship for the first time at the end of the 1957/58 season. In a tight race for the title, the club finished ahead of Upton Colliery (the reigning champions) and Retford Town in the seventeen-team competition. The team had to win its final two fixtures to lift the title, a 7-1 rout of Pilkington Recreation in the penultimate match setting up a game on the last day of the season against Briggs Sports. After twice going behind, Grimethorpe emerged 5-3 winners in a tense finale to the season, in front of a large crowd. This was something of a turnaround for the club, as two years earlier, it had been on the verge of folding following a poor showing in the 1955/56 season, with gates being way below break-even level and the club's survival resting on the three to four pounds a week brought in by the voluntary levy funds from the local colliery workers.

At the club's presentation supper in June 1958 the club captain Syd Normanton stressed that the success was not only down to the club's players, but also its hard-working committee, as well as the Ladies' Committee. The club was then treated to music courtesy of the famous Grimethorpe Colliery Institute Band.

An interesting feature that featured the Grimethorpe club appeared in the *South Yorkshire Times* on Saturday 16th August 1958, '*It must come as an eye-opener to many of soccer's more casual followers that a club of the comparatively junior status of the Sheffield Association League can find itself with a players' wages and expense bill of over a thousand pounds! Here indeed, is the serious business of soccer and the adequate answer to those who, quite understandably, often ask 'Why can't we run a team?' Grimethorpe Athletic Club's balance sheet contained this figure. They were Sheffield Association League champions last season, and it was interesting to see how the 'gate' figure moved up by £110 to £177 – as mark of support for a winning team. But that's little enough return for a championship side with a bill like this to face. Grimethorpe are yet another club to be absorbed within the Miners' Welfare scheme. They will compete this coming season under the title, Grimethorpe Miners' Welfare.*'

Upton Colliery reclaimed the Sheffield League title the following season, with Grimethorpe close behind in another close finish to a league competition that belied its 'city league' status, being arguably the premier competition in the county below the Yorkshire League. A reserve team, meanwhile, operated in the Doncaster Senior League, but retained the 'Athletic' part of the title until the following summer.

However, more success was to follow when, in the 1959/60 season, Grimethorpe won the Sheffield & Hallamshire Cup for the first, and only time, with a 3-2 victory in the final against Denaby United, then a Midland League club, at their own Cemetery Road ground, in front of a post-war record attendance of 2,000. The final was Denaby's fourth match in five days, and despite leading twice, goals from Leadbeater, Gray and Storrar enabled Grimethorpe to come from behind to win the cup.

The Grimethorpe and Upton teams did not renew their rivalry for the 1959/60 season, as the former had made the jump up to the Yorkshire League, with its reserve team taking its place in the Sheffield league.

The move upwards proved - at least in the short-term – to be a success as the Yorkshire League Division Two title was won at the first attempt, on goal difference ahead of another new club Bridlington Town. The club's total of 109 goals in just 28 matches was the difference between the two rivals. After finishing fifth in the league's 18-team top division in the 1960/61 season - behind champions Sheffield Wednesday reserves, Stocksbridge Works, Farsley Celtic, and Retford Town, the Grimethorpe bubble burst.

The Yorkshire League was reorganised into three divisions in the summer of 1961, with the First Division reduced to just 16 teams. Grimethorpe finished 13th, and then bottom of the division in the following two seasons, culminating in relegation back to Division Two. With mounting costs, the club could not afford another promotion challenge, and at a time when a number of notable sides also dropped out, the club resigned from the Yorkshire League after the 1964/65 season. Its final two Yorkshire League campaigns yielded 10th and then 11th positions, enough to see the club in the bottom half of the league on each occasion.

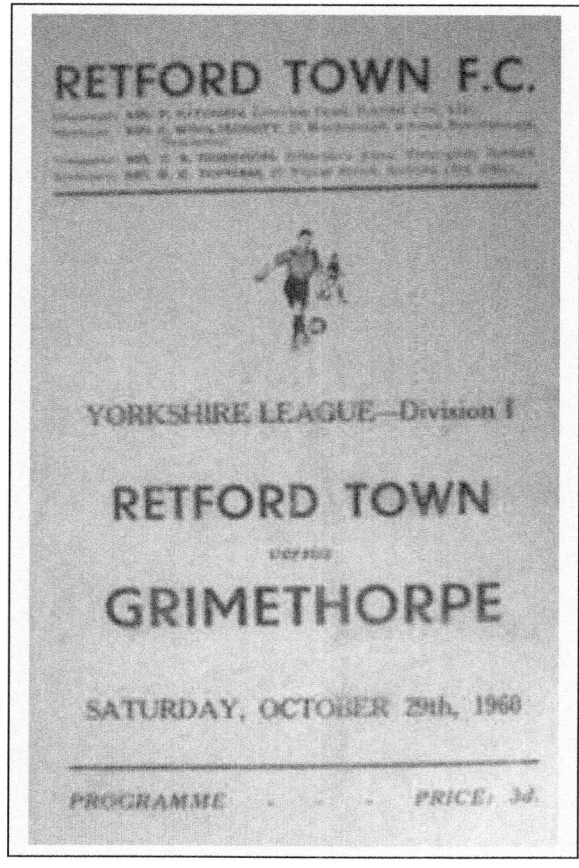

Grimethorpe fielded its first team in the Doncaster & District Senior League during the late 1970s, a resurgent side winning the Division One title in 1976/77 before winning back-to-back Premier Division titles in 1977/78 and 1978/79.

The club was again in a position to re-join the Yorkshire League for the 1980/81 season, entering Division Three and winning promotion at its first attempt, finishing fourth behind Bradley Rangers, Harrogate Town, and the Sheffield team Yorkshire Water Authority (Southern). The team then finished twelfth of sixteen teams in Division Two, in what would be the Yorkshire League's final season. Bottom placed Kiveton Park had only two points less than Grimethorpe at the season's end, such was the close nature of the bottom half of the league.

In 1982 the Yorkshire League merged with the Midland League to form the Northern Counties East League (NCEL), and Grimethorpe were among the founder members of the new competition. This brought with it a new era in terms of the increasing importance of ground grading, and the provision of suitable stadiums for paying spectators. As a result, many of the new league's founding clubs were either forced to leave the league or suffer demotion to lower divisions over the following few years as the competition's management rigorously enforced ever stringent conditions. In addition this was an exodus of clubs to the Central Midlands League for political reasons that had more to do with the tensions created by the National Coal Strike that decimated the region in 1984 and 1985 than it did football. The upshot of all this was that Grimethorpe won back-to-back promotions in the mid-1980s to reach the NCEL's Premier Division in 1987, despite having finished way off what would normally be a promotion position in each case.

Three seasons were spent in the Northern Counties (East) League's Premier Division, each with a lower finishing position than the season before, resulting in relegation back to Division One for the 1990/91 season. However, after six league defeats, and a heavy loss at home to Bradley Rangers in the FA Vase the club withdrew from the competition, again citing financial problems, and a lack of support.

Despite the closure of the Grimethorpe Colliery in May 1993, which had at times employed as many as 6,000 workers, a re-formed Welfare club joined the Sheffield & Hallamshire County Senior League for the 1993/94 season, immediately winning two successive promotions to reach the Premier Division for the 1995/96 season. Given the catastrophic effect the closure of the pit had on the village, which was dependent almost entirely on coal mining, this was no mean feat, given that the massive economic downturn in the community would had had a knock-on effect on the village social and sporting climate. The unemployment rate for much of the 1990s was above 50%, so football was certainly not top of the local population's priorities. With no money from paying spectators at this level, the club's existence, like others, was certainly on a hand-to-mouth basis, with support at the Athletic Ground measured in the dozens.

After finishing in third place in the league in the 1995/96 season, and reaching the Sheffield & Hallamshire Senior Cup final – losing 0-1 to Stocksbridge Park Steels at Emley's Welfare Ground - the club joined the Central Midlands League, winning promotion in its debut season in the competition to reach the uniquely (at least at the time) titled Supreme Division. After four years in that league, Grimethorpe again resigned and disbanded, due to a continued lack of finance.

However, in 2002 the club was resurrected yet again in the Sheffield & Hallamshire County Senior League, surviving for just one season before again folding. Given that by 1994 Grimethorpe was declared the most deprived village in Britain it is no surprise that a village club has been unable to maintain a place in the Football League System/Pyramid.

Since then, several Grimethorpe teams have played on the same Welfare ground, including more recently the Grimethorpe Sports/LLUK club which moved up to the County Senior League from the now defunct South Yorkshire League. The ground is now known as the Love Life Sports Ground, with an emphasis on youth development and coaching there. The Love Life company was founded in 2018 by former Barnsley FC player Bruce Dyer.

### Grimethorpe League Record

**Yorkshire League record**

| Season | Division | P | W | D | L | F | A | Pts | Pos |
|---|---|---|---|---|---|---|---|---|---|
| 1959-60 | Division Two | 28 | 22 | 1 | 5 | 109 | 37 | 45 | 1/15 |
| 1960-61 | Division One | 34 | 15 | 10 | 9 | 85 | 64 | 40 | 5/18 |
| 1961-62 | Division One | 30 | 9 | 6 | 15 | 60 | 86 | 24 | 13/16 |
| 1962-63 | Division One | 30 | 6 | 6 | 18 | 40 | 89 | 18 | 16/16 |
| 1963-64 | Division Two | 28 | 13 | 2 | 13 | 61 | 64 | 28 | 10/15 |
| 1964-65 | Division Two | 28 | 10 | 3 | 15 | 45 | 60 | 23 | 11/15 |
| 1980-81 | Division Three | 30 | 14 | 9 | 7 | 54 | 29 | 37 | 4/16 |
| 1981-82 | Division Two | 30 | 7 | 9 | 14 | 39 | 42 | 23 | 12/16 |

**Northern Counties (East) League record**

| Season | Division | P | W | D | L | F | A | Pts | Pos |
|---|---|---|---|---|---|---|---|---|---|
| 1982-83 | Div 2 North | 26 | 8 | 10 | 8 | 36 | 32 | 26 | 6/14 |
| 1983-84 | Div 2 North | 26 | 8 | 9 | 9 | 38 | 39 | 25 | 9/14 |
| 1984-85 | Div 1 Central | 30 | 12 | 6 | 12 | 59 | 53 | 42 | 10/16 |
| 1985-86 | Division Two | 30 | 12 | 7 | 11 | 50 | 48 | 40 | 7/16 |
| 1986-87 | Division One | 34 | 13 | 4 | 17 | 60 | 65 | 43 | 12/18 |
| 1987-88 | Premier Div | 32 | 11 | 9 | 12 | 46 | 49 | 42 | 9/17 |
| 1988-89 | Premier Div | 32 | 8 | 5 | 19 | 38 | 59 | 29 | 15/17 |
| 1989-90 | Premier Div | 34 | 7 | 3 | 24 | 40 | 90 | 24 | 17/18 |
| 1990-91 | Division One | *withdrew* (6-0-0-6-4-23-0) | | | | | | | |

**Sheffield & Hallamshire County Senior League record**

| Season | Division | P | W | D | L | F | A | Pts | Pos |
|---|---|---|---|---|---|---|---|---|---|
| 1993-94 | Division Two | 26 | 23 | 2 | 1 | 93 | 20 | 71 | 1/14 |
| 1994-95 | Division One | 26 | 17 | 7 | 2 | 73 | 28 | 58 | 1/14 |
| 1995-96 | Premier Div | 26 | 15 | 4 | 7 | 54 | 36 | 49 | 3/14 |
| 2002-03 | Division Two | 26 | 11 | 9 | 6 | 56 | 44 | 42 | 7/14 |

**Central Midlands League Record**

| Season | Division | P | W | D | L | F | A | Pts | Pos |
|---|---|---|---|---|---|---|---|---|---|
| 1996-97 | Premier Div | 34 | 23 | 7 | 4 | 104 | 26 | 76 | 2/18 |
| 1997-98 | Supreme Div | 30 | 10 | 4 | 16 | 36 | 53 | 34 | 12/16 |
| 1998-99 | Supreme Div | 36 | 3 | 7 | 26 | 27 | 92 | 16 | 18/19 |
| 1999-00 | Supreme Div | 36 | 12 | 7 | 17 | 54 | 70 | 43 | 12/19 |

# Grimethorpe in FA Competitions

**Grimethorpe United** first appeared in the FA Cup in the 1904/05 season, when it enjoyed its best ever run. Huddersfield were defeated 4-1 at home in a Preliminary Round tie, before victories over Mirfield United (3-1 at home, following a 1-1 draw), Thorpe Hesley (4-1 away from home), and Newark (3-2 at home), before a 1-4 defeat at Gainsborough Trinity in the Fourth Qualifying round. This wasn't as close to the first-round proper as one might expect, as there were three further qualifying ties to be played before that stage. Hull City and Denaby United inflicted heavy defeats on Grimethorpe in the next two seasons, before another good run in the 1907/08 season. Thorpe Hesley were defeated 4-2 at home in the Preliminary Round before a tie that took three games to settle with Kilnhurst Town. Kilnhurst won the initial First Qualifying Round tie 3-1, but Grimethorpe successfully appealed. The 'replay', also at Kilnhurst, was abandoned in extra-time with the score at 2-2, before United won the home 're-replay' 4-0. Wath Athletic were also defeated 2-1, to set up a Third Qualifying Round tie at home to Rotherham Town. Town won 4-0, and defeated Grimethorpe again in its next FA Cup entry in the 1909/10 season after United had knocked out Silverwood Colliery and Hoyland Town.

One more FA Cup entry was made by Grimethorpe United, in the 1911/12 season when it went down 1-2 to Redfearn's in an Extra Preliminary Round tie.

**Grimethorpe Colliery Institute** was in the 1914/15 draw, although with War breaking out, both they and their opponents, Sheffield FC, scratched from the competition. The team entered again for three seasons from 1919-22, with the first of those being the most successful, with home wins over Parkgate Works 6-0 and Silverwood Colliery, 2-1 before a 0-3 loss at Kimberworth Old Boys.

Colliery entered the competition again between 1927-34, winning only two ties, before scratching from the 1934/35 season, ironically against Sheffield FC, following the club's demise.

**Grimethorpe Rovers** entered the FA Cup in 1939/40, and then between 1945-47, but only won one tie – that a 6-1 home replay against Wombwell Main in a 1946/47 Preliminary Round tie. Rawmarsh defeated them one round later. The following season, as **Grimethorpe Athletic**, the club made it through three rounds – defeating Barton Town (away) 4-3, Thurnscoe (a walk-over) in preliminary round ties, before a 4-2 victory at home to Lysaght's Sports. Sadly, Norton Woodseats thrashed the club 7-1 at their ground in the Second Qualifying Round. The same club put Athletic out the following year, and only one more tie was won, the Athletic's final season in the tournament, 1952/53 seeing a 3-1 win at home to Sheffield in a First Qualifying Round tie, before defeat at Denaby United at the next stage.

**Grimethorpe Miners Welfare** did not enter the FA Cup, but were regular entrants in the **FA Vase**. Little success was achieved even at this level, with the club's best run also occurring in its debut season in the competition, 1982/83. Warrington team, Rylands were defeated 3-0 in a home replay in the Preliminary Round, before a 3-2 home success against Skelmersdale United. Gresley Rovers were defeated on their own ground to set up a Third Round tie at home to north-eastern side Easington Colliery, who won 2-1. Only two more ties were won before the 1990/91 season, when the side went down 0-5 at home to Huddersfield's Bradley Rangers before resigning from the league. Two more entries, between 1997-99 brought further defeats to Thackley and Hallam.

For those familiar with the *Viz* comic strip character *Billy the Fish*. The fictional arch-rivals to his Fulchester United team are Grimethorpe City. Any link with real life Grimethorpe teams ends there.

# Heeley
# 1862-99
## *'Both goals stand on two hills'*

The long-gone Heeley FC made a major impact in the Sheffield district during the 1860s and 1870s, winning local silverware and producing an England captain in the process. For a few years towards the end of the Nineteenth Century it could claim to be on a par with the very best teams in the Steel City before a momentous decision was made to revert to amateur status.

The club was founded as far back as 1862, as Heeley Christ Church FC, by members of Heeley Parish Church, which itself had been founded in 1846. There were claims in later years that Heeley FC had been formed even earlier, in 1860, but this seems to have been due to an error printed in the local press, which in turn was down to an error on the part of a secretary of the football club. One of the club's earliest reported matches took place on Monday 29th December 1862, in which Christ Church was defeated by two goals and three rouges to nothing by Mackenzie FC. At this time, in matches under Sheffield rules, rouge flags were placed an additional four yards each side of the goal. If the ball was kicked between the rouge flags and subsequently touched down then the team scored a rouge. If the score (in terms of goals scored) was tied at the end of the game then rouges could be used to decide the winner.

*Sheffield Independent, 8th October 1864*

The 'Christ Church' part of the name was dropped around February 1865, as the local press began to refer to 'Heeley Football Club'. At this time all fixtures were still friendly fixtures, with no league or cup competition to aim for. Even the first FA Cup final was still seven years away.

On the final Saturday of 1866, Heeley FC organised its annual Christmas Paperchase from the Ball Inn at Upper Heeley. This was a popular pastime and was an early form of cross country running, whereby two 'hares' would set off, leaving a paper trail for the 'pack' (ie, the rest of the runners) to follow. A distance of twelve miles was covered, and there were nine 'successful participants' who completed the course, before they all sat down to an excellent dinner at the Waggon & Horse Inn the following Tuesday, where prizes were awarded. T Downing took home a 'handsome timepiece' for being first home. Other prizes included a teapot, a cruet set, a writing table, a cigar case, and a penknife. During the summer months, it was not uncommon for Heeley players - as well as those from other football clubs – to take part in local athletics events, particularly in the shorter running events. The Christ Church sports themselves were held in the month of April in the early 1860s.

Heeley FC became a founder member of the Sheffield Football Association at the end of January 1867, and then took part in the ground-breaking Youdan Cup, a 12-a-side competition, held between 16th February and 9th March 1867. Heeley lost 0-2 in the first round to the eventual winners, Hallam, at Sandygate Road.

In 1872 the club's colours were all-white with narrow grey hoops on the shirt, however by 1879 they had switched to salmon pink/puce and black hoops, white shorts, and black socks, with a red cap. From 1881 the club played in violet and black. The club had 70 members in 1877. By 1880 that number was 250, reflecting its rising status.

A far as a home ground was concerned, Heeley FC is known to have played on a ground 'opposite the Tilt' in 1864 and also a field in what was known as Wellsbrook Park (which may well have been the same ground), before a move to a sloping field at Meersbrooke Park around 1876. The club dressing rooms were not on the ground at the latter venue, but the *Sheffield Daily Telegraph*, in its Monday 19th February 1877 edition, describes the field of play thus, 'The ground is one of the largest in Sheffield. It is not only a great length, but its lateral limits are also very expansive. This, coupled with the fact that both goals stand on two hills, with a deep valley between, makes it one of the most trying grounds to play on in the district, and no one can calculate which direction the ball will take when it comes in contact with the ground.'

By 1881 the club had its headquarters at the Red Lion, which was used until a move to the nearby White Lion in 1887. One year later the club was at the Crown Inn, also in the same vicinity.

The established Ball Inn ground on Myrtle Road was also being used by the 1879/80 season, and remained in use by the club right through to the 1890s. The site of this ground is now covered by Myrtle Crescent. By 1893 a ground on Chesterfield Road was being used by the nomadic club, before a return to The Ball Inn venue, which had also been used at one time by The Wednesday FC, itself a team with its origins in Heeley via its long-gone Olive Grove Ground.

Heeley FC took no time in embracing competitive football once it had been introduced to the district. The club lost the first ever final of the Sheffield & Hallamshire Senior Cup at Bramall Lane, losing 0-4 to fierce rivals The Wednesday after extra-time on Saturday 10th March 1877. It would not be the first time that it would be losing finalists in this competition. *The Sporting Chronicle* reported the 1877 final the following Thursday,

SHEFFIELD ASSOCIATION. FINAL CUP TIE. SHEFFIELD WEDNESDAY v HEELEY. *The final cup tie for the valuable silver cup given by the Sheffield Football Association was played at the Bramall lane ground, Sheffield, on Saturday last, and resulted, after one of the most magnificent matches ever witnessed, in favour of the Wednesday. The weather, though cold, was fine, and the match was looked forward to with such interest by the general public that fully 7,000 people were present. At five minutes past three o'clock, Heeley, having won the toss decided on defending the pavilion goal, with a strong wind in their favour. As soon as the ball was set in motion they bore down on the Wednesday goal, and after playing fifteen minutes their efforts were rewarded with the first* score, followed immediately afterwards by two more. Up to half time no further score resulted, but on changing ends the Wednesday, with the advantage of the wind, soon placed two to their credit, and a third some time subsequently. The latter goal equalised matters, and when time was called the match ended in a tie, but in agreement they then played extra half hour, fifteen minutes each way. Wednesday, with the wind, failed to score, but got a goal after changing ends, and thus won after a most exciting match, having altogether secured four to their opponent's three goals. For Wednesday, the brothers Clegg, Ling, and Bishop played magnificently, the spectators being so delighted with the last named that they carried him off the ground shoulder high ; while for the vanquished, Andrews, Deans, Hunter, and Tomlinson tried all they knew to save defeat, the first never showing to better advantage than on the present occasion. HEELEY – J E Deans (captain), J Linley, J Hunter, T Leslie, J Thorpe, H G Barringham, P Andrews, F Brownhill, T A Tomlinson, J Tomlinson, R Martin, and W Beard.

Three other finals, that were lost in this competition are as follows;

1878/79 final - The match, on Saturday 29th March 1879, was lost 1-3 to Thursday Wanderers, a team which was in all but name that of Sheffield FC. A crowd of between four and five thousand saw Heeley, who had defeated Hallam 4-2 in the semi-final on the same Bramall Lane ground, outplayed throughout.

1879/80 final - On Saturday 20th March 1880, Heeley went down 1-3 to Staveley at the Sheaf House Ground. Heeley had been strong favourites to win the tie, but for the second season in a row, were outplayed by the winning team.

1883/84 final - Two years after having won the cup for the first time (see below), Heely made the final again, but went down 0-2 to Lockwood Brothers in front of over 4,000 spectators on a fine, sunny day at Bramall Lane. However, Heeley were not sole cup runners up this season, as a new, short-lived, rule forced the losing finalists to play the semi-finalist that had lost out to the eventual winners, necessitating a 'second place' match with Middlesbrough. Following a draw in Sheffield, Heeley refused to travel to Middlesbrough for the replay, resulting in Middlesbrough receiving the medals for second place rather than Heeley.

1885/86 final - Two years further on, and Heeley lost another final, this time 1-2 against Mexborough at the Old Forge Ground, Newhall. Poor weather prior to the tie meant that the attendance was only around 2,000.

However, the cup was won for the first and only time in the 1881/82 season. The Pyebank club was defeated 5-0 on Saturday 25th February 1882, at the usual final venue, Bramall Lane. Despite the driving wind and rain, 3,000 spectators turned out for the one-sided tie. Interestingly, the two umpires for the final (additional to the match-day referee), J C & W E Clegg, were both in the Wednesday team that had defeated Heeley in the first final five years earlier.

The *Sheffield Independent* provided a lengthy report on the final of Sheffield's most prestigious competition of its time,

SHEFFIELD FOOTBALL ASSOCIATION. THE CHALLENGE CUP – FINAL TIE. HEELEY v PYEBANK. *The final tie for the Sheffield Association Challenge Cup was played on Saturday at the Bramall lane ground. The weather was very unfavourable, a brisk wind blowing over the ground and a drizzling rain falling. No doubt these circumstances combined to considerably reduce the attendance; but there was a very large assembly notwithstanding, some three or four thousand spectators putting in an appearance. The ground had been well rolled previous to the commencement of the game, but the going soon became extremely soft not- withstanding. The Heeleyites were strong favourites, odds of 6 and 7 to 4 being freely wagered in their favour; but still the Pyebankers were not without friends, and there were not a few of the onlookers who predicted that even if they did not quite pull through, they would, at any rate, make a strong fight for it. Anticipations in this respect were most signally upset, as the Heeleyites, after scoring a goal in the first half, had matters mostly their own way in the second, and ultimately won by five goals to none. We believe the result was not entirely unexpected by the Pyebank* team themselves. They had been practising nearly the whole of the previous week, but had not an extreme amount of fancy in their own favour. They, however, entered the field fully determined to try their utmost, and, though defeated, it is highly honourable to their club that they were so successful as to get into the final at all. We rather suspect, too, that some of their men hardly played up to their usual form on Saturday. Whether it was that they were somewhat strange to the ground, or that the going was too soft for them, we cannot say; but we certainly expected to see Rhodes, Green and Rodgers play better than they did. They tried their best, no doubt, and perhaps hardly got so much opportunity of performing as they might have done. Betts, Stevens, Jones, and R Kirk, in our opinion, excelled for the losers, and it might have been, if all had exhibited the dash of Betts and Kirk, that the result would not have been quite so serious. Hulley, Simpson, and Hall played fairly and no more, and as to the remainder they scarcely maintained their previous reputation. There can be no doubt the Heeley victory was well deserved. They have in previous years struggled hard to secure the Cup, having no fewer than three times got into the Final without absolutely obtaining their great object. It was quite evident that they were bent on winning on Saturday Hunter, W Moss, Whitham, Winterbottom, R Martin, Jacques, and others played in magnificent style for them, and after the first half the result of the match was never in doubt. The victory is a decided 'feather in the cap' of the Heeley team, and their prominent supporters, Mr John D Harrison, Mr John Barton, and others are thoroughly to be congratulated upon the manner in which, through thick and thin, they have stuck to the fortunes of the old club. The following were the teams, and as will be gathered by the initiated, both clubs had got their most formidable representatives together:– Heeley – J Tomlinson (goal), J Hunter (captain), V Moss, T Moss, T A Tomlinson. W E Jacques, R Martin, J Wyld, I Swallow, J Whitham, H Winterbottom. Pyebank – T Kirk (goal), J Stevens, W Betts, M P Jones, J Simpson, C Hall, C Green, R Kirk, E Rhodes, T Hulley, H Rodgers (captain). Umpires – Messrs. J C Clegg and W E Clegg: referee, Mr W P Dix. The Pyebankers were attired in scarlet jerseys, while those of Heeley were violet and blue.

A detailed one thousand-word, blow-by-blow report of the match followed, as was the norm in this day and age.

The following season, Hallam's junior team were Sheffield Minor Cup winners. The Heeley XI defeated Cobden Juniors 12-0 in the semi-final, and then went on to defeat Lockwood Brothers 3-1 in the final at the Newhall Ground on Saturday 24th February 1883.

## Heeley in the FA Cup

Heeley's first season in the national knock-out competition proved to be its most successful, with a run through to the last fourteen (yes, fourteen, with seven going through to the following round), without having actually left Sheffield. A 5-1 victory over crack works team Lockwood Brothers, also from Sheffield, on Monday 17th October 1881, was followed by an equally impressive 4-0 win at Sheffield FC in the second round, played on Saturday 26th November. The club was then one of seven teams to receive a bye through to round four, and it was at this stage when the run ended, losing 1-3 at The Wednesday on Saturday 21st January 1882 in front of over 4,000 spectators. All three of Heeley's ties were actually played at Bramall Lane, which offered better facilities as well potential revenue, rather than at the usual home venues of the clubs drawn as home teams. The *Sheffield Independent* referred to the ties as 'National Association Challenge Cup' fixtures.

The following four seasons saw Heeley knocked out by teams from Nottingham: Forest in 1882/83 (2-7) and 1884/85 (2-4), Rangers in 1885/86 (1-6 at home) all in the Second Round, and Notts County in the First Round in 1883/84 (1-3). With the introduction of preliminary rounds, Heeley was forced to start at the First Qualifying stage in 1888/89, which brought the club a record five ties. Home victories over Redcar (6-1), South Bank (2-1), Ecclesfield (3-1) and Owlerton (4-1), the latter of who ended cup a year earlier, brought a first round tie at Walsall Town Swifts. Heeley's first away trip of the competition sadly ended up in a 1-5 defeat. A 0-1 defeat at Sheffield United in a Second Qualifying Round tie in 1889/90 proved Heeley's last ever FA Cup tie. The club appeared in the FA Cup for the following two seasons.

but decided against travelling to Long Eaton and Grantham in late 1890 and 1891 and subsequently scratched from both ties.

*****

The club was clearly operating as a professional outfit during the 1880s, and given its high status in the city, was able to attract some of the best players in the country. However, in the summer of 1888, facing possible financial peril, it was decided that Heeley FC would revert to amateur status. It was a turning point for the club, which would no longer be able to attract star players and had to rely on prestige alone to attract its players, and local support. In August that year Heeley officials notified the local press that its prospects for the coming season were very fair, and that there was still plenty of vitality left in the club. In the short-term that was true, but with the introduction of league football its status would continue to be diminished.

Heeley's introduction to league competition was in the 1891/92 season, with a place in the Hallamshire League, a competition ranked lower than the Sheffield & District League, which had been founded two years earlier. Fifth place was achieved that season, but with the top four moving on for the following season, Heeley found the lower standard of competition to its liking. The team finished top of the league at the end of 1892/93 in what was in-effect a three-horse race between themselves, Rotherwood Rovers, and Norton Woodseats. However, the league championship final was lost by a single goal to Rotherwood on Saturday 29th April 1893. Despite the season's success, the club had now opted not to enter the FA Cup competition, given that there was little chance of success.

The Hallamshire League did not actually have a trophy to award its league champions, until Frank S Hatchard, a local politician, donated a trophy to the league in August 1893. However, it seems that the trophy ended up in possession of the Sheffield Alliance League instead, which was renamed the Hatchard League during the 1893/94 season. It was this competition in which Heeley took part that season, albeit without success.

The club was crowned Hatchard League champions at the end of the 1894/95 season. Parkgate United were defeated 3-0 in the championship final on Saturday 20th April 1895 at Ecclesall Road in front of a large crowd. Two days later the Sheffield Independent carried the following report of the match;

### HATCHARD CUP FINAL TIE. HEELEY V PARKGATE UNITED

*These teams met at Ecclesall-road in splendid weather and before a large number of spectators to play off for the above cup. Heeley kicked off, but Parkgate immediately got possession and gained a foul which caused some difficulty to the Heeley men in clearing. Parkgate again got dangerous, but Munks came with a timely kick and cleared. A pretty run by Hill was stopped by Wesson, and directly after Fox shot the wrong side of the post, Heeley at this time were having the best of the exchanges, the Parkgate defence being well tested, but it remained sound, Wesson and Hepworth showing splendid form. A good run by the Heeley front line ended in Hill shooting through with a beauty, thus giving Heeley their first goal. After this Parkgate showed up a bit and seemed to have a chance, but a foul against them when close in spoilt it, and the game grew more exciting, each custodian in turn having to display his ability. A good shot by Hutchinson just skimmed the Heeley bar, and a run down to the Parkgate goal ended in Fox scoring a second goal for Heeley after Wesson had cleared from Mifflin and F Jenkinson. Play up to half time was fast and exciting when Heeley led by two to nothing.*

*The second portion opened pretty even, and some good defensive work was shown by both teams and for Heeley the Brothers Hazlewood played a sterling game all through. Parkgate attacked fiercely and Fox was compelled to bestir himself with a beauty from Sutton. At length Heeley broke away, and the result of good forward play was a third goal being added to their score by Hill, with a shot which Beadman had no chance whatever with. Although three points behind, Parkgate were not discouraged, and they attacked determinedly, and would probably have got through bad it not been for the grand defence of the Heeley men, in which F Hazlewood was conspicuous. Once*

Hutchinson for Parkgate missed only by inches, and another shot from Holmes gave considerable difficulty to Fox, and a foul to Heeley was cleverly stopped by Hepworth. Parkgate pressed hotly, but could not get through, and a good game ended as under :– Heeley 3 goals, Parkgate United 0 goals. Heeley– Fox, Clarke, F Hazlewood, Munks, E Hazlewood, T Birkinshaw, T Jenkinson, F Jenkinson, Hill, Fox, and Mifflin.

Heeley spent the 1895/96 season in the Sheffield Minor Cup League. It is clear that the club was happy to stay in local competition, retaining its strictly amateur status after its problems in 1888. At the club AGM at the Wagon & Horses on Wednesday 19th August 1896 (at which the club founding date of 1860 was erroneously cited), a balance of over £3 was shown, with The Ball Inn ground confirmed as still being the club's home.

It seems that the Minor Cup League was incorporated into the new Sheffield Alliance League for the 1896/97 season, with Heeley winning the league's Division Two title, ahead of Owlerton and Rotherwood Rovers. However, the former defeated Heeley in the championship play-offs. The Alliance only had one division the following season, one which was a struggle for Heeley, the club finishing towards the foot of the eleven-team table.

The club did not join a league for the 1898/99 season, and it seems that it was by now more or less moribund. There was a special meeting of the Heeley Football Club held at the Sheaf House Hotel on Wednesday 8th February 1899. The advertisement in the local press merely stated 'Important Business', as it is likely that a decision to disband the club at the end of the season was made. There may have been a small debt by this point, but the club's demise, which went unreported, could well have been due to other factors, such as a lack of individuals to run the team or ground availability problems. A last match was possibly the friendly fixture with local rivals Heeley Friends at the Sheaf House Grounds on Tuesday 4th April 1899. Heeley won the match 5-1. This site is now partially covered by Lowfield School, just south of Bramall Lane.

### Heeley Football Internationals

John 'Jack' Hunter is the biggest name to have played for Heeley Football Club. Hunter, a butcher and silver cutler in his native Sheffield, played for various local clubs, which included Providence, Sheffield Albion, The Zulus, as well as Heeley. He won all of his seven England caps whilst playing for Heeley, having originally joined the club as a 16-year-old in 1868. His first international appearance was at Hampden Park, Glasgow against Scotland on 2nd March 1878, a match in which the England team was humiliated in a 2-7 defeat. He later captained his country, in a 0-1 defeat against Wales at Alexandra Meadow, Blackburn, on 26th February 1881.

After a short spell with The Wednesday, Hunter was appointed manager of a public house in Blackburn and as a result he joined Blackburn Olympic in 1882 as player-coach. As a centre-half, he made a huge impact there, guiding his team to a historic FA Cup win at the end of the 1882/83 season against Old Etonians. Olympic came from behind to become the first northern

John 'Jack' Hunter

team to lift the cup, win a 2-1 success after extra-time. Not bad for a team that wasn't even considered the top team in Blackburn at that time.

Hunter remained with Olympic until 1887, before joining rivals Blackburn Rovers. After a short spell playing for the club, he became assistant trainer and groundsman at Ewood Park, as well as continuing as a licensee in Blackburn. Hunter also had a short spell as coach to Cheshire side New Brighton Tower, helping that team rise from the Lancashire League to the Football League. He died of consumption on 9th April 1903, aged 51.

Peter Andrews, another Heeley player, was a Scottish international who played against England in 1875 (a 2-2 draw, in which he scored) and who was possibly the first Scottish player to move to England to play football. He moved south for reasons of work rather than football itself as professionalism had not yet been established.

Edwin Buttery was another notable Heeley player in the club's early years. He was a reserve for two England friendlies in March 1882, but remained uncapped.

### Other notable Heeley teams

**Heeley Friends**
Playing on a ground at Black Bank, this team has undoubtedly been the most successful Heeley side through the years, albeit at a very low level of the game. The Friends club first appeared in the 1892/93 season in the St Pauls' YMFS League, a small competition between local church teams. The team became champions and moved on to the Sheffield Sunday Schools League for the 1893/94 season. The club was still in existence, and winning league titles, in the mid-1950s.

It total, the club won the Sheffield Sunday Schools League on eight occasions; in 1901/02, 1907/08, 1914/15, 1923/24, 1929/30, 1930/31, 1932/33, and 1933/34, the Sheffield Friends Adult School League in 1910/11, 1912/13, and 1920/21, and the Sheffield Bible Class League in at least 1932/33, and 1954/55 (when it achieved the league and cup double) as well as the Heeley Charity Cup in 1923/24, 1928/29, and 1933/34. The latter local competition ran from 1921-39.

**Heeley St Peters** was the biggest local rival of Heeley Friends, with that club also lifting various league titles. The club also played in the Sheffield Sunday Schools League from 1893.

**Heeley Amateurs**
The Heeley Amateurs club competed in the Yorkshire League for twelve years during the 1960s and 1970s, yet never actually had a ground of its own. Reliant on groundshares, the club played at the likes of Beighton Miners Welfare, Dinnington, and Staveley before leaving the league in 1977.

A reserve team played at Killamarsh during the 1970s, and between 1967-69 played in the East Midlands Regional League. In the early 1970s it switched to more local competition in the Hatchard League.

| \multicolumn{8}{c}{Heeley Amateurs - Yorkshire League record} |
|---|---|---|---|---|---|---|---|---|
| Season | Division | Position | P | W | D | L | F | A | Pts |
| 1965/66 | Division 2 | 7/15 | 28 | 13 | 6 | 9 | 56 | 62 | 32 |
| 1966/67 | Division 2 | 15/17 | 32 | 7 | 6 | 19 | 53 | 97 | 20 |
| 1967/68 | Division 2 | 5/17 | 32 | 20 | 3 | 9 | 62 | 49 | 43 |
| 1968/69 | Division 2 | 2/17 | 32 | 21 | 5 | 6 | 81 | 25 | 47 |
| 1969/70 | Division 1 | 18/18 | 34 | 5 | 7 | 22 | 45 | 90 | 17 |
| 1970/71 | Division 2 | 11/14 | 26 | 6 | 6 | 14 | 33 | 64 | 18 |
| 1971/72 | Division 2 | 14/15 | 28 | 7 | 5 | 16 | 32 | 66 | 19 |
| 1972/73 | Division 3 | 15/15 | 30 | 8 | 2 | 20 | 44 | 77 | 18 |
| 1973/74 | Division 3 | 5/16 | 30 | 16 | 4 | 10 | 75 | 45 | 36 |
| 1974/75 | Division 3 | 10/16 | 30 | 8 | 7 | 15 | 47 | 65 | 23 |
| 1975/76 | Division 3 | 13/16 | 30 | 10 | 4 | 16 | 43 | 63 | 24 |
| 1976/77 | Division 3 | 15/16 | 30 | 7 | 9 | 14 | 38 | 63 | 19 |

It is hard to imagine a club that was reliant on groundshares away from the locality it represented would have gained much support at the gate. Even less so for a reserve team playing in a competition outside its immediate area.

Heeley Amateurs played three ties in the FA Amateur Cup, but lost each one – 0-4 at Sheffield Tube Works in a 1966/67 First Qualifying Round tie, followed by two Preliminary Round tie exits at home to Swallownest Colliery Welfare (0-5) in 1967/68, and Clipstone Welfare (2-3) in 1972/73. The club did not enter the FA Vase, which effectively replaced the Amateur Cup.

# Hull Brunswick
# 1894-1973
### *'The oldest team in Hull'*

Designed by Samuel Musgrave in Italianate style, The Brunswick Wesleyan chapel, on Holderness Road, Hull *(pictured, left)* was built in 1877 at cost of £4,500.

The Hull Brunswick Association Football Club, the team that was formed by members of the chapel, was in existence for almost 80 years, yet it was little known outside the local region for much of its existence.

Although a cricket team of that name was already in existence, Brunswick Wesleyans FC was formed in September 1894 by J T Ferens, a prominent figure in the town and within the local Methodists.

A newly formed rugby club was advertising free dates in the local press during that September, with interested clubs urged to contact a W H Moorhouse of Carlton Terrace, Durham Street. However, by November, news of the rugby club had dried up (its team in a victory at Stoneferry on 20th October being *'poorly represented'* according to the local press), at the same time as Brunswick association fixtures began to appear in the *Hull Daily Mail*. The same W H Moorhouse was honorary secretary of the association club (as well as being a playing member of the team), so one can assume that the new club had decided to change codes after an unsuccessful stint trying out rugby.

Although the names of the players in each team are different, Brunswick's association team would also meet at Durham Street Institute before setting off by wagonette to the likes of Hessle. Home matches at this time were being played on a field off Holderness Road.

By December, the club had also formed a reserve team. The *Hull Daily Mail*, on Tuesday 11th December 1894, reported, *'This rising club…added another victory to their list on Saturday by defeating St Charles' by 5 goals to nil, and their second-string surprised St Philips' 2nd by 3 goals to 1. Brunswick, so far this season, have scored 11 goals to their opponents 3, and have not lost a match.'*

Members of the Hull FA by 1896 (as was a Brunswick White Star FC), the club quickly established itself as one of the strongest in the town. The 1896/97 season saw the first team play 20 matches, winning 9 and drawing 3, although all 6 defeats were against clubs outside Hull. George W Cook was by now club secretary, with Rev W M Spencer the club president.

In November 1896 the referee in a match between the reserve teams of Brunswick and Alexandra Swifts had forgotten to bring his whistle along, so he used a door key instead, *'by means of which he succeeded in guiding the players'*. Exactly how this worked was never explained.

Elected to the top division of the newly formed Hull & District League in the 1897/98 season, Brunswick finished fourth in an eight-team division, behind champions Beverley Barracks. A separate Brunswick AFC was also in division two (with its reserves in division three), although it is not thought to have been linked to the Wesleyans club. Fifth place was achieved the following season but during the 1899/1900 season Brunswick Wesleyans were one of several clubs who withdrew from the league, leaving only four teams in the competition by the turn of the new year. The team had not been disbanded however, playing friendly fixtures and holdings its Annual General Meeting in the local library.

Around the early 1900s, the club was playing from a field at Sutton Ings near Holderness Road. The plot of land was owned by the Kingston Wesleyan Church, and his would remain their home until Brunswick's demise in 1973. It is unclear as to whether the team has always played at that ground, as Holderness Road was referred to as home ground right from the start of the club.

Brunswick, by now more commonly referred to as Brunswick Institute, took part in the *Hull Times* Charity cup from the 1900/01 season. It also made a return to the Hull & District League for the 1901/02 season, winning the Senior Division title and also running a reserve team in the competition. This success was perhaps not as prestigious as it might have been, given that there were just three teams in the division that season, and as a result those that ran the league itself were not overly keen on publishing league tables. Beverley Barracks and Withernsea were the two other teams in the division.

The Hull & District Football Association became the East Riding FA during the summer of 1902, and Brunswick Institute was again in the senior division of what was now the East Riding League - now expanded to seven teams - the following season. The club started the season poorly, but results picked up in the latter half of the season, with a final finishing position of fifth. A reserve team was revived, in the league's second division that year.

Brunswick Institute continued to play in the Senior Division, and in the 1904/05 season managed to run three teams in the league. That year, another unrelated

### 1897/98 Inaugural Hull & District League

**Senior Division**

| | P | W | D | L | Pts |
|---|---|---|---|---|---|
| Beverley Barracks | 12 | 10 | 2 | 0 | 22 |
| Beverley C I | 12 | 8 | 3 | 1 | 19 |
| Dairycoates | 12 | 6 | 4 | 2 | 16 |
| **Brunswick Wes** | 12 | 4 | 3 | 5 | 11 |
| Holborn | 12 | 3 | 3 | 6 | 9 |
| Hessle | 12 | 3 | 1 | 8 | 7 |
| East Hull | 12 | 1 | 2 | 9 | 4 |
| West Hull w/d | | | | | |

**Division Two**

| | P | W | D | L | Pts |
|---|---|---|---|---|---|
| Holmes | 20 | 17 | 3 | 0 | 37 |
| Oriental | 20 | 17 | 1 | 2 | 35 |
| Diarycoates res | 20 | 13 | 5 | 1 | 31 |
| Harlequins | 20 | 8 | 4 | 8 | 20 |
| Hornsea | 20 | 8 | 2 | 10 | 18 |
| Barracks reserves | 20 | 6 | 6 | 8 | 18 |
| Brunswick | 20 | 6 | 6 | 8 | 18 |
| Holborn reserves | 20 | 5 | 4 | 11 | 14 |
| Beverley C I res | 20 | 3 | 3 | 14 | 9 |
| East Hull reserves | 20 | 3 | 2 | 15 | 8 |
| Hessle reserves | 20 | 2 | 2 | 16 | 6 |
| West Hull reserves w/d | | | | | |

**Division Three**

| | P | W | D | L | Pts |
|---|---|---|---|---|---|
| Oriental reserves | 18 | 17 | 1 | 0 | 35 |
| Sculcoates Amats | 18 | 14 | 1 | 3 | 29 |
| Harlequins res | 18 | 11 | 2 | 5 | 24 |
| Victoria Swifts | 18 | 9 | 6 | 3 | 24 |
| Excelsior | 18 | 9 | 3 | 6 | 21 |
| St Paul's CLB | 18 | 3 | 5 | 10 | 11 |
| Brunswick reserves | 18 | 5 | 1 | 12 | 11 |
| Granville | 18 | 3 | 3 | 12 | 9 |
| Holmes reserves | 18 | 3 | 3 | 12 | 9 |
| Southcoates | 18 | 1 | 3 | 14 | 5 |

### 1902/03 East Riding League

| | P | W | D | L | F | A | Pts |
|---|---|---|---|---|---|---|---|
| Hull City | 12 | 9 | 1 | 2 | 35 | 8 | 19 |
| Barton St Chad's | 12 | 5 | 4 | 3 | 13 | 14 | 14 |
| Beverley Barracks | 12 | 6 | 0 | 6 | 16 | 23 | 12 |
| Withernsea | 12 | 5 | 1 | 6 | 27 | 20 | 11 |
| **Brunswick Inst** | 12 | 4 | 3 | 5 | 11 | 23 | 11 |
| Beverley | 12 | 3 | 4 | 5 | 16 | 21 | 10 |
| St Mark's | 12 | 1 | 5 | 6 | 11 | 20 | 7 |

*Brunswick reserves finished 6th of 11 teams in Division Two*

Brunswick AFC were the Division 4C winners. The 1906/07 season proved less successful, however, with the Brunswick Institute team relegated for the first time since its formation.

Around this time, Alf Spring, later a director of Hull City and president of the East Riding FA was an player with the club.

By the outbreak of World War One, the club was running four teams in a new competition, that of the East Riding Church League. Its first team won the championship of the league in the 1913/14 season, winning 15 of its 16 league matches and scoring 62 goals in the process. The Church League was first entered in the 1911/12 season, one in which the Institute had been pipped for the senior league title at the death by St Mark's, another former East Riding League club. The club's reserve team was also successful, being Division Two champions in the 1912/13 season. The club was by now running teams each of the league's divisions.

Hull Brunswick was revived after the conclusion of hostilities, in September 1919, taking up a place in in the East Riding Amateur League. The title was won at the first attempt, and the team remained unbeaten throughout the league season. The only loss that season was to Shipham's in the East Riding Senior Cup. The title was won again in the 1921/22 season, as was the Hull & District Sunday School League title by the club's Boys team. The first team continued to play in the East Riding Amateur League right up to the outbreak of World War Two.

One huge success for Brunswick Institute was the lifting of the East Riding Senior Cup, on Thursday 6th May 1926 at Boothferry Park, with their 2-1 victory over Bridlington Town being considered a shock result. H Sutton scored both Institute goals from the penalty spot. The same season the East Riding Amateur League's Dispensary Cup final with Dairycoates was drawn. That cup was also won in 1922/23 (Reckitt's defeated in the final) and 1923/24 (BOCM defeated 1-0 in the final).

A Brunswick Institute rugby union club played its first fixtures in 1927, although it did not survive as long as the soccer team, which really rose to prominence after World War Two.

Hawthorne White Star was the dominant side in the East Riding Amateur League in the early 1930's, although Brunswick almost ruined that club's two-season unbeaten record in the League Cup final at Anlaby Road on Thursday 4th May 1933. White Star won 1-0, but were second best during much of the first half. Cooper, the losing captain, in what was a *'gesture of goodwill and sportsmanship'*, went to the Hawthorne dressing room after the game to congratulate the team on its success.

The 1946/47 season was significant in that the team not only won the East Riding Amateur League title, but won it with a 100% league record and also won the league cup, defeating North Ferriby United 5-1 in the final at Anlaby Road, on Friday 25th April 1947. Hanson scored a hat-trick that night, along with one from Symes and an own goal. The league title was also won in each of the following three seasons. There was a late finish to the County Cup competition, with Brunswick losing out to Hull City reserves after extra-time in an exciting final, played on Saturday 7th June. Institute took the lead in the 93rd minute through a goal from Howarth, only for Hull to hit back with three goals before the final whistle.

The East Riding Senior Cup was won again however in 1947/48, when Bridlington Central United were defeated 3-1 in a replayed final. The original final took place on Thursday 29th April at Boothferry Park, but was abandoned after only 25 minutes due to hail and torrential rain. With several players in an almost state of collapse due to the conditions, there was no alternative but to abandon the final for the first time in its 44-year history, with the Bridlington team leading through a third minute goal. The replay, on Saturday 8th May saw no such distractions, with the trophy added to the league title and league cup competitions which had been retained. This was the only time Hull City didn't win the cup between 1935 and 1952. The last time an amateur club had listed the trophy had been in 1926, ironically by Brunswick themselves. Hull City defeated Brunswick 3-1 again in the 1952 final, while Brunswick went on to win the cup for the final time in the 1967/68 season.

Given the strength it had shown in the East Riding League, Brunswick Institute took an ambitious step up, and was admitted to the Yorkshire League in 1961. At the time it was reported in the local press that 'Brunswick are the oldest member of the league, and the oldest club in Hull'. An appropriate name change to Hull Brunswick FC meant that all references to the Wesleyan Institute were now gone from the club name.

### Hull Brunswick - Yorkshire League Record

| Season | Division | P | W | D | L | F | A | Pts | Pos |
|---|---|---|---|---|---|---|---|---|---|
| 1961/62 | Division Two | 26 | 10 | 4 | 12 | 59 | 52 | 24 | 9/14 |
| 1962/63 | Division Two | 28 | 17 | 4 | 7 | 85 | 48 | 38 | 4/15 |
| 1963/64 | Division One | 30 | 9 | 9 | 12 | 47 | 62 | 27 | 9/16 |
| 1964/65 | Division One | 30 | 7 | 2 | 21 | 42 | 92 | 16 | 15/16 |
| 1965/66 | Division Two | 28 | 15 | 3 | 10 | 70 | 66 | 33 | 6/15 |
| 1966/67 | Division Two | 32 | 25 | 3 | 4 | 105 | 40 | 53 | 1/17 |
| 1967/68 | Division One | 32 | 14 | 9 | 9 | 50 | 45 | 37 | 7/17 |
| 1968/69 | Division One | 34 | 6 | 7 | 21 | 51 | 78 | 19 | 16/18 |
| 1969/70 | Division Two | 34 | 20 | 6 | 8 | 103 | 52 | 46 | 4/18 |
| 1970/71 | Division Two | 26 | 13 | 7 | 6 | 46 | 36 | 33 | 5/14 |
| 1971/72 | Division Two | 28 | 11 | 7 | 10 | 48 | 32 | 29 | 6/15 |
| 1972/73 | Division Two | 30 | 12 | 6 | 12 | 53 | 43 | 30 | 9/16 |

Although never one of the most successful teams in the semi-professional competition, the Brunswick club was easily able to hold its own. Its most successful season was its 1966/67 campaign, when it bounced back from relegation two seasons earlier to win the Division Two title, scoring 105 goals in 32 league matches in the process.

### Hull Brunswick in FA Competitions

Brunswick were **FA Cup** entrants between 1965 and 1972 (missing just the 1970/71 season). The team made it to the Third Qualifying Round of the national cup competition on one occasion, that being the 1969/70 season, defeating Winterton Rangers and Barton Town (the latter after a replay) before going down to Scarborough, then flying high in the Northern Premier League. The only other two victories were against Yorkshire Amateur in the First Qualifying Round in 1965/66 (a 0-6 defeat at Bridlington Trinity followed), and then against Bridlington Town in a replay three years later (before a narrow defeat at Selby Town).

The **FA Trophy** was also entered twice (rather than the FA Vase). While a Yorkshire League Second Division team would have had little hope of success in this competition, it would offer the opportunity of a tie with one of the non-league 'big boys' once the qualifying rounds had been overcome. Brunswick defeated Ashby Institute 1-0 in the First Qualifying Round in 1969/70 before losing 0-4 at Denaby United. The club returned to the competition in 1971/72, losing 2-3 at Winterton Rangers at the first stage.

There was also very little for Hull Brunswick to shout about in the **FA Amateur Cup**. Despite being highly successful in the East Riding Amateur League following World War Two, the club made no impression in the competition, with only four out of 21 ties being won during that time.

Brunswick's best run came in the 1937/38 season, although it still fell short of the First Round proper Hall Road Athletic (4-1) local rivals Brunswick Avenue Old Boys (3-0 on the Old Boys ground at Chanterlands Avenue) and Rawmarsh Welfare (2-1 in a replay) were overcome before a disappointing 1-2 home loss to Manchester side Urmston in the Fourth Qualifying Round.

The club failed to win any of its ties in its final nine years in the competition, losing 1-4 (away) and 0-5 (at home) to Thackley in its final two appearances in 1959/60 and 1960/61.

\*\*\*

The Brunswick Chapel was demolished in 1960, and replaced by a new Holderness Road Methodist Church in 1962. The football club, however, continued.

Despite enjoying its highest ever standard of football through the late 60s and early 70s the Kingston Wesley Church trustees gave the club (who played in navy and sky-blue stripes) notice that the ground was required for development in 1973. The club tried to have the decision reversed, without success, and was forced to fold as no alternative site could be found. It was a sad end for the club, which, despite having the usual financial pressures facing all teams at Yorkshire League level, was holding its own both on and off the pitch. Houses now cover the site near Charnock Avenue on the south side of Holderness Road, with nothing left of the large open playing fields that once lay there.

Colin Smith was chairman and manager at the time of the trustee's withdrawal of support, with Ken Smales reluctantly taking over as manager in the final season.

The Sutton Ings ground had single entrance on Holderness Road, and was never more than a basic enclosure with a pavilion consisting of a club room and changing facilities, and a refreshments hut. There were also training floodlights erected in the club's latter days. After Brunswick's demise, the post and rail pitch perimeter barrier was sold to North Ferriby United for £50.

Legendary Hull City goalkeeper Billy Bly was involved at committee level with Brunswick after his playing days ended, and Brunswick players Les Collinson and Brian Crispey went on to make 296 and 145 appearances respectively for Hull City.

The biggest transfer from Brunswick was in 1967, when the club sold local lad Gerry Ingram to Blackpool, who were at the time managed by the great Stan Mortenson, for the sum of £2,000. Ingram went on to represent Preston North End and Bradford City, before playing in the North American Soccer League in the 1970s for the Washington Diplomats, competing against the likes of Pele and Johan Cruyff.

*Bartholemew Road Map Football Card, 1970/71*

# Hull Town
## 1879-98
*'Forerunners of Hull City'*

The current Hull City AFC was founded in 1904, but its roots lie further back than that, with the formation of the Hull Town club in 1879.

It was at a meeting at the Crown & Cushion Inn, situated in the delightfully named Land of Green Ginger in the centre of Hull, on Saturday 4th October 1879 that Hull Town AFC was born. The twelve men present were all members of the Hull Town Cricket Club, and it was resolved to form a winter club under association football rules, rather than the dominant rugby football code. Significantly, the club colours of this new venture would be amber and black, colours still used today by Hull City.

Initially, only members of the cricket club could be involved with the new football club, which was to be run by a sub-committee, with a membership subscription set at half-a-crown (12 ½ p). There was an agreement made that the footballers would not use the square or in any way damage the cricket field. The newly elected club president was T W Hearfield, L W Wallgate vice president, with a J Kendal as treasurer, and J H Walker as honorary secretary.

Matches with Scarborough, Brigg, Beverley, Goole, and Lincoln were organised, with the first fixture on the Argyle Street cricket pitch on Saturday 11th October being an eight-a-side practice match between two sides selected by committee members F H M Summers and T Milner. Milner's team won by one goal to nil.

Beverley were among the first visitors for a competitive association fixture, on Saturday 1st November 1879. The match was widely reported, with the *Sheffield Independent* allowing coverage of the match, which resulted in a 1-0 victory for Hull, the club's first victory. The goal was scored shortly after half-time by Wimbush, with *'a pretty screw kick'*. It was reported that *'a large number of spectators assembled to watch the game, and seemed to thoroughly enjoy it, and good play came in for hearty recognition at their hands.'*

The club held an annual athletic sports day on the Argyle Street ground in at least 1880 and 1881 The 1881 event, held on Saturday 2nd July was reported as an unqualified success, with prizes totalling £100 offered for the nine events. The Argyle Street site is now covered by the current Hull City AFC stadium, the current football pitch overlaying what was the main cricket pitch, with a railway line to the east covering what was part of the old Hull Town football pitch. The site was actually more easily accessed from Anlaby Road than it was from Argyle Street, and in time it became known as that, the Anlaby Road ground once the professional Hull City had made it home.

The team was initially quite successful, and victories included a 9-1 home rout of Bridlington on 4th December 1880, but, despite entry to the FA Cup, it gradually became less prominent and by the time it was disbanded in 1887, very little interest was roused by its passing.

A town club was reformed for the 1889/90 season in the form of Hull Association Football Club. Its home fixture on 4th January 1890, against H J Reckitts (Swanland) was on a ground at Prince's Avenue, which is likely to have been in the vicinity of Pearson Park. The nearby George Hotel was used as changing facilities. Reckitts arrived late for the game but still won 4-0. By October 1890 the club was on a new ground to the rear of the Haworth Arms, Newland. A reserve team fixture on 11th October was met with the following evaluation in the pages of the *Hull Daily Mail*, 'Some good individual play was witnessed, but the combination was worth nothing, practically speaking and there was certainly too much squabbling. I advise the reserves, as well as the first team, to pass with better judgement and to dribble more. If they do these things there will of course be less wild kicking, now so much indulged in.'

### HULL (ASSOCIATION) FOOTBALL CLUB.
#### FIXTURES FOR 1891-2.

| First Team. | | Reserve Team. | |
|---|---|---|---|
| Oct 3 | Scarborough ..... A | Oct 13 | White Star ..... H |
| Oct 10 | Humber Trinity ... H | Oct 15 | Hull Victoria ..... H |
| Oct 17 | Grimsby T. Res ... H | Oct 17 | Pocklington ..... A |
| Oct 24 | Retford ..... H | Oct 24 | Filey ..... A |
| Oct 31 | Doncaster Rovers A | Oct 31 | St. Paul's Assoc ... H |
| Nov 7 | Wakefield ..... A | Nov 7 | Grim Britannia ... H |
| Nov 14 | Rothwell ..... H | Nov 14 | Grim All Saints ... A |
| Nov 21 | Leeds Albion ..... A | Nov 21 | Barton Reserves H |
| Nov 28 | Grim. All Saints ... A | Nov 28 | West-end Swifts A |
| Dec 5 | Doncaster Rovers H | Dec 5 | Ampleforth Col ... A |
| Dec 12 | Barton ..... A | Dec 12 | Scarbro' Reserves H |
| Dec 19 | Brigg Town ..... H | Dec 17 | Hull Victoria ..... A |
| Dec 26 | Louth ..... A | Dec 19 | H.M.S. Audacious A |
| Dec 28 | ..... A | Dec 26 | |
| Jan 2 | Scarborough ..... H | Dec 28 | |
| Jan 9 | Retford ..... A | Jan 2 | Scarbro' Reserves A |
| Jan 16 | Open ..... H | Jan 9 | St. Andrew's ..... H |
| Jan 23 | Grim T. Reserves A | Jan 16 | Barton Reserves .. A |
| Jan 30 | Wakefield ..... H | Jan 23 | West-end Swifts H |
| Feb 6 | Attercliffe ..... H | Jan 30 | St. Paul's Assoc ..... A |
| Feb 13 | Attercliffe ..... A | Feb 6 | H.M.S. Audacious A |
| Feb 20 | Humber Trinity .. A | Feb 13 | Grim All Saints .. H |
| Feb 27 | Leeds Albion ..... H | Feb 20 | Pocklington ..... H |
| Mar 5 | Cleethorpes ..... A | Feb 27 | ..... A |
| Mar 12 | Barton ..... H | Mar 5 | Goole ..... H |
| Mar 19 | Grim All Saints .. A | Mar 12 | St. Andrew's ..... A |
| Mar 26 | Cleethorpes ..... H | Mar 19 | |
| Apl 2 | Brigg Town ..... A | Mar 26 | |
| Apl 9 | Louth ..... H | Apl 2 | Filey ..... H |
| Apl 15 | ..... H | Apl 9 | |
| Apl 16 | Rothwell ..... A | Apl 15 | |
| | | Apl 16 | Goole ..... H |

*The fixture lists for both first and second elevens were pretty busy. However, twelve months later there was no regular reserve team and the first team had far fewer fixtures.*

The club considered itself the senior association team in town, which explains a letter sent to the editor of the *Hull Daily Mail*, and printed on Wednesday 5th October 1892. 'Sir, may I be afraid to ask, through this wide circulating paper, how it is that the Hull Town Association Football Club will not give St Paul's Association Football Club a fixture for the season? Is it because they think themselves too superior to play such a club as the Paulites, or are they afraid of getting a good thrashing if they do play them? I think for myself the latter is the case;

but putting these surmises on one side the secretary of Hull St Paul's has corresponded with the secretary of the Hull Town, and the only conclusion they can come to is that the secretary of Hull Town says that their reserve team will play St Paul's first. Now a question arises. Can Hull Town Association Football Club raise a reserve team? By the appearance of last Saturday at Leeds they could not raise a first eleven of their own, but had to obtain some of the Gough's eleven and the Paulites. The secretary of Hull Town is trying to persuade several of the members of the St Paul's club to join their club and play for them. Now, then, all I can say to the members of St Paul's club is, be true to your colours. Honour your captain, and stick to your club. By doing so you will see in time that the newly-formed Association FC will be the senior club of the town.'

The St Paul's club went on to play in the Hull & District League but never did become the senior club of the town.

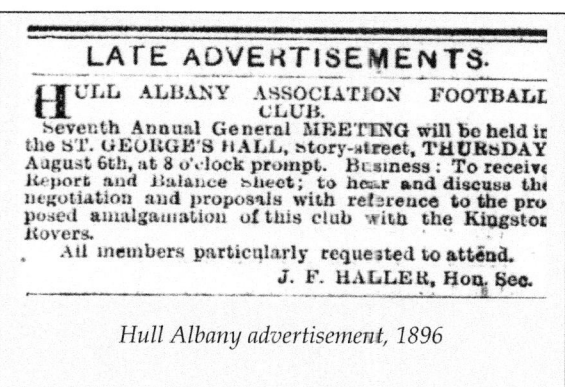

Hull Albany advertisement, 1896

Hull AFC took the old Kingston Rovers rugby ground on Hessle Road, its' third ground in its short existence, for its home fixtures in October 1892. Mr J Rushton was by now club secretary, with the club captain being A Rose. However, by January 1893 the club had cancelled all engagements, and subsequently folded, a mere five years after the failure of the first Hull town club. The fixture list for the season, printed in local newspapers in October 1892 had indicated only 15 fixtures had been arranged for the entire season, far fewer than twelve months earlier when its second string also had a busy schedule.

A Hull town team was again reformed when Hull Kingston Rovers, a club that initially stayed loyal to the Yorkshire Rugby Union during the great rugby split in 1895, amalgamated with the local association club Albany, itself founded in 1889. Albany had been using the Rovers' Craven Street ground since the beginning of the 1894/95 season. The result was, on 25th August 1896, a newly founded association section which was called Hull AFC but variously referred to as 'Hull Town'. Its first captain was W Robson, with J F Haller acting as secretary. The Craven Street ground was again made available on alternate Saturdays. A separate Hull Town Thursday club was already in existence at this time, playing in local midweek competitions.

The club's first ever fixture was a 1-2 loss at Park Avenue, Bradford on 5th September 1896. In its second season the club made the final of the Scarborough & East Riding Cup in 1896/97, losing 1-4 to Scarborough on Saturday 27th March 1897 on a ground at Malton. The Hull team put in a strong performance against opponents who had already defeated them easily that season, but were again well beaten on the day.

However, the defeat prompted the following letter to the editor of the *Hull Daily Mail*, which was printed the following Tuesday,

*Sir, – The decisive defeat the Hull Eleven in the final tie for the East Riding Cup, at Malton, must have come as a severe disappointment to a host of admirers, who were confident of the ability the Reds to land the Cup, and in no small degree to the losing players themselves. The reason of their defeat lies, in my humble opinion, to the fact that the Hull men had made no effort train, and took to the field in an obviously unfit state, presenting a marked contrast to the Scarborough Eleven, who had undergone course of training, and who were in the pink of condition, as was evidenced by the fact that they finished up quite fresh, while, on the other hand, the Hull men, after presenting a bold front during the most trying half, failed to stay, and were unable to take advantage of the wind, although only* one goal to the bad, in the second half. As the Hull men are likely to reach the final of another Cup Competition, I would suggest that they be taken away for a week's preparation previous to the final tie. No one is prouder pf the team than Mr Robson, and no one would be more than he should the Reds bring a trophy to Hull. Could he make some arrangement to act upon this suggestion; I venture to think the result would repay him - SPHEROID.

On Thursday 29th April, Hull made its second final appearance, this time in the *Hull Times* Charity Cup. In preparation for the final the Hull players did not, as suggested, spend a week away in preparation, but instead moved their practice sessions from Albany Road to the Boulevard, the venue for the final tie. Sadly, the team lost again, this time by two goals to one to Grimsby All Saints. This was much better performance than the previous month's final, with Hull unlucky not to equalise in the closing stages, which were marred by the All Saints players who *'resorted to the doubtful proceedings of kicking out on every available occasion,'* according to the local press.

By the close of its first season, the Hull club had played 22 matches, with 13 being won and six lost. Around 90 goals were scored. J F Haller was lauded in the local press for having not only kept the club afloat behind the scenes, but also for his performances on the field, being an ever-present in his team's cup-ties.

Sadly this success could not be built on. Despite Hull's reserve team advertising for fixtures by November 1897, playing its home matches at Newland, by the following summer the club had also disbanded. In its second, and final season, three cup competitions had been entered; the FA Cup, Scarborough and East Riding Cup, and the *Hull Times* Charity Cup, but once again success proved elusive. The final of the latter competition was reached again, resulting in a loss to Grimsby Rovers in front of a large crowd at the Boulevard on Saturday 23rd April 1898.

The Albany club itself was revived in 1901, ironically at the same time as the name of Hull City AFC appeared on the scene, one which was playing on the Hessle Road Locomotive ground at Dairycoates. The original City club played between 1901-03, with one W Hey as club president. This was not a newly founded club, however, as it had previously played in the top division of the Hull & District League (later renamed the East Riding County League) as Hull Comet (itself founded in 1899) – winning the title in the 1900/01 season, ahead of Withernsea.

The renamed club won the Beverley Hospital Charity Cup final in 1901/02 and 1902/03, although medals were not awarded to the players until the local MP Sir H Seymour King stepped in to donate some in 1903. The 1903 final saw Sculcoates Amateurs defeated at Station Road, the home of Beverley rugby club, on Saturday 4th April. Roslyn had been defeated in the previous years' final, in a replay on the same ground

The club was also the beaten finalist in the Scarborough & District Cup final, losing 2-3 to Scarborough Raincliffe 2-3 at Scarborough FC's Seamer Road ground on Saturday 18th April 1903. There was no close finish to the league this season, with City clear at the top all season. The club's reserve team withdrew from the league in March 1903, however.

The highlight of the season was – after having lost the previous season's final to Grimsby West Marsh Social, in a replay, its only defeat of a 26-match season) – the lifting of the '*Hull Times*' Charity Cup, defeating Grimsby St John's 3-2 in a replayed final at The Boulevard on Tuesday 28th April 1903. The following day, the *Hull Daily Mail* was glowing in its report of the evening's proceedings.

| 1900/01 Hull & District League | | | | | | | |
|---|---|---|---|---|---|---|---|
| *Division One* | P | W | D | L | F | A | Pts |
| **Comet** | 8 | 6 | 2 | 0 | 22 | 6 | 14 |
| Withernsea | 8 | 5 | 1 | 2 | 17 | 15 | 11 |
| **Beverley Church In** | 8 | 4 | 2 | 2 | 22 | 7 | 10 |
| East Hull | 8 | 1 | 1 | 6 | 11 | 20 | 3 |
| Beverley Barracks | 8 | 1 | 0 | 7 | 4 | 28 | 2 |
| *Patrington withdrew* | | | | | | | |

Comet reserves were Division Two winners for the second successive season, and were also unbeaten in the league

# FIRST TIME IN SEVEN YEARS
## 'HULL TIMES' CUP COMES TO HULL
### HULL CITY'S VICTORY

*The game on the Boulevard ground at the termination of the 'Hull Times' Cup final last evening was one of great enthusiasm, for the arrival of the time-limit found Hull City the winners of the trophy for the first time in the history of the Competition. Everyone seemed vastly pleased, because the winning of the cup will give 'soccer' in Hull an impetus which was required, after the fiasco of last year's final.*

*For a while there was only to be seen the crowd of some two thousand clustered around the stands that are above the dressing-rooms. Then the people parted, and down the narrow lane stepped briskly a tall, clean-shaven young man. It was Mark Andrews, captain of the City team – a sportsman whom all seemed to know, for they gave him a rousing welcome.*

*Next Mr E S Lewis (the President of the 'Hull Times' Charity Cup Committee) was seen handling the trophy, which had produced such a splendid battle. It was decked with a streamer of green ribbon, and at the sight a great cheer went up from all parts of the stand, and the crowd around. Led by the President, the hat waving and cheering were so vigorous that the sudden hush which came seemed a strange contrast.*

*Mr Lewis referred to the persistency of the Lincolnshire sportsmen, who had kept the Cup on the other side for so many years. He paid a tribute to both sides for the way they had played the game. It had been a great pleasure to the Hull men to meet the Grimsby team, for they had been worthy opponents, and for that reason the victory was all the greater. Grimsby had made a splendid fight on Saturday afternoon, and although defeated that night, he was sure they had the respect and best wishes of the supporters of the game in Hull for the future.*

*He then handed to cup to Mr Mark Andrews, Mr Lewis added 'I have great pleasure on behalf of the 'Hull Times' in presenting you with this trophy.'*

*Another babel of cheering followed before the Hull captain could reply. He remarked that at the moment he was the 'happiest man in Hull,' a rally which the crowd acknowledged with a god-natured laugh. The honour he had received was also that of the team, and he must add that he considered he had realised the highest ambition that could be attained in Association circles in Hull in receiving the handsome cup. He was sure that they would all join with him in thanking the 'Hull Times' for the trophy, and also Mr Lewis in coming down to present it (cheers).*

*Mr Lewis then called for cheers for the Grimsby team, and those accorded were as hearty as any.*

*Of the match, it should be stated that Grimsby had no intention of giving anything away, for they brought three reserves with them to make sure of a full team. Blanchard, too, was in splendid form considering the rough and tumble he experienced on Saturday.*

*The City men were also the same way inclined, for Hobbs, whose knee was likely to give out, was not included this time, 'Dodger' Ridsdill justifying his place amongst the forwards by a splendid goal. One of the backs – and they were an unusually safe pair – missed his kick. Hay centred smoothly, and Ridsdill racing up found the net with a shot of tremendous force that the goalkeeper could hardly have seen.*

*During the interval, Andrews, who had received a kick above the right eye, had the wound dressed. And his pluck in playing, with one eye covered, and without mistakes, won him sympathy and applause. One or two witty ones dubbed him 'Nelson'. Another plucky City man was Hay, who bundled in amongst the heavy weights with the agility of a dancing master, and set many tongues commenting.*

*Robinson was also responsible for several good things. Barlow was a tower of strength; on one occasion in the second half he placed up to Hay, but the St John's backs relieved, as they did successfully time and time, but Barlow jumped in and cleared his lines again.*

*About half and hour from the finish St John's bustled along vigorously, putting another man forward, and with such a strong attacking force they began to make an impression. This strategy put the visitors in a goal-scoring humour, and with only a point between the two it looked anyone's match. Andrews, though, was wonderfully safe, but seeing that he was handicapped it was surprising that he didn't put another man back.*

*Excitement was running hight towards the close, and it was with considerable relief that the call of time was heard, with the score 3-2 in Hull's favour.*

*The victory was duly celebrated at the Arts and Sports Club last night by the holding of a smoking concert, which was largely attended.*

An ambitious application to join the Midland League was turned down in 1903, and the club hoped it would not have to rely on the rugby club at Dairycoates for its home matches in the future. A suggestion that the club should also enter the FA Amateur Cup was also mooted in the local press. The club wound up its second season with a dinner - again at the Hull Arts and Sports Club - in June, with Sir King, who described the club as *facile princeps* (to much applause), as the special guest.

The decline in association football in Hull over the summer was described locally as a *'football phenomenon'*, as several prominent junior clubs folded. Not least, the Hull City club. The name, despite the club's lofty ambitions, failed to reappear in any competition, and this was seemingly unreported even in the local press. The reason for its sudden disappearance, and the lack of a story in its passing, may well have been due to apparent ongoing efforts to create a professional club in the city. In June 1904, Alfred E Spring, the president of the East Riding Football Association outlined at the association's AGM, his hopes of, and ongoing efforts towards, a professional club in the city of Hull, one that would be able to play on a ground with better potential than the Dairycoates enclosure. Those efforts did come to fruition with the birth of the professional Hull City AFC that year, one which of course lives on to this day.

| 1902/03 East Riding County League | | | | | | | |
|---|---|---|---|---|---|---|---|
| Division One | P | W | D | L | F | A | Pts |
| **Hull City** | 12 | 9 | 1 | 2 | 35 | 8 | 19 |
| Barton St Chad's | 12 | 5 | 4 | 3 | 13 | 14 | 14 |
| Beverley Barracks | 12 | 6 | 0 | 6 | 16 | 23 | 12 |
| Withernsea | 12 | 5 | 1 | 6 | 27 | 20 | 11 |
| Brunswick Wes | 12 | 4 | 3 | 5 | 11 | 23 | 11 |
| **Beverley** | 12 | 3 | 4 | 5 | 16 | 21 | 10 |
| St Mark's | 12 | 1 | 5 | 6 | 11 | 20 | 7 |

### Hull Town in FA Competitions

Hull Town played two **FA Cup** ties, losing 1-3 at home to Grimsby Town in a First Round tie in the 1883/94 season, and the following season lost 1-5 at home to Lincoln City at the same stage.

Hull AFC was entered into the **FA Amateur Cup** for the 1897/98 season, its last, and was granted exemption to the Third Qualifying Round. Sadly, a 2-4 loss to Grimsby All Saints was the result.

Hull Albany also entered the FA Amateur Cup on two occasions, the 1895/96 and 1904/05 seasons, either side of its merger with the Kingston Rovers rugby team. Both games ended in defeat, 0-6 at Loftus in a Third Qualifying Round tie, and 2-3 at home to Hull Central Old Boys in the Second Qualifying Round.

# Kilnhurst
# 1876-1951
## *'First champions of the Sheffield League'*

Kilnhurst is a village in the Dearne Valley, south of Mexborough and Swinton, on the banks of the River Don and the Sheffield & South Yorkshire Navigation Canal. It grew up around the coal mining, ceramics, glass, brick-making and locomotive industries; none of which remain.

The first matches played by a Kilnhurst Football Club were reported in 1876. On Saturday 21st October, the nascent team lost 0-1 at home to Shiregreen, while on Saturday 10th November 1877, another match was reported on the ground of the Mexborough MS&L club, a team that was playing its first ever fixture. Kilnhurst lost that one 0-4. The match kicked off at 3.45pm and time was called at 6pm. This was in the days before the standard ninety minute match. The Kilnhurst club played, at the time, on the village Recreation Ground, which was shared with the village cricket club.

The first piece of silverware won by Kilnhurst FC came in the 1878/79 season when it won the Conisbrough Cup. Its youthful players, who were awarded silk badges for their cup final success, were described as *'both clever and determined'* in the *South Yorkshire Times*.

| 1878/79 Conisbrough Cup results | |
|---|---|
| First round: | Mexborough 2 Wath 0, Swinton 1 Conisbrough 0, Kilnhurst 6 Thrybergh 0 |
| Second round: | Kilnhurst 1 Mexborough 0, Swinton - bye |
| Final | *Saturday 29th March 1879 at Conisbrough:* Kilnhurst 1 Swinton 0 (Goalscorer: E Prince) |

Kilnhurst's 1879 AGM saw A Cuckson elected as secretary and G F Kell as President, with the captain being C F Thomas. In October of that year, an agreement was made with the village cricket club, whereby, with the cricket season having reached its conclusion, the football players could train on the cricket ground (on top of being able to play some matches there, provided that they kept off the square. This was not an uncommon arrangement for local cricket and football teams, with the latter quite often dependent on the good will of the cricketers.

The first match of that season for Kilnhurst, known locally as *The Wasps*, was a convincing win at home to Killamarsh, the match on this occasion lasting just an hour. The *South Yorkshire Times* correspondent was moved to write *'Players from a distance can rest assured that both fairness and good temper will prevail in any games played here.'*

*Sheffield Independent*, Tuesday 30th December 1879

*EFFINGHAM BRASS WORKS v KILNHURST (1st Teams.) A match between these teams was played on Saturday, on the ground of the former at Rotherham, and resulted in a victory for the home team by two goals to none. The visitors having won the toss, elected to kick with the wind, which was very strong. In spite of this the Kilnhurst citadel was constantly in danger, and was at last lowered by some really fine play on the part of the Brass Works forwards. Ends having been changed, the Brass Works had decidedly the best of the play, and throughout the last half the Kilnhurst goal was constantly in danger. Shot after shot was made, but they were ineffectual, on account of the excellent play of the Kilnhurst goal-keeper. After the Brass Works had scored another goal the visitors left the field ten minutes before time, which gave considerable dissatisfaction to the home team and spectators.*

The 1877/78 season also saw fixtures played by the Kilnhurst Alliance and Kilnhurst Wanderers clubs as the round ball game became increasingly popular in the district.

A Challenge Cup competition for local junior (in status) teams was promoted by Kilnhurst FC from the 1880/81 season. The cup itself was valued at 10 guineas, and among the later winners were:
1884/85: Ickles Bessemer (3-2 v Kimberworth Red Rose in the final),
1885/86: Kimberworth (3-0 v Kilnhurst Excelsior in the final),
1886/87: Darnall Rovers,
1887/88: Darnall Rovers (3-2 v Warren Vale in the final),
1888/89: Warren Vale (5-1 Sharrow in the final).

Possibly the most popular player in the Kilnhurst team was Charley Taylor. His return to the team in 1890 was hailed in the *South Yorkshire Times*, in a piece in its Friday 7th February edition,

*'Followers of the football game in this district will be delighted to hear that Charley Taylor, the famous back player, has returned to Kilnhurst. As a contemporary well states: – 'Taylor was ever a favourite throughout the locality, and his return to it will be heartily welcomed by all his old friends. He intends playing for Kilnhurst, and the Kilnhurst people are so sweet upon him that they are determined he shall play for no other club if they can possibly prevent it. People who know Taylor's abilities will admire their resolve. That Charley has taken up his residence in Kilnhurst was proved on Monday morning in last week when he commenced working at one of the local centres of industry. I wish him a long, pleasant, and successful stay amongst us.' I hope we shall soon have an opportunity of seeing him on the ball.'*

Charley Taylor had also played for the famous amateur clubs, Old Carthusian's, Old Etonians, and the London Caledonians. He passed away in May 1921, at the age of 55. At the time of his death his son, Charles, was playing as half-back for Mexborough.

Kilnhurst FC became a founder member of the Sheffield & District League in the 1889/90 season, along with Exchange, Attercliffe, Ecclesfield, Walkley, Clinton, Owlerton, and Eckington Works. Only two sides completed their complement of 14 fixtures, although reports in the local press of the time confirm that following a 6-2 defeat of Clinton on Saturday 15th March, Kilnhurst were the first league champions. It would appear however that no trophy was awarded to the team due to the unfinished nature of the competition.

The title was retained the following season, with a 5-1 victory at home against Mexborough on Saturday 11th April 1891 enabling Kilnhurst to pip Ecclesfield by just one point for the league championship. This time a trophy was awarded, donated by George Willey, and known as the *'George Willey Sheffield & District Football League Challenge Shield'*. This was a wooden shield covered in red hide with a metal centre with a football scene depicted. The players themselves each received a silver medal. The team did not lose a match on its own ground all season, and had a balance in hand of over £7 at the end its campaign, although by the middle of the decade the club was in debt. With performances on the field dropping off markedly after its league title in 1891, this would have led to lower gates, which in turn would have led to a reduction in payments and other expenses to players.

Kilnhurst failed to retain the title in the 1891/92 season. Despite getting the better of the other leading teams, crucial points were dropped against teams lower down the league table. This may have been due to the dissention reported in the ranks of the club, leading to several of its players, Charley Taylor included, sitting out some matches. The club's cause was made all the more difficult when Taylor suffered a badly broken arm at Eckington Works on Saturday 9th April 1892 and was forced to miss the remainder of the season.

The village correspondent for the South Yorkshire Times was moved to write in his weekly column, *'I hear Taylor's injuries, although severe, are going on satisfactory, but of course he will have no more football this year. Perhaps one of the worst abused men in the district, for what reason I cannot say, unless owing to his undoubted superiority to those opposed to him. Taylor has played in good company in his time. I recollect him playing for London at least once, and he was during the time resided in London, when the Kilnhurst Club felt his loss to no little extent, a regular player with that well-known club,* 'Old St. Paul's.'

### Kilnhurst FC league positions

| Season | League | Position |
|---|---|---|
| 1889/90: | Sheffield & District League | 1/8 |
| 1890/91: | Sheffield & District League | 1/8 |
| 1891/92: | Sheffield & District League | 4/10 |
| 1892/93: | Sheffield & District League | 8/14 |
| 1893/94: | Sheffield Challenge Cup League | 13/14 |
| | Sheffield & District League Div Two | 4/5 |
| 1894/95: | Sheffield Challenge Cup League | 12/15 |
| | Wharncliffe Charity Cup Lge – North | 4/5 |
| 1895/96: | Sheffield Challenge Cup League | 6/15 |
| 1896/97: | Sheffield Association League | 6/10 |
| 1897/98: | Sheffield Association League | 4/12 |

### Kilnhurst Town league positions in the Sheffield Association League

| | | | | | |
|---|---|---|---|---|---|
| 1904/05: | 4/7 | 1905/06: | 10/14 | 1906/07: | 4/13 |
| 1907/08: | 13/15 | 1908/09: | 15/15 | 1909/10: | 14/14 |
| 1910/11: | 10/14 | 1911/12: | 12/16 | 1912/13: | 4/15 |
| 1913/14: | 14/16 | 1914/15: | 6/13 | 1915/16: | 5/9 |

The club almost lost the use of its ground during the summer of 1892 after a fall-out with its treasurer, W H Barton. Barton himself had leased the ground from the owners, and in turn he sub-let to the cricket and football clubs. However, feeling undermined by the football club, whose secretaries had banked money without his knowledge, he duly withdrew permission for Kilnhurst FC to play there. A public meeting was held on 8th July at the village Co-operative Hall where various propositions were put forward regarding possible alternative venues (along with a suggestion that the cricket and football clubs should merge), but it seems that the matter was settled amicably in time for the forthcoming season.

As league positions worsened, respite came with a run through to the final of the 1892/93 Rotherham Charity Cup, although the tie was lost to Heeley. Runner-up medals were presented to the players at the club AGM, which was held at its usual venue, The Station Inn, in May 1893.

In December 1896 a specially organised ladies' committee organised a public tea and social evening, which included a dance, in order to help alleviate the debts. 150 sat down to the event, which raised a not inconsiderable £12 for the cause. These events would continue throughout the rest of the decade.

Kilnhurst concluded the 1897/98 season by lifting the Mexborough Montagu Cup, defeating Birdwell 1-0 in a re-played final. The original match, played on Saturday 16th April was lost 1-2, in front of 2,000 spectators at the perennial final venue at Mexborough. However, Kilnhurst successfully appealed against the result, due to inaccuracies on the Birdwell team sheet. This resulted in the Birdwell club being suspended for two weeks and its secretary for three months. The replayed final, two weeks after the first, saw Kilnhurst win 1-0 in front of a small attendance. Gladwin scored the winning goal in extra-time.

It seems that the club folded during the summer of 1898, despite a massively improved league showing, in which fourth place was attained in the twelve-team Sheffield Association League. The sudden departure of the club from the local scene is more than likely down to its poor financial position.

### Highthorn Mission & Kilnhurst Town

In the absence of a representative club bearing the Kilnhurst name, Highthorn Mission emerged on the scene in 1901. Highthorn itself was nothing more than a hamlet on the edge of Kilnhurst, adjacent to The Rock Tavern, which is likely to have been the football club's base. The home ground was the Old Forge ground in Kilnhurst, located around a mile away from Highthorn itself. The flood-prone ground was still in regular by use local teams up to the 1950's.

*Highthorn Mission, photographed around the time of its victory in the Montagu Cup final (photo sourced from www.montagucup.com)*

After a season in the Wombwell & District League, the 1902/03 season saw the club – now in the South Yorkshire League - reach the final of the Mexborough Montagu Cup, playing Sheffield Association League team Wath Athletic. Following a 1-1 draw in front of 2,000 spectators on Saturday 28th March, Highthorn went on to defeat the favourites 2-1 in the replay, on Saturday April 11th. The following Monday *Sheffield Daily Telegraph* was on hand to provide a brief report of the final,

*MONTAGU CHARITY CUP. REPLAYED FINAL. Wath v Highthorn* – This replayed final tie took place on the Mexborough Town ground, attracting another large gate, fully 4,000 spectators assembling. Wath started with the slope, wind, and sun in their favour, and assumed the aggressive. Highthorn occasionally broke away, and always looked dangerous, but despite every effort half-time arrived with nothing scored. Resuming, Highthorn went off with rare vigour, and for some minutes the Wath goal was in imminent danger of falling. Mansbridge, however, shaping wonderfully well. Mid-way through the half a sharp burst by the Highthorn right wing saw the first goal the game scored, the ball striking the Wath cross-bar beating Mansbridge. Wath played up spiritedly, but met with no luck, and Highthorn returning Nevitt scored a second, and apparently good goal, but the point was disallowed for off-side. Within a minute of this Wath equalised through the agency of Winstanley, who was hurt,. and had to leave the field. Bisby gave Highthorn the lead again with a grand shot, that beat Mansbridge all the way. Wath made effort to get on terms but were beaten back. Result:– Highthorn, 2 goals, Wath 1 goal.

Despite having been briefly suspended by the Sheffield & Hallamshire FA during the summer for non-payment of fines, Highthorn won the South Yorkshire League title in the 1903/04 season, ahead of its newly formed rivals Kilnhurst Town (A Kilnhurst Mechanics Institute FC was also in the competition that season).

The secretary of the new club was a Mr E Burkinshaw of Victoria Street, Kilnhurst. This is significant, as one Jack Burkinshaw, a wing-half, was playing for the team by 1906 before going on to enjoy a successful career in the Football League with the likes of The Wednesday (56 appearances, 8 goals), Bradford Park Avenue (23 appearances, 2 goals), and Accrington Stanley (31 appearances, 1 goal), as well as Grimsby Town (who he joined from Kilnhurst), Rotherham Town (two spells), and Swindon Town. He also turned out as a guest player for Barnsley during World War One, along with his brother. After leaving Stanley in the summer of 1922 Burkinshaw returned to the district to play his football, playing with Denaby United and Wath Athletic. In 1924 he moved to Chicago to play with the successful Chicago Bricklayers & Masons club.

Following a successful spell in the South Yorkshire League, both Highthorn Mission and Kilnhurst Town stepped up to the Sheffield Association League for the 1904/05 season. Despite there only being seven clubs in the competition this season, due to several clubs having withdrawn or become defunct, the standard was still far higher than South Yorkshire League. Highthorn finished fourth, with Kilnhurst only two points behind them, albeit bottom of the table on goal-difference.

It is interesting to note that Kilnhurst Town had the same nickname – *The Wasps* - as the previous club, and also made use of the same Station Inn as HQ. Its AGM on Saturday 8th July 1905 was a relatively sombre affair given the struggles to keep it afloat the previous season, however, the club had been able to pay off its small season's deficit and planned to run a reserve team in the Second Division of the South Yorkshire League. Kilnhurst had also attracted four players from the Highthorn club. One bone of contention was the number of people who would watch home fixtures free of charge from a vantage point on Victoria Street, rather than entering the ground.

Highthorn withdrew from the Sheffield Association League in March 1906. The club was bottom the expanded 14-team league at the time. In reality, a club representing such a small hamlet was always punching above its weight in the district's top league, and could not possibly have competed financially, particularly as Kilnhurst's town football team, which picked up a few more of the Highthorn players, had again established itself.

Kilnhurst Town continued in the same competition until it suspended normal operations for the War. The club finished in fourth place in 1906/07 and 1912/13, but most seasons were spent in the bottom half of the table, and finished bottom in two successive seasons between those high place finishes. Its final season was 1915/16, the club finishing fifth of six teams that completed the season, three others having dropped out late in the season (other league fixtures were played in the Wharncliffe Charity League, the club finishing seventh, and bottom).

The club did, however, win the Mexborough Montagu Cup on two occasions. In the 1906/07 final, Parkgate & Rawmarsh United were defeated 2-0 on Saturday 13th April 1907. Mr Lewis the match referee look set to postpone the tie but both teams were anxious to settle the resting place of the cup that day, despite the wretched weather conditions. *The Wasps* dominated the match, and goals from Nevitt and

Jack Burkinshaw ensured a 2-0 victory for Kilnhurst. A celebratory dinner was held for the winning team at the Station Inn on Victoria Street and fifty people sat down to a sumptuous meal provided by the hosts Mr and Mrs W C Taylor. Out of interest, the menu was: Tomato Soup, fish, roast beef, roast veal, York ham, roast ham, boiled mutton, roast chicken, boiled foul, veal pie, pigeon pie, royal pudding, fruit jelly, rhubarb tart, cheese, and celery.

Six years later – during the 1913/14 season - South Yorkshire Hotel (Mexborough) were turned over 6-1. In the Montagu Cup final. Kilnhurst's opponents played in the Licensed Victuallers League and were massive underdogs on the day. S Dawson scored four times for the winners.

Kilnhurst Town closed down in the summer of 1916, but was not revived after the war. The club was effectively replaced by a Kilnhurst United, which was founded two years after Town's demise. Other relatively short-lived clubs also appeared in local competitions during the 1920s.

United spent the 1918/19 season in the Sheffield Alliance League, before spending the following season with teams in the Rotherham Minor League and Swinton Alliance. They were joined in the Alliance in the 1920/21 season by Kilnhurst Athletic. United themselves played in the competition – as well as in the FA Cup - until the club folded in the summer of 1922.

The Mexborough Montagu Cup was won by another club from Kilnhurst. In the 1922/23 season, Kilnhurst WMC – of the Rotherham Licensed Victuallers & Working Men's Clubs League - defeated Sandhill Juniors 4-1 on Saturday 28th April in the final (following a 3-3 draw three weeks earlier), in front of 1,500 spectators.

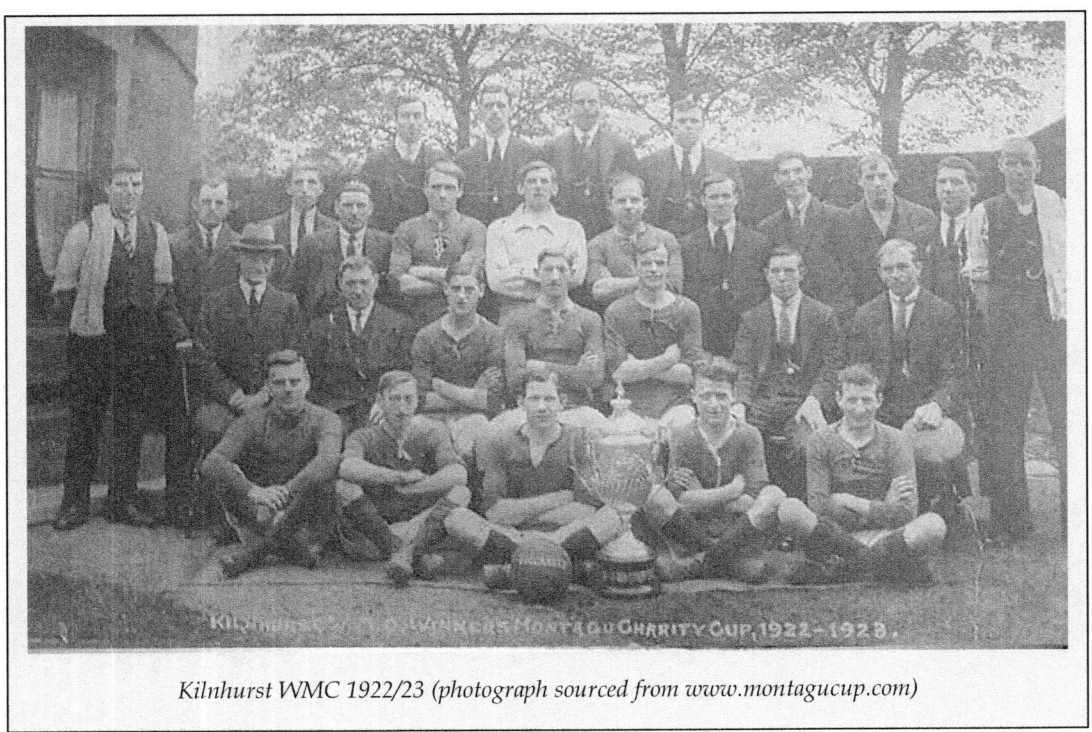

*Kilnhurst WMC 1922/23 (photograph sourced from www.montagucup.com)*

In the 1925/26 season, Kilnhurst Athletic tried its luck in the FA Cup, following a successful 1924/25 season in which it won the Rotherham Minor League Cup and Mexborough Cup competitions. Among its rivals between 1925-27 was the Kilnhurst Victoria club, which played its matches on a ground on Hooton Road. However, by 1928 Athletic had also folded up.

Following World War Two, Kilnhurst Colliery spent several seasons in the Sheffield Association League, and also entered the FA Cup between 1948-51. The league title was first won in the 1971/72 season (after having lifted the Division Two title the previous season), and again in 1973/74, when the club also won the Rotherham Charity Cup. This played on the same ground as previous and subsequent Kilnhurst clubs, although the Recreation Ground was by now known as the Welfare Ground.

## Kilnhurst teams in the FA Cup

The original **Kilnhurst FC** played thirteen FA Cup ties between 1890-98. Its first tie was a 5-4 victory at Doncaster Rovers in a Second Qualifying Round tie in the 1890/91 season, although that was followed by a resounding 2-6 loss at Staveley in the following round.

A First Qualifying Round tie with Sheffield FC in 1896 attracted a crowd of 2,000 to the Kilnhurst ground, the home team winning 3-0. However, Grimsby Town put Kilnhurst out in the very next round, the second time Grimsby had done this in three seasons. The most notable result in the club's history, however, came at the First Qualifying Stage in the 1897/98 season, when Bradford FC were defeated 3-1 at the Recreation Ground on Saturday 25th September 1897. The Park Avenue team had been expected to overcome the village side with some ease, but with the Sheffield district still being way ahead of the West Yorkshire region in terms of playing ability, this was never going to happen. Mexborough put Kilnhurst out in the very next round in front of a rather disappointing number of spectators.

The *Sheffield Daily Telegraph* carried good coverage of the victory over the Bradford team on Monday 27th September, 1897,

*Only a very small crowd, numbering about 300 persons, put in an appearance at this match on Saturday. The weather was all that could be wished for, the day being a delightful one, with a fresh breeze tempering the sun's rays, and meagre 'gate' must consequently be attributed to lack of enthusiasm on the part of the Villagers, and to the increased price of admission. Very little interest locally appeared to be taken in the match, consequent, no doubt, to the poor performances of the Kilnhurst players, and the only mild flutter of excitement was provided by the late arrival of the Bradford men. Owing to this cause the kick-off did not take place until ten minutes after the advertised time.*

*With a strong breeze blowing down the field, winning the toss meant something to the fortunate ones, as it also gave them the advantage of having the sun also behind them; it may be imagined, therefore, that when the Bradford representative got the better of the local men in the spin of the coin, the spectators didn't enthuse much. The home team, however, went away with a burst from the kick-off, and for a few minutes were decidedly aggressive, but passing spoilt their efforts.*

*A foul against Kilnhurst gave relief to the visitors, who now put on the pressure, and seven minutes from the commencement their centre forward, Matthews, forced the first goal. From this point the home team played determinedly, doing most of the pressing, and G Gladwin had hard lines not scoring with a capital shot, while almost immediately afterwards the Bradford goalkeeper was called upon to clear twice in quick succession. In fact, Harker was at this stage giving very good display between the posts. A couple of unproductive corners came to the home team, who were still on the aggressive, and then G Gladwin sent in a fast shot which went through, but the point was disallowed for off-side. Again the ball came back to Harker, but he managed to clear, half-time arriving with the score: – Bradford, 1 goal, Kilnhurst, 0 goal.*

*On the resumption, the home team took almost immediate advantage of the wind, and as the result of a piece of play amongst the forwards, W Gladwin made the scores equal three minutes from the re-start. Bradford now played up with more vigour, but though quick on the ball and kicking strongly, they lacked decision, and the forwards allowed themselves to be robbed the ball time after time. Desultory play in midfield ruled for a time, and then the visitors were slowly but surely forced back, their goal narrowly escaping downfall from the foot of Birkenshaw.*

*Play was hereabouts stopped for a couple of minutes, owing to Clarke getting kicked. On resuming, pressure on the visitors' goal was continued, and Harker was compelled to give a corner, which was taken Jessop, but the final shot went wide. Directly afterwards a free kick accrued to Kilnhurst consequent on Harker carrying the ball more than the two steps allowed by law, and from this Birkenshaw scored; whilst the ball had scarcely been set in motion again, when Ramsden notched a third point for the home team. Following this, play was a give and take character, and with nothing further scored either side, the game ended :– KILNHURST 3 goals. Bradford 1 goal. Teams:– Kilnhurst. – Hammond, goal; G Caterer and Hawcroft, backs; Bentham. Pepper, and Clarke, half-backs; Jessop, W Gladwin, G Gladwin, and Birkenshaw, forwards. Bradford. – Harker, goal; H Collinson and Isaac Smith, backs; Drennan, Duncan Menzies and N Thome, half backs; Garner, Ingham, Matthews, David Menzies, and Helmhirst, forwards.*

**Kilnhurst Town** played fifteen ties in the FA Cup, its success in the competition being no better than the previous Kilnhurst club. Rotherham Town put the club out at the Preliminary Round stage in its first season of entry, 5-1 in the 1906/07 season. Kilnhurst failed to register more than one victory in one season, although it did play five ties in the 1912/13 season – four of them against Industry Inn in the Extra Preliminary Round, three draws followed by a 2-1 success. The run was ended at the next stage when they went down 0-5 at Worksop Town. The same team defeated Kilnhurst 8-0 in the 1914/15 season, the latter club's last FA Cup tie.

**Kilnhurst United** was forced to start at the Extra Preliminary Round during the three seasons it entered the competition. Darfield St George defeated the side 4-0 in the 1919/20 season, but United did manage to win their ties at the this stage the following two seasons, against Jump WMC (in a replay) and Sheepbridge Works, both at home, before defeats at Mexborough and Tinsley Park in the subsequent round.

**Kilnhurst Athletic's** one and only tie was a Preliminary Round home loss, 1-2 to Hemsworth West End, while **Kilnhurst Colliery** experienced defeat in each of its three ties, all at the Preliminary Round stage – 0-1 at Denaby United in the 1948/49 season, followed by a 1-2 loss at Hoyland Common Athletic and 0-3 loss at home to Beighton Miner's Welfare in the following two seasons.

*Sheffield Evening Telegraph - Monday 27th March 1893*

### FOOTBALL AS PLAYED AT KILNHURST. SPECTATORS V PLAYERS

*At the Rotherham Police Court this morning a case of interest to footballers came on for hearing.*

*A man named James Winstanley, Mexborough, was summoned by Charles Taylor and James Schofield for assault committed on the 11th inst. Mr W E Clegg who prosecuted, stated that the complainants were members of the Kilnhurst football team. Which was playing the Mexborough club at Kilnhurst on the date mentioned. Defendant was a spectator. During the course of the game one of the Mexborough men kicked a Kilnhurst player, as was said, with intent, but whether that was so not was immaterial to the case. The result was that two of the players came to blows, Schofield being assaulted. The other complainant, Taylor, attempted to put an end to the disturbance. Defendant then got over the barrier separating the spectators from the players, on to the field of play, struck Taylor in the mouth, and then, turning his attention to Schofield, gave him blow as well. On seeing this several of the spectators also climbed the barrier, and went on to the field in a body, with the result that the game was delayed for about twenty minutes, and an unseemly disturbance ensued. It was such persons as defendant who, instead allowing the proper officials to deal with any bother that might arise, interfered themselves, and caused disturbances which reflected discredit to all concerned and brought a very good game into disrepute. Since then defendant had admitted the offence, and pleaded with the committee to overlook it.*

*In the interests football, however, the committee felt bound to prosecute. Witnesses were then called for the prosecution. When Taylor was in the box Mr Hickmott, who appeared for the defence, sought to prove by cross-examination that the bother was due to Taylor and Schofield's irregular playing, that the spectators called to them to that effect, and that the prosecution was undertaken merely to stave off Taylor's suspension by the Association.*

*Mr Clegg, 'I may as well say, from my official position, that there has been no report to the Association about this match either one way or the other,'*

*Mr Hickmott, 'There will be – Witnesses for the defence contended that two of the players were kicking each other, and that it was that which led to the disturbance,*

*Mr Verelst (chairman), 'How long did this kicking last?'*

*A Witness, 'Three or four minutes,'*

*Mr Verelst' 'What was the referee doing?'*

*Witness, 'Nothing,'*

*Mr Verelst, 'He could not stop it, you mean?'*

*Witness, 'He never saw it.'*

# Leeds Ashley Road
# 1928-83
## *'Ralph Naylor's Lads'*

Many football clubs, both current and long-gone, have enjoyed thriving junior sections over the years, but few will have experienced the level of success in age-group competitions as Leeds Ashley Road FC. The club also enjoyed success at senior level, with its youth players going on to stay with Ashley Road once they had outgrown the club's junior set-up.

A team from the Harehills based Ashley Road Methodist Church in Leeds is said to have first played between 1904-24 (albeit sitting out 1914-18 due to World War One), although little is known about it as there are no records of a side going by that name joining any league competition. It is therefore probable that the team that was run from the church went by a different name, or played just friendly fixtures between those years.

The Ashley Road Methodist Church AFC, which first appeared in 1928 was founded by former members of the Ashley Street's Church Scout troop, and it was renamed Leeds Ashley Road in 1962. The club's early years were spent running just youth teams in local competitions, with no open-age side. However, between 1934-37 a team from Ashley Road took part in the Leeds Non-Conformist League. That league merged with the Leeds Churches League in 1938, with the team spending two more seasons in that competition before war broke out. At the end of the 1937/38 season, there was appearance in the league's Senior Cup final, but sadly a 1-3 defeat to Theaker Lane Methodists. An under 17 team was entered into the Leeds Minor League between 1936-39, gradually establishing itself as a leading light in the competition.

However, it was in the years after the war that the name of Ashley Road Methodists really began to make a mark, on a local, regional, and national level, all under the tutelage of Leeds schoolteacher Ralph Naylor. Following a season in the Leeds Combination, the club began life in the Leeds Red Triangle in prolific fashion, and by the close of the 1948/49 season had won a considerable number of trophies.

Among the phenomenal success in the 1948/49 season were:
Leeds FA Junior Cup (for under 18s) winners: defeating Seacroft Community 4-0 in the final, on Saturday 30th April at the Burton's Sports ground,
Leeds Minor Cup Winners: defeating Leeds Stormcocks in a replayed final 2-0 on Wednesday 4th May at Elland Road (following a 2-2 draw)
Leeds Red Triangle Division Two cup final winners: A 1-0 victory over Oulton YC at Elland Road, on Friday 6th May in the final
Leeds Red Triangle Division Two championship final winners: A 3-1 win against New Wortley St Mary's, on Saturday 7th May (the team had already won the Division 2A title) in the final

The team also won the All England Methodist Junior Cup in the competition's first year and several players were selected for the Leeds FA under 16 team (a trend that would continue throughout the decade). Another Ashley Road age-group team continued to play in the Leeds Minor League.

The following season Ashley Road made its first appearance in the West Riding Junior Cup final, losing 2-3 to Whitwood (a team which secured its fourth trophy of the season) in the final at Altofts on Friday 12th May 1950, in front of 3,000 spectators. As consolation, the Leeds Junior Cup was retained. Teams were still engaged, with success, in the Red Triangle and Minor Leagues. On 1st September 1949, when previewing the Red Triangle league season, the *Yorkshire Post* had remarked, '...*under the competent guidance of Ralph Naylor...the Ashley Road coaching schemes are a good example of their sound methods, for each lad receives individual attention throughout the year, while the services of some of the country's greatest players are obtained when the summer camp is held in Morecambe.*'

The club's Junior team also won Leeds Hospital Cup against Leeds United Juniors at Elland Road during the 1949/50 season, at which point Naylor was approached by Leeds United officials with a view to incorporating his teams at Elland Road and taking up a coaching role there. Naylor declined the offer, Ashley Road remaining a stand-alone club for the time being. Leeds United Juniors had swept all before them in the Northern Intermediate League that season, and had not expected to lose to Ashley Road.

An open-age team re-emerged for the 1950/51 season, albeit consisting of players who had been playing junior football until recently. Rather than fielding a side in the Red Triangle's open-age division, the team was accepted into the West Yorkshire League – unsurprising given the club's lack of success – and finished fourth in a 16-team division. The club, which was sharing its Selby Road ground with Whitkirk Wanderers, had failed in its application to join the league a year earlier.

| 1950/51 West Yorkshire League Division Three (top 5) | P | W | D | L | F | A | Pts |
|---|---|---|---|---|---|---|---|
| Leeds Electric | 30 | 23 | 4 | 3 | 103 | 44 | 50 |
| Burley Trojans | 30 | 21 | 2 | 7 | 124 | 72 | 44 |
| Farsley Celtic reserves | 30 | 17 | 4 | 9 | 102 | 74 | 38 |
| Ashley Road Meths | 30 | 17 | 3 | 10 | 81 | 51 | 37 |
| L.I.C.S. Sports | 30 | 17 | 3 | 10 | 77 | 53 | 37 |

In the Red Triangle League, the Junior team won the Division Two championship again after defeating Henry Barran YC 4-1 at Hudson Road and then beat Town Colts in the league cup final. The under 17 team in Division Three actually lost its two year unbeaten record when it went down 0-2 to Leeds Wanderers in the league cup final at Oldfield Lane, but the side did retain its league title. The league's division were, at the time, not based on ability, but on age – Division Two featuring under 19 teams, Division Three under 17's, and the top division being the open-age division.

Leeds Wanderers were defeated in Leeds Junior Cup final (under 18s) on Saturday 12th May at Skelton Road, Osmondthorpe, but an even bigger success for the Ashley Road team was its first West Riding County Junior Cup final success, against Town Colts on the same ground six days later. Victory was not assured in all finals however, with defeats to Leeds United Juniors in the Hospital Cup final on Tuesday 15th May.

| 1951/52 West Yorkshire League Division Three (top 5) | P | W | D | L | F | A | Pts |
|---|---|---|---|---|---|---|---|
| Farsley Celtic reserves | 28 | 21 | 5 | 2 | 96 | 31 | 47 |
| Ashley Road Meths | 28 | 21 | 4 | 3 | 107 | 45 | 46 |
| Farnley WMC | 28 | 19 | 3 | 6 | 110 | 58 | 41 |
| D.P & E (Otley) res | 28 | 15 | 5 | 8 | 95 | 55 | 35 |
| Harrogate Town res | 28 | 14 | 6 | 8 | 97 | 77 | 34 |

The 1951/52 season saw the open-age team finish a close second in the West Yorkshire League Division Three behind Farsley Celtic's reserve team (a team which actually earned itself a double-promotion to the first division for the following season). The League Cup final was reached that season too, but the side went down to Burton's Sports.

However, the club's youngsters proved successful again as the Ashley Road bandwagon marched on. The West Riding County Junior Cup was retained, in a replay against Doncaster district side Armthorpe Rangers (after 1-1 draw), and the All England Methodist Junior Cup was won for a second time. In the

Red Triangle, the Division Three side defeated Leeds United Colts 2-1 in the league cup final, although the Leeds Junior Cup final was lost 2-4 against their old foes Leeds Wanderers at Skelton road at the end of April.

The summer of 1952 marked a big change in the course of the history of Ashley Road Methodists. Ashley Road's senior team in the West Yorkshire League became Yorkshire Amateur 'A' in the summer of 1952. The two clubs had joined forces prior to the 1952/53 season, with eight Ashley Road players having turned out for the Yorkshire Amateurs Yorkshire League side the following season. The agreement was that Ashley Road - which had won 22 trophies in the past four seasons - would limit itself to junior teams only, with players moving on to the Yorkshire Amateur team when they were old enough to play open-age football. Each club retained its own organisation, but there was also a joint executive of the two clubs, with Ralph Naylor of course heavily involved.

This led to a dilemma for several players in February 1953. On Saturday 14th the West Riding FA required Ashley Road Methodists under 16s to play their County Junior Cup semi-final against Leeds UYMI on the Skelton Road ground. However, the same day Yorkshire Amateurs - consisting of the same set of lads - were due to play an FA Youth Cup fourth round replay against Doncaster Rovers at Bracken Edge. In the event, the weather saved the day, with both ties being postponed and re-arranged for different dates.

The number of Ashley Road lads who went on to play at Football League or senior non-league clubs could fill a book in itself. Just three of these were; Left winger Jack Overfield one of the club's best known players, who went on to play for Yorkshire Amateurs and then Leeds United, where he made 159 appearances, scoring 20 times; John 'Jack' Fountain, who went on to play for Sheffield United, Swindon Town and York City between 1949-63. In 1964 he received a jail term when involved in a betting scandal; and Bob Oates, who played for England's Youth team in April 1974 against Northern Ireland, at Prenton Park, Tranmere. He was the first non-league player to don an England jersey for 37 years. He later went on to play for Scunthorpe United, where he made 315 league appearances, before spending one final season with Rochdale in 1983/84.

*From left to right, Jack Overfield, Jack Fountain, and Bob Oates*

The 1950s continued with Ashley Road Methodists making its mark in each season. 1952/53 saw more success, with a third successive County Junior Cup win, courtesy of a defeat of Ravensthorpe Albion in the final. The Red Triangle team won a Division Three league and cup double, defeating Stormcocks 3-0 at Bracken Edge late in April to win the latter.

There was a rare defeat in the 1953/54 Leeds FA Minor Cup final, Ashley Road going down 1-3 to St Patrick's, but despite that, Red Triangle success was never far away with the club regularly making the headlines for wins such as that in February 1954, a 22-0 rout of New Farnley.

The West Riding County Junior Cup was won four more times over the years, at the end of the 1964/65, 1966/67, 1971/72, and for seventh and final time, 1972/73 seasons.

Having become independent from Yorkshire Amateurs by the mid-1960s, Ashley Road re-started its own open-age team in the Red Triangle before being accepted into the semi-professional Yorkshire League for the 1965/66 season. In all, seventeen seasons were spent in this competition. The first was a baptism of fire, with only Brodsworth Main below the club in the final Division Two table (a massive eleven points below, in fact). The 1969/70 season proved to be the club's worst ever in the Yorkshire League, with 16th position in an 18 team league seeing the club relegated to the re-formed Third Division. To be fair, only the top eight teams avoided the drop in the league reorganisation.

Promotion back to Division Two was achieved at the end of the 1971/72 season when the divisional title was won, three points ahead of Harrogate Town. A further promotion as runner-up (and nine places higher than their old friends Yorkshire Amateur) at the end of 1975/76 saw Ashley Road in Division One for the first time.

Following tenth place at the end of the previous season, team strengthening during the summer paid off as, for the first and only time, Leeds Ashley Road finished top of the Yorkshire League at the close of the 1980/81 season, two points ahead of Emley, and four ahead of North Ferriby United. One year later Emley turned the tables, with a two point difference between themselves, Guiseley, and Ashley Road.

As part of a wider restructuring of non-league football in the north of England, The Yorkshire and Midland Counties Leagues merged in the summer of 1982 to form the Northern Counties (East) League (In the same way that the Cheshire County League and Lancashire Combination merged to form the North West Counties League). However, with re-organisation came improved grading standards for those teams involved, and Ashley Road's ground at the time, at Temple Newsam, was nowhere near the standard for that required for the new league's Premier Division. So, despite its recent success, the club was faced with life in Division One (North), and with no chance of promotion due to its lack of floodlights and spectator facilities at its council owned pitch. The season was not a successful one, with Ashley Road, having lost many of its championship winning team, finishing well down the table in 10th place. At the end of the season, a decision to disband the senior team was made, and it has never been revived.

| Leeds Ashley Road - League Record 1965-83 | | | | | | | | |
|---|---|---|---|---|---|---|---|---|
| Yorkshire League | P | W | D | L | F | A | Pts | Pos |
| 1965/66 Division Two | 28 | 7 | 4 | 17 | 47 | 61 | 18 | 14/15 |
| 1966/67 Division Two | 32 | 13 | 4 | 15 | 53 | 67 | 30 | 10/17 |
| 1967/68 Division Two | 32 | 16 | 5 | 11 | 55 | 51 | 37 | 6/17 |
| 1968/69 Division Two | 32 | 11 | 10 | 11 | 55 | 65 | 32 | 10/17 |
| 1969/70 Division Two | 34 | 9 | 5 | 20 | 47 | 84 | 23 | 16/18 |
| 1970/71 Division Three | 28 | 10 | 7 | 11 | 48 | 41 | 27 | 9/15 |
| 1971/72 Division Three | 26 | 16 | 7 | 3 | 58 | 21 | 39 | 1/14 |
| 1972/73 Division Two | 30 | 15 | 5 | 10 | 57 | 37 | 35 | 5/16 |
| 1973/74 Division Two | 30 | 12 | 6 | 12 | 41 | 47 | 30 | 7/16 |
| 1974/75 Division Two | 28 | 9 | 5 | 14 | 32 | 37 | 23 | 12/15 |
| 1975/76 Division Two | 28 | 18 | 7 | 3 | 58 | 23 | 43 | 2/15 |
| 1976/77 Division One | 30 | 16 | 6 | 8 | 48 | 35 | 38 | 5/16 |
| 1977/78 Division One | 30 | 9 | 6 | 15 | 35 | 45 | 24 | 12/16 |
| 1978/79 Division One | 30 | 10 | 8 | 12 | 34 | 37 | 28 | 9/16 |
| 1979/80 Division One | 30 | 10 | 8 | 12 | 39 | 36 | 28 | 10/16 |
| 1980/81 Division One | 30 | 18 | 8 | 4 | 58 | 25 | 44 | 1/16 |
| 1981/82 Division One | 30 | 15 | 9 | 6 | 44 | 30 | 39 | 3/16 |
| Northern Counties (East) League | | | | | | | | |
| 1982/83 Division 1N | 26 | 7 | 6 | 13 | 30 | 44 | 20 | 10/14 |

The Ashley Road Junior set-up was not finished however, despite Naylor having retired several years earlier, and in 1984/85, and 1985/86, the club was back to winning ways. Ashley Road were Leeds Minor Cup winners in those two seasons, and as late as 1988/89 the same club had its name on the Leeds Sunday Junior Cup.

## Grounds

After World War Two the club spent a time playing at Manston Park in the Crossgates area of the city, before a move to another open ground in Roundhay Park. The open-age team made another move, sharing with Swillington Miners Welfare at the Miners Welfare Sports Ground on Wakefield Road, in the summer of 1965 when it was elected to the Yorkshire League, ironically replacing Swillington in the league.

A later move was made to the 'Pavilion' pitch at Temple Newsam Sports Arena, which was surrounded by a cinder running track. This ground had no spectator facilities and was very basic, which prevented the team from playing in the top division of the Northern Counties (East) League. It was surrounded by a cinder running track which for a while was used by Leeds City Athletic Club among others, before that club moved to improved facilities in the north of the city.

*Ashley Road's Temple Newsam ground in more recent times*

## Ashley Road in FA Competitions

Leeds Ashley Road played in the FA Amateur Cup, and then the FA Vase, which replaced it, between 1964-83. Its first Amateur Cup appearance, as a Red Triangle League team ended in a narrow 2-3 home defeat to West Yorkshire League side and future Yorkshire League opponents, Guiseley, which was certainly no disgrace. The only time Ashley Road progressed past the Second Qualifying Round was in 1972/73 season when home wins against Whitkirk Wanderers (4-1) and Yorkshire Amateur (2-0), was followed by a 3-3 draw at Ossett Albion. The home replay was lost 0-2.

The 1968/69 season was significant in that Hedon & Marfleet United were defeated at home in a preliminary round tie, by the remarkable score of 9-5.

The club's best run came in its second season in the FA Vase, 1969/70, when a run through to the Fifth Round – the last sixteen – brought the club back into the spotlight. The run started in the First Round, with a narrow 1-0 win at Whitkirk Wanderers, followed by another close game at Guiseley, which was won 3-2. Chadderton were defeated 2-0 at home in the Third Round, bringing a last 32 tie at home to Manchester side Wythenshawe Amateurs. The match ended 1-1, before a narrow 2-1 win in the replay. The Quarter-final tie was at home against Leicester team Friar Lane Old Boys, who won another tight game, 2-1.

Ashley Road's last Vase appearance was a 0-1 home loss to Blue Star (Newcastle) in a Second Round tie in the 1982/83 season.

A letter written by Ralph Naylor, the main man behind the Ashley Road Methodist Church AFC. Reference is made to the coaching camps that were run by the club at Morecambe. At the time, there was surely no bigger star than Stan Mortensen, the Blackpool and England centre-forward, who was one of those who helped out at the camps.

# LEEDS ASHLEY ROAD A.F.C.

Members of the Northern Counties Eastern Football League

TEMPLE NEWSAM SPORTS ARENA  Founded 1904

## LEEDS ASHLEY ROAD FOOTBALL CLUB

Surely one of the best known, well respected and longest established of amateur sporting organisations in this part of the world, Ashley Road shares with several famous soccer clubs (Aston Villa for one) the common ancestry of Sunday School sport — indeed, by many they are still referred to as "the Methodists."

The original club was formed in 1904, and apart from the closedown from 1914 to 1918, lasted until 1924. Revived four years later in 1928 by former members of the Church Scout troop, it has kept a continuous and vigorous existence ever since, except for the period of World War II, from 1939 to 1945. Eighteen of its playing members in 1939 lost their lives in the War.

Ashley Road's successes have been in the areas of junior football and of soccer coaching. Many of the present League side have graduated from the club's junior ranks. Over the years, all players and staff have been voluntary and unpaid, with a subscribing membership an integral part of the set-up. For years they dominated junior soccer in Yorkshire — for instance in the period between 1946 and 1952 they annexed over forty trophies — two All-England cups among them. Twice since then they have got into the last sixteen of the F.A. Youth Cup.

However, probably the greatest achievements of Ashley Road have been witnessed during the last two seasons, finishing County Cup semi-finalists and Yorkshire League Division 1 runners-up in 1982 and, even better, League Cup semi-finalists, County Cup finalists and Yorkshire League Division 1 champions in 1981.

Ashley Road's contribution to soccer over the past 80 years has been considerable — long may it continue.

**YOU GET MORE THAN JUST A DISCOUNT AT COMET**

Radio — Television — TV Rental — Video — Hi Fi — Photographic — Kitchen Furniture — Electrical and Gas appliances

# Leeds Malvern
# 1896-1924
*'Lesser lights'*

One of the lesser lights in Leeds and district football circles, Leeds Malvern's first reported fixtures were early in 1896, with several non-competitive matches played against local opposition in March of that year. The club was an offshoot of the well-established Beeston Hill Parish Church club, formed by several lads who didn't agree with that club's policy of only selecting players who attended the church. The South Leeds rugby team disbanded around that time, so Malvern took over their ground, which was situated behind the Tommy Wass Hotel on Dewsbury Road.

Friendly fixtures continued until the club joined the West Yorkshire League for the 1897/88 season. Playing in the South section of Division Two, the club struggled badly, winning only one of the ten fixtures completed and with only Leeds Cameron below them in the eight team table. The team, which is believed to have moved to a on pitch on Prince's Avenue, in the Soldier's Field / Roundhay Park area, disbanded at the end of the season through a lack of funds, with several of its team going on to play for Leeds Salem the following season. The Beeston Hill Parish Church club itself joined the West Yorkshire League at the same time as Leeds Malvern, being admitted to Division Two North and playing in the league until 1905.

The Leeds Malvern name was revived sporadically for friendly fixtures between 1901-08, and in the 1908/09 season, the team played mainly friendly fixtures from a home ground in Beeston, as well as competing in the junior Holbeck & District Cup. It reached the semi-final of that competition, losing 1-4 to Holbeck St Francis in the semi-final early in January 1909.

Leeds Malvern re-emerged in Division Two of the Leeds Amateur League in the 1919/20 season, winning the divisional title at its first attempt, and also winning the Leeds Amateur Cup, defeating Leeds Churchville 2-1 at Oldfield Lane, the Leeds Schools FA ground, in what was wretched weather on Saturday 10th April 1920. Churchill had won the cup in the final two seasons before the competition was suspended for the duration of World War One, and led by a single goal at half time, but goals from Foster and Lewis saw Malvern, who played down the slope in the second half, win its first silverware.

Just four days earlier, the Malvern team had surprisingly lost 1-2 to Prospect United in the Hoyland Smith Cup final at Airebank, Hunslet before 3,000 spectators.

The *Yorkshire Post* reported that there were three Malvern players in the Leeds United team that played its final Midland League fixture at Elland Road against Scunthorpe United on Wednesday 28th April 1920, although they were not named.

Malvern retained the Leeds Amateur Cup following season, although the 1920/21 cup final replay was held over until Wednesday 7th September 1921, with only players registered before the end of the season eligible to play. Malvern's opponents at Elland Road were Harrogate West Park, who put up a strong fight until a remarkable spell just before half time when Malvern's reserve centre forward Pybus scored no less than four times, three of them being headers. Three more second-half goals from Holt (2) and Maxfield were enough to see Malvern easy winners in the end. The teams had drawn 0-0 at the same venue on Monday 2nd May before 3,000 spectators.

On Wednesday 11th May 1921, Malvern defeated Morley St Andrew's 6-3 in the Amateur League's Sugg Cup final at the city's Goodman Street grounds. Malvern finished runners-up to St Andrew's in the league's Senior Division (South), St Andrew's themselves losing to North Division Prospect United in the league final.

Malvern played in the Leeds Amateur League's Senior Division in the 1921/22 season. Two points were deducted early in the season for a rule infringement, although that didn't really matter as the club finished mid-table and trophyless in the league. Yeadon Celtic won the title. A Malvern reserve team finished third of eight teams that completed the season in the league's Reserve Division.

On Saturday 13th May 1922, Malvern played the holders, Castleford & Allerton United, in the final of the Leeds Hospitals Cup on the ground of Castleford Town. This cup was at one time the premier cup competition in West Yorkshire, being initiated before the West Riding County Cup, although its prestige had waned somewhat by the 1920s. However, it was still highly regarded among Leeds clubs and their followers, although on this occasion two-thousand spectators went home disappointed as the game finished goal-less after extra-time. No replay has been traced.

However, despite indifferent results in the league, the 1921/22 season was the one that put Leeds Malvern on the national stage, with an amazing run in its first appearance in the FA Amateur Cup.

Local rivals Leeds Harehills were defeated 1-0 at home in the First Qualifying Round, and this was followed by a more convincing 4-0 defeat of Rawdon at the next stage. Another home tie at the third qualifying stage saw York team Acomb WMC defeated 4-1, before a much stiffer tie at Armley in the final qualifying round. Following a 1-1 draw, the replay was won 4-1, setting up a First Round proper tie with Darlington Railway Athletic. Following a 2-2 draw at home, Malvern thought they were through following a 3-2 win after extra-time at Brinkburn Road, Darlington, after having trailed 0-2 early in the game. However, due to a rule infringement the tie had to be re-played. Luckily, Leeds Malvern won 3-0 at the third time of asking on Tuesday 27th December 1921.

The club's Second Round tie was the most exciting of all. South Bank East End were defeated 4-3 at Elland Road, which had made available by the directors of Leeds United, on Saturday 7th January. Goals from Wilkins (2), Shires and Hara proved just enough in front of almost 5,000 spectators.

*Yorkshire Post,* Monday 9th January 1922

ENGLISH AMATEUR CUP – SECOND ROUND. LEEDS MALVERN ENTER NEXT ROUND:

'HAT TRICK' BY BROWN

*The 4,935 who paid £198 to witness this match at the ground of the Leeds United Club received value for their money, as in addition seven goals being scored, the quality the play was always good and often very exciting. Soon after the start looked very much as if the Leeds men were going run away with the men from South Bank, as they were two goals in front after only five minutes' play. The 'Bankers',' however, refused to be stampeded, and remainder the match was fought out amidst many fluctuations of fortune, but Malvern certainly earned their right to a place in the round.*

*The spectators had not long to wait for thrills. In three minutes Malvern forged ahead, Shires scoring from a well-placed corner by Holt, whilst a minute later Wilkins smartly put the local men further in front. An unproductive period followed, but eventually Brown scored for South Bank, and Wilkins obtained his second goal for Malvern, while Brown again rattled the home net for the visitors, the three goals having been obtained in as many minutes. At half-time Malvern were leading 3 goals 2.*

*Malvern re-opened with great dash, but could not penetrate the South Bank last line of defence until the game was well advanced, although awarded a penalty kick. Eventually, however, Hara (centre half-back) shot a clever goal for the locals, and Brown immediately replied for the 'Bankers' thus accomplishing the 'hat trick.'*

*Result: – Leeds Malvern 4 goals, South Bank East End 3 goals.*

The third round took Malvern all the way to the south coast to meet RMA Portsmouth, the Royal Marines Artillery team, on Saturday 11th February. A 1-1 draw, after extra-time, was the result after Buckley's first half header from a Shires cross for the Yorkshire team had given them the lead. With Elland Road unavailable, it was hoped that the Huddersfield Town ground at Leeds Road could be used, as Huddersfield Town had offered it free of charge, but the competition rules prevented teams from playing ties outside their own town, so its ground at Beeston Royds was used for the replay, held the following Saturday.

Malvern made the perfect start to the replay when Buckley scored after only five minutes, again from a Shires cross, but despite being the better team for long periods of the game, the 'home' team was defeated 1-2. The Navy team went down 0-1 at home to eventual winners Bishop Auckland in its Quarter Final tie.

The *Yorkshire Post,* on Monday 20th February 1922, carried a report of the game, a report that was perhaps rather harsh on the losers,

### THE AMATEUR CUP. THIRD ROUND TIE. LEEDS MALVERN v ROYAL MARINE ARTILLERY.

*After playing a very plucky game, in which they did appreciably more attacking than their opponents, Leeds Malvern were defeated in the replayed third round tie of the English Amateur Cup by the Royal Marine Artillery (Portsmouth). The game was played at Beeston Royds before a crowd of about 4,000. The gross receipts were £140 – but the ground is not properly enclosed, and a canvas screen, about 130 years long was blown down by the wind before the match.*

*Malvern took the lead after only five minutes. Shires, who, individually, was the beat forward on the field, making a tricky run along the left wing, and putting across a centre, from which Buckley scored. The home defence, under pressure, did not inspire confidence, Kelly, in goal, being distinctly nervous, and running recklessly out of goal., whilst he persistently used his feet instead of his hands. Graham, the right back, had no effective understanding with his half back, and allowed the opposing wing forward yards start in many attacks. The Marines equalised at the end of half an hour. Smoxall scoring during a scramble in front of goal, and five minutes later the visiting centre forward, obtained what proved to be the winning goal.*

*Thanks chiefly to the efforts of Hara, the centre-half, who opened out game with good judgement, Malvern had many simple looking opportunities of scoring; but Pybus, Buckley, and Wilkins- the latter particularly – in their anxiety, could nothing right in front of goal. The Marines defended very stolidly, and were the more powerful side in the closing stages. Result: U.M.A. (Portsmouth) 2 goals, Malvern 1 goal.*

There was a new competition for Leeds Malvern to look forward to the following season. In response to the formation of the Bradford-based West Riding County Amateur League, the Leeds football authorities backed the rebranding of the Leeds Amateur League's top division as the West Yorkshire Amateur League, of which the club became founder members in 1922.

The inaugural West Yorkshire Amateur League season in 1922/23 was a successful one for the club, with Malvern edging out local rivals Leeds Harehills at the top of the league upon completion of its regular league fixtures. However, the team lost-out in the top four 'Shield' play-offs to Yeadon Celtic, who then defeated Harehills in the final. Malvern was also successful in the Leeds & District Senior Cup, defeating Leeds Harehills 3-2 at Elland Road on Wednesday 25th April 1923 in what was *'a severe tussle'* according to the *Yorkshire Post*. The two rivals were to meet again only days later, drawing 2-2 in the league cup final on Saturday 5th May 1923. The replay was left over until the start of the following season, with Harehills, who had since moved up to the Yorkshire League, winning 2-1 on Wednesday 5th September.

Despite all of its success, and a bye straight through to the first round of the FA Amateur Cup due its success the year before, a 1-4 defeat at Eston United, Redcar, precluded any further progress for Malvern that season.

Sadly the Malvern team was only to last one more season. The team surprisingly finished the bottom half of the West Yorkshire Amateur League table for the 1923/24 season, and went out of the FA Amateur Cup at the first qualifying stage, losing 0-3 at fellow Leeds side Whitehall Printeries. Malvern did however reached the final of the league's Spartan Shield competition, but lost 1-2 to Garforth Athletic at the Black Road football ground on Saturday 15th March 1924. Malvern's second team was by now playing in the Leeds Alliance, one of a number of local league competitions that emerged between the Wars.

The West Yorkshire Amateur League disintegrated in the summer of 1924, as indeed did the Malvern club itself, only a year after having been league champions, and two years on from reaching the final stages of the national amateur competition. It is likely that the lack of a suitable ground may have led to this, although at the time of Malvern's demise, it is interesting to note that the club's great rival Leeds Harehills changed its name to Leeds City.

However, left over to the start of the following season was the final of the Beeston Charity Cup competition which Malvern had qualified to play in. A Leeds Malvern eleven was mustered for the occasion, defeating East End WMC 5-0 on Monday 15th September 1924, with goals from the appropriately named Shooter (2), Mitchell, Cook, and Teale, before the players once again went their own way.

The Leeds Malvern name was revived just before World War Two, with a team playing in the top division of the Leeds Red Triangle for the 1939/40 season, but sadly World War Two put paid to any chance that club might have had of establishing itself.

# Luddendenfoot
# 1911-1984
### *'Don't mention the FA Cup'*

The village of Luddenden Foot, better known in current times as Luddendenfoot, has a population of just under 3,000. It lies to the west of Halifax, in the Upper Calder Valley between Sowerby Bridge and Mytholmroyd, and below the village of Luddenden. Predominantly a textile village, the Rochdale Canal and railway station (the latter of which opened in 1840 and closed in 1962) enabled the village to prosper, with the River Calder and main Halifax to Todmorden Road (now the A646) enabling easy access despite the narrow, steep sided nature of the Calder Valley.

The original Luddenden Foot Football Club played under rugby rules, often using the local General Rawdon Hotel for its meetings and other official business, and is reported to have been 'flourishing' at its AGM in April 1882. The club was founded early in the 1880s and by the 1893/94 season was playing in the Yorkshire Rugby Union's 'Third Competition – Group B'. It was defunct by the end of 1900, along with many other teams in that competition, but reformed a few years later in the Northern Union (Rugby League).

Luddenden Foot Albions was the first association team to play competitive football in the village, with an appearance in the short-lived Elland & District League in the 1902/03 season. By 1904/05 Albions had moved on to the Halifax & District League after a season of playing friendlies, before moving quickly on to the Ackroydon League at in the summer of 1905, at the same time dropping the 'Foot' part of the name. Luddenden Foot St Mary's also spent the 1905/06 season in the Ackroydon League, which was one of a number of short-lived leagues in the Halifax district in the early years of the Twentieth Century.

A separate Luddenden Foot AFC took part in a 14-team Halifax & District League in the 1905/06 season, but disbanded at the end of the season despite finishing well clear of the bottom clubs..

By 1906/07 there was no shortage of local clubs. Luddenden Albions & Luddenden Foot St Mary's were in division two of the Halifax & District League. Luddenden Foot White Star played in the Halifax League's 'Combination division', having played in the Salterhebble League Junior Division the season before. A Luddenden Foot New Road also played friendly fixtures this season.

However, these clubs seem to have folded or reverted to friendly fixtures only around the same time as they were all missing after the summer of 1907, presumably due to the novelty of the 'new' sport in the district having worn off.

After a few years without a club of note, a new Luddenden Foot AFC was formed in the village in 1911 and it is this club that carved a name for itself over the years. Between 1911-14 & 1918-36 it competed in the Halifax & District League, although success was not immediate. Luddendenfoot Boys Brigade also ran football teams in the years prior to World War One.

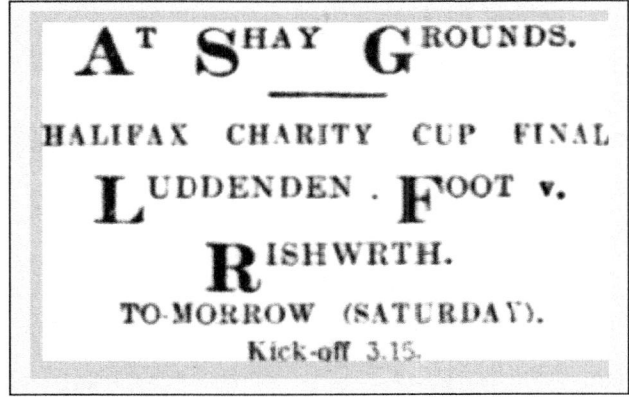

Luddendenfoot's first ever success was in the Halifax Charity Cup at the end of the 1923/24 season. In fact, the final was not concluded until September. The initial tie between Luddendenfoot and Rishworth at The Shay on Saturday 3rd May 1924 ended as a 1-1 draw after nearly three-hours play in mud and rain. The replay, on the Grantham Road ground of Boothtown AFC was played on Saturday 30th August, and that also ended in a tie, one goal each. A second replay, on the same ground, on Tuesday 2nd September was finally won by Luddendenfoot, thanks to a last minute winner from Senior. The team was treated to a civic welcome on their return to the village Institute.

*Halifax Evening Courier*, Wednesday 24th September 1924,

**Their First Trophy - Luddenden Foot Footballers Rejoice**

*Members and supporters of Luddenden Foot AFC. met last night in the Assembly Hall at the Institute for the purpose of celebrating the recent success achieved by the team in winning the Halifax Charity Cup, this being the first trophy which the local club has ever captured. There was a large and enthusiastic attendance, including a number of ladies, also old players and Coun. E E Cockcroft, JP, presided, and supporting him was the club president, Mr H Hellewell.*

*In a happy and encouraging address, the chairman congratulated the players on their success, and expressed the hope that they would have another successful season and bring further credit to the district. He spoke of the benefits of good, clean sport, and he hoped the local lads would always play the game in a true sportsmanlike manner.*

*The president said he was a strong believer in amateur sport, and the Luddenden Foot club could always depend upon his interest and support so long as they ran the organisation on sound, amateur lines, and played the game in a clean manner. Mr Hellewell congratulated the local lad, W Jackson, upon his advance in the football sphere, and trusted he would do well with the Stoke club. He then presented the cup to the captain of the team, B Senior, and the medals to the following players: B Spencer, W Lambert, W Wright, F Murty, W Jackson, W Little, W Halstead, J Hitchen, S Jackson, S Cryer, W Mundy (reserve), and B Senior.*

*On behalf of the players and officials of the club, he also presented a toilet set to W Jackson (his brother S Jackson, received the gift), who has left the club for Stoke AFC, coupled with best wishes for future success.*

*Mr. Frank Calvert, secretary of the Halifax and District AF League and secretary of the Charity Cup committee, addressed the company and congratulated the local club upon their success.*

*Mr J W Parker, club secretary, also spoke and expressed the thanks of the members to the president for his practical interest in their welfare. He mentioned that Mr Hellewell had paid for the engraving of the names on the medals.*

*The cup was filled, and all drank to the toast of 'Future success to the Luddenden Foot AFC.'*

*Luddendenfoot AFC 1923/24*
*The team is photographed with the Halifax Charity Cup*

The club also won the Halifax Association Challenge Cup at the end of the 1935/36 season, defeating Hipperholme & Lightcliffe 3-0 in the final on Wednesday 29th April 1936 at The Shay, after having defeated Mytholmroyd by seven clear goals in the semi-final. This is almost certain to have been the 'league cup final' although both this and the 'other' Halifax Cup final, played the same week were referred to as 'Halifax Association Cup final'. Luddendenfoot went on to lose to Boothtown in the 1936/37 and 1937/38 Halifax Association Cup finals

With the Halifax League in decline, and lacking strength in depth, the club made a move to the Bradford Amateur League in 1936, staying in this competition until the outbreak of World War Two. The strength of the club was apparent, with a runner-up position behind Bolton Woods at the close of the 1937/38 season. This proved a frustrating season for Luddendenfoot, as two cup finals were also lost.

*Halifax Evening Courier,* Monday 2nd May 1938

*BRADFORD SENIOR CUP FINAL. Luddenden Foot lost their second cup final in two days when they were beaten by three clear goals by Bolton Woods in the final of the Bradford Senior Cup competition, played on the Manningham Mills ground on Saturday night. Bolton Woods were worthy winners of a keen and interesting game. Luddenden Foot, who were without the services of Jackson and Wadsworth, gave a good display under the circumstances, but were obviously a tired team after their recent exertions. They had chances early on to win the match, including a penalty award in the first five minutes, which was not turned to account.*

*Two goals in arrears at half-time, any chance the locals had of winning disappeared when Thorpe was taken off with a leg injury. Luddenden Foot did well to hold their opponents to a goal in this half Ackroyd, T Hurl and Shackleton were best of the 'Foot' defenders but there was again a lack of punch in the front line where Beard and O'Shea were best. This is the fourth season running in which Bolton Woods have won the trophy. The cup and miniature trophies were presented by Mrs. Spencer, wife of a Bradford League committee official.*

Two days earlier, Luddendenfoot had been defeated for the second year running in the Halifax & District Cup final by Boothtown at the Shay.

The Bradford Amateur League title was won, however, the following season when Thackley were pipped at the post.

### 1939/40 Halifax War Time Association League
**Senior Section**

| | P | W | D | L | F | A | Pts |
|---|---|---|---|---|---|---|---|
| Holmfield | 12 | 9 | 2 | 1 | 66 | 17 | 20 |
| Luddendenfoot | 12 | 8 | 2 | 2 | 50 | 26 | 18 |
| Siddal Park | 12 | 6 | 1 | 5 | 40 | 38 | 13 |
| Stainland | 12 | 6 | 1 | 5 | 33 | 36 | 13 |
| Norland | 12 | 5 | 2 | 5 | 34 | 42 | 12 |
| Dean Clough | 11 | 2 | 0 | 9 | 19 | 45 | 9 |
| Asquith's | 11 | 1 | 0 | 10 | 19 | 51 | 2 |

The club lost its Holme Recreation Ground during the summer of 1939 when it was closed by the local council for tipping purposes. A new field at Ellen Royd was initially earmarked, but eventually a ground at 'The Astley's' near Tuel Lane Top was obtained. The rural site, close to Warley, and adjacent to Sowerby Bridge Church Institute Cricket Club is still being used as football pitches to this day.

Luddendenfoot's committee had planned to apply for membership of the West Riding County Amateur League, but with the ground issue not resolved, an application to the league arrived too late. With War breaking out, the team chose to join the Halifax League, which operated a special War-Time league and cup competition for the next six seasons. Luddendenfoot won the league in four of its six seasons, doing the league and cup double twice.

The following successes were achieved during this time:

1940/41: Luddendenfoot just pipped an Army XI and early leaders St Pauls' for the title in the 13-team league. The Army XI did defeat them 4-2 in the league's Robert's Cup final, however.

1941/42: The club finished behind Elland Brotherhood in the league, but won the Robert's League Cup.

1942/43: In a fifteen-team league, Luddendenfoot went through the entire season undefeated, and retained the Robert's League Cup.

1943/44: The club ran two teams in the league, the first team achieving the league and cup double for the second successive season, defeating Asquith's 3-0 in the Robert's Cup final.

1944/45: Luddendenfoot were easy winners of the league again, but did not win the league cup on this occasion.

In the summer of 1945, the team did finally take its place in the West Riding County Amateur League. It's run of success would continue in this higher standard of competition. But despite all of its league success, it should be added that in the years leading up to World War Two, Luddendenfoot endured what is possibly one of the worst set of results of any club in national competitions. Twenty three of

### Luddendenfoot in FA Competitions

**FA Cup**
*15 ties over 14 seasons*

1926/27: EPR Guiseley (H) 0-2
1927/28: PR Darfield United (H) 2-6
1928/29: EPR Horsforth (A) 1-7
1929/30: PR Farsley Celtic (H) 0-4
1930/31: Q1 Monckton Athletic (A) 1-9
1931/32: PR Frickley Colliery (A) 0-7
1932/33: PR Guiseley (A) 2-6
1934/35: PR Goldthorpe United (H) 1-5
1935/36: EPR Denaby United (H) 0-6
1936/37: EPR Bentley Colliery (A) 0-3
1937/38: EPR Farsley Celtic (H) 0-0, (A) 0-2
1938/39: EPR Yorkshire Amateurs (A) 1-3
1939/40: EPR Goole Town (A) 1-8
(competition abandoned following EPR)
1947/48: PR Bradford United (A) 0-1

**FA Amateur Cup**
*9 ties in 9 seasons*

1925/26: Q1 Liversedge (A) 1-11
1926/27: Q2 Guiseley (A) 0-7
1927/28: Q2 Horsforth (H) 1-5
1928/29: Q2 Guiseley (A) 1-3
1929/30: Q2 Knaresborough Town (A) 1-10
1930/31: Q2 Whitehall Printeries (A) 0-2
1931/32: Q3 Meltham Mills (A) 2-6
1932/33: Q2 Guiseley (A) 2-7
1936/37: PR Ravensthorpe (H) 2-4

*EPR = Extra Preliminary Round*
*PR = Preliminary Round*
*Q1/2/3 = First/ Second/ Third Qualifying Round*

its twenty-four ties in the FA Cup and FA Amateur Cup competitions ended in defeat, many of them heavy, and only a 0-0 draw with Farsley Celtic in the FA Cup in the 1937/38 season broke the duck. The results are worth including.

***

Luddendenfoot returned to The Holme after a fourteen-year absence enforced by the park's closure, on Friday 28th August 1953. The opening event was a match against a Halifax League team, which was followed by a social evening. In addition to The Holme, the reserve team also used a field at Kershaw House, off Luddenden Lane (the site of which is now covered by houses) as the local Boys Brigade's football club also had use of The Holme on alternate weekends. A ground at Town Lane, Warley had been used by the reserve the season before that.

A ground at Top Shutts had been earmarked by the club in case The Holme had not been ready on time. Those involved were desperate to leave their current ground, which, being close to Warley, was too far outside the village and had led to lower than hoped for attendances.

However, there were problems, as the club could not charge admission charges for its matches due to the park being owned by the Sowerby Bridge Urban District Council, which was a problem as the club was fined by the West Riding FA for not charging admission for its County Cup ties.

The team reached Halifax Association Challenge Cup final, at The Shay on Saturday 5th May 1956, after having defeated St Bernard's Rovers in a semi-final replay. However, Holmfield had the edge on the day and won 3-2.

In terms of the West Riding County Amateur League, Luddendenfoot had become one of the league's leading lights by the end of the 1950s, and enjoyed great success in the league and league cup, as well as lifting the county cup.

### 1960-61 West Riding County Amateur League

| | P | W | D | L | F | A | Pts |
|---|---|---|---|---|---|---|---|
| **Luddendenfoot** | 26 | 18 | 5 | 3 | 88 | 32 | 41 |
| Liversedge | 26 | 15 | 5 | 6 | 66 | 50 | 35 |
| Thackley | 26 | 14 | 6 | 6 | 87 | 52 | 34 |
| **Bradford Rovers** | 26 | 15 | 4 | 7 | 92 | 60 | 34 |
| Brook Sports | 26 | 14 | 4 | 8 | 85 | 58 | 32 |
| Thornhill Edge | 26 | 15 | 2 | 9 | 84 | 69 | 32 |
| Manningham Mills | 26 | 13 | 3 | 10 | 70 | 61 | 29 |
| Yeadon Celtic | 26 | 11 | 4 | 11 | 71 | 66 | 26 |
| Firth Sports | 26 | 8 | 8 | 10 | 53 | 63 | 24 |
| Lightcliffe | 26 | 9 | 6 | 11 | 57 | 74 | 24 |
| Birkenshaw Rovers | 26 | 7 | 3 | 16 | 63 | 93 | 17 |
| Golcar United | 26 | 7 | 1 | 18 | 61 | 83 | 15 |
| Rawdon Old Boys | 26 | 6 | 3 | 17 | 44 | 76 | 15 |
| Int Harvesters | 26 | 2 | 4 | 20 | 28 | 109 | 8 |

The league title was won no less than five times between 1960-1974, making the club one of the most successful in the competition: Titles were won consecutively in the 1960/61 and 1961/62 seasons (following two third place finishes in the seasons prior to these titles), and a decade later three times in four seasons; 1970/71, 1972/73, and 1973/74.

Despite losing three league cup finals, 1959/60 to Bradford Rovers, 1960/61 to Thackley, and 1970/71 to Silsden, there was some success in cup competitions for Luddendenfoot when, in 1972/73, it became West Riding County Cup winners, defeating Fryston 3-1 in the final, which was played at East End Park, Leeds.

The Halifax & District Cup was also won, when, on 1st May 1973, Hebden Royd Red Star were defeated 4-0 in the final, held at The Shay. On top of these successes, the West Riding County Amateur League cup was won in the 1956/57 season, when its great rivals Bradford Rovers were defeated in the final.

The 1974 title success was the last for Luddendenfoot in its current league, as it resigned from the County Amateur League at the end of the 1976/77 season.

Luddendenfoot's switched to the West Yorkshire League provided further success, with the club winning the league's first division title in both 1981/82 and 1983/84, although entry to the Premier Division was at the time by invitation only. Fellow Calder Valley club Hebden Bridge won the division one title in 1984/85, with Halifax AFC doing the same a year later, in a short period when Halifax district teams turned to that league instead of the County Amateur League. Willowfield Celtic also played in the West Yorkshire league during the 1990's, also playing out of Holmes Park, by which time Luddendenfoot FC had sadly folded.

The name has been revived at least once, most noticeably in the name of the team that swept up through the Halifax & District League to win the Premier Division title in the 2008/09 season before resigning from the league during the following season. The club had played as Golden Lion FC until the summer of 2006.

Holmes Park, which sits between the Rochdale Canal and River Calder is still used for football today.

# Manningham Mills
# 1909-88
### *'The mill team'*

Manningham Mills AFC was one of the best known names in Bradford amateur football for many decades, playing for much of its existence in the strongest league in the West Riding, yet its name is missing from the winners lists for all but a handful of seasons.

The thousands of employees of Lister's Manningham Mills supported an incredible range of social, cultural, and sporting activities, of which football was just one, the women's soccer team for a time becoming even better known than its men's counterpart. Between six and seven thousand employees of the mills contributed a small part of their wages to the recreational club there.

There were already well-established cricket (established in 1865) and cycling (founded around 1894) clubs operating under the Manningham Mills banner when the association football team emerged in 1909. Tennis, table tennis, snooker, bowls, and ballroom dancing were some of the other sports and pastimes on offer to the workforce.

The newly formed association football team was elected straight into the top division of the Bradford & District League for the 1909/10 season, alongside the likes of a reformed Girlington (the first association team to play home fixtures at Valley Parade), Silsden, Keighley Celtic, Horsforth, Windhill Parish Church, and local rivals Manningham AFC in a sixteen-strong league. The majority of clubs in the top division were by now well-established and ambitious organisations, so it can be assumed that the Mills side consisted of players of a high quality. However, the club disappeared as quickly as it had arrived, perhaps having overestimated its chances in the district's top division. The club generally struggled in the competition, with expense also a probable factor in the decision to fold the team. The paying of players was the norm for teams in the league, and any Mills players that made an impact would undoubtably have been enticed to clubs that offered financial incentives.

The team was reformed in 1912, with its team of young players all being workers in the Manningham Mills complex. The team played in the lower divisions of the Bradford Central League between 1912-14, a far more modest level than three years earlier, and one in which payments to players were not required. Competitive games were played in Manningham (Lister) Park, with the club's dressing rooms located in an outbuilding at the nearby Beamsley Hotel. Club practices were said to have been fitted in during the week in the workers' lunch hour. The team didn't play competitively from the 1914/15 season, and throughout World War One, though.

Just after World War One, the club moved to the new Manningham Mills sports ground, on Scotchman Road, adjacent to the mills. The grounds included cricket and football pitches, which still exist to this day, with a new stand erected on the football field by the end of the decade.

Friendly fixtures were played until a competitive return was made for the 1921/22 season, with a season spent back in the Bradford Central League. Mills then made the step up to the Bradford FA League in the summer of 1922. This was essentially a renamed Bradford & District League, but now of a lower status, particularly now that the West Riding County Amateur League had been formed that year, taking the best of the clubs in the city. These had since ceased paying players, this now being the norm in the Yorkshire League, which itself had been formed in 1920 for the more ambitious (semi) professional clubs in the county.

Manningham Mills spent the period between 1922-27 in the Bradford FA League, with the club's reserve team latterly playing in the Bradford Red Triangle. The first team finished just ahead of Birkenshaw at the head of the league at the end of the 1926/27 season, overhauling their rivals in April. The seven other sides in the competition finished way behind the two front-runners. The side were also losing finalists to County Amateur League side Thornton United in the Bradford & District Cup, going down 1-3 on Monday 25th April 1927 at Valley Parade.

The move up to the West Riding County Amateur League in the summer of 1927 illustrated the growing strength of the club, which became champions at the first time of asking. In its 22 league programme, only one point was dropped all season, and the team finished eleven points clear of runner-up, Yeadon Celtic. Remarkably, given the utter dominance of the team during that season, this was to be the only time that the club would win the title. Yeadon Celtic also finished runner-up to Mills in the Yeadon Hospital Cup, the league champions running out easy 5-1 winners in the final, which was played at Guiseley on Saturday 5th May 1928.

Boothtown and Yeadon Celtic finished above Mills the following season, with the team finishing way off the pace in subsequent seasons.

| 1927/28 West Riding County Amateur League | | | | | | | |
|---|---|---|---|---|---|---|---|
| | P | W | D | L | F | A | Pts |
| **Manningham Mills** | 22 | 21 | 1 | 0 | 90 | 31 | 43 |
| Yeadon Celtic | 22 | 14 | 4 | 4 | 90 | 53 | 32 |
| Farsley Celtic | 22 | 12 | 4 | 6 | 75 | 54 | 28 |
| Southowram | 21 | 12 | 2 | 7 | 66 | 52 | 27 |
| Guiseley | 22 | 8 | 8 | 6 | 73 | 60 | 24 |
| **Boothtown** | 22 | 7 | 10 | 5 | 70 | 61 | 24 |
| Blythwick | 22 | 8 | 3 | 11 | 66 | 81 | 19 |
| **Haworth** | 20 | 6 | 3 | 11 | 35 | 57 | 17 |
| Apperley Bridge | 22 | 5 | 4 | 13 | 56 | 69 | 14 |
| Thornton United | 21 | 4 | 4 | 13 | 48 | 82 | 13 |
| Keighley Parkwood | 22 | 5 | 2 | 15 | 56 | 94 | 12 |
| **Horsforth** | 22 | 5 | 1 | 16 | 51 | 82 | 11 |

Despite a poor showing in the league, Mills won the Bradford & District FA Cup for the only time in the 1933/34 season, defeating Bolton Woods, the Bradford Amateur League champions, in the final. The club's Scotchman Road ground had for some years, and would continue in the future, to host many end-of-season cup finals for local football leagues as well as the local football association.

The club then experienced something of a dramatic fall from grace. After a near-disastrous league campaign, the club left the West Riding County Amateur League at the end of the 1934/35 season, when only seven points were amassed in its twenty-two fixtures. Over one hundred goals were conceded, and only two matches won, although the club did avoid bottom position by finishing a point above Marsden, who also left the league.

By now the Bradford Amateur League had established itself as the top district league below the County Amateur League, and Mills were able to regroup in its top division. Tenth place in a fourteen team division marked an unsuccessful debut season in the competition, and although the team improved to 9th in the 1936/37 season, there were only eleven teams completing the season. Following another ninth placing, the 1938/39 season proved to be the worst ever for Manningham Mills FC. The side lost 21 of its 22 league fixtures, with only one victory, to finish well bottom of the league table, this just over a decade after its unbeaten season in the County Amateur League.

The 1939/40 season was disrupted by the outbreak of World War Two, and Manningham Mills initially played in the Bradford Amateur League's third division before shelving its open-age team. Junior teams continued to be fielded in the Bradford Red Triangle and the bizarrely titled Bradford Nig Nog League during the War. Despite the rather questionable title of the latter, at the time this represented a youth movement that sought to encourage the playing of sports and pastimes by local youths, and the league itself proved very popular for two decades or so after the War. The young team actually achieved a Nig Nog Junior league and cup double in the 1941/42 season, and Mills would continue in the league after

*Manningham Mills, 1947/48*. Back row: J Firm, G Whitford, L Atkinson, M Tordoff, D Keeton and H Jackson; Front row: D Coucom, D Racher, H Jennings, N Jackson (captain), S Smith and L Smith. To the left is J Watts and to the right, J Austin in the flat cap. Photograph courtesy of Paul Jennings.

hostilities had ceased. The club's cricket team also continued to operate in local competition during World War Two.

The side returned to the top division of the Bradford Amateur League - now titled the 'Premier Division' for the 1947/48 season, and finished in third place behind Keighley district teams Sutton United and Haworth in the 14-team league. Despite only finishing fourth the following season, the team was accepted back into the County Amateur League for the 1949/50 season, the fine facilities at Scotchman Road no doubt being appreciated as an asset to the league.

In an article published in the *Telegraph & Argus* on 21st June 2020, social historian Dr Paul Jennings (whose article *'Life at Lister's - Sport, sociability and culture at Lister's Mill, Bradford'* was published in *The Bradford Antiquary* in 2016) wrote about the Mills team during its successful 1947/48 campaign.

*'The team was re-organised after the end of the Second World War. My dad, Harry Jennings…remembered how those interested picked all the stones up from the neglected pitch and cut the grass ready to play again. The team all then worked at Lister's.*

*About the 1947/8 season: the club's chairman, W. (Willie) Bennett, wrote in the company magazine that they had been in the newly formed Premier Division of the Bradford Amateur League and 'finished among the leaders.'*

*They were runners-up in the Bradford and District Cup, beaten 3-1 by Salts at Valley Parade on April 26 but just four days later, on April 30, won the Bradford Amateur League Cup at Park Avenue, beating the United States Metallic Packing Company 4-1.*

*The club's president, director and future managing director of Lister's, Graham Watson, who will be well remembered not only for his work for Bradford, but for his legacies of land in the Yorkshire Dales and a superb collection of antiquarian books, presented medals to the players in the works canteen on June 1.*

*They then all adjourned to Lilycroft Working Men's Club, above the mill on Lilycroft Road, for dancing and entertainment provided by Lister's 'artistes' John Briggs (piano accordion and guitar), Alf Race (guitar) and Alf Illingworth (drums) with Cynthia Normington and Benny Moorhouse vocalists. The evening was 'one of the most successful and enjoyable during the history of the club'.*

| 1949/50 West Riding County Amateur League | | | | | |
|---|---|---|---|---|---|
| | P | W | D | L | Pts |
| **Bradford Rovers** | 26 | 20 | 2 | 4 | 42 |
| **Manningham Mills** | 26 | 18 | 2 | 6 | 38 |
| Liversedge | 26 | 15 | 5 | 6 | 35 |
| **Luddendenfoot** | 26 | 15 | 4 | 7 | 34 |
| **Boothtown** | 26 | 14 | 4 | 8 | 32 |
| Guiseley | 26 | 14 | 3 | 9 | 31 |
| Thackley | 26 | 13 | 3 | 10 | 29 |
| Thornhill Edge | 26 | 9 | 5 | 12 | 23 |
| Lightcliffe | 26 | 8 | 6 | 12 | 22 |
| Meltham | 26 | 7 | 6 | 13 | 20 |
| Salts (Saltaire) | 26 | 8 | 4 | 14 | 20 |
| Yeadon Celtic | 26 | 7 | 3 | 16 | 17 |
| Rawdon Old Boys | 26 | 5 | 4 | 17 | 14 |
| Ossett Albion | 26 | 2 | 3 | 21 | 7 |

Manningham Mills FC spent the rest of its existence, the best part of next four decades, in the West Riding County Amateur League. The team almost won the league again in its first season back, eventually finishing runners-up, four points behind Bradford Rovers, at the end of the 1949/50 season. The team finished comfortably ahead of the likes of Guiseley and Thackley, both of which would move on to a higher standard of football in the not-too-distant future.

In 1958/59, the club finished bottom of the twelve-team league, but such was the tightness of the bottom half of the table that season, one more win would have seen Manningham Mills finish in mid-table. Although no further league titles were attained, there were league cup final successes in 1965/66, and 1968/69. Additionally, in a period of sustained success the club's second team were Reserve Division champions in 1967/68, and 1968/69, also winning their league cup competitions five times, in 1968/69, 1969/70, 1972/73, 1975/76, and 1977/78.

Lister's Mills were in financial difficulties by the 1980s, facing stiff competition from overseas competitors and changing trends in the industry, and the football club itself found it harder to operate due to its lack of funding. The team lost its Premier Division status in the County Amateur League at the end of the 1985/86 season, and after two years in the league's second tier folded in the summer of 1988. The mills themselves were closed for good in 1999, but the buildings live on in all their glory having more recently been converted into private apartments.

The Scotchman Road ground was initially taken over by the re-formed Bradford Park Avenue, for its inaugural season in the County Amateur League, and who vacated the ground in search of a ground more suitable for entry into a higher standard of competition, at that time the Central Midlands League. The ground has been upgraded in recent years by former County Amateur League side Campion AFC, who now play higher up the non-league ladder on a ground that is now fully floodlit. The Manningham Mills cricket team is also no more, although the cricket pitch is also still in use today. 2006 saw the opening of a new £1.5 million club house and community centre on the site, under the banner of Manningham Mills Sports Association, of which Campion AFC is a partner.

**Manningham Mills' final season 1987/88 West Riding County Amateur League**

| Division One | P | W | D | L | F | A | Pts |
|---|---|---|---|---|---|---|---|
| VAW (Low Moor) | 24 | 17 | 6 | 1 | 71 | 22 | 40 |
| Farsley Celtic Res | 24 | 15 | 6 | 3 | 64 | 28 | 36 |
| Wibsey | 24 | 12 | 10 | 2 | 45 | 33 | 34 |
| Hall Green United | 24 | 12 | 7 | 5 | 50 | 25 | 31 |
| Mandela Santos | 24 | 10 | 6 | 8 | 46 | 40 | 26 |
| Lower Hopton | 24 | 9 | 8 | 7 | 47 | 43 | 26 |
| Otley Town | 24 | 10 | 2 | 12 | 50 | 69 | 22 |
| Wrenthorpe | 24 | 8 | 3 | 13 | 33 | 42 | 19 |
| Morley Miners | 24 | 5 | 9 | 10 | 28 | 45 | 19 |
| Blakeborough | 24 | 7 | 3 | 14 | 40 | 54 | 17 |
| **Manningham Mills** | 24 | 4 | 7 | 12 | 31 | 51 | 15 |
| Rawdon OB | 24 | 5 | 5 | 14 | 35 | 61 | 15 |
| Keighley Town | 24 | 4 | 4 | 16 | 29 | 56 | 12 |

*Tyersal - expelled*
*Manningham Mills reserves finished 11th out of 13 teams in the Reserve Division*

### Manningham Mills in the FA Amateur Cup

Mills reached the Second Round of the tournament on two occasions, the first after negotiating the qualifying rounds, and the second after receiving a bye to the First Round after its previous successful run.

A first appearance was made in the 1928/29 season, when easy victories over Sowerby United (5-1 at home), and Farsley Celtic (4-0 away), were followed by a heavy 0-8 loss at the hands of Yorkshire Amateurs in a Fourth Qualifying Round replay.

Farsley knocked the Bradford team out of the tournament the following season by eight goals to one, but when the sides met for a third consecutive season in the Second Qualifying Round in the 1930/31 season at Scotchman Road, Manningham's 3-2 victory was the first in a series of wins that took the club to the Second Round for the first time. Further victories at Guiseley (3-1), at home to Leeds side Whitehall Printeries and then Percy Main Amateurs (both 2-1) followed, before the Second Round tie at home to the famous Northern Amateurs side. Mills went down narrowly 1-2.

As a result of that fine run, Mills didn't have to play in the qualifying rounds of the 1931/32 competition, but were remarkably drawn at home to Northern Nomads again, this time in the First Round. The match again proved a close run thing, will Mills this time edging out their opponents 2-1 on Saturday 12th December 1931. The Nomads had a team consisting entirely of players with country representative honours, five amateur internationals, and four players who had recently represented the Football Association in other representative matches. However, it was the Yorkshire team that proved victorious on the day, with Gill heading home a Hawley cross in the first half, and McDermott converting a late penalty after the Nomads had equalised.

*The Shipley Times*, Saturday 23rd January 1932,

## MANNINGHAM MILLS BEAT NORTHERN NOMADS

What must have been the greatest football surprise in the country was staged in a Football Association Amateur Cup-tie at Scotchman Road, Bradford. The visitors were the Northern Nomads, the famous amateur team from the Manchester district, and such poor record have Manningham Mills, even in West Riding Amateur League games that not a person the district dared to hope for victory. For so important a fixture there was only a very poor attendance, this probably being partly due to the people expecting the visitors to outclass the opposition, but those who did attend were astonished with the great surprise the Mills had in store for their visitors. Admittedly on the run of the play the Nomads deserved at least a replay, but it was the Mills who gained the verdict on the stroke of time for a penalty kick taken in the last minute earned them a passage into the second round.

For the first ten minutes play was confined to midfield. Manningham then broke away the left. McDermott sent the ball along the goal mouth, but unfortunately the inside forwards were not in a position to accept a good chance. Manningham's backs were playing a sound game. They repeatedly checked the Nomads' forward movements, but on one occasion it was only a brilliant save by Ayres that prevented a score.

The Mills went ahead after 30 minutes' play when, from a centre by Howley, Gill headed into the net. They still held this lead at the interval to the surprise of the crowd, but the visitors improved after the interval, and certainly looked as if they were going to fulfil expectations and win by an easy margin. The Manningham defence thought otherwise, however, and gave the Nomads forwards little opportunity. Jones made two clever saves when severely tested by Norman and Mathers, while McDavid repeatedly checked dangerous onslaughts. The Mills repulsed two good efforts before Pitt equalised. Almost on time Manningham went ahead, McDermott converting a penalty kick

However, north-east team Stockton left Scotchman Road with a 2-1 victory in the Second Round, watched by a crowd of around 2,000 on Saturday 16th January 1932, of which two-hundred or so had made the journey from the north-east. McDermott had given the home team a first half lead, but Stockton proved just too strong on the day. At the time, Mills were struggling near the bottom of the County Amateur League, so their cup exploits were perhaps all the more remarkable.

The following Saturday, the *Shipley Times*, offered a detailed summary of events in what was described in the local press as the most attractive fixture offered to local football fans in recent seasons.

## MANNINGHAM MILLS LOSE TO STOCKTON

From the first, Manningham were the more aggressive, a neat forward movement on the right carrying play well into the Stockton quarters, and Newton was called upon to deal with a difficult shot from Knight. Two dangerous moves from the visitors were cleverly repulsed by Craven. On both occasions attacks by the home forwards followed but they were met with a strong defence in Thompson and Little. A corner kick then followed, to Manningham, but without result, for although the kick was well placed, the visiting defence hooked the ball away Despite one or two occasional breakaways by the visitors, Manningham continued to have the best of play, and after 25 minutes play they went ahead as the result of a clever goal scored by McDermott, who accepted a neat pass from Clayton.

Following this reverse, the visitors made two determined attacks, and the home backs had a difficult task in preventing Stephenson and Smith from breaking through. Manningham however were seldom in their own half, and despite the efforts of the Stockton half-backs they were apt to be dangerous on several occasions. Newton, the visitors' goalkeeper effected clearances of a clever character, Clayton sending in two hard shots. Towards the interval Manningham again attacked strongly, but without success, and on the run of play they deserved their slender lead in what had been a rather tame half. Had Gill, the Mills left-winger, made better use of McDermott's many passes, the interval lead might have been much bigger.

The second half opened at a very fast pace, both goals being visited quickly in return. A header from Coulthard three minutes after the interval brought the scores level and inspired Stockton with the result that their smarter *passing soon enabled them to gain the upper hand. Ayres, the Mills goalkeeper, however, made some amazing saves, and Stockton had much difficulty in securing the lead (through another goal from Coulthard). Well supported by Knapton, McDermott and Ayres took the honours in the Mills' eleven. Craven made some effective clearances at left back. Thompson defended well at right back for Stockton, whose experienced centre-backs contributed to Stockton's second half success.*

The Manningham Mills team that day was: *W Ayres, W Huggan, N Craven, J Taylor, W Myers, E Knapton, J Howley, E Mathers, S Clayton, T McDermott, and A Gill.*

Unfortunately, there was little else for the Bradford team to write home about in the Amateur cup. Guiseley put them out in the First Round in the 1932/33 season, after another exemption from the qualifying rounds, with a 4-1 success at Scotchman Road.

The club then left it almost three decades before entering the competition again, losing at home to Guiseley again in their return in the First Qualifying Round in 1961/62. A break was again made, with the club entering for four more seasons between 1967-71. Its only win was a 3-2 home success against Birkenshaw Rovers in 1969/70 before yet another home defeat to Guiseley in the First Qualifying Round. The final season of entry, 1970/71 saw another home loss 1-3 to Sheffield, following a 3-3 draw in South Yorkshire in the Preliminary Round.

The FA Amateur Cup was replaced by the FA Vase in 1974, but Manningham Mills did not enter the new competition.

# Methley Perseverance
# 1908-29
## *'In the dock'*

Methley is a village south-east of Leeds, within the area bounded by Leeds, Castleford, and Wakefield. The Wesleyan Chapel, later called Methley Methodist Church is located at Mickletown. The Foundation stones of this Chapel were laid in 1887 and it was officially opened in July 1888, playing a part in the social and sporting life of the villagers for many years since then.

Several junior teams, such as Methley Rovers and Methley Wanderers played in the early 1900s, with Methley United, playing in local competitions between 1904-10. In the 1919/20 season, a new United played in the strangely named – and short lived - Leeds Invinsa Alliance league's Senior Division alongside a strong line-up that included Altofts West Riding Colliery, Rothwell Parish Church, and Woodlesford, but was not in the competition the following season.

The church team, Methley United Methodist Chapel, spent one season in the Leeds Nonconformist League (in 1908/09), before the appearance of the Methley Perseverance club in 1911/12, which was placed in the B Division. The club was among the divisional front-runners along with the Hunslet UMC and Zion UMC clubs.

Perseverance made a big step up for the 1913/14 season, becoming founder members of the new Leeds Senior League, finishing 7th out of 13 clubs. However, there was one major success when the club won Leeds & District Cup, underlining its swift rise to prominence, by defeating Altofts Albion 2-1 in the final. Altofts had thrashed Beeston Hill Parish Church 6-0 in its semi-final which had been played on the Methley ground.

The 1914/15 Leeds Senior League season was Methley make a good start, as by 7th November the *Yorkshire Evening Post* reported *'Methley was one of the last villages in the south of Leeds to be won over to soccer football, but it must be admitted that the standard of play attained by the Perseverance Club of the Methley village is proving a revelation. A well-balanced side and much bigger in physique than the usual local elevens, their team have fulfilled eight Leeds Senior League games up to date with the loss of but one point. Of the 31 goals registered in their favour their speedy centre-forward, T Abrams, claims 17.'*

Fryston Colliery were eventual league champions with the Methley team, along with Rothwell Parish Church and Rothwell White Rose close behind. Some silverware was won, however, when Rothwell White Rose were defeated 2-0 in the final of the Rothwell Charity Cup on Saturday 17th April 1915.

Perseverance then closed down for the remaining years of World War One, but was resuscitated in the summer of 1919, playing on a field round at Cutler Lane, off Lower Mickletown.

The Leeds Senior League itself reformed as the West Riding Senior League for the 1919/20 season, of which Methley became founder members. The change of title was supported by the Leeds & District FA as a battle emerged between itself and the Bradford & District FA to form a county-wide league for amateur clubs. However, three clubs withdrew prior to the start of the season, leaving only six teams in the league, those alongside Methley being Castleford Town reserves, Horsforth, Harrogate, Marsden, and Rothwell Athletic. Methley made it through to the West Riding County Cup final that season, losing in a replay at Elland Road to Altofts West Riding Colliery, 0-1, in front of 3,000 spectators on Monday 26th April 1920. Sixteen days earlier the teams had drawn 1-1.

The West Riding Senior League grew to 14 clubs, rising again to 16 the following season, with Methley finishing 8th in 1920/21 and 7th in 1921/22. However, the highlight for the club was the lifting of the County Cup in both of those seasons.

The 1921 final at Elland Road was tight contest, with Methley defeating Horsforth 1-0 in front of 3,000 spectators on Monday 25th April. The winning goal was scored by Parker halfway through the second half, Horsforth having had the better of the first half. Just 48 hours after lifting the County Cup, Methley were back at Elland Road to win the Leeds & District Cup, defeating Altofts 1-0 in a replay.

The 1922 County Cup final resulted in a much more convincing victory for Methley, with Castleford & Allerton United defeated 3-0 in the Elland Road final, on Tuesday 18th April in front of 5,000 spectators. The match itself was said to have been quite a poor one, according to the following day's *Yorkshire Post*, its report going on to say,

*Castleford United head the West Riding chart, and have beaten the Perseverance twice in League warfare, on this occasion they were no match for their opponents. From beginning to end they were generally a side with little vitality, and a crude idea of the Association game. Methley, whilst not displaying the form of last season…at times glimpsed skill of moderate quality, but the play at no time raised great enthusiasm even amongst the club's followers, who supplied a greater portion of the crowd.*

*Play had only been running seven minutes when Church, the Castleford right-back, fouled Parkin, the Methley centre-forward in the penalty area, Maskill scoring from the 'spot' kick. This early reverse seemed to take the 'vim' out of the United players, and the Perseverance, who had the wind behind them, added to their total in thirty minutes through Charlesworth. The teams swung round with Methley leading by 2 clear goals. The cup-holders did well against the breeze, and increased their lead in seven minutes, Varley scoring after the ball had travelled along the Castleford crossbar from a shot by McCreadie, who was the best forward on the field. Methley's defence had one or two short periods of stress, but came through safely.*

The 1922/23 season saw a battle with eventual winners Altofts at the head of the table in a smaller nine-team West Riding Senior League. By now there were four 'county' leagues to choose from for West Yorkshire teams; the Yorkshire League, the Leeds-based West Riding Senior League, the Bradford-based West Riding County Amateur League, and also the West Yorkshire Amateur League (which had previously been the Leeds Amateur League). Methley's grip on the West Riding County Cup ended, with a 0-1 defeat in the semi-final to the eventual winners, Castleford & Allerton United, who thus gained revenge for that cup final defeat the previous season, at the Castleford Town ground.

However, in April 1923 the club was censured by the West Riding Football Association as its accounts had been kept in a very unbusinesslike manner. Also, vouchers showing what had been paid to both amateur and professional players had not been kept, and the club was ordered to improve matters and to pay the costs of the enquiry.

The West Riding Senior League folded in the summer of 1923, at which point Methley moved up to the Yorkshire League. Despite the step up in standard, the move could not have been more successful, with the club becoming champions at the first attempt, ahead of its great rivals Altofts, and just two points clear of its nearest challengers, Frickley Colliery. For a club from a village the size of Methley this was a phenomenal achievement, and one that would ultimately be unsustainable, considering the impending economic downturn which would affect attendances, gate receipts, and the ability of clubs this size to pay their bills, a good deal of which were payments to players.

The club was in a spot of trouble again at this time, with the club secretary told off for his criticism of the referee following a fixture with York City reserves, and the club was again in the dock when one of its officials was accused of inciting a player to strike an opposing player after a home game with Leeds Harehills on Easter Monday. The accusation could not be proved, so Methley went unpunished on this occasion.

Charlie Bentley was the captain of the successful Methley team around this time. Due to family commitments he had to turn down the offer of trials with Arsenal FC, but was also an excellent all-rounder with Methley Cricket Club.

The 1924/25 season was disappointing, with an eighth place finish in the league, although the club could call on a thriving ladies' working party operating on its behalf, holding dances and whist drives, one of which offered a ton of coal as a special prize.

**METHLEY PERSEVERANCE.**
Top row (left to right):—J. Greenwood, Dickenson, King, Guest, Walsh, W. Ray. Second row:—Clark, Wall, Pollard (captain), Abrams, Tillotson. Bottom: Burton, Henery, Pybus.

*Methley Perseverance, Yorkshire League champions, 1923/24*

The Yorkshire League was won again in the 1925/26 season, however, this time on goal average ahead of Selby Town, Perseverance scored a massive 99 goals in just 28 league games. Unfortunately at that point the bubble burst, and the final three years of the club's existence proved to be something of a struggle.

The 1926/27 season saw Methley finish down a lowly 13th in the 16 team league, and the following season the club was unable to fulfil all of its fixtures.

Four games, against Bridlington Town, Scarborough Penguins, and York City reserves, twice, were not played. Part of this may have been due to the fact that Methley had lost the use of its Cutler Lane ground during the summer, with a frantic search resulting in the club being accommodated at Oulton Welfare Sports Club from September 1927. On top of that, the club was suspended early in 1928 due to a non-payment of money owed to the league. That suspension was lifted on 22nd March, once the monies had been paid but only the woeful Wakefield City sat below Methley in the end of season final table.

The 1928/29 season was the club's first, and only, entry into the FA Amateur Cup, which underlined the fact that players were no longer being paid by the club. In December 1928 the club was again under a cloud when its secretary was suspended by the West Riding Football Association. Wilfred Hetherington alleged that several Bradford players had deliberately tried to cripple players from his own team in a match on 17th November, and that the match was a disgrace to Yorkshire League football. Methley's goalkeeper had been injured in an accidental collision with the Bradford centre forward, which Bradford went on to win by twenty goals to 1 (in fact Bradford scored a remarkable 191 goals in just 30 matches that season, dropping only 2 points all season, Methley finishing 6th in the 16 team division). Hetherington was ordered to withdraw his remarks and apologise to both the Bradford club and the league. Methley's response was rather unexpected – the committee duly elected a new club secretary, Mr Hetherington's wife!

Wilfred Hetherington's appeal was heard, and rejected, by the league's Appeals Board the following February. The following month the league referred the matter of Mrs Hetherington's role to the West Riding FA as it was felt that this appointment made a mockery of the suspension of Mr Hetherington. The County FA took no action over this matter and effectively left it to Methley to sort out.

### Methley Perseverance Yorkshire League record

| Season | P | W | D | L | F | A | Pts | Pos |
|---|---|---|---|---|---|---|---|---|
| 1923-24 | 34 | 24 | 6 | 4 | 84 | 24 | 54 | 1/18 |
| 1924-25 | 30 | 10 | 8 | 12 | 59 | 64 | 28 | 8/16 |
| 1925-26 | 28 | 20 | 4 | 4 | 99 | 36 | 44 | 1/15 |
| 1926-27 | 30 | 10 | 3 | 17 | 69 | 111 | 23 | 13/16 |
| 1927-28 | 20 | 2 | 2 | 16 | 24 | 67 | 6 | 12/13 |
| 1928-29 | 30 | 14 | 3 | 13 | 76 | 88 | 31 | 6/16 |

In 1929 Mexborough offered Methley a financial guarantee to switch the FA Cup tie between the clubs to Mexborough - who went on to win easily – which underlines the fact that the Methley club was clearly not in a healthy position financially. The move out of the village had obviously done the club no favours, and on the field it was no longer the force it had been.

By mid-December 1929 the club was second bottom of the league, with only newcomers Pontefract Borough below them. However, when the clubs met on 18th December, Methley defeated their hapless rivals 25-0. Pontefract started the game with only ten men, and later lost the services of their goalkeeper. The referee reported that in all his years as a player and referee, he had never seen such remarkable shooting as shown by the Methley players. The Pontefract team was subsequently fined five shillings by the league for failing to put out a full strength team (they resigned from the league following a 0-15 home defeat to Bradford City reserves in January) but, more significantly, this was Methley's last ever match. No other club can surely claim to have gone out on such a high

At this point the club was taken over by Huddersfield Town, in December 1929, becoming the Football League club's 'A' team. Arrangements had been made for Methley to retain its identity and to become Huddersfield's nursery club, but as contracted professionals were to be fielded by the Leeds Road side then the club was forced to take the Huddersfield name instead. The teams had past links, Town sending a team to Methley in May 1924 in order to play a benefit game for Methley player Pybus, who had been injured earlier in the season. What is interesting, however, is that permission to change the name of the

Methley club to Huddersfield Town 'A' by the Yorkshire League followed several letters in support of the change, a significant one coming from the Methley secretary, one Wilfred Hetherington.

## Methley Perseverance in FA Competitions

Methley Perseverance entered the FA Amateur Cup on just one occasion, and that was right at the end of its existence. With professionals having being dispensed with, the club couldn't have made a better start with 6-1 home thrashings of Guiseley and Knaresborough Town in the Second and Third Qualifying Rounds. However, in the following round Horsforth gained revenge for an FA Cup defeat a few weeks earlier by winning 2-0 on their home ground.

Success was only moderate in the FA Cup. In the club's first appearance in 1921/22 Horsforth were defeated 5-1 at home in an Extra Preliminary Round tie, but that was followed by a 0-2 loss in a replay at its great rivals Castleford & Allerton United. The 1925/26 season saw Methley return to the competition, but a 4-2 Extra Preliminary Round victory over South Kirkby Colliery was as good as it got as Wombwell thrashed them 8-0 at the next stage. Denaby United put paid to further progress in the 1928/29 season, defeating Methley in a second replay in the Second Qualifying Round, this after 3-2 wins away at Monckton Athletic and Cudworth Village in previous rounds.

Horsforth were again defeated, 2-0 in the 1929/30 season, again in an Extra Preliminary Round tie, but the financial inducement that led to the First Qualifying Round tie to be switched to Mexborough, saw Methley hammered 1-7. The same team had thrashed them 7-2 in the 1926/27 season.

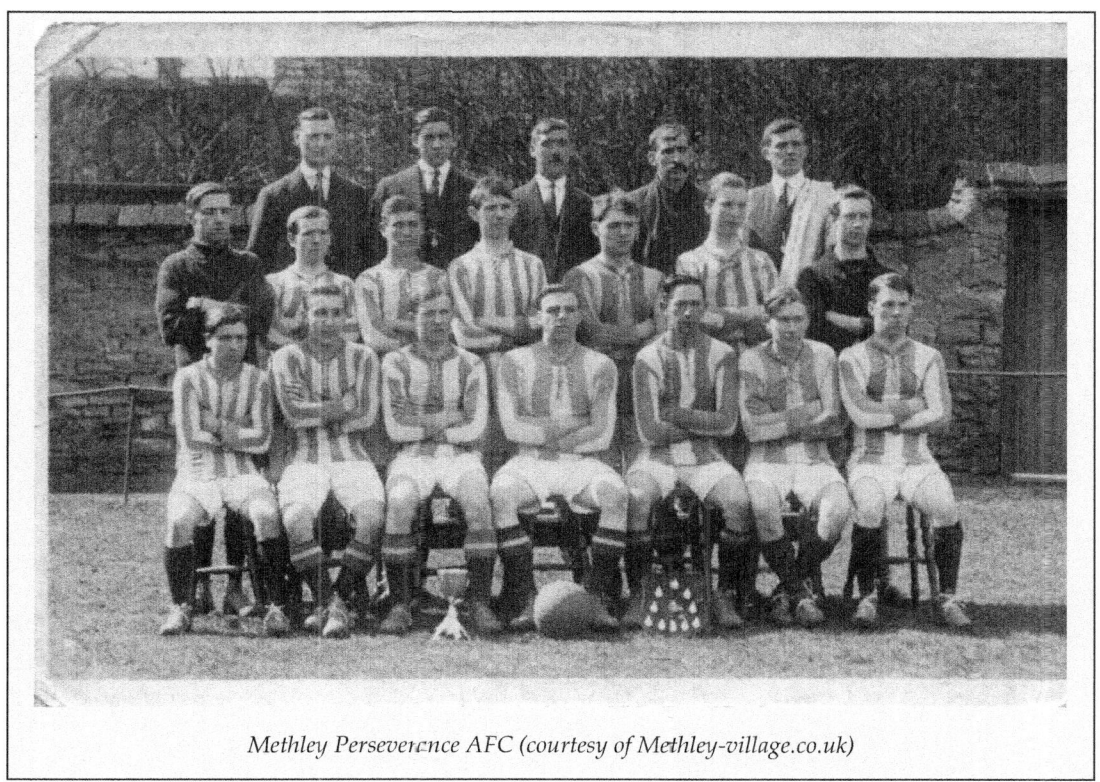

*Methley Perseverance AFC (courtesy of Methley-village.co.uk)*

# Methley United

It would be another twenty years before another club from the village really made a mark in local football. In the 1949/50 season a new Methley United came to prominence, as members of the Leeds Combination and Pontefract & District Leagues. By 1952/53 the club was in the top division of the West Yorkshire League, and were league champions at the end of the 1955/56 season. The club were runners up in 1954/55 (on goal difference only) and again in 1956/57, and remained in the top division of the league until 1975.

### 1955-56 West Yorkshire League

| Division One | P | W | D | L | F | A | Pts |
|---|---|---|---|---|---|---|---|
| **Methley United** | 30 | 22 | 5 | 3 | 98 | 44 | 49 |
| Swillington Welfare | 30 | 22 | 1 | 7 | 120 | 54 | 45 |
| East End Park WMC | 30 | 19 | 1 | 10 | 74 | 50 | 39 |
| Ferrybridge Amateurs | 30 | 16 | 5 | 9 | 92 | 66 | 37 |
| Ossett Albion | 30 | 17 | 2 | 11 | 80 | 63 | 36 |
| Rothwell Athletic | 30 | 14 | 6 | 10 | 84 | 71 | 34 |
| D.P. & E. (Otley) | 30 | 14 | 5 | 11 | 81 | 78 | 33 |
| Farsley Celtic reserves | 30 | 13 | 3 | 14 | 57 | 59 | 29 |
| Yorkshire Amateurs | 30 | 13 | 2 | 15 | 67 | 84 | 28 |
| Harrogate Town | 30 | 11 | 3 | 16 | 47 | 57 | 25 |
| Micklefield Welfare | 30 | 11 | 3 | 16 | 65 | 81 | 25 |
| Altofts Welfare | 30 | 10 | 3 | 17 | 91 | 93 | 23 |
| Fryston Colliery | 30 | 9 | 5 | 16 | 59 | 70 | 23 |
| Selby Town reserves | 30 | 10 | 1 | 19 | 61 | 92 | 21 |
| Carlton United | 30 | 6 | 6 | 18 | 58 | 100 | 18 |
| Harrogate Railway Res | 30 | 6 | 3 | 21 | 56 | 128 | 15 |

By the end of the 1950s, the club were regular entrants into the FA Amateur Cup. In the 1957/58 the club was successful in five qualifying rounds before reaching the First Round Proper for the first, and only, time. North Ferriby United, who were at home, were brushed aside 6-1 in a Preliminary Round tie, before a 2-0 home win against Swillington Miners Welfare, a narrow 3-2 victory at Liversedge, followed by a 7-1 win at Kingston Wolves and finally a 3-1 win at Armthorpe Welfare. Sadly, Durham City defeated Methley 6-0 in the First Round tie up in the north east.

The current Methley United club was founded in May 2002, playing in the same red and white colours as its predecessors, and also playing at one time on the same Savile Road recreation ground at Mickletown.

# Mirfield United
# 1897-1914
## *'If it wasn't for that team from down the road'*

Before the outbreak of World War One Mirfield United was perhaps - outside those that went on to Football League or Midland League status - the strongest team in the West Riding. Its folding was not down to a poor playing record, or particularly severe long-term debts, but due to the success of another club from down the road.

The club's president, and a player for them in the early days, was Richard N Wheatley, a member of a locally established mill owning family, who had presented the Wheatley Cup to the Heavy Woollen Football Association in 1898. The local FA have since then used the trophy for its district cup competition. Mirfield lost in the first Wheatley Cup final in the 1898/99 season – 0-1 v Morley at - but won the trophy in 1901/02 and again in 1902/03.

On Saturday 26th April 1902, at The Victoria Grounds, Savile Town, Mirfield trailed 0-2 to Saviletown Clarence at half-time, but overturned that score with the wind behind them. Brook Taylor and Thwaites both scored early in the second half, but Mirfield had to wait until three minutes from time before Brook Taylor struck the winner. The 1902/03 final was played at the same ground on Saturday 18th April, and resulted in a 2-0 victory over Dewsbury & Savile. This followed a seven goal victory over Heckmondwike Parish Church in the semi-final.

The club reached the final of the even more prestigious West Riding County Cup in the 1902/03 and 1904/05 seasons. In 1903 the side was defeated 1-0 by Altofts at Valley Parade, Bradford on Tuesday 14th April, following a 1-1 draw three days earlier at Dewsbury. On Saturday 15th April 1905 Bradford City themselves defeated Mirfield by a single goal at Beck Lane, Heckmondwike.

After a season playing friendly fixtures against local opposition, United were founder members of the Heavy Woollen League in 1898, winning the Senior League title in 1902 before joining the West Yorkshire League for the 1902/03 season. After taking a runner-up position in its debut season behind Altofts, Mirfield United won the title in its second season in the competition, ahead of Bradford City reserves (ironically after having played City's first team in the FA Cup), staying in the league until the summer of 1910, when the club was a founder member of the Yorkshire Combination, a (semi) professional competition containing the reserve teams of Football League teams as well as ambitious clubs such as York City, Halifax Town and Goole Town. During its four seasons at that level, the club finished runner-up once (1913/14 behind Bradford Park Avenue reserves), and in third place twice (1910/11 and 1912/13).

The club also made an unsuccessful bid to join the Midland League in the summer of 1912. The league expanded to twenty clubs that summer but despite three other Yorkshire clubs - Halifax Town, Goole Town, and York City – being admitted, Mirfield was unsuccessful.

### Heavy Woollen District League 1898/99 - Inaugural season

| Northern Division | P | W | D | L | F | A | Pts |
|---|---|---|---|---|---|---|---|
| Birstall | 14 | 12 | 1 | 1 | 71 | 12 | 25 |
| Morley | 14 | 8 | 4 | 2 | 55 | 26 | 20 |
| Batley Swifts | 13 | 7 | 2 | 4 | 32 | 41 | 16 |
| Pildacre Mills | 13 | 6 | 0 | 7 | 32 | 38 | 12 |
| Ossett reserves | 14 | 4 | 4 | 6 | 26 | 33 | 12 |
| Ossett GNR | 14 | 4 | 2 | 8 | 27 | 46 | 10 |
| Ardsley West End | 14 | 4 | 2 | 8 | 27 | 37 | 10 |
| Batley Institute | 14 | 2 | 1 | 11 | 15 | 52 | 5 |
| **Southern Division** | | | | | | | |
| Savile Town Clar | 18 | 14 | 3 | 1 | 55 | 20 | 31 |
| Dewsbury Juniors | 18 | 10 | 4 | 4 | 41 | 32 | 24 |
| Dewsbury Moor | 18 | 9 | 2 | 7 | 49 | 41 | 20 |
| Dewsbury Celtic | 18 | 7 | 4 | 7 | 43 | 51 | 18 |
| **Mirfield United** | 18 | 8 | 2 | 8 | 44 | 39 | 18 |
| Ravensthorpe Inst | 18 | 7 | 2 | 9 | 35 | 45 | 16 |
| Dewsbury St Matt | 18 | 6 | 4 | 8 | 38 | 42 | 16 |
| Boothroyd White St | 18 | 5 | 4 | 9 | 42 | 38 | 14 |
| Dewsbury Eightlds | 18 | 5 | 2 | 11 | 44 | 50 | 12 |
| Shepley Bridge | 18 | 4 | 3 | 11 | 38 | 54 | 11 |

*Savile Town Clarence defeated Birstall 3-0 in the championship play-off*

### Mirfield United in the Yorkshire Combination

| Season | P | W | D | L | F | A | Pts | Pos |
|---|---|---|---|---|---|---|---|---|
| 1910/11 | 18 | 11 | 3 | 4 | 41 | 31 | 25 | 3/10 |
| 1911/12 | 26 | 14 | 6 | 6 | 55 | 32 | 34 | 6/14 |
| 1912/13 | 24 | 15 | 6 | 3 | 63 | 25 | 36 | 3/13 |
| 1913/14 | 17 | 10 | 3 | 4 | 46 | 20 | 23 | 2/10 |

Mirfield United had no less than eight of its players - Todd, Ground, Rudge, Dyson, Duncannon, Mallinson, Smith, and Longbottom - selected for the Heavy Woollen District team when Sheffield Wednesday visited the Dewsbury ground in March 1903. However, despite their success, the club's pitch at the bottom of Station Road had been subject to some criticism, with the *Yorkshire Evening Post* in March 1901 describing it as '…*a very bad one: even last Saturday, with such fine weather, the ground was in a wretched condition, and the slope is, for a football ground, like a mountain side.*' This necessitated a move and, in August the same year, it was reported in the *Batley Reporter and Guardian* that a good ground behind the Savile Arms had been secured for the following season. This ground was shown on maps of the time and is now covered by Whitehall Avenue, with the public house standing adjacent.

The club's biggest cup success was in the 1910/11 season when it won the West Riding Cup in its third appearance in the final, and then retaining the trophy the following season. The 1911 final was played at Savile Town on Saturday 29th April when United ran out 5-1 winners against Allerton Bywater, only four days after an epic semi-final that included four replays against Morley, who they finally conquered 2-0 at Valley Parade, had been concluded. In the one-sided final itself, Stainsby scored a hat-trick, with MacGill and Waites also on target.

The club's 1912 final success against Halifax Town was also played at Savile Town, on Saturday 13th April. This time goals from Moon and Drake were enough to see the holders win 2-0.

The *Leeds Mercury* covered the game the following Monday,

MIRFIELD UNITED CUP WINNERS. *Scorers: - Mirfield United: Moon and Drake, Halifax Town: nil,*

*In the final of the West Riding Cup competition at Dewsbury, Mirfield United beat Halifax Town by two goals to nil. The first twenty minutes' play gave promise of an interesting struggle, but Halifax fell away, and although their opponents faced the wind and sun, the goal from Moon which enabled his side to cross over in front, more than fairly represented Mirfield's superiority*

*The second portion of the game proved an anxious time for Halifax, and Sutcliffe alone prevented a big score being run up against them. Drake added Mirfield's goal.*

*Mirfield throughout were faster and more methodical aide. Their forwards were a good line; whilst Moon and Horton, in the middle division, rendered valuable assistance. Donald Bell, however, the Harrogate back, who assisted Mirfield, was generally admitted to be the best man on the field.*

Mr J Connor, the president of the association, presented the cup and medals to the players. The 'gate' receipt were £17 10s.

Four day before this tie, Mirfield had been defeated 1-4 by Bradford City in the Bradford Charity Cup final, in a match played at Sandhall, Halifax.

Mirfield obviously had the finances to attract quality players, as players such as Haikings and Cotterill joined the club from Scarborough and Nottingham Forest respectively, while others, such as Trerham and Doggart had been full time Football League players in their heyday. Donald Bell, who signed for Bradford (Park Avenue) in October 1912, subsequently achieved fame as the only English professional footballer to be awarded the Victoria Cross for his bravery in the Somme in 1916, where he sadly lost his life.

*Donald Bell*

And yet, by the end of October 1914, it was all over. Having entered the Leeds Senior League for the 1914/15 season (the Yorkshire Combination having folded after just four seasons), the club was no more. The officers in charge of winding up the club cited financial concerns caused by the recent success of Huddersfield Town, in the same way that near-neighbours Morley FC had cited the success of Leeds City. Mirfield's last ever fixture was a 2-1 home success against Rothwell Parish Church on 17th October 1914. Ironically, the following month the league committee had to deal with claims from the defunct club that their opponents had used foul tactics in that game, and that poor refereeing had exacerbated this. Rothwell and the referee were exonerated of all blame, but it was a sad end for the club. Since then, several clubs have represented Mirfield since the War, but none have come close to the standard that Mirfield United achieved.

The *Yorkshire Evening Post* covered what was seen as a sad loss for the Heavy Woollen district in its 31st October 1914 edition, *'In Morley, Mirfield United and Heckmondwike the Heavy Woollen district for a long time claimed three clubs that held a prominent position in West Riding Association football. It is a matter of history now that the success of Leeds City quickly proved the undoing of the Morley club, and present appearances point to an early end of the Mirfield United club also. This contingency, it is believed, has been created by the success of Huddersfield Town. The resignation of the Mirfield club from the Leeds Senior League will doubtless come as a surprise to the local public, who for some time have looked upon the Mirfield organisation as part of the bedrock of West Yorkshire Association football. Financial stress has led the officials to take this course here intimated.'*

It is possible that Mirfield United moved grounds again prior to the outbreak of war. At the time of the club's demise, there was an established football ground just outside the village on Leeds Road, suggesting that the club had moved away from the Savile Arms ground. Local maps of the time do not show this ground but among the references is that in The *Huddersfield Examiner* on 10th May 1915, reporting, *'Never in the history of Association football locally has a ground been turned into such a good account as was the Leeds Road football field on Saturday afternoon, when the 12th Service Battalion of the Yorkshire Light Infantry halted on their way to St. George's Square. The display of enthusiasm was remarkable, and one could scarcely believe that in such a thickly populated neighbourhood there were hundreds of young men, physically fit and without encumbrances who had not answered the call of King and country.'*

Whichever ground was used, Mirfield hosted the West Yorkshire Cup semi-final between Leeds City reserves and Heckmondwike in March 1907. 3,000 spectators were in attendance and the £59 gate receipts were, at that time, a record for a semi-final tie. The Heavy Woollen FA also made use of the Mirfield ground for key cup ties, as well as representative fixtures against other district associations, with the match against Huddersfield in October 1902, probably taking place at Station Road (six of the Heavy Woollen team that day were Mirfield players).

*Pre-War Mirfield United, courtesy of Gerald Pollard & Eric Ellis*

### Mirfield United in the FA Cup

The club first entered the FA Cup in the 1903/04 season, defeating Royston United 2-1 away from home in a First Qualifying Round match, this following a 1-1 draw at home. Luck was against Mirfield in the following round, drawn away to the new Bradford City club that had just been elected to the Football League, but there was no disgrace in a 1-3 defeat on Saturday 17th October 1903, in front of 5,000 spectators at Valley Parade. The local and regional press was divided between those who considered City far more superior, if not wasteful in front of goal, and those who felt that the Mirfield team enjoyed far more of the play. Two examples are given below;

*Sheffield Daily Telegraph,* **Monday 19th October 1903**

*Mirfield won the toss, and played in the first half with the wind. The game was rather one-sided, although the Mirfield backs defended well. The Bradford forwards out played their opponents, and before the interval scored two good goals, and MacMillan also shot one cleverly. Other shots just missed. Mirfield had two corners, but they did not fructify. In the second half Bradford City continued to keep the game almost continuously in the Mirfield half, but the visitors' backs played exceedingly well, and number of strong attacks were well frustrated. Mirfield several* times, however, spurted, and from one rush Thompson scored for them with a hard 20 yards' shot. A keen game ended: – Bradford City, 3 goals; Mirfield, 1 goal.

*Bradford Daily Telegraph,* Monday 19th October 1903

*It was evident from the start that the Bradford City team were prone to underestimate the opposition from Mirfield and scarcely once throughout the game did they fairly settle down to their work. The Mirfield lads worked hard and showed an amount skill which certainly astonished both the Paraders and the Bradford public. From a City point of view, however, the game was not good one, and was further marred by unseemly and childish tactics on the part of some of the home team.*

Between 1904-13 little progress was made in the competition, with, at best, one qualifying round being successfully negotiated before defeat in the following round. Local rivals Morley FC were encountered four times, with honours shared, while Huddersfield Town were overcome 6-0 and 2-0 in the 1909/10 and 1910/11 seasons.

Ironically, United's last appearance in the FA Cup, 1913/14, was its best, with Heckmondwike overcome 1-0 at home, followed by away wins at South Kirkby Colliery (2-0) and Hebden Bridge (4-2). Halifax Town put an end to the run in the Third Qualifying Round with a 2-0 victory at home.

**Mirfield West End FC** was the next village club. Playing in the Heavy Woollen League directly after World War One, it then spent two seasons in the West Riding Senior League between 1920-22, finishing 13th of 14 teams and then 15th of 16 before unsurprisingly dropping out.

# Portsmouth Rovers (Todmorden) 1887-1928
## 'The team that didn't reach the First Round of the FA Cup'

There is a story going round that, in the dim and distant past, a tiny football club from just outside Todmorden battled its way to the First Round of the FA Cup. It's a remarkable story, but sadly, one that is just not true. What it true, is that this was indeed a much loved tiny club, one that played on a remote ground close to the border with Lancashire, and which was much missed following its sad demise between the Wars.

Todmorden is close enough to the Lancashire soccer hotbed to have been influenced by the 'new' code of association football, giving the town an ideal opportunity to get a head start on the rest of West Yorkshire. However, those teams that have represented the town through the years have barely managed to make it beyond district league level, with only Portsmouth Rovers having made it beyond that.

A Lydgate association club, which played its first match in January 1886, was possibly the first club in the town. Todmorden's strongest clubs, not surprisingly, were found along the Burnley Valley, to the north-west, and this included Portsmouth Rovers whose first fixture was against Burnley Union Star at its rural ground at Rattenclough on 17th Sept 1887. By the following year there were at least nine clubs in Todmorden, including four from the outlying village of Portsmouth itself (Britons, Blue Star, and Colliers, in addition to Rovers).

The first season of league football for Portsmouth Rovers was in the 1891/92 season, when it won the Burnley League, with near neighbours Todmorden AFC at the bottom. The two clubs would build a strong rivalry over the years, but the latter's on-off existence prevented it from achieving anything beyond the Halifax, Calder Valley, and Rochdale district leagues. Portsmouth Rovers itself won the Halifax League in 1906/07, having switched to the White Rose county to play its league football, with

> *Burnley Express*, Wednesday 12th December 1888
>
> *Myrtle Bank v Portsmouth Rovers*
>
> *A match between these clubs was played on the Wood Top Recreation Ground, Burnley, on Saturday. The visitors scored five goals to four, but it is alleged by Myrtle Bank that the Rovers left the field ten minutes before time because they were afraid of losing.*

Todmorden AFC the runner-up club, having also switched. Both would return to Lancashire league battles in the not too distant future.

Portsmouth Rovers, which had its headquarters at The Roebuck Inn, was ambitious enough to move up to a higher standard of football. Initially this move proved to be a great success. Despite finishing at the bottom of the nine-team league at the end of its first season in the North East Lancashire Combination, the club went on to win the title for three consecutive seasons between 1908-11, before moving up into the second division of the prestigious Lancashire Combination. In 1907/08 the club also reached the final of the Lancashire Junior Cup, losing out by a single goal to Skelmersdale United in the deciding tie at Accrington on Saturday 14th March 1908.

The following Friday, the *Todmorden Advertiser and Hebden Bridge Newsletter* carried a detailed blow-by-blow account of the tie, and this was prefaced by the following summary,

*The long-deferred final tie of the Lancashire FA. Junior Challenge Shield was played on the Moorhead ground at Accrington on Saturday, when Skelmersdale United and Portsmouth Rovers were the contestants. The tie had been the general topic of conversation among footballers in this district during the past week, the general consensus of opinion being that the Portsmouth team were in for severe drubbing, and that the only question was about the number of goals they would be defeated by. But the 'knowing ones' were very wide of the mark in their reckoning, for the Rovers put up a magnificent fight, and were somewhat unlucky to lose, the teams at the finish being only divided by the odd goal in three.*

*The Accrington Stanley ground was by no means in good condition, not having recovered from the recent heavy weather, and although the surface had been well rolled, in various parts it was of a very treacherous character. There was a capital attendance of spectators present, these being mainly drawn from the districts form which the teams hailed, and the colours of the clubs were very much in evidence.*

The teams met with a hearty reception on entering the playing area, the Portsmouth team being — Greenwood, goal; Fielden and T Sugden, backs; Pickles, Bulcock, and H Sugden, half-backs; Bestwick, Stott, Nesbitt, Dawson, and Hindle, forwards.

In order to maintain standards at Rattenclough that would match the team's on-field success, in 1910 the committee decided to raise funds for a new up-to-date pavilion on their ground, including a house-to-house collection throughout the district.

Portsmouth's reserve team was also successful in local competition, becoming 1910/11 Todmorden & District League champions, underlining the strength in depth at the club.

### Portsmouth Rovers in the North East Lancashire Combination

**1907/08**

| | P | W | D | L | F | A | Pts |
|---|---|---|---|---|---|---|---|
| Great Harwood | 16 | 11 | 3 | 2 | 48 | 36 | 25 |
| Darwen Woodfold | 16 | 9 | 4 | 3 | 46 | 26 | 22 |
| Nelson reserves | 16 | 7 | 5 | 4 | 59 | 43 | 19 |
| Accrington Stan res | 16 | 8 | 2 | 6 | 50 | 40 | 18 |
| Worsthorne | 16 | 5 | 4 | 7 | 43 | 41 | 14 |
| Brierfield Swifts | 16 | 5 | 4 | 7 | 34 | 49 | 14 |
| Rossendale Utd res | 16 | 6 | 2 | 8 | 30 | 45 | 14 |
| Holme | 16 | 5 | 0 | 11 | 45 | 61 | 10 |
| **Portsmouth Rovers** | 16 | 3 | 2 | 11 | 43 | 57 | 8 |

**1908/09** League & league cup double

**1909/10**

| | P | W | D | L | F | A | Pts |
|---|---|---|---|---|---|---|---|
| **Portsmouth Rovers** | 18 | 13 | 2 | 3 | 46 | 24 | 28 |
| Nelson reserves | 18 | 13 | 1 | 4 | 46 | 22 | 27 |
| Burnley Casuals | 18 | 10 | 1 | 7 | 41 | 41 | 21 |
| Brierfield Swifts | 18 | 9 | 2 | 7 | 47 | 34 | 20 |
| Baxenden | 18 | 9 | 2 | 7 | 42 | 42 | 20 |
| Barnoldswick | 18 | 8 | 3 | 7 | 43 | 37 | 19 |
| Padiham | 17 | 6 | 5 | 6 | 40 | 46 | 17 |
| Holme | 18 | 4 | 2 | 12 | 29 | 49 | 10 |
| Darwen reserves | 17 | 4 | 0 | 13 | 32 | 56 | 8 |
| Colne reserves | 18 | 4 | 0 | 14 | 44 | 60 | 8 |
| *Haslingden reserves w/d* | | | | | | | |

**1910/11** League & league cup double

### Portsmouth Rovers in the Lancashire Combination (Division Two)

| Season | P | W | D | L | F | A | Pts | Pos |
|---|---|---|---|---|---|---|---|---|
| 1911/12 | 30 | 6 | 5 | 19 | 51 | 86 | 17 | 15/16 |
| 1912/13 | 34 | 8 | 3 | 23 | 53 | 101 | 19 | 16/18 |
| 1913/14 | 34 | 8 | 3 | 23 | 53 | 101 | 19 | 17/18 |
| 1914/15 | 24 | 7 | 3 | 14 | 49 | 68 | 17 | 11/13 |

At the close of the 1913/14 season the club made the decision to drop out of the Lancashire Combination and play in the Blackburn Combination instead, in order to cut costs - specifically those related to the playing budget. However, when local rivals Hebden Bridge were elected in their place (themselves moving from the Yorkshire Combination), Rovers had a change of heart and decided to stay in the senior competition. Sadly, they struggled in the 1914/15 season, as they had done in each season in the league, with only Bacup below Portsmouth and Hebden Bridge in the final table. The league did operate during the war, but neither of the pair chose to take part.

Several outstanding footballers began their careers with Rovers, most notably goalkeeper Jerry Dawson, who went on to become an England international. Hailing from the village of Holme, just up the road from Portsmouth, he signed for Burnley in 1907 after having played for Portsmouth Rovers while working as a coal miner. He played over 700 times for Burnley although he missed the 1914 FA Cup final through illness. However, he was still awarded a winners medal because of his gentlemanly conduct. The night before the final, he admitted to his manager that he may not manage to complete the whole game, and in an era before substitutions were permitted, this would have caused problems for his club.

*Jerry Dawson*

Dawson's England debut came against Northern Ireland on Saturday 21st October 1921, at Windsor Park, Belfast. The game ended 1-1. His second, and final cap, came on Saturday 8th April 1922 when England went down 0-1 at home to Scotland at Villa Park, Birmingham.

After retiring from the game Dawson became a member of the coaching staff at Turf Moor, and played as a batsman in the Lancashire Cricket League for Burnley Cricket Club. His nephew Arthur Dawson also started his career with Portsmouth Rovers. He was also a professional football player with Burnley and Nelson.

### Portsmouth Rovers in the FA Cup

It is claimed that Portsmouth twice reached the First Round of the FA Cup around this time. However, this is not true as the furthest they got was the First *Qualifying* Round following successes in the Preliminary Round.

Rovers only won two FA Cup ties before World War One. In the 1910/11 season a 4-0 Preliminary Round success over Burnley Casuals (following a 1-1 draw away from home), was followed by a defeat at Barnoldswick United, 0-3, in the First Qualifying Round (certainly not the First Round proper). Three years later, Tottington were defeated 4-2 at home, before a heavy First Qualifying Round defeat at home to Southport Central, 1-9. The team's record in the competition after World War One was even worse.

*\*\*\**

As football returned to normality after the war, Portsmouth politely turned down an invitation to re-join the Lancashire Combination, and opted instead for local football, the club all too aware that its ground was by no means in a central location, and that attendances were often adversely affected by the inclement weather often experienced in the Burnley Valley.

In terms of success on the football field, that decision was proved a correct one, as the 1919/20 Halifax & District League title was won, with long-time leaders Stainland United overcome in the final weeks

### 1923/24 North East Lancashire Combination
(Shield Competition – 2nd half of the season)

| | P | W | D | L | F | A | Pts |
|---|---|---|---|---|---|---|---|
| Colne Carlton | 12 | 8 | 2 | 2 | 25 | 21 | 18 |
| Blackburn Rov 'A' | 12 | 6 | 3 | 3 | 19 | 23 | 15 |
| Barnoldswick Tn | 12 | 5 | 3 | 4 | 22 | 18 | 13 |
| Barnoldswick Pk V | 12 | 4 | 2 | 6 | 26 | 24 | 10 |
| **Portsmouth Rovers** | 12 | 4 | 2 | 6 | 21 | 25 | 10 |
| Earby | 12 | 4 | 1 | 7 | 19 | 22 | 9 |
| Burnley 'A' | 12 | 4 | 1 | 7 | 14 | 23 | 9 |

### 1924/25 North East Lancashire Combination

| | P | W | D | L | F | A | Pts |
|---|---|---|---|---|---|---|---|
| Clitheroe | 16 | 12 | 1 | 3 | 44 | 27 | 25 |
| Colne Carlton | 16 | 11 | 1 | 4 | 51 | 27 | 23 |
| Barnoldswick Pk V | 16 | 9 | 2 | 5 | 41 | 22 | 20 |
| Burnley 'A' | 16 | 7 | 5 | 4 | 31 | 26 | 19 |
| Blackburn Rov 'A' | 16 | 8 | 2 | 6 | 41 | 26 | 18 |
| **Portsmouth Rovers** | 16 | 3 | 6 | 7 | 26 | 35 | 12 |
| Walsden United | 16 | 5 | 2 | 9 | 25 | 42 | 12 |
| Earby | 16 | 3 | 2 | 11 | 16 | 42 | 8 |
| Knowlwood Utd | 16 | 3 | 1 | 12 | 25 | 50 | 7 |

*Hebden Bridge w/d*

### 1925/26 North East Lancashire Combination
(First competition)

| | P | W | D | L | F | A | Pts |
|---|---|---|---|---|---|---|---|
| Walsden United | 12 | 9 | 1 | 2 | 46 | 25 | 19 |
| Burnley 'A' | 12 | 7 | 2 | 3 | 43 | 19 | 16 |
| **Portsmouth Rovers** | 12 | 6 | 3 | 3 | 48 | 30 | 15 |
| Knowlwood Utd | 12 | 5 | 4 | 3 | 34 | 28 | 14 |
| Blackburn Rov 'A' | 11 | 4 | 2 | 5 | 31 | 25 | 10 |
| Low Moor | 12 | 2 | 2 | 8 | 20 | 39 | 6 |
| Accrington Colls | 11 | 0 | 2 | 9 | 9 | 59 | 2 |

of the season. What was remarkable about this success was that in mid-February, Rovers were second bottom of the ten-team league, and facing a massive fixture backlog, having only played five league games (only two of which had been won).

For the first, and only time, Rovers reached the semi-final of the West Riding County Cup that season, eventually losing 2-3 to Altofts at Exley, Halifax. The Halifax Charity Cup final was also reached that season, resulting in 1-3 defeat to its old adversary, Hebden Bridge, in front of 3,000 spectators at Luddendenfoot in April.

However, just weeks later, Stainland United were trounced 5-1 in the Halifax & District Cup final at the same ground on Saturday 1st May. The team was greeted by Cornholme Band when it arrived home, with *'See the conquering hero comes'* and *'England the land of our birth'* played through the village as it made its way to its headquarters, the Roebuck Inn. It was the last piece of silverware that would be won by the Portsmouth Rovers first team.

The club stepped up to the revived North East Lancashire Combination for the 1920/21 season, but there was little success in this competition throughout its stay, despite the league struggling for numbers, leading it to organise two separate competitions in order to give its team sufficient fixtures. Consequently, support for the club from the public began to wane further.

The 1922/23 season saw the Portsmouth's reserve team, in its final season, win the Calder Valley Challenge Shield and finish well up in the Todmorden League's top division.

Rovers again had only seven opponents in the league in its final season, 1925/26, and one of those failed to complete the season, so there were again two competitions organised. Walsden United won the first competition, while Burnley 'A' finished as champions of the 'Shield' competition which followed. It was no surprise when North East Lancashire Combination folded in the summer of 1926.

Rovers spent the 1926/27 season in the Padiham & District Amateur League, a move which proved successful, the team losing finalists in the league cup the Chadwick Shield - 0-1 to Rosegrove Unity at Lowerhouse - and also runner-up in the ten team top division, just two points behind Burnley Lads' Club. The team scored exactly 100 goals in its 18 league fixtures, 24 of them coming in 10-0 and 14-0 victories over the hapless Read United.

> PORTSMOUTH ROVERS A.F.C.—MEDAL COMPETITION, 1926 (approved by Lancashire F.A.).
> Open to Mills and Workshops, eight miles radius of Portsmouth Station. Twelve Gold Medals for Winners, and twelve Medals for Runners-up.
> Commence Monday, April 5th, 1926. Entries close Monday, March 22nd, 1926. Rules and full particulars, apply to J. LORD, 8, Station-parade, Portsmouth, near Todmorden. 130

For the 1927/28 season, Rovers made a move to the West Lancashire League, near neighbours Walsden United having done so twelve months earlier. This was a big step up in terms of playing strength from the Padiham League, but it was hoped that the higher standard of competition would attract more support. An application had been made to join a proposed Second Division of the Lancashire Combination, but with insufficient applicants, the league shelved the idea.

On Monday 2nd April 1928, an emergency meeting was held in the Labour Club, with T Ingham (club president) in the chair, in order to ascertain whether it was worth the club continuing. Despite a general feeling that there was little enthusiasm to continue running the team, its ground had never been in a better position in terms of facilities, having been properly fenced round, with a new covered stand erected and the dressing pavilion, pay box, and other equipment all in excellent condition. The meeting was unanimously in favour of continuing, a final decision being deferred until the adjourned AGM at the Roebuck on the 16th of that month. There it was underlined how little support there was at the gate, with the club continuing to survive on a hand-to-mouth basis, and a suggestion to drop into a more local league might change that. Sadly the Todmorden League was struggling with five clubs, not all which were in a position to complete their fixtures, leaving the league in a moribund state. The committee decided to at least continue until the end of season, the club finishing near the foot of the league with just six wins and three draws from its 30 fixtures. The club's final competitive win was a home success against Walsden on 11th February 1928.

Ironically, in May the final of the Portsmouth Rovers 'Medal Competition' attracted the largest ever gate for its final, but the club's final two competitive fixtures ended in 1-8 defeats at Adlington and Chorley reserves, its final home game being on 26th April, a narrow 2-3 defeat to Barnoldswick Park Villa, in front of a small crowd. On Tuesday 12th June 1928 the committee decided that would not be able to keep the club afloat for another season after all, and so the decision to disband the club was made.

The loss of a team playing in the likes of the West Lancashire League quite often goes un-noticed, but the club was genuinely missed by the local footballing fraternity. For months there were references in the local newspapers to the old club that had survived for over 40 years, with hopes that it might one day be revived. Sadly, Rattenclough would never see the likes again. The club sold its effects to Wilson Bros. Bobbin Works for £35, whose team took over the ground.

On 26th January 1929 a presentation was made, at the Roebuck, to long serving secretary Joshus 'Jos' Lord, who was given a Mahogany grand-father clock for his 23 year service to the club (he had actually played for the club in 1902 but a nasty injury finished his playing career). On the evening, John Webster Greenwood, a former player with the club recalled, *'there was a hill in the top right corner like a miniature grandstand and the river was many times higher than the ground. The dressing room was fairly warm being warmed by hot air at about*

### 1926/27 Padiham & District Amateur League

| Division A | P | W | D | L | F | A | Pts |
|---|---|---|---|---|---|---|---|
| Burnley Lads' Club | 18 | 15 | 1 | 2 | 73 | 35 | 31 |
| **Portsmouth Rovers** | 18 | 14 | 1 | 3 | 100 | 22 | 29 |
| Padiham St Matt | 18 | 13 | 2 | 3 | 83 | 29 | 28 |
| Rosegrove Unity | 18 | 8 | 4 | 6 | 48 | 53 | 20 |
| Lowerhouse Mills | 18 | 7 | 4 | 7 | 52 | 59 | 18 |
| Dean's Copper Wks | 18 | 7 | 2 | 9 | 52 | 52 | 16 |
| James Nelson's | 18 | 5 | 5 | 8 | 46 | 66 | 15 |
| Municipal College | 18 | 3 | 3 | 12 | 40 | 66 | 9 |
| Butterwth&Dicksn | 18 | 3 | 2 | 13 | 34 | 71 | 8 |
| Read United | 18 | 2 | 2 | 14 | 30 | 99 | 6 |

### 1927/28 West Lancashire League

| | P | W | D | L | F | A | Pts |
|---|---|---|---|---|---|---|---|
| Burnley 'A' | 30 | 23 | 1 | 6 | 106 | 53 | 47 |
| Lancaster Town res | 30 | 20 | 6 | 4 | 84 | 52 | 46 |
| Westhoughton Coll | 30 | 20 | 4 | 6 | 87 | 47 | 44 |
| Chorley reserves | 30 | 18 | 4 | 8 | 91 | 61 | 40 |
| Barnoldswick Pk V | 30 | 17 | 4 | 9 | 86 | 61 | 38 |
| Lytham | 30 | 13 | 8 | 10 | 76 | 95 | 34 |
| Leyland Motors | 30 | 15 | 3 | 12 | 77 | 67 | 33 |
| Adlington | 30 | 14 | 5 | 11 | 83 | 59 | 33 |
| Breightmet United | 30 | 13 | 7 | 10 | 64 | 64 | 33 |
| Blackburn Rvrs 'A' | 30 | 12 | 2 | 16 | 79 | 80 | 26 |
| Bury 'A' | 30 | 11 | 3 | 16 | 73 | 83 | 25 |
| Walsden United | 30 | 8 | 5 | 17 | 56 | 82 | 21 |
| Colne Town | 30 | 7 | 3 | 20 | 64 | 101 | 17 |
| Morecambe res | 30 | 6 | 5 | 19 | 51 | 91 | 17 |
| **Portsmouth Rovers** | 30 | 6 | 3 | 21 | 57 | 108 | 15 |

*Portsmouth Rovers 1904/05 © PHDA Todmorden Antiquarian*

### Portsmouth Rovers' final season West Lancashire League 1927/28

The results of the 33 matches played are as follows:—

| Date | Match | F–A |
|---|---|---|
| Aug 27 | Bury "A" (h) | 4–3 |
| Sept. 2 | Dick Kerr's, F.A. Cup (h) | 2–5 |
| " 9 | Chorley Res. (h) | 2–4 |
| " 23 | Westhoughton, W.L. Cup (h) | 2–3 |
| " 30 | Bury "A" (a) | 1–5 |
| Oct. 8 | Walsden, Lancs. Jun. Cup (a) | 2–3 |
| " 15 | Barnoldswick P.V. (a) | 2–4 |
| " 22 | Blackburn R. "A" (h) | 5–7 |
| " 29 | Colne Town (a) | 2–7 |
| Nov. 12 | Walsden (a) | 0–1 |
| " 19 | Morecambe (h) | 7–2 |
| " 24 | Darwen Res. (h) | 5–2 |
| Dec. 3 | Adlington (h) | 1–1 |
| " 10 | Lancaster Res. (a) | 0–2 |
| " 17 | Breightmet (h) | 1–3 |
| " 31 | Blackburn R. "A" (a) | 2–3 |
| Jan. 7 | Lancaster T. Res. (h) | 1–4 |
| " 14 | Darwen Res. (a) | 2–0 |
| " 21 | Leyland Motors (h) | 2–1 |
| " 28 | Burnley "A" (h) | 1–5 |
| Feb. 4 | Breightmet (a) | 4–4 |
| " 11 | Walsden (h) | 2–1 |
| " 18 | Lancaster T. Res. (Richardson Cup (a) | 0–2 |
| " 25 | Lytham (h) | 1–4 |
| Mar. 3 | Westhoughton (a) | 0–2 |
| " 10 | Burnley "A" (a) | 1–4 |
| " 24 | Lytham (a) | 2–6 |
| " 31 | Leyland (a) | 1–5 |
| Apr. 14 | Westhoughton C. (a) | 2–2 |
| " 21 | Morecambe (a) | 2–3 |
| " 26 | Barnoldswick P.V. (h) | 2–3 |
| " 28 | Adlington (a) | 1–8 |
| May 5 | Chorley Res. (a) | 1–8 |

Goals: For 62, against 116.

four cow pressure. If you were short of room to strip, well you pushed a cow a little further over...subscriptions were about 4s a week and anyone who got behind was left off the team.

A final act was completed in February 1929, when the former officials and committeemen of the club met at the Roebuck (where else) in order to dispose of the balance left in the club's bank account, £7 3s 7d. It was resolved, unanimously, to divide this equally between Reuben Jackson, who had been instrumental in getting the main stand erected, and the Todmorden division of the St John's Ambulance Brigade's building fund, due to the valuable service rendered during matches at Rattenclough over the years.

The Rattenclough ground was used by a number of the clubs until at least the late 1960s. There is little trace of the ground now.

# Rowntree's
# 1897-2013
## 'Relegated champions'

Rowntree's Football Club was one of York's best known amateur football clubs. In later years it was known as Rowntree Mackintosh FC and then Nestlé Rowntree FC – reflecting the ownership of the Rowntree's confectionery, a major employer in the city since 1862. The club was founded during Joseph Rowntree's ownership of Rowntree's.

A Rowntree's Employees football club was already in existence when the association side came along, playing the York & District Rugby Union League's Number Two Competition in 1896. The Rowntree company provided multi-sporting opportunities for its workforce, which, at its peak numbered over 20,000 in a way that Lister's Manningham Mills did in Bradford.

The Rowntree's Employees association section was one of nine founding members of the York Football League in 1897, but the league failed to get off the ground at the time. However, following meetings at the Pack Horse Hotel, Micklegate, over the summer of 1898, there was a second, successful attempt to get the league organised for the 1898/99 season. Rowntree's entered two teams in the new competition (along with Acomb, a club which is also featured in this book), and the club was in continuous membership of the league for well over a century, right up to its demise in 2013.

The 1899/1900 season saw the club entering teams in all three of the league's divisions, with the league title won for the first time at the end of the 1901/02 season (the first of its ten league titles). The club was in the running for the 1899/1900 title but a thumping 0-4 loss early in March 1900 at home to Ebor Wanderers, who retained the title, ended Rowntree's hopes. The Ebor team was the strongest team in the city at the time, and they went on to defeat Rowntree's 2-0 in the final of the York Faber Senior Cup on Saturday 20th April 1901, played on the city's Holgate ground.

| 1898/99 York & District League Inaugural season | | | | | | | |
|---|---|---|---|---|---|---|---|
| Division One | P | W | D | L | F | A | Pts |
| Ebor Wanderers | 10 | 8 | 1 | 1 | 39 | 9 | 17 |
| St Clement's | 10 | 7 | 0 | 3 | 41 | 5 | 14 |
| Selby | 10 | 5 | 1 | 4 | 18 | 19 | 11 |
| **Acomb** | 10 | 4 | 1 | 5 | 16 | 21 | 9 |
| **Rowntree's** | 10 | 4 | 1 | 5 | 20 | 27 | 9 |
| Ulleskelf | 10 | 0 | 0 | 10 | 6 | 59 | 0 |
| *Easingwold & St Crux clubs withdrew* | | | | | | | |
| *Division Two* | | | | | | | |
| St Clement's res | 10 | 8 | 1 | 1 | 32 | 8 | 17 |
| Heworth Parish Ch | 10 | 6 | 3 | 1 | 34 | 9 | 15 |
| Sycamore | 10 | 5 | 1 | 4 | 18 | 20 | 11 |
| **Acomb reserves** | 10 | 4 | 0 | 6 | 17 | 23 | 8 |
| Groves Wesleyans | 10 | 2 | 1 | 7 | 8 | 32 | 5 |
| **Rowntree's res** | 10 | 2 | 0 | 8 | 19 | 36 | 4 |
| *Selby reserves withdrew* | | | | | | | |

It seems that the Wanderers team disbanded during the summer of 1901, at the height of its success, which allowed Rowntree's to take full advantage by lifting its first league title the very next season.

Runner-up position in the league was achieved three times over the next few years - 1910/11, 1912/13, and 1919/20 – underlining the club's position as one of the district's strongest amateur teams. The factory also sponsored age-group teams too, with the Rowntree's Boys Club team also prominent in town (as was the Rowntree's Youth Club team, which went on to play in senior football some decades later).

As a result of its success, Rowntree's AFC became one of the founding members of the Yorkshire Football League in 1920/21. The club was one of those that taken part in initial talks in April and May 1920 at the Griffin Hotel, Leeds when the new league was rubber-stamped, going on to finish eighth in both of its seasons in membership. A reserve team did continue in the York League during this time.

Moving its first team back to the York League in order to save costs, the team again established itself with another runner-up position at the end of the 1929/30 season, followed by a second title one year later, ahead of the Northumberland Fusiliers and Ripon City clubs.

Rowntree's Boy's Club A.F.C. 1911-12

The club experienced a massive resurgence during the 1960s. After winning the league's second tier title in 1957/58, the league title was won no less than eight more times before the team stepped up yet again. The titles won were in 1963/64, 1964/65, 1965/66, 1972/73, 1975/76, 1978/79, 1980/81, and 1981/82.

In 1969, the team's name was changed to Rowntree Mackintosh due to the company's merger with Mackintosh's. The club successfully applied to join the newly formed Northern Counties (East) Football League for the 1982/83 season, meaning that the club had by then become founding members of three different leagues. The club was originally placed in Division Two North, having not competed the season before in either the Yorkshire or Midland Leagues that had merged to form the league. It was no surprise when the divisional title was duly won, the club finishing the season two points clear of Pontefract Collieries.

Upon promotion to the NCEL Division One, Rowntree's finished runners-up behind the Pontefract club. Runner-up position was achieved three more times in a de-regionalised Division One, in 1986/87 (behind Ossett Albion, but scoring over 100 league goals in its 34 fixtures), 1987/88 (just three points behind local rivals York Railway Institute, who were also denied promotion due to the lack of facilities at their ground) and 1988/89 (behind Sheffield). Rowntree's were repeatedly denied promotion to the league's Premier Division due to the unsuitability of its Mille Crux ground.

| Rowntree's AFC Yorkshire League record | | | | | | | | |
|---|---|---|---|---|---|---|---|---|
| | P | W | D | L | F | A | Pts | Pos |
| 1920/21 | 24 | 9 | 2 | 13 | 42 | 45 | 20 | 8/13 |
| 1921/22 | 32 | 14 | 9 | 9 | 60 | 44 | 37 | 8/1 |
| Northern Counties (East) League record | | | | | | | | |
| | Div | P | W | D | L | F | A | Pts | Pos |
| 1982/83 | 2N | 26 | 18 | 6 | 2 | 73 | 29 | 42 | 1/14 |
| 1983/84 | 1N | 26 | 16 | 2 | 8 | 59 | 43 | 34 | 2/14 |
| 1984/85 | 1N | 32 | 15 | 8 | 9 | 62 | 37 | 53 | 6/17 |
| 1985/86 | 1 | 30 | 16 | 5 | 9 | 67 | 45 | 53 | 4/16 |
| 1986/87 | 1 | 34 | 20 | 4 | 10 | 101 | 54 | 64 | 2/18 |
| 1987/88 | 1 | 30 | 20 | 5 | 5 | 74 | 35 | 65 | 2/16 |
| 1988/89 | 1 | 30 | 18 | 6 | 6 | 68 | 36 | 60 | 2/16 |
| 1989/90 | 1 | 28 | 18 | 7 | 3 | 63 | 23 | 61 | 1/15 |
| 1990/91 | 2 | 24 | 12 | 8 | 4 | 46 | 25 | 44 | 3/13 |

Rowntree's then won the Division One championship in 1989/90 – now bearing the name Nestlé Rowntree, after the takeover of their parent factory – but suffered the ignominy of relegation instead of the expected promotion. With ground grading becoming tighter as the league committee strove to improve facilities, Mille Crux's grading was now not adequate for the top two divisions.

After finishing third in the lower division in the 1990/91 season, and limited by its ability to improve its ground, the club decided to resign from the ever-shrinking league.

Rather than dropping back to the York League, the club sought the strongest league possible, and was accepted into the Teesside League for the 1991/92 season, when the club finished runner-up in the league behind Cassell Mall from Billingham. Had Acklam Steelworks not had three points deducted they would have won the league instead, but as it was finished fourth as just two points separated the top four clubs.

The Teesside League title was won in the next two seasons, however; in 1992/93 just ahead of Acklam Steelworks, and in 1993/94 - despite having three points deducted – ahead of Grangetown BC. A fourth season was spent in the league, culminating in a disappointing 8th place in the 16 team league, before a further move to the West Yorkshire League.

Invited to join the West Yorkshire League's Premier Division for the 1995/96 season, the Rowntree's team would now travel south for its home matches rather than northwards in the Teesside League. In its efforts to widen its influence further, and strengthen its top division, the league had invited a small number of prominent clubs to join its expanding Premier Division.

Rowntree's first West Yorkshire League season saw the club find no problem hitting the back of the net, with 102 goals scored in its 30 league fixtures. However, the club trailed champions Carlton Athletic, and runners-up Wakefield AFC in the final table. Consolation came in the form of winning the Premier Division League Cup, with Sherburn White Rose defeated in the final.

After two more top-four finishes, the club became West Yorkshire League Premier Division champions in the 1998/99, and 1999/2000 seasons. The first title was won with a seven point margin over the consistent Carlton Athletic and Beeston St Anthony's clubs, although the league cup final was surprisingly lost to Bradford/Keighley team Sandy Lane. There was a massive fourteen points separating Rowntree's from Beeston St Anthony's the following season, as the York team won 24 of its 28 league fixtures, scoring 100 goals in the process. Carlton won the title the following season, finishing six points ahead of Rowntree's. Sixth place was achieved in the 2001/02 season, with the club way off the pace, and a decision was made to again return to the York League as a cost-cutting exercise for the 2002/03 season, effectively replacing its reserve side in the competition.

No longer financed by the parent company, the club's return to the York League was not initially successful, with relegation from the top division in its second season back. However, an instant return was made by winning the Division One title at the end of the 2004/05 season to gain promotion to the Premier Division. Despite being relegated again in 2008, the club was back in the Premier Division when the end came.

In August 2013 the club withdrew from the league, 116 years after it had first joined it, citing a lack of players and continuing financial pressures, which included the withdrawal of funding by Nestlé Rowntree and the sale of its Mille Crux ground, which has now been incorporated into the York St John's sporting campus.

*The York Press*, Wednesday 14th August 2013

York football has lost its most historic club after Rowntree quit the York Minster Engineering Football League. The club, who have been part of the league since its foundation in 1897, have been forced to disband 'due to a lack of players and continuing financial pressures'.

During the 1980s and 1990s, Rowntree were York's most successful club – winning numerous trophies including the Northern Counties East League division two title at their first attempt in 1983. Four times runners-up in division one, they won the NCEL title in 1989/90, but were relegated back to division two because their Mille Crux ground did not comply with new regulations.

The club, which has produced the likes of York City players Neil Grayson, Andy McMillan and Andy Leaning, dominated both the Teesside and West Yorkshire Leagues before returning to the York Minster Engineering competition, where they had remained represented by a reserve outfit. Rowntree finished tenth in the premier division last year.

A league statement, ahead of this year's kick off on Saturday, said: "When the York Minster Engineering Football League kicks off this coming Saturday, it will be without its most historic and well known club."

"Rowntree's, who have been part of the league since it was founded in 1897, have been forced to quit due to a lack of players and continuing financial pressures.'

"Despite the continued hard work of Mick Hodgson and other members of the Rowntree's backroom and playing staff, the club has suffered several recent setbacks which have seen them left with no choice but to end their 116-year unbroken stay in the league – the only team with such a record.

"Unfortunately, the withdrawal of funding from Nestlé and the more recent loss of their Mille Crux home to York St John University have proven to be the final nails in the coffin of a club who can proudly claim to be ten times York League champions, and who won the Northern Counties East League division one as recently as 1990."

## Rowntree's in FA Competitions

Three **FA Cup** ties were played by Rowntree's, and all were lost: In 1919/20 - 0-5 at South Kirkby Colliery in a Preliminary Round tie, 3-5 at Halifax Town in the Extra Preliminary Round a year later, and then, in 1921/22 1-2 at Boothtown (Halifax) in the preliminary round.

Both of the club's **FA Amateur Cup** ties also ended in defeat – 1-4 in a Third Qualifying Round match in Cleveland at Skinningrove Ironworks in 1901/02, and then in 1903/04 2-4 at Ripon United in a Fourth Qualifying Round tie.

The **FA Vase** brought some degree of success, with at least some ties ending in victory for Rowntree's. The club entered this competition for six seasons between 1983-89, reaching the Second Round proper in its final season of entry 1988/89. Resounding victories over Coundon Three Tuns (4-1 at home), Esh Winning (4-0 away) and Northallerton Town (4-1 at home in the First Round) were followed by a narrow 0-1 loss at home to Dunston Federation Brewery.

The First Round proper was reached on three more occasions; in 1983/84, losing at home to Gretna (1-2) after wins at home to Stockton (4-3) and South Shields (4-1); 1985/86, losing 0-1 at home to Coundon Three Tuns after a 2-2 draw at Coundon, and in 1986/87 when a 1-0 home win over Fryston Colliery Welfare was followed by a disappointing 0-2 defeat at Nottinghamshire side Arnold Kingswell.

# Scarborough Penguins 1921-29
### *'Seaside rivals'*

In terms of oddly named football clubs, few could have reached such a high standard of football as North Yorkshire's Scarborough Penguins FC, a team which rose from local football to county league football, before being merged into its major rival.

Scarborough FC had formed as early as 1879, by members of the local cricket club, and since then had been, without doubt, easily the strongest team in town, which at the time numbered around 40,000. A Scarborough & District League was founded in 1892, lasting just two seasons before being revived in 1898, with Scarborough reserves among its number. Many local teams passed through the local competition without coming close to challenging the supremacy of the town team. However, for a short time during the 1920's things were a little different, as the Scarborough Penguins club briefly challenged its bigger and more established rival.

The Penguins club, founded by a group associated with the fishing industry, and which unsurprisingly played in black and white shirts was founded in 1921, the first chairman being C A Oxley, a council member of the Scarborough FA. Club secretary was B Pickup.

The Penguins club was elected straight into the top division (of three) in the Scarborough & District League for the 1921/22 season. Its first fixture, however, was a 3-0 win at Malton Town in a friendly, on 3rd September 1921. Two weeks later the club completed a 19-1 rout of the 5th Yorks Regiment side in the league.

The new team's home attendances varied between 500 and 1,000 at the Athletic ground, Seamer Road, the home of Scarborough FC, who were the main tenants of the council owned ground. Scarborough FC had decided not to run a reserve team that season, allowing the newly formed club to become sub-tenants.

There were 1,500 present at Seamer Road to witness a 2-3 defeat to Westwood in the Scarborough Cup on 4th March 1922. Westwood also knocked Penguins out of the North Riding Cup on Saturday 17th December 1921, and Penguins also lost in the Scarborough Hospital Bowl to Westwood's second team on Wednesday 26th April. However, the league title was won with a remarkable 100% record, 16 wins out of 16, with 90 goals scored and only eight conceded. The team finished ten points clear of South Cliff and twelve clear of Westwood, who had won the league the previous season.

Penguins also won the Scarborough Hospital Cup, defeating Whitby Town 2-1 on Saturday 29th April 1922 in front of 1,000 at Seamer Road. Whitby had led at half-time, but the tables were turned in the second half through goals from Hopper and Cashmore. Gate receipts of £55 were realised for the tie. Overall, one could say that the Penguins had certainly made its mark in its first season.

In the 1922/23 season, its second, Penguins won the Scarborough & District Cup, defeating Pickering Town 2-1 in the final on Saturday 21st April 1923. The Scarborough and District League title was also retained.

Scarborough FC were first played in a competitive match in a Hospital Cup quarter-final at Seamer Road during the 1923/24 season. Penguins lost 0-6 in front of 2,000 spectators. By now the club was based at Northstead, in the north of the town close to the old Scarborough to Whitby railway line. However, the roof was blown off the main stand there during gales on Saturday 3rd November 1923, although a new covered shelter was in place before the end of the season. The club won the Scarborough & District Cup again, 2-0 in a final replay against Pickering Town on Saturday 26th April 1924, as well as winning the league title for the third successive season.

Scarborough FC were twice winners of the local derbies played in the 1924/25 season, on both occasions at Seamer Road. Penguins went down 2-5 in an FA Cup tie on 6th September 1924 in front of 2,200 spectators and in the following April 1-2 lost in the Hospital Cup semi-final in front of 2,500. The team also lost Scarborough Junior Bowl final, 1-2 to Scarborough's Junior / 'A' team, at the end of April 1925, one year after the teams had twice drawn the previous season's final. The team also failed to win the league that season, the honour going to Whitby Whitehall Swifts instead.

By now the club was strong enough to step up a level, and prior to the 1925/26 season was elected to the Yorkshire League alongside Selby Olympia and a newly formed Brighouse (a club which sadly failed to complete its fixtures). The first fixture in the competition was at home to Fryston Colliery on Saturday 29th August, which was narrowly lost 1-2. Penguins also lost 1-2 at Scarborough in the FA Amateur Cup on 24th November 1925 in front of a crowd of 4,000. At the season's end, 8th place had been achieved, and a £150 profit made.

The 1926/27 season was significant because Scarborough Penguins found itself in the same league as Scarborough, and by the season's end had turned the tables by finished above them. Scarborough had dropped into the Yorkshire League following a number of poor seasons in the Northern League, culminating in the club being found guilty of making illegal payments to seven players in what was strictly an amateur league. The two derby matches in the league saw honours shared Penguins won 3-1 in front of a crowd of 6,600 at Seamer Road on Monday 27th December, but four months later, on Monday 18th April, Penguin's home match was switched to Seamer Road in order to accommodate a larger crowd. Scarborough FC won the return 5-1 in front of 6,000 spectators. The Penguins also lost 3-4 to Bridlington Town in the Bridlington Hospital Cup final.

Despite only finishing tenth in the Yorkshire League - five places and eight points behind Penguins - Scarborough FC was elected to Midland League at the end of the season. In reality, Scarborough FC but was a far better established club, which had a far bigger support base, and a far superior ground, and therefore a much bigger potential than their cross-town rivals.

Penguins' fall from grace was quite rapid. With Scarborough FC now a fully professional outfit, it was always going to be difficult for two professional teams to co-exist town in the town. A dire financial position was revealed at Northstead, resulting in the club retaining just two professionals during the 1927/28 season, with local amateurs making up the rest of the team. This culminated in a season of struggle near the foot of the league. A loss of £180 was made on the season, and although this was the first time that the club had made a loss, it was significant. At the club AGM in June, club president, James Johnson, bemoaned the fact that the weather had been fine for only two home matches that season, and this had clearly affected home attendances. There were obviously ground issues late in the season too, as home games versus Goole Town and Methley Perseverance were switched to Bridlington and Harrogate in the final weeks of the season.

The club was not ready to throw in the towel, however, fully intending to carry on in the Yorkshire League, and resumed its fixtures in the 1928/29 season. However, on Thursday 18th October 1928 at the Yorkshire League's monthly meeting, J Johnson, the Penguins representative reported the possible amalgamation of the two Scarborough clubs, and he wished to know what the league's stance on this would be. Subject to certain criteria being met, the Yorkshire League committee did not object to this, and a deputation was arranged to meet representatives of each club.

Eight days later, on 26th October 1928 the 'merger' (in effect, a takeover by Scarborough FC) was completed, when the 600 members of Scarborough FC confirmed its committee's recommendations with Scarborough reserves therefore taking over the remaining Penguins fixtures in the Yorkshire League. The Penguins committee decided to give any surplus funds from the club to the founding of a bed at Scarborough's new hospital.

**Scarborough Penguins Yorkshire League record**

| Season | P | W | D | L | F | A | P | Pos |
|---|---|---|---|---|---|---|---|---|
| 1925/26 | 28 | 12 | 3 | 13 | 56 | 68 | 27 | 8/15 |
| 1926/27 | 30 | 17 | 1 | 12 | 72 | 63 | 35 | 5/16 |
| 1927/28 | 23 | 5 | 2 | 16 | 56 | 82 | 12 | 11/13 |

(One game, against Methley, not played)

Scarborough FC 1926/27 record in the same league: 30 10 7 13 74 69 27 10/16

One day later the team went down 2-4 at Selby OCO, and the following Saturday (3rd November) went down 2-8 at Goole Town. This was the last recorded match that Scarborough Penguins first team played, as on 10th November, it was Scarborough reserves that fulfilled the away match at Hull City reserves, going down 1-7.

However – almost unnoticed outside the town - Scarborough Penguins Juniors, the club's second string, did not disappear the same time, fulfilling matches in the Scarborough & District League right up until the end of the 1928/29 season, when it then folded.

Scarborough Council later developed the Northstead ground into playing fields for the adjacent school in Maple Drive.

## Scarborough Penguins in FA Competitions

The club played in the **FA Amateur Cup** for three seasons between 1923-26. In each case they were given byes until the Second Qualifying Round. Penguins went down 0-4 at Carlin How Athletic in the 1923/24, and 1-2 to rivals Scarborough in 1925/26. Their only success was in the 1924/25 season when Grosmont were defeated 2-1 (following a 1-1 draw), before a 2-6 defeat at Loftus Albion in the Third Qualifying Round.

Entry into the **FA Cup** was made for five seasons, between 1924-29. Scarborough defeated them 5-2 in an Extra Preliminary Round in 1924/25 and 3-0 in 1927/28. In 1926/27, Stockton Malleable Institute defeated them in a Preliminary Round tie 1-3, and Loftus Albion defeated them 3-0 in a First Qualifying Round tie.

It was only the 1925/26 season that saw Penguins achieve a win in the FA Cup, Filey Town defeated 2-1 away following a 3-3 draw at Seamer Road. In the First Qualifying Round, the Penguins went down to Guisborough Belmont Athletic 0-2.

# Sutton United
# 1903-56
### *'Noisy neighbours'*

Sutton-in-Craven is a village in the South Craven district, roughly half-way between Keighley and Skipton. Its football team might not have played in the upper echelons of non-league football, but its level of success at local level has often been overlooked, with local rivals Silsden and Keighley Town usually attracting most attention locally.

There were several Sutton rugby teams such as Sutton Mills, Sutton Rovers & Sutton Parish in existence in the village during the 1880's, all being of a minor level and playing friendly fixtures only. A much more successful village club operated between 1891 and 1901, becoming joint winners of the old Bradford & District League in 1895/96 along with Thornton, and later playing in the 'Yorkshire Number 3 competition', where they struggled in such elevated competition. That season the club was said to have moved to a new ground close to the village cricket field. It eventually folded as the game went into decline in the region, but not before having turned to Northern Union' (today's Rugby League) in 1899, a full season before the professional Keighley club made that switch.

Sutton Forest FC was the first in the village to experiment with the round ball game in the early 1900s, and by 1904 the name of Sutton United had emerged, and it was this side that became a force in league football for almost half a century. In its early days, the club was closely associated with Sutton Baptist Church, one of the conditions of membership of the football team being attendance at the chapel or Sunday School. The fledgling side went undefeated in friendly fixtures in its first season, having secured a ground at the Vineries in the village.

Success was not immediate in competitive football for United, with a heavy defeat at Cullingworth in the first round of Keighley Charity Cup in 1904/05, and the team went out in inglorious fashion the following season to Silsden, with whom they would share a fierce rivalry in years to come. However, by the end of the 1905/06 season, the side were first ever Keighley & District League champions. Despite suffering defeat to their closest rivals Keighley Celtic in their penultimate game, a 3-1 victory at Wagon Lane, Bingley, over Bingley Town's second team on Saturday 28th April 1906 brought the title to the village for the first time.

The *Keighley News* reported, on May 5th, that *'A large crowd assembled at Cross Hills to await the return of the victors, and when the wagonette arrived about eight o'clock, with flags flying and the club colours waving, the players had an enthusiastic reception. Broadley* (the club captain) *was seized and carried shoulder high to the Liberal Club, which was crowded and where an impromptu concert was held to celebrate the occasion.'*

At its celebration evening held on a later date, Keighley League president E T Shearing congratulated the club and handed the championship shield and medals to the players. The medals, silver with an enamelled front bearing the league's inscription, were individualised with each player's name on the back.

Meanwhile, village rivals Sutton Forest had dropped the 'Forest' part of its title, and the club was also in the top division of the Keighley League. Despite a 0-11 hammering at Keighley Celtic in March, they more than held their own in that first season.

United, whose ground was probably the same as the one used by the old rugby club, were way off the pace at the end of the 1906/07 season, finishing below Sutton FC, who had benefitted from a number of players moving from the recently defunct Kildwick club, but they became the first and only Keighley district side to lift the ill-fated Airedale & Wharfedale Cup the following season when the club defeated St Patricks 6-1 in the final at Lawkholme Lane, the rugby ground being a popular venue for local association finals. Their passage to the final had included victories over Sutton FC themselves (4-0), Silsden Rangers (8-2) and Skipton Union Shed (3-2). The Sutton sides trailed Barnoldswick and Silsden in the league that season, and also saw local rivals Silsden finish way ahead of them at the end of the 1908/09 campaign.

*Sutton United 1908/09*

It was in cup competition that United really made its mark, however, winning the Keighley Charity Cup in both 1907/08 and 1908/09, and also the first ever Keighley & District FA Cup in the latter of those seasons. The first Charity Cup success was achieved after a replay with Silsden. After having drawn 3-3 in the initial match, United edged home 3-2 in the replay in front of a crowd of 4,000, a record for the final at the time, and where receipts totalled nearly £100 for the two games.

United then became the first club to successfully defend the Keighley Charity Cup when Cullingworth were thrashed 5-1 on Saturday 17th April 1909 season. Two days later the *Leeds Mercury* was among numerous newspapers that carried a report of the game,

'*SUTTON UNITED AGAIN WIN THE KEIGHLEY CHARITY CUP. On a rather soft turf, which later on became very sloppy, the final tie for the Keighley Charity Cup was decided on the Lawkholme-lane enclosure, between the holders (Sutton United) and Cullingworth. Sutton from the start played like men who meant to win. Moulding gave them the first goal by unluckily driving the ball into his own net, and Hardaker added second with a ball that first touched the upright. Guest and Riddiough followed with two more before half-time. Broadley in the second half gained a fifth goal for Sutton United, and Cullingworth could only notch a single, to the credit of Winscom. The Mayor of Keighley (Mr. J. Wharton) presented the Cup and medals to Sutton United and medals to Cullingworth, The attendance wars about 1,000.*'

A few weeks earlier, Sutton United had also become the first ever Keighley & District cup winners. The final of the inaugural competition attracted 2,000 spectators to what was the YMCA ground on West Lane, Keighley, and they were witness to second half headed goals from Hardacre and Green that saw off Fell Lane United.

Seeking a higher grade of competition, both Sutton teams, along with Silsden and Keighley Celtic defected to the Bradford & District League in the summer of 1909. It was not a successful move, with all teams finding that their peripheral position led to financial difficulties. Sutton FC themselves dropped into the Skipton Hospital League at the end of the season, and after another poor campaign in the lower standard of competition threw in the towel, as did the Skipton League itself, leaving just United to fly the flag for the village.

United dropped back into the Keighley League for the 1910/11 campaign, using local players only, but made no impression on the leading teams until Keighley Celtic had again left for pastures new. By now the leading teams in the Keighley district were prepared to import players from outside the region in their quest for success. Bigger clubs offered employment to their 'amateur' players, but this would be surprising in Sutton United's case, with probably expenses and one or two other 'perks' being offered instead. Future years would see United switch leagues several times in their search for appropriate competition, many of these changes mirroring those made by the likes of the Silsden and Keighley Town clubs. Sutton United was the 'noisy neighbour' that was forever threatening the dominance of the district's top two teams.

The 1911/12 Keighley Charity Cup competition saw Sutton United the victims of a local giant-killing at the hands of Sutton Highfield. Highfield knocked United out of the competition at an early stage. and not a lot is known about the club, save for the fact that they finished runners-up in the 'Junior Section' of the Keighley League that season, third the following year in an expanded division and folded on the eve of the 1913/14 season. It is quite possible that one or two of their players were tapped up by the senior team in the village, which went on to reclaim the Keighley League title in 1914. United did not defend its title however, as it was one of the first to withdraw without kicking a ball due to the onset of war.

Sutton United was reformed after the Great War, adopting the same red and white stripes of its predecessors. There was a new ground behind the village church, one which had been in use by the former Sutton Forest club. The side gradually re-established itself in the Keighley League, before being prime movers in the formation of the new South Craven League, encompassing some of the stronger teams in the Keighley and Skipton district. However, the club committee got the club into a spot of bother when, right at the start of the 1922/23 season they had a change of heart and decided to keep the first team in the Keighley competition, placing their reserves in the new league instead. Their argument was that the rules of the new South Craven League disbarred players from outside a set radius playing for them, thus rendering them unable to field a full strength team in that competition. But with sanctions hanging over them, the United committee changed its mind again and instead placed their reserves in the Keighley League. The damage had been done though, with the defeats suffered by their reserves in early South Craven fixtures costing them the title.

Feeling that they had 'missed the boat' by not joining the new West Riding County Amateur League instead, a successful application was made to that league for the 1923/24 season, which meant a third different league in three seasons. There was also another ground move, literally to other side of the wall, sharing playing surfaces with the Kildwick Parish Cricket Club on Holme Lane. With their respective seasons overlapping, this caused a few early fixtures in their new league to be cancelled. The season turned out to be anything but successful, with only Silsden below United at the end of the season as the Keighley district sides struggled badly (Parkwood finishing just above them). So Sutton United changed leagues again.

Along with Silsden and Parkwood, United turned again to the South Craven League, edging out Parkwood to win the 1924/25 title, and they won it again in the 1928/29 season when they remained unbeaten in the league. Despite that unbeaten tag, the club still needed to avoid defeat in their final game to win the title. This was against nearest challengers, Cowling, who led 2-1 going into the final minute when United's Howson scored a dramatic equaliser, meaning that the Sutton side won the title in the last minute of the season.

The 1924/25 campaign saw an overdue cup success, when Carleton were defeated 4-1 in the Charity Cup final, when Newbold bagged an impressive hat-trick in front of 2,500 spectators at Lawkholme Lane, and the final was reached again the following year, when United were this time defeated by the odd goal in seven by Parkwood FC.

Keighley League side Steeton were defeated 4-0 in a replayed 1926/27 Keighley & District Cup final, played on another popular local cup final venue at Parkwood. Heavy rain fell throughout the game, and as a result only 400 or so spectators saw United win easily.

Two more cup finals were played against arch-rivals Parkwood FC (who would eventually be renamed Keighley Town, and who played on the Parkwood ground, later renamed the 'Beckside ground', and one that would later become Keighley Greyhound Stadium). There was a 4-1 success for United in the 1927/28 Charity Cup, before a resounding 6-1 revenge victory for Parkwood in the 1929/30 District Cup. Following a District Cup final defeat of Cowling the following year, it was another eight years before another cup final victory, and then, like the local buses, two and a half came at the same time. Silsden were defeated 3-2 in a 1938/39 District Cup final replay, Keighley Town had been routed 12-1 in the semi-final, and when the Charity Cup final with Steeton was also drawn, the two clubs shared the trophy. The Keighley League 'Victory Shield' competition was also won for the first time, during that 1938/39 season, a Laycock hat-trick helping Sutton to a 6-4 success against Morton.

In the meantime, Sutton United had, along with the usual suspects, again been at the forefront of the formation of another new league, this time the Airedale & Craven League. A higher standard of football was again the aim, although the County Amateur League had proved to be *too* high a standard. In the three seasons that this league operated - between 1931-34 – United finished fourth, second, and then finally as champions, ahead of Settle United. A 5-2 defeat of Silsden in the final game of the season was enough to clinch the title, although the same opponents had defeated them in the Charity Cup final.

The league fell apart following its third season, so Sutton United, along with old rivals Keighley Town and Silsden moved again, to the senior division of the Bradford Amateur League. The trio remained in this competition for another three years, until 1937, when they returned to the Keighley League.

## Airedale & Craven League tables

### 1931-32

| | P | W | D | L | F | A | Pts |
|---|---|---|---|---|---|---|---|
| Silsden | 26 | 22 | 2 | 2 | 120 | 38 | 46 |
| Keighley Town | 26 | 20 | 3 | 3 | 170 | 42 | 43 |
| Nelson Amateurs | 26 | 19 | 3 | 4 | 100 | 57 | 41 |
| **Sutton United** | 26 | 17 | 3 | 6 | 78 | 55 | 37 |
| Colne Town | 26 | 15 | 3 | 8 | 118 | 63 | 33 |
| Grassington | 26 | 13 | 0 | 13 | 94 | 86 | 26 |
| Skipton United | 26 | 12 | 2 | 12 | 57 | 77 | 26 |
| Thwaites Brow | 26 | 11 | 2 | 13 | 63 | 101 | 24 |
| Cowling | 26 | 7 | 6 | 13 | 59 | 78 | 20 |
| **Haworth** | 26 | 6 | 3 | 17 | 50 | 69 | 15 |
| Cononley | 26 | 5 | 5 | 16 | 47 | 98 | 15 |
| Ingrow Crotona | 26 | 6 | 2 | 18 | 66 | 123 | 14 |
| Settle United | 26 | 4 | 6 | 16 | 49 | 92 | 14 |
| **Gargrave Town** | 26 | 4 | 2 | 20 | 37 | 66 | 10 |

### 1932-33

| | P | W | D | L | F | A | Pts |
|---|---|---|---|---|---|---|---|
| Keighley Town | 24 | 19 | 3 | 2 | 126 | 53 | 41 |
| **Sutton United** | 24 | 16 | 4 | 4 | 74 | 38 | 36 |
| Colne Town | 24 | 17 | 2 | 5 | 89 | 53 | 26 |
| Settle United | 24 | 15 | 5 | 4 | 90 | 48 | 35 |
| Silsden | 24 | 13 | 4 | 7 | 95 | 57 | 30 |
| Nelson Amateurs | 24 | 12 | 4 | 8 | 77 | 61 | 28 |
| Grassington | 24 | 10 | 2 | 12 | 75 | 85 | 22 |
| Steeton | 24 | 9 | 3 | 12 | 67 | 79 | 21 |
| Skipton United | 24 | 6 | 5 | 13 | 52 | 77 | 17 |
| Carleton | 24 | 6 | 3 | 15 | 36 | 75 | 15 |
| Cononley | 24 | 5 | 2 | 17 | 53 | 93 | 12 |
| Thwaites Brow | 24 | 4 | 2 | 18 | 51 | 94 | 10 |
| Cowling | 24 | 3 | 3 | 18 | 32 | 102 | 9 |

### 1933-34

| | P | W | D | L | F | A | Pts |
|---|---|---|---|---|---|---|---|
| **Sutton United** | 24 | 20 | 2 | 2 | 93 | 27 | 42 |
| Settle United | 24 | 19 | 2 | 3 | 132 | 50 | 40 |
| Silsden | 24 | 16 | 3 | 5 | 98 | 42 | 35 |
| Steeton | 24 | 13 | 3 | 8 | 93 | 74 | 28 |
| Colne Town | 24 | 13 | 2 | 9 | 88 | 84 | 27 |
| Keighley Town | 24 | 11 | 4 | 9 | 76 | 77 | 26 |
| Skipton United | 24 | 10 | 5 | 9 | 67 | 55 | 25 |
| Grassington | 24 | 8 | 5 | 11 | 59 | 74 | 21 |
| Cononley | 24 | 7 | 4 | 13 | 54 | 90 | 18 |
| Earby Victoria | 24 | 6 | 4 | 14 | 70 | 83 | 16 |
| Barnoldswick Tn res | 24 | 6 | 1 | 17 | 51 | 101 | 13 |
| Addingham | 24 | 5 | 1 | 18 | 54 | 96 | 11 |
| Carleton | 24 | 2 | 4 | 18 | 42 | 123 | 8 |

A promising first season in the Bradford League saw Sutton finish in the top half of the table, behind Silsden, but well ahead of Keighley Town, and also reach the league cup final. Another bright season was experienced in the 1935/36 season, with Keighley Town thrashed 8-2 during the campaign, but the following season saw Sutton struggling at the wrong end of the table. It was nevertheless a massive shock to local football when a decision was made in January 1937 to disband the senior team with immediate effect, retaining only the young reserve team that was competing in the second division of the Keighley League. That team finished joint top of the table with Morton but lost the title in a play-off. The reason for dropping down was a cost cutting exercise, leading to senior players, who earned basic match fees or other inducements, leaving the club.

The 1937/38 season saw Sutton United fielding two teams in the Keighley & District League. The first team made no impression on the leaders during the season, but did win the Craven Morrison Cup with a defeat of Craven League champions Carleton in the final.

One year later Sutton finished runners-up in the league behind Steeton who retained their title. However, it was Sutton who threw the title away, after having enjoyed a 100% league record by Christmas 1938. After being held to a 2-2 draw by Steeton at Holme Lane, the team began to regularly drop points, which Steeton were happy to take advantage of.

As consolation, United won one and a half local cup competitions that season, the District Cup and Charity Cup (the latter of which was shared with Steeton).

On top of the cup successes in the 1938/39 season, the Sutton United reserve side which had moved to the Craven League, surprisingly lifting the title ahead of Lothersdale Athletic. By now the club was one of those calling for a revived Airedale & Craven League. The idea never got off the ground, but it was clear that the club was stuck in the middle between local football and county level competition.

Times were hard, with the country enduring the onset of war, the club, (along with the Craven League), went into hibernation during the summer of 1939, choosing not to compete in the War-time Keighley league and cup competitions, and remained dormant until 1946.

Upon re-formation Sutton United achieved an unprecedented level of success before a sharp decline and oblivion in 1956. Entry was made to the Craven League in 1946, but only one season was spent in that company as the title was won, as well as the Keighley & District Cup when they saw off old rivals Silsden 2-0 in the final.

The *Barnoldswick & Earby Times* carried an interesting acccunt of proceedings the previous weekend between Earby and Sutton United on Friday 10th January 1947,

*Unhappy Incidents at Earby. SUTTON WON AFTER GRIM DUEL. Earby Victoria 2, Sutton United 3.*

*Sutton United remained firmly at the heels of Gargrave in the Craven League championship after their game at Earby on Saturday, but their victory adds no distinction to their record. It was dirty game and all the blame for that does not rest with Earby. There was more tripping, more elbowing, and more goalkeepers than has been seen on the Punch Bowl ground before. There were the beginnings of more fights, too, more stoppages of play, and far more reversed decisions. The referee did not rule with a rod of iron, and the game suffered. Nearly half of the playing area was in mud; that in itself was enough to prevent good football. The ball was sluggish when it bounced out more often than not it did not bounce. In these conditions the visitors did well to set about with robust kicking which gained them ground as no other method could.*

Sutton United, 1947

A return to the Bradford Amateur League was made for the 1947/48 season, and along with Keighley League champions Haworth heady heights were again achieved, as the two local sides left the other twelve sides trailing in their wake. Led by George Walker, only two league defeats were suffered, and with Haworth dispatched 6-0, United had an eight point gap between themselves and the Worth Valley side by the season's end. Progress was also made in the County Cup, where the fifth round was reached and a second successive Keighley & District Cup also went their way as two goals from Fisher saw off new Keighley League champions Guardhouse 2-0 in front of 3,000 spectators at the Keighley Town ground. Sutton had thrashed Silsden 11-1 in an earlier round.

After all that, the 1948/49 season was something of a disappointment, with a mid-table position finish in the league, although Worth Village Albion were defeated 3-2 in a third successive District Cup final success. The first tie produced a thrilling 3-3 draw in front of a crowd of 3,000, while 4,000 returned to Lawkholme Lane to see the Holme Lane side win.

United didn't win the Keighley Cup the following year, preferring to enter the Bradford & District Cup instead (going out disappointingly to Dick Lane United) but a return to league form saw a third Bradford Amateur League title in four years as United finished the 1949/50 season seven points clear of their closest challengers. They were top right from the start of the season, opening with a 7-0 rout of Wyke Old Boys, and benefitting from the goals of Jack Hindle, brother of former Keighley Town and Leeds United stalwart Tommy. The presence of Cononley Brass Band couldn't stop Sutton going out of the County Cup in a home replay against Kirkheaton Rovers, but overall the season was viewed with much pride. It was certainly not known at the time, but ever again would such success be encountered by the club.

Photograph (year unknown) showing the villages of Crosshills and Glusburn. The former ground of Sutton United is clearly shown, towards the bottom right hand corner. The village of Sutton-in-Craven is just to the left of the photograph.

With the demise of Keighley Town following their disastrous entry into the Yorkshire League, United was undoubtedly the top side in the district again, and entry to the West Riding County Amateur League for the 1950/51 season was no surprise. However, the side's experience matched that of their previous season in the league over a quarter of a century earlier, and the step up proved too big a step. Notwithstanding the huge amount of travelling incurred, the team just wasn't strong enough, and another position one off the bottom was all it could achieve. It was a tough campaign, highlighted when three players needed hospital treatment after a league cup tie against Salts. With key players retiring or leaving for pastures new, and finances in need of strengthening, the club dropped back into the Craven League.

Despite a third place finish in the 1951/52 Craven League, when they finished just behind Gargrave and Cowling, and victory in the Craven Burton Cup final with a 2-1 defeat of Rolls Royce in the final, the team was past its best. Re-entry into the Bradford League for the 1953/54 campaign proved to be the beginning of a rapid slide as the club resigned from the competition in October 1953, reporting a shortage of players. The reserve team that operated in the Keighley League – itself now a shadow of its former self – was now the first team for the rest of the season. Only Silsden's third team sat below United and bottom place, with the club seemingly on its last legs. The following season saw a Sutton Textiles side operating in the Keighley League, with United fielding a side in the Keighley Minor league only, before the United name returned to senior football for one final season. The team's swansong was a 2-6 loss to league champions Worth Village in the Victory Shield (league cup) final, after which, in the summer of 1956, Sutton United slipped quietly from the scene.

The old football ground now sits below the South Craven School site, with Crosshills FC currently based a stone's throw away on the other side of Holme Lane, and until recently Sutton Juniors FC using the school playing fields.

# Wombwell
## 1880-1933
### *'A tale of two teams'*

The period between 1880-1933 actually encompasses several different 'Wombwell' clubs, including three versions of Wombwell Town, as well as various incarnations of the separate Wombwell Main colliery-based team. The first 'town' club has its roots back in 1883 as Wombwell Clarence, folding in 1902, the second - entirely unsuccessfully - between 1907-09, and the third from 1920-33 (and there have been several others since then). Competing with these, at various times, was not only the Colliery team, but also a number of other shorter-lived but significant junior (in status) clubs.

The first record of organised football in the vicinity is during the 1880 'Wombwell Feast & Sports' gala which was held on 20th & 21st September, with football hosted at the Wombwell Main Cricket Ground. Fours team entered a football tournament, these being; Ardsley, Hoyle Mill, Low Valley, and **Wombwell Main**. On the Monday, Main defeated Ardsley, with Hoyle Mill defeating Low Valley. The 'final', played a day later saw Hoyle Mill defeat Wombwell Main. No other details were given in the report in the *Barnsley Chronicle*.

The following month the Wombwell Main Cricket & Football Club commenced its first association football season, and after a practice match on Monday 18th October, the footballers were defeated 0-1 at Darfield Wanderers later that week. On Saturday October 23rd, a home game was played against Ardsley Red Rose, which was won 3-0. A football pitch was eventually established close to the cricket ground, but at the other side of the railway, although the football section of the club seems to have been a rather informal entity for the first few years of its existence, with only a few fixtures reported during the 1880s.

Later in the decade, Wombwell Temperance was one of several short-lived early association teams in the town. This club emerged early in the 1887/88 season. In October 1887 its committee consisted of; President John Whitlam, vice president B Malpass (himself president the following year), secretary G H Atkin (Mssrs Kaye & Marshall the following year), treasurer A J Wroe, and captain T Fletcher. Its first match that season was against Brampton on 8th October 1887.

The Temperance football club was running two teams 1888/89 season, at the end of which the club had just over £1 7s in the bank. However, the club seems to have folded around the summer of 1889.

Wombwell Clarence was another local club, with matches played between 1883-88. Its first match was possibly that on 20th October 1883 at Hoyle Mill, when it lost a *'very slow game'*, according to the *South Yorkshire Times*, 1-2. The team line-up in a 3-1 victory over Kingstone Place on Saturday 8th December 1883 was: *Goal: G Turton, Backs: T Kilner (captain) & C Littlewood, Half-backs: Hanson, Stanger, Honsly, Centre: Wilson, Noble, Hargreaves, Forwards: Prine, Wasnigton, (spellings as given in the newspaper).* The Clarence cricket club renamed itself Wombwell Cricket Club in May 1884, but the football club did not, although the Clarence name disappeared from the football fixtures in the summer of 1888.

However, the Wombwell Cricket Club became known as 'Wombwell Town Cricket and Football club' in August 1888. This organisation could well have absorbed the Clarence club, as there was an S Kilner involved in the decision to adopt football in the winter months. The football team, naturally, became known as **Wombwell Town** FC. A 0-0 draw against Wombwell Temperance Thursday 25th October 1888 was amongst its fixtures.

By the 1890/91 season, the club was fielding two teams on a Saturday, and in 1891/92, Wombwell Town's Junior team reached the final of the Barnsley Junior Cup. After a 6-2 defeat of St Peter's in its semi-final at Queens Gardens, Barnsley, the team was also successful in the final, winning a tighter match 4-3 against Kilnhurst, at Oakwell.

By August 1892 the club was advertising as a 'professional team' for fixtures in the local press. Club secretaries at this time were Thomas Thornsby & J W White, with headquarters at The Horse Shoe Inn, and it had a membership of 70. For the 1892/93 season the Barnsley Senior and Junior cups were both entered, and the club originally intended to play in the South Yorkshire League. However, a late change saw Wombwell Town in the second division of the Hallamshire League instead, possibly to avoid playing in the same competition as Wombwell Main. Late in the season the first team lost in the semi-final of the Barnsley Charity Cup, to St Peter's.

**Wombwell Main United** appeared in the 1888/89 season, the colliery team's headquarters being at the Sir George's Arms, with a William Bennett as secretary. The club initially grew quickly, as the following season it was running two teams, and added a short-lived third team for 1890/91 (the reserve teams being known as Wombwell Main Rovers and Swifts) At the club AGM in August 1892, it was reported that there was £21 in bank, and in October that year the club was advertising for three professional forwards in the local press.

The club dropped the 'United' suffix for the 1892/93 season, its first team playing in the Sheffield Alliance, with reserves in the lesser South Yorkshire League. Runner-up position was achieved in the former, Main drawing 1-1 in the deciding match at home to Elsecar in front of 1,000 spectators. G Thompson of Elsecar was ordered off the field 15 minutes from time, leading to a 20 minute stoppage but it was they who became champions. There was an opportunity for the club to merge with Wombwell Town at this time, with the aim of creating a really strong village club, but the colliery team chose to find its own path to success.

For the 1893/94 season, both Town and Main competed in the Sheffield & Hallamshire Minor Cup League competition, while Wombwell Main had also retained a team in both the South Yorkshire League and Sheffield Alliance. Wombwell Town reached the final of the Barnsley District Charity Cup, but lost 3-6 to its old rivals Barnsley St Peter's at the Dearne Athletic grounds.

**Town Go It Alone**

Main lost the use of its ground in the summer of 1894, but chose to disband rather than merge with Town, who took the pick of its players. The Main cricket club moved to a new ground in 1895, however Being the 'colliery' team it is understandable why it chose to keep its own identity, and later years would see the name of Wombwell Main back in local football. By now several other 'junior' clubs had emerged in the town.

It was left to Wombwell Town as the only 'senior' club in the town though. During the 1894/95 season Town competed in the Northern division of the Sheffield Shield, essentially a 'second division' of the Wharncliffe Charity Cup League. Despite struggling in the league, the first team won 23 out of its 38 fixtures that season and capped it all with the capture of the Sheffield Minor Cup, defeating Rotherwood

Rovers 4-0 in the final, which was played at Carbrook. There was 'tea and social evening' in late June 1895 to commemorate winning the cup, with reports in the local press describing the club as *'flourishing'*.

The 1895/96 season saw Wombwell Town in the Sheffield Challenge Cup League, where it finished in ninth position in a 15 club competition. This was the strongest league in the district, the team playing against the likes of Mexborough, Chesterfield Town, and the reserve teams of the Sheffield clubs United and Wednesday. Other fixtures were played in the 'Sheffield New League', a four team competition, alongside Kilnhurst, Elsecar, and Hoyland Silkstone, although the club finished at the foot of the table.

The top league in the district was reorganised as the Sheffield Association League for 1896/97, with Town enduring a disappointing season at the foot of the table. It fared better with a mid-table finish in the Wharncliffe Charity Cup League which it had joined in the summer.

The 1897/98 saw the first team continue in the Sheffield Association League and reserves in the Barnsley Minor Cup (which was of course, a league competition, in line with many other South Yorkshire Leagues). By now the Guide Post Inn and Alma Inns were also being used for some clubs meetings. A debt of just over £1 18s was reported at the end of the season, which wasn't considered too worrying at that time.

The season was more successful, with Town finishing level on points with Parkgate United at the head of the Sheffield league, but losing the deciding championship match 0-3, played at neutral Carbrook on Saturday 23rd May 1898. The reserve team were also league runners-up behind Birdwell's second team.

The 1898/99 season looked like it could be a turning point in the history of Wombwell Town as it became the champion club of the Yorkshire League in its only season in the competition. The league had been founded the season before, bringing together the best teams in what is now West Yorkshire with the reserve sides of the top Sheffield and district teams. The team was welcomed home from its 4-0 win at Bradford late in April by Wombwell Brass Band, and the side did not drop a single point at home all season. Sadly the league all but fell apart at the end of the season, when all of the latter teams withdrew following two seasons of complete dominance. The reward for its title – a complimentary supper at the Guide Post Inn on Thursday 15th June 1899, where gold medals were awarded to the players.

Wombwell Town also finished fourth in the Sheffield Association League that season, the club turning out its first team in this competition as well as the Yorkshire League.

It was something of a surprise then, when the 1899/1900 season saw Town struggling. In the Sheffield Association League it could only finish eighth out of nine clubs, while in the Wharncliffe Charity Cup league it finished ninth and bottom. It is likely that such a turnaround in fortunes was due to a cost-cutting exercise that saw reduced payments to players, due to debts carried over from the previous season.

Town used the old ground near the Guide Post at New Wombwell for the 1900/01 season, and improved to finish just below mid-table in an expanded 15 team league (There was no Wharncliffe Charity League, the competition being played as a straight knock-out competition instead). The club's old ground at Station Road was prone to flooding which led to the temporary abandonment of that site.

> *Sheffield Daily Telegraph*, **Monday 11th March 1901**
>
> *On Saturday a foot race was decided, which had been brought about in consequence of a dispute between two players in the Wombwell Town Football Club as to which of the two players, Edgar Sykes and James Dyer, was the swiftest runner. They were matched to run from goal to goal for £10, the distance being 113 yards. Sykes got away well, Dyer stumbling in getting off his mark, Sykes winning by a yard.*

Town returned to the Station Road ground during the 1901/02 season however, but it proved to be the last for the club in its current guise. A first win in the Sheffield Association League didn't come until the end of October, a 3-2 home success against Hunslet, who could only muster ten men for the fixture. The club's worsening financial situation led the team to field amateurs only, and to make use of local talent, but in front of meagre crowds it could not make the game pay. In later years, it was reported in local newspapers that 'administrative difficulties' had played a part in the club's demise. Therefore, Wombwell Town dropped out of the league at the end of February 1902 – less than three years after being crowned Yorkshire League champions. Its reserve team had been playing in the South Yorkshire League, and also dropped out – although Wombwell Rising Star, another famous old club continued in that competition. Several other local junior teams were to be found playing in the Wombwell & District and Denaby & District Leagues at this time.

Even fund raising efforts could not save Wombwell Town, the attendance at a concert at the local Congregational Showroom in April was affected by the inclement weather, and as a result there was no club the following season.

*Wombwell Town c1901*

**Wombwell Main Return To Fly The Flag**

With the Town club now defunct, there was no senior football in Wombwell. **Wombwell Main** reformed, as a strictly amateur club, in time for the 1901/02 season, playing in the Second Division of the newly formed Wombwell & District League alongside six other teams. It appears Main joined the competition late in December, at a time when the division was restarted following withdrawals and the arrival of new clubs. At the end of the season, the club won the Barnsley Borough Cup, defeating local rivals Wombwell St Mary's in the final, played in Wombwell, on 'Mr Taylor's field, between the canal and the railway', according to the *Barnsley Chronicle*, on Saturday 22nd March 1902. A crowd of between 400 and 500 saw the only goal of the game scored in the first half, when a St Mary's defender inadvertently put through his own goal. There was an unfortunate incident during the second half when Main's Sykes was ordered off the field for striking an opponent. With the crowd swarming onto the field as a result of this, the game was delayed by twenty minutes while order was restored.

However, according to the same newspaper, *'There were great rejoicings up Wombwell Main way in the evening, two wagonettes being hired, and the players driving round all that neighbourhood, displaying the much coveted trophy. The people shared in the enthusiasm, and proceedings were for a time rather lively.'*

Main appeared in the Wombwell League the following season, in its single seven team division, but with that competition folding in the summer of 1903, a new league was sought for the 1903/04 season, and this was to be the Barnsley Minor Cup league. The club played second fiddle to Wombwell Rising Star in that competition, however. Rising Star, in existence since 1894, and based at the Guide Post ground, defeated Wentworth in a second replay to win the Barnsley Challenge Cup, and also finished runner-up in the Barnsley Minor League, losing 1-2 to Hoyland at the Guide Post Inn ground.

A reserve team was re-introduced for the 1904/05 season, with headquarters at the Sir George's Arms. The growing strength of the reformed club was apparent when it became Barnsley Association Minor Cup champion, holding a four point lead at the end of the season in the league competition. However, the club still had to play off against the second placed Grimethorpe United in order to win the title. They did this in a replay (following a 0-0 draw). At ninety minutes in the replay, the score stood at 1-1, necessitating extra-time. After fifteen minutes each way the score was 2-2. Therefore, the sides played another ten minutes each way, with no score, another 5 minutes each way, then another quarter hour each way, followed by ten more minutes each way, with Wombwell Main finally getting a third, and decisive goal! Rising Star finished well up the table again that season.

On top of that, Wombwell Main also lifted the Barnsley Challenge Cup, defeating South Kirkby in the final, but lost the Barnsley Beckett Hospital Charity Cup final 0-1 to Rockingham in front of 3,000 spectators at Hoyland on Saturday 1st April 1905.

The following four seasons all brought cup final success, as the club continued its fine run. The 1905/06 season saw Main finish in mid-table in the Barnsley Minor League, with Rising Star right at the bottom, but was in cup competition where silverware was easier to come by. Four cup finals had been reached by the end of the season;

In the Barnsley Beckett Cup, Barnsley Minor League champions Elsecar Athletic were defeated 2-0 at Dillington Park, Worsboro' Common in the final. The Rotherham Charity Cup final saw Goldthorpe Institute edged out 2-1 after extra time, in a replay at Wath. In previous rounds, Sheffield All Saints, Oxford Street, Parkgate, and Rotherham Town had been defeated. There was another narrow cup final victory in the Mexborough Montagu Cup, with South Kirkby beaten 2-1, in front of 3,000 spectators at the Mexborough Athletic Grounds. However, the Walton Charity Cup final was lost to Darfield.

The 1906/07 season saw Wombwell Main win no less than FIVE cup competitions during a busy end of season schedule After Main finishing at the head of the Barnsley Minor League, the Grimethorpe United club was defeated 4-2 in the Minor Cup final (following a 1-1 draw). The same club was defeated 4-0 in the Barnsley Challenge Cup final, also at Oakwell, in front of almost 3,000 spectators. Brunswick Mission were defeated 4-2 at Wath in the Rotherham Charity Cup final, after victories over Chapeltown Central, Thorpe Hesley and Heeley Friends in earlier rounds. To add to these successes, Mitchell's Main colliery team were defeated 2-1 in the final of the Walton Charity Cup at the Guide Post ground, and Darfield defeated 4-0 at Wath in the Winstanley Cup final. The team enjoyed a most satisfactory post season ham and tongue tea and concert at the colliery's Wesleyan Chapel at the end of May.

*Turton, Wombwell Main captain in 1906*

After having initially withdrawn from the Barnsley Minor League, Wombwell Rising Star replaced Staincross after a few weeks of the 1906/07 season. Unfortunately Star dropped out of the league for good at the season's close.

The 1907/08 season opened with a new Wombwell Town club joining Wombwell Main in the Barnsley League. This revival lasted only two seasons, with the team rooted at the bottom of the league for the duration. It is likely that the side used the Guide Post ground for its fixtures. The Main, however, continued to win cup competitions. Hoyland Town were defeated 1-0 at Oakwell in the Barnsley Minor Cup final at Oakwell, and Darfield United 2-0 in front of 2,000 spectators at the Guide Post ground in the Walton Charity Cup.

Despite finishing at the head of the league again, Main lost the Minor Cup final to Hoyland Town, but Darfield United were again defeated in the Walton Charity Cup, again at the Guide Post, this time 2-1 after a 1-1 draw. The replay was kicked off by champion boxer 'Iron' Hague.

Main spent just one more season - 1909/10 – in the renamed Barnsley Association League. No honours were won, the club having initially applied to join the much stronger Sheffield Association League, but for whatever reason this move was never made. Despite having almost £24 in hand at the start of the season, it was the last for this second incarnation of Wombwell Main FC as the club dropped out of the league in the summer of 1910. No reason was reported, but its demise was likely down to a lack or withdrawal of funding from the colliery sports club.

There were eight Wombwell teams in the Barnsley Sunday School league during the 1911/12 season (including Wombwell Main Wesleyans, which was a separate club), so football was by no means dead in the town.

Wombwell Main AFC returned in August 1913, playing in the Barnsley Association League for two seasons - winning the title in the 1914/15 season - and again during 1919/20 when football resumed after World War One (The club also competed in a wartime Barnsley Senior League competition). The team won the Barnsley Association Cup at the end of its first season back, defeating Cortonwood BC. On Easter Monday, 13th April 1914, at Oakwell, the sides drawing 1-1. The replay three days later saw Main win 2-0. And that wasn't the end of Main's new success, Birdwell were defeated 2-0 in the 1915 final. The club regrouped in the Barnsley Junior League between 1919-23, initially playing second fiddle to Wombwell Recs, who lost in a championship final in 1922. The league's Division Three title was won by Main in 1922/23, to but the club seems to have folded again at that point. By then, however, there had been new developments…

| 1908/09 Barnsley Minor League | P | W | D | L | F | A | Pts |
|---|---|---|---|---|---|---|---|
| **Wombwell Main** | 18 | 13 | 3 | 2 | 46 | 17 | 29 |
| Hoyland Town | 18 | 11 | 5 | 2 | 48 | 14 | 27 |
| Hoyland Silkstone | 18 | 10 | 3 | 5 | 43 | 22 | 23 |
| Darfield United | 18 | 10 | 3 | 5 | 38 | 19 | 23 |
| Elsecar Main | 18 | 11 | 3 | 4 | 37 | 25 | 23 |
| Monckton Ath res | 18 | 8 | 3 | 7 | 33 | 24 | 19 |
| **Grimethorpe Utd** | 18 | 8 | 2 | 8 | 37 | 36 | 18 |
| Birdwell | 18 | 4 | 2 | 12 | 26 | 42 | 10 |
| Mitchells' Main | 18 | 3 | 2 | 13 | 16 | 43 | 8 |
| **Wombwell Town** | 18 | 0 | 1 | 17 | 11 | 93 | 1 |

## A New Era - Town Return

*South Yorkshire Times*, Saturday 24th January 1920

WOMBWELL'S FOOTBALL ENTERPRISE
*Proposal to Establish a Midland League Club*
COMMITTEE APPOINTED TO FUND A GROUND
*Suggested Start Next Season*

'Proposals which promise to culminate in decisions of vital importance and interest in sporting circles in the Dearne Valley, and, especially in the township and district of Wombwell, were discussed at a meeting held at the Royal Oak Hotel, Wombwell, on Wednesday evening. For some time, the feeling has developed locally that Wombwell is not sufficiently enterprising in the matter of sport, and it has been subject of general comment that the town has no football club which is anything like commensurate with its size and importance. Not only from a sporting point of view, but also from a business standpoint, prominent local sportsmen have argued that Wombwell is sadly lacking in initiative not to provide attraction in the town for the thousands who leave the district whenever there is a draw in one of the neighbouring towns.

It was to discuss the establishment of a really good class football club in the town – probably a Midland League club – that the meeting was held on Wednesday evening. The movement has a strong and influential backing, and there are good hopes that it will succeed in its object.

There were present at the meeting, Coun. A E Allott in the chair, and Messrs. F Hudson, Seed, Lythe, Calvert, Crossley, Flowers, H V Wroe, Edgar Wroe, Luther Holmes, S Smith, D H Roberts, G Steele, A Stenton, W Beardsall, J Ogden, J G Taylor, G Guest, R Clarke, H White, A Hunsley, and others.

They were met together that evening to talk over the question of the formation of a really good football club for Wombwell. With all due respect to other clubs in and round about the township, they had no team that could compete with, nay, such teams as Barnsley or Mexborough, a team that would keep at home the people who at present leave the town in hundreds to see football outside. It was really an astonishing fact that with a population of 20,000 they had no really first-class club. The number of small teams which were doing well in their own class of football, but who, unfortunately, were not of sufficient distinction to keep the people at home, showed that they had the material for making tip-top players. Such a team as he (Mr Allott) described, would, he thought, be a benefit to the town generally. It would provide healthy outdoor sport for those who played, and fresh air for those who liked to watch a really good game of football. It would keep the people at home, and if the people stayed at home they would spend money at home. That, of course, would benefit the trade of the town. No doubt their greatest difficulty would be experienced in obtaining a suitable ground. That had been the trouble with other football clubs in the town in the past. They had plenty of fields, but they were all too low down and susceptible to floods. Other fields they had been able to get in the past required fencing, and these were impossible on account of the expense.

Mr Seed enquired what was the title they propose to give the new club. The old Wombwell Town finished up in debt, and they could not start a new club in the old name without taking over their liabilities.'

Mr Harold Wroe, of Hough Lane, Wombwell, was appointed secretary at the meeting, with several possible sites for the new club discussed; land behind houses on Summer Lane which had been earmarked for housing, and was close to the Rectory, being a strong preference, given the fact that it was both dry and well-shielded. Two crofts that faced the schools on Kings Road were also suggested, as well another at the top of Main Street, behind the houses in Summer Lane Extension.

The application to join the Midland League unfortunately failed, but the club was instead welcomed into the newly formed Yorkshire League, and also into the Sheffield Association League.

The ground issue was solved when land off Hough Lane was procured. This is the same site *'on Summer Lane'* that had been discussed.

The *Star Green 'Un* reported, on Saturday 28th August, *'The new ground has undergone such wonderful transformation that it is difficult to believe that it was ploughed up only five months ago. The accommodation which the directors are providing for the home and visiting players, not forgetting the humble referee, looks like being second to none in the Yorkshire League.'*

The club, hereon named 'Wombwell FC' was assisted by county cricketer, Roy Kilner, who had occasionally appeared as half-back for Preston North End during the war.

In August, the company was floated, with the object of *'promoting and carrying on the business of a Football and Athletic club, in all the branches thereof, and to promote the practise and play of football, cricket, and other Athletic sports, games, and exercises of every description.'* A sum of £535 in £1 shares was immediately subscribed to.

The new club's first competitive fixture was on 4th September 1920, a 1-1 draw at home to Fryston Colliery in front of 4,000 spectators. By the end of the season, only Bradford (Park Avenue) reserves stood between Wombwell and the inaugural Yorkshire League title. Wombwell surged up the league in the second half of the season but finished three points behind the Bradford club. Average gates were just short of 3,000, with 4,000 present for the visit of Worksop Town in the FA Cup. On Christmas Day 1920, 6,000 witnessed the local derby at home to local rivals Wath, Wombwell equalizing with a late penalty to earn a 1-1 draw, and only 48 hours later another 7,000 packed into the ground to see the league Bradford (Park Avenue) reserves win 2-0, Wombwell's first league defeat of the season.

Another application was made to join the Midland League, which had lost three clubs to the new Third Division (North) of the Football League, and, along with three other clubs from the Yorkshire League, the Wombwell club was this time successful. This was hardly surprising given the large attendances the club had attracted during its successful season in the Yorkshire League.

Despite having struggled badly in its debut season in the Sheffield Association League, Wombwell's reserve team replaced its first team in the Yorkshire League for three seasons between 1921-24. In fact, a much strengthened reserve team finished fourth in the expanded seventeen team league at the end of the 1921/22 season.

The club's first Midland League season was relatively successful both on and off the field. A profit of over £46 was made over the season, which saw a mid-table finish amid a trade depression that was affecting the region quite badly. A crowd of over 4,930 attended the FA Cup tie at home to Doncaster Rovers on 24th September 1921.

The following season was less successful, and the club reported a loss of £94 on the 1922/23 season amid a heavy fall of almost £1600 in revenue. Net revenue in the Sheffield Association Cup was down by two-thirds, despite the club having won the competition. A 1-1 draw in the final with Mexborough at Oakwell on Saturday 9th April 1923, was followed by a replay at Wath on 16th April, which was won 2-0, before 4,000 spectators.

The financial situation worsened, and in February 1924 the Wombwell FC Supporters Club called a meeting with the club officials to consider proposals for reviving interest in the club from the local townspeople. The summer of 1924 saw the reserves withdrawn from the Yorkshire League, and a purely amateur team, consisting of locals, entered into the Barnsley Association League instead.

Wombwell dropped to the foot of the Midland League during the 1924/25 season, the reserves also struggling at the foot of the local league. The adjourned AGM was held at the Royal Oak on Monday

17th August, with another £128 lost on the season. This figure would have been far worse had a Shilling Fund not brought in £90, although the club by now owed £359 in total to the bank.

A new stand was purchased by the Supporters Club during the summer of 1926, this being large enough to accommodate up to 500 spectators, bringing seating capacity up to 1,250 – a figure above the previous season's average gate. The club had just finished in mid-table in the Midland League, but this was to be the last time that it finished anywhere other than near the bottom of the league.

With the financial position of the club worsening every year, club officials were forced to pay the train fares to send the team to venues such as Newark for Midland League fixtures from their own pockets. Fifty-game league seasons were endured between 1928-1930, with revenue from games continuing to fall.

Alfred E Allott, a former schoolteacher, and who was one of the prime-movers behind the formation of the club in 1920, was appointed club chairman in July 1928. Sadly, he could do little to improve either performances on the field, or gate receipts, which were by now usually only £20 or so for home fixtures.

It was reported at the club AGM in August 1930 that transfer fees, totalling £650, had saved the club, which planned to run a reserve team in the Sheffield Association League again the following season. Had it not been for the relentless efforts of the Supporters Club then Wombwell FC may well have folded up before it did. In addition, the other Midland League clubs kept their patience with Wombwell, who had to seek re-election to the competition on several occasions. The directors of the club spent over £130 of their own money trying to keep the club afloat during the 1931/32 campaign, and as a precaution against doing so too late to avoid financial penalties, the club resigned from the league. This resignation was later rescinded, but it underlined the dire position had found itself in. It was recognised that the trade depression, and the consequent lack of means of acquiring a 'ready-made' team, was having an effect on club finances and fortunes on the field. That didn't stop a number of Wombwell players from being signed up by Football League clubs however, and by the end of the 1920s the list included; Jack Johnson (Leeds United), Willie Wood (Oldham Athletic), Jack Smith & George Crownshaw (Huddersfield Town), Albert Smith (Leicester City), Walter Bennett (Portsmouth), Sam Hadfield (Sheffield Wednesday), Len Hopkinson and George Raynor (Sheffield United).

On Thursday 23rd March 1933, a decision to again withdraw from the Midland League at the end of the season was made at a sparsely attended meeting of shareholders of the club, with a further meeting organised for 20th April to wind up the club completely. There was to be no way back this time. By the end of that season, the club had shipped 196 goals in its 44 league fixtures, of which only four did not end in defeat, with the ground subsequently taken over by a greyhound company.

Ironically, a new, albeit short-lived junior league was formed for the 1933/34 season based around Wombwell – one of the teams in its inaugural season being Wombwell Main FC, which would achieve success the following season by winning the Barnsley Association League title, with a 2-0 defeat of Highstone United in the league final on Thursday 2nd May 1935. That club would continue to play football, on-and-off, during subsequent seasons, in competitions such as the Doncaster and Barnsley leagues, until stepping up to the Sheffield & Hallamshire County Senior

| Wombwell FC league record | | | | | | | |
|---|---|---|---|---|---|---|---|
| Season | P | W | D | L | F | A | Pts | Pos |
| **Yorkshire League** | | | | | | | |
| 1920/21 | 24 | 16 | 4 | 4 | 67 | 18 | 36 | 2/13 |
| **Midland League** | | | | | | | |
| 1921/22 | 42 | 16 | 9 | 17 | 60 | 66 | 41 | 12/22 |
| 1922/23 | 42 | 12 | 14 | 16 | 50 | 63 | 38 | 15/22 |
| 1923/24 | 42 | 12 | 10 | 20 | 47 | 74 | 34 | 18/22 |
| 1924/25 | 28 | 5 | 8 | 15 | 31 | 59 | 18 | 15/15 |
| 1925/26 | 40 | 14 | 9 | 17 | 73 | 89 | 37 | 12/21 |
| 1926/27 | 38 | 7 | 6 | 25 | 57 | 111 | 20 | 19/20 |
| 1927/28 | 44 | 12 | 7 | 25 | 70 | 107 | 31 | 20/23 |
| 1928/29 | 50 | 12 | 8 | 30 | 80 | 136 | 32 | 25/26 |
| 1929/30 | 50 | 15 | 9 | 26 | 76 | 116 | 39 | 21/26 |
| 1930/31 | 46 | 9 | 9 | 28 | 74 | 129 | 27 | 23/24 |
| 1931/32 | 46 | 14 | 9 | 23 | 81 | 99 | 37 | 20/24 |
| 1932/33 | 44 | 2 | 2 | 40 | 32 | 196 | 6 | 23/23 |

League from the latter in 1996. Among the trophies won were the Senior League's Premier Division championship in 1998/99, 2001/02, 2002/03 & 2007/08, as well as several other titles. These included the Barnsley Junior League 1964/65 (and the league's Junior league title in 1981/82), and several successes in the Barnsley Nelson League (Division One 1973/74, Division Two 1979/80, Division Three 1977/78, Associate Division 1954/55 & 1955/56). The club has also run a Sunday League team at times, and in total has won the Mexborough Montagu Cup on six occasions in the last quarter of a century; in 1997/98, 2000/01, 2001/02, 2002/03, 2006/07, & 2008/09 (losing three finals since then). The Barnsley Beckett Hospital Cup has also been won by the Sunday league side several times.

Other short-lived teams from the town have also tasted moments of success through the years in Barnsley & district minor league competitions.

## Grounds

Several grounds in the town have been used by the various Wombwell clubs. However, two in particular have been most prominent.

**The Guide Post** – the ground, at New Wombwell, was used by several local clubs after the demise of Wombwell Rising Sun, and was still in use during the 1920s by clubs such as Guide Post FC, Cortonwood Wesleyans and Wombwell Ivy Leaf.

**Hough Road** – other local teams, such as Alma Inn in the mid-1920s, used the ground when Wombwell FC was not using it. It soon became a greyhound stadium, with the first meeting for dogs in May 1934, not long after Wombwell FC had disbanded. It was used for this purpose until 1972, being demolished soon after its closure. The site is now mostly covered by the King's Oak Primary School.

Wombwell Main Colliery, circa 1920

## Subsequent Wombwell 'town' teams

### Wombwell Athletic

Athletic initially played at Ings Road, New Scarborough before moving to Hough Lane, and in the 1945/46 season joined the Yorkshire League, winning the title in its first season. The club also won the league cup with a 6-1 rout of Goole in the final, played at Selby. A huge total of 103 goals were scored in just 28 league matches, with a nine point cushion ahead of Thorne Colliery. A third success was the lifting of the Sheffield & Hallamshire Senior Cup that season, defeating Harworth Colliery 2-0 in the final, which was played at Wath.

Success eluded the club after that remarkable season. The team finished runner-up in the Yorkshire League in the 1949/50 season, but three years later suffered relegation to division two. Its final season, 1955/56 saw the club placed 12$^{th}$ out of 14 in the lower division.

Athletic was kept afloat by Harold Bonell, who objected strongly to the abandonment of the Athletic club and subsequent move to Low Valley in 1956.

### Wombwell & Darfield

A breakaway club from Wombwell Athletic, this club emerged in the summer of 1956, and replaced Athletic, which was left unable to continue by the break-away, in the Yorkshire League at the start of the 1956/57 season. The new club played at the George Hotel ground at Low Valley, which had previously been used by Houghton Main FC. Interestingly, a Fred Bonell was one of those behind the breakaway club.

Five unsuccessful seasons were spent in the bottom three of Yorkshire League's second division before being replaced by another new club, Wombwell Sporting Association in the summer of 1961.

### Wombwell Sporting Association

Wombwell SA proved much more successful than the Wombwell & Darfield club, becoming Yorkshire League Division Two Champions in its second season, 1962/63.

The team then went on to become Yorkshire League champions in both 1964/65 and 1965/66. By 1971/72, however, the club found itself back in Division Two, with a further relegation at the end of the 1973/74 season to Division Three. It remained in this division – apart from just one season in Division Two in 1978/79 – until it became founder members of the Northern Counties East League in 1982/83, where it spent six seasons in the lower divisions.

For the 1988/89 season, a further drop in status saw the club in the Central Midlands League Premier Division, struggling in that competition before a further rebrand in 1990, when it became Wombwell Town. The club entered FA Vase 1975/76 as Wombwell & District FC.

### Wombwell Town

Town continued to play in the Central Midlands League, in the Supreme Division, until 1993/94 when it joined the Sheffield County Senior League. Following a third place in the Premier Division, the club withdrew at the end of the 1999/2000 season. Its home ground was the Recreation Ground on Station Road. In 2018, another new Wombwell Town was formed, playing in the Sheffield County Senior League.

## Wombwell in FA Competitions

National competitions have provided Wombwell-based teams with very little success. Wombwell FC, Wombwell Athletic, Wombwell SA, Wombwell Town, and Wombwell Rising Star have all taken part in the **FA Cup** without really making an impression.

Wombwell FC made it to the First Round of the competition in the 1930/31 season, going out at that stage at home to Wellington Town (who became Telford United in 1969) 0-3, following a goal-less draw down in Shropshire. This had followed wins over Frickley Colliery (home, 3-0), Mexborough Athletic (home, 1-0), Yorkshire Amateurs (home, 3-2), and Whitby United (away, 3-2) in the qualifying rounds.

The club had made it to the Fifth Qualifying Round in the 1921/22 season, before losing 0-2 at Worksop Town. Wombwell Rising Star entered the FA Cup just once, the club's only game a 1-3 defeat at Sheffield FC in a Preliminary Round tie early in the 1904/05 season.

There has only been one appearance by a Wombwell team in the **FA Vase**, and that was during the 1975/76 season when Wombwell & District FC ( actually the Wombwell SA club) defeated Redfearn National Glass (from Monk Bretton) 2-1 in the First Round, only to go down 0-1 to Brigg Town at home in the Second Round. The same club is the only one from the town to have taken part in the **FA Trophy**, north-eastern team Boldon Colliery Welfare defeated 3-2 at home in the First Qualifying Round, before a 0-4 defeat at Bridlington Trinity (following a 1-1 home draw).

No club from Wombwell competed in the old FA Amateur Cup.

# York City
# 1887-1915
## *'Versions one and two'*

The current York RLFC was formed in the city in 1868 as 'York Football Club', initially playing both association and rugby football codes. Different fields were used for practice as the club did not have its own venue, although a ground opposite the main stand at the York racecourse is known to have been used. In a short time however, the Rugby section became prominent, eventually going over to the Northern Union in 1901, having initially stayed with the Rugby Football Union during the great split of 1895, and eventually becoming York RLFC. The association sector was very short-lived and there is nothing to suggest that association practice was anything other than between club members.

The next attempt to form a York City came club came right at the end of the 1886/87 season. Despite a relatively high profile inception, this club seems to have faded away as quickly as it had first appeared.

*Yorkshire Evening Press*, Saturday 28th May 1887

*AN ASSOCIATION CLUB FOR YORK. Association football, which in York in the past has been at a discount, in likely in the future to take a prominent position in local athletic games. Though several weak attempts have been made to introduce the game, nothing of definite nature was established until towards the close of last year, when number of enthusiasts held a meeting at Mr J H Freeman's in Clifford-street, York. It was then proposed and agreed that Mr H Tripp should be president, and among the vice-presidents selected were Lord Wenlock, Mr A E Peace, MP, Major-General Daniell, and Mr J R Wood. J B Freeman was elected captain; Mr McFetridge vice-captain; Mr Butler, treasurer; Mr G Morrall, secretary. The membership numbers about fifty at the present time, and when the knowledge of the game becomes more general the interest attaching to it will without doubt attain to a popularity in fair comparison to Lancashire on the one hand and Cleveland on the other. The ground selected by the club by club is that situate in Leeman-road in which the initiatory match will be played on Whit Monday.*

The club joined the Cleveland FA, and set Whitby Challenge Cup entry in its sights.

*York Herald*, Tuesday 31st May 1887

*FOOTBALL ASSOCIATION GAME IN YORK. Though it may appear to be an inappropriate period of the year to introduce Association football into the ranks of local athletic games, the York City Association have acted wisely in playing their initiatory match towards the close of the regular season. The conspicuous absence of Association play in York and the vicinity has been apparent, notwithstanding the great and deserved popularity of the Rugby game, and should the former class of play take a prominent position there need be no fear of unfortunate clashing. Reference has already been made in these columns to the formation of the club, and it is satisfactory to know that the playing members made a really good 'show' against the Gainsborough team yesterday after-noon on the Leeman-road ground. There was only a moderate attendance of the general public, counter attractions and want of knowledge of the game contributing to this materially, but those present had the advantage of witnessing a well contested match, in the course of match the home players gave great promise of future good playing.*

Pattinson kicked off on the part of the visitors, and the home men quickly returning the play obtained a corner from which, however, they derived no advantage. Some good passing was then shown, and the ball was neatly put through by Marshall, who thus drew first blood for the home team. After some open play the visitors claimed hands from an advantageous position, but the York backs saved well, and some smart play followed, Marshall putting in some good work, and after one unsuccessful attempt he again rushed the leather through, thus putting on the second goal for the untried players. From this point the visitors began to show better form, and although Marshall looked like scoring again the ball was sent out and Pattinson smartly rushed it under the horizontal.

Gainsbro' continued to make a strong attack, but were well responded to by the York men, who were, however unable altogether to hold their ground, Pattinson once more scoring and equalising the score before the call of half-time. In the second half of the game the visitors showed their greater experience and superiority, and after obtaining a 'corner' they shot the leather through for their third goal, Pattinson again scoring. Immediately afterwards Hind was instrumental in putting on a goal for the visitors, and then some lather clever heading and passing by Gainsbro' culminated in one more goal being obtained by Pattinson. A couple of corners were then secured by the visitors, but the home men put in some good defensive play, Marshall doing good service before hands were allowed to Gainsbro', and soon after one more goal was well earned by the visiting team. Some fairly equal play followed until Capes earned the leather through, putting on the seventh goal for Gainsbro'. Then the York men tested the opposing goal-keeper, who ably responded and sent the game back, which was again returned by a capital dribble the shot at goal by Freeman just failing Continuing to play well, the home men pressed strongly, and scored a third goal. From this point the play was fairly interesting, but neither side gained any advantage, and at the call of time the visitors were in a majority of seven goals to three.

York City : Goal, F J Newey ; backs, W Freeman and Bartt ; half-backs, G Morrell, H Freeman, and C Mitchell, forwards (right wing), J H Freeman, Hughes (centre), McFetridge (left wing), Ellison, and H Marshall.

Keen to improve on its members experience, at least one match was played in the close season, a home fixture against York Athletic on Monday 28th June 1887, which was won 2-0. This is unsurprising given the club's formation being so late in the season.

The *York Herald,* on Saturday 1st October 1887, reported on the AGM of the York City association club, which had been held the previous Monday at Lawson's Refreshment Rooms, on Parliament Street, with about 40 members present. Several new members were enrolled, although Mr Hughes, the club captain tended his resignations as he was leaving the area, and he was replaced by G N Burtt for the remainder of the season. Matches had been arranged with Scarborough Town, Keighley, Whitby, and several York schools.

York lost 1-3 at Keighley on Saturday 22nd October, when the configuration of the pitch there was said to have led the York forwards to misjudge their shots on goal. There was also a successful application to play in the Scarborough & East Riding Challenge Cup, with a first round tie against Oliver's Mount School at Scarborough. The tie was played on the Recreation Ground on North Marine Road on Saturday 26th November 1887, and resulted in an easy win for the home side, by five goals to two.

The club then folded – after having been in existence for only six months or so. Whether it was general apathy, precipitated by the loss of Hughes, a lack of support from the local public, or disenchantment following poor results we shall probably never know, as the club's passing certainly didn't receive the attention that was given in the local press that it had received on its inception.

A York Wednesday association club arrived in 1894, playing on a ground behind The White House, The Mount. Several other minor teams also came and went in the city during the 1890s, The York & District League finally got off the ground in 1898, and the York Football Association followed in 1900, without there being a representative team for the whole town at the time.

**Northern League tables featuring Ironopolis**
*(Including the team's results against other teams in the final two columns)*

| 1908/1909 | P | W | D | L | F | A | Pts | H | A |
|---|---|---|---|---|---|---|---|---|---|
| Bishop Auckland | 22 | 14 | 5 | 3 | 67 | 29 | 33 | 1-5 | 1-10 |
| South Bank | 22 | 15 | 3 | 4 | 61 | 34 | 33 | 2-1 | 2-7 |
| Stockton | 22 | 10 | 6 | 6 | 46 | 29 | 26 | 0-7 | 1-2 |
| Crook Town | 22 | 10 | 6 | 6 | 49 | 40 | 26 | 4-0 | 0-5 |
| West Hartlepool | 22 | 11 | 2 | 9 | 50 | 35 | 24 | 0-4 | 1-0 |
| Grangetown Ath | 22 | 9 | 3 | 10 | 47 | 53 | 21 | 3-1 | 0-4 |
| Darlington St. Aug | 22 | 8 | 4 | 10 | 48 | 52 | 20 | 3-3 | 0-5 |
| Scarborough | 22 | 9 | 1 | 12 | 45 | 56 | 19 | 1-5 | 1-3 |
| Saltburn | 22 | 6 | 6 | 10 | 33 | 42 | 18 | 0-0 | 4-4 |
| West Auckland | 22 | 6 | 4 | 12 | 32 | 46 | 16 | 2-1 | 1-2 |
| **York City** | 22 | 6 | 3 | 13 | 31 | 73 | 15 | -- | -- |
| Leadgate Park | 22 | 6 | 1 | 15 | 30 | 50 | 13 | 2-0 | 2-4 |
| | | | | | | | | | |
| 1909/1910 | | | | | | | | | |
| Bishop Auckland | 22 | 15 | 3 | 4 | 67 | 37 | 33 | 3-3 | 1-8 |
| South Bank | 22 | 13 | 4 | 5 | 50 | 26 | 30 | 1-3 | 0-4 |
| Stockton | 22 | 13 | 3 | 6 | 68 | 34 | 29 | 1-2 | 1-4 |
| Darlington St. Aug | 22 | 12 | 2 | 8 | 41 | 35 | 26 | 3-3 | 0-2 |
| West Auckland | 22 | 9 | 4 | 9 | 35 | 35 | 22 | 0-4 | 1-2 |
| Crook Town | 22 | 8 | 4 | 10 | 45 | 43 | 20 | 3-1 | 1-3 |
| Scarborough | 22 | 8 | 4 | 10 | 43 | 49 | 20 | 2-2 | 0-5 |
| West Hartlepool | 22 | 8 | 4 | 10 | 32 | 40 | 20 | 1-1 | 1-4 |
| Knaresborough | 22 | 8 | 4 | 10 | 43 | 58 | 20 | 6-4 | 1-6 |
| Saltburn | 22 | 7 | 4 | 11 | 28 | 46 | 18 | 0-2 | 1-4 |
| Grangetown Ath | 22 | 6 | 2 | 14 | 30 | 44 | 14 | 4-1 | 5-3 |
| **York City** | 22 | 4 | 4 | 14 | 36 | 71 | 12 | -- | -- |

**York City league record**
*Yorkshire Combination*

| | P | W | D | L | F | A | Pts | |
|---|---|---|---|---|---|---|---|---|
| 1910/11 | 18 | 5 | 3 | 10 | 17 | 38 | 13 | 8/10 |
| 1911/12 | 26 | 8 | 4 | 14 | 37 | 70 | 20 | 8/14 |

*Midland League*

| 1912/13 | 38 | 16 | 6 | 16 | 69 | 80 | 38 | 10/20 |
|---|---|---|---|---|---|---|---|---|
| 1913/14 | 34 | 13 | 5 | 16 | 48 | 60 | 31 | 12/18 |
| 1914/15 | 38 | 12 | 7 | 19 | 45 | 72 | 31 | 16/20 |

*Reserves*
*Yorkshire Combination*

| 1912/13 | 24 | 8 | 2 | 14 | 44 | 64 | 18 | 10/13 |
|---|---|---|---|---|---|---|---|---|
| 1913/14 | 18 | 6 | 3 | 9 | 29 | 36 | 15 | 7/10 |

*York City's reserve team played in the York & District League prior to 1911*

It wasn't until 1908 that a second York City club was founded, following a meeting on Monday 30th March that year, which was presided by a J Biscomb. An amateur club from the outset, the honorary secretary was Mr Trees, one of those instrumental in setting up the club. A successful application to join the Northern League enabled the club to start its life at a very high standard.

Home ground for the new York City was on Holgate Road, on a ground at the end of Lindley Street and Murray Street. Use was made of a couple of open stands from York Racecourse, one of which was canvas-covered and could accommodate 300 people. According to 'Northern Goalfields', City registered an astounding 746 players with the league in its first three months.

The new club's first competitive game was at home to South Bank, which was won 2-1. It was a significant result, because South Bank were denied the title on goal average that season, and the two points gained by York went towards the club escaping bottom place at the season's end. Unfortunately the club could not avoid the wooden spoon at the close of its second season, but the side was hardly out of its depth and could not have been playing at a higher standard considering its short history.

A move was made to the Yorkshire Combination League in 1910, although little impact was made on the leading places in its two seasons in the competition.

A significant point in the club's history was when J E Wright took over a secretary from Mr Trees. He encouraged the club to hire its first professional player, Corrighan. Yorkshire Combination rules permitted the signing of one professional, which may well have been the main reason for the club's switch of league. However, Wright was also one of those behind the formation of a limited liability company that would run the club on professional lines in the summer of 1912. The chairman of this new company was Lord Mayor, Alderman Norman Green. Five shilling shares were issued as a means of raising finance, and a new ground – on an area of rough land - at Burton Stone Lane was procured, which was subsequently known as Field View.

Admitted to the professional Midland League for the 1912/13 season (and leaving a reserve team in the Yorkshire Combination). Peter Boyle, an Irish international full-back, and formerly of Sheffield United and Sunderland, was appointed player-manager. Also signed on was Roddie Walker, a full back from Hearts, and who had represented the Scottish League against the English League in 1910/11.

The first game at Field View was against league champions Rotherham Town. The opening ceremony was filmed, and later shown at the Empire Cinema and Victoria Hall in Goodramgate. The attendance that day was 5,000, charges on the gate being sixpence for men, half that for boys, and free for ladies. Season tickets were also on offer, at 7d 6d.

Despite the growing popularity of association football, the club struggled to gain a foothold amongst the sporting public, as York Football Club was still by far the most established of the two clubs. The York City ground was given a North v South representative fixture by the FA, but the match was poorly attended, and raised only £36. The club actually considered making an application to the Football League's Second Division at the 1913 AGM, and this was widely reported. In the event, that application was not made, and it is highly unlikely that it would have been successful given the club's lack of success.

An upward move had already been made in 1912 when the club entered the Midland League, which permitted the paying of all players, not just one individual. The league had expanded to 20 clubs, with Scunthorpe, Goole Town and Halifax Town also admitted to the competition.

Despite a comfortable mid-table place in its first season in the Midland League, the 1913/14 & 1914/15 seasons saw the team struggling at the wrong end of the table. However in August 1914, representatives of the club were invited to a meeting by the Nelson club to discuss the possible formation of a Third Division of the Football League, but the onset of World War One put paid to that.

City was still in the Midland League in 1914/15 before the competition was suspended. A few friendly fixtures were played during the 1915/16 season, but the club was liquidated in 1917 due to unpaid debts. The stand and club equipment were sold for £750, while Field View was turned into allotments, and has subsequently been built on. Although the club's debt was only £518 at the time, there was little chance of survival given that the stand had not been paid for and at least one creditor was chasing an early payment of the debt. Furthermore, on Friday 10th August 1917 the Official Receiver stated that, in his opinion, *'the insolvency of the company has been aggravated by the payment of extravagant sums to professional players and want of experience on the part of the management.'*

The current York City FC was founded in 1922, and was elected to the Midland League before being admitted to the Football League in 1929. The club initially played on a ground at Fulfordgate, Heslington Road, Fulford.

### York City in FA Competitions

The club entered the **FA Cup** between 1909-15. Its first tie resulted in a 4-0 thrashing of Scunthorpe United in a First Qualifying Round tie early in the 1909/10 season, although a 1-5 loss at Denaby United followed. The Third Qualifying Round was reached in 1912/13, although eight ties were played that season – including three against Mexborough Town (winning 3-2 in a second replay), and two against Scunthorpe United and Castleford Town, the latter defeating them 1-0 in the replay. City's best run came the following season, when victories over Lock Lane Woodville (Castleford), 10-0, Scunthorpe, Grimsby's Haycroft Rovers and Goole Town (in a replay) took the club to a Fourth Qualifying Round tie, and defeat, at home against North Shields Athletic.

The 1914/15 season saw York City go out to Goole Town 0-2 in the Second Qualifying Round at the fourth attempt, following two goalless draws and a 3-2 York City victory that was annulled due to York's inadvertent playing of an ineligible player.

York City entered the **FA Amateur Cup** for three seasons before adopting professionalism. The 1908/09 season saw a 2-1 home victory over Withernsea in the First Qualifying Round, before a victory at local rivals York St Paul's, 3-1. Following a 2-2 draw at Scarborough, the replay was lost 1-4. York St Paul's were again defeated on their own ground the following season, this time more easily, 7-1, before a really disappointing 1-5 loss at home to Hull Day Street Old Boys in the Third Qualifying Round.

The club's final season in the competition, 1910/11, saw its best run. Nether Edge Amateurs were defeated 6-1 at home in the First Qualifying Round, followed by a 6-3 success at home to Hull St Georges 6-3, a 3-0 success at home to 5th Northumberland Fusiliers and a 6-1 home defeat of Hornsea. This took City to First Round Proper, but sadly Crook Town put paid to any further progress with a 2-1 away victory.

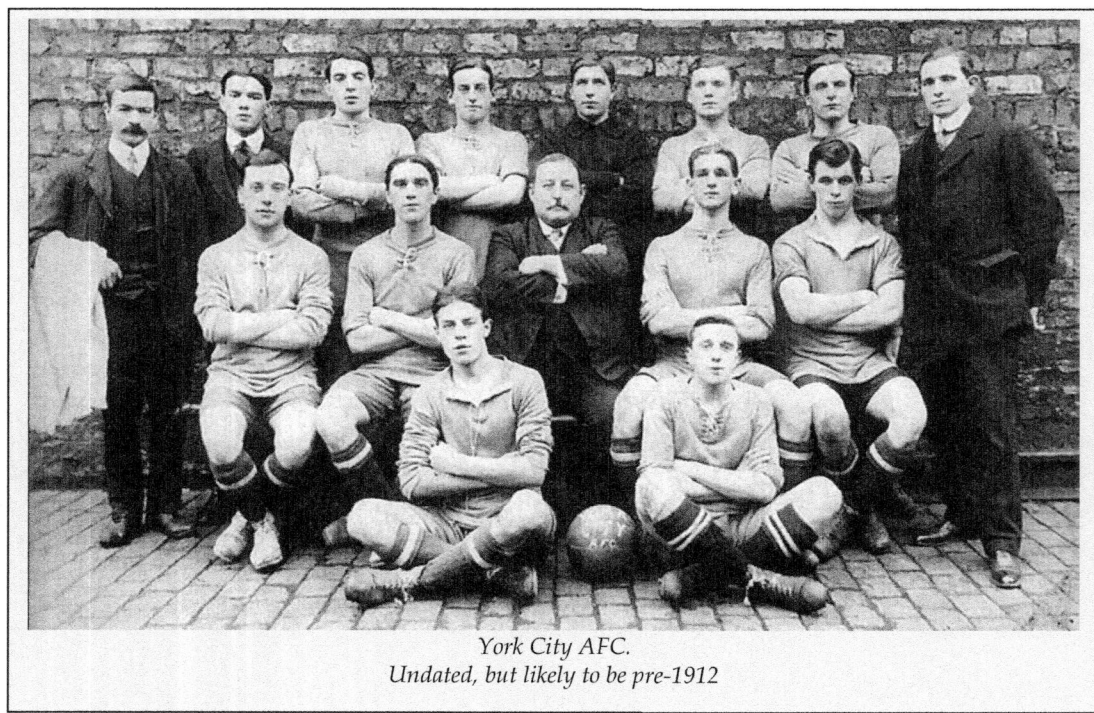

*York City AFC.*
*Undated, but likely to be pre-1912*

# Women's Football Pioneers of the 1920s

As mentioned at the start of the book, any history of football and football clubs involves the history of women in football, albeit a hidden one, in that the roles they often played in the running of clubs was usually behind the scenes, or in some supportive capacity. This has always tended to be overlooked particularly as such work was rarely reported in the local press. However, Yorkshire has seen a fair sprinkling of women's clubs is existence through the years, before the huge upsurge in the game from the late 1980s.

There were several exhibition games throughout the 1890s and into the early 1900s in cities such as Bradford, although these were not considered anything but novelty matches by the local and national press and by those who attended the matches.

During World War One, several matches were played to raise money for war funds and various charities, although one such instance on Saturday 7th April 1917 in Sheffield, resulted in an improvised grandstand collapsing, leading to injuries to several spectators, although only one was detained in hospital, having suffered severe concussion. Two months earlier, Oakwell, Barnsley had hosted a match between workers engaged at Barnsley Shell Factory and Vickers Ltd, Sheffield - attended by 4,000 spectators – in aid of the Barnsley Mayor's Soldiers Comforts Fund. The Barnsley team, which won 6-0 '*wore a neat costume of short skirts and tam-o'-shanters*', according to the *Sheffield Independent*.

There was little opportunity for the women's game to take off in Yorkshire following World War One the national FA declaring a ban of women's football being played on the grounds of any FA member club. This ban lasted from December 1921 to 1971 and was in response to the huge attendances being attracted to matches involving Dick, Kerr Ladies, who represented the Munitions Factory of that name in Preston. On Boxing Day, 1920 a reported crowd of 53,000 had attended Goodison Park with a further 14,000 locked out, for a game involving Dick, Kerr and St Helens Ladies, which raised £3,115 for charities. The Dick, Kerr club played several, mostly well-attended fixtures with Yorkshire teams in the early 1920s too.

The FA viewed the women's game as a threat, particularly as many lower division football league clubs could get nowhere near the gates that Dick, Kerr's could. The FA could happily ignore what they saw as a showground attraction but once the women's game began to make a name for itself then the blazers at the FA felt they had to defend their own interests. Their claims that football was not to the physiology of women have subsequently been shown to be untrue. There were also question marks over the proceeds from charity games played by women's teams, with claims that extravagant and often hidden expenses were siphoned off from the money raised. In short, no logical explanation for the ban was ever given, and the women's game suffered massively as a result

Receiving less negative attention was one Mary Jane Hodgson, who became one of the first women to become president of a (men's) football club, a role so played in the early 1900s at the Selby Mizpah club. However, her position was seen as something of a novelty at the time.

Amid the huge surge in popularity of the women's game were a number of Yorkshire-based clubs. The first properly organized ladies' football team in West Yorkshire was the **Huddersfield Atalanta** club, which was founded in 1920.

The Atalanta Sports Club, named after the mythological Greek heroine, who was abandoned at birth and reared by a bear, was formed towards the end of November 1920, when a group of like-minded women got together *'to provide games for the women of Huddersfield, to foster a sporting spirit, and a love of honour among its members.'* At that first meeting a committee was established under the chairmanship of Constance Waller, and the new club set about securing premises and raising funds. Despite being unable to find a suitable field, the local Education Committee agreed to allow the club to use the netball courts at a number of sites, which included Birkby Council School and the Girls' High School on Saturday afternoons and holidays. Therefore the club started out playing netball as well as football.

The *Huddersfield Examiner* recorded that *'the footballers thoroughly enjoyed themselves in spite of (or because) of the field being very muddy and slimy, and all are keen to play again. They were not so much playing the game as learning to kick the ball.'*

Later, the Sandhouse football field at Crosland Moor was secured for practices, between *golds* and *blues*, the first being on New Year's Day 1921. Teams of nine-a-side put on a display resulting in a 1-1 draw. On 5th February, twenty-four players turned up, the best number so far, this avoiding a small-sided practice match for the first time. By now the club was reported to have been also running a water polo side and a cricket eleven as well as the football team, with netball having seemingly been dropped, given that references to that sport had completely dried up.

Atalanta's first competitive association football match was at home to Bath Ladies at Leeds Road, the home of Huddersfield Town, on Good Friday, 25th March 1921. Of the Atalanta team, Rhoda Wilkinson, was among the more skilled players, later being selected to play at centre half for a combined Lancashire and Yorkshire team against the Dick, Kerr team at Leeds on April 6th.

The Huddersfield public had certainly caught on by now, with a massive 15,246 spectators turning up to see Atalanta win by a single goal. The winning team that day consisted of: Ethel Lee, Hilda Clarke, L. Barraclough, Minnie Kenworthy, Lily Mitchell, Stanley, Wilkinson, Edgely, Steele, Broadhead, Constance Waller.

The *Leeds Mercury* covered the match in brief the following day,

LADY FOOTBALLERS. *Over 15,000 Persons Witness Match at Huddersfield.*

*Enormous interest was taken in the match at the Leeds-road Ground, Huddersfield, between two teams of women footballers. The sides were the Atalanta Club, of Huddersfield, and Bath Ladies' Football Club. The latter side were eventually defeated, the Huddersfield ladies proving much superior to their opponents, despite the fact that their team has only been in practice a few weeks. Over fifteen thousand people were present, and enthusiasm high. The only scorer was Miss Broadhead, of Huddersfield, who obtained a goal.*

Another 8,000 spectators turned up at Thrum Hall, Halifax, on 25th April 1921, for a match against the well-established St Helens Ladies, which was in aid of the Halifax Ex-Servicemen's Association, and provided gate takings of £300. Atalanta lost 1-3, after having trailed 0-3 at the break.

The club's next game couldn't have been any tougher, against Dick, Kerr Ladies themselves. Dick Kerr had played 52 competitive games already that season alone, and it was reported that their goalkeeper did not touch the ball during the whole of the game, which was played at Hillsborough stadium, Sheffield. Sheffield Mayor, Alderman Wardley, kicked off, and the mere 4-0 victory for Dick, Kerr's was regarded as a good result for the Huddersfield team.

With Leeds Road being re-turfed, the Fartown ground of the Huddersfield Northern Union club was used for a match against a French XI on 18th May, this team largely drawn from the multi-sport Fémina club in Paris, which had been founded in 1912, originally as gymnastics club for ladies. Before 3,832 spectators, the French team won 1-0, and £424 8s 6d was raised for the Mayor's Distress Fund. Four days earlier, Atalanta had been defeated 0-2 at Hull, on their White City ground. The match was followed by a celebratory dinner at the Masonic Hall, hosted by the Mayor of Huddersfield.

*Leeds Mercury*, Thursday 19th May 1921

*FRENCH LADY FOOTBALLERS. A team of French lady Association football players visited Huddersfield yesterday, and on the Fartown Northern Union ground in the evening played the Huddersfield Atalanta ladies, before crowd of 9,000. The effort was for the benefit of the Mayor's Distress Fund, for which during the present week an attempt is being made to raise £10,000, concluding on Saturday with a 'trail of pennies collection' in the streets.*

*The French ladies proved more skilful at most points the game, kept their positions better, and kicked with greater power and Judgment. The forwards were particularly smart. In the first half the Atalanta missed an open goal, and were a goal in arrear at the interval, Mdlle Brasquermond scoring after an individual effort from three-parts the length the field. Miss Minnie Kenworthy was injured on the head and took no part in the game after the interval. The French representatives had much the better of the game towards the end, but failed to add the score. The receipts totalled £424.*

For the opening game of the 1921/22 season Atalanta played **Hey's Brewery Ladies** of Bradford, at the Blakeborough FC ground (still in use today as the home of Brighouse Town). The match took place on

16th September 1921 but the score is unknown. Hey's Ladies, themselves suffered 0-9 and 1-4 defeats in charity games to the same Dick, Kerr team but the second defeat illustrated a marked improvement in their play, the crowd that day has reported as being between 4,000 and 10,000 in number. Factory teams were common at this time, as employers sought to improve the morale and working conditions of their workforces, and not just for the men, although most of the sporting and recreation facilities were intended predominantly for their use.

*Leeds Mercury,* Thursday 20th October 1921

*LADY FOOTBALLERS. Dick Kerr's Ladies beat Hey's Brewery Ladies by four goals to one at Valley Parade, Bradford, yesterday. There was an attendance of 4,000 spectators, and the receipts, amounting to £184, will be devoted to the Bradford Motor Lifeboat Fund. The Bradford ladies put up a capital game, and Dick, Kerr's defence was often hard pressed. J Harris, L Parr (2), and F Bedford scored for the Preston side end E Jackson, Hey's centre forward, netted for the losers.*

Hey's themselves were crowned Yorkshire Ladies' Champions in 1921, although it was clear that women's association football in the district had a long way to go. Other matches were played at various venues but regular games were played at the Greenfield stadium in Bradford which, being a multi-sport venue, managed to get around the 'ban' on women's football as the ground was not in ownership of any football team. As ladies' teams were also banned from using registered referees and linemen then that added an extra problem in terms of employing suitable match-day officials.

On 3rd October 1921, Atalanta took on Dick, Kerr Ladies for a second time. The match, again at Leeds Road, was kicked off by Alderman Woolven, Mayor of Huddersfield and Honorary President of the Atalanta club. It was a bad day for the locals, with the Preston team winning 10-0 in front of a disappointing 1,800 crowd, due no doubt to the inclement weather and early (5pm) kick-off. Only £110 was raised for the Cinderella Society that day.

The players and officials at Atalanta didn't really see that the ban, which began on 5th December 1921, would cause any great hardship to their club, which had its own ground by now, at Cowlersley, and wasn't intending to play more than the occasional match against outside opponents, being content to stage matches within the club membership for the most part.

The club affiliated to the new English Ladies' Football Association, founded in response to the ban, and two of the club's players, Whitwam and Barraclough, were selected to play in a match at Grimsby in 21st January 1922; Whitwam at right half for the English Ladies FA team, and Barraclough at left back for Grimsby.

Hey's were played again at Cowlersley, on Good Friday, 14th April 1922, with Hey's winning 4-2. The teams met again the following month in the semi-final of the Bradford Charity Shield, a seemingly one-off competition that also included **Keighley Ladies, Doncaster Ladies, Huddersfield Ladies** and **Huddersfield Alexandra**. Atalanta had been given a bye in the first round. The match was played on 17th May at the Greenfield Athletic ground at Dudley Hill, Bradford, with Hey's winning more comfortably this time, 4-0.

A couple of months earlier, Hey's had lodged an application with the Bradford Rugby Union club to use its facilities for a match against the French touring team. Quoted below is an example of the attitude shown toward ladies football, not just by the Football Association, but by the Rugby Union authorities too.

*Halifax Evening Courier*, Tuesday 14th March 1922

'WOMEN SHOWS' Lady Footballers Banned by Yorkshire R U

*Some pointed views regarding the playing of football by were made at a meeting of the Yorkshire Rugby Union at Leeds on Monday evening. Mr R Oaks said he had received a letter from the Bradford club requesting an application to play a match at Lidgett Green between French International Ladies and Heys Ladies.*

*Opposing the application Mr J Miller (Leeds) said that football, like lacrosse and hockey, was not the right for women, who when they tried to play it made a ridiculous exhibition of themselves. 'We must not encourage them,' he remarked, 'because football is not good for them or the game. These women footballers may be alright to look at but they cannot play football. They are not football matches but simply women shows.'*

*The Rev Huggard (Barnsley) said it was quite out of place for women to make an exhibition of themselves on football grounds. They respected, and, he hoped, loved their women, and therefore ought not to encourage them to do anything derogatory to their position, or anything that would be unseemly The application was refused.*

\*\*\*

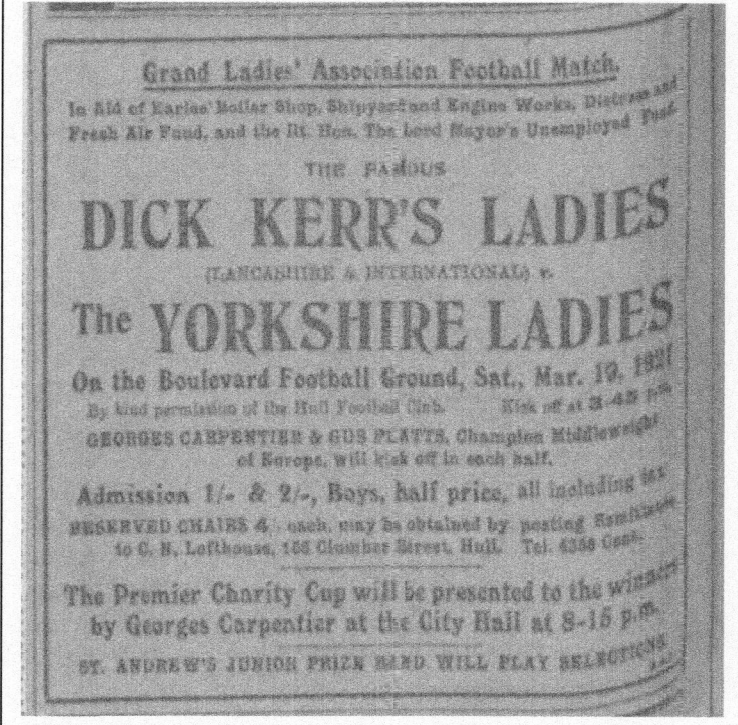

Atalanta Ladies also entered the first – and only - ELFA Cup competition which was launched in January 1922, and the club was given a local derby with the **Huddersfield Ladies** on Saturday 11th March at the Moor End ground, Lockwood. What was described in the local as *'the best girls' football match that has been played in Huddersfield,'* saw Atalanta emerge as 2-1 winners with goals from Edgley and Waller.

The second round brought a home tie at Cowersley against the Potteries side Chell on Saturday 22nd April, Atalanta winning 2-1. There was a bye in the third round so Atalanta were drawn against **Doncaster and Bentley** in the semi-final on 3rd June 1922. The tie took place at the City Athletic ground in Wakefield with the South Yorkshire team winning 4-0. The Doncaster team had already defeated Grimsby 7-1, Lincoln 20-0, and Manchester 3-2 in previous rounds - as well as Heys Ladies in a friendly - and met Stoke Ladies in the final on Saturday 24th June 1922 at The Cobridge Athletic Ground, Stoke, then the home of Port Vale FC. It had originally hoped that the final could be staged in Bradford, but no suitable ground could be secured, Cobridge's use as a multi-sports venue meaning that it could be utilised. The Stoke team won the game 3-1 in front of a crowd that would have been predominantly local.

The team had started the 1921/22 season as 'Doncaster Ladies', consisting mainly of employees of the firewood works at Arksey, and coming to prominence when it played a number of matches in aid of the local soup kitchens during a recent coal dispute. The club's main support came from nearby Bentley, hence the addition of that village in the club's title.

The ELFA itself folded later in 1922, as the Atalanta players reverted to internal practice matches before fading away. In 1926 Broad Oak cricket club, Linthwaite acquired a new wooden pavilion for changing rooms and scoreboard, bought from the Atalanta club, at a cost of £144. Hey's Ladies played few games after 1922 and by 1925 had also faded away. Even the Doncaster and Bentley club found it hard, and having no competition to aim for, were also defunct within a short time of their cup final appearance.

One year after the formation of the Atalanta club, **Manningham Mills Ladies** (also known as Lister Ladies) appeared. Dick, Kerr's defeated them 6-0 at Valley Parade in April 1921 in front of 14,000 spectators, and again by 11 goals later in the season but this works team did not last as long as its cross-city rivals Hey's.

Keighley Ladies played its first game in September 1921, on a ground on Aireworth Road, against the Heys team, who won easily 12-1. In May 1922, a 1-6 loss resulted at Moor End against Huddersfield Ladies, before the Keighley team appears to have folded as no more matches have been traced.

Women's football didn't die out completely once the effects of the ban began to strangle the game, but for many years competitive matches were few and far apart. A Sheffield Ladies' team visited Hoyland recreation ground on Monday 4th October 1926 to play the local ladies team. The home side won 2-0. Sheffield was used as a venue for representative fixtures in later years.

*Patrick Brennan has written an excellent detailed history of the Atalanta Ladies team. His work, from 2008 can be found at www.donmouth.co.uk/womens_football/huddersfield_atalanta.html*

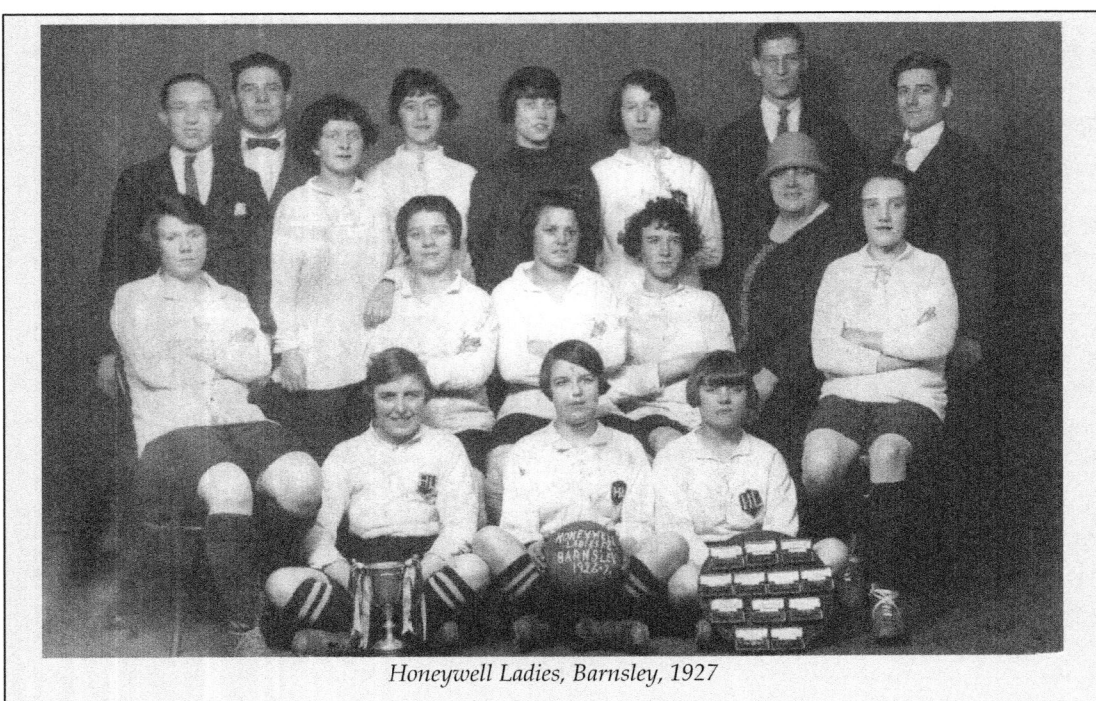

Honeywell Ladies, Barnsley, 1927

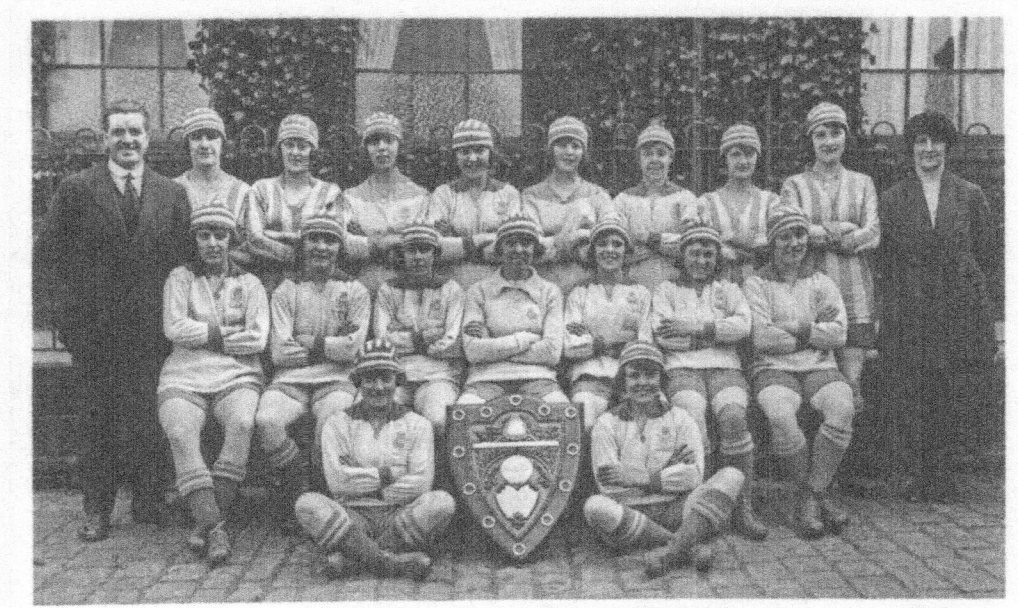

HEY'S BREWERY (BRADFORD) LADIES' A.F.C.
RECORD 1921-22. WINNERS YORKSHIRE LADIES' CHAMPIONSHIP, WHITEHEAD LIFEBOAT SHIELD, FIVE-A-SIDE YORKSHIRE TOURNAMENT.
TWO DRAWN GAMES WITH DICK KERR'S FOR ENGLISH LADIES' CHAMPIONSHIP.
BRADFORD

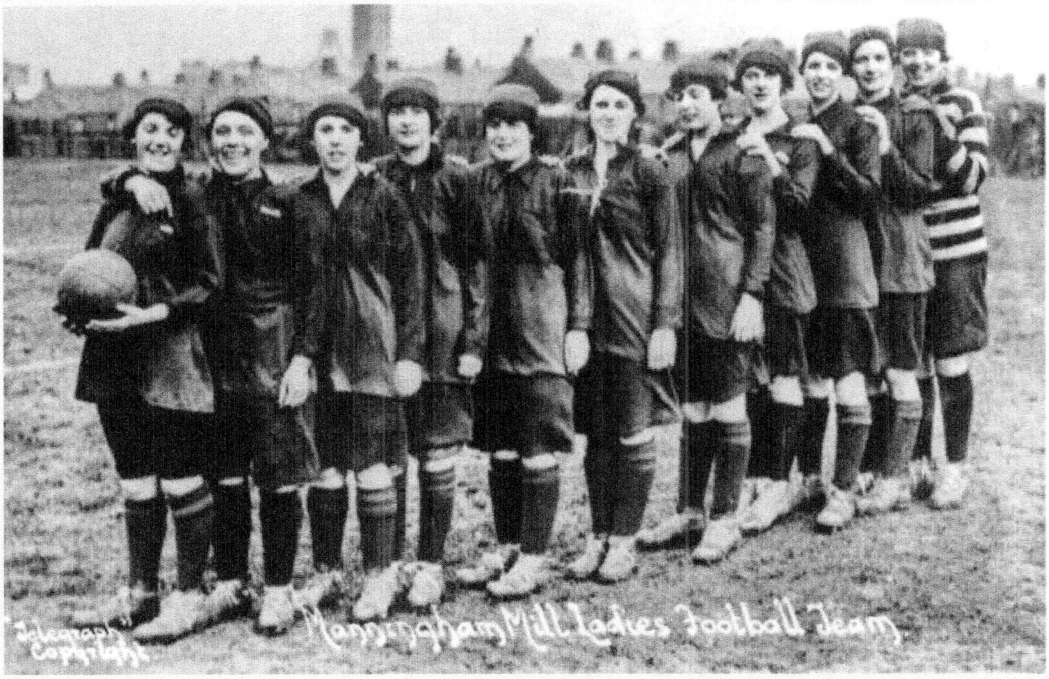
Telegraph Copyright
Manningham Mill Ladies Football Team

*Manningham Mills Ladies*

# Brontë Ladies
# 1968-1996

Doncaster Belles has been the highest profile of all the Yorkshire clubs in the women's game, but far less is known about the other team from Gods Own Country that has graced the top levels of the game.

The Brontë Ladies club was founded by Bradford City FC director Bill Roper in 1968, and initially played home games at Marley, Keighley until its entry to the Women's FA Premier League in 1991. Initially playing in minor Yorkshire competitions and friendly fixtures, the club joined the North West League in 1973 in order to play regular competitive football. Women's football was becoming more organised and the North West League was considered the strongest in the North of England, its clubs by no means confined to the geographical area its title suggested.

The first reported match involving the side was a charity game against Sutton Ladies (a one-off team from the nearby village of Sutton-in-Craven) to raise money for the kidney unit at St James' Hospital in Leeds. Brontë won 2-1 and the proceeds of £120 far exceeded expectations. Less successful was a later game against a team of 'TV Wrestlers' that raised a mere £40 for the new Leisure Centre sports hall. Led by Marion Reape, and including the likes of Marion Illingworth, Brenda Peel, and the youngsters Wendy Potter and Maureen Kelly, the side started to get themselves noticed with some notable performances. Early successes included a Bradford League 5-a-side tournament, where Brontë's junior side finished runners-up.

A first North West Counties League Cup final was reached in the 1974/75 season, Stocksbridge defeated 7-3 in the Quarter Final and holders Ossett 2-0 in the Semi Final, thanks to a double strike from Julie Turner in front of the England selectors. As a result, Reape and Potter were invited to the England trials later in the year, both narrowly missing out on international selection. The following year saw Brontë in the Semi Final of the Townsend Cup competition at Rotherham. From a field of sixteen teams, the Keighley side defeated Woodbeck (Derby) 5-0, Nottingham Rangers 1-0, and drew 0-0 with Star Inn (Rotherham) in their group games. Only one goal was conceded in the tournament, and that was enough to knock them out as another Nottingham team, Car Fasteners defeated them by a single goal in the last four. Later in the season, both Brontë Ladies and Brontë Girls won their respective 5-a-side competitions at Parkside Sports Centre, Bradford, with 2-0 victories over Fairfax and Sutton respectively in their finals. In total, 64 goals were scored by the teams in the tournament (only one was conceded), with Maureen Kelly leading the way with eleven. With so few organised women's teams at the time, small-sided competitions enabled regular competitive fixtures to be maintained.

The senior side established itself further as the '70s progressed, playing on the famous old Marley 'Centre Pitch' at Keighley, which was the sports ground's prestige field, normally only used for local cup finals and representative fixtures. The pitch was surrounded by a cinder running track, with several steps of terracing along the sports pavilion side, a wooden building that housed several changing rooms and offered a little cover for spectators.

County 5-a-side tournaments were dominated, with Wendy Potter scoring 11 of her side's 28 goals en-route to a 2-0 final victory over West Park Rangers in the 1976/77 competition. Denholme had been turned over to the tune of 13-0 in the Semi Final. The title was later retained with a 7-1 success against St George.

Back in the North West League, Ulverston Dynamoes were thrashed 22-0, with double figures also being recorded against Stakepool (18-0 & 17-0), BAC Warton and Lancaster. Unfortunately Preston North End's two convincing victories over Brontë enabled them to lift the 1976/77 league title instead. As consolation, the North East Regional 5-a-side competition was won instead, with an emphatic 6-0 defeat of Sheffield in the final. There was certainly a lot of travelling to be done in the league, but there was no alternative for Brontë, as an organised 11-a-side league in the White Rose county was still a long way off.

Several former Brontë players helped to form the short-lived Nab Wood Ladies in 1977, the same year that Brontë defeated their own girls team in the final of the Sunblest-5-a-side competition at Parkside Bradford. The new club joined Brontë in the North West League, the Keighley team at last lifting the league title, after two successive second places, at the end of the 1978/79 season. Again, there were double figure victories that season, Cumberland coming off worst at the end of a 15-0 scoreline. The title was sealed with a 3-1 victory over Preston North End, and for the first time the last sixteen of the Women's FA Cup was reached. Queens Park Rangers proved too strong for Brontë in that competition, in a game played at the Otley Town FC ground, due to the unavailability of Marley. Further success was achieved when Brontë Girls won the league's Second Division title, and then Robin Hood Ladies were thrashed 11-0 in the final of the County 5-a-side competition.

There was by now no doubting the fact that Brontë were among the top sides in the North of England as their phenomenal run of success continued. The ARCO 7-a-side tournament at Hull was annexed during the 1979/80 season, with St Helens defeated in the final, and later in the campaign there were four Brontë players in the league representative side against the North East. Eileen Lillyman meanwhile became the club's first ever international, selected for the England team that faced The Netherlands There was almost a league cup success that season too, but keen rivals Preston North End proved victorious in a final held over from the previous campaign. Nab Wood found that Brontë were less than charitable in a league game however, as the established side won 15-0. Perhaps the only disappointing event of that season was the burning down of the cricket pavilion at Marley, Brontë having made use of that building – rather than the main sports pavilion - as changing facilities for its home matches

The 1980/81 season saw another runners-up spot in the league, for both first and second teams, but the league cup had been won five times in total before the early '90s. Brontë even tasted success in international competitions. Two years after winning an invitation tournament in Benidorm, the side returned to Spain towards the end of the 1981/82 season to defeat top Majorcan sides Atletico V vero 6-0 and Santa Maria 4-0.

Brontë made the Quarter Final of the FA Cup during the 1987/88 season, losing out to the crack Merseyside team and eventual finalists Leasowe Pacific 0-6 at Bebington Oval, on The Wirral. Pacific would go on to win the FA Cup twice in subsequent years.

When long-serving manager Chris Beaumont left, former England International Patricia Firth became player-coach. The first player to score a hat-trick for England's women's team, Firth had lengthened her career by becoming a goalkeeper, and this is the position she played with Brontë. In 1988/89 Firth's team made it even further in the national competition, winning through to the semi-final of the Women's FA

Cup, after a shock win over the fancied Millwall Lionesses 3-2 in the Quarter Final. Sadly they missed out on an appearance at the televised final at Old Trafford, losing 3-0 to Friends of Fulham at Sincil Bank, Lincoln.

Brontë must have been a hard team to break down, its defence boasting the talented Clare Taylor, Scottish international Lorraine Kennedy, and of course England international Eileen Lillyman.

*Brontë Ladies, 1988 (courtesy of Edna Smith)*

It was no surprise therefore that Brontë was among the clubs invited to become founder members of the FA Women's League in 1991, although this necessitated the need to play on an enclosed ground that the club could guarantee the use of, of which there were none at the time in Keighley, with Marley being a multi-sport, multi team venue. Therefore a move was made to the Salts FC ground in Saltaire, Shipley. This ground was by no means fully enclosed but offered more privacy, and an ability to charge a gate.

Success in the new league was instant, The Division One North title was won at the first attempt, earning the side promotion to the top tier of ladies' football, among the likes of Arsenal and Doncaster Belles. The side was not disgraced, but could not avoid relegation in its one season in the Premier Division. Following three full seasons back in the Northern Division, the last of which was something of a disaster, the club folded during the 1996/97 campaign, unable to compete financially with the bigger clubs that were reaping the benefits of the explosion of interest in the women's game.

Among the best known Brontë Ladies players was Clare Taylor, who also enjoyed a football career with Liverpool Ladies FC and Huddersfield Town. As well as being a top quality footballer, Clare was also one of the UK's most successful women cricketers, representing England 121 times and also playing for Yorkshire and New Zealand's Otago State. In 2000 she was awarded the MBE for her services to cricket and later moved to New Zealand.

The Marley centre pitch is long gone, but competitive football is still played on the site, with the current artificial pitch that now overlays the site hosting Steeton, ironically, now members of the men's North West Counties League. The Salts FC ground is still very much in use and has also undergone improvements in recent years..

## FA Women's Premier League Tables featuring Brontë

### 1991/92 Division One North

|  | P | Pts |
|---|---|---|
| **Brontë** | **14** | **25** |
| Sheffield Wed | 14 | 22 |
| Davies Argyle | 14 | 17 |
| Wolverhampton | 14 | 12 |
| Spondon | 14 | 11 |
| Sunderland | 14 | 11 |
| Cowgate Kestrels | 14 | 10 |
| Villa Aztecs | 14 | 2 |

### 1992/93 National Division

| Arsenal | 18 | 34 |
|---|---|---|
| Doncaster Belles | 18 | 32 |
| Knowsley United | 18 | 23 |
| Wimbledon | 18 | 21 |
| RS Southampton | 18 | 17 |
| Ipswich Town | 18 | 17 |
| Stanton Rangers | 18 | 13 |
| Millwall Lionesses | 18 | 8 |
| Maidstone Tigresses | 18 | 8 |
| **Brontë** | **18** | **7** |

### 1993/94 Division One North

| Wolverhampton | 18 | 40 |
|---|---|---|
| Sheffield Wed | 18 | 40 |
| Abbeydale | 18 | 29 |
| **Brontë** | **18** | **28** |
| Cowgate Kestrels | 18 | 28 |
| Villa Aztecs | 18 | 27 |
| St. Helens | 18 | 22 |
| Langford | 18 | 17 |
| Nottingham Argyle | 18 | 16 |
| Kidderminster H | 18 | 12 |

### 1994/95 Northern Division

| Villa Aztecs | 18 | 37 |
|---|---|---|
| Cowgate Kestrels | 18 | 36 |
| St Helens Garswood | 18 | 36 |
| Sheffield Wed | 18 | 31 |
| Ipswich Town | 18 | 28 |
| **Brontë** | **18** | **27** |
| Langford | 18 | 24 |
| Kidderminster H | 18 | 14 |
| Nottingham Argyle | 18 | 11 |
| Solihull Borough | 18 | 10 |

### 1995/96 Northern Division

| Tranmere Rovers | 16 | 44 |
|---|---|---|
| Huddersfield Town | 16 | 39 |
| Garswood St Helens | 16 | 31 |
| Sheffield Wed | 16 | 30 |
| Langford | 16 | 17 |
| RTM Newcastle K | 16 | 13 |
| Notts County | 16 | 13 |
| Kidderminster H | 16 | 13 |
| **Brontë** | **16** | **2** |

### 1996/97 Northern Division

Brontë Ladies withdrew

**GRAND ASSOCIATION FOOTBALL MATCH.**
YORK WEDNESDAY v. SCARBORO' ST. MARY'S.
On the Ground, CLEMENTHORPE, by kind permission of St. Clement's F.C.
Kick-off 3-30. Admission 2d.
The proceeds will be given to the "Yorkshire Herald" War Fund.

**GRAND ASSOCIATION FOOTBALL MATCH.**
YORK WEDNESDAY v. SCARBORO' ST. MARY'S.
On the Ground, CLEMENTHORPE, by kind permission of St. Clement's F.C.
Kick-off 3-30. Admission 2d.
The proceeds will be given to the "Yorkshire Herald" War Fund.

**GRAND FOOTBALL MATCH.**
VALLEY GROUND, MEANWOOD.
BUSLINGTHORPE VALE v. ROTHWELL HAIGH.
Admission: Gents 4d., Ladies 2d.
Meanwood Cars pass Ground.

**Grand Football Match.**
MYTHOLMROYD v. THORNHILL LEES (West Riding League) at Mytholmroyd TO-MORROW, Sept. 3rd, at 3-30. Admission 9d., Ladies and Boys 5d. each.

**GRAND FOOTBALL MATCH.—TO-DAY.**
TEST MATCH REPLAY (BEATTY LEAGUE).
On CAMMELLS' GROUND, SHIREGREEN.
WARD'S SPORTS v. BALFOUR'S ATHLETIC.
Kick-off 6 p.m. Admission 6d. Boys 3d.

**Grand Football Match.**
MYTHOLMROYD v. STAINLAND (joint leaders of the Halifax and District League), at MYTHOLMROYD TO-MORROW (Saturday) at 3 p.m. Admission 5d., Ladies and Boys 3d. A collection will be made on the field at the interval for the benefit of Grace.

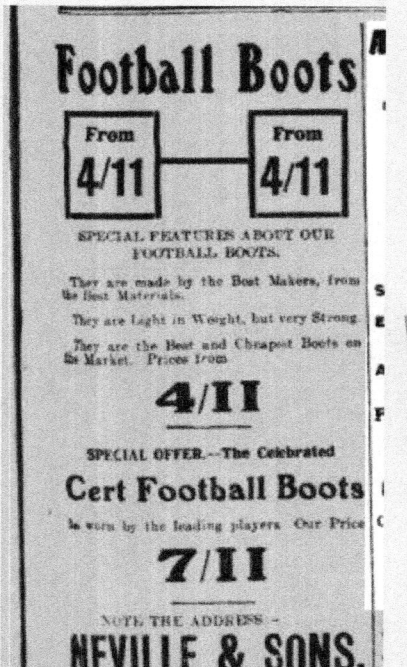

**Football Boots**
From 4/11   From 4/11

SPECIAL FEATURES ABOUT OUR FOOTBALL BOOTS.

They are made by the Best Makers, from the Best Materials.
They are Light in Weight, but very Strong.
They are the Best and Cheapest Boots on the Market. Prices from

**4/11**

SPECIAL OFFER.—The Celebrated
**Cert Football Boots**
as worn by the leading players. Our Price

**7/11**

NOTE THE ADDRESS—
**NEVILLE & SONS,**
Boot and Shoe Dealers,
Clothiers and Outfitters,
6, College Street.
ROTHERHAM.

# Other Notable Clubs

Several long-lost clubs within the Bradford district are covered in *Late To The Game* (indicated with *), so I have just included brief details of these clubs here. The complete history of the many different **Keighley AFC** and **Keighley Town** clubs, as well as **Keighley Central** are covered in great detail in *Keighley's Soccer History*, so I have purposefully left those clubs out.

## Acomb

Acomb, a suburb of York has not had a particularly glorious footballing history. However, its association football team was significant in that it was a founder member of the Yorkshire League in 1920.

An association team did play in the vicinity in 1883, with the *York Herald* reporting on a match played on Saturday 24th February 1883 at home to Ulleskelf. Home, on this occasion, was a field kindly lent by a Mr Holmes. *'Acomb won the toss and elected to play with the wind. The first half of the match was uninteresting. Acomb, aided by the strong wind, kept the ball in their opponents' ground, but failed to secure a goal. After half time, the wind having dropped, the playing was fast, and Acomb soon scored their first goal, and in a short time secured a second. Ulleskelf now made a rush, and succeeded in getting a shot at Acomb's stronghold, which, however, was stopped by the goal-keeper. The play was now loose on both sides, and at the call of time Acomb were winners by two goals to nothing.'* The Acomb captain on the day was E Wallace. It would seem that this club did not last long and the following year saw the emergence of rugby in Acomb, with the formation of Acomb Football Club, which had its headquarters at the Marcia Inn.

In early January 1885, several local newspapers reported that a young man named Duff had broken his collar bone while practicing on the Acomb football field. This happened through a fall which he sustained *'after being collared in running.'* The rugby football club seems to have become defunct during the 1895/96 season.

A new Acomb Association Football Club is said to have been a founder member of the York Football League in 1897 along with clubs such as Bishopthorpe, Easingwold, Ebor Wanderers, Rowntree's Ulleskelf, York St. Clements, York Trinity, and York Wednesday. However, the league failed before a ball could be kicked, and local clubs had to wait another twelve months before a district league was founded.

The formation of the York League (42) took place on the evening of Monday 28th March 1898, and on offer to the champion club was a cup worth twenty-guinea cup donated by H H Riley-Smith of Toulston Lodge, Tadcaster. Acomb placed its first team in Division One, and a reserve team in Division Two.

By the 1899/1900 campaign, Acomb was running three teams in the competition, one in each division, with Ebor Wanderers and Sycamore being respective winners of the top two leagues.

The club fielded a team in the York & District League until 1920, although between 1914-19 the club went into abeyance due to World War One. By 1901 the club was known as Acomb Parish Church, winning the league's Division Two championship in 1913/14. The following season the club had become Acomb Working Men's Club, reflecting the fact that it was no longer under the jurisdiction of the local church.

| Acomb WMC Yorkshire League Record | | | | | | | |
|---|---|---|---|---|---|---|---|
| | P | W | D | L | F | A | Pts | Pos |
| 1920-21 | 24 | 8 | 3 | 13 | 43 | 66 | 19 | 9/13 |
| 1921-22 | 32 | 18 | 1 | 13 | 61 | 86 | 37 | 9/17 |
| 1922-23 | 30 | 4 | 4 | 22 | 42 | 108 | 12 | 16/16 |

Along with fellow York sides Rowntrees and York YMCA, Acomb became a founder member of the Yorkshire League in 1920. The club was far more successful in the new league than York YMCA, which had stepped up from the second tier of the York & District League. That team was way out of its depth and finished both of the first two seasons way adrift at the foot of the league, the second of which it conceded a remarkable 239 goals in just 30 league matches. Acomb spent three years in the Yorkshire League, but left after having finished bottom in 1922/23, unable to compete financially with the bigger clubs in the league.

Acomb WMC was back in the York League for the 1923/24 season before being replaced as the village club by the likes of Acomb AS (Division Two winners 1925/26 & 1926/27), Acomb Carr Lane, (Division Two winners in 1931/32) and Acomb AFC (Division Two winners in 1935/36).

Acomb teams have produced several notable players over the years, including George Lee, who signed for York City in 1936 scoring 11 goals in 37 matches for the Minstermen, before going on to play for Nottingham Forest (76 appearances, 20 goals), and then West Bromwich Albion (271 appearances, 59 goals), with who he won the FA Cup in 1954.

In the **FA Cup,** Acomb lost 0-8 at home to Mexborough Town in a 1914/15 Preliminary Round tie. After the War, the team drew 1-1 at home to Frickley Athletic at the same stage in the 1920/21 season, but scratched from the replay. The club's only other appearance saw a 2-5 Extra Preliminary Round defeat at Halifax club Boothtown in the 1921/22 season.

Four ties were also played in the **FA Amateur Cup**. In 1920/21, Selby Olympia were defeated 6-1 at home in the Second Qualifying Round, but this was followed by a 0-2 loss at Scarborough. One year later, Guiseley were defeated 5-1 at home, also in the Second Qualifying Round, before a 1-4 loss at Leeds Malvern.

# Airedale *

Formed in July 1897, Airedale emerged as one of the early leading lights of the game in the Bradford district.

The side originally played on Spier Fields (sometimes referred to as Spy Fields), on Moorside Road in Fagley, although references also refer to 'The Tower Grounds' in the Lister Lane area of Fagley. It is likely that these were one and the same ground which was considered too small and far removed from a populous centre, necessitating the short removal to a new ground at Undercliffe Cricket Club. The club was a founder member of the Bradford & District League, where its first team played between 1899-1902 (and were champions in 1901/02 ahead of the first Bradford City AFC), its second team then played in the league during the 1902/03 season.

Nicknamed *The Terriers*, the club's sudden demise was barely mentioned in the local press. It is possible that the club overstretched its resources or lost the use of the cricket ground after playing the 1902/03 season in the West Yorkshire League. However, given the massive focus directed at events at Valley Parade that summer, there is a strong argument to suggest that the club folded as a result of this, their own plans to become the city's leading club thwarted by the introduction of the professional Bradford City club.

There was a relaunch of the Airedale club in time for the 1906/07 season, re-joining the West Yorkshire League and entering the FA Amateur Cup for the first, and only, time. However, the club was defunct again by the start of the following season after having initially notified the West Yorkshire League that it intended to play in the Bradford & District League for the following season in order to reduce its running costs.

# Batley

Playing at Mount Pleasant, 'Batley AFC' – an offshoot of Batley Cricket, Athletic & Football Club – had flown the flag for the town in the early years of association football in the district. The team was founded in 1896 and had started the 1897/98 season in the West Yorkshire League, but failed to complete its fixtures, having disbanded during the season. The parent company pulled the plug late in November 1897, due to a *'lack of public interest and support'*. The team had suffered some heavy defeats, winning only one match since the start of the season, and, with poor form shown by the players. However, the committee was not entirely blameless for, according to a report in the *Batley News*, *'they have done little, if anything to foster a love for the game, and the players have been provided with most indifferent tackle'*. The same report proffered, *'there can be little doubt but that the course of a year or two a team will be available worthy to bear the town's name, and who will uphold its prestige in the Socker world as do the fifteen in Rugby circles.'* That prophecy never came to pass.

Batley Swifts was a local rival of Batley AFC. Swifts had been formed earlier, in 1895, and played on Healey Lane and then, from 1896/97, at Upper Batley Cricket Club. However, in 1899 the club was in trouble for non-payment of Heavy Woollen league fees, failing to fulfil fixtures against local opposition and then failing to pay the referees expenses. The club, along with its forty registered players, was suspended until the resulting fines were paid. The club secretary, a Mr Brearley, was moved to write to the local FA to express his dissatisfaction over the way he felt his club has been treated, and declared that the Swifts were washing their hands of the local association and would from then on play friendly fixtures only.

Football in the town was not yet finished as, back in the Heavy Woollen League for the 1900/01 season, was a new 'Batley AFC' - interestingly with a certain Mr Brearley on its committee, and H Barker as club president. A ground at Carlinghow had been secured for the season although, prior to 1901/02. the former Batley Casuals ground at Batley Field Hill - also known as 'Lamplands' - which was said to have been in excellent condition, had been secured. The club itself was again reported as being 're-formed' in the summer of 1901, and its Vice-president was Alderman J W Blackburn. A Fred Blackburn, most likely a close relative, was given the role of club 'skipper' that season. The club's finances were said to have been healthy for the club's second campaign, although more support at the gate was hoped for.

One year on, the club was again 're-formed', this time as 'Batley Rugby Union and Association Football Club,' with Alderman Blackburn continuing as a vice-president. It was a rare case of a town's representative football club (albeit in different incarnations) having had links with clubs from both rugby codes, the latter being very much an amateur organisation. It would seem that the Rugby Union section was newly formed, having thrown in their lot with the 'socker' players rather than to risk going it alone, at a time when Northern Union was very much the biggest winter sport in the region.

Batley AFC left the Heavy Woollen League and disbanded in the summer of 1903, just one year after the amalgamation with the rugby club, with the likes of Batley Speedwell, Casuals, and St Mary's taking its place in the league over the next few seasons. By 1906 a new Batley Swifts was playing friendly fixtures, but that club was short-lived. The Rugby Union club, however, continued for just a little longer and in August 1904 moved to Mount Pleasant to share with Batley C&FC club after the latter had disbanded its second team. It was a rare instance of both rugby codes playing on the same ground without objection from the authorities.

A Batley Tuesday club was founded in August 1900, and was not in any way related to the senior Batley AFC, and relations between the two clubs were not good.

There has been no real attempt to establish a 'town' team for Batley, and similar attempts at nearby Birstall have also failed. Birstall Parish Church AFC was a founder member of the West Riding County Amateur League in the 1922/23 season, but the club dropped out of the league after just one season, having finished 12th of 16 teams.

In recent times, Batley Town joined the West Riding County Amateur League in 1997, playing home fixtures at Mount Pleasant. Despite a promising first season when third place in Division Three earned the club promotion, immediate relegation followed, and the club folded during the 2000/01 season. At this time, Howden Clough FC, of the West Yorkshire League, is arguably the most established club in the area.

## Bowling * and Bowling Albion

The original Bowling association club played its home fixtures at the well-established Usher Street ground, Bradford, on alternative weeks to the established Bowling Football Club which was a member of the Northern Union. Having playing informal matches on the ground for some time the rugby club decided to adopt the association team formally in April 1897. The parent club was in serious financial trouble at the time, and the introduction of association football at Usher Street may well have been an attempt to relieve these financial pressures.

Bowling AFC played in the professional West Yorkshire League between 1897-99 but withdrew in March 1899 due to a lack of interest and inability to raise a team as well as the financial burdens associated with travel to away fixtures. In November 1899 it was reported that the club had been suspended by the West Yorkshire FA for not payment of fines, the suspension applying to recent officials as well as players. The Bowling Football Club was also wound up soon afterwards, while its players went on to play for other local sides in the Bradford district.

Almost two dozen teams from the Bowling district had played in local competitions by the onset of World War Two. Bowling Albion made the biggest impact, albeit for a relatively short time. The Albion name was used intermittently between 1904-35, although that name was not always one that attracted the best headlines. In the 1906/07 season, the club, which was playing in the Bradford Alliance, was censured by the West Yorkshire FA in October 1906 for the foul language used by its spectators. At the same time, its player, Ansty was suspended until January 1st for striking a linesman and kicking an opponent.

The 1920s saw the emergence of a successful Albion side. The 1920/21 season saw the club make the final of the Bradford & District FA Cup, despite playing in the Second Division of the Bradford & District League, losing 1-3 to Calverley on Monday 25th April in front of 2,500 spectators at Valley Parade.

In the 1921/22 season, the club's first, and only, entry into the FA Cup saw Harrogate defeated 2-1 at home in an Extra Preliminary Round, before a 0-3 defeat at Frickley Colliery.

Founder members of the West Riding County Amateur League for the 1922/23 season, the club moved from its ground at Back Lane, Bowling to the Greenfield ground at Dudley Hill, one of the most prominent sporting grounds in the city at the time. That season proved its most successful.

In the space of twelve days at the end of the season, Bowling Albion played 11 league matches and secured 18 points out of a possible 22 — an astonishing feat, but as the team had also and taken part in two cup-ties within that period, then that would equate to more than one match per day. The club won the first ever West Riding County Amateur League title, pipping Apperley Bridge by just two points, and on Thursday 10th May 1923 also won the Bradford Hospital Cup with a 2-0 defeat of Birkenshaw in the final at Park Avenue, Bradford.

| 1922-23 West Riding County Amateur League | | | | | | | |
|---|---|---|---|---|---|---|---|
| | P | W | D | L | F | A | Pts |
| **Bowling Albion** | 30 | 22 | 6 | 2 | 78 | 21 | 50 |
| Apperley Bridge | 30 | 19 | 10 | 1 | 68 | 23 | 48 |
| Calverley | 30 | 16 | 9 | 5 | 61 | 27 | 41 |
| **Boothtown** | 30 | 17 | 4 | 9 | 83 | 45 | 38 |
| Liversedge | 30 | 16 | 6 | 8 | 61 | 39 | 38 |
| Thornton United | 30 | 12 | 10 | 8 | 51 | 42 | 34 |
| Cleckheaton | 30 | 14 | 5 | 11 | 69 | 51 | 33 |
| Scholes Athletic | 30 | 14 | 5 | 11 | 51 | 33 | 33 |
| Wibsey | 30 | 13 | 4 | 14 | 52 | 50 | 30 |
| Silsden | 30 | 10 | 6 | 14 | 49 | 66 | 26 |
| Bingley Town | 30 | 8 | 10 | 12 | 44 | 65 | 26 |
| Birstall Parish | 30 | 9 | 5 | 16 | 47 | 60 | 23 |
| **Haworth** | 30 | 8 | 4 | 18 | 53 | 67 | 20 |
| Greenfield Athletic | 30 | 6 | 4 | 20 | 39 | 95 | 16 |
| Ings House | 30 | 5 | 3 | 22 | 41 | 94 | 13 |
| Thornhill Lees WMC | 30 | 2 | 7 | 21 | 24 | 93 | 11 |

The following season, Albion could only finish 13th in the league, and suffered a 1-13 loss to Boothtown in the West Riding County Cup, having lost several players during the season. The club dropped down into local league football at the end of that season.

Albion tried its luck in the FA Amateur Cup during its two County Amateur League seasons. In the 1922/23 season a 1-0 victory at Garforth in the First Qualifying Round was followed by a 2-0 home win over Thornton United, before a heavy 2-5 loss at Wibsey at the third qualifying stage. A 0-1 loss at Rawdon saw the club exit at the first stage the following season.

The 1927/28 season saw a 16-1 rout of Frizinghall Congs in January in a Bradford Red Triangle Division Three fixture, and the following season Albion were defeated by Hillside Rovers in a play-off for the Bradford City League championship. The club was back in the Red Triangle (also known as the YMCA League) by the early 1930s, as well as running an under 18 team in the Bradford Amateur League's Junior Division, enjoying the assistance of Ellis, a Bradford City reserve player, but by 1935 had apparently folded.

# Dewsbury & Savile

One of a number of exhibition games, organised to further the interest in association football in the West Riding, took place on Saturday 15th September 1883 in Dewsbury, featuring the well known and established Darwen and Blackburn Olympic clubs. This match attracted a large crowd, including many who had journeyed by train from East Lancashire. Darwen defeated their neighbours, and FA Cup holders, 4-2, and, although not stated in the local press, it is likely that the venue was Crown Flatt, the home of the local rugby football club, which had been in use since 1876. This did not, as hoped, lead to the immediate formation of a successful club in Dewsbury, but the town did not have to wait long for the code to take hold in what was a strong rugby stronghold

The Dewsbury & Savile AFC was founded in the summer of 1896, following a meeting that had taken place on Thursday 25th June 1896 at the Kings Arms Hotel. The meeting consisted of a number of association football enthusiasts who were keen to establish the sport in the town. Mr E Brook had been voted to the chair and the large gathering voted unanimously to approach the Dewsbury & Savile Cricket and Football Club. The secretary *pro tem*, C Holdsworth, had written to a number of existing clubs in the district asking for a copy of the rules, among other things, but had only received a reply from the Halifax club, who gave their encouragement to the new venture.

With its acceptance by the Dewsbury & Savile C&FC, the new team had lofty ambitions, and competed in the West Yorkshire League during the 1897/98 season, finishing joint second in a five-team league with Ossett, and behind Altofts. The team played on the Crown Flatt ground along with the rugby football club (and which had formerly been used by the United Clerk's Cricket Club).

However, 1898 is significant in that the association section broke away from the parent club and moved to a new ground at Savile Town, known as The Victoria Ground. The Dewsbury & Savile rugby football club had stayed loyal to the English Rugby Union in the Great Split of 1895 but had found little success, and the sport is said to have been abandoned completely halfway through the 1897/98 season, having been played at Crown Flatt since 1876. A new rugby football club, this time affiliating with Northern Union, was formed in the summer of 1898, continuing to play at the same ground.

The semi-independent association club became one of the three new teams elected to the Yorkshire League in 1898, playing as 'Dewsbury AFC'. The competition proved too strong for the new team, which finished bottom of the ten clubs, with only one win from its 18 fixtures.

The Victoria Ground had previously been used by the Dewsbury St Paulinus club, was later used for West Riding and district association cup finals. While it was being prepared, the adjacent cricket field was used for home fixtures. Sadly, the new ground's inauguration on Saturday 12th November 1898, a Yorkshire League match against Sheffield, was marred by the death of a visiting team player, 20-year-old Joseph Edward Eadon, who suffered a suspected heart-attack during the match, which caused its premature abandonment of the game (He was erroneous referred to as a home team player in my previous book). His body was covered by the overcoats of two of his team-members, and carried shoulder-high on a board to the Dewsbury club headquarters at the Savile Town Hotel. It transpired later that the steelworker had a pre-existing heart condition and was in no fit state to actually take to the field that day.

The club's second Yorkshire League season saw only five clubs take part after the Sheffield & Hallamshire teams withdrew en-masse, leaving just West Yorkshire clubs left in the competition. Dewsbury finished bottom again, with just one win from its eight fixtures. There was a newly reformed senior section of the West Yorkshire League for the 1899/1900 season, with Dewsbury electing to play in this competition too. Some matches actually doubled up as both Yorkshire and West Yorkshire League fixtures. Dewsbury finished mid-table in the Senior Division (South) but both leagues closed down at the end of that season. The association club was struggling to pay its way, and at the club AGM on Monday 23rd April 1900 the outgoing football secretary, C Holdsworth, was more or less left to plead with the Dewsbury & Savile C&FC to keep it going, despite its inability to – as yet – fully pay its own way.

The local Heavy Woollen League had been formed in time for the 1898/99 season, and this contained many local Dewsbury teams. Indeed Dewsbury AFC reserves competed in the league's second season, but Dewsbury AFC initially decided against putting its first team in the Heavy Woollen League for the 1900/01 season, and also withdrew its second team from the competition, preferring to play just friendlies and cup ties instead. The club also became known as 'Dewsbury & Savile AFC' again, reflecting its dependence on its parent body.

The Heavy Woollen Football Association's knock-out cup, The Wheatley Cup, still competed for today, was donated by Richard Nevin Wheatley, a former captain of the Dewsbury association team, and at the time linked with the Mirfield United club. He was one in a line of Wheatley's who had given charitable donations and gifts to worthy causes in the district for many years, and also served as President of the Heavy Woollen FA from its formation in 1898 until 1920, save for a short time during the 1907/08 season. He was also president of the hugely successful Mirfield United club at one point. The inaugural Wheatley Cup competition was played on successive weekends throughout March and April 1899, with 21 teams entered, and with Morley defeating Mirfield United 1-0 in the final.

Dewsbury & Savile were winners of the cup for the first time at the end of that 1900/01 season, defeating Morley 4-1 on their own Victoria ground on Saturday 13th April 1901. A first half brace from Skelton went part way to ensuring a comfortable victory.

Dewsbury & Savile C&FC agreed to absorb the Dewsbury Corinthians association club in April 1901, as well as to allow the Old Dewsburians rugby club to ground-share at the Victoria Ground. The Corinthians would thereby become the association section from now on, and in the absence of a county league, a decision to join the local competition instead was also made (The Old Dewsburians ground-share did not last long, and a new Corinthians breakaway club was playing friendly matches by 1902 before quickly fading away).

Surprisingly, the club did not initially build on that cup success, finishing down in 11th place (of 12 teams) in the 1901/02 Heavy Woollen League, its cup winning team from the previous season having moved on and been replaced by the Corinthians players. Local rivals Dewsbury Celtic finished way ahead in runner-up spot - losing a play-off with Mirfield United - and Dewsbury St Matthew's also finished above them in the final table.

For the 1902/03 season, Dewsbury & Savile enjoyed an influx of players from the strong Savile Town Clarence club, which was now surprisingly defunct, as well as a few from Thornhill Lees. The season proved much more successful, with the league title won, and another Wheatley Cup final appearance. Sadly, this was lost 0-2 to Mirfield United, who, like Dewsbury Celtic, had stepped up to a reformed West Yorkshire League. Celtic played on a field at Cemetery Road and had headquarters at The Star Inn, failed to complete the season and promptly folded after a relatively short existence, in which it had clearly overstretched itself.

Late in 1903 the Midland Railway Company, which owned the Victoria Ground decided to use the land, which was leased by a local farmer to the football club, for its own use. The club was therefore given until 1st November to vacate the field. The railway company compensated the football club to the tune of £175, while an adjacent field was provided for the rest of the season in order for the club to be able to complete its home fixtures that season.

A new permanent ground was leased from the same farmer, a Mr Ponder, situated opposite the Savile Hotel, and at the time bordering Mill Street West. This field still exists as an open space adjacent to what is now West Street in the town.

A return was made to West Yorkshire League competition for the 1903/04 season, and the club's run lasted longer than that of the Dewsbury Celtic club. The team finished 10th in the 12 team league, and the following season finished in the top bunch of clubs, albeit well behind Bradford City reserves (winners), and Heckmondwike (runners-up) before dropping out of the league at the end of the season.

The club still had aspirations of becoming one of the district's leading clubs, but storm clouds were on the way.

The club made the headlines for the wrong reason, albeit through no fault of their own, during October and November 1904 when several teams refused to travel to Dewsbury due to a small-pox epidemic that had broken out in the town. The minutes of a West Yorkshire Football Association meeting on Wednesday 14th December 1904, as recorded in the *Yorkshire Post*, reflect the headaches that were caused by postponed fixtures.

*Football matters arising out of the small-pox scourge still prevalent in Dewsbury still cause not a little trouble to the Committee governing the West Yorkshire Association. Two claims made by the Dewsbury and Savile Club for broken engagements on account of the epidemic came up for discussion at the meeting of the Executive.*

*The more important one was against the Leeds City Club, which had before been discussed. This claim was for the sumo of £13 18s 3d for a broken engagement on October 15. The Leeds organisation declined to receive Dewsbury and Savile at Holbeck, and having been previously ordered to pay Dewsbury's expenses, now contested the chief items which had been placed against them. These were fares and players wages amounting to £3 14s.*

*It was urged by the representatives of the Leeds City Club that if the match had been played Leeds City would have been acting quite contrary to the health authorities of the city, and they could not afford to do that. If they did they would run the risk of losing the support of some of the leading citizens to who thy looked for help towards floating a first-class professional Association club in the city.*

*After a short discussion the Executive decided to allow the claim, subject to the proper receipts being sent by the Dewsbury Club to the Association secretary.*

*The next claim made by the Dewsbury and Savile club was against Oulton for £9 0s 3d, including gate money taken in and returned to the spectators, amounting to £4 6s 9d. It was stated that the Dewsbury players turned up together with the referee, but Oulton failed to do so. Dewsbury now withdrew their claim for gate money, and it was decided to allow Dewsbury a sum of £3 19s 3d.*

The small-pox epidemic caused the Dewsbury & Savile club financial problems on more than one level. With the step up to the West Yorkshire League the team was now fully professional (in this day and age it would be classed as semi-professional, with players being paid wages and expenses per match), and the loss of home fixtures meant that not only was there no revenue coming into the club, but also that the players were unable to be paid for matches that were cancelled. This led many to look elsewhere for 'employment.' The cancelled matches were completed in the new year, but at a financial cost at the gate to the club.

**Selected Heavy Woollen Wheatley Cup finals:**
1900/01: Dewsbury & Savile (4-1 v Morley)
1902/03: Mirfield United (2-0 v Dewsbury & Savile)
1903/04: Dewsbury Albion (2-1 v Morley)
1907/08: Northorpe (3-1 v Dewsbury & Savile)
1910/11: Drighlington (1-0 v Dewsbury & Savile)

Given it's problems the previous season, it is perhaps no surprise that the Dewsbury & Savile club again reverted to playing friendly fixtures only for the 1905/06 season, a policy that was continued the following year too.

A short return was made to the West Yorkshire League for the 1907/08 season, albeit in the Second Division, and as a purely amateur club. The club was warned by the league committee by October 1907 that its ground should be marked out properly, as referees had reported confusion over the pitch markings. The problem was that by now hockey was also being played on the ground, leading to two sets of markings. Despite finishing in mid-table in the 14 team division, the league was forced to dispense with Division Two when many of its clubs (in particular those from Wharfedale) withdrew due to the expenses incurred, particularly from travelling. Unable to compete with the stronger clubs in the district, Dewsbury & Savile once again reverted back to local football.

With many of the stronger clubs in the Heavy Woollen district having folded in recent seasons, the Wheatley Cup competition also lost a little of its early status. The Dewsbury club made the final for a third time during the 1907/08 season, but a 1-3 loss to Northorpe was the result.

1908/09 saw the club back in the Heavy Woollen League. Only a decade earlier the club had been competing in the top association league in Yorkshire, but having never been able to compete with the best, in terms of finance or success on the field, its status had gradually declined to the extent that is was by now just one of a number of junior clubs in the district.

Dewsbury & Savile's final success, of sorts, was in reaching the final of the Wheatley Cup at the end of the 1910/11 season, the final played at Heckmondwike on Monday 17th April 1911. However, this match was lost, by a single goal, to Drighlington, despite the Dewsbury team having been well on top in the second half. The club was still competing in the Wheatley Cup right up to the outbreak of World War One, although its status had dropped even further by then, and the Heavy Woollen League itself had been discontinued due to a lack of numbers. The association team was revived in 1919 at a minor level before fading away completely.

The association team's parent body, the Dewsbury & Savile Cricket and Football Club, also ran hockey, tennis, and bowling sections, and these were unaffected by the gradual decline in the football team, which could not expect to be subsidised by the other sports. Hockey, in particular, proved popular following World War One.

Dewsbury Northern Union club actually considered relocating to the Savile Town football ground in 1914, with a special meeting held at Crown Flatt on Saturday 23rd May where the recent negotiations with the Dewsbury & Savile club were discussed. A decision was eventually reached whereby that the rugby team stayed put, at least until 1991.

Among other pre-War Dewsbury clubs, Dewsbury Albion enjoyed its brief moment or two of glory when the club completed the Heavy Woollen League and Cup double in 1904. The following season the club lost a championship play-off to local rivals Boothroyd Rangers 0-2 after the clubs had tied at the top of the table, but by the summer of 1906 the club had folded.

Dewsbury & Savile Football & Cricket Club does still exist, but its sporting clubs have long gone. The cricket club was later amalgamated with Whitley Lower CC to form what is now the current Hopton Mills Cricket Club, its famous old ground and nearby football field abandoned around 1990. Both have since come back into use but there is little evidence of the fine grandstand at the cricket ground or of the facilities at the football ground.

Of the many individuals associated with the association football in Dewsbury prior to the outbreak of World War One, Samuel Knowles was perhaps the best known. He moved to the Dewsbury area as a boy, and playing both rugby and cricket for the Dewsbury & Savile club. After a short spell in Leicester, he returned to Dewsbury and helped to form the Heavy Woollen & District FA, the first district association football in the region, at the Kings Arms, Dewsbury. After being suspended by the Heavy Woollen FA, following suspected financial irregularities, he turned his attention to Bradford, where he played a part in the formation of Bradford City AFC. Knowles was also a vice-president of the West Yorkshire FA and President of the West Yorkshire Referees Society, also performing duties as a member of the Football League Referees Society. He passed away aged 68 in July 1939.

Charles Marsden was also a well known and respected cricketer, official and rugby union player with the Dewsbury club, was another who was instrumental in the formation and running of the Dewsbury & Savile association club. He died in February 1940, aged 83.

# Gargrave

The Craven district has lost some significant clubs over the past decade or so; Skipton LMS, Skipton Bulldogs, Embsay and Gargrave to name but a few. The latter, representing the village that lies some four miles north-west of Skipton has achieved success in different eras, and its ground lies virtually intact, stand *et al*, waiting for a new club to emerge.

The original **Gargrave AFC** first played competitive football in the 1905/06 season, when it joined the Craven Amateur League, which had been founded twelve months earlier. The runner-up position was achieved in its debut season, behind Skipton United in a ten team division.

After finishing in third and fourth place in subsequent seasons the club left Craven Amateur League in the summer of 1908, switching to the local Skipton Hospitals League, in effect replacing its reserve team in that competition. The 1909/10 season saw the first team finish as runner-up to Earby Amateurs in the Senior Division, with its reserves finishing at the foot of the Junior Division. On 28th August 1909, the club became a founding member of the Craven & District Football Association.

Unfortunately Craven football was at a low ebb by 1911, with the initial surge in interest in the sport now on the wane and the Skipton Hospitals League disbanded in the summer of that year. Gargrave FC also seems to have gone with it as there are no reports of any team playing competitively again until 1913.

In the Craven Football Association's Centenary publication, published in 1908, there is reference to a **Gargrave Celtic** being in existence in around 1910. This team is said to have played on a ground close to the church. A lady spectator was evidently banned from the ground for threatening players and the referee with an umbrella. Skipton Celtic and Glusburn Celtic clubs played in local competitions around this time, but the Gargrave club didn't, and may well have been a youth team.

**Gargrave Swifts** played in the re-formed Skipton & District League during the 1913/14 season finishing runner-up to Niffany Rovers in the eight team competition, but withdrew during the following season. On Saturday 24th October 1914 Cononley's Tom Watson unfortunately suffered a left leg fracture on the Gargrave ground in a league match between the sides, a significant event in the days before modern medicine. The club's folding was less significant, and hardly noticed as War-time priorities took precedence.

There was no competitive football in the village during World War One. The association game in the early days was played on several locations around the village; a field below Goffa Mill, fields above the Anchor Inn, Chapel Croft (known today as Swire Croft) during the late 1920s, and Neville Road, before the village club settled on its present position alongside the Leeds to Liverpool Canal off Skipton Road.

Gargrave AFC was revived for the 1919/20 season, but its Skipton & District League campaign was far from successful, a 0-12 defeat to Laurie's Own, a team from Barnoldswick, in late October 1919, underlining its struggles.

The South Craven League was founded in time for the 1922/23 season, and Gargrave became a founding member, finishing in mid-table. The following season they were joined in the competition by **Gargrave Athletic Works**, the local rivals finishing 7th and 9th respectively in the twelve team league.

The club renamed itself Gargrave Town in the summer of 1924, and placed sixth out of 13 teams to finish the 1924/25 season. The 14th team, the one that dropped out during the season, was Gargrave Athletic Works.

After having been among the front-runners in the 1926/27 season, albeit trailing runaway winners Keighley Parkwood by some distance, Gargrave's improving squad came good for the 1927/28 campaign. With Parkwood having moved on, the team were South Craven League and Craven & District

Cup winners, dropping only 3 points all season, and winning the ten team league well ahead of Skipton LMS.

Gargrave Town's second string played in the South Craven Intermediate League at this time, a competition for teams with an average age of 21.

With key players having moved on, Gargrave struggled in subsequent years in the South Craven League, finishing second bottom of the league in both 1928/29 and 1930/31. The South Craven League itself folded in the summer of 1931 as it was absorbed into the new Airedale & Craven League. The 14-strong competition comprised the strongest clubs in those districts as well some east Lancashire opposition, and it proved far too big a challenge for Gargrave, who finished bottom in the league's first season, and failed to complete some of its fixtures.

A second blow for the club was the closure of Airebank Mill, a major employer in the village. The cotton mill, one which had been established in 1780. This left the club short of players and as a result, it was forced to fold again.

A **Gargrave Unemployed** team is said to been around from 1933, reflecting the economic problems experienced around the county. Similar teams were formed in all of the main towns in the Aire Valley too.

The American medical supplies company Johnson & Johnson took over Airebank Mills in 1934 and brought new life to the village in terms of employment. It was no coincidence that **Gargrave Institute FC** was the next attempt to provide football for the locals. Founded the same year as the mill takeover, the club joined the new Craven & District League, finishing in third place in the Second Division in its debut 1934/35 season.

Promoted to the top flight, the club then achieved the league and cup double in the 1935/36 season, a remarkable achievement for a club revived less than two years earlier.

Institute joined the Nelson, Colne & District League (itself founded in 1928) for the 1937/38 season. This would be the first time a club from the village had hopped over the border to play in Lancashire, and it wouldn't be the last. It proved a successful switch, with the team winning 14-1 at Nelson Technical School early in October 1937 and going on to finish in runner-up spot in the league's top division, behind Jimmy Nelsons Sports Club. On top of that the club won the league cup. The 'Sir Amos Nelson' cup final against Earby Victoria was played at Barnoldswick on Thursday 28th April, and was won 5-3 – this after Gargrave had lost 1-4 to the same opposition in a league fixture just over two weeks earlier.

Gargrave recovered from a poor start to the following campaign to challenge in the top half of the table, but were no match for Earby, who ran away with the league title. The club was all set to play in the league in the 1939/40, season alongside another Gargrave club, **Johnson & Johnson Sports Club**, which had been newly elected to the competition, but ultimately both chose to withdraw due to the outbreak of World War Two.

Gargrave played friendly fixtures during the War, but afterwards it enjoyed a first golden period. The 1946/47 season saw victory in the Craven Cup, with Bentham defeated 1-0 in the final, which was played at Hellifield.

The following season the Craven League title itself was won after Gargrave defeated Cononley 5-2 in a play-off, the teams having tied for top place at the end of the season.

In the summer of 1948 the club again left the Craven League to play in Nelson, Colne & District Amateur League again as **Gargrave Community Council.** However, this move was relatively short-lived, as was the 'Community Council' part of the club name, and by the end of the 1951/52 season Gargrave AFC had achieved the Craven League and Cup double, just edging out Cowling and Sutton United to win the title.

In 1953 the club's current ground was bought by the Coulthurst Trust, a charity set up in the name of the prominent local family, and handed over to the village. The village hall is also maintained by the trust.

Following league cup success for both first and second teams, Gargrave became league champions again in the 1955/56 and 1956/57 seasons, but this was followed by a decline that saw the club struggle for the next two decades, firstly in the top division of the Craven League, before relegation to the league's second tier.

An unsuccessful experiment with Sunday Football in the 1973/74 season - Gargrave Celtic lost eleven out of its 12 matches in the Keighley Sunday Alliance Second Division – saw that idea dropped after just one season, and by the end of the 1978/79 season the club was bottom of Craven League's Division One (the league's second tier), with only two wins from its 28 games.

However, with other teams dropping out of the league, Gargrave FC was spared relegation and didn't look back. Just two season later, the club finished as Division One runners-up behind Colne team Rock Rovers – earning promotion to the league's Premier Division for the 1982/83 season. There was no stopping the side now, becoming 1982/83 & 1983/84 league champions, dropping only three points in each season, both of which saw them finish above runner-up Steeton.

An exciting end to the 1984/85 season saw Gargrave finish runners-up in the league to Barnoldswick United on goal difference, and just a point ahead of Haworth. A decision to move back into Lancashire football this time to the East Lancashire League was made in the summer of 1985. This league covers the same area as the old Nelson, Colne & District League and was seen as a step up from the Craven & District League. The club could have opted for the West Riding County Amateur League, but that would have involved far more travelling.

There was a move back to the Craven League for the 1991/92 season. Gargrave replaced its reserve team in Division One and duly won the divisional title, also reaching the league's TAP Trophy final which was narrowly lost 2-3 to Oxenhope. In 1991 the club won the Craven FA Cup with a 2-1 victory over Rolls Royce, and retained the trophy the following season.

Life back in the Craven Premier Division proved immediately successful, with the title won in its first two seasons back, 1992/93 and 1993/94. Gargrave were crowned 1992/93 Craven Football League champions after a thrilling match against their nearest rivals Embsay in April. Gargrave needed a point to take the title and achieved this by coming from behind four times to draw 5-5. Among the Gargrave scorers that day were Andy Geary and Dale Hoyle, two of the West Riding's top amateur players of their day. Gargrave also won the league's new Northern Plant Hire Cup that season, defeating Keighley Lifts 4-1 in the final.

In 1994 Gargrave stepped back up to the East Lancashire League again, winning the Division Two title and then finishing runner-up in the top division to Oswaldtwistle in the 1995/96 season. Dale Hoyle finished joint leading goalscorer in the league that season.

1995 saw the club win the Craven Cup again defeating Barnoldswick United in a replay at the Rolls Royce Sports Ground, Barnoldswick. The East Lancashire League Division Two Cup was also won that season. Embsay were defeated 2-1 when Gargrave again won the Craven Cup in 1997. However, the following season the Craven Cup final, played at the Rolls Royce sports ground in Barnoldswick, was lost 2-5 to Barnoldswick United, after the original tie had to be called off just minutes prior to kick-off due to a snow storm.

There was a great run in the 1995/96 West Riding County Cup run, when the club made it all the way to the semi-final, losing 1-2 to eventual winners Storthes Hall at the West Riding County FA ground at Woodlesford.

However, all good runs come to an end, and after finishing fourth in the East Lancashire League in the 1996/97 season the rot set in, as players moved on. Eleventh place in a twelve team division would have meant relegation at the end of the 1998/99 season, but instead Gargrave went back to the Craven League, where it was offered a place back in its Premier Division. Sadly the club could only amass a total of three points, from a win and a draw, from its 20 league matches back in the local league and finished well adrift of the rest of the teams at the end of the 1999/2000 season. Two years later another relegation followed, with again only one victory achieved in the league all season, to see the club at the lowest level in its history.

The club then achieved a double promotion back to the Premier Division. Following a third place finish in Division Two, the Division One title was won at the end of the 2003/04 season. The club managed to re-establish itself in the Premier Division, winning the league's Morrison Cup in the 2006/07 season, and in the 2008/09 season finishing league runner-up to Long Lee Juniors.

The football club joined with the adjacent village cricket club to form Gargrave Sports Association in 2005, which has charity status.

Gargrave's reserve team was by now making a name for itself, winning the Division Two title with an unbeaten record in the 2006/07 season (also winning the Craven League's Norman Pratt Trophy the season before, defeating Settle United reserves 5-1 after extra-time), and then the Division One title the following season, with Long Lee in second place. However, the reserves were unable to be promoted due to the first team being in the Premier Division (escaping relegation by one position that season) and so the teams were 'swapped', with the reserve team becoming the first team, and vice-versa. This explains the sudden return to form of the Gargrave FC first team in the 2008/09 season.

Other club honours included, the Northern Plant Hire Trophy in 2004/05, Cononley Sports defeated 2-1 in the final, and Morrison Cup winners in 2006/07, when Skipton Town were defeated 3-1 in the final, which was played at Settle late in April

In April 2005, Gargrave's Dennis French was presented with an award by the Football Association for 50 years service to the game. Dennis joined Gargrave as a player in 1946 and joined the committee two years later, filling most club official positions during his time with the club.

'Gargrave Footballers'
Year unknown

Relegation back to Division One followed two years after the club's final runner-up spot in Craven League's Premier Division in 2009, but by the 2015/16 season the club had regained its Premier Division status. However, all was not well, and with its reserve team having already been dispensed with, the club was unable to raise a team for three fixtures, and finished second from bottom at the season's end. Gargrave was saved from relegation due to Cononley's withdrawal during the season (bottom team Grindleton switched the East Lancashire League at the season's end) but there was bad news to come as the new season approached.

A statement on the club website on 3rd August 2016, brought news that the club was to drop out of the league.

*'The Craven FA and the Craven League have both been informed that Gargrave AFC are withdrawing from all competitions in the forthcoming season. The decision has not been taken lightly but due to lack of players there was no alternative. Despite the power of social media, word of mouth, website and local awareness we have insufficient players coming forward to field a regular side. A small number of players are available on a regular basis but their numbers were not sufficient to allow for injuries and unavailability. These committed players held a meeting after their training session on Tuesday evening and reluctantly agreed that they had no option but to fold.*

*The officers at Gargrave Football Club would like to acknowledge these players and the support they have given to the club, some for many years and some for a few latterly. In particular special mention must go to Jonathon Chapman who has given tremendous service to Gargrave AFC both as a player and a Manager.'*

The club has not yet been revived, although a new club, Gargrave United, running junior teams, was founded in 2019. Its home ground is the Parish Football Field, at Low Green.

## Girlington *

This was the first association football club to play home games at Valley Parade, Bradford, as tenants of what was then Manningham Football Club. Girlington AFC was founded by A H Grunberger who fulfilled several roles for the club, including those of secretary and financial secretary.

The club's first two seasons saw it playing friendlies, initially playing at a ground at Four Lane Ends, before moving to Duncombe Street, off Ingleby Road. Its headquarters at this time was the nearby Red Lion Hotel. A new ground at Thornton Road was used for the 1898/99 season.

The club become founder members of the Bradford & District League in 1899 and were champions in the league's first two seasons, 1899/1900 and 1900/01. The following season the club won the Bradford District Cup, after having lost the previous two finals. To cater for a growing number of spectators, Girlington's home matches were played at Valley Parade from 1901. This move undoubtedly attracted more spectators but, with both rugby and soccer being played on the same pitch, wear and tear of the turf increased, and several games were cancelled because of this.

Things were not well behind the scenes, but it was still a surprise when the club disbanded in the summer of 1902 despite being accepted into the West Yorkshire League. In January 1903, there was a failed effort to reform the side, but the club did reform in time for the 1907/08 season though, playing in the second division of the West Yorkshire League. The following season the club was back in the top division of the Bradford & District League before fading away before World War One.

# Goole Loco

*Goole Loco 1911/12*

Never more than a junior team (in status) the team is photographed following its most successful season. Locos defeated Goole Primitive Methodists, a team they also beat into second place in the Goole League, to win the Goole & District Junior Cup in the 1911/12 season (this after having lost the previous final 1-2 to Swinefleet). Such was the team's dominance in the local league that season, it took until the first week in March before its first point was dropped, a 2-2 draw with St Mary's at Old Goole. The league final, played between the top two teams, at the Pleasure Grounds, the home of Goole Town FC, was won 4-2.

The team also reached the final of the Castleford & District FA Cup, losing 1-2 to Allerton Bywater in the final. This followed a 3-2 win over a strong Lock Lane Woodville in the semi-final, and is perhaps the club's greatest achievement.

The club was a founder member of the Goole League in 1908, but didn't play in that competition's predecessor, the Thorne & District League. It would seem that the club, despite its success, folded in the summer of 1912. A revived club played in the Goole Senior League between 1929-31, along with a separate Goole LMS team, but was not successful, finishing in the lower reaches of the league on both occasions.

# Guardhouse Sports Club

*Guardhouse SC 1934/35*

This club, formed in 1929, enjoyed much success locally during the 1930s, winning the Keighley & District FA Cup three times in succession. Steeton were defeated 2-1 in the 1935 and 1937 finals (the latter in a second replay), and Keighley Town defeated 3-0 in 1936. Silsden ended the Guardhouse run of success in the 1938 final.

After sharing the 1932/33 Keighley League title with Ingrow United, Guardhouse won it outright in 1934/35 and 1936/37, before returning after World War with three further league titles in four years in the later 1940s and early 1950s.

The club's second team was also successful, winning the Keighley League's Division Two title in 1934 and 1935, and also winning the league's Victory Cup competition in 1935. The photograph shows both first and reserve teams with the four trophies won in that 1934/35 season. The team folded in 1951.

# Guiseley Celtic

Guiseley Celtic, whose headquarters were at the New Inn, was the undisputed top team in the town in the game's formative years. The club won the Airedale & Wharfedale Senior Cup twice, and enjoyed a successful history in local and county leagues. The club, known locally as *The Tigers*, emerged in the 1901/02 season, playing friendlies. Its first foray into league competition was a tentative one, joining the Bradford Alliance for the 1902/03 season. However, the club won the league's First Division title in its only season in the competition, a success that earned it acceptance straight into the top division of the Bradford & District League. Two seasons (1903-05) were spent in the First Division of the stronger competition, before a further step-up, to the West Yorkshire League.

In March 1905, there was a proposal to merge the Guiseley Celtic and Menston clubs in order to create a club strong enough to compete at West Yorkshire League standard, making alternate use of the football grounds in each village. In the event, despite both committees agreeing to the merger, and anticipating crowds of around 2,000 the following season, both remained separate entities. The proposed Wharfedale United was dead, and both teams separately joined the county league for the 1905/06 season instead.

The 1905/06 season proved the club's most successful so far, finishing as Division Two champions at the end of the season, and earning another step up into the county's premier league competition. By now a professional club, with players paid for playing, runner-up position was achieved in the 1906/07 season behind Heckmondwike. After the teams had tied on points, it took two play-off games and a single goal to defeat the Wharfedale club in the decider, played on Saturday 27th April 1907.

The *Leeds Mercury* printed the following match report the following Monday.

### GUISELEY CELTIC BEATEN IN WEST YORKSHIRE DECIDING MATCH

*The contest between Guiseley Celtic and Heckmondwike for the championship of the West Yorkshire League, which had resulted in a draw at Bowling a fortnight ago, was replayed on Saturday evening, at Valley Parade, before about 2,000 spectators. Both teams were evidently determined to avoid a repetition of the disappointment of the original match, and displayed energy which an English League team would be proud. Guiseley started with rush, but Heckmondwike soon began to press, and for a long time kept the 'Celts' busy defending. In fact, during the greater part the game play was at the Guiseley end, and but for the good defensive work by the backs, Heckmondwike might have heaped up a merry little score.*

*Judging by the yell which rent the air as Joel the Heckmondwike centre forward, sent the ball into the net from a centre by Rogan, it would appear that the 'Wikes' had brought the best part of their township's population with them.*

*At the re-opening Heckmondwike still pressed, but both teams appeared to be fagged, and for some time their play was 'sloppy.' They brightened up a bit in time, and Guiseley began to be more the aggressive than they had been in the first half; but, although they tried hard, their efforts came to nothing, and when, amidst the greatest excitement, the whistle blew for time, the result remained : – Heckmondwike, one goal; Guiseley Celtic, nil.*

*Jeffreys, Heckmondwike's right half back, played a good game, and others conspicuous were Bruckner, McAndrew, and Rogan. On the Guiseley side, Dunnington, Sunderland, Murphy, and Beck showed good form. After the match medals were distributed to the men of both the winning and the losing teams Mr. Alfred Ayrton, ex-chairman of the Bradford City Club.'*

In all, the club won 20 of its 31 league and cup matches that season, with leading scorer Dunnington having scored 25 of his team's 85 goals during that time. The same player was, along with team-mates Kenworthy and Kneeshaw, were selected to play for the West Yorkshire representative team against its East Riding counterparts in Hull during the season.

The following season, the club's last in the West Yorkshire League, saw a sixth place finish.

The Airedale & Wharfedale Cup was the forerunner of the current Wharfedale FA Cup, and it ran for three seasons. Celtic won the first final, at the conclusion of the 1905/06 season, defeating Menston 2-0 in the final, which was played at Cottingley Bridge, Bingley on 31st March 1906. Special trains, offering reduced fairs, were run from Ilkley, the large crowd seeing Guiseley winning with late goals from Sunderland and Beck.

The following Friday, the *Wharfedale & Airedale Observer* reported,

*'On arrival at Guiseley station the Guiseley representatives received a tremendous ovation. The inhabitants of the town gathered in overwhelming numbers at the outskirts of the station. and when the train conveying the triumphant players steamed into the station a most animated seem was witnessed. Great enthusiasm prevailed on all sides, and the players were greeted with tremendous cheering. Conveyances had been provided for the victorious team, and their supporters, and headed by the Guiseley Brass Band, with hundreds of cheering spectators bringing up the rear, the players were taken in triumph to the New Inn, the headquarters of the club. During the evening several members. including Mr. Rhodes (president of the club) delivered brief speeches of congratulation to the players. Afterwards a torch-light procession was formed through the town. and the rejoicings were kept up to a late hour.'*

The 1906/07 final was played at Otley on Saturday 20th April 1907, with Bingley defeated 3-0 in front of what was estimated to have been the largest attendance to date on that ground.

At the club AGM at the New Inn on Wednesday 29th May 1907, it was revealed that £106 15s had been paid to players in the season just gone, leaving the club £44 in the red, although only £14 of that debt had been accrued in the past twelve months. The Airedale & Wharfedale Cup alone had accounted for £12 of that.

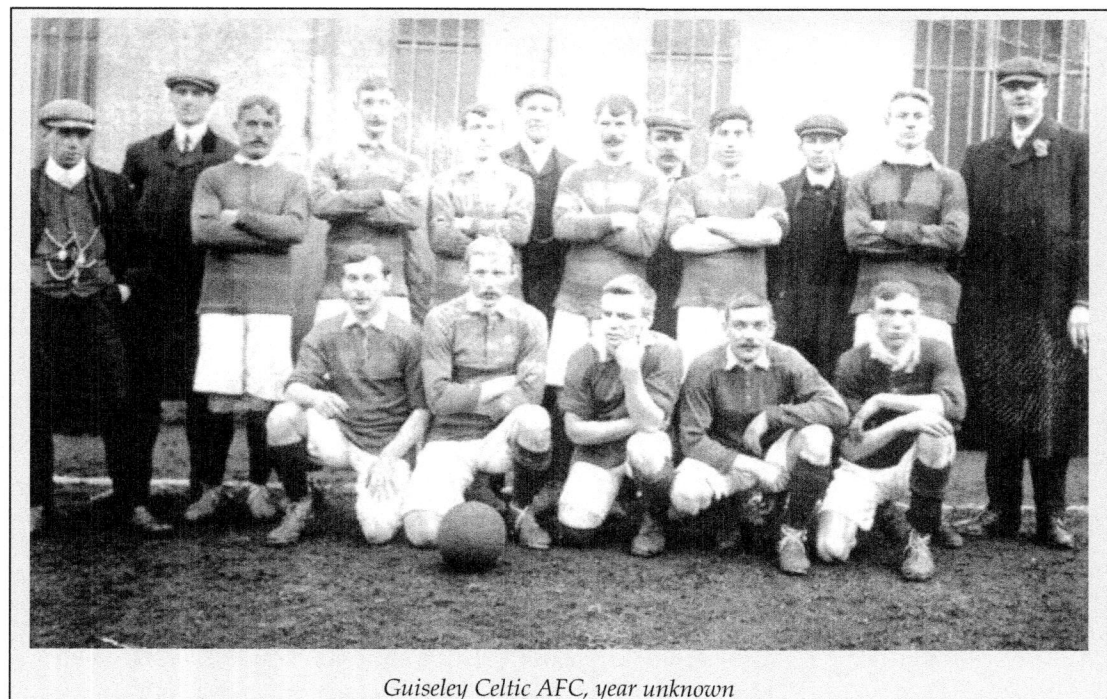

Guiseley Celtic AFC, year unknown

With the Airedale & Wharfedale Cup being such a loss-making exercise for the Celtic club, it was not entered for the 1907/08 season, the competition's last, and Celtic's committee chose to enter the FA Cup instead.

In the national competition, local rivals Swaine Hill United were defeated 2-0 at home in the First Qualifying Round replay, this after an entertaining 3-3 draw. Mirfield United were then defeated 2-1 on their own ground, again in a replay following a 1-1 draw at Guiseley. Worksop Town ended the run, with a narrow 3-4 victory at Guiseley in the Third Qualifying round, a match that was Celtic's last in the competition.

However, the costs of operating at such a high level began to take their toll, in particular the payments to players, and so Celtic dropped back into the Wharfedale League, where just three paid players per team were allowed, for the 1908/09 season, playing alongside local rivals Guiseley St Oswald's. Sadly, the club disappeared completely in the summer of 1909, despite its committee – which included President J H Ives, treasurer H G Procter (who was also treasurer of the Wharfedale League), and secretary F Clapham - intending it to just go into 'hibernation'. Celtic had been one of many teams of its status that overstretched itself, and that proved to be its downfall.

In Guiseley Celtic's absence, Nethermoor-based Guiseley Victoria (who had almost become Celtic's reserve team in the summer of 1908, and whose headquarters were at the town's Woolpack Inn) contested the Wharfedale Cup final at the close of the 1909/10 season (losing 0-8 to Horsforth), before rebranding itself as 'Guiseley AFC' in time for the 1910/11 season, with several old Celtic players said to have thrown in their lot with them. That club is of course still in existence today.

# Haworth

The village of Haworth is best known for its literary heritage in the form of the Brontë sisters. Their home at what is now the Brontë Parsonage Museum alone accounts for almost 100,000 annual visitors from around the world. Less well known is its local football team, which, despite its best efforts over the years, has never made its mark beyond the local football scene.

The first properly organised association team in the village was Haworth Midland FC, a team consisting of railway employees, who played on a ground at Marsh Top. It took part in the first Keighley Charity Cup competition to be held under association rules in the 1904/05 season, but went out 2-9 to eventual winners Silsden in Round One. Ironically, the last team to win the Charity Cup under its previous guise as a rugby competition was the Haworth Rugby Club.

The club was in the 1905/06 Keighley & District League in that competition's inaugural season, finishing 11th of the 12 teams that finished the season (a reserve team dropped out of its division during the season). The club finished bottom of the league's top division the following season, with a separate Haworth FC in Division Two (a Haworth Albion club having dropped out prior to the season), but both seem to have folded during the summer of 1907.

A number of other clubs appeared in the village before World War One, all playing briefly in the Keighley League's second tier, these being; Haworth Albion (1908/09), Haworth Athletic (1909-11), Haworth Wesleyans (1912/13), and Haworth Church (1913/14). These are all likely to have been linked.

Following the War, Sladen Valley, a team that played on a ground between Haworth and Stanbury emerged in the Keighley League in the 1919/20 season. It finished in fourth place in the top division before moving to West Lane, Haworth and thus renaming itself Haworth FC. The club won the league title at the end of the 1920/21 season, ahead of Keighley Town, and with an unbeaten league record.

Sladen Valley did itself reform between 1921-23, again playing league fixtures at West Lane, and winning the Keighley & District FA Cup in its second season before folding.

Despite only finishing fifth in the Keighley League in 1921/22, Haworth FC became a founding member of the West Riding County Amateur League in the summer of 1922, at the same time retaining a reserve team in the Keighley League. Nine seasons were spent in the County Amateur League, its best position being fifth in a 14-team division at the end of the 1928/29 season, this only two years after having finished at the foot of the league. Haworth also finished 6th from 16 teams in the 1923/24 season, but most seasons were spent in the lower half of the table. There was also a move away from West Lane around this time, to a new field behind Haworth Old Hall, close to the bottom of the famous village Main Street. The Fleece Inn, on Main Street itself, was also used as club headquarters.

Between 1926-28 another team operated out of the village, that of a revived Haworth Wesleyans. The club won the Keighley League's Division Two with ease in its first season, winning 26 of its 27 league fixtures and scoring 161goals in the process. Rather than stepping up to the league's top division, a move was made instead to the stronger South Craven League, where it finished the 1927/28 season in fifth place, out of ten teams, and also reached the final of the Keighley & District Cup, going down 2-7 to Cowling in the final. The club did not reappear the following season, although given the improved campaign that the senior Haworth FC enjoyed in 1928/29 it can be assumed that the Wesleyan club was absorbed in to that club.

Following two disappointing seasons at County Amateur level, Haworth FC became founding members of the Airedale & Craven League for the 1931/32 season. Although this was a step down in status, this new competition brought together the better teams in the Keighley and Craven districts. However, this was also a disappointing season, with Haworth finishing down in 10th place in a 14 team competition. Struggling with finances, and support, the club disbanded at the end of that season.

The Keighley Charity Cup was won twice by this particular Haworth FC. Parkwood were defeated in the 1926/27 final, and Cowling 3-1 (following a 2-2 draw) four years later.

The next club to appear in the village was Brontë Rovers, who also used The Fleece as headquarters and the Old Hall Ground for its home matches. Three seasons were spent in the Keighley League between

*Action from the 1921 Haworth v Cullingworth Keighley Charity Cup final replay at Lawkholme Lane, the home of Keighley RLFC, which was played in front of 3,000 spectators. Cullingworth won 2-1, following a 1-1 draw on the same ground.*

1936-39 (third place in 1936/37 being its best finish) before World War Two caused football in the district to more-or-less shut down.

Haworth FC was revived in 1946, its return to local football proving initially successful as the club won the Keighley League, winning all but two of its 18 fixtures. Attendances in the league were usually around the 300-500 mark, higher than those at the games of the struggling Keighley Town, playing down the road in the Yorkshire League. The period between 1947-54 was spent in the top division of the far stronger Bradford Amateur League. The 1947/48 season saw Haworth in the runner-up position behind Sutton United, which was ultimately its best showing in that competition.

By 1950, the club committee was keen to see facilities at the Old Hall Ground improved. The playing area was said to be uneven and 'badly shaped', so a 'Ground Improvement Committee' was set up to oversee any developments. Unfortunately, a lack of finance prevented any real improvements being undertaken, and following a disappointing 10th place (from 13 teams) at the conclusion on the 1953/54 season, the club again closed down. Significant silverware had been won by the club by then, notably a 5-2 thrashing of Bingley-side Eldwick in the final of the 1950/51 Keighley & District Cup final, played at the Parkwood Greyhound Stadium.

Haworth Sports FC followed, emerging in the 1956/57 season when it finished third in a nine-team Keighley League, prompting a switch for its second - and ultimately final – season to the Craven League. However, with weeks of the start of the 1957/58 season, Haworth had resigned from its new league following a 1-15 loss to Oxenhope, citing a lack of support and finance for its demise, and leaving a struggling second string to see out the season in the Keighley League before the club once again folded.

Keighley & District League Medal, awarded to E Kitson

Another two-season effort proved entirely inglorious, with the 1961-63 incarnation enjoying two seasons of struggle in the Craven League, the club's home ground by now being established on Butt Lane. However, Haworth Youth Centre FC fielded two age group sides in the Bradford Red Triangle between 1963-65, before dropping the 'Youth Centre' part of the name shortly after moving into the open-age Craven League. Fourteen seasons were spent in the Craven League, with the club finishing runner-up in the Premier Division in its final season in the league behind Colne United in the 1985/86 season.

Third place in the Premier Division was achieved three times, twice during the late 1960s and again in 1984/85. The latter season finished in dramatic fashion. Going into the closing stages of the season, Haworth actually looked like it would do the 'treble' of successive titles after having won the Division Two and then Division One titles over the previous two years. The side needed one win from their final three games to become champions, only to pick up a single point. Cononley destroyed Haworth's dream, winning 3-1 in the final

Haworth FC, 1947. The team is photographed with the Keighley & District League's 'Butterfield Shield'.

game to avenge a league cup final defeat only four days earlier. This left the emerging Barnoldswick United as champions, on goal difference from Gargrave, and with Haworth just one point in arrears.

Haworth stepped back up to the West Riding County Amateur League in 1986, albeit in the league's third tier, while maintaining a reserve team in the Craven League. By 1990/91 the club was running three teams, although the first team could only finish a lowly 14th, third from bottom, in the County Amateur League, prompting its withdrawal from the league for one season. The Keighley & District Cup was won during the 1989/90 season, with Crosshills defeated 2-1 in the final, which was played at Lawkholme Lane. A late winner from Richard Clarkson proved the difference between the teams.

Following a fourth place finish in the Craven League in the 1991/92 season, the first team was again placed in the County Amateur League the following season. However, the season was a disaster, with both first and second teams finishing bottom of the league, each of them conceding over 100 league goals (the third team having been dispensed with). This was the last time a Haworth team would play in this competition.

The former Old Hall Ground at Haworth. The adjacent quarry is now a car park, the football pitch itself now covered by housing. Haworth Main Street runs across the top right hand corner of the photograph.

Six and a half seasons were spent in the Craven League before Haworth FC folded early in the 1999/2000 season. The 1994/95 saw a Division One league and cup double, as well as promotion to the Premier Division, achieved. The divisional title was won on goal difference from Barnoldswick Park Rovers. The club established itself back in the Premier Division – finishing fourth in 1996/97 – but by the time the 1999/2000 season arrived the club was struggling. A reserve team had already been dispensed with, and there was little interest in the club, either from a playing point of view or from the local population. The main cause of this was the inadequacy of the club's Butt Lane base, which was no longer of the standard required. This had necessitated a move to the Marley sports fields in Keighley, which meant that support from the villagers dropped off as well as from local players. Sadly, the club has never been revived.

The field on Butt Lane is still used by the local Primary School, while the Old Hall Ground has long been built over with houses. The West Lane ground is still used for sport, being the home ground of Haworth Cricket Club. The original site at Marsh Top, however, is still a farmers field.

Brontë Wanderers was founded 1996 with aspirations of being based in Haworth, but was sadly unable to realise it ambitions. Despite the club progressing from the Craven & District League to the County Amateur League, the club was forced to play all of its home fixtures at Marley. Following failed attempts to bring Butt Lane up to standard, the club folded prior to the 2012/13 season.

# Hebden Bridge

With the town's rugby team experiencing financial difficulties, Hebden Bridge AFC rose to prominence between 1902-11 in the Halifax & District League. It had been formed in 1901, competing in its first competitive season in the newly formed Calder Valley League, which contained teams such as Monument Mystics, Todmorden Swifts and Pudsey Rovers. Vale Swifts won the championship, with Hebden Bridge finishing seventh in the nine team league.

The club moved to Calder Holme in 1907 just as the incumbent rugby team, despite their brand-new tenant's assistance in trying to wipe out its debts, was forced to suspend operations due to those debts amounting to £60.

The club also fielded a 'first' team in both the Rochdale League and the Calder Valley League during the 1908/09 season meaning that, along with Mytholmroyd and Portsmouth Rovers, they had plenty of fixtures to fit in. However, it was the club's 1909/10 campaign that was its most successful season as the side won a clean sweep of the Halifax League (edging out Mytholmroyd after a championship play-off), Halifax & District Cup (3-1 v Sowerby Bridge in the final) and the Charity Cup (2-0 v Norland in the final), with Greenlees scoring 29 goals that season and Lomas close behind with 25.

The Charity Cup was also won in the 1910/11 and 1911/12 seasons, 3-1 against Sowerby Bridge in the former, and 1-0 against Halifax Town reserves in the latter.

The town's rugby club reformed in 1910 but, with the association team now established at Calder Holme, it was forced to relocate to a ground above the village at Nell Carr, and then relocate again to a more convenient site, sharing at Mytholmroyd AFC.

The 1911/12 season also brought success for the club's second string, the reserves being winners of the Hebden Bridge & District League Cup, defeating Stubbing Holme 4-2 in the final, although they were pipped to the league title by Lydgate United. The reserve team also enjoyed a fairly successful 1913/14 season, finishing runner-up in both league (to Ridge Rangers) and cup (losing 0-1 in a replay to Hebden United) competitions.

Having left it too late to join the Yorkshire Combination in 1911, a season was spent in the Bradford League (1911/12) which offered a higher standard of competition to the Halifax League, but incurred additional cost as teams from out-with the city had to pay half the fares from Bradford Station of the visiting teams.

The following summer, the county's premier club competition welcomed the club, but the season was one of struggle. Bridge found it difficult to attract the better semi-professional players to the Calder Valley outpost and finished bottom in its second season (1913/14) in the Combination. The club's best run in the FA Cup came this season though, going out in the Second Qualifying Round at home to Mirfield United (2-4), following earlier victories over Thornhill Lees Albion (4-0) and Calverley (5-1), following a 2-2 draw at home).

At Christmas 1914 the club's players were informed that expenses would be reduced to two shillings per match, with the promise of the further two shillings that they were receiving before Christmas if the club's financial position were to improve. The club at this time was renting its Calder Holme field for £20 per annum from the Lancashire & Yorkshire Railway Company.

Hebden Bridge became the first Calder Valley team to reach the final of the West Riding Cup competition in the 1912/13 season, losing 0-2 to Morley in the deciding tie on Saturday 12th April at the Clarence Ground, Kirkstall, Leeds (*see section on Morley FC for the match report*).

> **HEBDEN BRIDGE ASSOCIATION FOOTBALL CLUB.**
>
> THE ANNUAL GENERAL MEETING of the above Club wil be held at the Neptune Hotel, on Monday Evening, July 14th, 1913. To commence at 8-15 prompt. All persons interested heartily invited.

A switch was made to the Lancashire Combination for the 1914/15 season, where the club would renew its rivalry with Todmorden neighbours Portsmouth Rovers in the league's second tier. Sadly, and due mainly to its precarious financial position, the club struggled in its new surroundings and closed down in the summer of 1915 for the remaining duration of the war.

The club re-joined the Halifax & District League in the summer of 1919, and played in the league's top division, maintaining a reserve team in the competition from 1920, without winning any silverware. The 1922/23 season was significant in that Hebden Bridge was one of only four teams that completed the season in Division One, alongside Stainland (the winners), Heptonstall, and Mytholmroyd.

Showing ambition, the club's first team entered the West Riding Senior League in 1920, playing in that competition until it closed down on 1923. The league was seen as a stepping-stone to the newly formed Yorkshire League, and the Calder Valley club was certainly not overawed, finishing fourth in a fourteen-team division (behind winners Altofts) in the 1920/21 season, and third in an expanded 16-team league one year later (behind winners Castleford & Allerton United). Its third season, 1922/23 saw mixed results, and a sixth place finish in a nine team division.

The West Riding County Amateur League had been founded in 1922 and it was to this league that Hebden Bridge turned to for the 1923/24 season when the West Riding Senior League disbanded due to a lack of numbers. The club finished runners-up behind Liversedge in a strong 16-team league. At this point, the club, certainly on the field, was the strongest in its history, but sadly it was unable to sustain such prowess.

In order to cut down on travelling, and to reduce costs, the club at this point again switched allegiance to the Red Rose county, moving into the North East Lancashire Combination for the 1924/25 season, with its reserve team remaining in the Halifax League. However, both teams were withdrawn from their leagues during the season, the reserves around Christmas 1924, and the first team late in the season. Neither were struggling in their respective competitions at the time, but financial difficulties were reported in the local press. The club was also suspended by the Lancashire FA for its inability to pay fines for not fulfilling fixtures in the Combination. It was a sharp fall from grace for a club that had established itself as the strongest in the Calder Valley and – Halifax Town aside – the wider Halifax district.

However, the club's debts were paid off by a new organising committee as an effort to revive the club was made in 1929, with Hebden Bridge FC officially revived in August of that year.

*Todmorden Advertiser and Hebden Bridge Newsletter - Friday 30th August 1929*

PREPARATIONS FOR THE SEASON

*The officials of the Hebden Bridge Association Football Club are losing no time in making their preparations for the coming season, and there is a spirit of enthusiasm on all hands. Mr J W Parker has been appointed chairman of the committee, with Mr. Sutcliffe Greenwood as vice-chairman; the tackle is being overhauled, a players' meeting is to be held to-night 7.45, at the headquarters used for the Workshop Competition, and a practice match has been fixed for to-morrow night at Calder Holme, when a collection will be made instead of a fixed charge.*

*In a circular sent out to residents the Committee state: 'By voluntary effort a considerable debt left by the old club a few years ago has been entirely cleared, and it has been decided unanimously at a public meeting to revive the club on a strictly amateur basis. Negotiations have resulted in the Calder Holme field being rented at an economic figure, and there is every prospect, with the help of subscribers, of a successful and interesting programme in the Halifax and District League and its Cup Competition. The revival of Association football has been generally welcomed, for a football club is a valuable asset to the town, and since the last club suspended activities the loss of the sport has been felt by many people, especially as the club won notable successes in the past. A scheme of schools football is also in contemplation, and as this will give local schoolboys their first opportunity of playing organised games at Calder Holme, the committee will give the scheme their hearty, support.'*

The re-formed club's first match was on Saturday 14th September 1929, a 2-4 loss at home to Sowerby United in front of *'a large number of spectators'*, in a league match. Despite not winning any silverware, the club made a profit of £112 in its first season back, one in which it finished third in the Halifax League. The club's end-of-season Workshops competition for local sides had proved highly profitable and was deemed a massive success. In fact, the club chairman, Parker, as moved to say at the club's AGM at the end of June 1930 that the club *'had had a jolly good first season.'*

The 1930/31 season, however, proved highly successful, with the side seeing off closest rivals and near neighbours Heptonstall to lift the league title, and also winning the Halifax & District FA Cup, defeating Sowerby United 2-1 in the final, which was played on the 25th of April 1931 at The Shay in torrential rain. Holden scored both goals for the winners that day. However, history was to repeat itself as the club again suffered a sharp decline, one that would again lead to its folding.

It was no surprise that the club decided to apply for membership of the West Riding County Amateur League for the 1931/32 season but the season was a disappointing one, with a 10th place finish and with only a poor Pudsey Town below them at the end of the season. Bridge won only three league matches, and gates were well short of those experienced in the Halifax League, which is where the club returned for the 1932/33 season.

However, life back in the Halifax League did not last long, as Hebden Bridge found it difficult to raise a full team at times, and despite being in a comfortable mid-table position, withdrew from the league early in 1933. It was decided to concentrate on the reserve team instead for the rest of the season, one that had just joined the Todmorden & District League. The team finished fourth in the competition, but at the end of the season the club was again defunct.

There have been some attempts to form a successful Hebden Bridge team since World War Two, all of which have played at Calder Holme. Probably the most significant was the team that performed successfully in the West Yorkshire League during the 1980s. After winning the Division 3A league and cup double in 1981/82, the team won the Division Two title the following season, the Division One cup in 1983/84, and then the Division One league and cup double in 1984/85. Sadly, the club's ground, now a council owned recreation ground, could not expect to have achieved the standards necessary for what was then an invitation only Premier Division, and within a few seasons the club had also folded. The former Wadsworth United club have since then used the ground for Halifax League fixtures, and from 2021 Hebden Bridge Saints' senior men's team are using the pitch for its home matches in the Yorkshire Amateur League.

# Heckmondwike

The Huddersfield & District League was founded in September 1898. Among teams in its inaugural season were Heckmondwike Casuals, formed the previous season, who went on to finish runner-up behind the first champions, Honley. The club switched over to the Heavy Woollen League in 1901, fielding a team in the Junior South Division (alongside the Heckmondwike Parish Church team) rather than the Senior league, a competition which contained the Heckmondwike Swifts club, one which played on a ground on Cemetery Road and which had also been founded in 1898. Both Swifts and Parish Church had joined the Heavy Woollen League in 1899.

Casuals stepped up to the Senior Division for the 1902/03 season, alongside the Swifts, who surprisingly withdrew in December 1902. However, by the following season, the Casuals name had also disappeared

Heckmondwike AFC was founded in 1903. Following a meeting on Monday 28th April 1903, the club was organised over the following days, with its first president a Dr Prior (who promised to guarantee £10 towards expenses) and its Honorary Secretary, a W H Allerton of Littletown. The new club opportunistically took over the Beck Lane ground of the town's former Northern Union football club when the latter succumbed to its financial problems. That club had intended to 'reform' as an association club, but was basically beaten to it by the new organisation.

Heckmondwike Casuals threw in their lot with the new club – not surprising given that the Casuals had had their ground suspended the previous May until it was 'properly equipped' - but the Heckmondwike Parish Church club, playing at a ground on Walkley Lane, chose to remain separate. The new organisation applied successfully to the West Yorkshire League for membership.

Heckmondwike AFC was immediately successful, being West Yorkshire County Cup semi-finalists in its first three seasons, and losing finalists in two of those (1903/04 and 1905/06). In league competition, the club was runner-up in the West Yorkshire League behind Bradford City reserves in 1904/05 and 1905/06, but became champions in both 1906/07 and 1907/08.

The 1903/04 County Cup final was played at Valley Parade, Bradford, on 16th April 1904. Only eleven days earlier Heckmondwike had defeated their cup-final opponents Altofts 1-0 in a league game. The *Yorkshire Post* on Monday 18th April reported that *'The game was not a good exhibition of the Soccer code, numerous chances of scoring being missed by both sets of forwards. Nervous excitement was manifested throughout, and a draw would have been correctly indicated the merits of the opposing teams.'* Altofts won the trophy for the third successive season thanks to a second half goal direct from a corner.

The 1905/06 final was also lost by a single goal, this time to Bradford City reserves, at the Park View ground, Upper Armley, Leeds on Saturday 14th April. The following Monday the *Leeds Mercury* reported that *'The Bradford team were in better condition, cooler, and more resourceful than the losers, and having once taken the lead they held it tenaciously, and deserved to win.'*

*Free Critic*, of the *Leeds Mercury*, penned this complimentary piece on the club two days prior to the final.

HECKMONDWIKE FOOTBALL CLUB. ITS RISE AND PROGRESS.

*The Heckmondwike FC is a striking example of the effect of excellent management in a football club. Commenced three years ago in a hotbed of Rugbyism, its progress has been most rapid. Three times have the team reached the semi-final of the West Yorkshire Cup, and on Saturday next they will try to wrest from Bradford City Reserves the proud honour of holder.*

*Their form has not been of the 'flash-in-the-pan order', for whilst doing so well in the Cup Competition they have been league runners-up two years in succession to Bradford City. Dr Prior, the president, is a most enthusiastic worker, who does not believe being a mere figure-head. He is never so happy when actively engaged in working for the club, and to see him on the 'line' will convince one that his heart is in the game. He never shirks putting his foot down upon shady play of any kind, and the record of the Heckmondwike Club will bear comparison with any.*

*The rise in prominence of the club was coincident with the coming of J Fielding, the centre forward, who soon revolutionised the front rank. Another player of inestimable value to the club is McAndrew. He has been associated with them from the commencement, and a coach, as well as player has done much to bring the club to its present position.*

*The team at the present time is at its best. Wrightson in goal is equal to anyone in West. Yorkshire outside Leeds City and Bradford City. Holmes and Dryden are proving reliable backs, and on form are quite up to average Second Division football. The club has a strong half line, McAndrew and Pruckner being the stars. Forward, Ackroyd, the captain, stands out as the most accomplished player, though Hogan, Goodall, and Chadbourne run him close.*

The club did win the Heavy Woollen FA's Wheatley Cup competition in the 1905/06 season however, defeating Thornhill Lees Albion 2-1 in a re-played final, following an objection. Heckmondwike won the original match 4-1 at Mirfield on Saturday 7th April 1906. However, following the game their opponents, the holders of the trophy, complained that the winning goalkeeper Wrighton had not played four qualifying matches prior to the first round of the competition. Despite the fact that that there had been no complaints in previous rounds, the final was ordered to be replayed on Easter Tuesday at Savile Town, Dewsbury. Heckmondwike did threaten to boycott the replayed match unless suitable financial arrangements were made, and it was agreed that both teams would get 25% of the gate takings for the match.

There was much ill feeling for the replay, with the referee forced to suspend proceedings while some spectators were ejected from the ground by the police. Upon the final whistle, the Heckmondwike players refused to attend the re-presentation of the cup at the Savile Town grandstand, still aggrieved at having had to re-play the match.

Great strides were made by Heckmondwike in the West Yorkshire League, winning the title in 1906/07 by the narrowest of margins. They, and Guiseley Celtic, tied for points at the end of the season, necessitating a 'play-off' at Birch Lane, Bradford which was drawn 3-3. A second play-off, at Valley Parade on the evening of Saturday 27th April 1907, resulted in a narrow 1-0 victory in front of 2,000 spectators, the club's centre forward Joel scoring the decisive goal in the first half of the game.

Both Heckmondwike and Guiseley clubs were the senior teams representing small towns and were heavily investing in out-of-town players to boost their hopes of success. Within a few years, overstretching would account for the demise of both these and many other small-town clubs across the region.

Twelve months later Heckmondwike retained its league title, with a comfortable lead over Castleford Town at the end of the season. The most noteworthy result that season was perhaps the club's 18-0 rout of bottom club Swaine Hill United in February 1908.

The Wheatley Cup final was again reached in the 1908/09 season, but Thornhill Lees Albion gained revenge for its controversial defeat three years earlier with a convincing 3-0 win in the tie. It had taken Heckmondwike four matches to dispose of Thornhill Edge in the semi-final. They won the first game 3-0 but were forced to replay the match after having played an ineligible player. The replay ended 1-1, with Thornhill winning the replay of the re-match 3-0. However, Heckmondwike successfully appealed this result, resulting in a fourth match, which was won 2-1 after extra-time.

Heckmondwike first entered the English FA Cup competition in the 1904/05 season, and in 1906/07 had made the Third Qualifying Round following wins over Mirfield United, Darfield United, and Castleford Town, before a 3-5 loss at home to Denaby United. However, the 1909/10 season brought with it an embarrassing 0-11 home loss to Huddersfield Town in a Preliminary Round tie, played on Saturday 18th September 1909.

Despite finishing adrift of the top clubs in its 1908/09 and 1909/10 West Yorkshire League campaigns, it was no surprise that Heckmondwike FC became a founding member of the new Yorkshire Combination in 1910, and remained members in all four seasons that the league ran. However, the club surprisingly made no impact among the leading teams in the new competition, although the team did lift the Leeds Hospitals Cup during the 1913/14 season with a 2-1 victory over Fryston Colliery in the final, held at Castleford on Saturday 21st February 1914.

The club's second season in the Combination finished with the club right at the bottom of the league, and by the time the league disintegrated in the summer of 1914, the club was no longer the force it had been.

As football in many cases closed down for the war, Heckmondwike made a surprise, but ultimately successful application to join the Midland Counties League for the 1914/15 season. It was hoped that a higher standard of competition would attract bigger crowds and therefore higher income, but given the current circumstances, the club was clearly overstretched and, clearly out of its depth. The team failed to fulfil several fixtures and finished adrift at the foot of the table.

The team was captained by former Hull City and Sheffield United striker Jack Smith, but as early as September Sheffield's *Star Green 'Un* football columnist *Tatler* commented that *'I'm afraid he is not so great a capture as they seem to think.'*

The club found itself in trouble with the league as early as October for having arrived at Scunthorpe a man short on the 8th of that month, for which it was fined 10s 6d at the following month's league meeting. By then, the £10 deposit that the club should have paid to the league upon its election to the competition had still not been paid. Heckmondwike were given seven days to pay its deposit, but by the December meeting, had still not done so, incurring a further fine of one guinea.

Other fines followed, while on the field things were not going much better. The team was routed 1-11 at Lincoln City in a rearranged fixture on Wednesday 28th April 1915, the situation summed up in the *Sheffield Daily Telegraph* the following day, *'Only four Heckmondwike players turned up, the other players, it was said, being engaged on war munition work. The remainder of the team was composed of local lads, mostly Army men, including one wounded soldier, who seemed very anxious to don football apparel.'* The match had originally been scheduled for 20th March, but only one Heckmondwike player had turned up for the match.

By the end of the season, Heckmondwike finished 20th, and bottom, in the league, seven points behind the nearest club, Hull City reserves. Amazingly, five matches were won during the season, with one drawn, but just 30 goals were scored in its 38 matches, with 169 conceded.

Ironically, the team had enjoyed its best ever run in the FA Cup during the 1914/15 season, reaching the Fourth Qualifying Round. Wins were achieved over local opposition; Clarence Iron & Steel Works, Castleford Town, Rothwell White Rose, and South Kirkby Colliery (in a replay) before a 0-2 home loss to Shirebrook signalled the club's last ever tie in the competition.

At a Midland League EGM on 29th May 1915 it was decided to formally expel the club from the competition due to its debts to clubs they had failed to play, and to league funds for accrued fines. In reality, the club was all but defunct anyway, and it was not revived after the war. It proved a sad end to a club that had promised so much in its first few seasons.

In the absence of a 'town' team in Heckmondwike, local league clubs Brighton Street WMC and Heckmondwike Spen both achieved Wheatley Cup success in future years, the former winning the competition three times in succession (1934, 1935 & 1936), and the latter twice (in 1945 & 1946, after having lost the final in 1944).

In recent times the Beck Lane football ground has since been used by Huddersfield Town AFC and is currently the home of Littletown AFC.

*Beck Lane, the former ground of Heckmondwike FC*
*© Ian S - geograph.org.uk/p/3957755*

# Horsforth

The Horsforth association club first emerged around 1900, competing in the Junior section of the Leeds & District League between 1904-07, alongside the likes of Horsforth Rovers, Horsforth United and Horsforth Cragg Hill. A Dr Bailey was the club president at this time and continued in that role for most of the club's existence.

There was a step up to Senior status in 1907 when the club entered the West Yorkshire League taking its place in Division Two, where it finished 10th in a division consisting of 14 teams. However, 1907/08 wasn't a good year financially for the club, with its committee making the decision to drop out of the West Yorkshire League after just one season and into the newly formed Wharfedale League for the 1908/09 season instead. This would lead to massively reduced travelling expenses.

An earlier attempt to form a Wharfedale League had failed four years earlier, but the new competition was a success, with Horsforth taking the title. That season, Horsforth also won the Bradford Hospitals Cup (defeating Bierley St John's 3-0 in the final), and the Wharfedale FA Cup. On top of that, the Horsforth reserve team were Leeds & District Junior Cup final winners (following a walkover in the final against Hunslet Zion, who were disqualified for having taken part in an unaffiliated medal competition). The reserves were also runner-up in the Wharfedale League's Second Division.

This was certainly a golden era for the club. This was underlined by four Wharfedale FA Cup wins in six years, including resounding 8-0 and 6-0 final victories over Guiseley Victoria and Burley in 1910 and 1913. Barnoldswick United was defeated in the 1909 final, and Apperley Bridge 3-0 in the 1914 final although the latter victory would by no means be the club's biggest success that season.

The club also made the final of the Leeds & District Cup, losing the 1909/10 final 2-4 to Allerton Bywater, but twelve months later won the Bradford & District Cup with a 2-1 victory over Sunfield Rovers in the final.

A switch was made back to the Leeds & District League (this time in the Senior section) for the 1912/13 season, in a league in which only six teams completed the season. Horsforth lost out narrowly to Benson Lane Red Rose at the conclusion of the season, although the club did win the Leeds Workpeople's Hospital Cup that season.

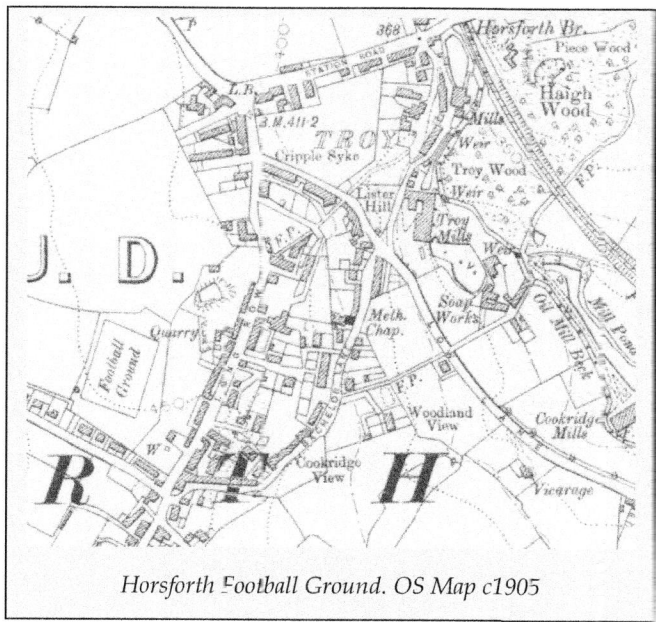

*Horsforth Football Ground. OS Map c1905*

Horsforth AFC then became a founder member of the Leeds Senior League for the 1913/14 season, attaining third place by the season's end. However, it's biggest achievement to date came in the West Riding Junior Cup Final at Elland Road on Friday 10th April 1914, when a second half-header from Isles was enough to defeat Fryston Colliery.

**WEST RIDING JUNIOR CUP.**

**FINAL TIE WON BY HORSFORTH.**

Horsforth and Fryston Colliery yesterday competed in the final of this tournament, which was instituted in 1897, the cup being the premier trophy of the West Riding until the introduction of professionalism into the district, when another competition was brought into being. The match took place on the Leeds City ground, and the "gate" produced the sum of £53 18s. 4d. In the early stages of play the game promised to be of good quality, in spite of a strong wind, as the ground was in capital condition, but about half-way through the first half a heavy rainstorm swept the field, and the subsequent exchanges deteriorated considerably, probably owing to the greasy state of the ball and the turf. Horsforth won the match in the second half by the only legitimate goal scored in the match, but had Fryston taken half the chances that came their way—and good ones, too—they would probably have been the victors.

Fryston were lucky enough to obtain first use of the elements, but Horsforth opened the game in fine style. Playing good football all round, they gave one the impression that victory would ultimately attend their work. Isles quickly shot over the bar, and Swailes drove the ball low into the hands of Stead. Play continued to run in their favour for some time, but ultimately Dyer changed the trend of the ball, and after running it down the field sent across to the right, where both Burns and Gedney bungled chances in turn. In addition to bad shooting, Fryston's forwards were continually getting off-side, and thus neutralising effective mid-field work. Isles played a good centre forward game for Horsforth, and Burt, the Fryston centre, all but got the ball home, Greenwood having to be very smart to save an effort by him near half-time, while Burn and Gedney were again at fault on the Fryston right. Half-time arrived with the score-sheet blank.

On the resumption, with the wind at their backs, Horsforth went to the attack with much smartness. The Fryston defence was quite equal to the strain, however, and turned defence into attack, but again allowed a chance to slip by, Dyer shooting erratically. Riley later missed an opportunity for Horsforth. Hereabouts Fryston were undoubtedly having the better of the game, although they seldom exhibited penetrative force. But at the end of about twenty-five minutes' play the unexpected happened, and Horsforth not only gained the lead, but kept it. The goal was scored by Isles, who got between the opposing backs with the ball in his possession. Seeing the danger, the Fryston "goalie" came out in an attempt to save, but Isles headed the ball beyond his reach, and into an empty goal it went. Encouraged by their success, Horsforth played well for the remainder of the game, and succeeded in getting the ball into the Fryston net on two other occasions, but each time the off-side rule had been infringed. Result:—Horsforth 1 goal, Fryston Colliery none. Teams:—

Horsforth—A. Greenwood, goal; F. W. Hudson and A. Stead, backs; R. Simm, S. Davies, and A. Rogers, half backs; P. Riley, W. White, F. Isles, A. Swailes, and S. Roo, forwards.

Fryston Colliery—S. Stead, goal; C. Frost and W. Baker, backs; F. Biggins, G. Whetton, and J. Burnell, half backs; R. Burns, S. Gedney, J. Burt, J. Plant, and J. Dyer, forwards.

*Yorkshire Post match report of the 1914 West Riding Cup final, which had taken place the previous evening.*

Following World War One, the Leeds Senior League's top division was relaunched as the West Riding Senior League. Horsforth appeared in all of the league's four seasons. No silverware was won in this competition, with the team occupying a mid-table position in each season. The club's reserve team did win the Wharfedale League title in the 1922/23 season though, underlining the club's strength in depth.

The club also won the Wharfedale Cup twice more, at the end of the 1919/20 and 1920/21 seasons. The latter final was attended by a crowd of 4,000, who saw the club defeat Otley Parish Church 4-0 at Guiseley on Saturday 23rd April 1921. The 1919/20 competition was actually won by Horsforth's reserve team, who defeated Apperley Bridge 4-3 in the final, played at Rawdon, also in front of a crowd of 4,000.

In the summer of 1923, Horsforth FC was forced to find a new league when the Senior League folded, so it turned to the West Yorkshire Amateur League, again finishing in mid-table. However, that league also fell apart at the end of the season. Luckily, Horsforth was accepted into the West Riding County Amateur League for the 1924/25 season, where it spent the following seven seasons.

| 1929-30 West Riding County Amateur League | | | | | |
|---|---|---|---|---|---|
| | P | W | D | L | Pts |
| **Horsforth** | 22 | 17 | 3 | 2 | 37 |
| Yeadon Celtic | 22 | 14 | 4 | 4 | 32 |
| Wibsey | 22 | 12 | 6 | 4 | 30 |
| Farsley Celtic | 22 | 12 | 3 | 7 | 27 |
| **Boothtown** | 22 | 12 | 1 | 9 | 25 |
| **Manningham Mills** | 21 | 8 | 7 | 6 | 23 |
| Guiseley | 21 | 10 | 2 | 9 | 22 |
| Blythwick | 22 | 8 | 2 | 12 | 18 |
| Keighley Parkwood | 22 | 8 | 2 | 12 | 18 |
| **Haworth** | 22 | 4 | 5 | 13 | 13 |
| Southowram | 22 | 3 | 5 | 14 | 11 |
| Pudsey Town | 22 | 2 | 2 | 18 | 6 |

The club generally struggled in this league. Despite finishing 6th in a twelve team league in the 1926/27 season, the club finished rock bottom in the following two seasons, but in each case was re-elected at the league AGM at the end of the season.

In a dramatic turnaround, Horsforth finished the 1929/30 season as league champions, finishing ahead of Wharfedale rivals Yeadon Celtic at the head of the table, meaning that the club was arguably the strongest amateur team in the West Yorkshire district at the time. However, the title obviously came at a price. Despite the league being purely amateur, with payments to players strictly prohibited, there were mounting financial problems at the club, reportedly due to a lack of support. Over £19 in arrears with its rates, and unable to pay, the club was forced to approach the local urban council in order to find a solution in February 1931. The solution was that the club was excused payment of its debt, but with an ever worsening economic climate, the club's financial problems were not over.

Horsforth AFC 1929/30

The following season saw the club down in 8th place in an expanded 14 team league, and in order to cut costs further dropped into the Leeds League for the 1931/32 season. A return was made to the County Amateur League in the 1932/33 season, but Horsforth finished bottom of the twelve team league, and at the end of the season was wound up.

Horsforth Woodside and Horsforth Unemployed went on to represented the town in the Wharfedale League in the next couple of seasons, although both were short-lived. Several 'Horsforth AFC' teams have existed during the years since then, although none have been related to the original club.

However, the Horsforth St Margaret's Football Club was founded in 1921, and although there have been seasons when a senior side was discontinued, the club has achieved much success over the years, and currently operates boys and girls teams at all age groups.

The old Horsforth rugby football ground was located close to the Long Lane / Lee Lane junction, the site now covered by Greenbank Avenue. It is highly likely that Horsforth AFC used this ground for many years, although use was also made of the ground at New Road Side, which was also used by Horsforth United.

Horsforth played over twenty FA Cup ties, although its only victory in the competition was in its first tie, a 1-0 victory at Sheffield in the First Qualifying Round in the 1907/08 season. Worksop Town defeated Horsforth in a replay in the following round. The club then entered the competition each season between 1910/11 and 1930/31 (war years apart) but failed to win a single tie.

# Ingrow United

*Ingrow United, year unknown*

This Keighley team was a big rival to Guardhouse *(featured earlier)*. In the 1932/33 season, Nelson Amateurs were defeated in the Keighley Charity Cup final, although surprisingly the team never made the final of the Keighley & District Cup. The Keighley League title was shared with Guardhouse after two drawn matches in the title decider at the end of the 1932/33 season, but the title was won the following season, with a two point lead over Guardhouse.

Ingrow St John's (founder members of the Keighley League), Ingrow Wesleyans, and Ingrow Parish Church all played in the local league prior to World War One. A previous Ingrow United also played in the Keighley League between 1910-12, initially playing on a field opposite the old Fell Lane Hospital (shared with Keighley Celtic and Fell Lane Juniors) before moving to a ground at Hermit Hole for its second season.

After the War, Ingrow Celtic, Ingrow Mission, a briefly reformed Ingrow St John's, and Ingrow Crotona all played in local competitions at a time when there was a huge surge in numbers of clubs at grassroots level.

Ingrow United emerged in 1930, a likely merger between the Mission and Crotona clubs, which had competed in the South Craven Combination the previous season. United was initially successful in the Keighley League but by the outbreak of World War Two had been relegated to the league's Second Division.

The club reformed in 1948, with a first team in the Bradford Amateur League and reserves in the Keighley League. After resigning from the Bradford league in 1951, following three seasons in its top divisions, the 1951-52 season was spent with one team in the Keighley League. Winning just one of its 18 league fixtures, the club folded at the end of the season.

The club's field is now covered by the bottom part of Oakbank School playing fields, its now walled up entrance on Ingrow Lane still being visible. The sloping ground was in the area close to the junction of Ingrow Lane and Bracken Bank Avenue.

# Menston

Association football came to Menston around 1894 when the village football club, that had previously played rugby fixtures, switched codes to the 'new' form of football. Opponents in the latter part of 1895 included Harrogate St Peter's and Leeds Northern, the latter at the 'Malt Shovel Ground'. Whether this was referring to the home ground of Menston or Leeds Northern is not known.

The *Wharfedale & Airedale Observer* reported on a match played at The Oak Avenue Ground, Burley-in-Wharfedale on New Years Day 1898 between 'Burley Old' and Menston Association Football Club, played under rugby rules, that suggests the club was happy to play both codes, depending on its opponent's preference. The club president was Gordon Prince who was a member of all of the sports clubs in the village, including the bowling, tennis, and cricket clubs.

Competitive football for Menston began in 1896 when the club entered the West Yorkshire League, which was just running two Junior (in status, not age) divisions. Initially the team was placed in North Division alongside Bradford reserves, Eldon (Leeds), Halifax Thursday, Leeds reserves, Leeds Cameronians, and Otley.

Menston defeated Otley 4-2 on 19th September 1896, but the *Wharfedale Observer's* match day correspondent was moved to write, 'the good movements of the team were neutralised by the inability of the players to move on the sodden ground, which was little short of quagmire. We would advise the Menston team, if they wish to gain the respect of visiting teams, to procure a better ground, and to play game less noisily, and with less reference to fisticuffs. A careful perusal of the rules of the association game of football would likewise prevent repetition of the amusing blunder made by one of the Menston players during the second half. Considering the state the ground, which in some parts was six inches deep in mud, the Otley team did well to prevent a larger score being put up against them'.

There were obviously problems with spectators during the match too, as, following a report from the match referee, the Executive Committee of the West Yorkshire FA later order to the match to be re-played, with Menston ordered to pay the train fair of the Otley team.

The following season was spent in Division Two (North), which lay below a reintroduced Senior Division. Fourth place was achieved in the eight team division.

The club's opening match of the 1898/99 season was away at Cardigan Fields, when they were defeated 0-3 by Leeds United, a team that actually failed to see out the season. The league had again reorganised, combining senior and junior sections, and dividing its teams into Northern and Southern Divisions. Menston achieved the runner-up spot in the former, ahead of Harrogate, but well behind Ossett, a team that won the league with a 100% record (Altofts achieved the same feat in the Southern Division).

However, as district leagues began to spring up around the county, a move to the more local Bradford & District League was made in 1900. At the same time, the West Yorkshire League disbanded through a lack of numbers. The Menston side was still ambitious though and, despite having to withdraw during the 1901/02 season, returned the following season, and won the league's First Division title in the 1903/04 season. The championship ended in controversy when Menston were awarded four points for un-played fixtures against St. Jude's, lifting them two points above newcomers Guiseley Celtic. Despite appeals from the Guiseley club, Menston were awarded the title. That summer an application was made to re-join a re-formed West Yorkshire League but on this occasion the club was turned down, leaving the club to play in the Bradford League for another season.

The club was finally re-admitted to the county league in the summer of 1905, in a Second Division that consisted predominantly of Wharfedale clubs. Sadly, less of an impression was made this time around and, after finishing at the bottom of the league at the end of the 1907/08 season, the team chose, along with all the other Wharfedale teams in the league, to join the new Wharfedale & District League. The reduction in travelling and a hoped-for increase in support would help the finances of the club, which at the time was £8 in the red. Another change at this time was that the club reverted to playing an all amateur, local team, the players paying a subscription to play for the club rather than the other way round.

Menston AFC was revived in 1910 after a season in abeyance and, by the summer of 1911, the club was reporting a healthy bank balance, and having been unbeaten all season on their home ground, had turned itself around. However, there were problems procuring a suitable field on which to play for the coming season and it seems that the club went into long-term hibernation in the summer of 1912.

Several Menston AFC incarnations have existed since the Wars. Menston St John's were members of the old Wharfedale League in the 1950s & 60s, while Menston Rangers played in the Bradford and Leeds Red Triangle Leagues in the 1990s.

## Monckton Athletic

Monckton Colliery (1878 - 1966) was located seven miles north east of Barnsley, and one mile east of Royston railway station, to the west of Lund Hill Lane. The site was recently occupied by the Monckton Coke and Chemical Works, which closed in 2014. The company sports ground was to the east of Lund Hill lane where the current sports pitches are.

The football team, Monckton Athletic, was a mainstay of the Barnsley Association League from 1906 until World War One (the league was known as the Barnsley Minor League until 1909). Between 1908-11 its first team moved up to the Sheffield Association League, leaving a reserve team in the Barnsley League

The 1909/10 season proved very successful, with the club lifting the Sheffield Association League title, and the second team becoming joint champions of the Barnsley Association League. Having finished level on points with Hoyland Town in the latter, the two met in a play-off to decide the winners, but after a 2-2 draw the title was shared.

The Sheffield Association League title also went right to the wire, with Monckton overhauling Wath Athletic and Parkgate & Rawmarsh United in the final weeks of the season, winning on goal average from the former. This represented a dramatic rise to prominence for the club, which had been formed only four years earlier.

However, the title was won at a cost. The following season the club was suspended by the county FA and its records expunged from both leagues, despite being in contention in both, the Barnsley League team being in second place at the time.

The last Sheffield League match was a 2-0 win against Rotherham County reserves on Saturday 11th February 1911. It seems that the club had been suspended until fines and claims (match fees for referees included) had been paid, representing yet another case of a local club overstretching itself. Success in the Sheffield League was reliant on good quality players, and these did not come free. The Bullcroft Colliery incident featured in this book illustrates the implications of clubs paying players they could not afford. The fines were not paid, and a decision to close down the football club was made by its parent body in charge of sport at the colliery.

Football returned for the 1912/13 season, with all debts settled, and the entry of a team in the Barnsley Association League. H Hutchinson, who had guided the affairs of the Royston Midland club for several seasons, was brought as secretary in to assist the club, and he was keen to stress that the club would be *'starting on small lines'*, perhaps alluding to the scale of expense involved in winning the league in 1910. The new club trainer was a J Bottomley. The new team's first match was a 1-0 victory at Hoyland Town, one in which their 17-year-old goalkeeper Downing impressed with a fine performance.

There was also a run through to the semi-final of the Barnsley Challenge Cup in that first season back, which was lost 1-2 to Royston Midland on Saturday 8th February 1913.

The revival was short-lived though, as Monckton Athletic FC did not operate in competitive football the following season, and rugby union was played at the ground instead, having already hosted an exhibition game between Barnsley and Wakefield in April 1913. The football team did play the odd match in the Barnsley Medal Competition that season, but hostilities put paid to any opportunity to start up the club properly again for a few years.

As local sport recovered from the ravages of War, the Monckton Athletic club was back for the 1918/19 season, with a team in the Barnsley Senior League and a reserve team in the Barnsley Junior League. The first team enjoyed a successful season, reaching the final of the league championship, going down 1-3 to Darfield at Oakwell on Monday 21st April 1919, having led 1-0 at half-time.

Monckton were defeated finalists again in the 1919/20 season, this time in the Barnsley Challenge Cup, going down 1-2 to Ardsley Athletic at Oakwell on Tuesday 6th April 1920, before 2,500 spectators, but it did not need to wait much longer to win more silverware.

A crowd of 10,000 saw Monckton win a cup final at last, the Barnsley Beckett Cup, in which Prospect United were defeated 1-0 at Oakwell on Friday March 25th 1921. Four days later, the club won the Barnsley Challenge Cup in yet another final played at Oakwell, where Cudworth Old Village were defeated 2-0 in front of 6,000 spectators.

The club then went on to win the Hemsworth Hospital Cup on Thursday 14th April, when Houghton Main were defeated 1-0 in the final, in front of 3,500 spectators at Hemsworth.

The attendance figures for the two Barnsley cup finals are staggering when compared to district cup finals in this day. Local sport was booming in the years after the war, and this was reflected not only in the huge attendances seen at district level, but also in the number of teams, and league competitions, that were formed around this time.

The 1921/22 season saw the club maintain its position as one of the best in the Barnsley district, although during the season the club was reprimanded for the behaviour of its junior supporters, who pelted the referee with missiles following a Sheffield & Hallamshire Cup semi-final tie, which was lost to Eckington Works.

The Barnsley Cup was retained, with a 3-1 win against Prospect United on Wednesday 19th April 1922 at the usual venue. The Beckett Cup final took three games to decide, before Prospect United got the better of Monckton in May, winning 2-1. Monckton had needed three games to see off Hoyle Mill United in the semi-final, trailing 0-2 at half time in the second replay, played at Dearne, before coming back to win 4-2.

The Hemsworth Hospital Cup final against Grimethorpe was drawn 1-1 on Monday 1st May 1922. No replay has been traced.

The following season brought even more success. The Beckett Cup was lifted for the second time in three seasons with a resounding 6-0 defeat of Hoyland Common Wesleyans on Monday 2nd April 1923 in the final. Cudworth Village were defeated 2-1 in the Royston Charity Cup final on Saturday 12th May 1923, and to top it all, the club was crowned Barnsley Association League champions

It was no surprise when a successful application was made to the Yorkshire League at that league's AGM on Saturday 16th June 1923, along with the likes of Methley Perseverance, Leeds Harehills, Altofts WRC and York City reserves. In the event, this again led to the wholesale paying of players in order facilitate the move upwards.

Monckton's Yorkshire League debut couldn't have been tougher with the visit of league champions Bradford Park Avenue reserves, who won 2-0 on Saturday 25th August 1923. However, a fine fourth place was attained in the 18-team league, the highest placing the club would achieve. More significant, however, was that the season ended brought with it a credit balance of £4 10s. This looked fine on paper, but perhaps masked the fact that the club owed a significant amount in wages to its players – something which may well have been 'hidden' from the balance sheet.

This may well go some way to explaining why the 1924/25 season was in such stark contrast to that of previous seasons, with Monckton finishing rock bottom of the league. Despite a narrow 1-2 defeat to league champions Brodsworth Main in the final of the Goole Charity Cup on Saturday 9th May 1925, the team struggled all season, with many players from the previous season having moved on.

### Monckton Colliery Yorkshire League record

| Season | P | W | D | L | F | A | Pts | Pos |
|---|---|---|---|---|---|---|---|---|
| 1923/24 | 34 | 17 | 8 | 9 | 71 | 41 | 42 | 4/18 |
| 1924/25 | 30 | 8 | 3 | 19 | 40 | 59 | 19 | 16/16 |
| 1925/26 | 28 | 11 | 7 | 10 | 84 | 82 | 29 | 7/15 |
| 1926/27 | 30 | 11 | 2 | 17 | 58 | 94 | 24 | 12/16 |

Two more seasons were spent in the Yorkshire League, with the club making no impression on the leading teams, but staying clear of the bottom positions. The club's resignation was sent to the league at the end of April 1927, with arrangements in place for the team to drop back into the Barnsley League.

The Barnsley Association League offered the club an opportunity to again cut its costs drastically and also operate with a massively reduced playing budget, and even with these self-imposed restrictions in place it struggled back at this level. At the end of the season the club was placed bottom of the ten-team league. An under 18 team in the Barnsley Intermediate League performed a little better.

Having regrouped, things did improve. The 1930/31 Barnsley Association League campaign went right to the wire between South Hiendley and Monckton. Having finished their 16-game programme with almost identical records, the teams needed two play-off games to decide the winners – Monckton losing 0-7 at Dearne on Saturday 18th April in the 'replay'. Two weeks earlier, Monckton had been heavily defeated by the same team in the Royston Cup final, 0-4 on this occasion, just days before the first league championship final was drawn.

The period between 1931-35 was spent back in the Sheffield Association League. The 1933/34 season saw the club among the league leaders, but ultimately trophyless, but the following season was another of struggle which led to Monckton returning again to the Barnsley League.

In the years leading up to World War Two, there was further local success;

1932/33: Finalists in the Beckett Cup, losing 0-2 to Platts Common at Oakwell in front of 3,500 spectators on Saturday 14th April 1933.

1935/36: Finalists in the Beckett Cup, losing 0-1 to Darton Welfare at Dearne in front of 1,400 spectators on Tuesday 14th April 1936.

1936/37: Beckett Cup winners, defeating Mapplewell Bethel in final, this following a massive 11-1 defeat of Worsbrough Bridge Athletic in the semi-final.

Barnsley League champions, winning the league final 4-2 against Mitchell & Darfield on Saturday 24th April 1937. The team averaged six goals per game in its league matches.

1938/39: In a season when George Hollis club continued in his role as club secretary for the 22nd successive year, Monckton Athletic won the Royston Charity Cup and Beckett Cup competitions.

Mitchell's & Darfield were defeated 5-0 in the Barnsley Beckett final, played on Saturday 15th April 1939 at Oakwell. Carlton were defeated 4-1 in the Royston final.

*South Yorkshire Times - Friday 21st April 1939*

### *Monckton Get Another Five in Beckett Final*

*Whether it was an enforced re-arrangement, a tricky wind, or the fact that Mitchell's look upon this historic pitch as their 'bogey' ground, it is hard to say, but there is no gain saying that they never looked to have the beating of Monckton in their grasp in the Beckett Cup final on Saturday. The absence of Cook and Seddon (injured) led to a re-shuffling.*

*A strong wind blew in favour of Mitchell's, but it proved more hindrance than a help, passes missing their objective by yards. Over-kicking gave the Monckton defence plenty of time to clear. The number of goal kicks taken by Cocke in the Monckton goal, would give the casual observer the impression that Mitchell's were doing all the attacking, whereas the boisterous breeze was chiefly responsible.*

*Although the ball was seldom out of the Monckton half for the first twenty minutes, there were only two shots that looked dangerous, Plant, after beating Stephens and Priestley, firing over the bar from close in, and Ellis being equally unlucky, after Neale and McHale had paved the way for a lovely chance. Monckton, after feeling their feet, went in for the ground passing called for in the conditions prevailing, and after Stott had twice disappointed by failing to shoot from close in, he tipped the ball to MILLS, Monckton's well-built centre-forward, who 'nodded it in. Mitchell's again appeared to be top side, but Cooke was never in trouble with any of the long balls, some of which dropped in front of him to bounce over the bar. From a side that had scored 63 goals in 15 league games, the Mitchell's shooting was amazingly erratic.*

*The second half saw Mitchell's go nearer opening their scoring when, in their first really well-engineered attack, Rowe, Cobb and Ellis found Cooke. Priestley, Webster, and Crossley with all their work cut out to clear the danger. Davies was the man who cut short Mitchell's aspirations, however! He went away from the firing zone with the ball, and tackled by Brownbridge, he deftly fed Cartwright, who slipped it across for MILLS to put past Gibbs again. There was little between the sides, both ends being visited in turn, up to the last quarter of an hour, when Monckton simply ran away with the game. Maurice Priestley twice went through, and the attack was rewarded by two goals in less than two minutes. CARTWRIGHT, taking the wing berth, got the first, and Stott put the ball at the feet of LUMB for another. STOTT had been making openings galore but never offering to shoot himself until, with only seven minutes to go, he again weaved his way through and scored.*

*Introduced by Mr J W Hirst, the Mayor of Barnsley (Ald. Cassell) congratulated both sides on their clean, sporting display, and said though the victory had been somewhat one-sided, he hoped that he or his successor would have the pleasure of handing the trophy to Mitchell's and Darfield next year. He also spoke of the good object of the competition and of the great work of the Barnsley Beckett Hospital. The Mayor handed the cup to the captain, Cartwright, and replicas to the teams. Both Cartwright and Rowe replied.*

Monckton began the 1939/40 season in the Barnsley Association League but with local football reorganised in the light of the outbreak of War, the club fielded teams in the Barnsley Minor League and Nelson League competitions instead. Cudworth Village, a team that had been unbeaten in the league all season, and which had defeated Monckton twice already that season, were defeated 4-2 in the Beckett Cup final on Saturday 11th May 1940.

The following season, with its one team playing in the Minor League, the Barnsley Challenge Cup final was lost to Grimethorpe Rovers (although there has been no report of the final traced). The team then finished runners-up in the league, on goal average to Birdwell Rovers, in the 1941/42 season.

The club continued in the Barnsley League after the war, and continued to enter the FA Cup for a few seasons afterwards.

Monckton's first FA Cup appearance was in the 1907/08 season, resulting in a 1-3 loss at Rotherham Town in a Preliminary Round tie. Twelve months later, Parkgate United were thrashed 12-0 at the same stage, before Monckton lost at home to Wath in the following round, after extra time.

The club's best run came in the 1930/31 season, when Cudworth Village were defeated 3-2 at home, before a 9-1 defeat of Luddendenfoot in the First Qualifying Round. A 3-4 loss at Yorkshire Amateurs saw the mini-run ended in the very next stage.

A last appearance, in the 1948/49 season, saw a 1-2 Preliminary Round loss to Firbeck Main Colliery.

***

### Monckton Colliery
### West Yorkshire League winning seasons

| 1968-69 *Premier Division* | P | W | D | L | F | A | Pts |
|---|---|---|---|---|---|---|---|
| **New Monckton Colliery** | 26 | 18 | 5 | 3 | 67 | 23 | 41 |
| Keighley Central | 26 | 17 | 6 | 3 | 72 | 27 | 40 |
| Whitkirk Wanderers | 26 | 13 | 8 | 5 | 54 | 53 | 34 |
| Keighley Shamrocks* | 25 | 12 | 7 | 6 | 40 | 33 | 32 |
| **Methley United** | 26 | 12 | 4 | 10 | 63 | 54 | 28 |
| DP&E (Otley) | 26 | 10 | 6 | 10 | 65 | 55 | 26 |
| Rothwell Athletic | 26 | 9 | 8 | 9 | 41 | 50 | 26 |
| Snydale Road Athletic | 26 | 9 | 6 | 11 | 48 | 50 | 24 |
| Yorkshire Copper Works | 26 | 10 | 3 | 13 | 45 | 49 | 23 |
| Altofts | 26 | 9 | 4 | 13 | 37 | 51 | 22 |
| Fryston Colliery* | 25 | 7 | 6 | 12 | 37 | 53 | 21 |
| Salts (Saltaire) | 26 | 7 | 3 | 16 | 31 | 56 | 17 |
| East End Park WMC | 26 | 5 | 6 | 15 | 30 | 60 | 16 |
| Ardsley Celtic | 26 | 7 | 0 | 19 | 36 | 73 | 14 |

* Keighley Shams & Fryston not played – points shared

| 1970-71 *Premier Division* | P | W | D | L | F | A | Pts |
|---|---|---|---|---|---|---|---|
| **New Monckton Colliery** | 24 | 17 | 5 | 2 | 75 | 31 | 39 |
| Fryston Colliery | 24 | 14 | 6 | 4 | 45 | 32 | 34 |
| Whitkirk Wanderers | 24 | 11 | 8 | 5 | 42 | 29 | 30 |
| Leeds Athletic | 24 | 13 | 4 | 7 | 54 | 38 | 30 |
| Swillington Welfare | 24 | 13 | 3 | 8 | 42 | 35 | 29 |
| Altofts | 24 | 12 | 5 | 7 | 35 | 32 | 29 |
| Crabtree Mann (Otley) | 24 | 11 | 5 | 8 | 57 | 44 | 27 |
| Keighley Central | 24 | 8 | 5 | 11 | 37 | 47 | 21 |
| **Methley United** | 24 | 6 | 6 | 12 | 42 | 41 | 18 |
| East End Park WMC | 24 | 7 | 4 | 13 | 42 | 46 | 18 |
| Ardsley Celtic | 24 | 6 | 3 | 15 | 39 | 73 | 15 |
| Snydale Road Athletic | 24 | 6 | 1 | 17 | 38 | 72 | 13 |
| Salts (Saltaire) | 24 | 2 | 5 | 17 | 23 | 51 | 9 |

Monckton Colliery FC - also referred to as New Monckton Colliery from the mid-1960s – was the successor to Monckton Athletic. The club played on a ground a couple of miles to the north-east of the old colliery site, at the Ryhill Welfare Ground, and with its headquarters at the Ryhill Liberal Club. The club secretary was L Jones of Havercroft.

The club rose to prominence, not in the Barnsley or Sheffield leagues, but in the West Yorkshire League, playing in that competition with the permission of the Sheffield & Hallamshire Football Association. With its close proximity to Wakefield, it has not been uncommon for Barnsley district teams to play in West Yorkshire competition through the years.

Division Three South winners in the 1959/60, season and Division Two South winners in 1960/61, the club spent fifteen seasons in the top division of the West Yorkshire League (Division One was renamed Premier Division in 1964), finishing as champions twice and runner-up twice more.

There was a gradual improvement up to 1963/64, when the club finished third, behind Snydale Road Athletic, and Guiseley, and also won the league cup for the first time when the team, which included 38-year-old comedian and former professional footballer Charlie Williams in its team, defeated Fryston 4-0 in the final. Two seasons later, however, the team finished 11th and bottom (although one club had withdrawn during the season). A place in the league's Premier Division was, at the time, by invitation only, and Monckton regained its place in the top flight, achieving runner-up position just twelve months later. Thackley became the 1966/67 league champions, finishing just one point clear of Monckton, both finishing well ahead of third placed Keighley Central. The league cup was also won in 1967/68 and 1968/69.

The latter season actually saw Monckton complete the 'double', pipping the Keighley side by one point to win its first title. Central ran away with the championship in the 1969/70 season, but the title was regained by the Colliery team the very next season – 1970/71 – and the Sheffield & Hallamshire Junior Cup was also won for the one and only time that season too. As players moved on though, the club gradually lost its dominance over most of its rivals and in the 1975/76 season lost its place in the Premier Division after finishing well adrift at the bottom.

By now the club was fully independent and the days of being funded by the colliery, which had shut a decade earlier, were only a memory, and after finishing down in 12th place in the 14-team second tier, the Monckton club faded away.

# Morley

Its not often that a successful football club is forced to fold straight after its greatest achievement, but that was sadly the case with the original Morley AFC

Morley AFC played on the ground at Scatchered Lane adjacent to the cricket field. The club was formed around 1898, not long before the Morley Cricket & Football Club temporarily abandoned rugby due to its precarious finances. The new association club was successful from the start, winning the 1898/99 Wheatley Cup, with a 1-0 victory over Mirfield United in the final, played on Saturday 22nd April 1899 at Dewsbury. A late winner by Schofield in an entertaining match was enough the bring the club its first silverware.

The next two Wheatley Cup finals were lost, 1-2 to Saviletown Clarence in 1900, and 1-4 to Dewsbury & Savile in 1901. The club also played in the Heavy Woollen League from its inception in 1898, winning the title with an unbeaten record in the 1899/1900 season after winning the 'North' division, well ahead of Pildacre Mills, and then the league championship with a 3-1 victory over 'South' division winners Dewsbury Celtic.

In the summer of 1902, Morley stepped up to the West Yorkshire League, staying in the competition until 1909. Its first season saw Morley and Mirfield United edged out by the eventual champions Altofts, but in subsequent seasons Morley did not make an impression on the top of the table, although neither did it struggle in this competition. Debts associated with running a side in the competition were reported to have been wiped out in the summer of 1904 thanks to contributions from a number of local gentlemen. The club also won the prestigious Leeds Hospitals Cup in the 1905/06 season, with an easy 6-1 thrashing of Glasshoughton in the final, played on 21st April 1913 at Castleford.

Morley returned to county league football in 1910, after having had a year out in order to wipe off its latest debts, and joined the newly-formed Yorkshire Combination, finishing in mid-table for three seasons from 1910-13. The club and enjoyed what was easily its best run in the FA Cup during the 1911/12 season. Entry to the national competition had first been made for the 1903/04 season, when a 0-3 defeat at Rockingham in a Preliminary Round tie was the result, but the club's run in 1911/12 too it to the Fourth Qualifying Round. Leeds United were defeated 3-1 in the Preliminary Round, followed by victories over Calverley United (1-0), Mirfield United (2-0, following a 0-0 draw), and South Kirkby Colliery (1-0), before a 1-2 defeat at home to Castleford Town in a replay (following a 1-1 draw).

This run was in contrast to Morley's only FA Cup tie in the 1905/06 season, a 0-11 loss at Leeds City in a First Qualifying Round tie.

However, winning the West Riding County Cup was undoubtedly the highest point achieved by Morley AFC, a 2-0 victory over Hebden Bridge played at the Clarence Ground, Kirkstall on Saturday 12th April 1913.

The Leeds Mercury carried a report of the match the following Monday,

*MORLEY'S CUP TRIUMPH. After a fast and exciting game, Morley beat Hebden Bridge by two goals to nil in the final of the County Junior Cup, at Kirkstall, on Saturday, this being the first trophy they have secured since they won the Leeds Hospital Cup tan years ago.*

*It was unfortunate for the losers that Moon, one of their best forwards, was compelled to leave the field early in the game through the result a collision with one the Morley players. Morley's rear division played an important part in attaining the verdict, and, singularly, it was a movement started by Whittingham, one of their backs, that led up to Naylor scoring their first goal. Green, the Morley custodian, cleverly saved a penalty from the foot of Martin. Hardy looked putting his side level terms before the interval, for after beating the opposing backs was left with only Green to beat, but shot high over the bar.*

*Aided by the breeze in the second portion, Hebden Bridge, in spite of being man short, gave their opponents an anxious fifteen minutes. Then Sherman, seizing upon momentary hesitation in the Hebden defence, placed the ball to Laing, who, being unmarked, had little difficulty registering another goal.*

*Morley deserved their victory, their forwards proving the more effective. Martin, the Bridge left half, was about tbs best player on the field, whilst Hardy tried hard to make up for Moon's absence from his side. Mr J Connor, the President of the Riding Association, presented the cup and medals after the game.*

Sadly, following its greatest success, the club folded in August 1913, citing a lack of support due to the sporting public transferring their affections to Leeds City FC. It was hoped that the club would be reformed in the near future but that never came to pass, due in no small way to the outbreak of war. Harold Wainwright was the club president when the club disbanded with debts of around £80. Former goalkeeper John Green landed himself in court when he sold lottery tickets to raise money to reduce the debt, presumably from his tobacconist shop. He was fined 10s for his efforts.

Morley United briefly made a name for itself the following season, reaching the Wheatley Cup final , where it lost to Thornhill Lees Albion 0-3, following a 1-1 draw, and taking part in the FA Cup (losing 1-2 at West Vale Ramblers in a Preliminary Round tie). However, the War put paid to any progress that the club might have made.

The well-established Morley Town successfully flies the flag for the town at the current time, but the football history of Morley could well have been very different had Morley AFC been able to ride out its financial crisis before the outbreak of World War One.

# Mytholmroyd

Originally founded as Mytholmroyd Juniors, the 'Juniors' suffix was dropped in 1899, when the association section of the club joined the Halifax & District League. The club had been formed in 1877, originally playing rugby, and reaching the final of the Yorkshire Challenge Cup twice - winning it in 1900 and losing in 1904 (both matches being played at Claro Road, Harrogate) before turning wholeheartedly to association football. The club folded in August 1923, and for much of its existence used the Royal Oak Inn as its base.

The club's first real success as an association club was in the 1900/01 season, when it won the Halifax & District League's cup competition, defeating Sowerby Bridge 3-0 in the final on Saturday 13th April 1901 at the St Augustine's ground at Highroad Well. The 1907/08 Halifax Cup final was lost 2-4 to the same opposition.

As rugby floundered, the round ball game became much more prominent in the Calder Valley, and as a result the village adopted this sport as its most popular pastime.

The 1908/09 season saw the club fielding teams in the Rochdale, Halifax, and Calder Valley Leagues – finishing runners-up to Portsmouth Rovers in the latter - but was in trouble with the authorities late in the season. On Friday 5th February 1909, the *Todmorden & District News* carried a report of unruly scenes at the club,

UNRULY FOOTBALL CROWDS AT MYTHOLMROYD.

THE GROUND SUSPENDED A MONTH. *A meeting of the West Yorkshire Commission was held the Central Hall Cafe, Halifax, Tuesday evening, Mr Skinner presiding. Mytholmroyd spectators were reported on two counts for assaulting referees. The first complaint was made by the President the league, Mr G H Mitchell, who refereed in the match between Mytholmroyd and West Vale Ramblers on January 23rd. Mr Mitchell reported that he had received a kick on the calf of his right leg, and that the assault took place on the field. He also reported the spectators for assaulting Luke Smith, the West Vale right full-back, who, at his request, walked behind him on the way to the dressing-room. Luke Smith, wrote Mr. Mitchell, was most brutally kicked by several spectators when about twenty yards from the gate of the field. His most serious injury was a kick on the right leg, and he had to be assisted to the dressing-room, where his leg was both bathed and bandaged. Most of the Mytholmroyd players ran off the field immediately the whistle blew for time. A few of the Mytholmroyd committee did their best to prevent any injury being done or any assault taking place. Mr Mitchell, Mr L Smith, and a Mytholmroyd representative gave evidence before the commission. Mr Mitchell said a small knot of spectators were really to blame rather than the whole of them. These spectators were bringing the Club into disgrace by the language they used, and the inciting manner they had of calling on the players. Mr Woodhead, who was referee in the match last week between Mytholmroyd and Halifax Trinity, also reported the spectators for assault. Mytholmroyd had a counter-complaint, alleging incompetence on the part the referee, and stating that he had made insulting remarks during the game. Evidence was given in this case by Mr Woodhead. and the Mytholmroyd representative. The referee stated that was told at half-time that 'If Mytholmroyd didn't win he knew what his lot would be.'*

*After due consideration of the cases, it was decided that the Mytholmroyd ground be suspended for one month. The Mytholmroyd representative stated that they had stopped several people from attending their matches. If they persisted in this action they would have no spectators at all. They had tried their best to preserve order, but they would have to have mounted police on the field do so.*

On Saturday 7th May 1921, the team won the Halifax & District Cup, defeating Eastwood at Hebden Bridge in the final. The *Todmorden Advertiser and Hebden Bridge Newsletter* provided an excellent report of the match;

*MYTHOLMROYD WIN THE TROPHY. This match was played at Calder Holme last Saturday, before a large crowd. Mr S Robinson was the referee, and the teams were –*

*Mytholmroyd: Nutter; Cockcroft and Carter; Pickles, Greenwood and Hanson; Crossley, Shaw, A Sutcliffe, H Sutcliffe and Helliwell. Eastwood: Barker ; J. Stansfield and Greenwood; Rae, Mitchell, and E Stansfield; J Hughes, Hodgins, Fielding B Lomas, and W Lomas.*

*Eastwood put up a valiant struggle, especially in the first half. An early attack by Mytholmroyd soon placed the Eastwood goal in danger, and Shaw had hard lines in striking the bar after taking a pass from T Helliwell. After a fine sprint W Lomas centred too far up, and play returned to the Eastwood end again, where Barker cleared a header from H Sutcliffe. Fielding carried play forward, but Carter cleared his shot for goal with a well-timed kick. Play was fairly even, but Royd showed a nicer style and were quicker on the ball, and now they took the lead. H Sutcliffe going through and passing to A Sutcliffe. who scored with a well-placed shot, much to the jubilation of the Royd supporters. Eastwood continued to have a fair share of the attack, and Carter and Cockcroft were often called upon. Fielding reached close range, but Nutter easily cleared the shot. The Royd halves co-operated well with their front line, Hanson being conspicuous. From his pass Shaw had a nice shot cleared by Barker. Then Eastwood found success. Rae placed a free-kick well forward, and after a skirmish in the goal-mouth a corner was conceded. A splendid flag-kick by W Lomas dropped the ball in the Mytholm goal-mouth, and Hodgins tapped it into the net, making the scores equal. In later play Fielding had a header for goal smartly cleared by Carter. Then Royd attacked and this time successfully; a capital centre by Crossley resulted in a melee in the goal-mouth, and Shaw netted from close range. At half-time the scores were: Mytholmroyd 2, Eastwood 1*

> **Mytholmroyd Football Club.**
> PERSONS TRESPASSING in the Football Field will be PROSECUTED without further notice.

*The weather, which had been very unsettled, now broke down, and a heavy downpour commenced. Play had been keen in the first half, and a good pace had been maintained, but after the interval the players relaxed their efforts a little. and the game was not so keenly contested nor so interesting as it previously had been. W Lomas attacked for Eastwood, but was deprived by Carter when reaching close range. The Eastwood goal-keeper played a splendid game, and his competence probably saved Eastwood from a more decisive defeat. He fisted a beautiful shot front H Sutcliffe aver the bar. and cleared one from F Greenwood in equally fine style. Although Mytholmroyd were now having most of the attack their backs were by no means idle, and Nutter was called upon on more than one occasion. Fielding reached close range but Nutter ran out and cleared, and Hodgins had a strong shot for goal stopped by Carter. At the other end Royd had hard lines, H Sutcliffe striking the post after a fine dribble, while a few minutes later Crowley had a strong shot for goal fisted out by Barker.*

*Result: Mytholmroyd 2, Eastwood 1*

*CUP AND MEDALS PRESENTED. After the match the cup and gold medals were presented by Mr Fred Rawson to the winners' captain, C Cockcroft. Mr Rawson complimented the Mytholmroyd team upon their display, and said the committee were wise in bringing the final to such a convenient centre. The game had been a hard one, but was played in a very sportsmanlike manner. He hoped Eastwood would be so fortunate as to win the cup next year. The Royd skipper made a suitable response. The silver medals for the runners-up were presented to W Mitchell, Eastwood's captain, who said he was convinced that the better team had won, as they were the better trained team. Later the Mytholmroyd players had tea at Webster's cafe, and then spent an enjoyable half-hour at the Neptune Hotel. Leaving there about 7 o'clock they had  triumphal tour in a char-a-banc, provided by Mr Fred Greenwood. They first went through Mytholmroyd, then on to Cragg Vale. and at the Robin Hood Hotel they had their first fill of the Cup, then down to Luddenden Foot, and back to the White Lion. where they spent the rest of the evening, the party breaking up about 11 pm.*

Along with other clubs in the upper Calder Valley, Mytholmroyd tended to switch between leagues either side of the Yorkshire/Lancashire border. In the 1910/11 season it was in the North-East

Lancashire League, but was back in the Halifax League by 1914. During World War One the club's ground was requisitioned in order for fruit and vegetables to be grown, which led to the club using the field of the village hockey club at Calcene when it was revived in 1919. Following its success in 1921, Mytholmroyd went on to play its final two seasons in the West Riding Senior League. The 1921/22 season actually saw the club reach the Semi Final of the County Cup competition, defeated by eventual winners Methley Perseverance in a replay.

The club's final three fixtures were all against Stainland. On Saturday 28th April, Mytholmroyd defeated their opponents 2-0 to win the Halifax FA Cup final in front of 2,000 fans at The Shay, before the teams drew 0-0 in the Charity Cup final on the same ground amid mud and heavy rain one week later.

Stainland then won the replay 1-0 on Saturday 19th May 1923, and that was the last fixture played by Mytholmroyd FC. Following the demise of the West Riding Senior League, the club had intended joining the West Riding County Amateur League for the 1923/24 season, but a debt of £41 and an inability to form a new committee that summer led to its disbanding instead.

Mytholmroyd AFC 1920/21

# Oakworth Albion

It took a little longer for the round ball game to take-off in the Aire Valley than it did in many other parts of the West Riding, but it was even later that the sport was played competitively in the village of Oakworth, a couple of miles south-west of Keighley and lying at the edge of the Worth Valley.

It wasn't until 1909 that the first association football club appeared in the village, Oakworth FC spending just a single season in Division Two of the Keighley & District League, alongside the likes of Beechcliffe, Wesley Place United and Morton Athletic. The team finished just one off the bottom in the ten team division.

Oakworth Albion first appeared in the Junior Division of the Keighley League in the 1911/12 season. One year later a senior team was added, that team finishing as runner-up in the Second Division behind Cononley, but opted not to play in the top division for the 1913/14 season.

The Division Two title was won at the second time of asking, with an unbeaten record and ahead of Parkwood FC, a team that would become major rivals over the next few years. A field at the edge of the village at Denby Hill was used at this time, one that was likely shared with one or more of the informal teams that were playing occasional matches, Oakworth Low Bank FC being one of the more significant.

After an uneventful season for both senior and junior teams in the top division of the Keighley League in 1914/15, Albion closed down due to the outbreak of World War One. In the 1919/20 season the club was revived in the 'Average Age 21' section of the second division, finishing third behind both Parkwood and Victoria Park.

Now playing on what was known as the 'Pleasure Ground', 1920/21 turned out to be the club's most successful season to date. All 18 league fixtures were won in Division Two B, well ahead of Victoria Park, and then Albion defeated Division Two A winners Parkwood – who had also won their section with a 100% record - 4-1 in the divisional final.

Parkwood, who would later become Keighley Town, ran away with the Division One title the following season, Albion being one of only two sides to defeat them. The Oakworth team finished ninth in a 14-team league - although two teams (including an older incarnation of Keighley Town) dropped out before the end of the season. Home matches this season were played at Wide Lane, on the field adjacent to what is still Oakworth Cricket Club.

Another ground move followed, this time back at Denby Hill for the 1922/23 season. Wide Lane remained a football and rugby ground for many years, with Slack Lane FC likely to have been using it when Albion vacated. Fourth place in the league was an improvement, but the highlight of the season was Oakworth Albion's appearance in the Keighley Cup final at Lawkholme Lane. Gilstead St Wilfrid's, Oxenhope Church, and then Parkwood were defeated in early rounds, before Eastwood were defeated 4-2 in the semi-final, played at West Lane, Haworth.

Sladen Valley, the team that played home fixtures at West Lane, were encountered in the final. Despite leading through an early goal from Brown, it was the Haworth team that won the cup with a 3-1 victory.

By now Slack Lane (with 2 teams) had been joined temporarily by Oakworth White Star, and then a new Oakworth Lane Ends as rival clubs to Albion. However, both Albion and Slack Lane folded in the summer of 1924, leaving Lane Ends and then Oakworth Church to fly the flag in the village in the lower divisions of the local league.

Oakworth Albion re-emerged in the summer of 1928, again playing in the Keighley League. The club sat out the 1930/31 season, but after that began to make a name for itself, appearing in four league cup finals in five seasons, winning the final on three of those occasions.

Oakworth Albion also appeared in the final of the Skipton Hospitals Cup in the 1933/34 season, losing to Settle United in the final.

**Oakworth Albion in Keighley League 'Victory Shield' finals**
1932/33: won 4-2 v Wilsden
1933/34: won 5-2 v Thwaites Brow
1935/36: won 4-2 v Cullingworth YMCA
1936/37: lost 1-4 v Guardhouse Sports Club
1951/52: won 3-1 v Oxenhope Church

Albion finished at the top of Keighley League's second division at the end of the 1932/33 season, finishing runner-up in the top division three years later (this after a one season spell in the newly formed Craven League). In the worsening economic climate, the number of locals clubs had declined sharply since the early 1920s, and Albion again became one of those that closed down in the summer of 1937, despite its recent successes. Its final seasons were spent playing home games in a field behind Gill Clough Farm, off Slaymaker Lane with a nearby barn used as rudimentary dressing rooms, and then, from 1936 on a ground on Goose Cote Lane, on the site of what is now the Oakworth Juniors FC playing fields.

Ten years after having folded, Albion was again resurrected in time for the 1947/48 season, with a first team in the Keighley League, and a reserve side in the Craven League. Two years later, both first and second teams were playing in the same division, as the Keighley League committee decided to run with one division of 18 teams. The experiment was unpopular with the clubs involved, with few teams completing a full programme of fixtures (despite one club dropping out during the season).

Oakworth Albion, 1932/33, photographed with the Keighley & District League Division Two shield and the league 'Victory Shield'

Oakworth Albion was once again dormant during 1950/51 and again in 1952/53, most likely due to problems securing a ground, yet in the season in between the club lifted the Keighley League title! The league was in a spot of bother that season, with only seven teams down to take part. This situation was worsened when St Joseph's withdrew before Christmas. The league programme was played in two halves, with the winners of each 'half' of the season playing off for the overall league title. This wasn't necessary however, as Albion won both halves to make a play-off unnecessary. The club then achieved the league and cup double when Oxenhope Church were defeated 3-1 in the Victory Cup final.

The Keighley League was also dormant during the 1952/53 season, but when it – and Oakworth Albion – re-emerged the following season its champion club was no longer a major force. The 1953/54 season also saw an Oakworth Albion team entered into the second division of the Bradford Amateur League, and the final table for that competition shows Oakworth having lost all 20 of its fixtures. However, with no fixtures traced beyond the first few weeks of the season, it does seem that Albion dropped out of the league during the campaign, concentrating on its Keighley League team instead. An Oakworth Albion team stayed in this league until 1956, reaching league's Jubilee Cup final in the latter of those seasons. Sadly a 0-6 loss to Central Youth Club in that match was not the result that was hoped for.

Two more seasons were spent in hibernation, before a revival in 1958 that saw Oakworth finish second and then third in the Keighley League, a competition that was by now weak in comparison with other competitions. The Craven League was now attracting more clubs from the Keighley district and in 1963 the Keighley League closed for good.

Oakworth made the switch to the Craven League in 1960 but suffered relegation from Division One in its first season back in the league, finishing one off the bottom, in 15th place, and conceding 135 goals in its 26 fixtures (teams did not play all of the other teams twice). The following season was an improvement, losing the Division Two championship in a top four play-off final to Oxenhope's reserve team, this despite having finished ahead of their rivals at the end of the regular season. Between 1962-65, Albion struggled in the leagues' top division, but with a new Premier Division formed for the 1965/66 season, Oakworth's poor record meant that it was to remain in Division One. Initially the club yo-yo'd between the Premier Division and Division One, but by 1973 Albion found itself down in Division Two, which consisted mainly of reserve teams of higher division clubs. Two seasons were spent at this level before the club was promoted back to Division One for the 1975/76 season. That season proved the last for the ailing club, which folded for good in the summer of 1976.

By the time of its demise, Oakworth Albion was not even playing fixtures in the village. Following another spell at Gill Clough, and later in a field behind Oakworth Social Club, the club had been forced to relocate to Marley Playing Fields in Keighley due to the inadequacy of facilities at the grounds in the village. In an era when running showers and adequate changing facilities became mandatory, the club could not afford - or indeed expect to get permission to install – these facilities at its rented grounds, so a relocation to Marley was the only viable option. Ironically, near neighbours Haworth FC would also suffer the same fate within a couple of decades, as support from the local community, and overall interest in the club could not be maintained when playing away from the club's home village.

Oakworth did have a senior team again between 2005-2013 when Oakworth Juniors created an open-age team. The club played in the Craven League, playing on what became a railed-off pitch on the club's Goose Cote Lane playing fields. An unsuccessful application was made to join the West Riding County Amateur League before the senior team broke away from the club, reforming as Broomhill FC, and playing in the same league until the summer of 2021, when it folded. Oakworth Juniors FC, however, continues to have a strong presence today.

# Pontefract

## AFC, Garrison, United and others…

Several local newspapers reported that an association football club had been formed at Pontefract Barracks in connection with the King's Own (Yorkshire) Light Infantry in early March 1889. The team intended to tour Yorkshire to play fixtures principally in towns where the regiment had been recruited from. Both the Garrison team, and a separate Pontefract AFC (who enjoyed a successful first season, playing friendlies throughout the 1893/'94 season), were founder members of the first West Yorkshire League in 1894, although only Garrison took part the following season. However, they too dropped out in the summer of 1896, with their remaining players, it was suggested in the local press, throwing in their lot with Pontefract AFC - who had, presumably, been playing friendly fixtures during the 1895/96 season. This is perhaps unlikely given that the army team will have had several other options open to them, not least their responsibility to the forces, and that, also, the town club itself had only minor status after dropping out of the league.

A rugby team had been founded in Pontefract in 1880, folding for the first time in 1894 before reforming soon after, and in June 1896 merging with the association team. Fixtures at the Skinner Lane ground were played on alternative weekends. With no West Yorkshire League the following season, it seems that friendly fixtures will again have been on the cards for the association team, which faded away despite the huge upsurge in interest in the game locally.

In 1897/98 a reformed Garrison team was to take part in the senior division of the West Yorkshire League but it dropped out before playing any fixtures, although the club did continue to play, successfully, in the Castleford & District League, and less successfully in the Leeds & District League, before the war. The town's rugby team briefly took up residence at the Garrison Football & Cricket Field in 1903, after leaving Skinner Lane (and via a short stay on a ground at Park Avenue), before a final move to nearby Halfpenny Lane in December 1904. This ground was on the site of what is now the Prince of Wales Hospice, not far from the old Barracks. Precisely two years later, the club folded. The Pontefract AFC was still playing friendly fixtures in the 1902/03 season, with a 0-4 loss to the Garrison team in a local derby in January 1903 among them.

Between 1900-04, the Garrison held a competition between the two regiments at the barracks. The Yorkshire Light Infantry and the York & Lancaster's played a series of five matches to decide the winners of the shield that was presented by a Colonel Clark. The Garrison also had a cricket team in local league competition and ran a range of other sports teams, with an athletics festival during the summer.

Pontefract Town, formed in 1905 through the merger of Pontefract Victoria and Pontefract United, was the next association team to show ambition but it failed to progress beyond local competition before it also it folded.

Pontefract Borough, playing at Willow Park, off Baghill Lane, was the next club to step up to the Yorkshire League. Having competed in the FA Cup in the 1927/28 season while still a Castleford & District League club (losing 1-7 at home to Altofts WRC on Saturday 3rd September 1927 in an Extra Preliminary Round tie), Borough stepped up to the Yorkshire League for the 1928/29 season.

The team's first season in the Yorkshire League was nothing short of remarkable. Despite finishing bottom of the 16 team league, Borough did win seven of its 30 fixtures and scored a total of 76 goals during the season, three more than runners-up Selby Town. However, 148 goals were conceded, meaning that on average, 7.5 goals were scored in matches involving Pontefract Borough (assuming the figures are correct that is, many league tables around this time often being inaccurate in that wins and losses, and goals for and against throughout the whole division don't tally). In a season where high scoring became the norm, due mainly to the recent change in the offside rule, Bradford Park Avenue reserves scored 191 goals in winning the title that season.

In the FA Cup, the club provided the district with its biggest shock as the club won 2-1 at Midland League side Wombwell in a Preliminary Round tie. However, Cudworth put Borough out in the First Qualifying Round, winning 3-1 at Willow Park, following a 1-1 draw. There was cup joy, however, as Pontefract Borough defeated Hemsworth White Rose 1-0 in the Pontefract Infirmary Cup final on Saturday 4th May 1929.

Unfortunately the 1929/30 season was a disaster, with the club withdrawing from the Yorkshire League after having played 18 matches, of which only four points were obtained. The club promptly folded, although the Borough name has been revived in more recent times.

There have been many Pontefract-based teams through the years, among those that played at county league level - albeit below the Yorkshire and Northern Counties East Leagues - are the following:

Another Pontefract United was top team in the town in the years leading up to World War Two. Formerly known as Tanshelf Gems, the club changed its name after having secured a new ground on Ackworth Road. That team played in the West Yorkshire League after World War Two, alongside Pontefract Collieries. When the Collieries club later folded, United merged with a local junior club and took on the Collieries name itself. In recent times, this club, based just off Skinner Lane, has of course established itself in the national league system.

Pontefract Town Athletic and Pontefract Corinthians also played in the West Yorkshire League in the 1970s, as did Pontefract Borough in the mid 1980s. Pontefract Town played in the competition from 1990 until 2005, playing at the Barracks Playing Field.

Pontefract Labour were also in the West Yorkshire League 1995, after having been in the Selby League. Playing at Willow Park, the club was renamed Pontefract Sports & Social in 1999, playing in the Premier Division between 2000-06, but withdrew from the league during 2009/10 season. The club has since been reformed.

Pontefract AFC joined the West Riding County Amateur League in 1991, becoming Pontefract Borough in 1996. This club folded in the summer of 1999 after finishing well below the other clubs in its one season in the Premier Division. The team initially played at Pontefract Park, adjacent to the Racecourse, but by the mid 1990s had relocated to Ferrybridge Park, Castleford Lane, Ferrybridge.

# Selby

## AFC, Mizpah & Olympia

A Selby AFC was first referred to in the local press in March 1892 when an '*interesting match*', according to the *York Herald*, took place at The Bowling Green ground between York Commercial College and Selby. The result was a 1-1 draw. It seems that either the town's first association club faded away relatively quickly, because there is nothing else traced regarding this club, or that the match was an experimental one played by the Selby Football Club, which was well established in rugby circles at the time.

A new Selby AFC was founded in September 1896 at the town's Young Men's Institute, with a James R Foster serving as secretary *pro tem*. W F Lee was later elected as club chairman. Initially, friendly fixtures were played against other local clubs before the club became a founder member of the York & District League in the 1898/99 season, with teams in both the First and Second Division. But, after reporting a slight deficit over the season, the club was wound up in August 1899, with a new club, Selby Londesborough formed in its place. However, the 'new' club was referred to as plain 'Selby' during the 1899/1900 York League season before itself folding by 1901.

A brand new, and ultimately successful attempt to form a Selby AFC was made on 10th June 1902 at the town's Mellanby's Vaults, with M Scott elected as the club's first chairman. The club won the Barkston Ash Cup in the 1905/06 and 1906/07 seasons, and was also runner up to Halton United in the first

*Selby AFC 1905/06 (courtesy of David Haddock)*

Templenewsam Charity Cup competition, losing the final 3-2 in January 1908 at Whitkirk, after having led 2-0 at one stage in the first half.

Selby AFC reached its first Barkston Ash Cup final in the 1902/03 season, its first, when they were soundly defeated 0-4 by Whitkirk. The 1904/05 cup victory was achieved with a 4-0 victory over South Milford in the final, which was played on Saturday 20th April 1905 at the Garforth Parish Church ground. The tie was over by half time, with Selby team having scored all of its goals in the first half. The following season, Halton United were defeated 4-2 in the final on their own ground on Saturday 21st April 1906.

Selby AFC soon had rivals as Selby Mizpah, an established rugby club in the town, converted to soccer in the summer of 1903. Both teams played in the Barkston Ash League in their early years but Mizpah took the decision to pay their players and field a team in the West Yorkshire League between 1906-10. The club held its own, and following a mid-table placing in its debut season in the league, it achieved a fine third place in the 1907/08 season, behind Heckmondwike and Castleford. However, the club's final season, 1909/10 saw the club struggle in a league that contained just seven clubs (the league itself folding at the end of the season).

Both clubs put teams in the York & District League as well as the Barkston Ash League in the years leading up to the war, with Mizpah also entering the FA Cup, with little success, between 1908-10. Its first tie resulted in a 1-8 loss at Grimsby Rangers in the First Qualifying Round, while in 1909/10 a 7-2 win at home to Hull Day Street Old Boys in the Preliminary Round, was followed by a 2-7 loss at home to Grimsby Rovers.

Despite having reverted to amateur status since leaving the Yorkshire League, the Mizpah club was £45 in debt by January 1912. Lord Londesborough (Lord of the Manor of Selby) donated £1 to the club's cause, as did local politician Geo R Lane Fox, who also wrote a sympathetic letter to the club's secretary. It seems that these financial problems were too great for the club, which folded soon after.

Mizpah did win the Barkston Ash Cup on one occasion, defeating Halton United 2-1 in a second replay in the 1908/09 final, played on Wednesday 28th April 1909 at Selby. The first replay, played at Garforth, had ended in controversy when the referee awarded Halton a late penalty for handball, which was duly converted to leave the score at 2-2. The referee was mobbed by Mizpah supporters at the final whistle, and required a police escort in order to reach the dressing room safely.

MR. ARTHUR CAMPEY.

Just 24 hours before lifting the Barkston Ash Cup, Mizpah had won a cup competition outright for the first time, winning the Selby & District Cup, by defeating the Army Ordnance Corps team 3-1 in the final, which was played on Mizpah's Bowling Green Ground.

Two years earlier, Mizpah and Selby AFC had shared the Selby & District Cup, following two drawn games in the final (Selby reserves had won the first ever final in this competition in 1904).

John 'Arthur' Campey, who joined Mizpah as a 16-year-old, went on to make a name for himself. He helped Mizpah to local success before moving on to Knaresborough, then in the Yorkshire Combination. Campey then went on to spend a season with Leeds City's second team, Goole Town (Midland League), and then Southern League Walsall (1913-16), where he became the first player for that team to score 30 goals in a season, as well as appearing for Falkirk during the 1915/16 season. He was later the club trainer at Bradford Park Avenue and then Leeds United.

The Mizpah club was one of the few to have a female president, in Mary Jane Hodgson. The word Mizpah is Hebrew and simply means a 'lookout' or a 'watchtower' - Mizpah monograms were applied to Protestant prayer books and gravestones from the 1870s.

The Selby AFC and Selby Mizpah teams played at the same ground as the original club; James Street Recreation Ground, also known as The Bowling Green. The site still exists, adjacent to the Morrisons Supermarket. The current Selby Town AFC was founded after the War, in 1919, and played on the same ground until 1951.

Selby Olympia Cake & Oil was another local club of note. The team played in the Yorkshire League between 1925-31, and was known simply as Selby Olympia until 1926 (and as Olympia Mills from 1952), and played in the York League before, during and after its spell in the Yorkshire League.

Its best season in the Yorkshire League was its second, finishing in sixth place out of 16 teams. However, that was the only time the club finished in the top half of the league, and with the economic climate hitting clubs hard, the first team reverted back to York League football after six seasons in the county competition.

Three York League titles were won, by its second team in 1926/27, 1927/28, and the first team in 1931/32. The club left the league in the summer of 1966, but returned in 1980, as Selby Olympia WMC, playing in the York League to this day.

The Olympia club played two FA Amateur Cup ties, losing 1-6 at Acomb WMC in a Second Qualifying Round match in the 1920/21 season, and again in 1924/25 when it lost 1-4 at Whitehall Printeries in a Preliminary Round tie. Twenty-six FA Cup ties were played between 1920-35, although its first resulted in a 1-10 rout at Bradford side Apperley Bridge in the 1920/21 season, and its second, a 0-7 loss to Hull Dairycoates four years later. Its first win came in the 1925/26 season when Marfleet were defeated 5-0 at home in the Extra Preliminary Round before defeat, again, to Dairycoates.

Marfleet were thrashed 8-0 twelve months later at the same stage of the competition, before a 4-0 win over Grimsby Rovers, and a 2-1 success against Goole Town saw the club into the Second Qualifying Round, where they lost to a single goal at Scunthorpe United, this following a 0-0 draw. The club also made it to the same stage one year later. It's last match in the competition was a 0-1 defeat at Marfleet in the 1934/35 season.

**Selby Olympia / OCO Yorkshire League record**

|  | P | W | D | L | F | A | Pts | Pos |
|---|---|---|---|---|---|---|---|---|
| 1925/26 | 28 | 8 | 5 | 15 | 66 | 75 | 21 | 12/15 |
| 1926/27 | 30 | 15 | 4 | 11 | 67 | 46 | 34 | 6/16 |
| 1927/28 | 24 | 9 | 2 | 13 | 49 | 60 | 20 | 8/13 |
| 1928/29 | 30 | 9 | 7 | 14 | 77 | 96 | 25 | 10/16 |
| 1929/30 | 26 | 5 | 5 | 16 | 41 | 70 | 15 | 13/14 |
| 1930/31 | 22 | 7 | 1 | 14 | 51 | 75 | 15 | 10/12 |

# Upton Colliery

The village of Upton lies north-east of Barnsley and north-west of Doncaster, close to South Elmsall. Its colliery had a relatively short existence, with work on the site beginning in 1924, and closure just 40 years later following an explosion 20th May 1964 and geological faulting in the seams.

The colliery football club was founded on Monday 18th August 1930, at a meeting at the Upton Arms Hotel. A large number of interested parties were present, the title of the new club being 'Upton Colliery Athletic Football Club.' Initially a B Moulton was elected secretary, and it was suggested that two teams be formed, one in the Doncaster Red Triangle, the other in the South Kirkby & District League. Playing members were signed on and the search was on for a ground on which to play.

The ground that was procured became known as the Colliery Ground, and was located close to the Upton Colliery site. The new club was actually reorganised in January 1931, its new list of officials including; F Rich (chairman), F Weatherall (secretary), W Chadwick (treasurer), B Cook (captain).

In the event, just one team was put out in the club's first two seasons. Its debut season was spent in the 14-team South Elmsall League, where it finished 11th. The club's second season, 1931/32, saw an improved position in what was now a 16-team league, Upton finishing just above mid-table.

The 1932/33 season saw the club operating in two leagues for the first time. While retaining a team in the South Kirkby League (which was in effect a renamed South Elmsall League), a team was also entered into the Doncaster Senior League. The latter competition was somewhat farcical, with Upton having completed its 16 fixtures before Pilkington and Worksop had completed even half of theirs. Around this time, a promising young player called George Ashall played for Upton, before moving on to Frickley Colliery and then into the Football League between 1935-47 with Wolverhampton Wanderers (84 league appearances, 14 goals) and Coventry City (62 league appearances, 10 goals)

| Doncaster Senior League 1932/33 | P | W | D | L | F | A | Pts |
|---|---|---|---|---|---|---|---|
| Hatfield Main | 16 | 11 | 2 | 3 | 48 | 31 | 24 |
| South Kirkby | 16 | 11 | 0 | 5 | 51 | 35 | 22 |
| Pilkington Recs | 16 | 9 | 2 | 5 | 45 | 40 | 20 |
| Brodsworth Main | 16 | 8 | 0 | 8 | 55 | 39 | 16 |
| Hemsworth White Rose | 16 | 5 | 4 | 7 | 46 | 48 | 14 |
| Thorne Amateurs | 16 | 6 | 2 | 8 | 29 | 37 | 14 |
| Bentley Colliery | 16 | 6 | 1 | 9 | 41 | 61 | 13 |
| **Upton Colliery** | 16 | 4 | 3 | 9 | 33 | 41 | 11 |
| Worksop Town | 16 | 4 | 2 | 10 | 29 | 45 | 10 |
| **South Kirkby & District League 1932/33** | | | | | | | |
| Sth Kirkby Common Rd | 20 | 18 | 0 | 2 | 117 | 18 | 36 |
| South Kirkby Coll | 20 | 16 | 0 | 4 | 100 | 37 | 32 |
| **Upton Colliery** | 20 | 13 | 1 | 6 | 79 | 35 | 27 |
| Oxford Juniors | 20 | 11 | 3 | 6 | 44 | 39 | 25 |
| Brodsworth St Michaels | 19 | 9 | 1 | 9 | 85 | 54 | 19 |
| Moorthorpe | 19 | 8 | 3 | 8 | 38 | 66 | 19 |
| Carr Lane | 20 | 7 | 3 | 10 | 36 | 52 | 17 |
| Harcam | 20 | 7 | 3 | 10 | 40 | 60 | 17 |
| South Kirkby Juniors | 20 | 6 | 0 | 14 | 45 | 104 | 12 |
| Hemsworth YMCA | 20 | 3 | 2 | 15 | 35 | 83 | 8 |
| Toll Bar | 20 | 2 | 0 | 18 | 26 | 95 | 4 |
| *Hemsworth Vic & Hemsworth Albion both withdrew* | | | | | | | |

After only three years in existence, Upton joined the Yorkshire Football League in 1933, along with near neighbours South Kirkby Colliery, using mainly the same set of players from the previous season, plus a few additions. Mr S L Criddle was by now acting as both chairman and secretary of the club. Its first Yorkshire League match was on Saturday 26th August 1933 at home to Leeds United 'A', and this resulted in a convincing 4-0 victory in front a large number of spectators. The club finished in fourth place at the end of the season, two places behind its local rivals in the 13-team league.

A reserve team was entered into the Pontefract League for the 1933/34 season, the strength in depth of the club underlined in its 21-0 victory over Brown's Pottery on Saturday 3rd March 1934, which was at the time a league (and club) record, and its first league defeat did not come until February. The Pontefract Infirmary Cup was won by the side, Ackworth defeated 8-1 in the final, played on Saturday 5th May at the Frickley Colliery ground.

Having left the South Kirkby League, Upton Colliery was replaced in that competition by two short-lived teams, Upton Rangers and Upton Juniors, reflecting the growth of the new colliery village.

The 1934/35 season proved to be Upton's best. With the Yorkshire League expanding to 18 clubs, the competition was increasing in strength again following several lean years. Upton challenged at the top of the league all season, finally losing out on the title on goal average to Selby Town. The club had looked likely champions, but a 0-3 loss to struggling Thorne Colliery late in April proved decisive.

Upton made the headlines early in the 1935/36 season, but not for the right reasons. Several local newspapers carried the following story,

Doncaster Invitational Cup final - Saturday 2nd May

UPTON SUSPENDED - SHEFFIELD FA'S DRASTIC ACTION
*A bombshell was dropped on Upton Colliery FC, the Yorkshire League club, on Tuesday, when the club was suspended by the Sheffield F.A. Emergency Committee for not having paid its affiliation fees to the County FA. The secretary reported that he had been put to a great deal of trouble with the club, who were setting at defiance the rules of the Association. The meeting decided that the suspension be put into operation as from Tuesday (1)th September), a very serious view being expressed at the manner the club had carried out its duties. That the suspension was a 'storm in a teacup' was the hint conveyed by Mr S L Criddle, manager of Upton Colliery and secretary of the club, to the 'Times' yesterday. He explained that the club sent in the affiliation fee a fortnight late,*

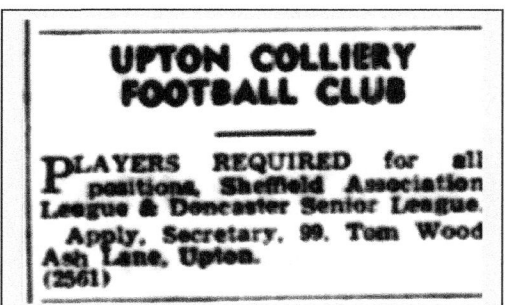

*and it appeared that as a result the fee was doubled. It was only a matter of half-a-crown, and this was sent by the next post after receiving a reminder from Sheffield. He received the receipt yesterday (Thursday) morning, but he had not been officially notified of the suspension, and as he could not accept any Press report the club would play its home match with Huddersfield Town 'A' tomorrow.*

The Huddersfield match, due to be played on 14th September did not take place, but the suspension had been lifted by the following week.

Upton finished eighth and then third in its following Yorkshire League seasons, losing out to York City reserves on goal average for the runner-up spot the 1936/37 season (Goole Town were champions that season). The club also won the Sheffield & Hallamshire Senior Cup that season, defeating Thurnscoe Victoria 4-3 a thrilling final, which was played at Hampden Road, Mexborough on Saturday 20th March 1937.

*The South Yorkshire Times*, on Friday 26th March 1937, carried an extensive report of the final, the first part of which is reproduced here,

GLORIOUS FINAL - WITH ALL THE TRADITIONAL FLAVOUR - UPTON TAKE A LATE LEAD AND THWART THE VICS
*This is one of those delicate situations. Fifteen hundred soccer fans can't all be wrong. But cutting out the most rabid favour carriers I guess two-thirds of them couldn't quite make up their minds who deserved the cup at Hampden Road on Saturday. It was a great game – traditional hustle and bustle, replete with every ounce of zip and energy that go to make these tourneys so attractive. But I don't think I have seen two more evenly balanced teams in a final.*

DIFFERENT INGREDIENTS
*The scales balanced with different ingredients. Thurnscoe were essentially bustlers and pacemakers. There was little orthodox about their work: it was whole hearted 'go-getter' stuff, the type of which produced a goal for them*

### Renown Upton Colliery Footballers

*Top left: Clarrie Jordan*
*Top right: George Ashall*
*Bottom: Charlie Williams*
*(source unknown)*

within the first minute of the game. Real football. And it was a type which never flagged. They were bustling away as hard as ever even at the final whistle. Upton on the other hand, were more stylish and academic. They had a great pull at half-back. In fact, if this brilliant trio had allowed Thurnscoe's worrying forwards to 'rattle' them in the early phases of the game there's no knowing just how many goals Bloomfield and company might have accounted for. But throughout the whole of the ninety minutes they stood like Gibraltar – as imposing and almost as impregnable. Haigh, the centre-half, was one of the most brilliant of the twenty-two players on the field: he seemed to dog the footsteps of every one of the Thurnscoe forwards and still find time to ply his wingmen with grand through passes.

However, the summer of 1937 proved a turning point in the fortunes of the club, which was by now heavily in debt.

In April 1937 the club received a £10 grant from Barnsley FC for the signing of outside-left A Brewer (Sunderland had paid £50 for the signing of Griffiths two years earlier), and this had helped the Upton sports clubs with the considerable expense it had endured relating to the laying down of two football pitches, two cricket pitches, with the enclosing walls, stand, dressing rooms and 500 yards of fencing.

Despite having a settled team, with several players having been with the club since its first season in the league, the loss of three key players to a higher level of football , including Eric Humphrey to Rotherham and Stanley Clayton to Notts County weakened the team, which was increasingly reliant on local players in order to reduce costs. Manager of the colliery and club secretary S L Criddle was forced to step down from his roles due to work commitments, and he was replaced by George Ball, who was head lampman at the pit.

Given that Upton represented the smallest village in the Yorkshire League, large attendances for home games could never be expected, and rather than two to three thousand expected at the larger clubs, Upton could only attract a handful of spectators for home matches. The resulting lack of finance, even after voluntary contributions by working miners at the pit (who gained free admission to home matches), meant that the club's high placings in the league was never going to be sustainable. The 1937/38 season saw the team plummet to 18th place in the 20-team league (South Kirkby Colliery had also tumbled, from fourth the previous season to 17th), with only Bradford Park Avenue 'A' (on goal average) and Altofts below it. Significantly, however, the club was temporarily free of debt at the close of its cost-saving season.

An improvement to ninth place followed in the 1938/39 season, and club was quietly confident of maintaining a top half placing in the league the following season. However, a 1-7 home loss to league champions Sheffield Wednesday 'A' on Saturday 26th August 1939 was not an ideal start, and the league was subsequently suspended due to the outbreak of World War Two. In early December, the team was defeated 1-6 by Frickley Athletic in the Sheffield & Hallamshire Senior Cup, by which time the club had reverted to playing fixtures in the Doncaster Senior League.

Upton Colliery did reach the Mexborough Montagu Cup final at the end of the 1941/42 season, going down 2-4 to Manvers Main, who won the cup for the third year in succession, at Denaby. The attendance for the final was disappointing, raising only £23, prompting the Denaby United club to hand back the ground percentage it was due as a donation.

One player of interest for the Upton Colliery club at this time was Charlie Williams, who went on to play over 150 games for Doncaster Rovers (scoring once) between 1948-59, before going to become one of Britain's best loved comedians in the 1970s & 80s. Clarrie Jordan was another who made his mark, playing for Upton for the club until 1940. He went on to play for Doncaster Rovers (48 goals – including scoring in 10 consecutive games in 60 league appearances) and then Sheffield Wednesday (92 league appearances, 36 goals).

Joe Shaw worked briefly as a coalminer at Upton and also played for Upton Colliery FC, before moving on to playing football full time with Sheffield United, where he made a massive 714 appearances (632 in the Football League) between 1945-66. He went on to manage York City from 1967 to 1968 and then Chesterfield from 1973 to 1976. Three years after his death in 2007 the club erected a statue in his honour outside Bramall Lane.

### Upton Colliery Yorkshire League Record

| Season | P | W | D | L | F | A | Pts | Pos |
|---|---|---|---|---|---|---|---|---|
| 1933/34 | 24 | 11 | 6 | 7 | 63 | 54 | 28 | 4/13 |
| 1934/35 | 34 | 24 | 4 | 6 | 88 | 46 | 52 | 2/18 |
| 1935/36 | 38 | 19 | 5 | 14 | 78 | 75 | 43 | 8/20 |
| 1936/37 | 36 | 20 | 9 | 7 | 108 | 69 | 49 | 3/19 |
| 1937/38 | 38 | 11 | 5 | 22 | 59 | 91 | 27 | 18/20 |
| 1938/39 | 38 | 16 | 6 | 16 | 78 | 76 | 38 | 9/20 |
| 1946/47 | 38 | 2 | 3 | 33 | 46 | 188 | 7 | 20/20 |

Upton Colliery did not immediately re-join the Yorkshire League after World War Two, re-joining in the 1946/47 season, one year after local rivals South Kirkby Colliery. The season proved disastrous, with the club stuck at the bottom of the league with only seven points from its 38 matches, and conceding 188 goals in the process. Unsurprisingly, the club withdrew from the league after just one season back, having witnessed pitiful home attendances as well as results.

However, this was not the end for the club, which regrouped in the strong Sheffield Association League. The Sheffield & Hallamshire Senior Cup was won for the second time at the close of the 1949/50 season, when Beighton Miners Welfare were defeated 5-3 in another exciting final at Tickhill Square, Denaby, on Saturday 6th May 1950.

The club won the league title four times in the space of six seasons during the 1950s: 1953/54, 1955/56, 1956/57, and 1958/59, on each occasion deciding not to re-apply to re-join the Yorkshire League. The top clubs in the Sheffield League were considered strong enough to have competed strongly in the Yorkshire League, and with Upton winning much more often in its current league, its committee was happy for it to stay put.

Around 1955 the club moved to a new ground at Quarry Lane, which was paid for and prepared by the National Coal Board. However, with the colliery itself closing in 1964, the football club also fell by the wayside.

Upton Colliery continued to compete in the FA Cup even after it had left the Yorkshire League, reaching the Third Qualifying Round on three occasions.

Its first season in the competition was in the 1936/37 season, when Huddersfield district side Meltham Mills were overpowered 8-1 in an Extra Preliminary Round tie, this after a 2-2 draw at Meltham. Upton lost at home to Worksop Town in the following round.

Ravensthorpe were thrashed 7-2 on their own ground the following season, before Upton won a Preliminary Round replay at Farsley Celtic 2-2, following an exciting 4-4 draw. A home loss to Frickley Colliery put paid to any progress, and the club went on to lose at the first stage in its next eight entries into the national competition, and this included a 1-9 thrashing at Bentley Colliery in the 1949/50 season.

Frickley Colliery became a bogey team for Upton, when its fellow colliery team defeated it three seasons in succession, twice at the Third Round stage, in 1951/52 and 1953/54. However, a 4-3 home win over Frickley in the 1954/55 season, was followed by a 3-2 win at home to Sheffield, before a 0-2 loss at Denaby United – this being the final time the Third Qualifying Round was reached.

Upton's final five ties in the FA Cup were all lost, beginning with Frickley Colliery (who else) in the 1955/56 season, and ending with a 5-2 defeat at Farsley Celtic in the 1959/60 season.

The club ceased to operate sometime around 1964, when the colliery itself was closed. The old colliery ground is still used for local football today, although unrecognisable to the site that existed during Upton Colliery's tenure there. The Quarry Lane venue is of course still in use, with rugby league and football pitches on the site.

**Bradford Red Triangle Football League**
*League Cup Final*

GATEHOUSE F.C.
V
GREEN LANE Y.C.

FRIDAY 6th May 1988. K.O.

ECCLESHILL UTD. F.C. GROUND

PLUMPTON, WROSE, BRADFORD

Admission 50p. O.A.P. &

---

**V. A. W. LOW MOOR A. F. C.**

OFFICIAL PROGRAMME

---

PROGRAMME 10p

**FRECHEVILLE COMMUNITY**
ASSOCIATION FOOTBALL CLUB
SILKSTONE ROAD

V
BRIGGTOWN
MARCH

Official Programme

---

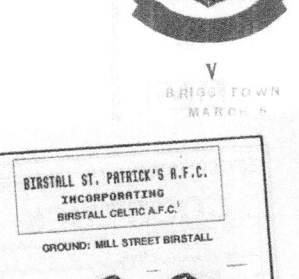

**BIRSTALL ST. PATRICK'S A.F.C.**
INCORPORATING
BIRSTALL CELTIC A.F.C.
GROUND: MILL STREET BIRSTALL

BIRSTALL CELTIC A.F.C.
VERSUS
FIELD A.F.C. RESERVES
SATURDAY 8.10.94
K.O. 2.30pm

20p

---

ASSOCIATED DEVELOPMENTS
INNS & TAVERNS
*are pleased to Sponsor*

**GRATTAN FOOTBALL LEAGUE CUP FINAL**

Friday 7th May 1999
at Thackley A.F.C., Ainsbury Avenue
Kick Off 7.00pm

LOCAL HYGIENE F.C.
V
WOODEND RANGERS A.F.C.

Admission £2.00     Cons. £1.00

# Gallery

### Armley Amateurs

This short-lived club played in the Leeds Red Triangle during the 1922/23 season. The club played in local league competition between 1913-25, although it was dormant during World War One.

### Clifton AFC (Brighouse)

### Harewood AFC (Leeds)

## Sheffield (West District) Postmen's FC

The team is pictured in 1908 with the Postmen's Cup, a competition that was also won two years earlier.

Also shown here is a rare Baines Shield from the early 1920s that features Sheffield GPO

## Wadsley Bridge Wesleyans

This club was a founder member of the Sheffield Free Churches League in the 1902/03 season,

It re-entered the league in 1911, its membership ending in 1914. The club failed to win any silverware during its short existence. Wadsley Bridge Church FC played in local competitions during the 1920s.

# Hedon

*Hedon 1908/09*

The Holderness League was founded in December 1908, with its first fixtures played in January 1909. The deciding match in the championship took part on Battery Ground, Paull, on Monday 19th April 1909 between the home team and Hedon. Peter Everingham scored the only goal of the game for Hedon after only five minutes. Twice during the game the ball was kicked into the Humber, and on the first occasion a boat was sent out to rescue it. One of the Paull supporters waded into the water up to his shoulders in order to recover it the second time.

# Yeadon Park Rangers

*Wharfedale & Airedale Observer,* Friday 22nd April 1910

YEADON PARK RANGERS' SUCCESS. The Yeadon Park Rangers, whose ground is at Whack House, have exhibited consistently good form throughout the season, a statement which is proved by the fact that they tied with Woodhouse Salem for the championship the Farsley and District League. The deciding match was played at Farsley last Saturday, when the Rangers came out on top. In the first half, the game was suspended for a short time while the referee sent off two players for a bout of fisticuffs, and the teams crossed over each credited with a goal, the scorers being Hook and A Robinson. In the second half, Yeadon Park registered another goal, and thus ran out winners two goals to one.

The club's ground was described as being at Brewery Lane the following season, with the newly founded Swaine Hill Crescent (an offshoot of Yeadon Park Rangers) also playing on the field. Rangers entered the Wharfedale League for the 1913/14 season, but by October 1913 had withdrawn from the competition and promptly disbanded.

# Ardath Photocards

In an era when, in order to promote increasing sales among sporting fans, cigarette companies would produce sports cards, containing photographs, portraits, or caricatures of famous teams and individuals. Ardath was one such company, and in 1936 produced several sets of photocards consisting of football and rugby teams. The 'C' series of cards consisted of 110 different Yorkshire teams, and alongside those cards featuring the region's professional football and rugby league teams were a good number that featured amateur teams too.

Ardath Cards were interesting in that some of the teams featured had disbanded in the summer before the cards were actually produced. Reliant on information from the clubs themselves to send it their own team photographs, and also to provide brief details of the club itself, along with a list of players on the photograph, some cards featured factual errors.

A selection of the 'C' series cards, along with brief histories of each club, are featured here.

## Ainsty Builders

The club were Ainsty League champions in the 1935/36 season, remaining undefeated in all competitions, and also winning the Hospital Cup and York Junior Cup competitions that season. Ainsty moved to the York & District League in the summer of 1938, and returned to that league in the 1947/48 season, after having been dormant due to World War Two. The team initially played in Division Three, but resigned during the 1950/51 season while in Division Two.

## Balfour Sports

Composed of employees of the Arthur Balfour & Co Ltd, based at the Capital Steel Works, the club played at the company's sports ground at Whirlow Bridge in south-west Sheffield. The ground – formerly known as Bestwick Park - was officially opened on Saturday 11th July 1931, although parts of the sports ground had been used for a short time before that. Previously, a ground on Millhouses Lane had been used by the company teams.

On its new ground, the football team entered the Sheffield Works League, playing in the competition between 1931-33. The following two seasons were spent in the Sheffield Friendlies League - first in Division Four and then in Division One (no doubt due to team strengthening). The club then moved on to a new league.

Fourth place was achieved in its first season in the South Yorkshire League in 1935/36, and the club was also in the same league the following season. A switch back to the Sheffield Friendlies League was made for the 1937/38 season, with the team placed in Division One of the six-division competition. Unfortunately the team struggled badly, and lost 17 of its 20 fixtures, drawing the remaining three. Yet another switch occurred during the summer of 1938, with the team accepted into the Premier Division of the Sheffield Sports & Athletic League. The club again finished at the foot of the table, but did win two of its matches in the twelve team league.

**1935/36 South Yorkshire Amateur League**
```
Rotherham YMCA     26 23  1  2 121  26 47
Sheffield Teachers 26 20  4  2 100  38 44
Broom Sports       26 14  8  4  93  51 36
Balfour Sports     26 15  3  8 104  64 33
Sheffield YMCA     26 14  4  8  86  52 32
Sheffield Club     26 10  7  9 102  85 27
Ravens             26 13  1 12  78  80 27
Spartans           26 10  4 12  71  83 24
ND Ramblers        26  8  3 15  63  93 19
Sheffield Bankers  26  8  3 15  72 107 19
Municipal Officers 26  7  4 15  63  96 18
Sheffield University 26 7 1 18  43  97 15
Barnsley Optimists 26  4  5 17  58 111 13
Old Staveleyans    26  3  4 19  62 134 10
```

The club re-emerged after World War Two back in the Sheffield & District Works League. Balfour were Beatty League champions 1945/46, which was essentially a second division of the Works League. There would be no switching of leagues every season or so at this time. The sports ground is still in existence as the HSBC Sports Ground.

## Barugh Coalite

The UK's first commercial Coalite plant was opened at Barugh, Barnsley, in 1927. The company ran several sports team, including cricket and soccer. The latter were members of the Barnsley Nelson League in the 1935/36 season, also becoming Pickering Cup winners that season. This cup competition was in aid of the Darton Old People's Treat Fund. The club were also winners of the untraced Bristow Cup competition

## Bishop Monkton

The club was runner-up in the Ripon & District League in the 1934/35 & 1935/36 seasons, winning the league Cup in both of those years. It was founded by A Wood, who became club president in 1934. There was a Bishop Monkton club until relatively recently.

## British Dyestuffs (Huddersfield)

The British Dyestuffs club were Huddersfield & District Works League champions in 1934/35, and Hoyle Cup winners in 1935/36. A Dyestuffs team was also playing in the Huddersfield League when it was revived for the 1935/36 season, the club having played in that competition from 1928-32 before its suspension due to a lack of teams.

## Brunswick Methodists

The Brunswick Methodist FC is said to have been established in 1900, although it did not come to prominence until 1933. Playing at High Storrs Road, Sheffield, the club was a members of the Sheffield Churches League and Sheffield Sunday School League. In the 1935/36 season, the club was runner-up in both leagues, and won the Bible Class league title. Brunswick had also won the Sheffield Churches League in 1933/34.

**1936/37 Sheffield Bible Class League Division A**

| | | | | | | | |
|---|---|---|---|---|---|---|---|
| Brunswick Mission | 18 | 12 | 5 | 1 | 75 | 34 | 29 |
| Brunswick Meths | 18 | 14 | 1 | 3 | 76 | 36 | 29 |
| St Vincents | 18 | 11 | 3 | 4 | 59 | 28 | 25 |
| Allen Street Meths | 18 | 10 | 2 | 6 | 68 | 45 | 22 |
| Gleadless Meths | 18 | 7 | 3 | 8 | 47 | 66 | 17 |
| Grenoside Ch S 'A' | 18 | 5 | 5 | 8 | 36 | 62 | 15 |
| Birley Carr Inst | 18 | 5 | 4 | 9 | 49 | 55 | 14 |
| Sharrow Lane Meth | 18 | 5 | 2 | 11 | 45 | 65 | 12 |
| Ann's Road Meths | 18 | 3 | 3 | 12 | 34 | 67 | 9 |
| Heeley Friends | 18 | 2 | 4 | 12 | 32 | 64 | 8 |

On Monday 26th April 1937, Brunswick Methodists again won the Sheffield Bible Class League final against Grenoside Church Sports 'B' (who had won Division B) at the Midland Athletic Ground on Norfolk Road, after having initially finished level on points with local rivals Brunswick Mission at the top of Division A. The top two in each division had qualified for the play-offs. It seems that the club was not revived after World War Two, although by the late 1950s a Brunswick Trinity was playing in the Bible Class League.

## Cole Bros. Sports

Members of the Sheffield & Hallamshire Thursday Friendly League, the club first took part in the competition between 1928-30, and then 1931-33. The team finished eighth in its return to the league in a fifteen team division in the 1935/36, season, enabling it to take a place in the league's first division when it was expanded to two divisions for the 1936/37 season. After finishing 11th in the league, the club either folded in the summer of 1937 or changed its name.

## Crookes Congregational

Founded in 1933, the club finished third in each division in the Sheffield Friendly League for three successive years. In the 1935/36 season, the club was runner-up in the A J Sanders competition (the only competition run by the league in which a trophy was awarded), losing 4-5 to Woodseats Methodists at the Niagara ground on Saturday 7th March 1936, having trailed 0-5 at one point in the match. The team dropped out of the league in the summer of 1938. In the 1920s, there were various other sporting clubs associated with the church, including a cricket team and women's hockey team.

## Dore

The club lifted the Sheffield Amateur League title in 1935/36 After finishing runner-up in Division Two behind Fulwood, the club won the play-offs for the top two clubs in the league's two divisions. Fulwood were defeated 2-0 in the semi-final before a 4-1 success against Division One side Thurcroft in the decider, played at Shiregreen on Saturday 18th April 1936.

*Sheffield Independent,* Monday 20th April 1936

*Dore won the Sheffield Amateur League in rather convincing manner, beating Thurcroft 4-1 in game that was one of the most pleasing seen by a large crowd in the Shiregreen area this season. From the start the play of both sides was good, though the wind at times played strange acts with the lively ball. Dore, with the advantage in the first half were two goals up before the interval, Truswell and Ward scoring, Thurcroft doing some real good defensive play. After the change round Dore went further ahead. Burnell heading a capital goal Thurcroft, after this, missed two fine chances. Then to add iron the lot, Orridge failed with a spot kick, which Walker saved in masterly style. Pickering later made amends and scored, but Burnell, from a great solo effort, made the issue safe.*

*Walker, the Dore goalkeeper, gave an outstanding exhibition which won him great credit, and Bedford, the left back, was a player who did great work. Thurcroft had far more of the play in the closing stages, but could not get the ball into the net. The success of Dore is their first honour in the competition, and at the close Mr J Andrew presented the trophy.*

L Burnell, who scored twice in the final, was the team's star player, one who had recently played for the Sheffield & Hallamshire FA Representative team. Dore FC's home ground was next to the Church Hall on Townhead Road. The club continued to play in the Sheffield Amateur League until 1939, after which time World War Two disrupted local and national sporting events. Dore had originally joined the league in 1930, and despite struggling in its first season in the league, quickly established itself as one of the stronger clubs in the competition. Following World War Two, a revived club went on to play in the South Yorkshire Amateur and Hope Valley Leagues.

### Eborcraft United

This team took many of its players from Holmes & Co (York) Ltd. In the 1933/34 season, its first in the competition, it became York & District League Division Three (Group Two) winners, but was not promoted. At least three more seasons were played in the league's lower divisions without success before the club folded.

### English Electric (Bradford)

This club was founded in 1920, and played at Thornbury on a ground that was later used by Phoenix Park in the Northern Counties East League.

The club were Farsley & District Inter-Works League winners in the 1935/36 season, although this was by no means the strongest competition it played in, as its first team played in the Bradford Combination and Amateur leagues during the 1930s. Two seasons were spent in the Combination's Senior Division between 1930-32, before re-emerging in the Bradford Amateur League in 1933. Sadly the club, withdrew from the league's First Division during 1936/37 season.

Bradford Electric FC was admitted to a new Section B in the West Riding County Amateur League for the 1953/54 season, winning the divisional title the season after. The club finished fifth in the top division in the 1955/56 season, repeating that position a year later in an enlarged 18 team single league.

Unfortunately the 1957/58 season proved a struggle, and the club withdrew from West Yorkshire's top league at the end of that season.

### Sharow

The village team of Sharow played in the Ripon & District League during the mid-1930s. It was the winner of the Ripon Charity Cup in 1935/36, and beaten finalists the season before. The league championship was won with ease in the 1936/37 season.

## Kildwick Athletic

The original Kildwick FC played in the inaugural Keighley Charity Cup in 1904/05, before becoming a founder member of the Keighley & District League in 1905/06, its first team finishing bottom of Division One, and its reserve team withdrawing from Division Two during the season. Several of its players moved to near neighbours Sutton FC that summer, but after a one year hiatus the club returned for a season, spending 1907/08 in the Skipton Hospital League before folding.

Kildwick Old Boys *(photographed below)* was founded around the summer of 1908, playing in the Keighley & District League from 1910 before withdrawing early in the 1914/15 season due to the onset of war. Upon its resumption, the club played in the same league between 1920-22, winning the Division Two title in 1920/21, but struggling in the league's top division the following season. Two seasons were then spent in the South Craven League between 1922-24 (with its reserve team playing in the Keighley League in 1923/24)

The club was reorganised as Kildwick Athletic in the summer of 1924, with another switch to the Keighley League for 1924/25, and then back to the South Craven League the following season. It seems the club folded in the summer of 1926, although Kildwick Juniors played in the 1926/27 South Craven Junior League, finishing runner-up in the league after having lost a championship play-off with Silsden Juniors. That team was not around the following season.

However, Kildwick Athletic was reformed in 1933, and at first played in Division Two of the Skipton & District League in the 1933/34 season. The following season was going to be spent in the Keighley & District League, but a late switch saw the club join the newly formed Craven & District League instead, where it spent two seasons in its Second Division – finishing runner up in the league and league cup in the first of those seasons, and winners of the division in 1935/36. Despite featuring on one of the 1936 Ardath Cards, the club folded again in the summer of 1936, so the Ardath card featured a team that no longer existed.

# Skipton Christ Church

In an advertisement placed in the *Yorkshire Post* on 16th September 1876 by the Skipton Christ Church Football Club, there was a wish to arrange football matches for the forthcoming season, with the statement, *'Will play according to either Rugby or Association Rules'*. If any association matches were played, interested clubs having contacted the Christ Church Secretary, Geo W Cragg, they certainly went unreported. But given the town's proximity to the association hotspot located around East Lancashire, it is maybe no surprise that there was an intention to play whatever code their opponents chose.

The Christ Church association team was active in local league and cup competitions in the early 1900s, although not continuously. The team played in the Skipton Hospitals League between 1908-10, and Skipton Junior League 1913/14, without achieving any real success, but after World War One re-formed and joined the top division of the Keighley & District League for the 1921/22 season.

The club's first team finished fourth in the league's 14 team division, with its reserves playing in Division Two. For the 1922/23 season both first and second teams became founder members of the South Craven League, the former becoming that competition's inaugural champions, just one point ahead of Sutton United.

The league reverted to one division for 1923/24 so the reserves returned to the Keighley League. The first team were champions of the South Craven League again, however. With Sutton United having moved on, the Skipton side remained unbeaten in its league programme and well clear at the top of the final table.

The following season the club finished down in fifth place in a much stronger league, won by the returning Sutton United, ahead of Keighley Parkwood (later Keighley Town). The reserves withdrew mid-season from the Keighley League, and in the summer of 1925 the club closed down again.

The club was re-formed and re-emerged in the South Craven Combination in the 1931/32 season. This league was for teams with an average age of 21. Christ Church finished bottom of the ten team league, with only one win all season. The league essentially became the Skipton & District League in the summer of 1932, and the club played in this competition until the formation of the current Craven & District League in 1934. Despite being Division C winners 1935/36, the club folded yet again in the summer of 1936, resulting in another example of an Ardath card featured a team that was no longer in existence.

## Skipton Christ Church in the South Craven League

**1922-23**

**Division One**

| | P | W | D | L | Pts |
|---|---|---|---|---|---|
| Skipton Christ Ch | 16 | 11 | 3 | 2 | 25 |
| Sutton United | 16 | 12 | 0 | 4 | 24 |
| Cowling | 16 | 8 | 5 | 3 | 21 |
| Carleton United | 16 | 6 | 6 | 4 | 18 |
| Gargrave | 16 | 5 | 4 | 7 | 14 |
| Cononley Institute | 16 | 3 | 7 | 6 | 13 |
| Skipton Niffany R | 16 | 5 | 3 | 8 | 13 |
| Kildwick Old Boys | 16 | 4 | 1 | 11 | 9 |
| Grassington | 16 | 1 | 5 | 10 | 7 |

**1923-24**

| | P | W | D | L | Pts |
|---|---|---|---|---|---|
| Skipton Christ Ch | 22 | 20 | 2 | 0 | 42 |
| Hellifield | 22 | 14 | 3 | 5 | 31 |
| Marton | 22 | 11 | 4 | 7 | 26 |
| Settle | 22 | 11 | 4 | 7 | 26 |
| Carleton United | 22 | 12 | 1 | 9 | 25 |
| Cowling | 22 | 11 | 3 | 8 | 25 |
| Gargrave | 22 | 8 | 4 | 10 | 20 |
| Cononley | 22 | 9 | 1 | 12 | 19 |
| Gargrave Ath Wks | 22 | 9 | 1 | 12 | 19 |
| Kildwick Old Boys | 22 | 6 | 4 | 12 | 16 |
| Grassington | 22 | 3 | 4 | 15 | 10 |
| Embsay | 22 | 1 | 3 | 18 | 5 |

**1924-25**

| | P | W | D | L | F | A | Pts |
|---|---|---|---|---|---|---|---|
| Sutton United | 24 | 19 | 3 | 2 | 115 | 18 | 41 |
| Keighley Parkwood | 24 | 18 | 3 | 3 | 109 | 30 | 39 |
| Earby reserves | 24 | 14 | 4 | 6 | 88 | 37 | 32 |
| Carleton United | 24 | 15 | 1 | 8 | 101 | 45 | 31 |
| Skipton Christ Ch | 24 | 14 | 2 | 8 | 56 | 37 | 30 |
| Gargrave Town | 24 | 12 | 4 | 8 | 55 | 54 | 28 |
| Cowling | 24 | 13 | 1 | 10 | 59 | 48 | 27 |
| Cononley | 24 | 9 | 4 | 11 | 39 | 73 | 22 |
| Embsay | 24 | 8 | 4 | 12 | 68 | 80 | 20 |
| Grassington | 24 | 7 | 1 | 16 | 38 | 86 | 15 |
| Silsden | 24 | 4 | 7 | 13 | 36 | 90 | 15 |
| Skipton LMS | 24 | 3 | 2 | 19 | 31 | 94 | 8 |
| Skipton Belle Vue | 24 | 2 | 0 | 22 | 19 | 141 | 4 |

*Gargrave Ath Works w/d*

## Wetherby Junior Imperial League

The club were runners-up in the Harrogate & District League in 1935/36, and League Cup finalists, and also finalists in the Ripon Senior Charity Cup that season too. The side played in the league between 1932-39.

## Wetherby Rovers

Established in 1920, the Wetherby Rovers club played in the Harrogate & District League, becoming Division Two winners in the 1934/35 season. A team was also entered in the Harrogate & District Half Holiday League during the mid-1930s. In 1949, Rovers merged with Wetherby AFC, to form the current Wetherby Athletic.

## Woodthorpe Amateurs

This team was a member of the Sheffield Public Parks League in the 1935/36 season, finishing in third place in the 1935/36 season (runners-up according to the Ardath Card). The Ardath card refers to the club also winning the Rudyard League and league cup although this competition has not been traced. The Public Parks League ran between 1933-40, and was for teams that played on public parks or council owned grounds. It would seem that by the card the Ardath Card was printed, Woodthorpe Amateurs was no more as the club was not in any league the following season.

**Sheffield Public Parks League 1935/36**

|  | P | W | D | L | F | A | Pts |
|---|---|---|---|---|---|---|---|
| Burlington Sports | 18 | 12 | 3 | 3 | 66 | 29 | 27 |
| Boundary Sports | 18 | 11 | 5 | 2 | 65 | 29 | 27 |
| Woodthorpe Amats | 18 | 10 | 6 | 2 | 38 | 27 | 26 |
| Woodbourne Rov | 18 | 11 | 0 | 7 | 59 | 41 | 22 |
| Park Sports | 18 | 10 | 2 | 6 | 55 | 41 | 22 |
| Cottam Sports | 18 | 6 | 6 | 6 | 53 | 40 | 18 |
| Bradfield Villa | 18 | 4 | 5 | 9 | 36 | 57 | 17 |
| Prince of Wales Spts | 18 | 5 | 2 | 11 | 36 | 62 | 12 |
| Stanhouse Rovers | 18 | 3 | 1 | 14 | 35 | 71 | 7 |
| Walkley | 18 | 2 | 2 | 14 | 21 | 67 | 6 |

*Mappin Social, Harwood House, Tansley United Rose, and West End Sports, all w/d*

## Yorkshire Traction Sports

Part of the Barnsley-based multi-sporting club, the association football team was a member of the Northern Counties Traction Sports League, finishing in fourth place in the 1935/36 season. The Scottish Motor Traction Cup is said to have been won that season, however. This competition has not been traced, although the Yorkshire Traction team did play its Edinburgh counterparts in January 1931 in aid of the local Beckett Hospital. This match could well have been an annual event.

# Who Won What?

Looking back at 1936, when those Ardath cards were produced, its interesting to look back at just how many different, long gone competitions there were. On Wednesday 13th May 1936 the *Sheffield Independent* rounded up its coverage of the football season with the following list of winners:

## Sheffield Area
*Sheffield Challenge Cup*: Denaby Utd, r/u: Worksop T
*Sheffield Junior Cup*: Fulwood
*Sheffield Assoc Lge*: Rawmarsh Welf, r/u Norton Wds
*Sheffield Amateur League*: Dore, r/u Thurcroft Main
*Sheffield City League*: Crookes WMC
*Sheffield Junior League*: Woodhouse Hill WMC
*Sheffield Intermediate League (16-18)*: Woodburn Alliance, (14-16): St Vincent's
*Sheffield Parks League*: Boundary Sports
*Sheffield Central League*: Central Thursday
*Sheffield Central Cup*: Central Thursday
*Thursday Friendlies League*: Thursday Athletic, r/u Rotherham Butchers
*Sheffield Sunday School League*: Birley Carr Institute
*Sheffield Churches League*: Birley Carr Institute, (Junior Section): Brunswick Mission
*Sheffield Adult Schools League*: Hareshead Friends
*Sheffield Adult League Cup*: St Vincent's
*Sheffield Bible Class League*: Brunswick Methodists
*South Yorkshire Amateur League*: Rotherham YMCA, r/u Sheffield Teachers
*Sheffield Sports League*: Netherthorpe Institute
*Sheff Sports League (Senior Section)*: Gleadless HIMW
*Sheffield Friendlies League*: Oughtibridge Sports
*AJ Sanders Memorial Cup*: Woodseats Methodists
*Wragg League*: Crookes WMC
*Sheffield Works Cup*: Steel, Peach & Tozers
*Sheffield Works Premier League*: Atlas & Norfolk
*Sheffield Works Beatty League*: J Wood's Sports
*Sheffield Works Haig League*: Hampton's Sports
*Sheffield Works Drake League*: Atlas & Norfolk
*Barber Shield*: Hillsborough Park Methodists
*Attercliffe Alliance Cup*: Crookes WMC
*Darnall Medical Aid Cup*: Catcliffe Juniors, r/u: Aqueduct WMC
*Heeley Charity Cup*: Nether Edge
*Tinsley Charity Cup*: Tinsley Park WMC

## Barnsley Area
*Association League*: Ardsley Athletic
*Junior League* Division One: Royston High Street United, Division Two: Worsbrough B O B
*Nelson League* Div 1: Park Rangers: Div 2: Cudworth St Mary's, Div 3: Wentworth, Div 4: Ward Grn Ath
*Nelson Associate League* Div One: Parkhill Sports: Div Two: Wombwell Blythe Street
*Sunday School League*: Mapplewell Bethel
*Sunday School Junior Shield League*: Carlton Meths
*Intermediate League*: Birdwell Rovers
*Beckett Hospital Cup*: Darton Welfare
*Barnsley Charity Cup*: Ardsley Athletic

## Doncaster Area
*Doncaster Invitation Cup*: Upton Colliery
*Doncaster Charity Cup*: Pilkington Recs v Rossington Main – final played in September
*Doncaster Junior Cup*: Rossington Main
*Doncaster Thursday League Cup*: Massarella's
*Doncaster Royal Infirmary Shield*: Edlington Rgrs
*South Kirkby League*: South Kirkby Common Rd OB
*Bentley League Knock-Out*: Owston Park Rangers
*Goole & Thorne Cup*: Dunscroft United
*Stainforth League*: Dunscroft United reserves
*Stainforth League Cup*: Dunscroft United reserves
*Harworth League Cup*: Harworth Athletic
*Harworth League Mullins Cup*: Harworth Comrades
*Thorne Nursing Cup*: Hatfield Town
*West Riding CC Cup*: Doncaster West Rid Division
*Doncaster Red Triangle League*: Dunscroft United
*Bentley League* Division One: Woodland Amateurs, Division Two: Pegler's Sports
*Hartell Shield*: Owston Park Rangers

## Rotherham Area
*Rotherham Senior League*: Canklow Hotel, r/u: Dalton Old Village
*Rotherham Minor Lge*: Maltby PC, r/u: Maltby Main
*Rotherham Association Junior League*: Wilton Lane Sports, r/u: Holmes Hotel
*Rotherham Intermediate League*: Rotherham YMCA Juniors, r/u: Guest & Chrimes
*Rotherham Challenge Cup*, r/u Maltby Main, r/u Maltby Parish Church
*Rotherham Association Challenge Cup*: Maltby Main, r/u: Steel, Peech & Tozer
*'Wake' Challenge Cup*: Canklow Hotel, r/u: Holmes Hotel
*Rotherham Charity Cup*: Canklow Hotel, r/u: Thurcroft Main
*Rotherham LV & WMC League*: Holmes Hotel, r/u Canklow Hotel
*Rotherham & District Works League*: Habershon's Welfare, r/u Jenkin's Sport
*Rotherham SS & Churches League*: Clifton Methodists, r/u Mosbrough Trinity, Subsidiary Competition: Clifton Methodists 'A', r/u: Mosbrough St Paul's 'A'
*Rawmarsh & District League* Division 'A': Sandhill Athletic, r/u: Newhill, Division 'B': South Ward Welfare, r/u: Sandhill Athletic
*Rawmarsh Challenge Cup*: Math Main, r/u: Newhill
*Maltby Senior League*: Bramley PR, r/u: Maltby Main
*Rotherham Schools Athletic Association*: 'Early Cup': Rotherham Boys, r/u Rother Valley Boys, 'Blyth Schools Shield': Rawmarsh New Senior School, r/u: Oakwood Senior School
*Aston Nursing Association Cup*: Dinnington Athletic, r/u: Kiveton Park Colliery
*Woodhouse 'Kelly' Cup*: Swallownest, r/u: Catcliffe J

# Bibliography

**Books - Football Histories:**
**A History of Sheffield Football 1857-1889,** Martin Westby, 2018 edition
**Football in Sheffield,** M Liversidge & C Eyre, 2016
**Gone But Not Forgotten,** Dave Twydell, various editions,
**Football League – Grounds for a Change,** Dave Twydell, 1991
**In A League Of Their Own – Cricket & Leisure in 20th Century Todmorden,**
      Frida, Malcolm & Brian Heywood, 2011
**Northern Goalfields,** Brian Hunt, 1989,
**A Century of City – The Centenary History of Hull City AFC 1904-2004,** Mike Peterson, 2005
**Still United, The History of Rotherham United,** Gerry Somerton, 2008
**Rejected FC Volume 3,** Dave Twydell, 1995
**The Best of Bradford Amateur Football,** Ronnie Wharton, 1987
**A Pick of the Best of Bradford Amateur Football,** Ronnie Wharton, 1989
**The Grounds of Rugby League,** Trevor Delaney, 1991
**Grounds For A Change,** Dave Twydell, 1991
**York City – A Complete Record 1902-1990,** Dave Batters, 1990
**Round About Bradford,** William Cudworth, 1876
**The Life of Charlotte Bronte,** Elizabeth Gaskill, 1857
**Football's Secret History,** 3-2 Books, John Goulstone, 2001
**Football, The First Hundred Years,** Adrian Harvey, 2007
**Keighley Past & Present,** Robert Holmes, 1858
**The Origins of Football Debate: The Grander Design and the involvement of the Lower Classes,**
      **1818-1840**, Peter Swain, Sport in History, 34:4, 2014
**History of Football,** Francis Peabody Magoun, 1938
**Denaby United 1895-1995, One Hundred Years of Football,** Barrie Dalby & David Snodgrass, 1995
**Scarborough FC, The Official History, 1879-1998,** Steve Adamson, 1998
**One Hundred Years of Local Football, A Short History of the Heavy Woollen District FA,** Peter
      Hodgson, 1998
**Coals, Goals and Ashes, Fryston Colliery's Pursuit of the West Riding County FA Challenge Cup,**
      David P Waddington, 2013
**Some Sheep are on the Pitch,** Celebrating One Hundred Years of the Craven District Football
      Association, 2008

**Books - FA Competition Results:**
**The FA Cup Complete Results,** Tony Brown, 1999
**The FA Vase Complete Results,** Tony Brown, 2005
**The FA Trophy Complete Results,** Tony Brown, 2005
**The FA Amateur Cup Complete Results**, Fred Hawthorn, 2009
*Details of these books can be found at www.soccerdata.com*

**Newspapers:**
Athletic News, Barnoldswick & Earby Times, Barnsley Chronicle, Batley Reporter and Guardian Beverley & East Riding Reporter, Beverley Echo, Beverley Independent, Bradford Daily Telegraph, Bradford Weekly Telegraph, Burnley Express, Burnley News, Craven Herald & Pioneer, Daily Gazette for Middlesbrough, East Riding Telegraph, Eastern Morning News, Hull Daily Mail, Keighley Herald, Keighley News, Leeds Mercury, Northern Echo, Penistone Stocksbridge and Hoyland Express, Sheffield Daily Telegraph, Sheffield Independent, South Yorkshire Times and Mexborough & Swinton Times, Sporting Chronicle, Todmorden Advertiser & Hebden Bridge Newsletter, Todmorden & District News, Wakefield Advertiser & Gazette, Wharfedale Observer, Yorkshire Evening Post, Yorkshire Evening Press, Yorkshire Post, Yorkshire Sports, York Herald, York Press,

**Websites:**
League tables: nonleaguematters.co.uk
Statistical information: fchd.info
Old football kits: historicalkits.co.uk
Old newspapers: britishnewspaperarchive.co.uk
Old Victorian football maps: archiuk.com
https://mexborough.dearnevalleyhistory.org.uk/
www.montagucup.com/
www.methley-village.co.uk/
www.hull-city-history.org.uk/beverley-church-institute.php
http://hullcitysupporterstrust.com/hull-brunswick-the-disappearance-of-a-football-club/
https://womensfootballarchive.org/2017/10/11/players-pat-firth/
Atalanta Ladies: www.donmouth.co.uk/womens_football/huddersfield_atalanta.html
Brunswick Chapel: www.genuki.org.uk/
Yorkshire base map: d-maps.com
West Yorkshire Archive Services: http://wytithemaps.org.uk/

**Thanks to:**
Philip Rhodes (West Riding County Amateur League information), John Rowan (Mexborough), Bill Thackray (Methley Village website), Edna Smith, Paul Jennings (Manningham Mills), Derek Kettlewell, Chris Brook.

## ALSO BY ROB GRILLO

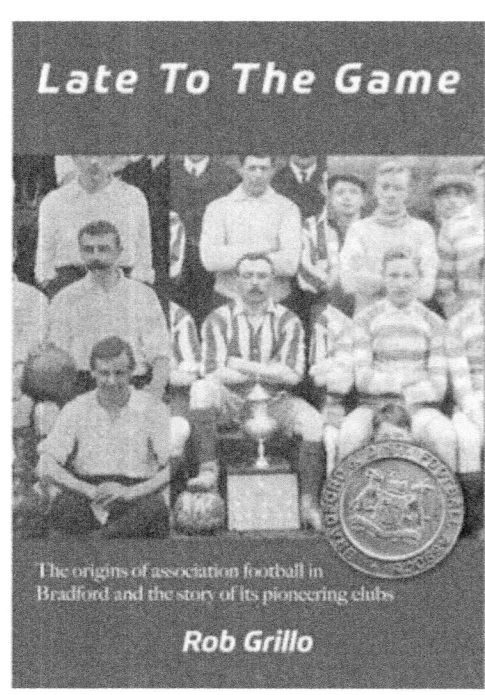

### Late To The Game
The origins of association football in Bradford and the story of its pioneering clubs

Available from
www.bantamspast.net
www.robgrillo.co.uk

### A Noble Winter's Game
The early years of association football in Yorkshire's West Riding

Available from
www.robgrillo.co.uk

**Also by Rob Grillo**

Crusty Farmers With Pitchforks - *West Yorkshire's early running clubs, runners, and races*

Anorak On The Pennine Way - *Trials, tribulations & pratfalls along Britain's best known long-distance route*

Is That The 12" Remix – *'80s music and music fanatics*

Keighley Cricket, Trying Times, & Keighley's Soccer History - *local sporting histories*

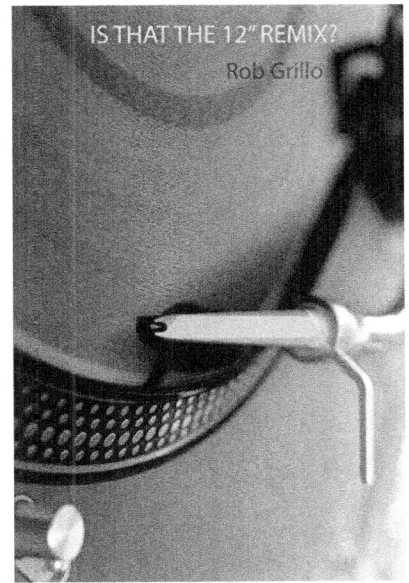

Printed in Great Britain
by Amazon